Security Intelligence with Sumo Logic

Your guide to an effective security detection and response program with the Sumo Logic platform

Bogdan Kireeve
Chas Clawson

<packt>

Security Intelligence with Sumo Logic

Copyright © 2026 Packt Publishing

All rights reserved. No part of this book may be reproduced, stored in a retrieval system, or transmitted in any form or by any means, without the prior written permission of the publisher, except in the case of brief quotations embedded in critical articles or reviews.

Every effort has been made in the preparation of this book to ensure the accuracy of the information presented. However, the information contained in this book is sold without warranty, either express or implied. Neither the authors, nor Packt Publishing or its dealers and distributors, will be held liable for any damages caused or alleged to have been caused directly or indirectly by this book.

Packt Publishing has endeavored to provide trademark information about all of the companies and products mentioned in this book by the appropriate use of capitals. However, Packt Publishing cannot guarantee the accuracy of this information.

Portfolio Director: Vijin Boricha
Relationship Lead: Anindya Sil
Project Manager: Gandhali Raut
Content Engineer: Shubhra Mayuri
Technical Editor: Nithik Cheruvakodan
Copy Editor: Safis Editing
Indexer: Tejal Soni
Production Designer: Ponraj Dhandapani
Growth Lead: Ankita Thakur

First published: January 2026
Production reference: 1290126
Published by Packt Publishing Ltd.
Grosvenor House
11 St Paul's Square
Birmingham
B3 1RB, UK.
ISBN 978-1-83588-976-3
www.packtpub.com

Contributors

About the authors

Bogdan Kireeve has been at Sumo Logic for three years and has been able to bring his cybersecurity experience to help expand Sumo Logic's footprint in Europe. Having previously worked at Elastic, Bogdan is familiar with the landscape of technologies that operate within the security and observability spaces and helps prospects and existing customers navigate it. Prior to Sumo Logic and Elastic, Bogdan consulted on security projects for large banks, working with security teams to mitigate threats during digital transformation projects, as he holds the AWS Solutions Architect and AWS SysOps Admin certifications and has experience with penetration testing and attacker methodologies.

Chas Clawson has been part of the Sumo Logic story for over six years. As Sumo's very first security-focused SE, he helped shape the company's security GTM strategy after the Factor Chain and JASK acquisitions that helped Sumo become a leading SIEM solution with CSE. Before joining Sumo, Chas spent years consulting for three-letter agencies in D.C., including the NSA red team, later moving into the commercial world as a SOC architect for HPE and an MSSP, now part of Optiv. Chas holds SME-level credentials and certifications, a master's in cyber information systems, and currently teaches cyber courses at UMGC.

About the reviewers

From Seattle, Washington, **Jake Lee** has 6+ years of experience in solutions engineering, cloud computing, data analytics, and cybersecurity. Throughout his career, Jake has developed proficiency in **Amazon Web Services (AWS)**, **Google Cloud Platform (GCP)**, and Microsoft Azure cloud services, designing and validating solutions spanning SIEM, application monitoring, and performance observability. Today, Jake works as a solutions architect at Sumo Logic and helps organizations detect, investigate, and respond to security and operational issues at scale.

Krity Kharbanda is a dedicated cybersecurity professional with a strong foundation in application security, data analysis, and machine learning. As a senior application security engineer at ServiceNow, she focuses on building secure-by-design solutions across cloud and containerized environments, empowering teams to scale safely through DevSecOps automation.

Driven by innovation, collaboration, and impactful problem-solving, she is committed to advancing modern security practices and strengthening the resilience of enterprise technology.

Table of Contents

Preface — xi

Free benefits with your book xvi

Part 1: Understanding Sumo Logic and the Convergence of Security and Observability — 1

Chapter 1: Introduction to Sumo Logic — 3

Overview of Sumo Logic 4

Digital transformation • 6

Complexity and attack surface • 6

Noise • 7

Controls and mitigations • 7

Growing attack surface • 7

Core features and capabilities of Sumo Logic 9

The modern architecture of Sumo Logic 13

Summary 14

Get this book's PDF version and more 15

Chapter 2: The Role of DevSecOps — 17

in Modern Security 17

Definition and principles of DevSecOps 18

Overview of the six DevSecOps principles • 19

Principle 1: Shift left security with Security as Code • 19

Principle 2: Continuous monitoring and continuous deployment • 21

Principle 3: Collaboration and shared responsibility • 23

Principle 4: Automated security testing • 24

Principle 5: Compliance automation and vulnerability tracking • 26

Principle 6: Security awareness and transparency • 27

First-principle thinking for DevSecOps • 29

Why DevSecOps matters and what happens when it's missing 30

Adapting to an evolving threat landscape • 30

Security as a business enabler • 31

Example: SolarTech Corp • 32

How does Sumo Logic help make security a business enabler? • 34

Risk mitigation and cost efficiency • 35

How does Sumo Logic help mitigate risk in a cost-effective way? • 36

Speed without sacrificing security • 37

Where does Sumo Logic help with increased speed of development? • 38

AIOps • 38

Building a security-first culture • 46

Where does Sumo Logic help? • 47

Adapting to an evolving threat landscape • 48

Where does Sumo Logic help? • 49

Improving collaboration across teams • 50

Summary **51**

References **51**

Get this book's PDF version and more **52**

Chapter 3: Measuring Security Outcomes and Performance — 53

Why does measuring performance matter? 54

The impact of security investments and metrics • 54

Aligning security with business goals • 56

Differing views – two examples • 56

Continuous security • 57

Start-left • 58

KPIs, SLIs, SLOs, what? How to define your performance criteria 59

SecOps KPI examples • 60

DevSecOps KPI examples • 62

SLIs and SLOs • 64

Defining the measurement process for your KPIs, SLIs, and SLOs • 64

Step-by-step guide • 65

Measuring these criteria with Sumo Logic • 75

Summary **79**

References **79**

Get this book's PDF version and more **80**

Part 2: Getting Started with Sumo Logic — 81

Chapter 4: Setting Up Your First Collector — 83

Creating a Sumo Logic instance and basic setup 84

Ingesting operating system logs 86

Table of Contents

Preface xi

    Free benefits with your book xvi

Part 1: Understanding Sumo Logic and the Convergence of Security and Observability   1

Chapter 1: Introduction to Sumo Logic   3

    Overview of Sumo Logic 4

        Digital transformation • 6

        Complexity and attack surface • 6

            Noise • 7

            Controls and mitigations • 7

            Growing attack surface • 7

    Core features and capabilities of Sumo Logic 9

    The modern architecture of Sumo Logic 13

    Summary 14

    Get this book's PDF version and more 15

Chapter 2: The Role of DevSecOps   17

    in Modern Security 17

    Definition and principles of DevSecOps 18

        Overview of the six DevSecOps principles • 19

            Principle 1: Shift left security with Security as Code • 19

            Principle 2: Continuous monitoring and continuous deployment • 21

            Principle 3: Collaboration and shared responsibility • 23

            Principle 4: Automated security testing • 24

            Principle 5: Compliance automation and vulnerability tracking • 26

            Principle 6: Security awareness and transparency • 27

        First-principle thinking for DevSecOps • 29

    Why DevSecOps matters and what happens when it's missing 30

        Adapting to an evolving threat landscape • 30

        Security as a business enabler • 31

            Example: SolarTech Corp • 32

How does Sumo Logic help make security a business enabler? • 34

Risk mitigation and cost efficiency • 35

How does Sumo Logic help mitigate risk in a cost-effective way? • 36

Speed without sacrificing security • 37

Where does Sumo Logic help with increased speed of development? • 38

AIOps • 38

Building a security-first culture • 46

Where does Sumo Logic help? • 47

Adapting to an evolving threat landscape • 48

Where does Sumo Logic help? • 49

Improving collaboration across teams • 50

Summary **51**

References **51**

Get this book's PDF version and more **52**

Chapter 3: Measuring Security Outcomes and Performance — 53

Why does measuring performance matter? **54**

The impact of security investments and metrics • 54

Aligning security with business goals • 56

Differing views – two examples • 56

Continuous security • 57

Start-left • 58

KPIs, SLIs, SLOs, what? How to define your performance criteria **59**

SecOps KPI examples • 60

DevSecOps KPI examples • 62

SLIs and SLOs • 64

Defining the measurement process for your KPIs, SLIs, and SLOs • 64

Step-by-step guide • 65

Measuring these criteria with Sumo Logic • 75

Summary **79**

References **79**

Get this book's PDF version and more **80**

Part 2: Getting Started with Sumo Logic — 81

Chapter 4: Setting Up Your First Collector — 83

Creating a Sumo Logic instance and basic setup **84**

Ingesting operating system logs **86**

Table of Contents iii

    Setting up a Linux Installed Collector • 87

        Choosing the operating system • 90

        Running the install command • 91

        Adding our first source • 93

        Configuring the source • 95

        Viewing the logs • 96

    Setting up a Windows Installed Collector • 98

        Adding our Windows source • 100

        Configuring the Windows Event Log source • 100

        Viewing the Windows logs • 102

Ingesting operating system metrics **103**

    Finding the metrics source • 103

    Configuring the metrics source • 104

    Viewing the metrics • 105

The App Catalog **107**

    Quick Linux app setup • 110

Summary **111**

Get this book's PDF version and more **112**

Chapter 5: Ingesting Data   113

Data collection methods **114**

    Hosted Collectors • 114

        Setting up AWS CloudTrail • 116

        Setting up Microsoft Office 365 • 120

    The Universal Collector • 124

    Infrastructure as Code (IaC) collection • 125

        AWS Observability • 125

        OpenTelemetry collection • 127

        Setting up an OpenTelemetry Collector • 128

        Setting up an OpenTelemetry Collector through an app in the App Catalog • 136

        Setting up Application Performance Management (APM) for a Python application • 142

        Instrumentation • 143

        Setting up a Real User Monitoring (RUM) collection • 145

        Setting up an OTLP/HTTP source • 150

        Bringing it all together • 151

Parsing **152**

    Field Extraction Rules (FERs) • 153

        FER best practices • 155

Best practices for data ingestion 156
Using source categories properly • 156
When and why to use partitions • 156
How to use Role-Based Access Control (RBAC) • 158
How to pre-process your data • 161
How to use ingest budgets • 161

Choosing your ingestion strategy 163
Small organizations (1–50 devices) • 163
Mid-sized organization (50–2,000 devices) • 163
Large enterprises (2,000–100,000+ devices) • 163
Highly regulated or air-gapped environments • 164

Summary 164
References 164
Get this book's PDF version and more 165

Chapter 6: Analyzing Data   167

Querying logs deep dive 167
Navigating Log Search • 168
Log results in the UI • 173
Aggregation results in the UI • 174
Problems with querying • 175
Querying • 176
Query basics • 176
Querying problems resolved?... • 182
Different queries for different teams • 182
LogReduce/LogCompare • 188
Live Tail • 193
Lookup tables • 196
Subqueries • 201
Mobot • 205

Log search optimization 212
Why is search optimization important? • 212
Key concepts • 213
Scan • 213
Retrieval • 214
Compute • 214
Using scopes to reduce scan • 214
Using keywords to reduce retrieval • 216

Table of Contents v

    Using extracted fields to reduce retrieval • 217

    Using scheduled views to speed up searches • 220

  Compute time: best practices • 223

Summary 226

References 227

Get this book's PDF version and more 228

Chapter 7: Metrics   229

What are metrics and how do you collect them? 229

Querying metrics deep dive 231

  Are metrics that important for security? • 232

    Benefits to a security team and examples • 232

    Best practices for combining metrics and logs • 234

  Navigating Metrics Search • 235

  Querying metrics • 240

    Example 1 – server CPU spike • 240

    Example 2 – application spans and traces • 243

Summary 245

References 245

Get this book's PDF version and more 246

Chapter 8: Alerting, Monitoring, and Visualizing Data   247

Monitor overview 249

  Building an alert monitor • 251

    Monitoring security logs • 251

    The ARP • 265

Visualizing data 272

  Building our first dashboard • 272

    Panel #1 – top 10 users • 272

    Panel #2 – outliers in failed logins • 275

    Dashboard configuration • 279

Summary 292

References 293

Get this book's PDF version and more 293

Part 3: Cloud SIEM and the Security Ecosystem   295

Chapter 9: Cloud SIEM   297

What does Cloud SIEM do? 298

Visibility • 298

Context • 298

Noise • 299

Next-gen SIEM architecture • 299

The data model • 300

Getting data into Cloud SIEM 302

The data pipeline • 307

Parsing versus mapping • 308

Enrichment • 308

Records, signals, and insights 309

What's a record? • 309

Record types • 310

What's a signal? • 312

The importance of entities and tracking "Bob" • 314

Suppression • 317

What's an insight? • 318

SIEM rules – configuration and usage 321

Rules ready to go • 321

Search versus rule • 323

Match rules • 326

Authentication with MFA • 326

Alerting on traffic to certain countries • 328

Identifying a phishing email • 329

Threshold rules • 331

Aggregation rules • 332

Outlier rules • 335

First-seen rules • 338

Chain rules • 340

Creating the signal • 344

On Entity • 344

Severity • 344

Tags • 345

Rule tuning • 346

The MITRE ATT&CK coverage matrix 348

The foundation – rules • 348

The matrix • 349

Summary 351

References 351

Get this book's PDF version and more 352

Chapter 10: The Insight Engine — 353

From signals to insights.. 354

    Deduplication and suppression • 355

        Suppressed lists: Fine-tuning signal suppression • 356

    Signal clustering • 357

        Setting the severity • 357

        Criticality • 358

    Entity activity score • 361

Navigating an insight: Deep dive 362

    The Insights UI • 363

        Metadata • 364

        AI investigation • 370

        Insight timeline • 372

        The story • 376

Cloud SIEM audit app: Deep-dive analytics on your SIEM solution's DNA 378

Real insights and use cases 382

    A phishing scenario • 382

    A ransomware scenario • 393

Custom insights 400

Cloud SIEM best practices 402

Summary 403

References 403

Get this book's PDF version and more 403

Chapter 11: The Automation Service and Playbooks — 405

Why automation matters 406

    Automation in Sumo Logic • 407

Creating and managing playbooks 408

    App Central • 408

        Integrations • 411

        Playbook templates • 417

    Creating a playbook • 418

        Testing your playbooks • 432

        How to Connect Playbooks • 435

Real-world examples of automated responses 438

Gmail phishing • 438

Changes in user accounts • 439

Summary **441**

References **442**

Get this book's PDF version and more **442**

Part 4: Advanced Topics and Future Trends — 443

Chapter 12: Bringing a Security Intelligence Program to Life with Sumo Logic — 445

Cyber threat intelligence: beyond feeds and PDFs 445

Types of threat intelligence • 446

Tactical • 446

Operational • 447

Strategic • 447

Priority information requirements • 448

Decision-making with threat intelligence • 449

OODA loop • 450

Cyber Kill Chain • 451

F3EAD • 452

Sumo Logic as the nucleus of actionable intelligence 456

Building a security intelligence program with Sumo Logic: a cross-team model • 457

Establishing intelligence flow • 458

Operationalizing intelligence across teams • 460

Evolving intelligence maturity • 462

Implementation • 463

Intelligence feeds ready to go • 463

Bring your own feed • 465

STIX/TAXII collection • 466

Intelligence API • 472

Cloud SIEM rules • 474

Dashboards and dissemination • 475

Summary **476**

References **477**

Get this book's PDF version and more **477**

Chapter 13: Compliance and Reporting — 479

Using Sumo Logic for compliance management 479

Holding yourself and vendors accountable • 480

'Show me' culture: turning promises into proof • 480
> Practical accountability checklist • 481

Generating reports and audit logs 482

Step 1: Don't reinvent the wheel, raid the App Catalog • 483
> Deploying a hosted collector • 485
>
> Adding a Microsoft Office 365 source • 485
>
> Checking that logs are coming in • 487
>
> Installing the app • 488

Step 2: Build auditor-ready master dashboards (by mixing panels) • 489

Step 3: If required, schedule the evidence so proof shows up on time • 491

Step 4: Log the logger to prove SIEM governance • 495

Step 5: Align retention with the rules you're under • 496

Step 6: Share broadly, safely • 497

Ensuring regulatory (continuous) compliance 498
Summary 499
References 499
Get this book's PDF version and more 500

Chapter 14: The Future of Security Intelligence   501

The future of intelligent security 502

The intelligent SOC • 502

What actually makes an SOC intelligent • 504

Why an intelligent SOC matters now • 505

The evolving role of AI in security 505

The new frontiers of risk: shifts in attacker strategy • 506
> Non-human identities (NHIs) • 507
>
> Shadow AI • 508
>
> Supply chain and CI/CD • 511
>
> Deepfakes • 512
>
> Cognitive overload • 513

AI as a co-analyst • 514
> Where AI actually helps today • 514
>
> What AI should not be asked to do • 517
>
> Explainability • 518
>
> The economics of defense • 519

How Sumo Logic applies AI to modern security operations • 519

Preparing for what comes next 520

Instrumenting decisions, not actions • 520

Assume non-human activity dominates • 521

Focus on correlation, not signals • 522

Keep humans in the loop, but reduce load • 522

Measure what matters • 523

Other emerging trends and technologies • 523

Internet of Things (IoT) • 523

Multi-agent AI attacks • 525

Automated vulnerability research and exploit development (VRED) • 525

Summary **526**

References **527**

Get this book's PDF version and more **527**

Chapter 15: Unlock Your Exclusive Benefits 529

Unlock this Book's Free Benefits in 3 Easy Steps 530

Step 1 • 530

Step 2 • 531

Step 3 • 532

Need Help • 532

Other Books You May Enjoy 534

Index 537

Preface

Cybersecurity is a difficult thing to get right. In a world where security practitioners are swimming in a deluge of data, where controls and processes need to be iron-clad in order to be effective, and with less visibility than ever before, security teams need help with the fundamentals.

Sumo Logic is a DevSecOps platform that enables teams to centralize their data, make sense of it, and understand what's happening quickly. DevSecOps is becoming vital to the defensive posture of a business because it naturally brings together the units that are responsible for operational monitoring, like all the limbs of a body working in unison.

DevSecOps on its own has a range of advantages that we tap into throughout the book:

- Better communication internally
- Unified goals for security, compliance, and operations
- Improved responsiveness and adaptivity to modern threats

With this theme in mind, we discuss how Sumo Logic can be placed at the heart of operations within an organization to help build an intelligent security program as quickly as possible. Sumo Logic's focus on speed and simplicity is incredibly useful here, and we approach the implementation of Sumo Logic in chunks.

First of all, we'll acquaint you with DevSecOps and the steps on how to practically embrace it within a business. This is followed up by an initiation into Sumo Logic and the first steps for using it – different methods of collection and initial analysis.

Then, we dive deep into analytics, the bread and butter of the platform – gaining actionable intelligence from streams of telemetry. We cover different analytical methods, both visual and textual, using a range of tools and internal features that allow the user to break data down in numerous ways. This is done from both an observability and a security perspective.

We then progress into security-specific themes such as Cloud SIEM, rules and insights, threat intelligence, and compliance that help to practically solidify all of the parts discussed up to that point to bring it all together.

Finally, we look at the future of intelligent SecOps and where we think it's headed, to give you a good understanding of what to expect and how to start thinking about your security processes to align yourself and your team for future threats.

The book will guide you through ways of making the most of this powerful technology and also best practices on how to get the best results. Working with Sumo Logic every day and speaking to myriad customers in the industry has given us the tools and knowledge to help bring this to users and future users of Sumo Logic to help bolster their cybersecurity efforts. We wanted to share our experience and hope that readers benefit.

Who this book is for

This book is primarily for security practitioners, operations, and DevOps teams, but can also be utilized by SOC and DevOps managers to help enable their teams to make operational and security arms come together seamlessly.

What this book covers

Chapter 1, Introduction to Sumo Logic, explains what Sumo Logic is and the modern challenges that it seeks to solve within operational teams.

Chapter 2, The Role of DevSecOps in Modern Security, elaborates on how to approach DevSecOps from a security perspective in order to leverage tools such as Sumo Logic to improve visibility and communication across the business.

Chapter 3, Measuring Security Outcomes and Performance, helps you to use Sumo Logic in order to quantify your operational efficiency. It is important to measure how you're doing in order to get better, and this is what we cover here.

Chapter 4, Setting Up Your First Collector, gets you going with the platform and sets up an initial collector to start ingesting data into the platform.

Chapter 5, Ingesting Data, covers the different ways that are available in Sumo Logic to help ingest all the MELT telemetry types in detail, so you can achieve maximum visibility across your business.

Chapter 6, Analyzing Data, showcases how to query your logs to analyze your data in depth and in different ways. We cover multiple scenarios covering observability and security use cases to help you in a practical way.

Chapter 7, Metrics, covers how to query your metric data and where metrics as a telemetry type sit within the DevSecOps paradigm, with examples to explain how to analyze this data type effectively.

Chapter 8, Alerting, Monitoring, and Visualizing Data, is a walk-through of how to use monitors to create alerts. We'll run through it end-to-end so you can apply it to your own data. We'll also cover dashboards and different visualization methods in this chapter, so you can express whatever data you want to see as a query.

Chapter 9, Cloud SIEM, provides a deep dive into what happens under the hood of Cloud SIEM. We cover the data model, SIEM rules, and how records, signals, and insights work together to help your security team. Finally, we cover the MITRE ATT&CK Coverage Matrix, which is used to improve your security posture over time.

Chapter 10, The Insight Engine, explains how the insight engine, the superpower of Cloud SIEM, works in detail and how we can use insights to focus on key threats and investigate them.

Chapter 11, The Automation Service and Playbooks, covers automation capabilities in Sumo Logic and how we can use playbooks to respond to incidents and other events. We'll also explore the process of putting a playbook together from scratch so that you can apply this to any scenario you want.

Chapter 12, Bringing a Security Intelligence Program to Life with Sumo Logic, puts threat intelligence into perspective and explains how Sumo Logic finally turns into the beating heart of your operational teams. We cover how to make intelligence actionable and how to engage other teams in the business to create a mature security program.

Chapter 13, *Compliance and Reporting*, explores the compliance use case, so crucial to many security teams now, and how you can use Sumo Logic to help monitor and track compliance across all the business telemetry we collect.

Chapter 14, *The Future of Security Intelligence*, looks forward to the future of security and how users of Sumo Logic are well-placed in order to defend against modern and future threats. We talk about example scenarios and how to prepare for the future.

To get the most out of this book

- You need to have a Sumo Logic environment:
    - If you are already a customer, you have what you need to put these concepts into practice. Note that a lesser-known feature in Sumo allows for parent/child tenants for a prod/dev setup where both draw from the same pool of credits.
    - If you don't have an existing Sumo Logic tenant, go to `https://www.sumologic.com/sign-up/` and get a free 30-day trial. *Note that the free instance does not provide access to premium features such as Cloud SIEM or Cloud SOAR. The core platform is included.*
    - If you are not a customer but are serious about testing the full capabilities with your own production data and tool stack, Sumo Logic will gladly work with you to do a full-scope proof-of-value. Impressively, you can stand up a near production-ready environment in less than 4 weeks.
- You need to have a basic understanding of log analytics, SIEM, or security operations: Sumo Logic provides free training within the product and through the Sumo Logic Academy. Setting up a free trial and going through training will give you a great hands-on experience that coincides with this book. Today, certifications include the following:
    - Sumo Logic Certified Fundamentals User
    - Sumo Logic Certified Search Mastery User
    - Sumo Logic Certified Admin
    - Sumo Logic Certified Logs for Security Analyst
    - Sumo Logic Certified Cloud SIEM Practitioner
    - Sumo Logic Certified Metrics Analyst
- A virtual lab (optional): Depending on your time and goals, there are amazing open source or community-built virtual environments or labs that will help you stand up the infrastructure needed to generate metrics, events, logs, and traces to feed into Sumo Logic. Here are a few:
    - OWASP WebGoat and Juice Shop: The full OWASP Top-10 in one app; runs via Docker or Node.js. Great for web attacks, auth abuse, file uploads, and so on.
    - Atomic Red Team: Hundreds of ATT&CK-mapped "atomic" tests; dead simple to run and trigger endpoint/Sysmon logs.

- Stratus Red Team: "Atomic for cloud" (AWS/Azure/GCP/K8s) to detonate cloud-native attacks.
- DVWA (Damn Vulnerable Web App): Ultra-simple PHP/MySQL target; many prebuilt Docker images.
- MITRE Caldera (+ Emu plugin): Automated adversary emulation platform with ready adversary profiles.

Download the color images

We also provide a PDF file that has color images of the screenshots/diagrams used in this book. You can download it here:https://packt.link/gbp/9781835889763.

> This book contains images and screenshots that may not be readable in certain formats or print sizes. These images are included for illustrative purposes only, to support conceptual understanding. Any important information relevant to such images has been included in the text itself.

Conventions used

There are a number of text conventions used throughout this book.

`CodeInText`: Indicates code words in text, database table names, folder names, filenames, file extensions, pathnames, dummy URLs, user input, and Twitter handles. For example: " Using `sum(_count)`, the count will now return row counts, not the sum of the original count."

A block of code is set as follows:

```
(_index=sumologic_audit_events) OR
(_index=sumologic_system_events)
| avg(insight.timeToDetection)
| round(_avg / 3600) as _avg
```

Any command-line input or output is written as follows:

```
pip install opentelemetry-distro==0.47b0
```

Bold: Indicates a new term, an important word, or words that you see on the screen. For instance, words in menus or dialog boxes appear in the text like this. For example: " In Sumo Logic, search optimization is driven by three core concepts: **scan**, **retrieval**, and **compute**. "

> Warnings or important notes appear like this.

> **Tip**
>
> Tips and tricks appear like this.

Get in touch

Feedback from our readers is always welcome.

General feedback: If you have questions about any aspect of this book or have any general feedback, please email us at customercare@packt.com and mention the book's title in the subject of your message.

Errata: Although we have taken every care to ensure the accuracy of our content, mistakes do happen. If you have found a mistake in this book, we would be grateful if you reported this to us. Please visit http://www.packt.com/submit-errata, click **Submit Errata**, and fill in the form.

Piracy: If you come across any illegal copies of our works in any form on the internet, we would be grateful if you would provide us with the location address or website name. Please contact us at copyright@packt.com with a link to the material.

If you are interested in becoming an author: If there is a topic that you have expertise in and you are interested in either writing or contributing to a book, please visit http://authors.packt.com/.

Free benefits with your book

This book comes with free benefits to support your learning. Activate them now for instant access (see the "*How to Unlock*" section for instructions).

Here's a quick overview of what you can instantly unlock with your purchase:

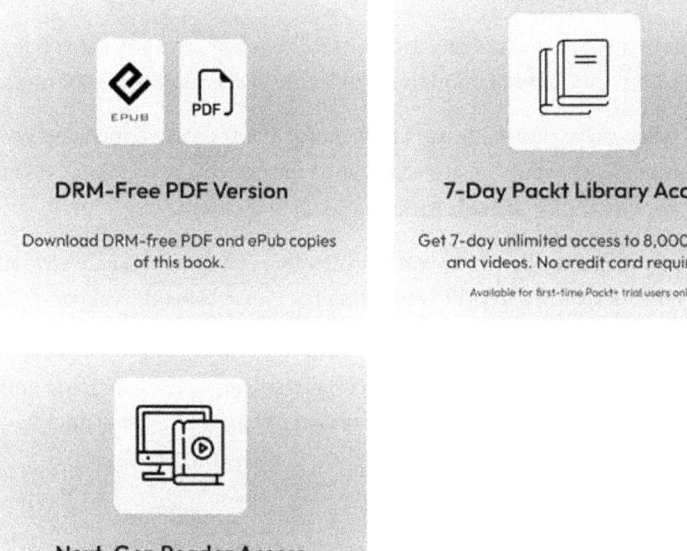

How to Unlock

Scan the QR code (or go to `packtpub.com/unlock`). Search for this book by name, confirm the edition, and then follow the steps on the page.

Note: Keep your invoice handy. Purchases made directly from Packt don't require one

Part 1

Understanding Sumo Logic and the Convergence of Security and Observability

In this first part of the book, you'll learn about the modern challenges that Sumo Logic helps to address as a DevSecOps platform, and we'll also talk about how security and observability are coming together. Not only that, but we'll discuss *actionable* ways for you to implement the points we discuss across your teams and wider business, especially if you plan on using Sumo Logic as your central platform of choice.

This part of the book includes the following chapters:

- *Chapter 1, Introduction to Sumo Logic*
- *Chapter 2, The Role of DevSecOps in Modern Security*
- *Chapter 3, Measuring Security Outcomes and Performance*

1
Introduction to Sumo Logic

Sumo Logic is a modern, cloud-native SaaS log analytics platform that centralizes all text-based log and event data, transforming raw noise into actionable insights and automating the detection and resolution of security, operational, and business challenges.

When it comes to analytics platforms, one of the most critical capabilities is the ability to centralize and aggregate data from across the entire enterprise ecosystem. Getting critical system telemetry into a single view is often more challenging than you would think. I was once told by a customer, "*I keep asking for a single pane of glass, but what I'm given is a single glass of pain.*" Sumo Logic aims to change such experiences with its ability to easily onboard, visualize, and correlate data. Of course, there's a lot more than dashboards to the platform and a lot of nuances to take into account when it comes to the practical benefit of this technology.

Let's start with where Sumo Logic came from and look at the evolution of the platform over more than a decade to see how it has managed to stay agile, modern, and at the cutting edge of log analytics over the years. As we look at this in greater detail, we'll cover the key features of the platform to give you an understanding of the core capabilities.

The following topics will be covered in this chapter:

- Overview of Sumo Logic
- Core features and capabilities of Sumo Logic
- The modern architecture of Sumo Logic

> **Note**
>
> **Your purchase includes a free PDF copy + exclusive extras**
>
> Your purchase includes a DRM-free PDF copy of this book, 7-day trial to the Packt+ library (no credit card required), and additional exclusive extras. See the *Free benefits with your book* section in the *Preface* to unlock them instantly and maximize your learning.

Overview of Sumo Logic

To understand how Sumo Logic was born, it's helpful to go back in time and explore the history of **log management** (**LM**) as a technology. Don't worry—there won't be a test at the end of this history lesson!

Centralized security analytics, often referred to as **Security Information and Event Management** (**SIEM**), is surprisingly recent. The first iterations appeared as upgrades from simple log aggregation servers in the late 1990s and were used primarily by the largest companies. These systems began to include alerting and filtering mechanisms to reduce *false positives*, events that cause a signal but don't present any threat, from **Network Intrusion Detection Systems** (**NIDSs**). This technology enabled organizations to find, track, and manage actionable security events on their networks. The push for LM gained momentum with government regulations such as the following:

- The **Health Insurance Portability and Accountability Act** (**HIPAA**) of 1996
- The **Gramm-Leach-Bliley Act** (**GLBA**) of 1999
- The **Federal Information Security Management Act** (**FISMA**) of 2002
- The **Sarbanes-Oxley Act** (**SOX**) of 2002
- The 2004 **Payment Card Industry Data Security Standard** (**PCI DSS**)

It wasn't until 2005 that Gartner formally coined the term SIEM in a 2005 Gartner report titled *Improve IT Security with Vulnerability Management*. Companies with tens, hundreds, or thousands of devices generating daily logs needed solutions that could handle the vast quantity of data. These logged events had to be managed in a way that ensured they were safely stored, archived, and easily accessible.

Fast forward to today, and log analytics still focuses on the value and visibility gained from collecting and storing the massive amounts of data generated by modern networks and cloud workloads. For security alone, the average large enterprise typically has between 40 and 70 different tools in use. This proliferation of tools can lead to challenges with integration, management, and visibility, often referred to as *tool sprawl*. From this digital exhaust, it's common to see environments logging thousands of **events per second** (**EPS**), generating gigabytes or even terabytes of data each day.

Sumo Logic was built from the outset to solve this challenge as a cloud-native, elastically scalable, machine data analytics platform providing real-time insights into various aspects of IT operations, security, and application performance.

Founded in 2010 by some of the original SIEM pioneers, the platform is tailored to handle the complexities of modern IT environments, which often include a mix of cloud, on-premises, and hybrid infrastructures. Sumo Logic's core value lies in its ability to process, analyze, and visualize large volumes of log and metric data from diverse sources, enabling organizations to achieve a high level of security intelligence, operational efficiency, and compliance.

The aim of the game is to help with making sense of data, and lots of it. We're looking at security intelligence and, as *Figure 1.1* illustrates, from a security perspective, the breadth of context that Sumo Logic can ingest from many different sources in your environment to consolidate, correlate, and cluster data to identify threats.

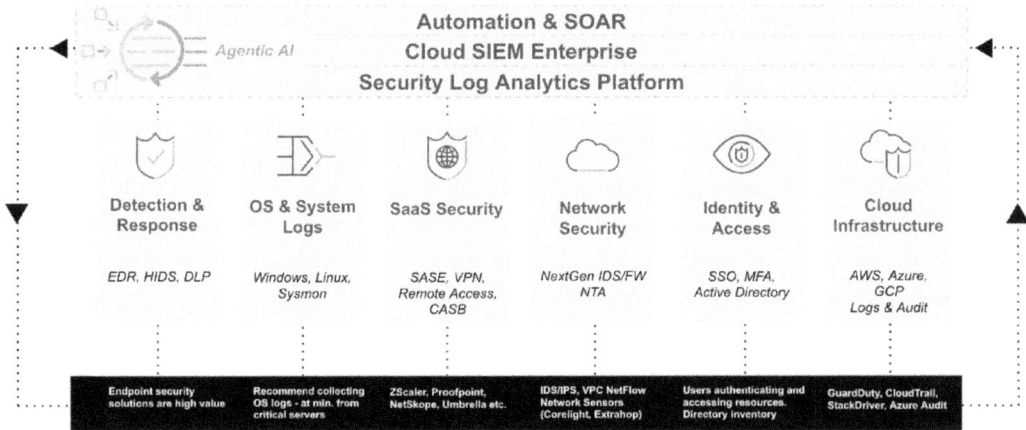

Figure 1.1 – Recommended security data sources to use for automatic correlation

One thing that Sumo Logic does really well is work with data from anywhere. It's completely vendor- and data-agnostic. This means that, unlike many other security tools, it can ingest data from typical security sources such as operating systems and cloud environments like AWS, Azure, and GCP, as well as from development tools such as GitHub, Jenkins, or Argo CD, to cover all development, security, and operations use cases. Great sources to include are the following:

- Cloud and network infrastructure logs
- Container and Kubernetes logs and metrics
- Application logs and traces
- CI/CD pipeline logs and metrics

What's the benefit here? You get to bring those sources of data that have typically been out of reach for security teams and tap into them for vital security context. Where once teams were tasked with finding the "needle in the haystack," now they are asked to find the needle in the needle stack! To do this, you need to have all the log data accessible and searchable *at scale*. That's the versatility of Sumo Logic.

Two of the most common business challenges that we encounter when speaking to customers are navigating rapid digital transformation and the increasing complexity of data and business environments. In fact, complexity impacts multiple layers of a business; complex environments lead to ever-increasing challenges in site reliability, application uptime, monitoring, security detection and response, and the growing stack of tools trying to make sense of this deluge of data. Many of these challenges are unavoidable in our digital age due to growing amounts of data and rapidly evolving technical requirements. However, businesses can reduce friction by modernizing their tooling and how they monitor and manage modern workloads.

The impact of digital transformation and complexity is discussed in detail next.

Digital transformation

Most organizations are now aiming to transform their businesses and realign them with modern standards, architectures, and technologies. One of the concerns is that these requirements are forever shifting. New technologies and standards are constantly being set as industries and operating models are modernized. It makes it a challenge just to keep up! Further, keeping up involves dedicating a lot of internal or expensive external resources to conducting labor-intensive planning, coordination, and implementation across the business. The larger the organization, the bigger and more complex the projects.

There are a few specific challenges that arise:

- **Lack of visibility and control**: Businesses in this day and age desperately need visibility. There are more moving components, more supply chains, more endpoints, and more IoT challenges and mobile devices than ever before. Having the data for these disparate systems scattered across siloed data locations and tools makes the business blind to operational issues and security incidents. This results in a weak response to an incident, both operationally and from a cybersecurity perspective.
- **Rising costs**: The reality is that the technology costs of innovation continue to rise for everyone. Much of these costs come from tooling, and one thing that larger enterprises have is a vast amount of tools that have been procured, sometimes for individual use cases and nothing more, but have stayed present in the ecosystem and are incurring costs for licenses, data usage, seat uses, and so on. Consolidating technology into multi-purpose platforms has been a massive driver for businesses as they look to improve their bottom line, as well as freeing them from the huge administrative efforts of operating and maintaining dozens of tools.
- **Lack of democratized, data-driven decisions**: When data is dispersed around the business, it is hard to get the full picture. Often, teams can see only a portion of the data they need, and extracting data from other departments and system owners introduces unnecessary friction. When conducting digital transformation projects, the democratization of data is paramount. By analyzing logs across applications, infrastructure, and security systems, organizations can identify performance issues, detect threats, and uncover usage patterns in real time. This visibility enables leaders to make smarter, faster decisions based on evidence rather than assumptions.

Complexity and attack surface

With increasingly inordinate amounts of data being sent and processed around the world, it can be overwhelming to understand where the critical data is, where it lives, what the dependencies are, and how the business consumes all of this information to achieve its goals.

In addition, the proliferation of *shadow IT* and, more recently, *shadow AI* is a bigger problem than ever. **Shadow IT** refers to the use of information technology systems, software, or services within an organization without explicit approval or oversight from the IT department, often leading to security and compliance risks. Deploying a server used to mean procuring the equipment and then *racking and stacking* it in a data center somewhere. Now, with a click of a button (or, more often, through automated code), developers and engineers can spin up an endless number of cloud systems and services. They have been given the keys to the digital kingdom. With this rapid growth of IT systems and the sensitive data they contain, organizations must retain visibility of their digital assets in increasingly complex environments.

So, what are some of the problems that arise from complexity? Let's get into it in detail.

Noise

All of this new technology is spewing out mountains of log telemetry, but not all data is useful, and what even is a good *signal-to-noise* ratio? The more complex an environment, the more difficult it becomes to monitor and analyze all of this data. Current technology stacks consist of multi-layered architectures comprising many moving components. Hundreds of Kubernetes clusters, thousands of Pods and nodes, dozens of applications, hundreds and thousands, if not millions, of visitors to apps and interacting with AI agents, firewalls generating gigantic amounts of data, and let's not forget one of the most critical aspects—employees logging in from absolutely anywhere in the world. Most organizations do not have the ability to monitor the *entire* ecosystem, and even if they do achieve that, trying to battle through the load of noise generated by their business is chaotic at best. Sumo Logic can ingest all this data and provide ready-made dashboards, monitors, and security rules for these different datasets, making it easy to make sense of the noise. And fortunately, it allows customers to match the value of the data to different data tiers, with the cheaper tiers coming in at pennies on the dollar while still being *hot* and *searchable* (more on this later).

Controls and mitigations

As compliance and governance challenges continue to grow, technology has become an increasingly critical area of concern for organizations worldwide. Compliance for its own sake is a reality, but it also represents a baseline set of controls that organizations must have in place. Falling out of compliance can present an immediate and significant risk to the business. Implementing the right controls and mitigations across complex environments, spanning multiple clouds, on-premises systems, and diverse teams, can be daunting. Sumo Logic helps simplify this challenge by leveraging raw logs and telemetry data to continuously monitor compliance controls, enhance visibility, and keep the organization aligned with regulatory and security requirements.

Growing attack surface

The bigger and more complex the environment, the more technology and stakeholders are involved. This increases the surface area of attack. You have the typical attack vectors, such as phishing and client-facing attacks, but also distributed environments that have their own admin users, power users, and normal user activity that has to be monitored. What is considered *normal* differs from environment to environment, day to day, and user to user. Therefore, tracking all of this behavior, in real time, is a colossal endeavor. In Sumo Logic, it's possible to correlate data across all your data sources in one platform, using one universal language and syntax, with almost 1,000 pre-created security rules covering modern attack techniques. Machine learning and UEBA rules allow for capturing anomalies and linked behavior in your environment that is worthy of investigation.

Sumo Logic is positioned to address these modern challenges because of the design, architecture, and capabilities of the platform, which we'll cover shortly. *Figure 1.2* presents an illustration of how Sumo Logic sits in the middle of People, Processes, and Technology at an organization and acts as a unifying layer:

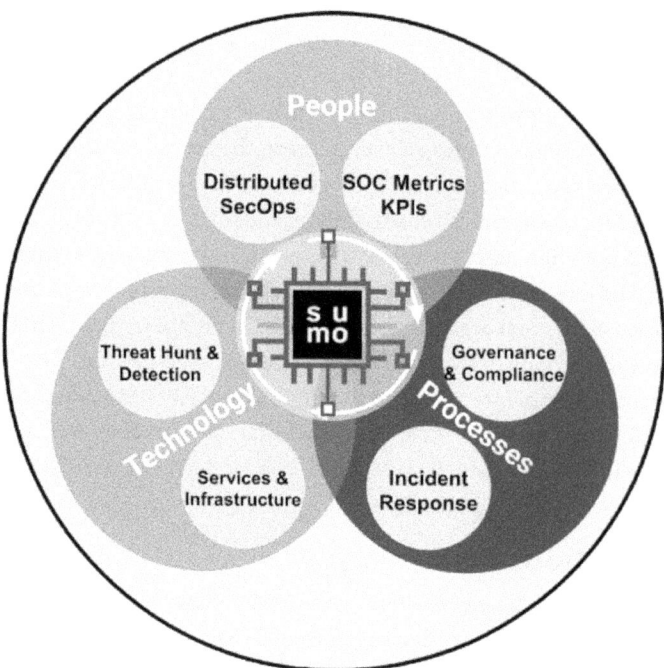

Figure 1.2 – Sumo Logic and the triad of People, Processes, and Technology

At the center is Sumo Logic, serving as the intelligent hub that connects and enhances all three pillars. The *People* domain focuses on distributed SecOps teams and measurable SOC metrics to drive accountability and performance. Expertise and collaboration of teams are essential for successful monitoring and improving the cybersecurity posture of an organization. Sumo Logic facilitates this by providing a unified UI, bringing together cross-functional teams to identify and resolve issues and incidents in real time.

Processes encompass governance, compliance, and incident response workflows that ensure operational discipline and rapid reaction to threats. It's important to have processes that are consistent, scalable, and aligned with best practices. Sumo Logic helps by automating the ingestion and collection of logs, metrics, and traces from across the IT estate into one single place. Then, through the use of analytics, dashboards, and monitoring, it enables analysts to not only put these processes into motion but also track how well they are working, something we will visit in *Chapter 3, Measuring Security Outcomes and Performance* when we look at measuring outcomes. This also reduces the risk of human error and ensures that security and operational incidents are addressed as quickly as possible.

Technology underpins threat hunting, detection, and resilient service infrastructure. Sumo Logic itself is cloud-native and highly scalable and supports hybrid data, ingesting data from all around the organization. A real-time **analytics engine** with machine learning and anomaly detection powers Sumo Logic. AI and agentic capabilities are also leveraged in the platform in a smart way, targeting aspects of usability where speed and context are paramount.

Core features and capabilities of Sumo Logic

In this section, we'll talk about the key parts of Sumo Logic and start setting the scene for when we build on these concepts later to create a cybersecurity program. The following isn't an exhaustive list of features, but those that will be pivotal to understanding why you can build a cybersecurity program around Sumo Logic and how exactly it can help with that:

- **Deep search and query**: A comprehensive query language allows for complete data manipulation, which is incredibly important when you need to extract vital insights from your data quickly. This includes over 70 query pipe **operators**. Query operators are the core building blocks you use to search, filter, transform, and analyze log data. They function much like commands or functions in a programming language, telling Sumo's search engine what to do with the ingested data and how users can visualize and gain insights from the log data. We will be exploring querying throughout the book, but we will take our first look at it when we reach *Chapter 4*, *Setting Up Your First Collector*.

- **Centralized data store**: Sumo Logic serves as a central log data store, often referred to as a security data lake, by unifying data from across an organization's entire digital ecosystem into a single, scalable, cloud-native platform. It collects and normalizes logs, metrics, and traces from applications, cloud services, and infrastructure, enabling security and operations teams to analyze everything in one place. Acting as a trusted "source of truth," Sumo Logic's architecture supports petabyte-scale ingestion, indexing, and retention. This centralization breaks down data silos, improves visibility, and provides the foundation for modern threat detection, compliance, and observability use cases, all powered by real-time analytics and AI-driven insights.

- **Dojo AI and Mobot**: Sumo Logic's Mobot uses foundational generative AI models delivered through AWS Bedrock to take the hard work out of querying your data. There is no need to learn a query language. Just ask what you want to see in natural language.

  For instance, you may have a typical SQL-based query such as this:

  ```
  sumo.datasource=windows deployment.environment=* host.group=* host.name=*
  ""channel":"Security"" (4624 or 4625 or 4771 or 4776 or 4768 or 4769)
  // 4624 - Login Success, 4625 or 4771 - Login Failures, 4776 - Domain Controller
  - Credential validation, 4768 - A Kerberos authentication ticket (TGT) was
  requested, 4769 - A Kerberos service ticket was requested
  | json "event_id", "keywords[0]", "channel" as event_id_obj, Keywords, channel
  nodrop
  | json field=event_id_obj "id" as event_id
  | where event_id in ("4624", "4625", "4771", "4776", "4768", "4769") and channel
  = "Security"
  | if (Keywords matches "Audit Success", "Success", "Failure") as outcome
  | timeslice 15m
  | count as attempts by _timeslice, outcome
  | transpose row _timeslice column outcome
  ```

Here is how it looks on the platform:

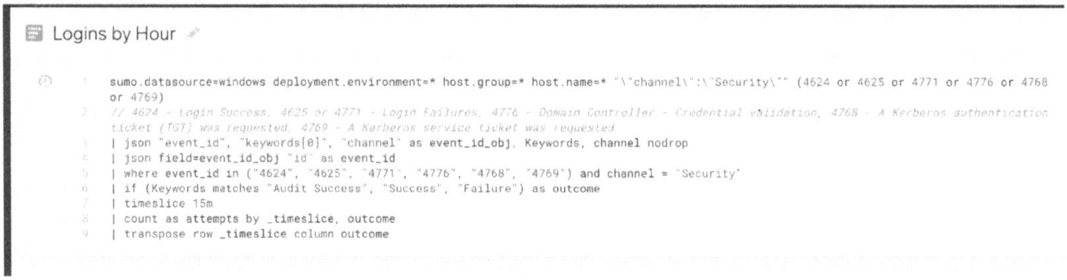

```
Logins by Hour

sumo.datasource=windows deployment.environment=* host.group=* host.name=* "\"channel\":\"Security\"" (4624 or 4625 or 4771 or 4776 or 4768 or 4769)
// 4624 - Login Success, 4625 or 4771 - Login Failures, 4776 - Domain Controller - Credential validation, 4768 - A Kerberos authentication ticket (TGT) was requested, 4769 - A Kerberos service ticket was requested
| json "event_id", "keywords[0]", "channel" as event_id_obj, Keywords, channel nodrop
| json field=event_id_obj "id" as event_id
| where event_id in ("4624", "4625", "4771", "4776", "4768", "4769") and channel = "Security"
| if (Keywords matches "Audit Success", "Success", "Failure") as outcome
| timeslice 15m
| count as attempts by _timeslice, outcome
| transpose row _timeslice column outcome
```

Figure 1.3 – Typical query syntax that users use when searching for things

This could be changed to a more natural way of interacting with your data, such as the following, which is the same request as the previous one, but much quicker to type out:

Find me all events that have "Microsoft-Windows-Security-Auditing" or the Microsoft event code of "4720", extract the json to focus on the security channel and add the username, domain name and computer from the event. Find the username, domain name and target subject name from the event data in the message and order by date in a table

- **Schema-on-read with schema-on-write**: In data systems, **schema-on-read** (or **schema-on-demand**) means the data is stored in its raw form, and structure is applied when you query it. This provides flexibility where analysts can interpret the same data in different ways without re-ingesting it. Schema-on-write, on the other hand, enforces a defined structure before data is stored, ensuring consistency, validation, and faster query performance for known use cases. Sumo Logic uniquely combines both approaches: it performs search-time parsing (schema-on-read) that allows ad hoc exploration and dynamic field extraction, while also maintaining a centralized parsing engine and data model (schema-on-write) for standardized analytics, dashboards, and cross-source correlation. Having both is crucial as it provides the agility to investigate anything while still maintaining governance and reliability for operational and security insights.

- **Out-of-the-box content**: Hundreds of Sumo Logic "apps" mean there are ready-to-go dashboards, monitors, and queries for many different technologies, from databases to firewalls to servers and more. Once again, you get to reduce time spent on the platform while increasing the value from your data.

- **Threat intelligence**: All of your data points in Sumo Logic are cross-referenced with high-fidelity threat intelligence provided by CrowdStrike and Intel 471 at no cost. Updated every 24 hours, this will provide you with game-changing context during any investigations and incidents, meaning the time it takes for you to understand the threat is reduced. Threat intelligence is used within both the real-time rules as well as search-time enrichments (threat lookup operator).

- **Query-based and real-time anomaly detection**: Sumo Logic provides two complementary methods for anomaly detection—**real-time rules** and **scheduled query-based detections**—giving security teams both speed and flexibility. The real-time rules engine continuously evaluates incoming data streams, instantly creating **signals** when defined patterns or thresholds are met. This is ideal for high-priority, time-sensitive threats. In contrast, scheduled query-based detections run at defined intervals, using complex or resource-intensive searches to uncover hidden or evolving patterns, which is perfect for trend analysis, insider threat monitoring, and compliance reporting. By combining both detection modes, Sumo Logic empowers analysts to balance real-time responsiveness with deep, contextual analytics, ensuring that both immediate threats and subtle anomalies are efficiently identified and acted upon.

- **Cloud SIEM**: Cloud SIEM is the pinnacle of advanced security analytics in Sumo Logic. It runs on advanced, proprietary machine learning algorithms that track sequences of events and signals caused by entities, and the insight engine clusters threat activity automatically. We'll get to the SIEM later, in *Chapter 9, The Cloud SIEM*.
- **Automation**: Automation is built into the fabric of Sumo Logic. It's not a separate module that you have to buy. It's called the Automation Service. You can automate simple to complex remediation processes with a low-code/no-code playbook canvas with drag-and-droppable actions. *Figure 1.4* presents an example of an incident response process involving VirusTotal:

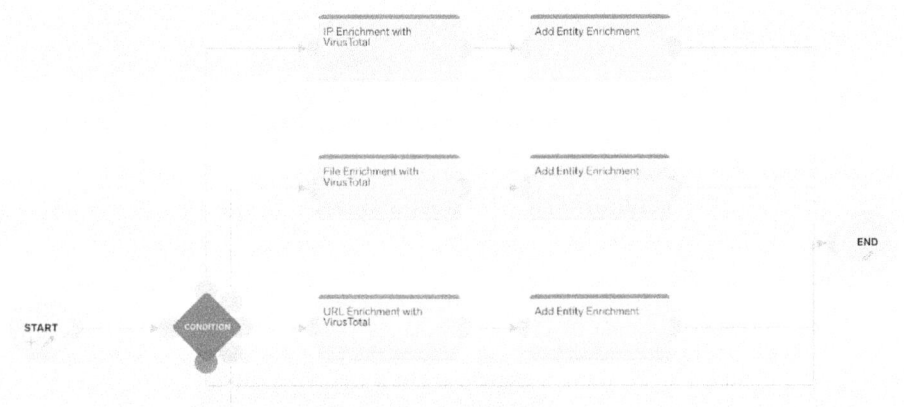

Figure 1.4 – A set of actions in a VirusTotal enrichment playbook

- **Infrastructure metrics**: As mentioned earlier, Dev and Ops in DevSecOps are crucial to the context that can be derived from an outage or incident, so Sumo Logic has all the capabilities of ingesting infrastructure metrics. Through the use of OpenTelemetry, collecting metrics is incredibly straightforward, whether it be for individual servers or containerized architectures in Docker and Kubernetes. Through dockerized collectors or, for Kubernetes, through the use of a Helm Chart, you can be up and running within minutes with an out-of-the-box dashboard like this:

Figure 1.5 – An example dashboard providing insights into a Kubernetes cluster

- **Application metrics/traces**: Traces are, once again, a vital piece of the puzzle. With the help of OpenTelemetry, it's possible to instrument applications and bring them into an OpenTelemetry-compliant platform such as Sumo Logic for analysis. The typical trace views that you're used to, all in one place, will look like the following:

Figure 1.6 – An example of span analytics in a trace to see application behavior

Seeing individual traces and spans in the context of logs they generate is important, but you can also see all the relationships of services in your application architecture that are crucial to understanding dependencies and problems as they arise in real time, as shown in the following figure:

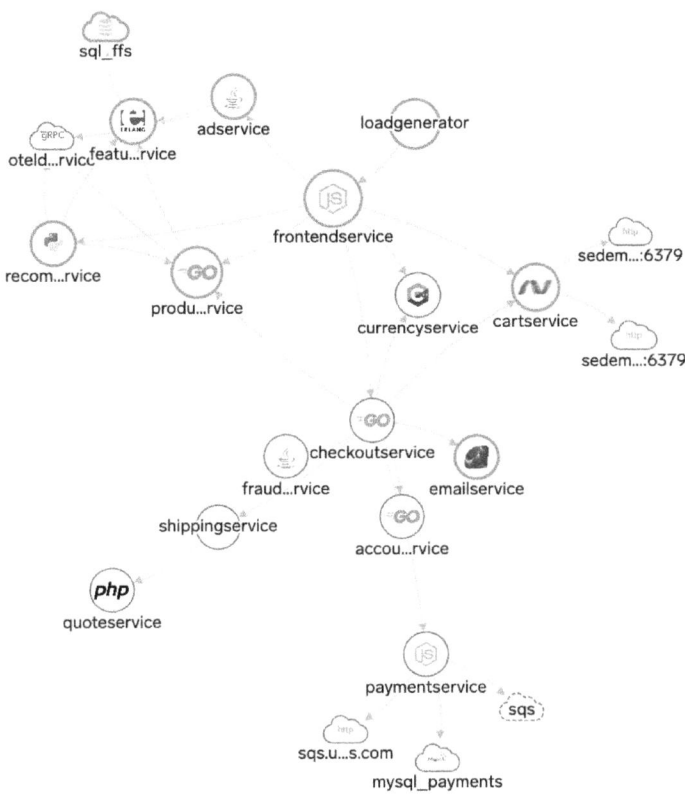

Figure 1.7 – An example of an application with its constituent microservice components

The modern architecture of Sumo Logic

So, how does a platform such as Sumo Logic deliver so many different services at scale? It was built from day one as a cloud-native, multi-tenant, microservices SaaS running on AWS. Its distributed architecture elastically scales up (and down) on demand, spinning up additional compute and networking as ingestion or query load rises, while maintaining resiliency and fault tolerance across the fleet. Behind the scenes, a modular design (dozens of independent microservices) lets Sumo ship frequent updates with minimal downtime, which is crucial for always-on security and observability workloads. To put the massive scale into perspective, Sumo Logic has over 2,000 customers worldwide with 175,000+ active users that use the platform to analyze 3.5 exabytes of data (3+ quadrillion records) and deliver tens of millions of real-time insights daily.

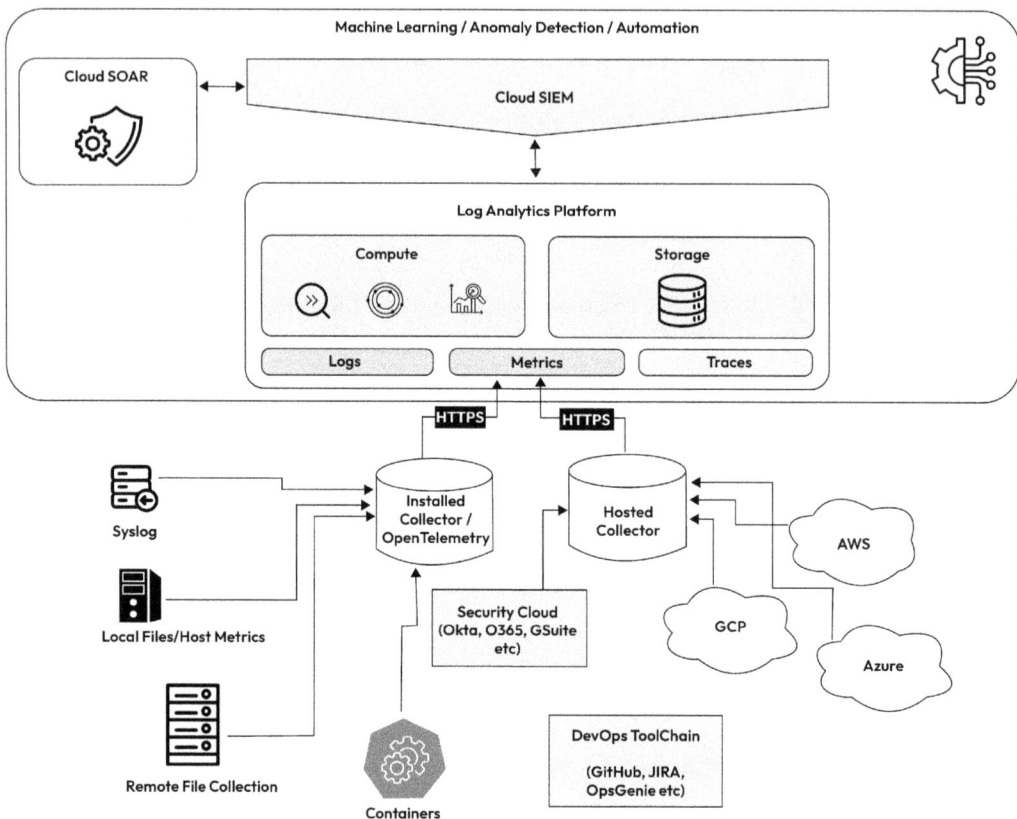

Figure 1.8 – Sumo Logic's modern, scalable, and agile architecture

This design allows customers to analyze data—whether through queries, dashboards, or monitors—at high speed, while storing massive volumes of logs cost-effectively in S3. It truly delivers the best of both worlds, performance and affordability, without the need for complex data tiering. However, for organizations that want additional cost optimization, Sumo Logic also supports tiering between frequently and infrequently accessed data, giving customers the flexibility to balance cost and performance, especially when scan-based pricing isn't the ideal model.

Summary

In this chapter, we've highlighted what Sumo Logic is and where it has come from as a technology.

We covered, briefly, some of the key and commonly occurring challenges for businesses in our modern age, such as digital transformation and complexity, and then moved on to how Sumo Logic has evolved over the years and the types of features it has incorporated to help address these problems.

In the next chapter, we'll take a look at the DevSecOps concept and philosophy, including why it's so integral to any business and cybersecurity strategy, and why we even label Sumo Logic as a *DevSecOps platform* to begin with. To make DevSecOps work, teams need the right technology to support not only technical processes but also the wider business. We'll cover not only these wider business elements in *Chapter 2, The Role of DevSecOps in Modern Security* but also why, with its modern architecture and capabilities, Sumo Logic is perfectly positioned for this.

Get this book's PDF version and more

Scan the QR code (or go to `packtpub.com/unlock`). Search for this book by name, confirm the edition, and then follow the steps on the page.

Note: Keep your invoice handy. Purchases made directly from Packt don't require an invoice.

2

The Role of DevSecOps

in Modern Security

In this chapter, the goal is to introduce you not only to *why* DevSecOps matters and the philosophy behind it, but also *how* to actually operationalize it with Sumo Logic at the center of your workflow. You may already be familiar with the term *DevSecOps*, but it remains surprisingly nebulous for many organizations. Even when teams conceptually *understand* it, they often struggle to approach it in a systematic way or extract meaningful business value from it.

DevSecOps is the practice of embedding security directly into the software development and operations process instead of treating it as a separate, last-minute step. It means building, testing, monitoring, and securing applications continuously so vulnerabilities are caught early and fixed faster.

There are a few challenges that we will be discussing in this chapter, such as the technology shift. Implementing DevSecOps requires modern tooling and automation platforms that support continuous delivery, continuous monitoring, and integrated security feedback loops. This represents a significant departure from how traditional operations teams have worked for the last two decades.

Further, new processes and governance structures must be codified to reinforce the new collaborative dynamic between development, security, and operations. This includes the use of shared runbooks, unified observability practices, and open communication channels across technical and management teams. Teams often need clear justification for why these changes matter. Shifting responsibilities left, adopting shared ownership models, and embracing rapid iteration can feel uncomfortable without strong leadership, measurable outcomes, and the right incentives.

This chapter will discuss how you can go about starting to make the transition to a modern, agile way of operating and meet the requirements necessary by using Sumo Logic, because, as mentioned in the previous chapter, Sumo Logic is a DevSecOps platform and naturally facilitates this transition for businesses and teams.

The following topics will be covered in this chapter:

- Definition and principles of DevSecOps
- Why DevSecOps matters and what happens when it's missing

Definition and principles of DevSecOps

DevSecOps is an evolution of **DevOps**. At its core, DevOps is a set of principles and cultural practices that help organizations embrace agility, continuous improvement, and shared ownership across development and operations. These principles, rooted in the *Agile Manifesto*, include the following[1]:

- Deliver usable, working software on a frequent and predictable cadence, ideally every few weeks, and preferably on the shortest cycle that still maintains quality
- Ensure that business stakeholders and development teams collaborate continuously, working together daily throughout the project
- Regularly pause to evaluate how the team can improve, then adjust processes and behaviors to become more effective

The *Agile Manifesto* marked the starting point as a recognition that the traditional, heavy, linear way of building software was too slow, too siloed, and too brittle for modern business needs. DevSecOps extends DevOps by making security a first-class citizen within this agile, iterative ecosystem.

However, it's important to acknowledge that there is no single, universally accepted definition of DevSecOps. Different organizations interpret it differently depending on their maturity, tooling, regulatory needs, and organizational culture. That said, a practical and modern definition looks something like this:

DevSecOps is a set of cultural principles, technical practices, and shared responsibilities that integrate security into every phase of the software development life cycle (SDLC), from design to development, deployment, and ongoing operations, all while preserving the speed, collaboration, and agility that DevOps enables.

> To benefit from this book, you don't need to know about the SDLC or have applications within your environment that you own.

What has also made DevSecOps difficult to apply universally is that several limiting factors have historically held organizations back. Until recently, most tooling wasn't capable of supporting a true DevSecOps operating model. Core capabilities such as **continuous security testing**, **automated policy enforcement**, **scalable observability**, and **real-time risk scoring** simply weren't accessible or integrated enough to be practical.

Additionally, DevSecOps requires cultural and organizational change. Many teams are entrenched in legacy processes and traditional "this is how we've always done it" workflows. Resistance to change, unclear ownership boundaries, and siloed communication channels make cross-functional collaboration difficult—yet this collaboration is foundational to DevSecOps success.

Another factor is the fragmented and reactive nature of toolchains. Most companies have accumulated a patchwork of open source and commercial tools over time, often purchased reactively in response to short-term issues. These disconnected stacks create data silos, duplicated effort, inconsistent visibility, and operational friction, making it hard to implement cohesive DevSecOps practices.

> Historically, organizations lacked the telemetry and frameworks needed to quantify DevSecOps effectiveness. This is partly a technology challenge, but also a strategic one: success requires measurable security and delivery outcomes. We'll explore this in more detail in *Chapter 3, Measuring Security Outcomes and Performance*.

Thus, the key objective of DevSecOps is to integrate security proactively into every aspect of the software delivery and operations process while maintaining openness and transparency with internal teams, customers, and stakeholders.

> Although it may sound counterintuitive to some, stronger security is only possible when everyone in the organization works together. Security cannot be the sole responsibility of the security team, nor can it be treated as something that is bolted on at the end.

Security must be a shared commitment across engineering, operations, product, and leadership. This philosophy aligns fully with the mission of Sumo Logic and the organizations that rely on it.

Overview of the six DevSecOps principles

Let's take a look at the six main principles of DevSecOps in detail, with a bonus one at the end.

Principle 1: Shift left security with Security as Code

In the military, the concept of "getting left of bang" refers to taking proactive measures to prevent an attack or incident before it occurs. On a timeline of events, *bang* represents the critical incident, and moving left means anticipating threats, detecting early warning signals, and taking action long before the situation becomes catastrophic.

In the context of DevSecOps, shifting left is a direct parallel. It means integrating security measures at the earliest possible stages of the SDLC rather than waiting until the code is written or the application is already running in production. By introducing security during design, coding, and testing, teams can identify vulnerabilities before they mature into real risks. This approach reflects the same prevention-first mindset as *getting left of bang* and requires strong collaboration across engineering teams to truly succeed.

However, shifting left is not only a cultural or process-oriented change. It also requires an architectural approach that makes security both scalable and repeatable. This is where Security as Code becomes essential. Historically, security was often treated as a final checkpoint before deployment, which created bottlenecks and delayed releases. Modern development cycles move far too quickly for manual review gates. To embed security early in a practical and sustainable way, organizations must codify their security controls, policies, and checks so they can run automatically on every commit, build, and deployment.

Security as Code: preparing for automation

Security as Code is the practice of codifying security controls, policies, and checks directly into your development processes. This includes writing security guardrails as configuration files, **Infrastructure as Code (IaC)**, policy-as-code frameworks, automated security tests, and more.

By treating security controls like any other piece of code—version-controlled, peer-reviewed, and automatically tested—teams can dramatically improve consistency and reduce human error. Let's take a look at some different patterns and how they can bring together a continuous security pipeline.

Infrastructure as Code

IaC allows teams to define cloud resources in version-controlled templates rather than through manual configuration. Tools such as Terraform and CloudFormation make it possible to enforce secure defaults, apply consistent configuration standards, and automate the deployment of entire environments. This reduces human error, eliminates configuration drift, and ensures that security, operations, and development teams all work from the same validated infrastructure patterns. IaC also supports automated scanning and policy checks, allowing security to be verified before changes ever reach production.

As organizations expand usage of AI agents to generate, review, and optimize infrastructure definitions, having everything expressed as code becomes even more valuable. AI agents can only reason about configurations that are structured, reproducible, and machine-readable. IaC provides the foundation for this automation, allowing AI systems to propose secure patterns, identify misconfigurations, or validate compliance much faster than manual review processes.

Policy and Access Control as Code

It might be surprising, but many organizations still manage access rules and compliance requirements using spreadsheets or ad-hoc documents. This creates blind spots, makes audits painful, and leads to inconsistent enforcement across environments. A modern DevSecOps approach treats both policy and Access Control as Code. While these concepts are different, they work best when used together.

Policy as Code tools, such as **Open Policy Agent (OPA)** and Cerbos, allow teams to express business and security rules in a structured, testable, machine-readable format. These rules might define who can deploy to production, which configurations are allowed in Kubernetes, or what conditions must be met before an infrastructure change is approved. Policy as Code provides the logic that governs how systems should behave.

Access control managed as code works at a different layer. Tools such as Terraform IAM modules or AWS Identity Center allow teams to define identities, roles, and permissions through version-controlled configuration. This ensures that access is consistent across environments and fully auditable. When identities and permissions are expressed as code, changes are reviewed, tracked, and validated just like any other development change.

Together, these two disciplines create a stronger and more predictable security model. Policy as Code defines the rules for what is allowed. Access Control as Code defines who is allowed to do it. When both are codified, organizations gain traceability, automated enforcement, reproducible environments, and a single governance model shared across development, operations, and security teams. This combination also improves collaboration because decisions are transparent, reviewable, and enforced consistently across the entire stack.

Continuous validation

The security checks we codify must be validated continuously through automated testing and rapid feedback loops. We will explore this more in *Principle 4*, but the foundation starts here. Modern teams rely on static analysis, configuration scanners, secrets detection, and compliance tests that run automatically inside development workflows. When these checks execute on every commit, build, or infrastructure change, security issues are caught early, and shift left becomes real.

AI is now strengthening this process even further. New AI agents, such as AWS's Security Agent and DevOps Agent, can automatically review code, analyze configurations, detect insecure patterns, and recommend or even generate fixes before the code reaches production. These agents operate directly within the SDLC, performing many of the validation steps that previously required manual review. By combining codified security checks with AI-driven analysis, organizations gain continuous validation that is both scalable and highly accurate.

That's how we shift left!

The role of Sumo Logic

Sumo Logic supports the shift-left approach and the practice of Security as Code in several important ways.

First, the platform is built API-first, which allows nearly every configuration, security control, and operational component to be automated through IaC workflows. The official Terraform provider[1] makes it possible to define collectors, data routing, parsing, enrichment, insights, alerts, dashboards, and role-based access directly in code. This helps teams place their monitoring and security guardrails alongside the same version-controlled infrastructure that powers their applications.

Sumo Logic also becomes part of the early development feedback loop by ingesting telemetry from build pipelines, code repositories, infrastructure provisioning tools, and security scanners. This early visibility allows teams to identify issues long before they reach production. Developers can trace problems back to specific commits, pipeline stages, or configuration files, which dramatically shortens the remediation cycle.

AI is beginning to expand these capabilities even further. Sumo Logic's Dojo AI initiative introduces agents that can help analyze logs, generate queries, surface anomalies, and support investigations automatically. The upcoming **Model Context Protocol (MCP)** server deepens this integration by allowing developers to interact with Sumo Logic directly from their IDE of choice. Through natural language, developers can ask for recent error logs, understand the root cause of a failing build, or request a suggested query to validate a hypothesis, all without leaving their development environment.

The result here is that teams can catch issues earlier, remediate faster, and continuously improve their security posture, all while moving at the speed of modern development. Shifting left is about changing when security happens. Security as code is changing when it happens. Working together, they give teams the power to make security a natural and automated part of their daily operations.

Principle 2: Continuous monitoring and continuous deployment

In any modern DevSecOps program, visibility is non-negotiable.

Continuous monitoring and **continuous deployment** are tightly coupled principles that create a fast feedback loop across the entire SDLC. Together, they enable teams to move quickly, deploy safely, and respond rapidly to security or operational issues.

Modern systems are complex, distributed, and dynamic. Whether you're running in the cloud, in containers, or on hybrid infrastructure, things are always changing. This only adds to the architectural and data complexity that modern businesses face. Continuous monitoring gives teams real-time awareness of what's happening in their environment. We're not just collecting logs and metrics for compliance; it's about enabling rapid detection of issues, understanding user behavior, and ensuring system health.

From a security perspective, continuous monitoring helps detect the following:

- Misconfigurations introduced during deployment
- Suspicious user activity or privilege escalation
- Vulnerabilities in dependencies or infrastructure drift
- Anomalies in network, application, or API traffic

On the other side of the loop is **continuous deployment**—the practice of shipping small, incremental changes frequently and reliably. To do this safely, teams need high trust in their monitoring systems. Without monitoring, continuous deployment becomes reckless.

The role of Sumo Logic

Sumo Logic is built for this type of continuous feedback loop. Due to its nature as a centralized platform for logs, metrics, and traces, the platform helps organizations build the real-time visibility required for both continuous monitoring and continuous deployment. It allows out-of-the-box integration with tools across the SDLC, such as **GitHub**, **Jira**, **Jenkins**, **Bitbucket**, **PagerDuty**, **OpsGenie**, and more.

Teams can track key DevOps metrics such as **DevOps Research and Assessment** (**DORA**) metrics (deployment frequency, lead time, change failure rate, mean time to repair (MTTR)), correlate build and deployment events with infrastructure and application performance, monitor user activity and system behavior in real time, and detect anomalies automatically using built-in machine learning.

Figure 2.1 shows an example of a development and delivery dashboard available out of the box within Sumo Logic, giving teams immediate insight into how well they are delivering and where improvements can be made:

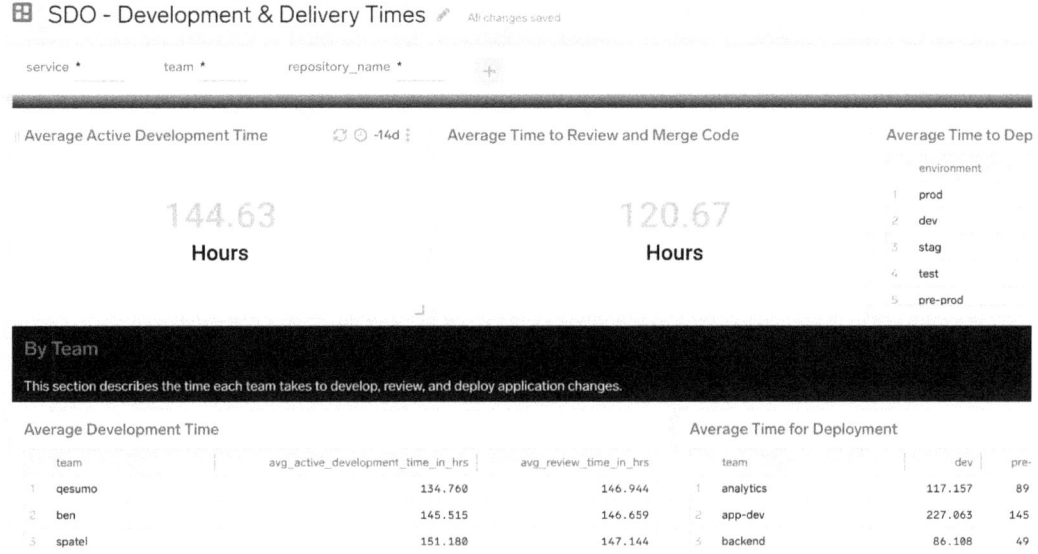

Figure 2.1 – An out-of-the-box dashboard in Sumo Logic that tracks development metrics

Continuous monitoring and deployment are the engine of modern DevSecOps, enabling teams to move fast without losing sight of security, reliability, or performance. How do we make this engine run as smoothly as possible? By making this everyone's business, which means collaboration is paramount.

Principle 3: Collaboration and shared responsibility

Tools are only one building block of DevSecOps; another is *culture*. No amount of automation or monitoring will succeed if teams work in isolation. Security, development, and operations teams must work together, not just at handoff points, but throughout the entire software life cycle. This is what collaboration and shared responsibility are all about. Those silos need to come crashing down!

Historically, security was seen as "somebody else's job." Developers built features. Operations teams ran the infrastructure. Security swooped in late in the process to raise concerns, and were (even now are) often seen as blockers rather than enablers. DevSecOps completely flips this old way of thinking on its head.

There is no need to "swoop in" anymore. If integrated earlier in the process, security becomes a shared responsibility embedded into daily work and owned by everyone. As we'll see, introducing security earlier into the process does the opposite of blocking everything. It opens communication between teams and lets feedback flow freely without blame (things indeed get heated when it comes to making sure that code is secure, released quickly, and keeps the business running).

The role of Sumo Logic and a unified platform

Technology can grease the wheels here, so to speak, by creating a *shared source of truth*. Sumo Logic enables this collaboration by bringing together data from across the business—application logs, infrastructure metrics, security events, user activity, and more—into a single platform.

When everyone is looking at the same data, the following happens:

- Conversations change from "Whose problem is this?" to "How do we fix this together?"
- Security becomes more accessible as developers see how their code behaves in production
- Operations teams gain visibility into security events and compliance data
- Security teams can contextualize risks and map to real operational impact

Ultimately, collaboration and shared responsibility are about trust, communication, and shared goals. Sumo Logic doesn't create a DevSecOps culture, but it removes friction, enabling teams to work better together. I'll leave you with this: security can no longer be a separate department at the edge of the organization. In a DevSecOps world, security is part of how teams build, ship, and operate software together.

Principle 4: Automated security testing

Once your security processes and controls are codified, and teams are collaborating effectively and sharing responsibility for security, the next natural step is automation. We need to scale all this goodness across the organization and validate continuously.

Manual security testing doesn't scale in modern environments because releases happen too fast, code changes daily, and infrastructure evolves constantly. That's why automated security testing is a cornerstone of DevSecOps.

Automated security testing is a continuous practice embedded into the software delivery pipeline that checks every commit, build, and deployment for vulnerabilities. We have one goal, which is to make this testing as routine and invisible as unit testing, happening automatically every time. Let's look at some approaches that facilitate this goal:

- **Static application security testing (SAST)**: Scanning code before execution to catch insecure functions and logic flaws early is like a little grammar checker for your code.
- **Dynamic application security testing (DAST)**: These are tests that run applications externally, simulating real attack behavior. You might have penetration testers doing their thing, but this is like a pentester checking the public-facing elements of your application from the outside.
- **Interactive application security testing (IAST)**: This approach observes applications during runtime and combines static and dynamic insights. Imagine a security camera checking on the internals of your app as it's being used or tested.
- **Software composition analysis (SCA)**: Quite straightforward but always useful, SCA detects vulnerable third-party dependencies in your build. A fantastic example was the Log4Shell, where a small logging library called Apache Log4j allowed a remote code execution with a single line of text. The impact was huge, and SCA would've picked up the vulnerable components.

When automated within CI/CD pipelines, these tests create a continuous feedback loop. Vulnerabilities are identified early, prioritized quickly, and rarely reach production, which means faster and cheaper fixes, which everyone loves.

Continuous assurance

Automated testing is about more than speed, it's also about consistency and repeatability. Not many people want to do this manually anymore; it is error-prone and takes up valuable time. An often-forgotten benefit of automation is that it provides clear metrics that drive improvement. This is key to DevSecOps, as we'll see in *Chapter 3*, and there are a number of integration capabilities that support this.

For example, let's take GitHub Actions. Sumo Logic has out-of-the-box integrations for GitHub, as well as similar sources such as Jenkins and GitLab CI, to give you views across activity around your code scanning, as in this dashboard:

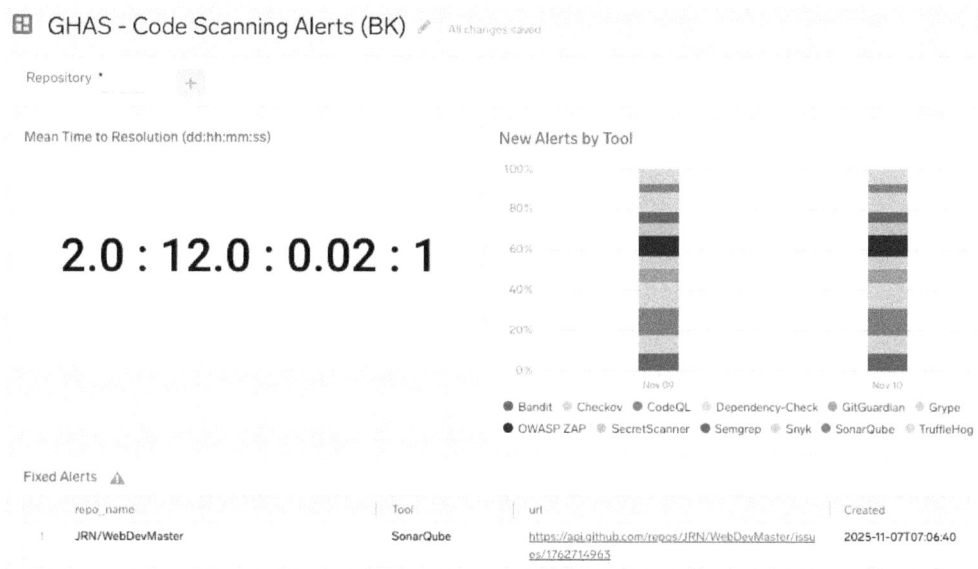

Figure 2.2 – Code scanning alerts to have a security lens on your pipeline earlier

This type of output highlights alerts raised by these code scanning tools in one single location, and it's possible to layer automation on top in Sumo Logic to respond in various ways. What this does is shift security teams from the *gatekeepers* in their traditional role to *enablers*, working closely with development teams before things escalate.

The role of Sumo Logic

While Sumo Logic isn't a security testing tool itself, it plays a critical role in helping teams operationalize and contextualize security testing results. Sumo Logic can start helping by ingesting this type of data into the same place as the rest of your data, and after which you can unlock the following benefits:

- **Correlation**: Build pipelines, deployment events, production telemetry, and application testing results. Having sight across all of this in one place means nothing is missed
- **Visualization**: Track visual anomalies or status/health monitors with the help of dashboards.
- **Automation**: Use Sumo Logic's automation service (more on this in *Chapter 11*) to automate response workflows, for example, creating tickets, notifying teams, and triggering playbooks.

The goal here is to turn static testing into *actionable intelligence*, where we can view this data alongside infrastructure metrics, user activity, and other telemetry. This provides incredible context; imagine your CI/CD pipeline events correlated with runtime metrics from your applications and infrastructure, with access to user behavior and security views.

Principle 5: Compliance automation and vulnerability tracking

As systems scale, so does complexity, and with that complexity comes risk.

In modern environments, managing compliance and tracking vulnerabilities manually is not only inefficient; it's also impossible. I remember working with a large organization that was using spreadsheets for its vulnerability tracking and security posture, full of macros and colors. Their remediation time for *high-risk* vulnerabilities was over six months! That's why compliance automation and vulnerability tracking are foundational to a mature DevSecOps program. If you happen to be in an industry that has tighter regulations, such as the financial services industry or the health and medical fields, then even more so! And things get even more stressful.

Vulnerability tracking at scale

Compliance automation means continuously checking your environments for misconfigurations, insecure settings, or violations of internal security policies and doing it *proactively*. This means using tools such as **Cloud/Kubernetes Security Posture Management** (**C/KSPM**) or other vulnerability management tools that inspect IaC, container configurations, and more. What are the benefits of doing this?

- Reduce audit overhead
- Catch risks before they escalate
- Help teams enforce baseline standards across rapidly changing systems

Capturing all of these compliance events and vulnerabilities at scale cannot be done without central visibility. You need fast correlation with an asset inventory to aid in understanding context.

The role of Sumo Logic

While Sumo Logic does not have a full-blown CSPM capability, it is…CSPM-esque. When ingesting data from your cloud environments into Sumo Logic, it's possible to combine log analytics with anomaly detection and an automation service working side by side to ensure misconfigurations are caught and remedied as soon as possible.

Integrating with third-party tools such as Qualys VMDR provides a cloud security, compliance, and vulnerability management solution across your IT infrastructure. *Figure 2.3* is an example of one such dashboard.

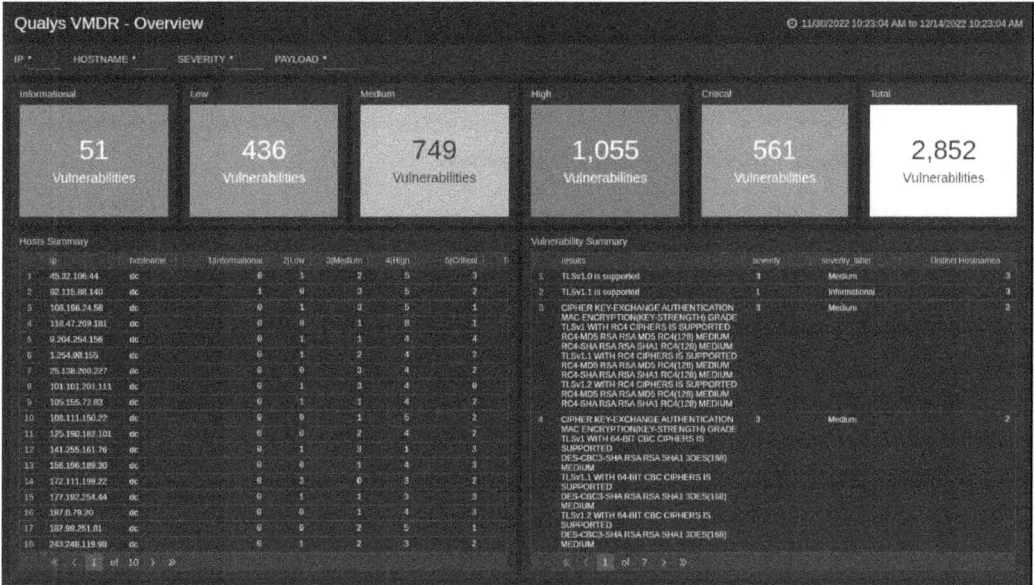

Figure 2.3 – A dashboard for Qualys VMDR that tracks vulnerabilities and feeds into compliance automation processes within Sumo Logic

This is one of a handful of views available to users and teams, ready to go.

Don't forget about key compliance frameworks such as NIST, PCI-DSS, and ISO 27001. The basis for all the monitoring required to comply with these standards is, you guessed it, logs. These logs tend to come from all your services, accounts, and devices, and when stored in the same place as all your other data, you get to hit multiple birds with one stone.

We can summarize this principle by saying compliance is no longer a periodic checklist; it's a continuous process. With the right visibility and automation in place, teams can track vulnerabilities, enforce standards, and respond before issues become incidents.

Principle 6: Security awareness and transparency

Transparency is achieved by seeing the complete picture behind any changes, modifications, or differences in machine code or user behavior in the ecosystem—in one word, **logs**. Logs capture the truth behind an event, and having logs as the underpinning foundation behind all of your data and how teams use it results in reduced time to comprehend what happens, as well as quicker troubleshooting and investigations.

Technology doesn't secure organizations, people do. Even with the best automation, testing, and monitoring in place, security ultimately depends on people making good decisions. That's why building security awareness, supported by transparency, is a core principle of DevSecOps. We need to create a culture where teams have access to the data they need to make these good decisions, and also turn mistakes into learning opportunities instead of a blame game. If you've ever worked in an operational team before, you know how unrealistic this might sound! With time, effort, and persistence, though, we can start to see a bigger and bigger shift.

Security awareness, as we've mentioned previously, is everyone's responsibility. It's not just about running annual phishing tests and compliance modules, even though they do help. Open communication is required to make this principle a core one; this is facilitated by a unified platform, and one key data type: logs.

In a DevSecOps world, logs become the ultimate source of truth. They capture **what happened**, **when it happened**, **who or what was responsible**, and **why it happened**.

The role of Sumo Logic

Sumo Logic enables this transparency by helping you ingest logs, metrics, and traces from across your environment and creating a unified view of systems, users, and activity. Dashboards give real-time visibility into security, operations, and user activity across all of this data, and this leads to quicker investigation, response, and learning time for your teams. What's behind the dashboards? A robust and universal querying language that was designed for data analytics. On top of this, everything is powered by machine learning and anomaly detection to capture anomalies and strange behaviors across all of your data sources.

Figure 2.4 is an example of a dashboard that is available out of the box for users who are bringing in a wide range of data sources—network, vulnerability, system, and user activity data in this case:

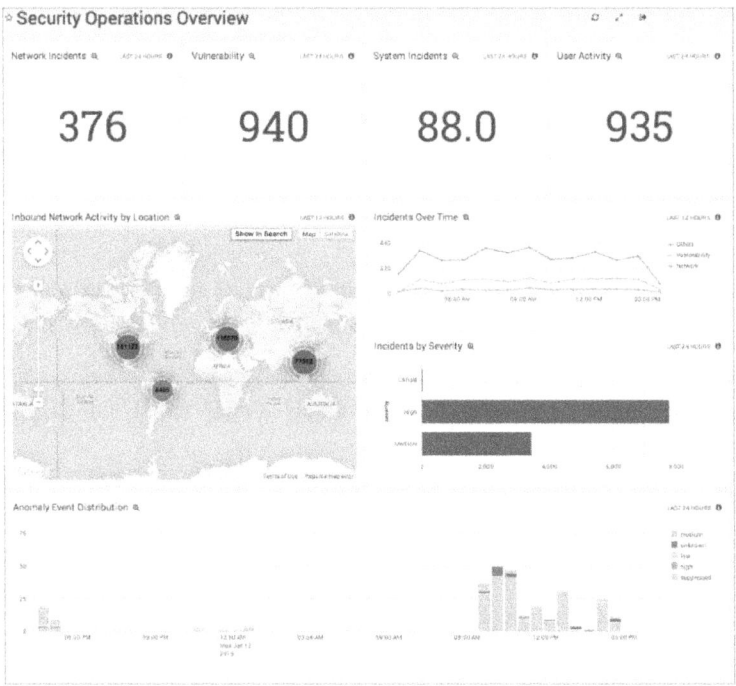

Figure 2.4 – A dashboard showcasing a security-focused overview of operations

Such a dashboard allows teams to bring a varied set of sources together and layer several key capabilities on top of each other for advanced insights. Let's look at these capabilities:

- **Comprehensive analytics**: Sumo Logic allows you to find any information you need from your structured and unstructured logs, and logs are the best source of context a business has

- **Anomaly detection**: Apply anomaly detection to all your logs, metrics, and traces to identify problems quicker, correlating it with, you guessed it, logs
- **Automated correlation and clustering of security events**: Any suspicious patterns of behavior seen across the environment are turned into insights

Now that the six principles of DevSecOps have been covered in detail, the only thing missing is a principle that binds all of them together. It is a central, atomic principle for cybersecurity and DevSecOps and is thus discussed after all six, next.

First-principle thinking for DevSecOps

All too often in cybersecurity, we focus on tools, tactics, and technology without asking the most important question: Why are we doing this? Are we buying another **endpoint detection response** (**EDR**) solution because it's needed or because it feels like progress? Are we building an in-house threat intelligence team because of business needs or fear of missing out?

This is where first-principle thinking is essential. I borrow here from Rick Howard's excellent work, *Cybersecurity First Principles*[2], where he distills the security mission down to its atomic core:

> *"Reduce the probability of material impact due to a cyber event over the next three years."*

What I love about this principle is that it's so clear and unmistakable in its intent. It's also measurable, as there is a clear before and after within a timeframe. Finally, and very importantly for the whole DevSecOps concept, is that it is universal. It can be understood and translated to many different teams, which opens up the floor to collaboration and transparency. This principle is *atomic*, meaning that the problem cannot be broken down any further than this. Every decision, strategy choice, or technology purchase and implementation should roll up into this atomic goal. It should be the North Star.

Now, in *Cybersecurity First Principles*, Rick Howard talks about DevSecOps as a *tactic* that achieves one of the five strategic pillars of meeting the first principle: **Zero Trust**, **Intrusion Kill Chain Prevention**, **Resilience**, **Risk Forecasting**, and **Automation** (DevSecOps here!)

Automation is the DevSecOps tactic and is directly related to what we've been talking about in this chapter so far. From a security perspective, automation is essential for SecOps teams to adapt to a changing threat landscape. It's fallen behind DevOps in that sense purely because developers and operational teams have been automating code deployments, server administration, and many other things since the early 2010s.

Google assigned the job of server management to its developers rather than the IT team, and **site reliability engineers** (**SREs**, as we know them today) were born[3], which heavily influenced the DevOps movement. The first team at Google was put together in 2003, but in actual fact, sysadmins have been using software and tools to automate operations stuff since the 1990s, but that's a conversation for another day. What's important is that from 2010 to 2015, there has been a lot of evolution in the DevOps space, which resulted in a tectonic shift that made operations teams leaner, more effective, and capable of making the best use of technology. Security teams, in comparison, were still searching for logs in a command line.

Security still has a lot of catching up to do. Embracing DevSecOps is key because it helps to bridge this gap not by radically changing how security teams think but by embedding them into the same operational and automation mindset that has driven DevOps success.

Throughout this book, we'll see how Sumo Logic can serve as the foundation for building this type of security program. The platform is not just a tool for collecting logs or generating dashboards; it's a platform that enables automation, visibility, and response at scale.

If the goal is to reduce the probability of material impact, then the practices we've explored so far, supported by Sumo Logic, become the tactics that help get us there.

Covering the principles so far puts us in the right headspace to approach a lot of the problems that we'll be tackling throughout the book by using Sumo Logic. The points we've just made feed into the next logical question: why is following these principles and addressing them important? Engaging in different approaches and trying something new is always difficult in cybersecurity, mainly because change can be costly and hard. However, if we know that every step we take reduces risk in a meaningful, measurable way, we're already doing better than most teams out there. Let's take a look at the exact reasons why it's worth you and your organization pursuing a DevSecOps approach.

Why DevSecOps matters and what happens when it's missing

We've taken a look at the underlying principles of DevSecOps and the first principle of cybersecurity, which lets us align what we're doing with the outcome. Let's now take a look at the importance of making security integral to operations across the business and even look at some practical scenarios to bring it together. It's important to consider that in the world we live in, with exabytes of data being generated every day and data becoming increasingly interconnected, the previous models of separate security, operational, and development teams are being challenged. The beauty of DevSecOps is how these operational teams are brought together into one symbiotic entity that allows for maximum versatility, creative thinking, and operational performance. There are four important parts to this, as described here:

- Security as a business enabler
- Risk mitigation and cost efficiency
- Speed without sacrificing security
- Building a security-first culture

Adapting to an evolving threat landscape

Even though DevSecOps encompasses all operational teams and their goals, this book is not only about security intelligence and building a security program with Sumo Logic, but the fact that DevOps is in a much better shape than security as a part of DevSecOps. Concepts such as IaC, containerization, and site reliability engineering have modernized operations a lot. Security is playing catch-up, and it's important to bring it into the progress that DevOps has made instead of creating something separate. Remember, *symbiotic* is what we're going for.

To bring DevSecOps to life, it's not enough to understand the principles, we have to understand why they matter to the business, and what happens when we get it wrong. The following sections dive into five areas where integrating security into the DevOps cycle drives real value, from enabling innovation to mitigating risk.

By the end of this chapter, I want us to be in a position where we understand how organizations used to operate before DevSecOps and how things transform after it's applied. I haven't thrown a table in here for a while, so let's look at one:

Phase	Without security integration	With DevSecOps
Planning and design	No threat modeling; isolated teams	Security engaged early; threat modeling applied
Development	No dependency scanning or secure coding checks	Automated SAST/DAST; dependency scanners
Testing	Late-stage fire drills for vulnerabilities	Security tests embedded in CI/CD
Deployment and monitoring	Reactive investigations; long MTTR	Real-time monitoring, anomaly detection, and fast response
Team collaboration	Blame games; siloed knowledge	Shared data, shared goals, and faster resolution

Table 2.1 – Organizations operating with and without DevSecOps

Now that we've set the scene, let's approach the integration of DevSecOps into your business.

Security as a business enabler

Injecting security into the wider business is no longer a technical necessity but also a strategic enabler for the business. Organizations that prioritize security can rapidly develop and iterate through product builds, innovate faster, and are more likely to gain a competitive edge. We will talk about this in a short while in the *Speed without sacrificing security* section.

This can be achieved by improving security processes at the beginning of the development cycle and introducing security tools that help with embracing the step toward security-conscious developers. By doing this, we can avoid costly breaches, build customer trust, and meet compliance requirements more effectively.

In a typical software development flow, more often than not, security is only really seen as a major consideration after development and during or after **Quality Assurance** (**QA**) and testing. *Figure 2.5* presents a typical workflow of the development process:

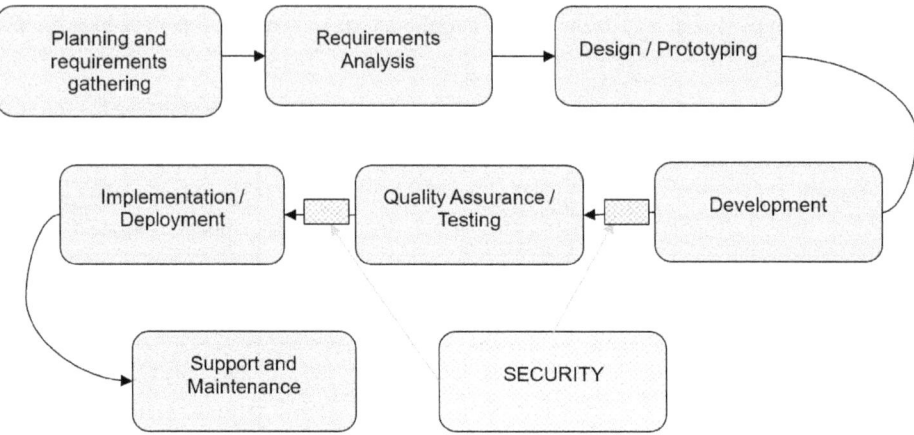

Figure 2.5 – A visualization of where security tends to be included in the development process

As shown in *Figure 2.5*, security activities (denoted by the checkered boxes) tend to be squeezed in toward the end of the development process, right before release, with teams desperately praying to the machine gods that there are no critical security flaws lurking in the code.

All the crucial early-stage planning, requirements gathering, design, and prototyping are left purely to the development team. This segregates security from adding value when it matters most and almost guarantees that issues will arise late in the process when they are the hardest (and most expensive) to fix.

If teams work in this way, and many teams do, they have to backtrack to cover any security holes in their applications and any testing that they've done. This causes a few issues:

- The application development process slows down or stops entirely while these issues are being resolved
- Tensions grow between the developers, the operations team, and security as these issues have to get ironed out to strict deadlines, with lots at stake
- Any issues encountered tend to be dealt with by duct-taping over problem areas without any consideration for long-term fixes because... no time!
- Teams that operate in this type of environment rarely have the luxury of time to create processes and focus on the longer-term, meaning that automation is never looked at, and barely anything improves

This is unsustainable. It causes arguments, complacency, and any positive change crumbles to a halt. Let's look at an example with a fictional scenario, where we learn about a development team that has learned the hard way about why it's important to shift left in security.

Example: SolarTech Corp

Consider a fictional company called SolarTech Corp. The development team here was working on a new customer-facing web portal designed to modernize the online shopping experience and integrate with a new loyalty rewards program. Like many organizations, security wasn't part of the early phases.

Security reviews only happened after development was "complete." Static analysis scans ran in QA. Threat modeling wasn't part of the process. When testing began, the security team uncovered multiple issues:

- Hardcoded API keys in the source code
- Misconfigured authentication flows vulnerable to bypass
- Outdated third-party libraries with critical vulnerabilities

Fixing these wasn't quick or easy. The development team had to unpick completed work, and security became the bottleneck. This led to deadlines slipping and frustrating everyone to no end.

The turning point

Leadership realized that change needed to happen. A few key changes were made, such as embedding security champions into dev teams from day one.

These security champions enabled threat modeling to happen during the initial planning stages of the application. On top of this, automated security tests (SAST/DAST) were brought into the CI/CD pipeline, and IaC checks became commonplace before app releases were deployed. Sumo Logic was used as a central space for visibility to aggregate a lot of this telemetry.

The result

By the time QA started on the next release, a few key points were noticed:

- Security issues were dramatically reduced
- Misconfigurations were caught in the pipeline, not in production
- Developers moved faster because they weren't constantly backtracking
- Security became a proactive partner, not a reactive bottleneck

Security didn't end up slowing them down; it made them faster and more resilient. With this example in mind, let's take a look at *Figure 2.6* to see what this could look like:

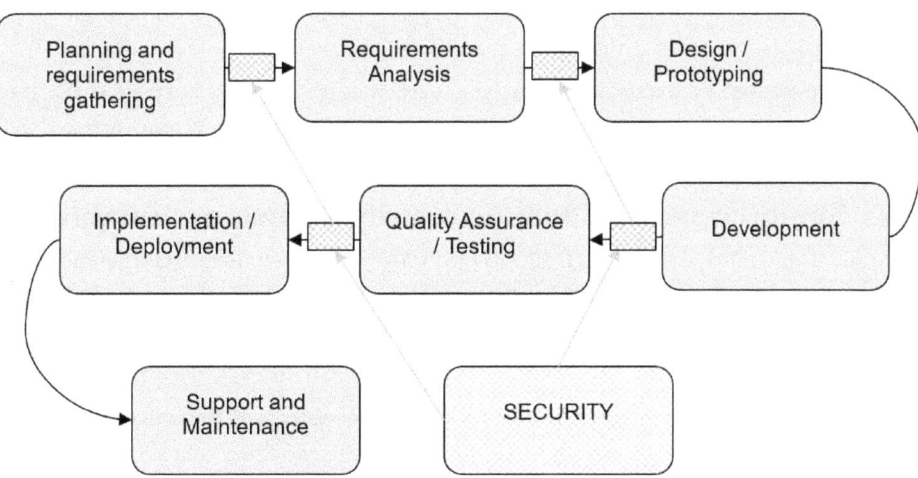

Figure 2.6 – A visualization of where security should be included in the development process

There are some key actions that can help you bridge the gap between *Figures 2.5* and *2.6* and get security coverage as effectively as possible. These are described here:

- **Introduce threat modeling for planning and requirements**: You can start to use open source tools such as OWASP Threat Dragon [4] to begin mapping threats and issues to various parts of the SDLC and help expose security requirements and user stories early. Dependency scanning tools, such as OWASP Dependency Check [5], can help ensure that you're staying on top of non-compliant or problematic dependencies in the code.

- **Integrate security checklists into the design/prototyping stage**: There are plenty of great resources for getting some solid, uniform security checklists for app development, starting with OWASP itself. We can use the OWASP **Application Security Verification Standard** (**ASVS**) [6] as a great starting point. IaC security tools, such as validation in Terraform [7], ensure that deployments of code and infrastructure conform to certain internal development and security standards.

- **Automate CI/CD testing**: Automate static and dynamic scans using various tools. OWASP has a great database of SAST and DAST tools that are open source or premium on their website [8]. For containerized environments, scan containers early and often during build steps.

- **Build cross-team awareness**: Get developers trained on security with entry-level training completely for free, with, once again, OWASP [9]. I find it's such an underutilized resource, and a lot of the content is accessible at no cost. Get your developers, DevOps, and SecOps teams collaborating more actively! Get them on calls, and discuss important areas of the business and phases of planning. Get security architects involved, too. There are lots of ways to bring these people to the table.

- **Incorporate a software bill of materials** (**SBOM**): Learn from the poor souls who had to go through the SolarWinds and Log4Shell attacks and use tools such as Syft or Trivy for containers, or CycloneDX and SPDX for compiled apps. Tie the output into CI/CD pipeline data, such as Github Actions, and you have a verifiable software inventory for every build. Use SCA tools to scan these SBOMs (this is starting to sound ridiculous, I know) and pull the output, usually JSON format, into Sumo Logic for correlation and alerting. Bosh. Less firefighting, easier compliance, and massively reduced risk.

A lot of these practices are achieved outside of Sumo Logic, and they are more of a business challenge than a technology challenge. You'll need to plan for training, enablement, and testing new processes and tools as part of it, but it'll be worth it.

How does Sumo Logic help make security a business enabler?

Even though Sumo Logic isn't a native SAST, DAST, or IAST tool, it can ingest metadata from these solutions, meaning that you can aggregate this information along with your pipeline build events (Jenkins, GitHub, Bitbucket, etc.). So, in addition to capturing DORA metrics, it's possible to align that with your security events coming into Sumo Logic to identify any suspicious or malicious behavior within your development processes.

The app in Sumo Logic that lets you integrate is called **Software Development Optimization** (**SDO**). It accelerates release velocity, improves reliability, and comprehensively monitors your software development pipelines with industry-leading metrics and actionable insights generated automatically from development tools such as Jira, GitHub, Jenkins, PagerDuty, Bitbucket, Opsgenie, and more. Here's an example from one of the DORA metrics dashboards shown as part of the SDO content that comes ready to use out of the box:

Figure 2.7 – A dashboard in Sumo Logic that looks at DORA metrics

Going back to our first principle—reduce the probability of material impact due to a cyber event over the next three years—we need to put ourselves into a position to reduce the chances that something will go wrong, and more importantly, reduce the probabilities of impact. We're looking at mitigating risks. We're going to cover the topic of mitigating risks with some real-world examples to help us put things in context and see where things go wrong so that we can use Sumo Logic to avoid making the same mistakes.

Risk mitigation and cost efficiency

When late-stage security fixes are identified and vulnerabilities are found post-release, it's a pain that no one wants to deal with. It impacts the following:

- Speed of development and re-release
- Cost of redeploying engineering effort
- Compliance efforts

It's crucial to integrate security into early-stage development to help identify pre-release vulnerabilities. The biggest reminder of this is the SolarWinds Orion breach of 2020[10]. It was huge, everywhere in the news, and rightfully so. A sophisticated adversary managed to breach the SolarWinds network around January 2019 [10], where a prolonged reconnaissance period led to attackers identifying key servers that would assist with the code deployment process.

This attack demonstrated the fact that security didn't have visibility across key areas within the SolarWinds estate. When Orion was first developed, it used a software build-management tool called ToolCity, which orchestrated the building of software by spinning up a bunch of **virtual machines** (**VMs**). If there was a failure during the build process, which is not an uncommon thing, a VM would be spun up that would contain a memory dump and a "snapshot" of everything during the build process. The adversaries realized that this existed and deployed a tiny malicious file on this machine that allowed them backdoor access into the environment, letting them return time and time again.

The investigators, a team from Mandiant, found this key bit of evidence and dubbed it *Sunspot*, but the lesson is that a company that doesn't have complete visibility of its entire environment and its assets like this will end up in an awkward situation. Even worse, an attacker could be dwelling somewhere already.

Now, the reason this was such a huge event is that it impacted around 18,000 customers, with the potential of affecting up to 33,000, based on various reports. These businesses had assets that were stolen, with further extortion in some cases, including a vast swathe of government and federal entities. The software was very popular and was used to connect to other parts of a network as it monitored services, helped to patch systems in bulk, and had a few other useful features. Attackers could leverage this to exponentially scale the accesses they had within different customers. These customers were compromised themselves, where assets were stolen, and further attacks and extortion took place. SolarWinds was just the epicenter of this global event, with tens of millions of dollars lost across all of these businesses.

This was a supply chain-driven attack, and the supply chain has become an incredibly dynamic attack vector since, with adversaries getting very creative around supply chains, different tech stacks, and communication technologies. Following DevSecOps principles can avoid scenarios like this , with organizations staying on top of versions and releases in development cycles. Sumo Logic helps with this by tracking all the metadata around these stages and where your applications are in line with those stages . This visibility gives all the operational teams the information they need to quickly see errors and pivot to the root cause to fix them.

While SolarWinds is the largest example in recent memory, there have been many others, including the breach of Codecov [11], where adversaries exploited the way that Codecov built and uploaded Docker images. Over 23,000 customers were affected. SolarWinds was a noteworthy attack due to the scale, method and impact of the breach. However, there are more recent events, such as the JetBrains TeamCity software supply chain attack[12]. The same team that conducted the SolarWinds breach targeted TeamCity, a CI/CD tool used by hundreds of thousands of developers to once again hit over 30,000 users of TeamCity. Someone didn't learn about the SolarWinds attack…oops.

How does Sumo Logic help mitigate risk in a cost-effective way?

If you look at SolarWinds, Codecov, DockerHub, and others, the root cause of the vulnerabilities lies in the fact that how applications and software are built has changed. There is more reliance on third parties, external providers, and other software as part of this process, and having sight of all these moving parts and how your developers are building their code is extremely important in mitigating the risk of attacks similar to those experienced by SolarWinds and Codecov. Sumo Logic exists to add visibility to the entire end-to-end flow, from CI/CD pipelines to release and all the monitoring and security efforts involved during and after this.

For example, you can use a dashboard as shown in *Figure 2.8* to monitor your pipeline, including any failures in deployment or errors in builds:

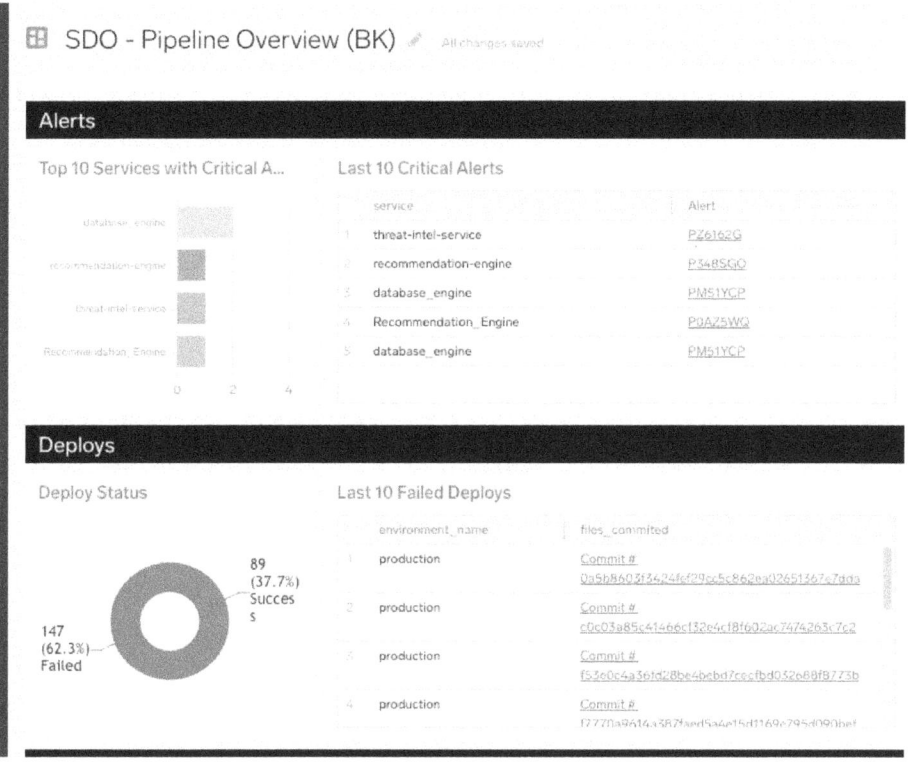

Figure 2.8 – A dashboard showing errors in deployment and code builds

This will help to keep track of any problems or failures early in the cycle, and they can be investigated quickly because, from here, we can pivot straight into the logs to find out why. Imagine if the SolarWinds Orion team could identify the build failure that caused the stranded VM to be created and linger in the system; they would have eliminated that attack vector as part of routine usage! This is what Sumo Logic is great at—improving the efficiency of the teams using it, driving the total cost of ownership down as tools are consolidated, and also helping to mitigate risks as they arise.

Speed without sacrificing security

Here's a common myth: if you keep placing security at each stage of the development process, it'll mean slower development. That's as wrong as thinking backups are optional. When done correctly, DevSecOps enables teams to move quickly without compromising security. This can be achieved by giving teams the ability to introduce the key concepts of **automation**, **continuous monitoring**, and **early testing** into their daily operating models.

Automation is a broad topic, but in this case, we're talking about automating the execution of different preventive and reactive testing to remain efficient and lean, in an attempt to reduce human error and inconsistency as much as possible. For example, imagine we identify suspicious behavior after receiving an alert about a developer pulling a library identified as *vulnerable*. We can automate the security response to that in Sumo Logic by suspending the user while we deal with the threat. On top of that, we could automate a vulnerability scan parallel to the preceding response. We'll talk about this some more in the following *Where does Sumo Logic help with increased speed of development?* section.

Continuous monitoring, as discussed earlier, turns noise into visibility. It gives you situational awareness because when a platform such as Sumo Logic ingests all those logs, metrics, and traces, patterns start to emerge, such as unusual API behavior, anomalous user activity, or infrastructure drift. It's how you spot early indicators of compromise, performance degradation, and a whole lot of other things before they turn into outages. Modern systems generate this firehose of data, and it makes the most sense to centralize it and have eyes on it all the time.

Finally, testing should be done often and early to stay on top of lapses in your security posture while developing applications. You can employ SAST and DAST tools out there, as well as developer best practices. The more you keep testing, the more data you feed into a platform such as Sumo Logic to help correlate with other sources in the end-to-end process, and the more likely it is that you'll identify something problematic early doors. Most importantly, testing early and often prevents testing after the fact, leading to reduced delays in launches and reduced threats identified in your applications. **Shift left!**

Where does Sumo Logic help with increased speed of development?

Sumo Logic will elevate your overall operational and security visibility by aggregating all of the preceding data sources and technologies in one place. It will provide you with a big magnifying glass that will let you zoom in on any inconsistency or issue across the beginning of your app development cycle, the CI/CD pipelines, and through to building, testing, and monitoring these applications. With all the context provided by logs, metrics, and traces in the same platform, it'll be easier to come to a resolution. Automation can be achieved across security and operational actions by leveraging Sumo Logic's automation service, with hundreds of integrations and the ability to create both simple and complex processes.

Next we'll look at AIOps and how Sumo Logic helps teams to align to this concept in a simplistic way.

AIOps

So, what is AIOps? The official definition given by Gartner is the following:

> *"AIOps combines big data and machine learning to automate IT operations processes, including event correlation, anomaly detection and causality determination."* [12]

I think the only thing missing from this definition is *advanced analytics*. A good way to make sense of all this big data is the ability to perform analytics on it for some end goal or to extract insights from it. If we were to visualize the AIOps loop for you, it consists of three steps. First comes **anomaly detection**, which requires you to have a mature solution that can learn your data, baseline it effectively, and help you find abnormalities. The next step is to find the root cause of the issue with the help of **log analytics** (not forgetting metrics and traces as invaluable context). With the help of a centralized data lake, operations teams have as much context as they need at their fingertips. Finally, we **automate** the response where possible and necessary to make teams more efficient with a flexible and versatile way of making this automation intuitive. These steps can be visualized like this:

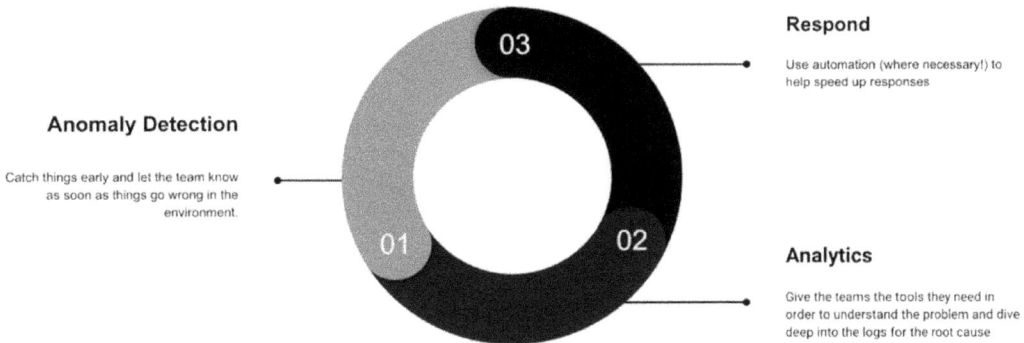

Figure 2.9 – The AIOps loop in three steps

AIOps helps teams find problems early and as quickly as possible with the discussed components. But how can you use Sumo Logic to help achieve AIOps? Let's take a look at each of these individual areas as part of the loop.

Step 1: Anomaly detection

Firstly, anomaly detection is built into Sumo Logic without you having to do much configuration to start using it. That's right: as long as your data is in the platform, you're able to apply machine learning operators to your data to start finding anomalies. There are two different ways in which we apply this **baselining**:

- Anomaly detection monitors
- Cloud SIEM **User Entity Behavior and Analytics (UEBA)** rules

These methods will be covered in greater detail in *Chapter 7, Metrics*, and *Chapter 9, Cloud SIEM*, but for now, here's a quick rundown.

Anomaly detection monitors allow you to create an event or behavior you're interested in. The platform learns about this behavior, and when it identifies activity that falls outside of thresholds that you can set, it will alert you. For example, a spike in the number of times a developer has pushed code to a certain repository. The algorithms used here can take concepts such as seasonality into consideration.

UEBA and machine learning rules in the cloud SIEM work in a similar, but more advanced way. Instead of learning about the baseline from the time you create a monitor, it will historically baseline your data (if you have the dataset in Sumo Logic) and apply anomaly detection to spot outliers.

While we cover the cloud SIEM later, let's focus on an AIOps scenario involving an anomaly monitor.

Let's say we have a monitor that is looking at anomalies in our cloud network traffic. We'll cover the monitor creation process in *Chapter 8, Alerting, Monitoring, and Visualizing Data*, but for now, we've isolated the behavior we want to monitor and just selected the option to get Sumo Logic to learn the baseline of activity automatically. This is done with algorithms that model the data for you, and this is all done with log data. As you can see in the following figure, it's also possible to use metrics for this:

Figure 2.10 – Choosing to monitor behavior with Sumo Logic's anomaly detection modeling

We're going to fast-forward to the triggering of this monitor, where we receive an alert that tells us an abnormality has been detected. In Sumo Logic, this alert can be sent wherever—Slack, Jira, Microsoft Teams, or any webhook—with any information you need and options to respond in different ways. Here is our alert in Slack:

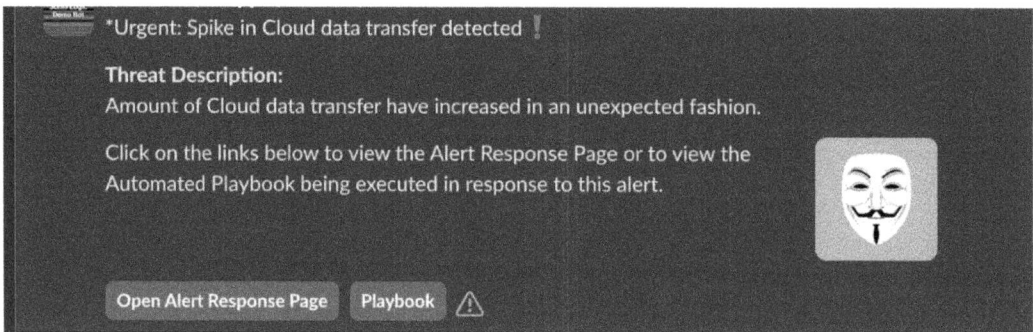

Figure 2.11 – Our Slack alert notifying us of the issue and giving some response options

If we click on **Open Alert Response Page**, we go to an area of the platform that helps the user understand the issue and provides some helpful context. Once again, we cover this in *Chapter 8*, but this leads us to *Step 2* of the AIOps loop, advanced analytics, where we try to hone in on the root cause.

Step 2: Advanced analytics

That brings us to the second step of the AIOps loop, advanced analytics powered by logs. Every view you're about to see originates from the same foundation, that is, structured logs continuously analyzed by Sumo Logic. Logs are what make anomaly detection possible because they're not just data; they're evidence.

Well, it's time to analyze, so let's get started! Our alert shows us this graphic, indicating a spike in traffic that was detected:

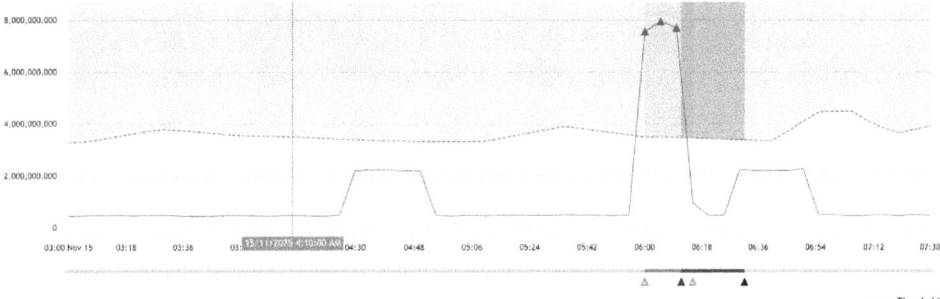

Figure 2.12 – An anomaly in our cloud network traffic has been detected by Sumo Logic

You'll notice the two blips on either side of this spike. These seem to be false positives because the anomaly detection algorithms used in Sumo Logic are able to dynamically adapt to nuances in your data, including seasonality. This means you avoid deviations from the norm that would typically trigger an anomaly. For example, if this spike happened every morning between 08:00 and 08:30, it would learn that this is normal behavior over time.

In terms of analytics, there are a range of options available. All of them are discussed in detail in *Chapter 8, Alerting, Monitoring, and Visualizing Data*, and these include querying your logs, metrics, and traces, looking at your data visually, being able to use pattern matching in your log data with an operator called logreduce, and comparing log events across time with logcompare. Additionally, from this **Alert Response** page, we can see related alerts and entities that are linked to this data. In this example, we've got a cloud network traffic dashboard that we can pivot into to identify some key information:

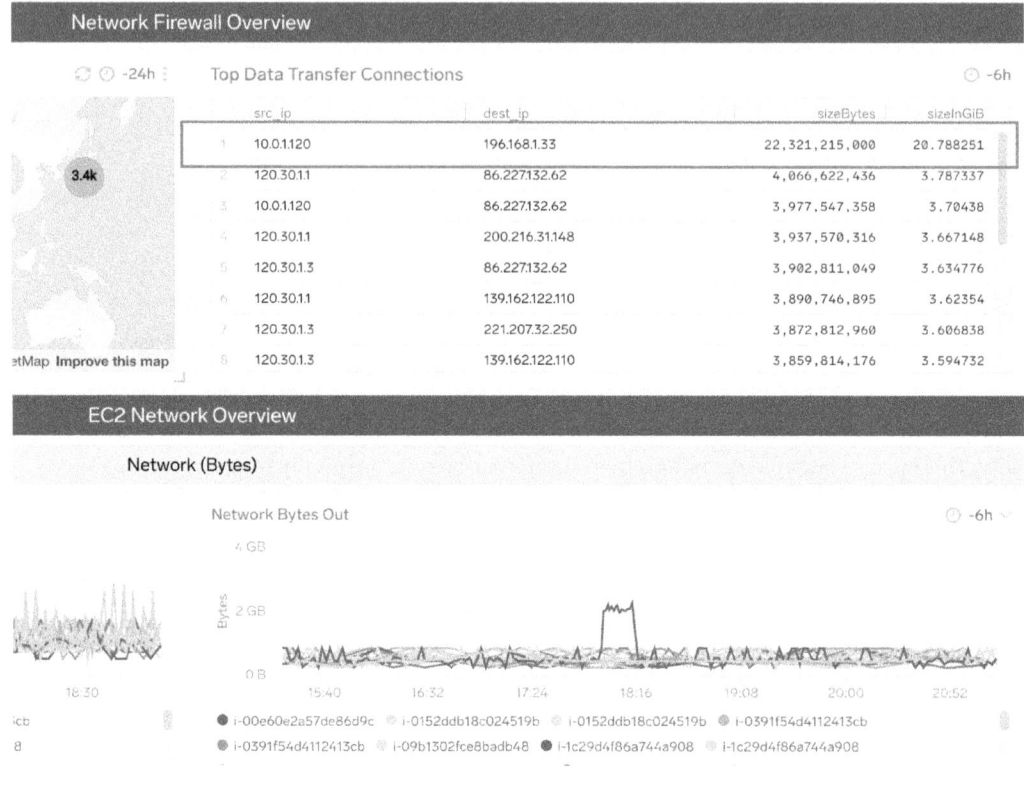

Figure 2.13 – We can open up a network dashboard related to this data from the Alert Response page

Instantly, we've been able to pivot into a graphical view that already has a breakdown of the highest traffic by IP. We can see the top entry is an IP address, **196.168.1.33**, that has transferred 20.7 GB of data in the last 6 hours compared to all the surrounding traffic, and immediately, we have our root cause. We can investigate this IP address further by just using it in a query:

Figure 2.14 – Looking for the IP address across our entire dataset

As Sumo Logic stores all your logs, metrics, and traces data in one place, you can search any term or entity across everything you have, which is great for correlating this information. Imagine not having to query your data from multiple places anymore! The text in *Figure 2.14* is quite small, but in the log message, it states the following:

Credentials created exclusively for an EC2 instance using instance role auto-updater-ec2-role have been used from external IP address 196.168.1.33

This isn't good news. We can investigate this case further, but at the very least, we should block this IP address while we look into it.

This takes us neatly to *Step 3* of the AIOps loop, response.

Step 3: Response

Response comes in many different forms. It can be based on the process, the severity of the event, or which entities are involved in the event, but one thing is true: being able to automate parts of a response in an intelligent way is the best way to remediate outages or threats. The problem is, not many teams are able to do this. It's due to a number of factors, such as being under-resourced, with no time to invest in automation. It could be a poor selection of tools that don't give the users the right usability.

Sumo Logic provides automation capabilities that are built into the platform, with no separate module to consider or any barriers to using it. It's just...there. Ready to help you take your team to the next level, whether you need to automate the blocking of an IP or a complicated sequence of activity. As part of our example, let's take a look at *Figure 2.15*, where we can see what playbooks are linked to our alert:

Figure 2.15 – The playbooks section of an alert, showing text and automated playbooks

As you can see, there is a way to manually define steps, which comes in handy when you want a structured process that anyone can read and access the steps to. This is handy as it is Markdown-based, which lets you add links to dashboards, like here, or add any other formatted information you need. Additionally, you can run an automated playbook, which can be seen at the bottom of this panel. In this specific scenario, we've got a playbook that does the following:

- Revokes the security group for an AWS inbound rule
- Alerts the SOC team on Slack

- Checks the IP address with an open source feed of information
- Creates a rule group to block the IP address

Figure 2.16 shows an AIOps loop in action with an example scenario:

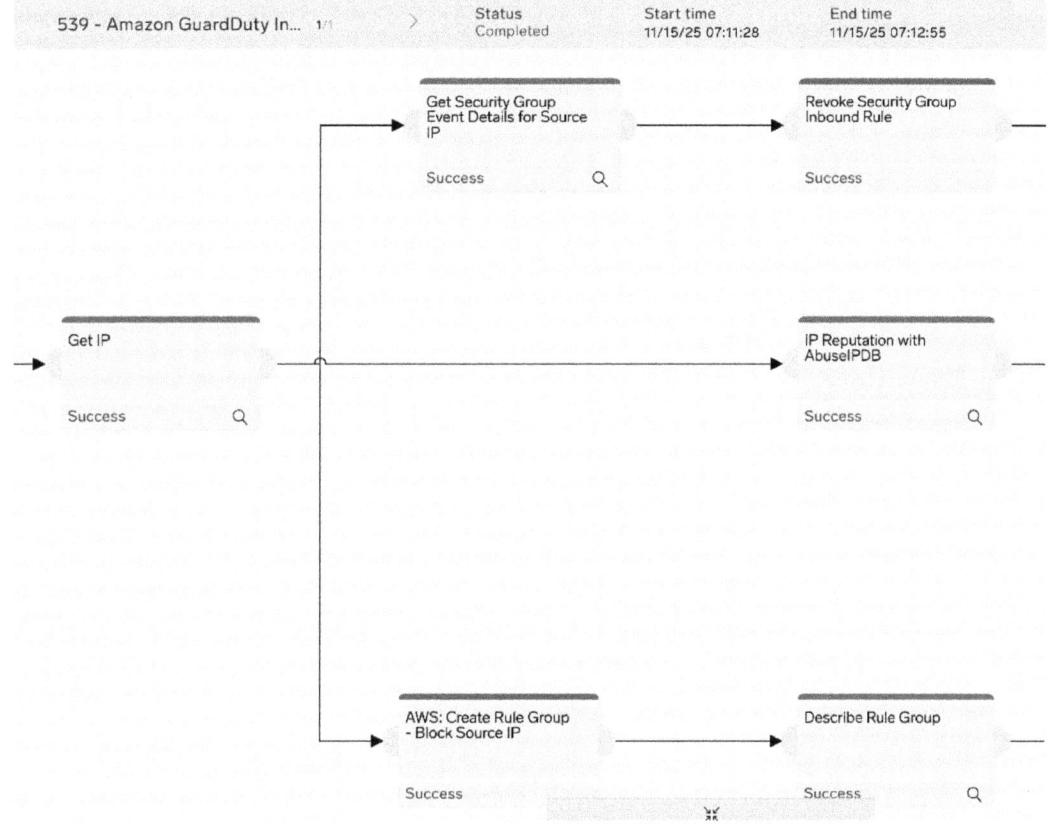

Figure 2.16 – The automated playbook example

Sumo Logic can apply this power of automation during the response process to all of your data, no matter where it has come from or what format it is in, making it incredibly easy to get started with and without the need to keep reviewing it and managing it.

Logs are the heartbeat of AIOps in Sumo Logic. They feed the anomalies, shape the entity relationships, and validate every log, metric, or trace you investigate. When you treat logs as your analytical foundation rather than a byproduct, you unlock true continuous intelligence. Tapping into AIOps in Sumo Logic has the potential to reduce downtime, improve speed and accuracy during incident response, and accelerate secure and compliant delivery of code. It is essential to any modern business operating in this landscape, whether across cloud-native or hybrid environments.

With AIOps covered, let's take a look at another crucial and arguably more difficult part of DevOps and DevSecOps: the culture.

Building a security-first culture

Implementing DevSecOps into your business is not just difficult because of the adjustments necessary from a technical perspective, but also because it requires a lot of *soft* changes across the teams. It's all about bringing teams together, bridging communication channels, and helping teams work on the same data to solve problems and resolve incidents. However, these softer cultural changes require quite a bit of planning and communication due to any number of things, such as biases, fear of change, skepticism, empire building, company politics, and other areas.

Nevertheless, there are a few steps you could take:

- Use management and internal channels to communicate about security issues and the steps being taken to drive security at an organizational level.
- Use metrics gathered from the security team to drive reporting (more on this in *Chapter 3, Measuring Security Outcomes and Performance*).
- Actively start to introduce technology and processes that impact your security posture. For example, a team could start by introducing a SAST tool into its process, then maybe expand and incorporate a DAST tool into the CI/CD pipeline. Changes like these are small but very impactful, and by doing this, the team will deliver results by catching errors early, identifying anomalies, and correlating results with security events.
Teams like tools that make their life easier, and unless they are absolutely in love with a particular technology, they will respect something that grants them more autonomy, flexibility, and speed. As users and teams learn of these enhancements, they start using them too, and you have this proliferation and increased adoption that ends up helping the business overall.
- Invest in security training for teams across the organization.
- Give team leads and practitioners who go above and beyond the power to make decisions around the security and DevOps capabilities that exist, and to take action where necessary.
- Start removing complexity where you can! As discussed in *Chapter 1* and at the start of this chapter, complexity is a big issue, and not only is it natural for things to get more complex, but sometimes processes can be over-engineered for no good reason. Sumo Logic is great at making things simple by having a single space for development, DevOps, and security data.
- Finally, eliminate silos and try to find a way to bring the typically disparate teams together to work on the same data and in the same place. We've just discussed AIOps in the previous section. These boundaries can start eroding by sharing visibility across your business data, which unlocks anomaly detection models to learn holistically across security, operations, and development data. This makes them even more powerful.

Where does Sumo Logic help?

When you ingest all your logs, metrics, and traces into the same platform and offer teams the opportunity to start using this data and tap into the surrounding context, teams start to see things and encounter situations that they're not used to. Let's cover a few examples I've personally encountered when working with different customers:

- **Scenario 1**: A user in the DevOps team, while checking the status of their Kubernetes containers, identifies a suspicious IP communicating with them. They run the IP on all the data in the instance and also cross-reference it with the high-fidelity threat intelligence feeds in Sumo Logic and see that it is linked to a threat actor group and has a high confidence rating. They then realize it's more than an operational issue, call a war room, and get the incident response team involved early. The result is quicker diagnosis and response. This would not have been possible before, as the teams would have been completely separate, and the process would have involved creating a ticket and taking up the SOC teams' time to investigate separately.

- **Scenario 2**: A member of the security team gets an insight in the SIEM tool that shows that an entity (a user from the dev team) has changed a few very important configurations on their AWS cloud environment, accessed a database with sensitive PII, and now data is leaving the firewall to an IP that is coming up as a hit on one of the threat intelligence feeds. The security analyst has access to all the data they need to run a complete investigation in one place without requiring any data from the dev team or communicating with them to arouse suspicion.

- **Scenario 3**: A developer is responding to an outage in the Kubernetes cluster and, after seeing the logs and metrics of the infrastructure correlated together, has run a query that separates normal logs from erroneous ones. They identify that the outage was due to the release of a new software version earlier that day. Someone in the DevOps team lets them know, but they're already aware of it and can work together to help resolve it.

Therefore, over time, as teams use the platform and realize they don't have to be siloed anymore, they can work with the same data, and it becomes much easier to do this cultural transition naturally instead of forcing it with tools that can't adapt to modern requirements. *Figure 2.17* is a visual representation of Sumo Logic and its ***monitor of monitors*** role.

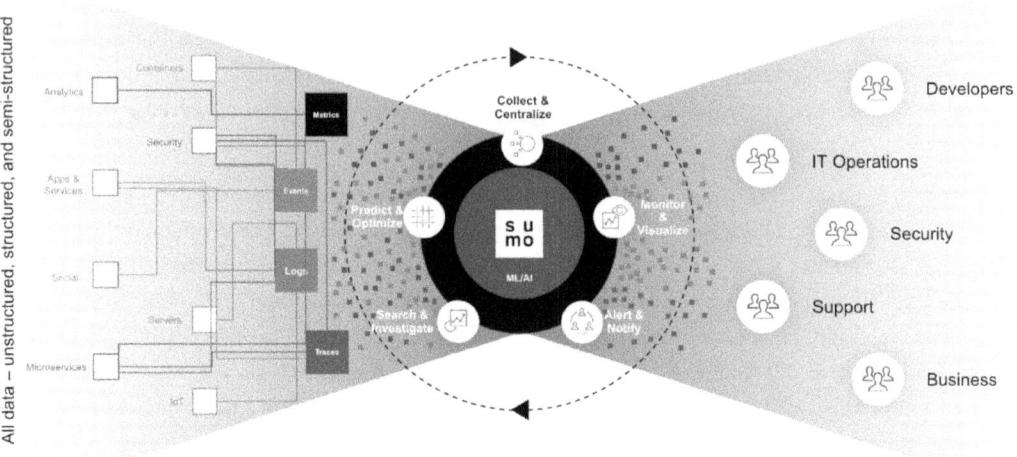

Figure 2.17 – A visual representation of the central role Sumo Logic plays in developing a security-first culture

Sumo Logic ends up at the heart of all operational activities and teams within a business because a lot of different data is sent there. This role naturally helps to start bringing teams together and working off the same sheet.

Adapting to an evolving threat landscape

Businesses have to adapt to one of the most actively evolving industries of all time: cybercrime. Criminals, from state-sponsored threat actor groups to ransomware groups, are dynamically changing their tactics daily based on what is working and what isn't. Based on this alone, integrating security into the wider business is extremely important. Breaches can obviously be financially damaging, with the average breach now costing $4.4m, as IBM reported in their 2025 Data Breach report [14], but they can also destroy trust in a brand and spell the demise of any business by, for example, wiping all the IP in a particularly malicious and destructive attack or releasing sensitive credentials publicly on a dark web forum or marketplace. Focusing on security allows for the identification of **zero-day attacks**, attacks that haven't been publicly seen before, supply chain attacks, which originate from communication pathways with suppliers, and other types of attacks and intrusions.

We live in a time where our businesses have sprawling technical ecosystems, covering multiple data islands [2].

> Note
>
> *Data islands* is a term coined by Rick Howard in his book that relates to the digital environments we now operate in: traditional data centers, mobile devices, cloud environments, and SaaS applications.

This means that the number of attack vectors available to an attacker has been the largest in history, and access to technology means that the innovation from attackers is constant and is also growing at the fastest rate it has ever grown.

Complete visibility across these data islands for businesses is no longer an optional strategy. It is a mandatory requirement not only for security but also for business operations. There are now too many digital elements within a business's services and technologies, so the impact of any outages is higher. User experience and customer experience are also extremely relevant, and the underlying hardware and software need to be running as reliably as possible to stop customers from going elsewhere or becoming unhappy that they can't order their clothes or favorite food on time!

Where does Sumo Logic help?

When working with Sumo Logic, you have complete visibility across your data islands, your security tools, your EDR tools, firewalls, zero-trust technology, **network/host intrusion detection systems** (**NIDSs/HIDSs**), cloud data, and so on. You also have access to excellent threat intelligence sources from day one. You can cross-reference all data across a feed built into the platform to quickly identify and verify whether strange, unknown, or unwanted indicators of compromise.

Let's take a look at the **Threat Intel Quick Analysis – IP** dashboard that comes out of the box. It summarizes any IP addresses that have been matched with the threat intelligence feed and brings back any curated context, such as the type of malware, stage in the kill chain, and any threat actor groups it's associated with. This is a fantastic resource because it can look across all your data sources simultaneously when cross-referencing against the feeds, as can be seen here:

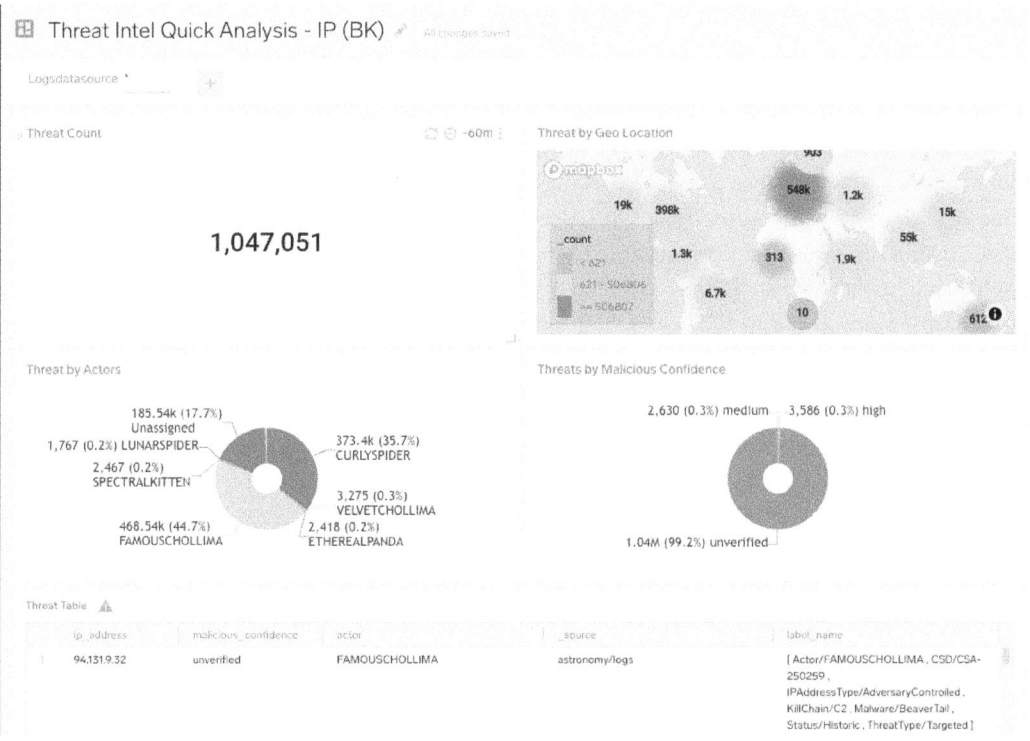

Figure 2.18 – A dashboard showing threat intelligence matches with data in the Sumo Logic across all of your data sources

The app provides these views across five different indicator of compromise (IOC) types:

- IP addresses
- URLs
- Domains
- Email addresses
- Hashes

This view relates to the IP address, and it adds a lot of value to both teams without threat intelligence, and those that have these capabilities in place. However, this is only one way of staying ahead of the evolving threat landscape. Another is to use a SIEM tool that is powerful enough to automatically correlate chains of activity seen across your entire business to identify malicious behavior. We'll see some great DevSecOps examples of this in *Chapter 10, The Insight Engine*, when we look at this type of capability.

Sumo Logic uses advanced anomaly detection and machine learning algorithms to help you stay ahead of evolving threats across your environment, no matter the log source or the amount of data you throw at the cloud SIEM. Whether it's infrastructure logs, endpoint logs, or application logs from your code repository, all of it can help to give you visibility into your environment and have the tools you need to analyze and remediate any problems that arise.

Improving collaboration across teams

One of the points made earlier, around building a security-first culture, was that teams need to work together, on the same data, and in the same place. This is important for several reasons.

First is **visibility**. Think about it, at this moment in time, most businesses have data separated away in distributed environments—some on the cloud, some on-premises, some in databases, and some in text files on a local machine. It's overwhelming, especially with the deluge of data that teams and businesses have to deal with. Visibility is hampered because teams have to constantly context-switch and work with different datasets. Imagine an environment where Ops teams can have visibility into the end-to-end chain of whatever activity they're monitoring or working on end to end, from an initial phishing email to data exfiltration from a VM in the cloud or from an error caused during deployment all the way to it impacting the performance of the application. Unlocking visibility means unlocking the performance of your team.

Another reason is **access**. Access to data is key to being able to take independence, ownership, and more importantly, action when it comes to problems in the environment. Teams have typically been slowed down by the necessity to ask questions at the most critical time, when they need to act. If a DevOps team encounters a suspicious user, they typically need to send an email or ticket to the SOC team if they need any logs from EDR solutions, firewalls, or audit tools but people are busy. There are all sorts of fires to put out, whether it be projects, other investigations, and incidents that all take time away from these requests. By improving access to data through an all-in-one centralized data lake, teams have the autonomy and self-reliance to act immediately. This makes the difference between a breach and a successful intervention.

Then we have **analytics**. If data lives in the same place, the same single source of truth for an organization, it's going to give teams a better understanding of the relationships behind that data. For example, if we have traces coming into Sumo Logic from an application, they're going to be related to certain logs. Those logs will be related to logs coming in from the infrastructure hosting the application, and those logs will also be related to the metrics from the infrastructure, too. Tying all this data together provides users with a comprehensive analytics capability, which will help them find answers to pressing questions under any circumstances. As machine learning and anomaly detection are heavily prevalent in Sumo Logic, it's easier to analyze and extract insights from data because it lives in the same place. Correlating data becomes easier because, you guessed it, it lives in the same place!

All of these point toward one end result—quicker investigation and response to outages and incidents in the environment. However, these considerations can also be taken as building blocks on the way to truly breaking teams out of silos and getting them to work together.

Sumo Logic customers find benefits from this model all the time. Recently, I spoke to a DevOps team that found security incidents quicker than their security team, housed a different SIEM and security stack, and their main issue was not treading on the security team's toes! Sumo Logic enabled this because it could then bring the teams closer together after they realized these operational gaps, and everyone ended up profiting from knowledge sharing and transparency. This conversation embodies the purpose of DevSecOps: aligning people, processes, and technology around shared visibility, so organizations can move faster securely.

Summary

In this chapter, you learned about the defining principles of DevSecOps, how to navigate the challenges that businesses face in the modern world, and covered practical examples of how you can start to use Sumo Logic to help adapt to these challenges. Here is a recap of the six principles of DevSecOps:

1. Shift-left with Security as code or "by design"
2. Continuous monitoring and continuous deployment
3. Collaboration and shared responsibility
4. Automated security testing
5. Compliance automation and vulnerability tracking
6. Security awareness and transparency

And the one principle that covers the very foundation of what we are trying to achieve with this book and with Sumo Logic: *Reduce the probability of material impact due to a cyber event over the next three years.*

Now we come to a different question. Having looked at how important DevSecOps is to the modern organization and how to use Sumo for it, how do we know that we are getting better? If we are going to bring these changes to our business, how can we see the value of them? That's what we'll be covering in *Chapter 3, Measuring Security Outcomes and Performance.*

References

1. https://registry.terraform.io/providers/SumoLogic/sumologic/latest/docs
2. *Howard, R., 2023. Cybersecurity First Principles*
3. https://itsvit.com/blog/05-2021-history-of-sre-from-far-2003-to-plans-for-2021-and-beyond/
4. https://owasp.org/www-project-threat-dragon/

5. https://owasp.org/www-project-dependency-check/
6. https://owasp.org/www-project-application-security-verification-standard/
7. https://developer.hashicorp.com/terraform/plugin/framework/validation
8. https://owasp.org/www-community/Free_for_Open_Source_Application_Security_Tools
9. https://devguide.owasp.org/en/07-training-education/
10. https://www.wired.com/story/the-untold-story-of-solarwinds-the-boldest-supply-chain-hack-ever/
11. https://blog.gitguardian.com/codecov-supply-chain-breach/
12. https://www.reversinglabs.com/blog/jetbrains-teamcity-software-supply-chain-attack-a-sunburt-redux
13. https://www.gartner.com/en/information-technology/glossary/aiops-artificial-intelligence-operations
14. https://www.ibm.com/reports/data-breach

Get this book's PDF version and more

Scan the QR code (or go to `packtpub.com/unlock`). Search for this book by name, confirm the edition, and then follow the steps on the page.

Note: Keep your invoice handy. Purchases made directly from Packt don't require an invoice.

3
Measuring Security Outcomes and Performance

Have you ever heard the saying, *If you can't measure it, you can't manage it*? Said another way, *What gets measured gets managed*. This principle is especially vital when building and maturing **Security Operations** (**SecOps**). Measuring what matters ensures that your efforts are effectively directed and impactful.

We've taken a look at DevSecOps, what it is, and how we can start to leverage the principles to create an organization that is coherent, agile, and connected through the usage of Sumo Logic. As we start to use the platform and start to look at our operations, questions such as the following pop up quite quickly:

- Do we know how quickly we are fixing errors in the pipeline?
- Do we know the impact an outage is having on our business revenue?
- Do we know how long it takes to investigate and remediate a phishing incident?
- Do we know how long it takes to investigate and remediate a malware incident?
- How long does it take to patch vulnerabilities in our Docker containers?

We need a way to answer these questions accurately and in a way that provides visibility and insight into how our teams are running and what tools they are using to support them. Why? Transparency. Building on top of the principles in *Chapter 2*, *The Role of DevSecOps in Modern Security* we want to have support from the top down in the organization, as well as across teams. Everyone needs to know what's happening because this helps to reduce operational errors and speeds up the time to investigate things. It's also good for budgets – we want to prove that we are extracting value from the tools we are using.

In this chapter, we will delve into the importance of quantifying the outcomes of your security and DevOps initiatives, followed by a focus on key performance indicators such as **Mean Time to Detect** (**MTTD**) and **Mean Time to Respond** (**MTTR**). We will cover quite a few different **Key Performance Indicators** (**KPIs**), **Service-Level Indicators** (**SLIs**), and **Service-Level Objectives** (**SLOs**), and explain the differences while we do so.

The following topics will be covered in this chapter:

- Why does measuring performance matter?
- KPIs, SLIs, SLOs, what? How to define your performance criteria

Why does measuring performance matter?

SecOps is often viewed as a non-revenue-generating part of a business, but its true value lies in cost avoidance and risk mitigation. A security incident can significantly impact a company through operational downtime, leading to lost revenue and reputation damage, resulting in the loss of customers. Business leaders need to reduce the potential impact of cyber events on the company's bottom line. Determining how much to invest in security versus profit-generating areas is a challenging task, especially since achieving total security is unrealistic. As security practitioners, it is our responsibility to quantify cyber risks and provide actionable metrics to decision-makers. This empowers them to make informed choices about resource allocation and determine the acceptable level of risk for the organization.

On the flip side, we have Dev and DevOps teams, who are seen as helping to generate revenue for the organization, and where performance criteria are clearer in terms of KPIs. If you're releasing code slowly and taking an age to remediate problems, that has a dollar cost attributed to it. Failures during code deployment, environments going down, or the team not being able to catch a faulty Kubernetes container that results in a crashed app are not good for business. It has direct financial repercussions on the business, so being able to monitor performance here also seems pretty critical!

From what we've covered so far, it's clear that there is a lot to keep track of. This is why measuring all of these elements and key metrics is so essential to not only the performance of all the teams involved but also to the overall security of the business.

The basis of any security strategy is for the decision-makers to be able to see and understand whether the controls, policies, and technologies are working and the business is deriving value. If you can't measure something, improving it with no clear data points is very difficult. Look at athletes – they know every metric about their body and their performance at all times. That's how they eke out incremental gains and improvements over time, and this is what we're going to help you with in this chapter.

A useful byproduct of focusing on metrics and KPIs is that it makes you and your teams more preemptive and proactive. Instead of just reacting to events as they occur and desperately putting out fires, your teams will know the status and current condition of everything. You will know ahead of time that an SLI isn't being met and this is causing problems upstream, or you'll know that a user is not doing something in a certain order or as part of a process. This section will outline what the impact of security investments and metrics is, how to align security with the business goals, and what part continuous security plays in all of this.

The impact of security investments and metrics

Imagine you're a SOC manager or lead who needs to build a business case for investing in a specific firewall that meets all requirements and boasts all the latest industry buzzwords. Alternatively, perhaps you've already secured approval to purchase the firewall, but now you're under significant pressure to justify the expense of this brand-new, costly piece of equipment. In both scenarios, it's essential to quantify the benefits and provide clear metrics to substantiate the investment. Here is a typical example of a conversation between a SOC manager and their CISO around the investments they're making into technology:

- **Chief Information Security Officer** (**CISO**): *How is the new firewall performing? You know, it accounted for a quarter of our budget this year.*

- **SOC manager (You)**: *It's fully operational and working well. We've blocked several suspicious activities flagged by our threat intelligence feeds.*
- **CISO**: *That's good to hear. Do we know how many threats we've blocked since its deployment? And how does it compare to last year?*
- **SOC manager**: *Well, I don't have the exact number at the moment. We'll need to review the firewall logs to provide an accurate count. I'll take that as an action item.*
- **CISO**: *Great. How long does it typically take to investigate and decide whether something should be blocked?*
- **SOC manager**: *I'm not sure, but Freddy handled the last investigation in approximately 15 minutes.*
- **CISO**: *"Approximately" 15 minutes? Is that pretty standard? What was it using our old network architecture? I have a meeting with the Chief Information Officer (CIO) in two days, and they want an update on how we're benefiting from our investments this year.*
- **SOC manager**: *Understood. I'll utilize Sumo Logic to gather the necessary metrics.*

The CISO is asking good questions. Defining, using, and understanding performance metrics is how teams arm themselves with information that helps to understand what each of their investments, actions, and reactions is doing in relation to the wider picture. An example of a KPI-based dashboard freely available out of the box in Sumo Logic is a security-focused one, such as this:

Figure 3.1 – An example SOC KPIs dashboard in Sumo Logic that captures performance metrics for security teams

This has a focus on MTTD, MTTR, and more, based on real data that the team is seeing. We'll come to those shortly.

If you remember, we made a point in *Chapter 2* where we mentioned that metrics and KPIs could be used as a way to shift the mindset of the organization to start embracing the DevSecOps philosophy. Performance metrics are key in that they get teams and individuals to be accountable and understand what they are trying to achieve.

Plus, management will love it as they will have data points to discuss and refer to during meetings. This brings us to the next point.

Aligning security with business goals

As mentioned earlier, aligning security measures with business goals helps prevent disruptions that could lead to downtime, revenue loss, or damage to the company's reputation – factors that are crucial for maintaining customer trust and competitive advantage.

Sometimes, the primary business objective is simply to meet regulatory compliance requirements necessary to operate legally. Demonstrating that no customer data has been compromised over a specific period, or consistently maintaining compliance with key regulatory frameworks such as GDPR, SOC 2, or PCI DSS, directly translates SecOps into business value. This not only protects the company from potential legal penalties but also reinforces its commitment to ethical practices.

Differing views — two examples

Let's take two fictitious companies.

Company A leverages analytic platforms such as Sumo Logic, which offer prebuilt dashboards specifically designed to map and monitor compliance with regulatory frameworks such as PCI DSS. These dashboards provide real-time visibility into the effectiveness of security controls and automatically generate artifacts that demonstrate adherence to specific compliance requirements.

When an auditor arrives, they can quickly access these comprehensive dashboards and reports, which showcase how each control is being met. The streamlined process allows the auditor to efficiently review and validate compliance without extensive intervention from the company's staff. This not only accelerates the audit process but also minimizes disruptions to the engineering and operations teams, allowing them to maintain focus on their core responsibilities. The ability to readily produce compliance evidence enhances the organization's credibility and reduces the risk of non-compliance penalties.

In contrast, *Company B* does not centrally collect data from its tooling for compliance monitoring and reporting. When an auditor comes knocking, the company must initiate a manual, time-consuming process to gather the required evidence. Engineers and system owners are pulled away from their primary duties to locate logs, compile data, and document the existence and effectiveness of security controls.

This ad-hoc approach can lead to several challenges:

- **Inefficiency**: Collecting and organizing evidence manually is labor-intensive and can significantly extend the duration of the audit
- **Inconsistency**: Without standardized reporting tools, the quality and completeness of the evidence may vary, potentially leading to gaps in compliance documentation
- **Operational disruption**: Redirecting technical staff to support the audit process can delay critical projects and impact productivity
- **Increased risk**: The likelihood of overlooking essential compliance elements rises when processes are not automated, which can result in audit findings or penalties

Ultimately, *Company B*'s lack of real-time visibility into the efficacy of security tools it's deployed, through real-time logging, creates a reactive environment where audits are more burdensome and stressful. This diverts valuable resources and potentially exposes the organization to regulatory risks.

By leveraging Sumo's prebuilt and customizable compliance apps, organizations can significantly enhance their ability to demonstrate adherence to regulatory requirements, streamline audit processes, and allow their teams to focus on strategic initiatives rather than administrative tasks.

Although compliance frameworks can sometimes be burdensome, it's important to remember that their ultimate purpose is to enhance your security posture and resilience. By adhering to these guidelines, you not only meet regulatory requirements but also strengthen your organization's ability to prevent and respond to security threats. Sumo Logic gives you the ability to map to various compliance frameworks – PCI/DSS, NIST, ISO, and others – in order to make sense of all the data you're gathering from across the business. Here's an example dashboard for PCI compliance for Linux machines:

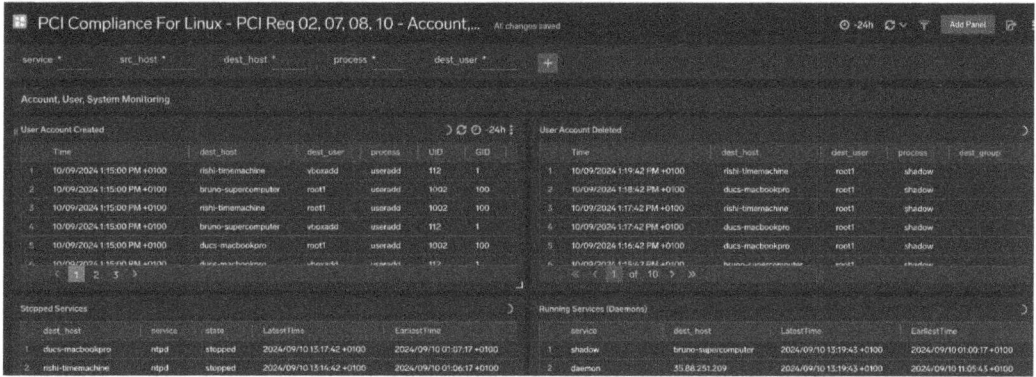

Figure 3.2 – An example dashboard of data useful for continuously monitoring compliance in line with the PCI standards

Additionally, as we'll see with Cloud SIEM, it's possible to apply real-time analytics to elements of the compliance framework that can be actively monitored, such as user logins, policy changes, admin actions, and so on.

Continuous security

Security teams cannot afford to sit back and coast, relying on existing information to help them try and identify new threats. Threats constantly evolve, and attackers are identifying new attack vectors very frequently, so monitoring key metrics such as MTTD, MTTR, and incident response times becomes crucial. Being able to have a way to improve over time for the team and individual users is very empowering and can be the difference between catching an adversary or not.

One thing that Sumo Logic does on top of all of this is a dynamic way of re-evaluating your rules, signals, and insights as they occur and based on how teams respond to them. It's a way of tuning the underlying rules mechanism without the usual labor-intensive approaches, which entail teams spending hours reviewing rules, looking at historic incidents and trigger context. The feature that makes this tuning possible is called the **Insight Trainer**, and it'll be discussed later in the book when we get to discuss the Insight Engine in *Chapter 11, The Automation Service and Playbooks* in more detail. However, here's a quick look at a small part of the **Insight**

Trainer dashboard, which shows the sources of our insights as well as how they go through the decision-making funnel:

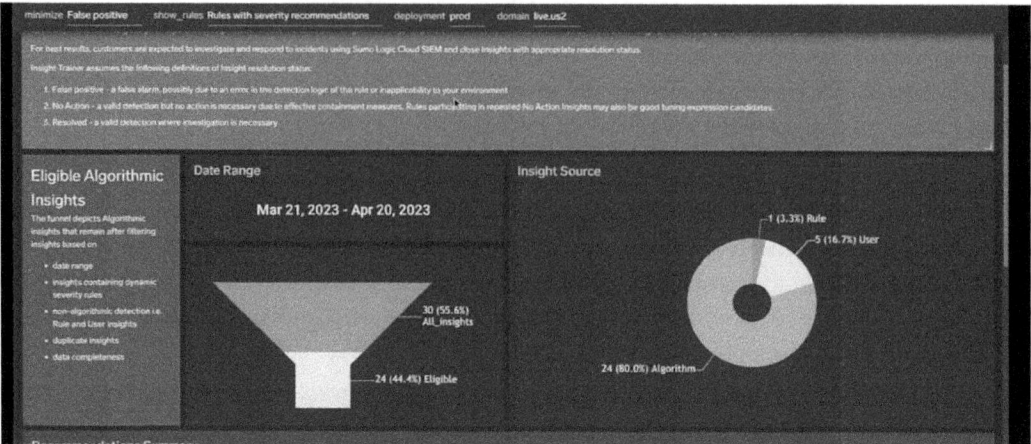

Figure 3.3 – The Insight Trainer dashboard

The goal here is what we all want help with – reducing false positives while simultaneously increasing the fidelity of our alerts. You don't want to be wasting time investigating the wrong activities, and having a stronger focus will improve some of the metrics we discussed earlier, such as MTTD and MTTR.

Continuous security is helpful to make sure your teams can stay on top of threats in your business. However, as we all know, prevention is better than a cure, so how can we start as *left* as possible to reduce the chance of events turning into threats? This is covered next.

Start-left

I know the very popular and common notion of shift-left has been mentioned a good few times already in this book, but as we're on the topic of continuous security, I wanted to go a step further. I think it's worth giving the spotlight to *start-left*. Many organizations are currently in the transition to shift-left, and it's a healthy process as it brings security into the process earlier. Some teams are going even further to start-left – it is the next iteration and a much stronger implementation of DevSecOps as it tries to inject security right at the very start of the process before anything else happens. Even better, we can measure this with high-impact outcomes such as the following:

- Reducing high-severity vulnerabilities making their way into production by x% within 6 months
- Security involved in 100% of new project kick-off meetings
- Architectural threat modeling performed for all major new services
- Time from new CVE disclosure to inventory of impact reduced to X hours
- Policies codified in **Infrastructure as Code (IaC)**/**Policy as Code (PaC)** increased by X%

Start-left success is measured not by how fast teams fix security issues, but by how rarely those issues are created in the first place. Now, how is this achieved? **Automation**. We can leverage feedback loops that have been built from starting to embrace AIOps (discussed in the last chapter) and components such as the Insight Trainer to start feeding into start-left practices.

DevOps and Dev leads should be enabling their teams by letting them use the right tooling to achieve this. We're talking about IaC, so tools such as Terraform, Ansible, and cloud-specific tools such as AWS CloudFormation, for example. We're also talking about compliance checks and the automated scanning (SAST, DAST) of applications, and CI/CD pipelines that generate observability data. The difficult part for any platform, including one like Sumo Logic, is giving *both* the SecOps teams and Dev/DevOps teams an environment that can make their jobs easier.

For developers, it's important to have developer-friendly tools that are nice to use and support things such as secure templates. The devs and engineers should want to use the technology! Fortunately, Sumo Logic is developer-friendly for many reasons – it's API-driven, supports automation and IaC, provides complete visibility from CI/CD pipelines for monitoring, identifies the root cause quicker, and many more practical and useful capabilities.

Some great ideas to get started on the *start-left* journey include the following:

- CI/CD pipelines should be blocking deployments where high/critical vulnerabilities are identified
- Deployments that haven't had enough test coverage should be blocked
- Bugs and vulnerabilities should be fixed locally before pushing code
- The same IaC or Docker images should be used locally, and these practices should be unified across the Dev team(s) right at the beginning

Continuous security is very important as it can truly redefine what it means to have a well-engineered, secure product design and build process. Most importantly, these changes bring about real, tangible advantages to a business, including competitive advantage, better products, and better user experiences. Performance criteria can be established around these efforts and fed back up to management and senior leadership to start to drive some great change across the business. Speaking of performance criteria, let's talk about how we actually go about defining it next.

KPIs, SLIs, SLOs, what? How to define your performance criteria

The reason defining performance criteria is difficult for most teams out there is that there is no structured, uniform process to follow, and there are so many potential KPIs to use. Going back to the introductory point of this chapter, you can't manage what you can't measure. If teams cannot define accurate success and performance criteria for their infrastructure, services, and processes, how can they know how good they are as a unit or as individuals? How do they know where the gaps are and where improvements need to be made? These are all crucial pieces of information that lead to the overall defense and security posture of the organization.

Before we jump into the process of defining performance-related metrics, I think a few definitions are in order:

- **KPIs**: KPIs are strategic metrics used to evaluate how effectively an organization is achieving its key business objectives. They are aligned with the organization's goals and are used to drive improvements.
    - **KPIs in SecOps**: KPIs in SecOps measure the effectiveness and efficiency of security operations in supporting the organization's broader business goals. They translate technical performance into business value.

- **SLIs**: SLIs are specific measurements that indicate the performance level of a particular service or system. They are quantitative metrics used to assess whether a service meets the agreed-upon standards, often defined in **Service-Level Agreements (SLAs)**.
    - **SLIs in SecOps**: SLIs typically measure the technical aspects of security services. They help in monitoring the health and effectiveness of security tools and processes. SLIs provide benchmarks for the performance of security services, ensuring that they meet the required operational standards to support overall security objectives.
- **SLOs**: An SLO is a *target value* or *range* for a service level that is measured by an SLI. It represents the desired level of service performance that a provider commits to achieving over a specific period. SLOs are used to set clear expectations and performance goals, often forming the basis of SLAs with customers or internal stakeholders.
    - **SLOs in SecOps**: The response time objective aims to respond to all critical security incidents within 15 minutes. The detection objective aims to achieve a true positive rate of 98% in threat detection.

We've covered the definitions of these important concepts, so let's dive into some examples of KPIs for SecOps and DevSecOps teams. In the following section, we will outline real examples where we plan to demonstrate how these have been implemented by us in our businesses, as well as when discussing performance criteria with customers. It's a natural conversation and extension from other use cases because as soon as customers realize the capabilities they have to measure operational performance in Sumo Logic, they want to make the most of it.

Let's start with SecOps measurement.

SecOps KPI examples

When looking at SecOps KPIs, we're interested in parts of the process that directly impact how security teams operate and how they stay on top of threats. There are multiple angles we can take when measuring this, from the straightforward and commonly known MTTR, all the way through to more nuanced KPIs such as *dwell time*. The following table covers some important KPIs, but remember, this is not an exhaustive list:

SecOps KPI	What does it do?	Why is it useful?
Mean Time to Detect (MTTD)	Measures the average time taken to detect a security breach or incident	Faster detection helps with faster response
Mean Time to Respond (MTTR)	Measures the average time taken to respond to a security incident once detected	Shorter response times reduce the risk of significant breaches
Mean Time to Recover/Contain (MTTR/MTTC)	Measures the average time required to fully recover from an incident	This measures the impact on operations and monitors efficient recovery

SecOps KPI	What does it do?	Why is it useful?
Number of incidents contained	Tracks escalated incidents contained without escalating into a full breach	This shows the effectiveness of containment as part of an incident response process
False positive rate	Measures the percentage of insights flagged as threats but identified as false alarms	False positives burden a team with extra work, making it harder to detect threats
False negative rate	Measures insights that were real threats but remained undetected	Tracking false negatives helps to make it clear how many incidents are being missed
Vulnerability detection and remediation time	Measures the average time taken from identifying a vulnerability to remediating it	Shortening this time reduces the attack surface and exploitation attempts
Patch management compliance	Tracks the percentage of systems and software that are fully patched and up to date	This ensures that known vulnerabilities are not left unaddressed
Access control violations	Tracks the number of incidents involving unauthorized access to sensitive systems and data	This measures the effectiveness of access controls and policies
Compliance adherence rate	Tracks the percentage of security controls that are in compliance with regulatory or organizational frameworks	This demonstrates that the compliance obligations are being met
Percent coverage	Tracks the percentage of devices (servers, workstations, mobile devices) that are under active monitoring	Higher coverage reduces blind spots
Dwell time	Measures the total time a threat remains undetected in the system	Reducing dwell time minimizes potential damage and data loss
Data Loss Prevention (DLP) incidents	Tracks the number of incidents where sensitive data has left the network	This helps ensure that data is not exfiltrated successfully during incidents
Percentage of incidents escalated	Tracks the number of incidents escalated from initial triage to stage 2 (or similar)	This helps to understand team capabilities and whether the escalation process is effective

SecOps KPI	What does it do?	Why is it useful?
Alert volume per analyst hour	Measures the number of alerts an analyst handles per hour	This helps assess workload distribution and identify potential bottlenecks or the need for additional staffing
Escalation rate	Tracks the percentage of incidents that require escalation to higher-level support or specialized teams	A high escalation rate may indicate the need for additional training or resources at the initial response level
Phishing success rate	Tracks the percentage of phishing attacks where users click on a malicious link	This helps to understand user preparedness and how much training should be delivered
Security control effectiveness	Tracks the percentage of attempted attacks that were blocked or mitigated by security controls	This ensures that security controls are working as intended and meeting SLAs

Table 3.1 – Useful SecOps KPIs that can be applied in practice

That's a fairly long list of KPI examples for a SecOps team, and even then, it isn't exhaustive. There are more ways of measuring performance within teams, but these are definitely the most popular ones. Take a look at some DevSecOps KPIs next so you can see the difference and the types of ways you can measure performance here.

DevSecOps KPI examples

Due to the nature of how DevSecOps straddles operations and security, you'll find that the KPIs are all about measuring the efficiency of the process when shifting or starting left. Additionally, you'll find there are some KPIs around the infrastructure that these teams manage from a security perspective as well. The following table presents the relevant KPIs:

DevSecOps KPI	What does it do?	Why is it useful?
Time to remediate security issues in code	Measures the average time it takes to fix identified security vulnerabilities in code	Reducing this time reduces the risk of deploying insecure code
Automated test coverage	Tracks the percentage of code covered by automated security tests	High coverage ensures that code is consistently and thoroughly tested for issues

DevSecOps KPI	What does it do?	Why is it useful?
Vulnerability recurrence rate	Measures how often previously remediated vulnerabilities reappear in code	This indicates the need for strengthening coding practices and better integrating security into the coding process
Build failure rate due to security issues	Tracks the percentage of build failures caused by security vulnerabilities identified during **Continuous Integration (CI)**	This ensures that security is built into the CI/CD pipeline
Mean Time to Secure (MTTS)	Measures the average time from detecting a vulnerability during development to deploying a secure fix	This ensures rapid remediation during the development life cycle
Open source component risk	Tracks vulnerabilities or risks introduced through third-party or open source libraries	Many modern applications run on open source components, which limits supply chain risks
Security debt	Measures the number of unresolved security issues or technical debt accumulated over time	This helps identify and prioritize the backlog of security-related work that needs to be actioned
Mean Time Between Security Incidents (MTBSI)	Measures the average time between security-related incidents across the development life cycle	This shows how frequently security incidents are occurring and assesses the security posture
Container and infrastructure vulnerability detection	Tracks the percentage of vulnerabilities detected in IaC and containerized environments	This helps ensure a secure container-based environment by minimizing misconfigurations
Security SLA compliance rate	Measures how often security SLAs are met for addressing vulnerabilities and incidents	This ensures that risks are remediated within acceptable timeframes

Table 3.2 – Notable DevSeOps KPIs that can be applied in practice

It's worth noting that it's not effective to use all of these KPIs! This is just a wide selection of different measurements that could help in one way or another to define team performance that adds value to the business. The maturity level of a team, or the business, defines the scale of measurement and what is measured, so you could potentially need anywhere from two or three KPIs to dozens across various functions. We have tried to outline the KPIs and how they are useful to help with this, but we'll see some examples shortly to frame this with some context. Before we do that, let's look at SLIs and SLOs.

SLIs and SLOs

In addition to KPIs, which track the performance of teams in line with business goals and objectives, SLIs and SLOs were designed to help with understanding and monitoring the performance of technical components. An example could be an uptime monitor on a website or the operating performance of a Kubernetes Pod or container.

Examples of SLIs within the security space include things such as the average click-through rate of a phishing email sent internally as part of business-wide security testing. These metric types sit at the operational level and are aimed at technical practitioners such as analysts, engineers, or ops teams.

Here is a handy table to quickly outline the differences between KPIs and SLIs:

Aspect	KPI	SLI
Focus	Business outcomes and goals	Technical service performance
Audience	Business leaders, executives, and teams	Engineers, operators, and system owners
Examples	Risk reduction, customer satisfaction	Uptime, error rate, response rate
Context	Measures overall success	Measures adherence to SLOs and SLAs
Granularity	Broad, organization-level	Narrow, system-specific

Table 3.3 – The differences between a KPI and an SLI

Defining the measurement process for your KPIs, SLIs, and SLOs

Creating measurements for SecOps and DevSecOps teams is not as straightforward as just getting a few KPIs and cracking on with business as usual. It's a team and business effort. It's a strategic process in that it takes planning, the correct stakeholders, the right tools, and, very importantly, the right mindset.

The issue with spinning up a few KPIs and letting a team get on with it is that it doesn't solve the overall problem, which is to create accountability and improve communication throughout the business, and align with the business. The best-case scenario with such an approach is that the team with the new KPIs actually benefits by becoming more efficient, quicker, and so on, but it'll all be in a vacuum. The process and outcome won't be shared or replicated by other parts of the business, and that isn't the modern, Agile approach we want.

In order to help with this, we can use a structured process that can be standardized across the business to roll out criteria across different teams. This will support cohesion and force teams and management to see the bigger picture. Conversations should be guided in directions such as the following:

- *If the DevOps team is being measured on security testing frequency, how about we align the SecOps team to both test more frequently and in a more structured way?*
- *Let's try to get ahead of vulnerabilities. If we measure the SecOps team on how quickly they identify and remediate vulnerabilities, we can tie that to a metric around vulnerability recurrence rates in the DevOps team.*

By involving as many stakeholders as possible in an organization-wide strategy like this, the measurements become clearer and more accurate, which results in actual value for the business and individual teams. So, let's look at how we can take a multi-stakeholder process like this and break it down into a set of steps.

Step-by-step guide

What follows is a visual step-by-step process that can be used to help your teams and business define and implement performance measuring criteria into your daily operations. The focus is on collaboration, transparency, and ownership, with the tone set by the senior layers of the organization. In each step, we'll cover the following:

- An overview of the step
- Aims and objectives
- Real-life examples of metrics that could be part of such a conversation
- Pitfalls and issues that teams could encounter at this stage, followed by ways to avoid or fix them

Here is the sequence of steps that make up this process:

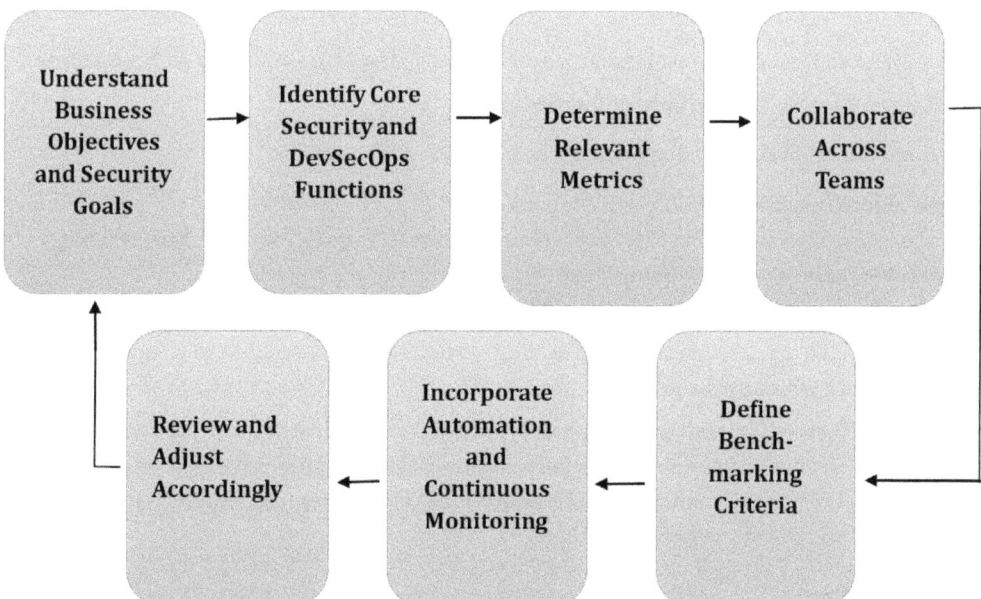

Figure 3.4 – The seven steps in the performance criteria definition process

Let's begin with the first step in this tricky transition, gathering the initial requirements.

Understand business objectives and security goals

The first step in creating effective performance measurement criteria is to align planned KPIs with the overarching business objectives. This alignment ensures that security metrics are not only technical but also directly contribute to achieving critical business outcomes.

At this stage, the conversation is high-level and focuses on gathering input from senior management to identify the most important business objectives. It also involves collaborating with technical teams to understand how their efforts support these objectives. Examples of business objectives might include the following:

- Customer trust: Maintaining data confidentiality and demonstrating commitment to security
- Uptime: Minimizing downtime caused by security incidents
- Compliance: Meeting regulatory requirements to avoid penalties and maintain market access
- Market expansion: Supporting new markets by ensuring scalable and secure systems
- Increasing revenue: Enabling secure, seamless customer experiences to foster trust and loyalty

Let's look at a real-life example.

Most customers I speak to have digital assets, a website, a store, and key business applications in finance, retail, and machine learning across many different industries. The primary concern for all of these businesses is customer experience, as it directly correlates with revenues, profits, and their brand reputation. I end up discussing uptime across infrastructure and applications all the time, as these tend to be critical for business; a corresponding security goal might be to reduce downtime caused by security incidents. For example, phishing attacks often disrupt operations, so the KPI could be as follows:

- Initial metric: Incident resolution time for phishing attacks is currently 45 minutes
- Target KPI: Reduce incident resolution time for phishing attacks to 15 minutes within 3 months

This makes the goal **specific**, **measurable**, and **actionable**.

Here are potential pitfalls of the KPI, along with planning tips to address them:

- **Vague objectives**: If business objectives are too broad (e.g., "Improve security"), it's difficult to translate them into actionable KPIs. We can use the **SMART** criteria (**Specific, Measurable, Achievable, Relevant, Time-bound**) to define objectives clearly to tackle this.
- **Lack of stakeholder buy-in**: Senior management may see security as a cost center rather than a business enabler. It's possible to present security goals as business enablers (e.g., uptime supports customer trust, which drives revenue).
- **Disconnect between business and technical teams**: Without clear communication, technical teams may not understand how their work supports business goals. Collaborative workshops with both teams to map technical work (e.g., threat detection) to business outcomes (e.g., minimizing data breaches) is a great way of bringing these teams together.

Identify core security and DevSecOps functions

To create meaningful performance measurement criteria, it's crucial to define the scope of your security and DevSecOps teams. This involves clearly articulating their functions, responsibilities, and the tools they use. By mapping out these elements, you ensure alignment with organizational goals and lay the foundation for measurable KPIs.

The main aspects to look into for this step are the following:

- **Defining team scope**: Are teams focused on threat detection, incident response, secure code deployment, or all of the above?
- **Clarifying framework alignment**: For example, does the SecOps team leverage frameworks such as MITRE ATT&CK for mapping threats and maintaining an internal threat knowledge base?
- **Taking stock of tools and technologies**: Identify and evaluate the tools that teams rely on to fulfill their functions.

This step is essential for laying out how teams contribute to business objectives (from the first step) and ensuring that they are equipped to succeed. You need to define the functions that these teams will be performing. It could be one or multiple of these, depending on the size of your organization:

- **Threat detection and response**: Using tools such as Sumo Logic to detect, analyze, and respond to threats and defining threats with the help of a frameworks like those from MITRE: ATT&CK (adversary perspective), D3FEND (defense perspective), ATLAS (AI threat landscape) and CWE/CVE (software vulnerabilities).
- **Code security and DevSecOps**: Ensuring secure software development and using **Software Bill of Materials** (**SBOM**) tools to track dependencies and vulnerabilities in-house and within the supply chain
- **Cloud security and compliance**: Using **Cloud Security Posture Management** (**CSPM**) and **Cloud-Native Application Protection Platforms** (**CNAPPs**) to maintain compliance and detect abnormalities across cloud infrastructure
- **Vulnerability management**: Using static and dynamic analysis, along with regular vulnerability management tools such as Qualys or Tenable, to prioritize and mitigate risks from vulnerabilities

This exercise isn't limited to just teams and their composition, but also the tools that are used in the day-to-day activities. Tools that cover the following areas are amazing for DevOps and SecOps teams alike:

- CSPM
- Pre-build scanning tools based on IaC
- SBOM
- Static and dynamic analysis
- CNAPP

Teams can unlock some tangible benefits when concentrating team functions in this way. When teams grasp their roles better, it's possible to shape much better KPIs, which can also have positive effects on job satisfaction and mental well-being.

> **Note**
> Being a member of a security team in this day and age is full of burnout and mental fatigue. Organizations with small teams sometimes have no choice but to wear multiple hats, and there are still KPIs that can help measure effectiveness.

Let's look at a real-life example involving vulnerabilities. Everything is packed with vulnerabilities, from npm packages in code to vulnerabilities in network devices, and patching them across the enterprise is hard. However, there are still ways of measuring how well you're doing to get better at it. For example, I worked with a team working for a retail customer, who had to maintain a very popular website. They built, tested, and deployed code frequently, as most developer teams do, but we ended up talking about how Sumo Logic can help improve their overall security posture, and we used the following KPIs:

- Initial metric: Current CVE rate in production is 3% of deployed applications
- Target KPI: Ensure that 90% of deployed applications have 0 CVE at deployment time within the next 6 months

As you can see, we flipped it so that we weren't looking at the **Common Vulnerabilities and Exposures** (**CVE**) present in production applications, but raised the standard to 0 CVEs in 90% of production apps. This is actually easier and less overwhelming to track, and in Sumo Logic, we can use the **Software Development Optimization** (**SDO**) app along with vulnerability management databases and tools to correlate and continuously monitor this information.

Here are potential pitfalls of this KPI, along with planning tips to address them:

- **Scope creep**: It should be quite easy to set some initial targets, but you may get stuck adding more and more items to your scope list when you get ideas. This is scope creep, and it is deadly. I've had conversations with teams that either had too much overlap, creating conflict and inefficiency, or took on too much, also causing problems. Have a clear focus across your teams to minimize the effects of scope creep.
- **Tool overload**: I've lost count of the number of teams that use the same tools as another team but don't communicate about it, or a team that uses different tools that do the same things, for example, multiple SIEM solutions. This is both inefficient and a complete waste of money for a business. Regularly audit your tools to prevent this, and also try to consolidate your tools wherever possible. We live in a time where technology is becoming more powerful, and a platform such as Sumo Logic can centralize your security, observability, and automation tools in one.

Determine relevant metrics

We've already covered metrics above in detail, but as the best builders say "measure twice, cut once", so we'll review the most important metrics here again to reinforce the concept. To ensure that metrics are actionable and insightful , it's essential to focus on both lagging indicators (measuring past performance) and leading indicators (predicting future outcomes). Leveraging tools such as Sumo Logic, which supports both logs and metrics in a single platform, enables continuous monitoring across systems, applications, and infrastructure.

Lagging indicators are types of metrics that look at historical performance and provide a snapshot of what has occurred. Examples include the following:

- **Mean Time to Detect (MTTD)**: The average time taken to detect a security breach or incident
- **Mean Time to Respond (MTTR)**: The average time taken to respond to a security incident once detected
- **False Positive Rate (FPR)**: The number of false positives the team has seen

Leading indicators focus on trying to improve a future event, so they help the team be as proactive, or pre-emptive, as possible. For example:

- **Percentage of security patches applied on time**: Patches applied within certain time windows
- **Training completion rates**: How many people have passed their phishing security training as a percentage of the business unit, team, or some other relative measurement

I helped a customer who was in the energy infrastructure space look at some KPIs for their environment from a security perspective, and I thought I'd share the examples of the lagging and leading indicators we came up with in this real-life example.

This customer had substantial energy infrastructure globally, so many separate **Operational Technology** (**OT**) environments, as well as more modern ones. OT environments are environments where software and hardware operate in tandem to monitor and control physical infrastructure. We were looking at implementing Sumo Logic as a central source of truth across all of the numerous data islands. I won't go over all our discussions – they were extensive, but I will share some interesting ones.

Let's look at lagging first.

This customer really wanted to revamp their cybersecurity and ensure that they had full visibility over everything, which is right in Sumo Logic's ballpark. As part of this, we covered lagging indicators that could help. One of the KPIs discussed was the following:

- **Initial metric**: Reduce MTTR for ransomware attacks
- **Target KPI**: Reduce MTTR for ransomware incidents in OT systems from 48 hours to 8 hours over the next 6 months by improving incident detection, isolation, and recovery processes

The reason for this KPI was that the business was worried about ransomware attacks due to many attempts on energy companies in the past few years, for example, the ransomware attack on Tata energy plants in 2022[1]. They were trying to improve on this front, but didn't have the technology to help, even though they had made a start on improving the processes and employing expertise. Sumo Logic helps them aggregate and correlate data across these OT environments, as well as the cloud, to identify potential ransomware events and reduce the time to response.

With leading indicators, we wanted to help the team implement steps to start being more proactive about their defenses. So we discussed the following:

- Initial metric: OT asset inventory coverage
- Target KPI: Achieve 100% of the inventory of OT assets and ingest them into Sumo Logic within 6 months

The purpose here was once again to make sure that the customer makes the most of having complete visibility of their OT environment in one place. This KPI would help to identify how well this is going and identify any gaps in coverage, too.

There are some common pitfalls here, namely, the following:

- **Too many metrics**: This happens very frequently. The number of metrics being used is usually very high, and teams get overwhelmed with tracking them all and stop after a time due to the load. Take a handful of metrics first, work them into your processes, and monitor them for a few months.
- **Metrics without actions**: When deciding on a KPI, ask yourself, "What decisions or actions will this data inform?" Ensure that the KPI you're setting will lead to changes in actions or behavior.
- **Unrealistic targets**: This is also a common one. Teams want to achieve too much too soon. Keep the metrics SMART and keep them realistic. Remember, each KPI should be *specific*, *measurable*, *achievable*, *relevant*, and *time-bound*.

Collaborate across teams

Effective KPI setting requires collaboration across multiple teams to ensure alignment, ownership, and successful execution. There's no point in even starting this if you're not going to take the courageous decision of bringing all of these teams together. Wipe the sweat off your brow and put your fingers on the keyboard to start writing those emails! While these teams may have different responsibilities and priorities, bringing them together helps create KPIs that reflect both technical realities and business outcomes. Involving senior stakeholders and technical teams ensures that KPIs are relevant, achievable, and support overall organizational goals. Oh yes, please don't forget the compliance and legal teams if necessary – they always get missed out of the fun.

Let's take a brief look at the reasons why collaboration is one of the most important things for this process and DevSecOps in general:

- Alignment: KPIs should reflect business priorities while remaining practical for teams to execute
- Shared responsibility: It encourages collaboration across silos such as Development, DevOps, SecOps, and Compliance to achieve a common goal
- Improved outcomes: Teams working together can identify interdependencies, share tools, and solve bottlenecks collaboratively
- Visibility: It ensures that senior leadership understands and supports the KPIs set by technical teams

Let's take a look at a real-life example that would entail multiple teams working together.

I encountered a customer once during a Proof of Value (PoV) that wanted to use Sumo Logic as a central data lake. Such a basic use case, you might think. It actually ended up unearthing some rifts in their operations. One of their criteria during the PoV was to "reduce production incidents caused by security misconfigurations." Sounds sensible, right? The issue was, they all thought this meant something different. There were four teams as part of this PoV: Engineering, DevOps, SecOps, and Compliance.

It just so happened that we discovered they had been trying to address this problem for a while already, except that all the teams were doing different things.

Engineering assumed this meant "fix IaC scripts," so they spent weeks rewriting Terraform modules. DevOps thought it was about "tightening Kubernetes policies," so they started experimenting with PodSecurity admission rules. SecOps thought "misconfigurations" meant IAM privileges, so they went off creating detection rules for risky API calls. Finally, Compliance assumed it was related to audit findings and prepared a report for ISO 27001 that focused on documentation gaps.

You might've guessed at this point that they weren't very successful at meeting this KPI and reducing their incidents, and you're 100% right. What was happening here is that the teams optimized for their interpretation of the KPI, not the actual problem. After digging into their logs and events, it turns out developers were spinning up containers with insecure defaults because no one agreed on baseline configurations. That is the cost of not collaborating. Lots of activity, zero progress.

During the PoV, we had the opportunity to get these teams together to test the technology and the success criteria. It was the perfect time for these teams to ask one simple question: "Where are security misconfigurations really entering our system?"

After an hour of honest discussion, an uncomfortable truth emerged: 80% of the misconfigurations came from developers copying outdated container templates. It had nothing to do with IAM, Terraform, or Kubernetes! After using this moment to align, the teams had a focus:

- Engineering adopted a new, secure base container image maintained by DevOps
- DevOps enforced image scanning at build time and rejected anything based on the old image
- SecOps created detections for drift and risky container behavior
- Compliance mapped the workflow to CIS and SOC2 controls to track the improvements

At that point, we had a real, SMART KPI: *Reduce production incidents caused by insecure container configs by 60% in the next 6 months by introducing secure base images, enforcing automated scanning in CI/CD, and implementing runtime drift detection.*

During the PoV, we noticed that the number of incidents caused by insecure container configuration dropped by 65%. Not because one team worked harder but because they were all working together on the same problem, with shared visibility and shared outcomes. That's the power of collaboration. However, as you can guess, pitfalls here arise mainly from poor communication between the teams involved, for example:

- **Lack of communication between teams**: This is the most common problem. Ensure that meetings are held regularly enough and have focused agendas to help decision-making and prioritization.
- **Misaligned priorities**: Teams might have different reasons for monitoring different metrics. Support discussions to make sure that teams are working together on solving their problems.
- **Lack of accountability**: Teams need to do what they say they're going to do and take responsibility for implementing these KPIs.

Define benchmarking criteria

So, now we have an idea of our business objectives, what functions the teams perform, and even some indicators with which to measure performance. We're in a good spot. What are we measuring against, though? With no clear baseline of what is *good*, we can't hope to see how we are progressing and improving over time. Let's take a look at why benchmarking is important.

Benchmarking is incredibly useful because it helps you do the following:

- Establish context: Provides a starting point for measuring progress
- Set realistic targets: Helps define what is achievable based on past performance or industry standards
- Track improvement over time: Highlights trends and deltas, enabling data-driven decision-making
- Align teams: Creates a shared understanding of acceptable performance levels

Luckily, you're not completely on your own when defining these benchmarks. There are a few options available. You could use an existing framework (unless you want to create your own), such as ISO 27001, NIST, or MITRE ATT&CK. You could also use industry reports such as the Verizon **Data Breach Investigations Report** (**DBIR**) for incident response teams, or the DORA *State of DevOps Report* for DevOps teams.

You could also access industry benchmarks to use as a reference point and an initial baseline based on company size, industry, and so on. Finally, you could use historical data to guide your teams. Try and analyze existing datasets that you have to see whether you can glean insights out of them. You can even use Sumo Logic to help you do this level of log analytics. Pair this up with anomaly detection in Sumo Logic to track these baselines of activity in real time to know when something deviates from that baseline as soon as possible.

Sumo Logic allows you to retain data for up to 13 years, meaning that if you are already using the platform and retain your data for at least 3–6 months, you probably have a lot of metrics around time taken to respond to alerts, investigation times, the downtime and uptime of applications, and so on. The ability to capture deltas between events of interest makes it easy to start putting a baseline together.

The most common benchmarking issues are as follows:

- **Unrealistic benchmarks**: Sometimes, depending on the source of data, a team might give themselves a mountain to climb. Keep it small initially, and use a bit of common sense as well to get a benchmark that is useful.
- **Benchmarking separately**: Teams might be benchmarking on their own, without communicating with other teams, which could impact the validity of the baselines.
- **Benchmarking validation**: Data sources around benchmarking have become easier to find now, but teams could still be using outdated benchmarks to feed the numbers.

With benchmarking in place, we should now have metrics that act as the foundation for our KPIs. We've made them SMART, so we have set out clear performance criteria. We've united our teams to discuss these metrics and now have benchmarks in place to know how and when we deviate. There are only a couple of steps left! The next step is starting to implement automation and continuous monitoring.

Incorporate automation and continuous monitoring

We have pretty much everything we need at this point. The purpose of this step is to define a method of consistently gathering and tracking the metrics that will drive the outcomes and performance of the teams in question. Automation and continuous monitoring are crucial for this because we can then gather performance data in real time, track progress toward KPIs without manual effort, identify and respond to deviations quickly, and share performance insights with senior stakeholders, preferably in a visual format, so the technology needs to have visualization capabilities.

We can use Sumo Logic for most of the requirements of this particular step based on how it centralizes data, along with all the capabilities that let you automate and monitor these logs, metrics, and traces. This is best explained with the following real-life example.

Here's our scenario. A DevOps team has set a KPI to achieve at least 10 deployments per day with 0 critical vulnerabilities in production consistently within 3 months. So far, it's a great SMART KPI, but there are a few things to note when implementing this from end to end:

- **CI/CD pipeline automation**: The team can use tools such as Jenkins or the GitLab CLI to automate deployment processes and integrate vulnerability scanning tools to block deployments with critical vulnerabilities
- **Continuous monitoring**: Set up a dashboard in Sumo Logic to track deployment frequency, vulnerability counts per deployment, and production application error rates
- **Alerting and reporting**: Create an SLO alert in Sumo Logic that can notify the team when daily deployments drop below 10 and when there are any critical vulnerabilities identified during production
- **Visualization**: The dashboards that are put together within Sumo Logic can be shared with key stakeholders in the business and all those who are accountable for delivering and improving on this KPI
- **Playbooks**: They can use Sumo Logic's automation service to run automated steps or processes if a critical vulnerability is ever identified, and because of how versatile it is, it can do anything from run Jenkins or GitLab actions all the way to initiating patching and remediation processes

The outcome of this process is that now the team has an actionable and useful KPI that can help them identify issues early and demonstrate compliance with KPIs, all while improving the security posture of the business.

However, there are a few interesting pitfalls with this process that all kinds of teams struggle with on a daily basis, namely, overcomplication of automation, alert fatigue, and monitoring in silos.

Overcomplication happens when teams try to bite off more than they can chew and quickly get overwhelmed trying to automate as much as possible. It is recommended that you start small and take one or two processes.

The alerts that should have been helpful in steering performance start to overpower the team; this is known as **alert fatigue**. Teams can use Sumo Logic's machine learning capabilities, where possible, to get the platform to learn about your data in real time, or at the very least, tweak the thresholds. Finally, if teams are using different tools to monitor all the different processes (that is, **monitoring in silos**), chaos ensues. They should aim to centralize monitoring in a common platform with a common toolset for more effectiveness and to obtain the visibility they need.

Review and adjust regularly

We've got the engine in motion now, and all we need to do is regularly review the performance metrics, make sure the KPIs are still SMART and tied to the business objectives, keep everything running smoothly, and improve operational performance. Here's a quick look at how to structure this:

1. **Set a review cadence**: This could be quarterly or bi-annual. For parts of the business that shift and change quickly, such as DevOps, quarterly is ideal.
2. **Evaluate performance against KPIs**: Identify which KPIs were exceeded, which ones were met, and which ones didn't do so well. Also, check your benchmarks to see whether they're still relevant.

3. **Lessons learned**: Analyze the KPIs and performance and understand where things went well and where they didn't. There's a lot to be learned from these day-to-day events. If there was a recent intrusion, how long did it take to contain? If it took longer than it should have based on the team's expertise and their tools, why did it take so long?

4. **Adjust KPIs**: Maybe you've learned that some KPIs are not very realistic. Change them slightly! It's a dynamic world we live in; goalposts can shift, but make sure there's accountability involved. If anyone can change KPIs on a whim without anyone else knowing or without a process, it means these KPIs are not valued and add nothing to the goals of the team and business.

5. **Communicate changes**: This is a super-important bit. Make sure all the stakeholders and teams as part of the KPI setting process are made aware, including senior management, who should be playing a role in this process anyway.

6. **Act on the changes**: Every great plan stays as only a plan without proper execution. Stick to the adjustments and commit to making sure you see the results of your hard work.

Let's look at a real-life example scenario where this type of change in relation to changing circumstances is warranted.

An airline customer who is conscious of their security has realized that there are lots of gaping holes in their defenses. They made a few solid investments into security technology and hired expertise, making significant progress with creating processes, automating them, and attaining visibility over their sizable estate.

Their initial KPI was something like this: *Reduce MTTR for all security incidents down to 2 hours from 5 hours within the next 6–12 months*.

That's a great KPI to start with, especially considering that some investments were made in the right areas to support this. However, their competitors in the industry have been getting hit with ransomware attacks, and that's a cause for concern. The team sits down and reassesses their KPIs and benchmarks after some high-profile attacks in the news and realizes there are changes to be made.

The original KPI was changed to the following: *Detect and respond to ransomware attacks within 1 hour of detecting suspicious file share activity*.

That is a review and readjustment done right! The team is flexible enough to change and adapt to changing circumstances and has historic performance data to back up their new targets and metrics.

We've now defined the measurement process in detail. We looked at the entire sequence from start to finish:

1. Understand business objectives.
2. Identify core security and DevSecOps functions.
3. Determine relevant metrics.
4. Collaborate across teams.
5. Define benchmarks.
6. Incorporate automation and continuous monitoring.
7. Review and adjust regularly.

These seven steps carry quite a bit of internal upheaval with them. In order to effectively adopt these steps, any business needs to have teams that are open to new ideas, willing to collaborate, self-reflect, and understand where they can improve and have the required management and technology resources to implement the process. This applies to businesses of the entire size spectrum, where some of the steps might be easier for certain organizations, and extremely delicate and time-consuming for others.

In the next section, we'll cover some more concrete examples of reliability management and performance monitoring with Sumo Logic's capabilities around SLO monitoring.

Measuring these criteria with Sumo Logic

We've covered some of the theoretical groundwork for performance criteria and their measurement, but let's see how it all comes together in a practical way using Sumo Logic. The platform can gather and ingest substantial useful metadata when it comes to KPI measurement, and several features and tools are available to you to help implement and continuously monitor all KPIs in one place.

As we mentioned both in the previous chapter and at the start of this one, there are many useful out-of-the-box views in the platform related to various KPIs and metrics, including some that have been covered so far. Once you've gone through the first three stages of the KPI development process, the SMART KPIs can be set in Sumo Logic to monitor, visualize, and report over time. There is a feature called **Reliability Management**, where SLIs, SLOs, and KPIs can be tracked over time across a vast range of variables. For instance, suppose you need to monitor your Insights in SIEM and ensure that too many false positives aren't occurring. You can reverse the logic and monitor the *true* positives, ensuring that your team is working on worthy incidents. Sumo Logic's SLO monitor screen looks like this:

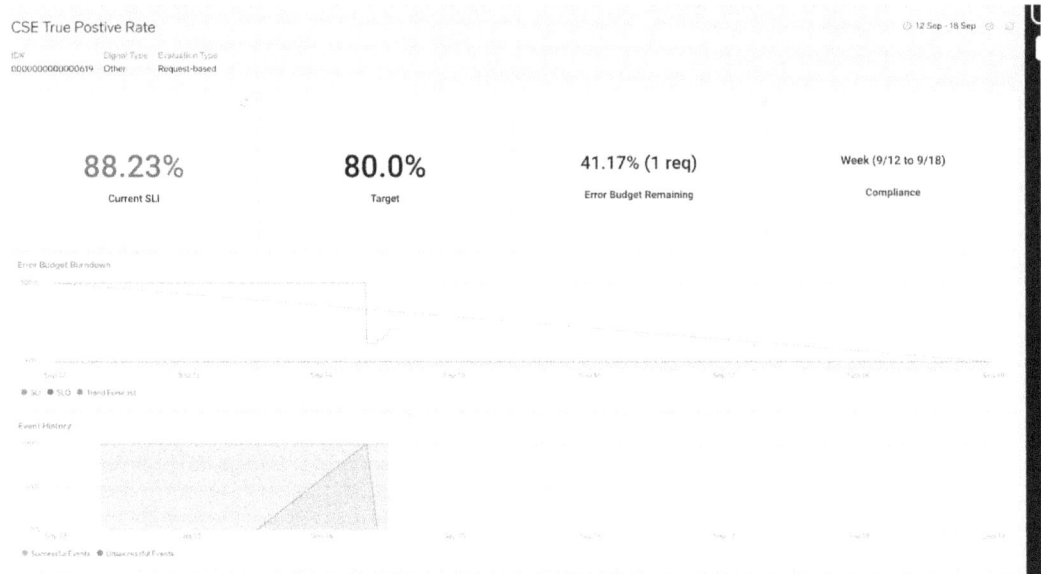

Figure 3.5 – An SLO monitor and dashboard that tracks Cloud SIEM Enterprise (CSE) True Positive Detection Rate

5 shows that we have a target of 80% for incidents that have to be true positives, and we are currently at 88.23%. What happens if this dips below 80? Well, the SLO monitors give you the option of defining an **error budget** and a **rolling compliance window** to define how this is tracked, and any failures in meeting the target will *burn down* a virtual budget to visually show you how well you are succeeding, or how badly you are failing at this particular KPI or SLI.

We can take another example, with an SLO dashboard that is monitoring the latency of a checkout service on a public-facing web application that the DevOps team is actively tracking. This SLO dashboard shows us how we are failing at keeping our checkout service below our key threshold:

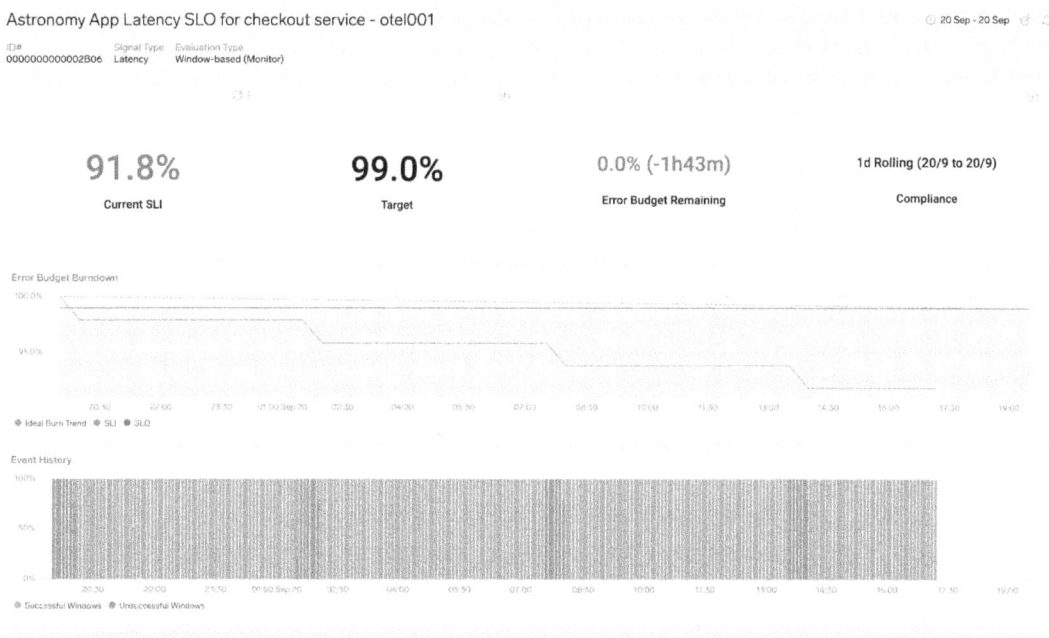

Figure 3.6 – SLO dashboard that shows checkout service is not below our key threshold

This example shows the same concept, but I've included the bottom panel of the dashboard, which is the **Historical Data** panel. This allows your team to track, *over the long term*, how well this particular KPI or SLI is being met:

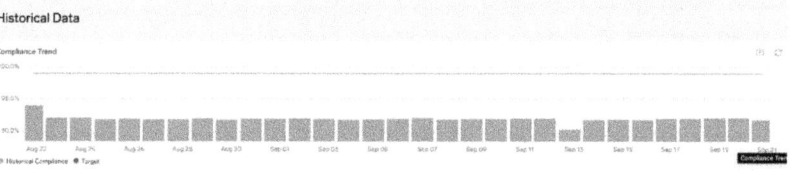

Figure 3.7 – Historical Data trend

Any glaring problems, such as, in this case, not being able to ever hit the target, help to realign the SLI and metrics to improve it. In this manner, Sumo Logic provides you with a way of measuring every aspect of your teams' business and technical requirements, allowing you to add value to the business and make teams more efficient in the process.

Let's not stop there! What if you want to measure some business KPIs around customer satisfaction, or things that have a direct impact on the business, such as customers abandoning their carts? You can create dashboards out of the metrics these applications are generating to keep track of this aspect, as shown here:

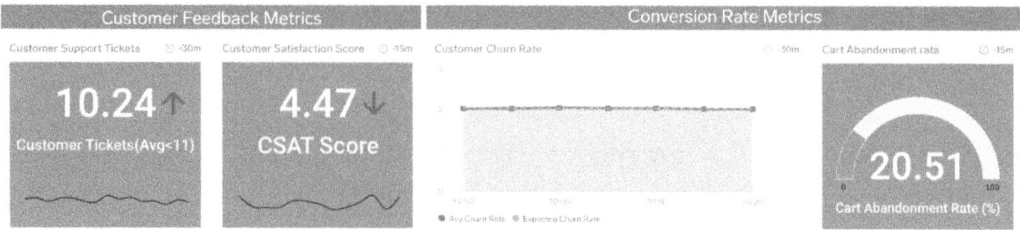

Figure 3.8 – Custom Feedback Metrics and Conversion Rate Metrics

And if we were to look at DevOps and DevSecOps with respect to pipelines and code development, you can use the SDO app in Sumo Logic for some out-of-the-box content that allows you to view a multitude of metric points and help Dev teams stay on track. We looked at an example of DORA metrics in *Chapter 1, Introduction to Sumo Logic* but if we were to don our SecOps hats and look at build failures to see whether it was due to a vulnerability or some other operational issue, we could easily use something such as the dashboard in *Figure 3.9*, which shows an SDO view focusing on **Alerts** as part of the pipeline process:

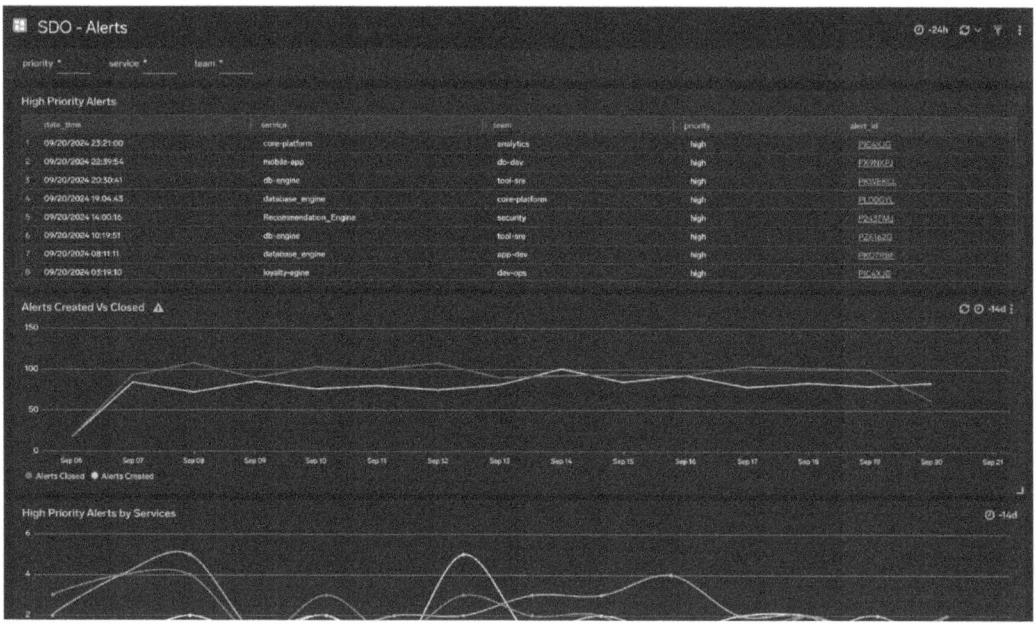

Figure 3.9 – An SDO dashboard showing alerts as part of the CI/CD pipeline

These are but a handful of examples; there is much more content to explore in Sumo Logic and much more value that you can derive from your data across DevOps, SecOps, and the wider business.

Summary

In this comprehensive chapter, we've explored performance criteria and metrics in detail. We started by covering why measuring performance in operations teams matters. It has multiple uses and advantages – helping to measure performance, to understand what's not working well and what is, and where improvements can be made. It can shed light on where investments need to be made by senior management and justify decisions across the operational spectrum of the business. Finally, it helps operational teams work together more closely, improving everything from decision-making and prioritization all the way to mental well-being and job satisfaction. The benefits are vast and game-changing.

We also covered what KPIs, SLIs, and SLOs actually are, providing definitions for each and examples of how to start utilizing some of the KPIs we discussed. These ranged from MTTR and MTTD from a SecOps perspective to minimizing vulnerable containers, minimizing technical debt from the environment, and many more.

Finally, we offered a step-by-step guide to defining this measurement process in your organization and how Sumo Logic can help you to continuously monitor and improve your teams, processes, and security posture with the help of various out-of-the-box dashboards and capabilities, such as SLO monitoring.

As it stands, we're tracking what's happening to our teams properly now and making sure they're working together and climbing the leaderboard to operational success. Drumroll, please! In *Chapter 4, Setting Up Your Fist Collector* we're going to dive into the Sumo Logic platform and start getting some quick wins by ingesting our first bit of data. Let's go!

References

1. https://industrialcyber.co/utilities-energy-power-water-waste/tata-power-data-being-leaked-by-hive-ransomware-group-after-negotiations-likely-fail/

Get this book's PDF version and more

Scan the QR code (or go to `packtpub.com/unlock`). Search for this book by name, confirm the edition, and then follow the steps on the page.

Note: Keep your invoice handy. Purchases made directly from Packt don't require an invoice.

Part 2
Getting Started with Sumo Logic

This part of the book is a primer on how to get started with Sumo Logic in a hands-on way. You'll learn how to start ingesting data into the platform across all MELT telemetry – metrics, logs, and traces, and then apply analytics on top of the data. We'll be doing a deep dive into analytics in this part also, covering the myriad ways of extracting insights out of your logs and metrics, both in queries and with visual analytics.

This part of the book includes the following chapters:

- *Chapter 4, Setting Up Your First Collector*
- *Chapter 5, Ingesting Data*
- *Chapter 6, Analyzing Data*
- *Chapter 7, Metrics*
- *Chapter 8, Alerting, Monitoring, and Visualizing Data*

4
Setting Up Your First Collector

Up to this point, we've been laying the theoretical groundwork, explaining DevSecOps, discussing frameworks and models, and learning how to begin implementing this massive shift internally within the business. Now we come to the practical side of things. Think of the next few chapters as recipes from a cookbook—a series of steps to take, what to do, how to do it in the best way, and bringing everything together and baking it into a nice analytical cake. Here is where we start looking at Sumo Logic in earnest. The aim is to take you through the entirety of the log analytics section of the platform to begin with. Sumo Logic, at its heart, is a data analytics technology, so there is a lot of ground to cover here. We'll start nice and easy from the very fundamentals, looking closely at data ingestion and management. This includes setting up our first collector in this chapter and what to keep an eye out for. These are crucial concepts when looking at improving visibility and reducing complexity. We can then move on to out-of-the-box content such as dashboards and diving deep into log analytics and observability.

It's worth defining what *observability* is and how it differs from security analytics. Observability refers to the ability to gain insights into the internal state of a system by analyzing the data it produces, such as **metrics, events, logs, and traces (MELT)**. It provides a holistic view of a system's performance and behavior, allowing teams to proactively detect and resolve issues. Log analytics is one part of the MELT observability puzzle. Security log analytics is even more focused, dealing with rich system and application logs, emphasizing correlation and context across the attack life cycle or kill chain across different data types to find anomalies and misuse, and leading threat analysis with a goal of faster time to detection, response, and remediation.

There are observability solutions that have logs as a source of power, and there are security solutions that are log-driven (SIEM solutions), but there aren't many platforms out there that do both of these things at a high level. Sumo Logic is a unified log analytics solution that puts logs at the heart of all of your data, and we will look at how to tap into this advantage as we go.

The following topics will be covered in this chapter:

- Creating a Sumo Logic instance and basic setup
- Ingesting operating system logs
- Ingesting operating system metrics
- The App Catalog

Creating a Sumo Logic instance and basic setup

Before configuring data sources or building detections, you first need a Sumo Logic instance. Sumo Logic is a cloud-native SaaS solution, which means that getting started is as simple as going to the website and starting a free trial. There is no need to provision the right level of hardware, plan the usage of the tool, and then muster teams to get it up and running. This is what a typical SIEM onboarding process *used to* look like. With Sumo Logic, it's very different.

Here are the steps for creating a Sumo Logic instance:

1. First, head to https://www.sumologic.com and click on **Start Free Trial** at the top right.

2. Then enter your email address, phone number, and region. Region is a very important choice because Sumo Logic complies with data residence regulations, such as **General Data Protection Regulation** (**GDPR**), so your data will live in the region you select and not leave. You have a few choices, as shown here:

Figure 4.1 – A list of regions available for Sumo Logic instances

> **Note**
>
> Note that there are some Sumo Logic regions available and comming soon for government and sensitive uses like **US FedRamp**, the **European Sovereign Cloud** and the **Swiss Data Center.**

3. When complete, you will receive an email to confirm your account. Fill in the required information about you and your company, and your account will be activated.

> **Tip**
>
> Don't worry too much about what you put in here. I think at one point I had a company called "*Monitor my kids' internet activity Inc.*"!

Now that your instance is created, you'll come to an introductory page that looks like this:

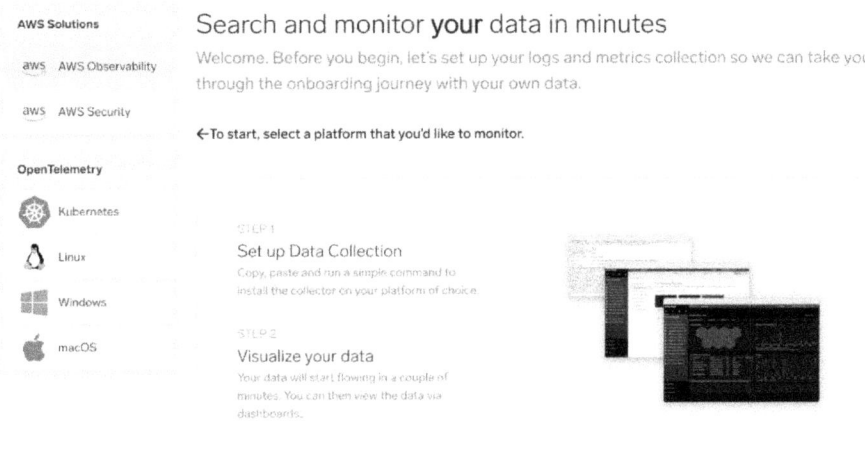

Figure 4.2 – The introductory page when you first log in to the platform

The introductory page of the UI helps you to start ingesting data. Since we are following this guide, we're going to skip this page for now.

1. Head to the three dots in the top-right corner and choose **Skip Onboarding (For Power Users)**.

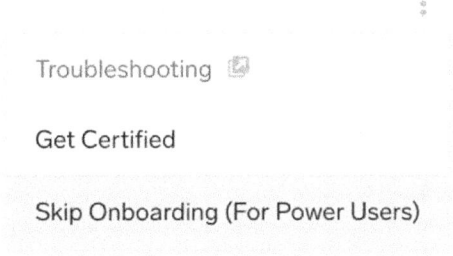

Figure 4.3 – Skipping the official onboarding process

Now we're in the main UI, and we can do anything we want to. I can almost smell that delicious analytical cake baking! We just need to get some sweet logs in here.

Whether Windows, Mac, or Linux, you can deploy a Sumo Logic collector on the system to start collecting logs and metrics and shipping them straight into your new trial instance. Some people refer to these collectors as *agents*, but I avoid that term as it has connotations of secret spying on everything happening on the system. However, collectors do that exact thing minus the secret part.

Enter **OpenTelemetry**, a vendor-agnostic collector that can collect various types of telemetry, route it, and transform it before shipping it off to data-hungry vendors (such as Sumo Logic). We'll talk more about this in *Chapter 5, Ingesting Data,* but just know that you have a choice between a traditional Sumo Logic collector and a newer, vendor-agnostic collector called OpenTelemetry, or **OTEL** for short. For now, let's get some quick wins.

Ingesting operating system logs

One of the quickest ways to get data into Sumo Logic is to ingest operating system logs and metrics. It's quite a straightforward process, and starting with it helps you interact with the platform as quickly as possible:

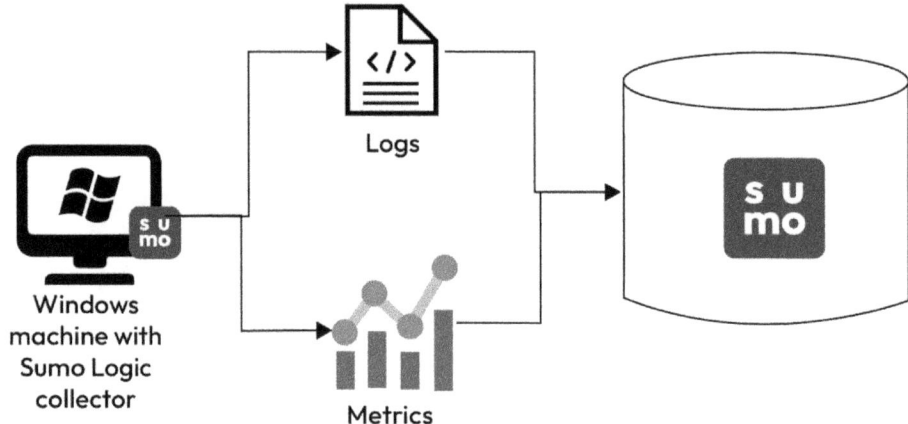

Figure 4.4 – Logs and metrics telemetry being sent from a Windows machine to Sumo Logic

Let's begin by setting up an Installed Collector on a Linux machine and covering the process as well as best practices.

Setting up a Linux Installed Collector

Head to the **Collection** section of the platform, which has a centralized data repository for all your data. You can get there by either clicking on **Data Management** in the left menu, followed by **Collection**, or using *Cmd + K* on a Mac or *Windows + K* on Windows; this will open the **Go To...** pop-up menu, where you can type Collection.

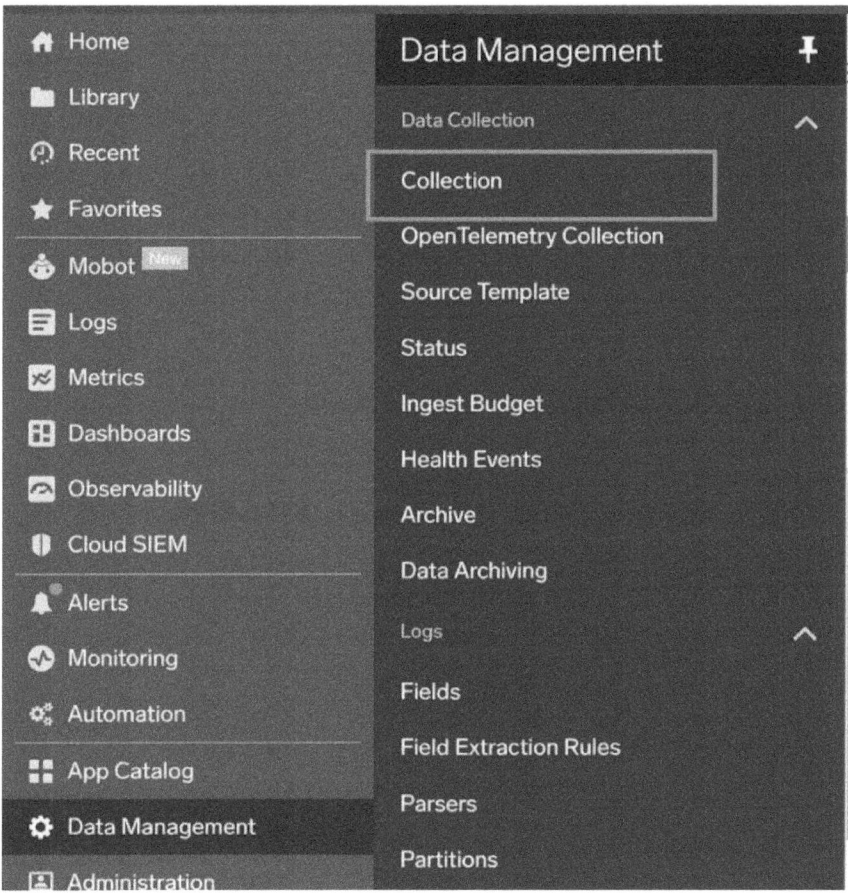

Figure 4.5 – The Data Collection section in the Configuration menu

You'll arrive at a **Data Collection** screen like this:

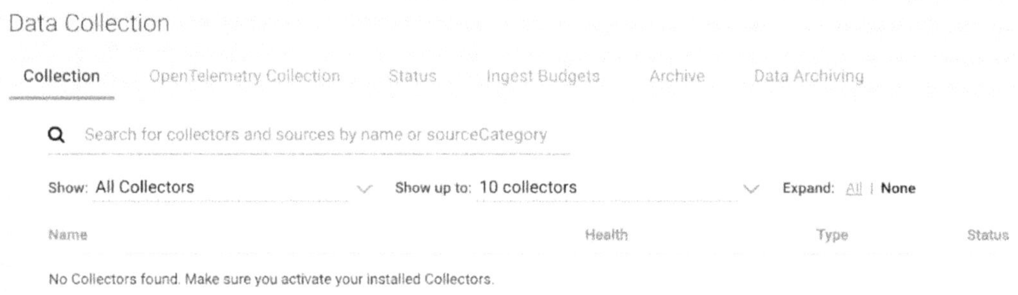

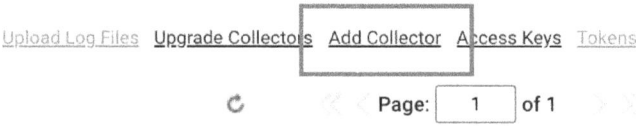

Figure 4.6 – The Data Collection UI, which we will be filling with collectors soon!

Let's add our first collector.

> **Note**
>
> You'll notice the **OpenTelemetry Collection** tab next to **Collection**; we'll cover this shortly.

To add a collector, look at the top right of this section and you'll see **Add Collector** underlined:

Figure 4.7 – The button to add an Installed or a Hosted Collector

When you click this, you are presented with two options: **Installed Collector** and **Hosted Collector**.

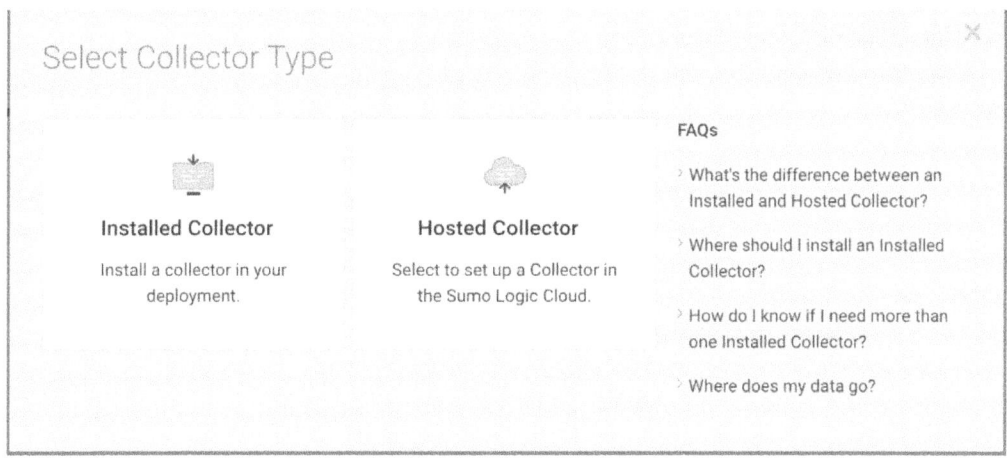

Figure 4.8 – The view where you choose which type of collector and data you need to be ingested

Sumo Logic is a hybrid data platform, meaning you can ingest something from an on-premises or local environment or from the cloud without issue. Your collector could be hosted in the cloud in either scenario, but these options are more about *who manages* the collection infrastructure.

Installed indicates you want to fully own the infrastructure and *install* it yourself, whether on dedicated systems, VMs, or your own cloud instances. The **Installed Collector** option is the best way of getting logs and metrics telemetry from a particular device, better than a Hosted Collector can. When deployed, you have access to any file, channel, or service data that you can forward to Sumo Logic for analytics.

Hosted simply means you are allowing Sumo Logic to *host* the collector on its own load-balanced, purpose-built cloud collector infrastructure. In this chapter, we will be focusing on Installed Collectors, but in *Chapter 5*, we will be covering all the other ingestion options, such as Hosted Collectors and OpenTelemetry collection. Hosted collectors are used when you are sending data over the cloud to Sumo Logic, whether it be from a hyperscaler such as AWS or Azure or from a source such as Zscaler or 1Password.

For now, get the collector installed locally by selecting **Installed Collector**.

Choosing the operating system

When selecting **Installed Collector**, you are presented with a list of operating systems that deploy a collector onto your machine:

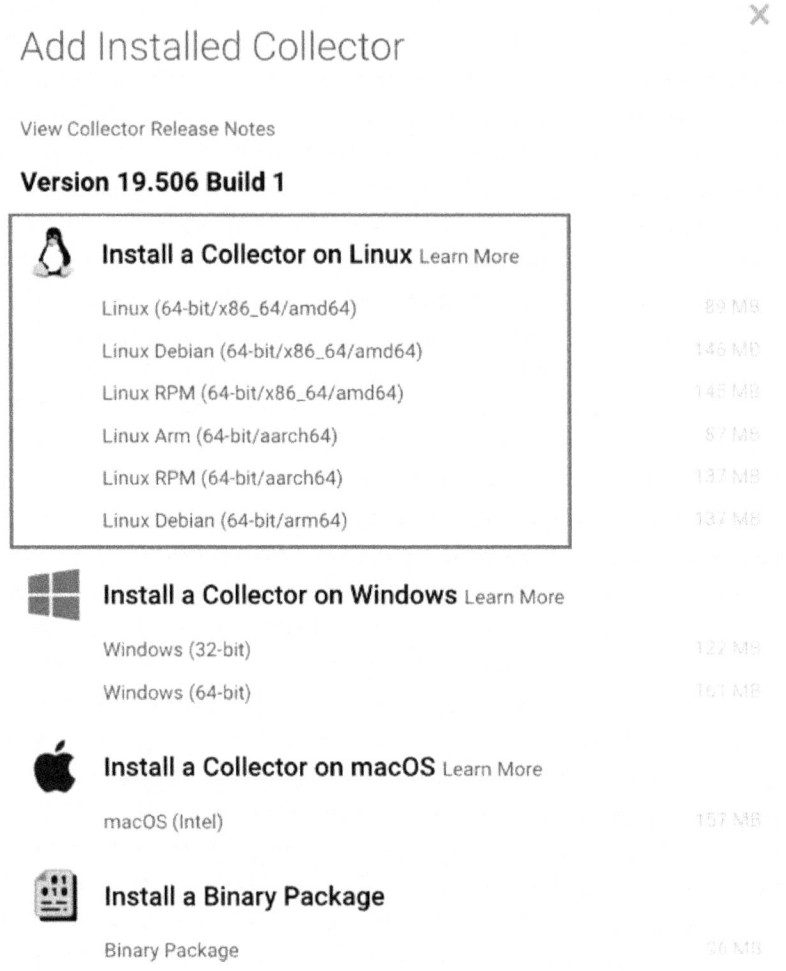

Figure 4.9 – Operating system options for the collector

You can click on the collector you want to install based on the operating system you are on. The example in this chapter (for both Windows and Linux) will deploy the agent on a server without a GUI but with a command line, because I will be installing these collectors on VMs. So, let's right-click on the **Linux (64-bit/x86_64/amd64)** binary and copy the link address. Then move to your Linux server and carry out a wget command, as shown next. The URL may be slightly different when you're doing this, but it'll be similar.

```
wget https://collectors.eu.sumologic.com/rest/download/linux/64 -O sumoCollector.sh
```

This is followed by a permissions change:

```
sudo chmod +x sumoCollector.sh
```

With the collector now downloaded onto your machine and executable, you can proceed to installation.

Running the install command

Now, before you run the binary, generate an access token that will help the collector associate itself with your Sumo Logic instance. The token has authentication hard-wired into it, which means authentication is smoother as we avoid using a typical username and password.

> **Note**
>
> Sumo Logic is a multi-tenant SaaS solution; that is, a lot of customers are sharing the same solution simultaneously. As such, each collector is strictly bound to only a single tenant or customer. This ensures there is no way for data to spill or be leaked across tenants or accounts, and this is accomplished through a variety of mechanisms, such as unique and rotating encryption keys.

In the top right of the collection page, two entries away from **Add Collector**, you'll see **Tokens**.

Click on it to create an installation token.

Go to **+ Add Token** in the top-right corner and create a token by giving it a name:

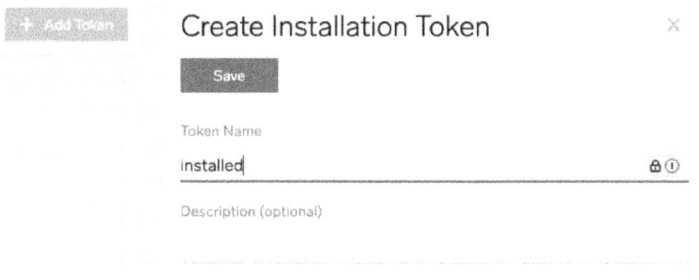

Figure 4.10 – Adding a new token

The outcome is a Base64 token string, which you can use as part of the installation string as shown here:

Figure 4.11 – The end result of adding a new token

Now, we go back to our Linux server, which in this case is an Amazon Linux 2 EC2 instance. Try to execute the binary by running the following command:

```
sudo ./sumoCollector.sh
```

Depending on the AMI you're using, it may provide you with an error that mentions missing Java packages. In my case, I didn't have the right **Java Development Kit (JDK)** on my machine, so I needed to rectify that first.

In this example, I ran the following command to install the JDK on my AWS EC2 Linux machine:

```
sudo dnf install java-21-amazon-corretto
```

Java 21 was the most recent version of Amazon Corretto at the time of writing, so we should have the latest Java libraries ready to go. This will be dependent on what flavor of Linux you opt for. As I'm on an Amazon Linux 2 EC2 instance here, this is a requirement, but if you're on an Ubuntu Linux machine, this mini-step won't be necessary. If you do run into any errors, a simple Google search will point you in the right direction.

So, once we've done that, we can install the collector with the following command. Adding your installation token is crucial here, as this will help to tie the collector to your instance and authenticate to your Sumo Logic instance:

```
sudo ./sumoCollector.sh -q -Vsumo.token_and_url=<installationToken>
```

The collector should deploy and complete with no issues. Refresh your browser, and the Installed Collector can now be seen in your collector list, as shown:

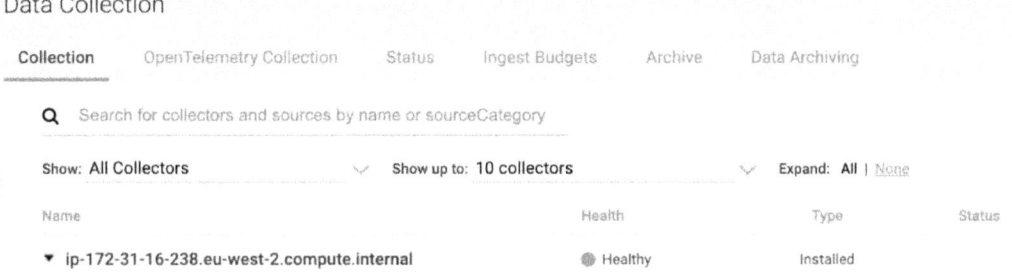

Figure 4.12 – The Installed Collector

Adding our first source

Now, we have the collector, but we need to add sources. Think of a collector as an empty parent container that sits wherever there is data to be ingested. The actual workhorses that bring in the telemetry and data are these **sources**. For example, a single collector could simultaneously bring in a wide variety of log data and listen in on multiple different network ports and log streams.

From the collection screen, where you should be now, find your new collector and go to the right side of the screen. Click on the **Add...** button, and then **Add Source**. You will be presented with a list of file sources that you can attach to the collector to start getting data in, as shown:

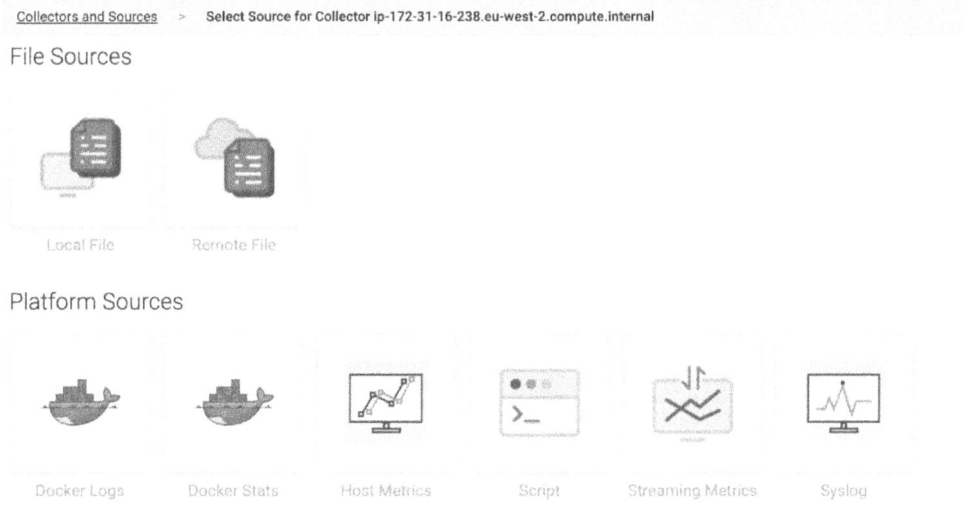

Figure 4.13 – The range of sources you can ingest from a Linux Installed Collector

As you can see in *Figure 4.13*, there are several options, from a basic log file ingest to syslog and host metrics. These are all useful in different ways. For instance, if you want to ingest log files from your server, you can use the **Local File** or **Remote File** option. If you have any applications that log to a particular file on your server, you can specify it and start monitoring the logs easily.

Syslog is a protocol that's used to ingest data when you want to have it somewhere useful instead of being lonely on a server somewhere. Syslog is great for a number of reasons, but it's usually easier to group, centralize, and ingest data into a SIEM solution via syslog natively. It can also stream in real time, as well as handling high volumes better than normal logging.

Host metrics will be covered in greater detail in *Chapter 7*, but metrics are great for understanding the health and operational capability of the device where the collector sits. How much CPU is it consuming at any given moment? How many network packets has it received in the last hour? These questions can be answered with metrics.

Further, if yours is a containerized server, you can ingest **Docker logs** and **stats**. We will be focusing on the **Local File** source in this example to get some log files into Sumo Logic, and before the end of the chapter, we'll take a look at metrics ingestion. The other most frequently used source is syslog, but we won't be setting up any syslog sources in this chapter.

Configuring the source

Let's go to **Local File** to send in some log files. You'll come across some fields for configuration. The main ones consist of giving this source the following:

- A name
- A file path
- A Source Category

These are the key fields to fill in for any new source. While **Source Category** isn't specified as a mandatory field with a red asterisk, it's incredibly important for data categorization. We will cover this next.

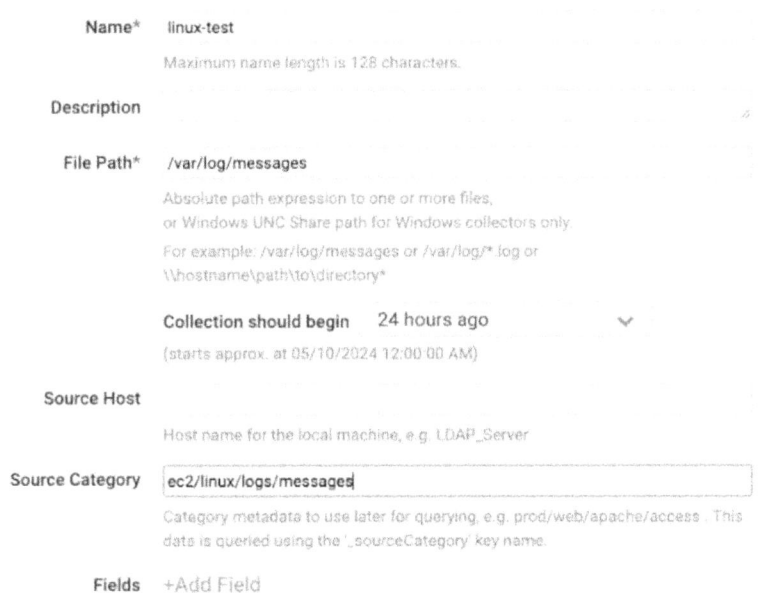

Figure 4.14 – The configuration of the Log File source with the key fields filled in

That should do it for now. **Name** and **File Path** are self-explanatory: the **Name** field gives a name to the source and **File Path** tells the collector where to look in your machine for the log files you've specified. You can use wildcards to specify multiple files within a directory or just reference multiple files here. What's this **Source Category** field, though? I'll give a quick explanation of the importance of this field.

> **Note**
>
> **Sumo Logic terminology – Source Categories**
>
> **Source Categories** are crucial to managing your data in Sumo Logic. A Source Category is a bit of internal metadata that allows you to categorize your data sources, which then allows you to easily use that data source in a query, in a dashboard, or even when deciding what teams and users can access what data with **Role-Based Access Control** (**RBAC**). We'll cover RBAC in the next chapter of this book, where we look at data ingestion best practices. We'll also cover Source Categories in greater depth a bit later

and in slightly more detail. Also, see this article for all the ways to leverage metadata tags in Sumo Logic: https://www.sumologic.com/blog/data-tagging-classification-enrichment/.

At the bottom of the configuration is a **Save** button. You want to finish the configuration; imagine setting up your first Sumo Logic collector and losing all that progress. Devastating.

Et voilà! Your source is created. Up to this point, we've downloaded the collector, installed it, and set up our first **Local File** source. Now we want to do the most important part—see the logs!

Viewing the logs

So, once everything is set up, you should be able to see logs coming through to Sumo Logic from your Linux server. Let's view them by looking at the **Collection** page. Hover over your new source and click on the document icon:

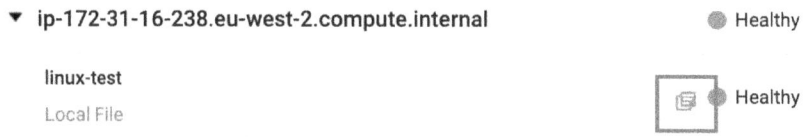

Figure 4.15 – This icon next to Healthy lets you quickly search the logs from this source

This automatically opens up the log query section and filters on the source in question, which is quicker than navigating to the log search section of the platform and typing in the Source Category manually. You should see something like this:

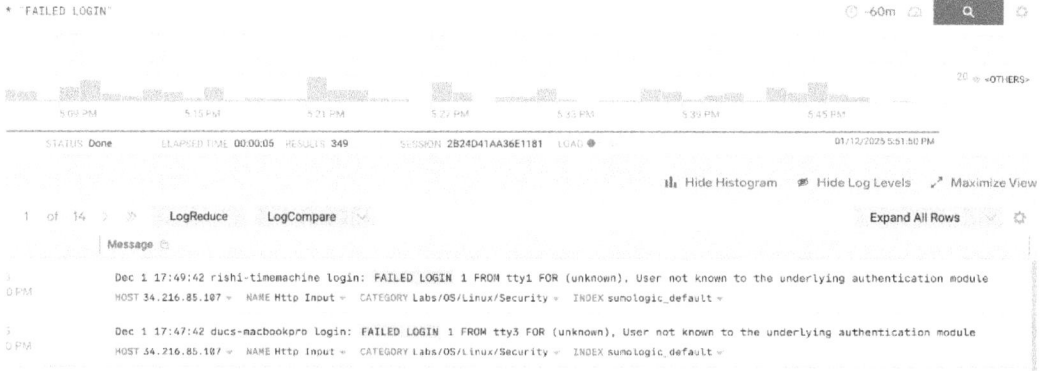

Figure 4.16 – The log search UI and an example of a log event

> **Note**
> Depending on your operating system, you may need to have internal logging already enabled. This was a fresh EC2 instance, so we had to install `rsyslog` and start the service before logs started coming in.

And just like that, we have data coming into Sumo Logic from Linux. Keep in mind, in order to DO something with this new data streaming in, you'll then have to browse the catalog and install the correpsonding apps for each data type. There are often multiple apps for the same data, in this case Linux logs, that you can choose from, each with a slightly different use case. More on this to come! Next, we'll look at the same process for Installed Collectors on Windows machines. Before we do that, I want to highlight a few things that you *didn't* have to do when setting up this collector:

- Concern yourself with indexes, light, heavy, or universal forwarders. A key mechanism of data ingestion and management in Sumo Logic is that you don't have to manage the index for each log or data stream. The data gets sent to one large, centralized data lake, which is managed by Sumo Logic, so your team doesn't have to do this, opening up time for more interesting things such as querying logs.
- Worry about mapping the data to a schema. Sumo Logic is schema-less. It runs on a "schema-on-read" model, and it can generate schemas on the fly for common data formats (JSON, Windows Event Logs, syslog, and more). It can also normalize data at ingest time, but more on that later.
- Set up any unnecessary preprocessing pipelines or worry about encryption keys for security when transporting data from the collector to Sumo Logic in the cloud.

From a log perspective, Sumo Logic makes it easy to ingest any unstructured or structured logs in this way. Further, if the data isn't parsed automatically by the schema-on-demand parsing, you get **Field Extraction Rules** (**FERs**) that help you parse the data any way you like, but we'll cover that in *Chapter 5, Ingesting Data*.

Let's jump into Windows!

Setting up a Windows Installed Collector

The initial steps for setting up a collector on a Windows machine are the same as Linux, up to the point where you choose the operating system. This time, you will choose **Windows (64-bit)**:

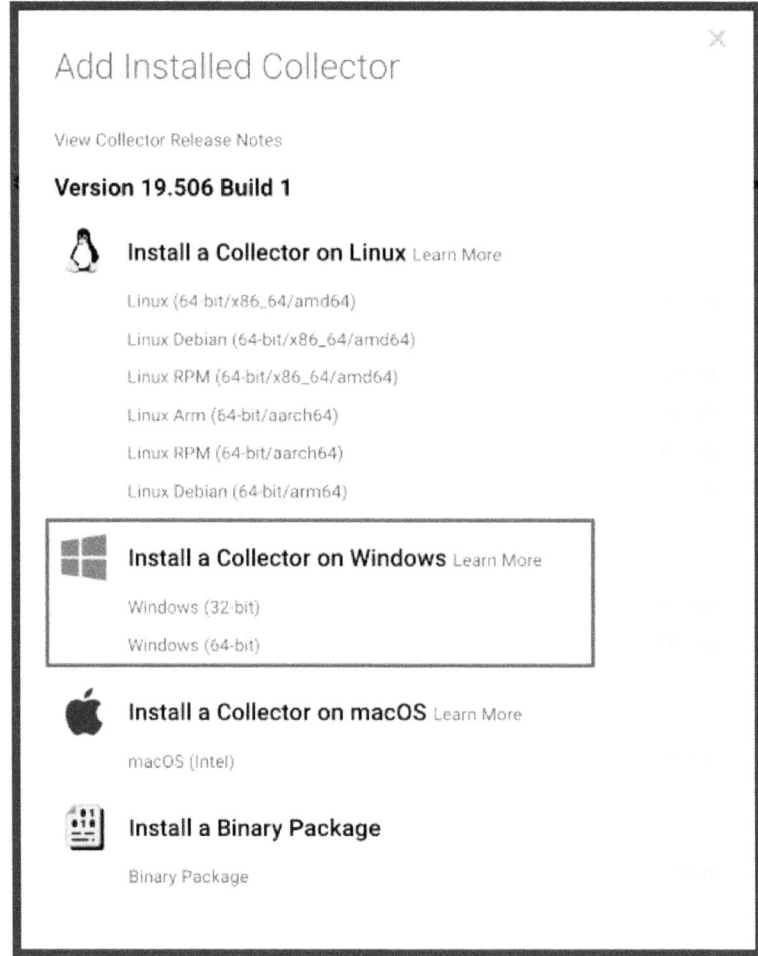

Figure 4.17 – The Installed Collector screen when selecting the Windows operating system

We'll need to be using a Windows device for this walk-through, so in my case, I've provisioned Windows Server 2025. Once the binary is downloaded onto the Windows device, you can run a similar command in PowerShell to the one we ran for Linux. Note that you can use the same installation token as you did for the Linux machine:

```
SumoCollector.exe -console -q "-Vsumo.token_and_url=<installationToken>"
```

The installation should take place without any issues, and you should then be able to see the Windows collector on your collection screen:

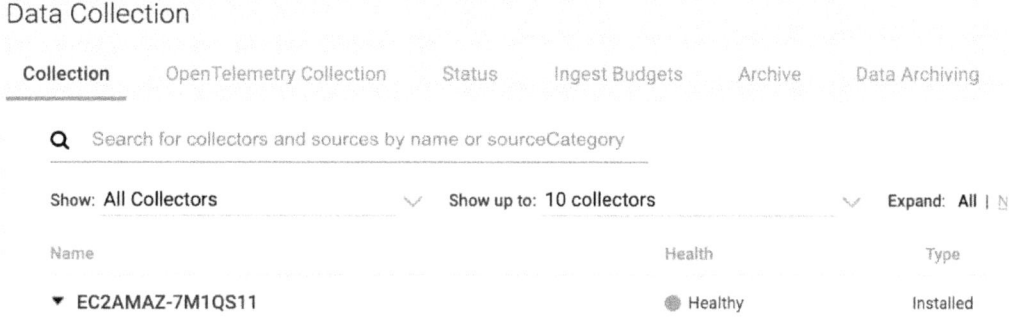

Figure 4.18 – Our Windows collector is now in the collector list

If you do experience any issues with the installation or deployment of your collector, there is a comprehensive troubleshooting section in the documentation, which you can refer to here: https://www.sumologic.com/help/docs/send-data/collector-faq/.

Also, let's not forget about Mobot! You can use the *Knowledge Agent* to ask about any problems you're having with the process. If we ran into a JDK problem earlier, we could've queried it with something such as, "I have tried to install a Linux Installed Collector but get an error about a missing Java Development Kit":

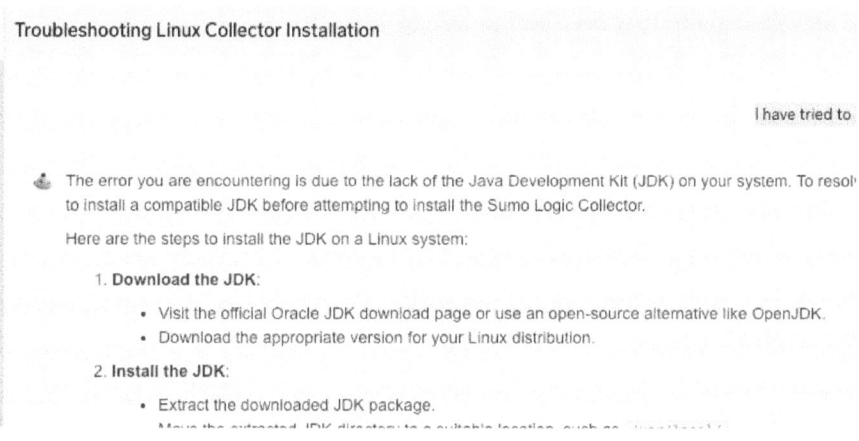

Figure 4.19 – Asking Mobot for help with Installed Collector deployment

Adding our Windows source

We've got the collector, and now we need to add our sources to it. You'll notice that when you go to the right-hand side and click **Add...**, then **Add Source**, there are three additional options presented at the bottom of the source grid:

- Windows Active Directory Inventory
- Windows Event Log
- Windows Performance

These sources allow you to bring in Windows-specific data types. Let's go with basic ingestion and get some Windows Event Logs into the platform.

Configuring the Windows Event Log source

You'll notice that this configuration page has a few more options to consider, so let's walk through them.

When you're planning your ingestion architecture, the first decision is how you want to collect logs: **locally** on each machine or **remotely** from a central server. Many customers start with a centralized collector that pulls logs from other devices on the network. This keeps the footprint small—one collector box, many sources—and is easy to maintain.

The alternative is deploying a collector directly on each machine. On the surface, this looks less scalable, but with configuration management tools such as **Ansible**, **Puppet**, or **Chef**, rolling out collectors to hundreds or thousands of hosts is straightforward. Both models work well; it really comes down to how your environment is structured and how much control you need over each endpoint.

For advanced users, note that there are technically four different methods to collect logs from Windows systems:

- Local collection via an Installed Collector
- Remote collection via an Installed Collector, where each system is identified by hostname
- Remote collection from **Domain Controllers** (**DCs**) using the DC discovery feature (**Domain Controller Mode**)
- Using Microsoft WEF/WEC to centrally collect logs to a single server using Microsoft's forwarding protocol, where our Installed Collector resides

We're not going to collect logs remotely here, but if you do opt for remote collection, you'll be able to enter your Windows domain, username, and password in the section that is no longer grayed out:

Figure 4.20 – Authentication options for remote collection on the network

Don't fill these in now, but they are an option for later if needed. Also note that when you select **Remote collection**, you can specify whether you'd like to activate **Domain Controller Mode** and collect events from the DCs visible on the network. This also sets the source as part of the Windows Entra ID inventory and detects any DCs on the network:

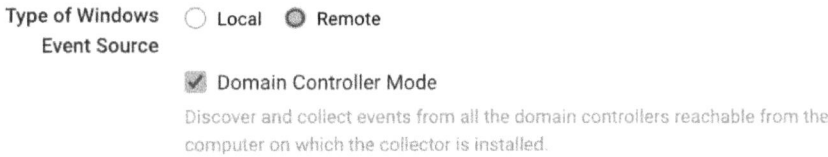

Figure 4.21 – Specifying Domain Controller Mode as part of remote collection

You can choose the event format to be either Windows legacy format or JSON. Sumo Logic can parse both with no problems and by default includes all the main event types and channels: **Application**, **Security**, and **System**.

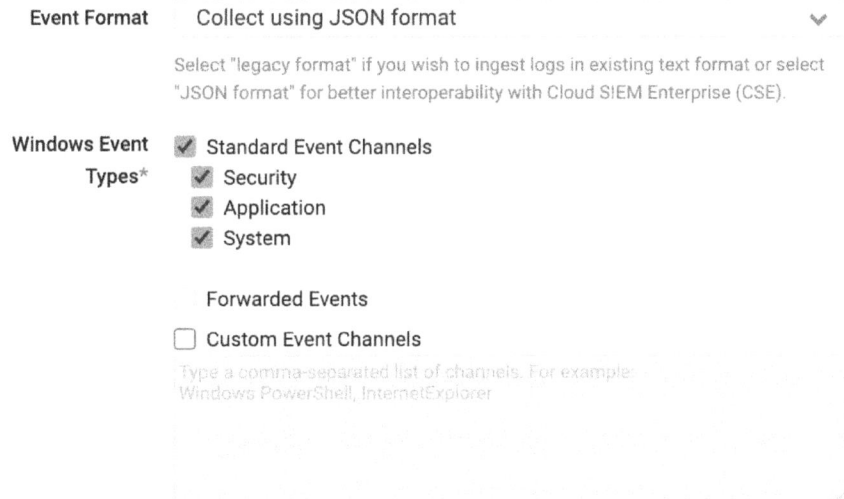

Figure 4.22 – Choosing the event format for our logs. Sumo Logic can accommodate older formats

You can also enter custom channels by checking the **Custom Event Channels** box. For example, if you log all PowerShell events, you would do so typically under a separate channel, which you can specify.

Once you've saved this configuration, the collector should start ingesting Windows Event Logs straight into Sumo Logic.

Viewing the Windows logs

Once activity occurs on the server, we'll get logs from one of the channels. To do a quick query on the source, point to the document icon next to the **Healthy** status column:

Figure 4.23 – Blue document icon to filter a quick log search on this source

This will then show you the logs that recently arrived on the platform, ready for viewing and analytics! Here is what I could see 20–30 seconds after setting the source up:

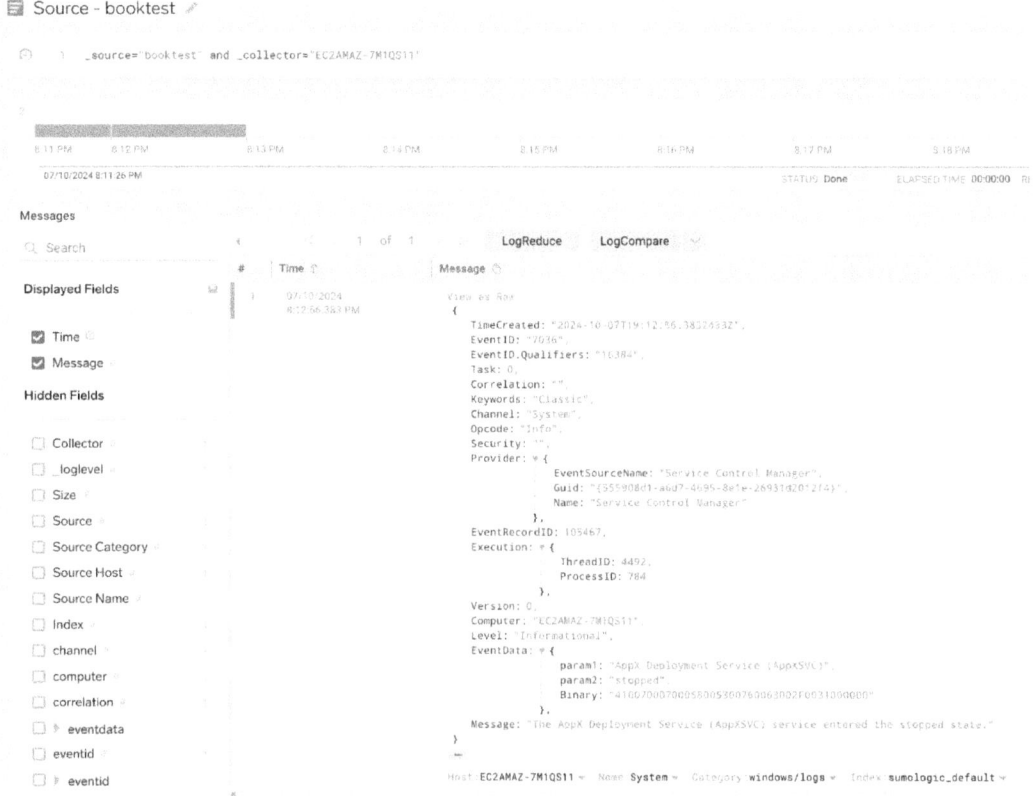

Figure 4.24 – An example event coming from our Windows machine

This log is from the **system** channel, which gives us changes in services that can be tracked and analyzed. It's particularly useful if there are services that shouldn't enter certain states but end up shutting down or being reactivated.

> You might be wondering about adding collectors on Mac devices. The process is quite similar to Linux, so we haven't included separate instructions.

You should now have a collector that is sending in log files to Sumo Logic, so congratulations on setting up your first collector!

We'll take a look at all the other methods of ingestion in the next chapter and bake more elements for our analytical cake; there are a lot of key ingredients still missing. So far, we've got the base of the cake that's just come out of the oven. Before we wrap up, let's cover metrics. They're incredibly useful and work perfectly with the logs to give you a full picture of what's happening.

Ingesting operating system metrics

It is worthwhile to cover how you can obtain metrics to supplement your logs. It's important to also monitor the state and health of your infrastructure, and metrics come in handy for that. Unlike OpenTelemetry collectors, which can ingest logs, metrics, *and* traces (we'll cover this in the next chapter), Installed Collectors only focus on logs and metrics. There are many metrics-focused views and dashboards that are packaged up within the apps in the App Catalog, so it's worth knowing how to quickly set these up. We'll cover the App Catalog and everything it has to offer in *Chapter 6, Analyzing Data*.

So, let's get some metrics in from our Linux machine and then discuss how we can achieve the same with Windows and Mac devices.

Finding the metrics source

Go back to your Installed Collector in the collector list and click on **Add...** and then **Source** on the right side of the screen. You will be presented with the sources available; this time, select **Host Metrics**:

Figure 4.25 – The Host Metrics source in the sources list

Let's look at the configuration involved to get those metrics streamed in.

Configuring the metrics source

The metrics configuration is very straightforward. The key fields here are as follows:

- **Name**
- **Source Category**
- **Scan Interval**
- **Metrics**

For this example, I've called my metrics source LinuxMetrics, given it a Source Category of linux/dev/metrics, and chosen a scanning interval of one minute. This value can be anything you want.

In the **Metrics** section, specify the metrics that you want to get from your operating system. The metrics come in five categories:

- CPU
- Memory
- TCP
- Network
- Disk

Within each category are a number of metrics that you can select from. For instance, spikes in CPU and memory usage are important because they can give indications that a device isn't behaving as expected. Whether this is due to an operational issue or something such as a cyber incident involving malware is something that is easy to investigate in Sumo Logic due to the context provided by metrics and logs over time.

Similarly, network monitoring is incredibly useful and can show how devices are performing at a network level. A great example is monitoring network packets inbound and outbound can reveal potential data exfiltration or beaconing attempts from a device to an external destination.

All you need to do is choose the relevant metrics and then hit **Save**.

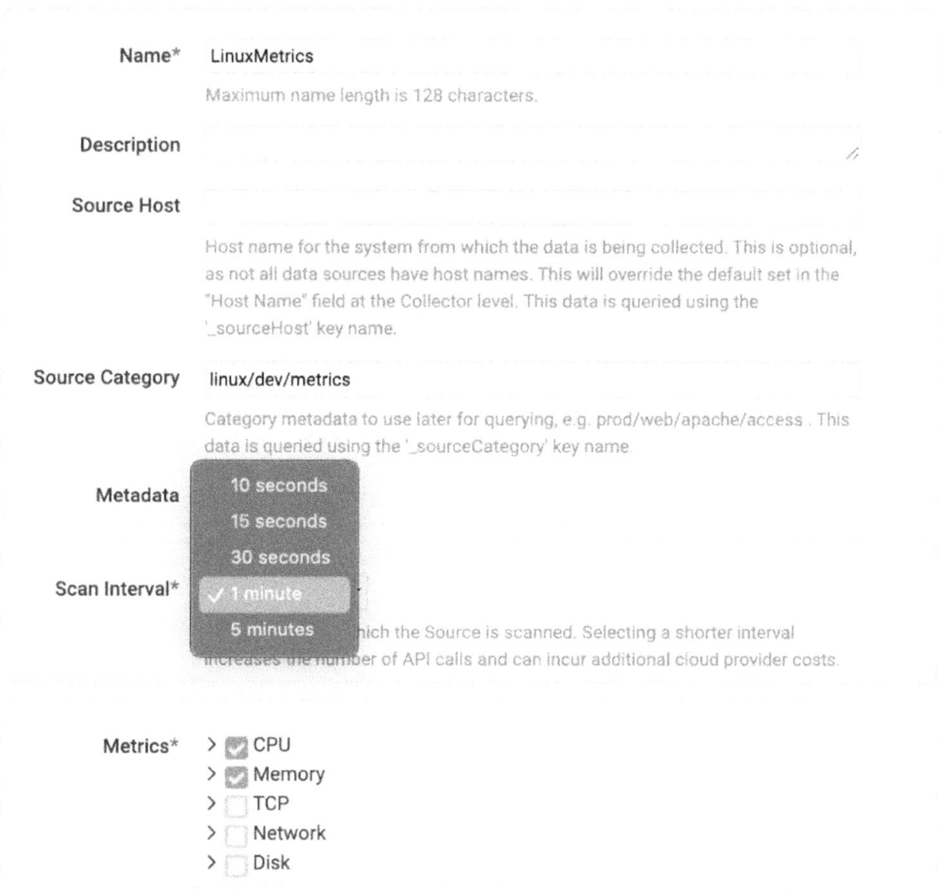

Figure 4.26 – The configuration for the metrics source

Viewing the metrics

To view the metrics from the source, do the same as you did for the logs. Hover your mouse to the left of **Healthy** and choose the metrics icon this time. It looks slightly different from the document icon, as shown here:

Figure 4.27 – The metrics icon

Once you click this, you will be taken to the **Metric** search UI with your source pre-filtered:

Figure 4.28 – The metrics UI view at a high level

You will see the **Chart** and **Time Series** options above the visual in the top-left corner. This is clearer in *Figure 4.29*. By default, **Chart** is selected, which illustrates the metrics in different ways based on the chart type selected (line, bar, heatmap, honeycomb, etc.), but clicking on **Time Series** will show you a list of all metrics that are being picked up:

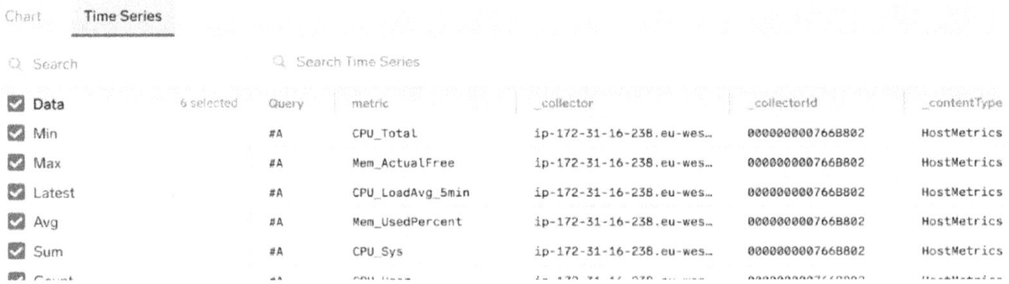

Figure 4.29 – Time Series view, which shows you all the metrics being collected

Now you can view your metrics and logs being collected from the machine. Happy days! We will explore both the log search and metrics search capabilities in greater detail when we explore the analytical capabilities of the platform in *Chapter 6, Analyzing Data*. I want to finish this process we've started with some useful information and views that you can access right now. There is an App Catalog in Sumo Logic that has hundreds of pre-built pieces of content for various sources, and we're going to set one up quickly now, so you can see your data in action.

The App Catalog

There are a lot of advantages to creating your own custom dashboards. You want to be using the data in the way that works best for you, which means you get more value from it. However, sometimes you don't want to be building out dashboards for basic, frequently monitored use cases. It still takes time, and let's face it, you just want to click a few buttons and have a lot of work done for you—who doesn't?! So, the App Catalog is packed full of hundreds of integrations with various technology types:

- IT infrastructure
- Compliance and security
- Microsoft Azure
- Amazon AWS
- Database
- DevOps
- Kubernetes
- Web server
- Sumo Logic
- Operating systems
- Storage
- Google Cloud Platform
- Tracing
- Sumo Logic Global Intelligence

Each of the technologies in these categories comes with out-of-the-box dashboards and queries that look for predefined use cases. In some cases, alerts are included, as in the case of the AWS Observability tools, but we'll talk about that shortly.

It's easily accessed from the left-hand menu under **App Catalog**.

We've already covered some examples in this book, namely the operating system ones, such as Linux and Windows, which come with great content. The other options available are also really powerful. For example, using Linux dashboards shows you what you're going to get, as shown:

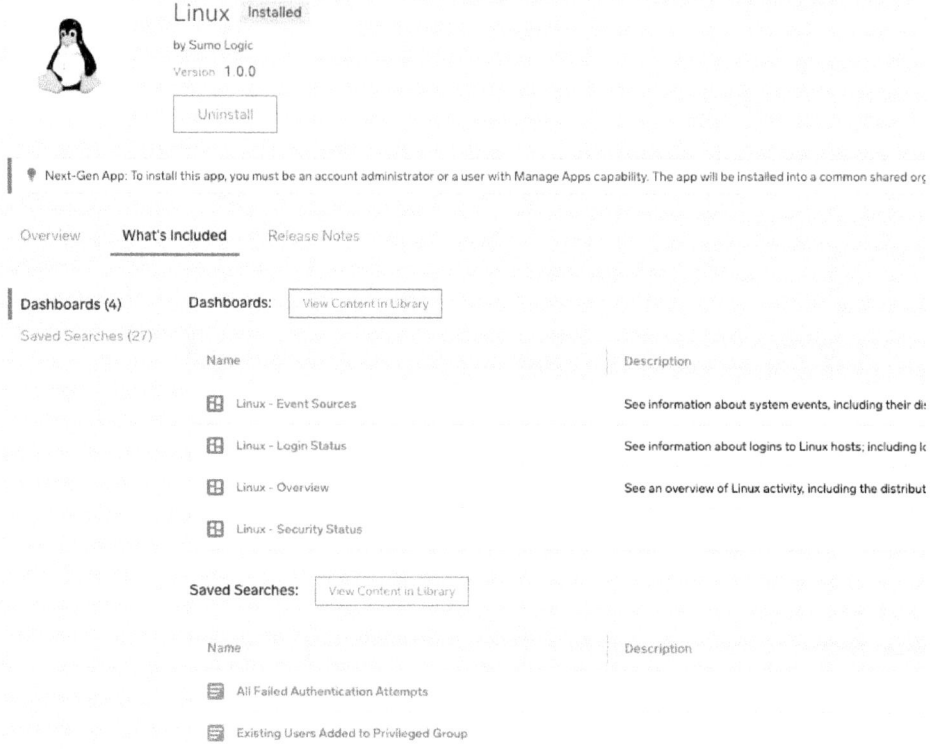

Figure 4.30 – The Linux dashboards and saved queries ready to go

The great thing about this content is that as soon as you point it at the source we set up earlier, the visuals start populating. This is because under each dashboard panel is a query, and these pre-created queries are running on the dataset they've been designed for, leading to some useful results. You don't have to do any work, just a few clicks to get something like this **Overview** dashboard that shows login trends within your Linux estate:

Figure 4.31 – The Linux Login Status dashboard

Each app has a step-by-step installation process that usually comes with prerequisite information before installing, and any configuration required on the technology to allow Sumo Logic to effectively understand the telemetry it receives from it. This culminates with the installation of content for that technology.

What we're looking for here is to help teams by doing the following:

- Speeding up the time from which they can extract value from their data
- Reducing the friction of having to quickly learn the technology to start creating useful, visual, data-driven approaches
- Making it easy to work in the Sumo Logic ecosystem

Up to now, we've covered a staggering amount of information on how to work with our data, namely because the options are so extensive and so versatile, so there are a lot of things to discuss and a lot of examples of where those capabilities come into play. In short, Sumo Logic provides the operational team with these options to make their jobs easier.

Quick Linux app setup

In this short section, we'll install the Linux app step by step to give you the same results with your data!

Head on over to the App Catalog and search for **Linux**. You'll see a few options, but we want to click on **Linux**, not **Linux - OpenTelemetry** (these OpenTelemetry apps will be covered in *Chapter 7*):

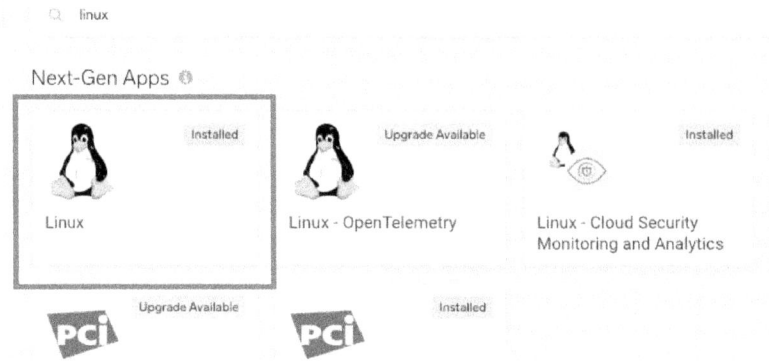

Figure 4.32 – Choosing the classic Linux app

Click the **Install App** button at the top, and then in step 1, choose **Next** in the top-right corner. You have the option of heading on over to the setup documentation, but we don't need that right now.

Step 2 is easy. You can choose from a range of metadata to help scope the data, but as long as you labeled your source with a Source Category, then **_sourceCategory** is definitely the recommended, and most used, option. The screen is presented here:

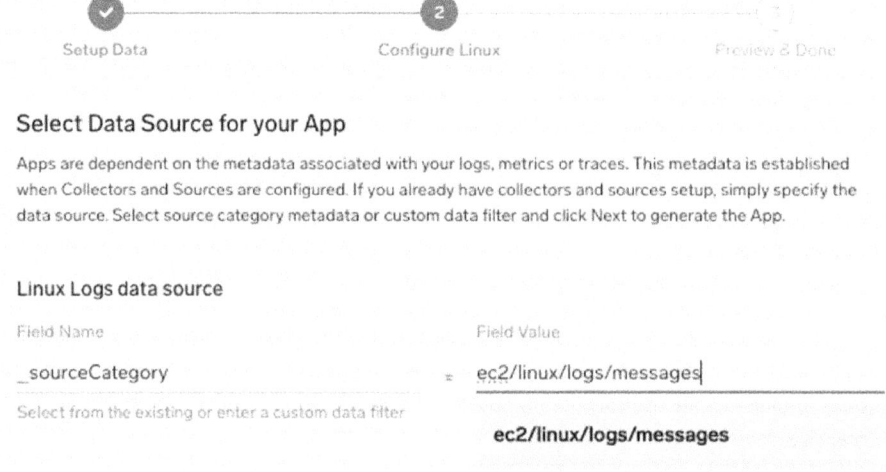

Figure 4.33 – Specifying where the data is located to help the app visualize your data

Click **Next** again, and you're done! Sumo Logic first installs the contents and then waits for data to come in from that source to populate the dashboard panels:

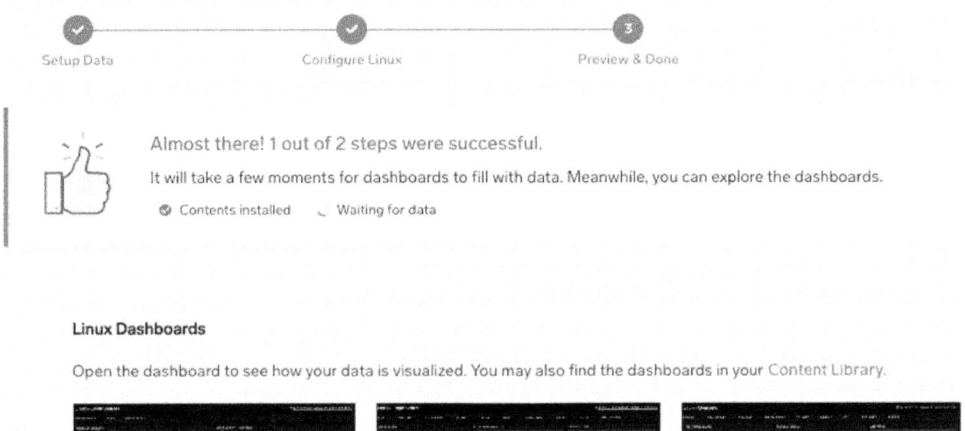

Figure 4.34 – Successful installation of the app

That wraps this chapter up quite nicely. We've gone from setting up our Sumo Logic instance to creating our first collector and adding a logs and metrics source to it, before finally installing an app that gives us insights into our data with minimal effort. This same concept applies to hundreds of different sources in Sumo Logic.

Summary

In this chapter, we introduced you to the steps required to easily set up an instance of Sumo Logic. Since Sumo Logic is a cloud-native SaaS technology, there are no servers to buy and set up in physical form, no virtual servers to provision, and no need to tinker with configuring an instance; all you need is to just click a few buttons.

We then demonstrated how you can quickly get some log files and metrics into Sumo Logic from a Windows or a Linux/Unix machine, such as a MacBook, to quickly get a feel for the process of basic data ingestion. We then finished by helping you set up an app from the App Catalog to instantly get insights into the logs and metrics telemetry.

The point to make is this—it's quick and easy to get your data into the platform to start *using* it. The key is to avoid a lot of the problems with typical data ingestion processes, such as schemas, forwarders, and data pipelines, and to start *extracting insights and value* out of your data, no matter the context, and as quickly as possible.

Sumo Logic is on a mission to show how different life is for businesses and teams that embrace complete visibility through one platform across all their logs, metrics, and traces. Businesses using the platform experience the following:

- Quicker return on investment. By using their data within minutes, they get to start making key operational decisions.

- By avoiding mapping data to schemas and manually managing it, teams can now spend that time proactively identifying and hunting for threats, ensuring that their systems are fully operational.
- A universal querying capability and language across all sources in a data-agnostic way means both less of a headache for teams working on multiple data islands and also a reduced time to investigate and resolve issues.

The next chapter will cover data ingestion in its entirety. We'll explore the other types of collectors, such as Hosted and OpenTelemetry collectors, and we'll cover how to get the other data types, such as metrics and application traces, into the platform. Further, we'll cover data ingestion best practices, parsing data effectively, and other useful and practical information when it comes to getting your important data into Sumo Logic.

Get this book's PDF version and more

Scan the QR code (or go to `packtpub.com/unlock`). Search for this book by name, confirm the edition, and then follow the steps on the page.

Note: Keep your invoice handy. Purchases made directly from Packt don't require an invoice.

5
Ingesting Data

Getting data into a big data platform is a process that typically comes loaded with questions. How long will data onboarding take? How many resources do I need to apply to the project? Do I need the vendors' help to migrate? How much will that cost?...and on and on the questions go. Depending on the size of your ecosystem, getting all the metrics, events, logs, and data flowing in can be a Herculean undertaking that takes months. Then we get into the technical requirements, which are vast: What log formats are accepted? Should we transform the data in the pipeline? How complicated are the schemas? How is the data indexed?

This is why a data ingestion strategy is crucial because it not only helps you make sense of your growing volumes of data but also makes it easier to manage in the long term. It's worth working with technology that makes your teams' lives as straightforward as possible. With your existing solution likely built and customized by users over the years, implementing a more modern tool with an updated approach to data ingestion and management can present both technical obstacles and social resistance, making it an uphill battle.

Sumo Logic addresses this issue. It enables quick onboarding with easy collection across three different collector types. When data onboarding is easy, especially in the early stages, it accelerates return on investment and time-to-value, and...happiness. Sumo Logic also works with any human-readable, text-based data format, and you don't need to map the data to schemas. Essentially, you receive insights from your data that help your team make decisions, instead of spending productive operational time configuring collection, schemas, and indexes. Further, streamlined configurations across data sources, even within Cloud SIEM, amplify these advantages.

We will be building on top of what we covered already in *Chapter 4, Setting Up Your First Collector*. We're going to be looking at ingesting some basic logs from your operating systems from a much wider range of sources. We'll cover Hosted Collectors in more depth, which allows cloud-to-cloud data ingestion, and also OpenTelemetry collection, which really opens up the playing field for all data types, such as logs, metrics, and traces, and allows us to expand the conversation out to DevOps, **Application Performance Monitoring (APM)**, and **Real User Monitoring (RUM)**.

By the end of this chapter, you will know all the methods of ingesting your telemetry into Sumo Logic, and when to use them, as well as how to make use of out-of-the-box integrations for your data sources. The following topics will be covered in this chapter:

- Data collection methods
- Parsing

- Best practices for data ingestion
- Choosing your ingestion strategy

Data collection methods

Using our analogy from *Chapter 4*, this is where we start adding additional ingredients and layers to our analytical cake. The previous chapter was the base, spongy, sweet, and strong enough to support the other ingredients, and we'll be building from there. I started this book by explaining that Sumo Logic helps with multiple key business drivers, and it does that by unlocking total visibility across the organization by centralizing all your data in one place. But how does data actually get sent to the platform? It is done through three flavors of collectors: Hosted, Installed, and OpenTelemetry Collectors. We covered Installed Collectors in *Chapter 4*, so let's dive into Hosted Collectors.

Hosted Collectors

Hosted is sometimes a confusing term because it's not always clear where the hosting happens. In this case, "hosted" means that the collector is hosted on vendor (Sumo) cloud resources. **Hosted Collectors** are agentless, so the collection infrastructure is wired into the platform itself, and you don't need to worry about deploying anything. Sometimes these are referred to as *cloud-to-cloud collectors* because they exist primarily to ingest data from cloud sources via webhooks and endpoints. It goes from one cloud source to the Sumo cloud destination. Most modern SaaS solutions have APIs to pull data out of their cloud solution for ingestion into external analytics platforms.

To add a Hosted Collector, we follow roughly the same process we did in *Chapter 4* when adding an Installed Collector, except this time, we'll choose a Hosted one. Go to **Data Management | Collection**:

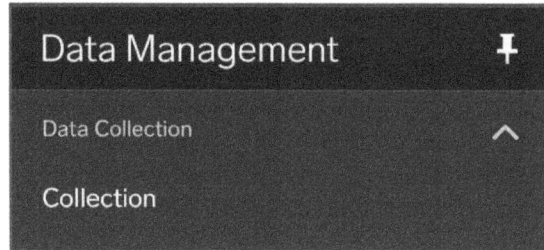

Figure 5.1 – The Collection section in the configuration menu

Then go to **Add Collector** at the top right of the sources list. Choose **Hosted Collector**:

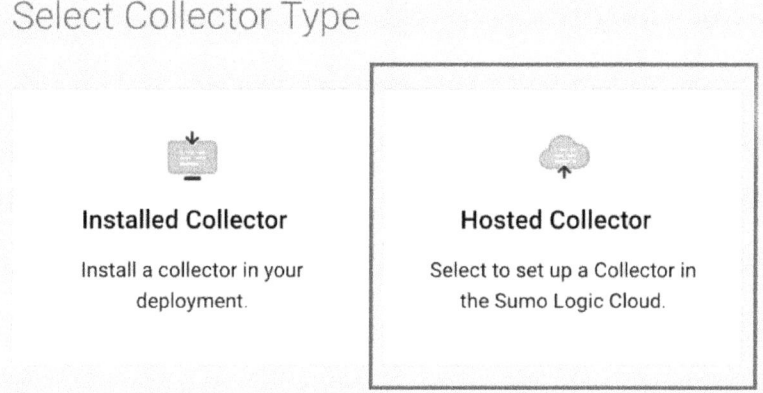

Figure 5.2 – Choosing the Hosted Collector option for cloud collection

This will bring up a window where you can enter the collector's name, and source category, assign it to a budget (covered later), and adjust **Time Zone** settings if needed. Give your collector a name and save it as shown here.

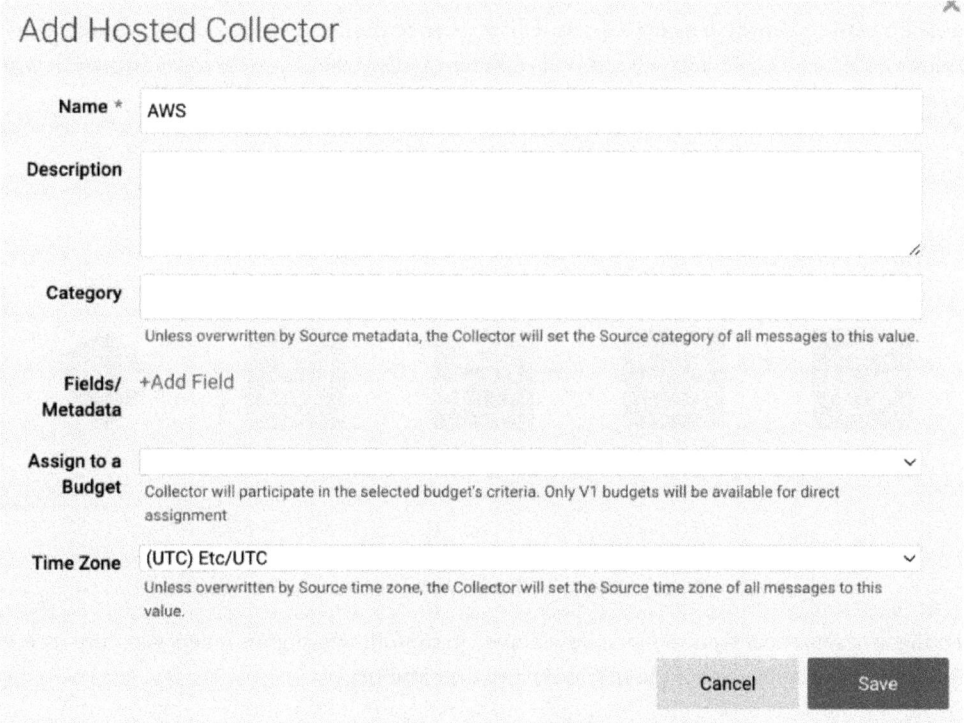

Figure 5.3 – Defining the Hosted Collector name

Sumo Logic will ask you if you want to add a data source to this new collector, click on **OK**.

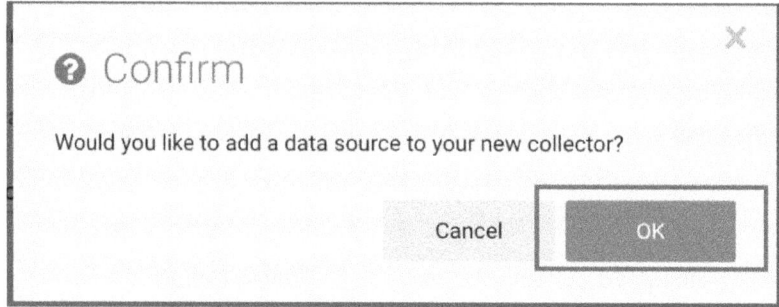

Figure 5.4 – Adding a data source to the new Collector

Strictly speaking, a Hosted Collector is just a parent container running in the cloud. Inside this collector, you can deploy any number of child *sources*. Example sources that fall into this category include **AWS data**, **Azure**, **Okta**, **Salesforce**, **Google Workspace**, cloud firewalls, and many others. Let's look at two different sources: AWS CloudTrail and Microsoft Office 365.

The next section takes you through setting up AWS CloudTrail from here.

Setting up AWS CloudTrail

Once you click on **OK**, as shown in *Figure 5.4*, you will be taken to the list of sources that are available with Hosted Collectors in Sumo Logic. You will see many different sources that allow for easy integration with Sumo Logic. Select **AWS CloudTrail** from the list, as shown here:

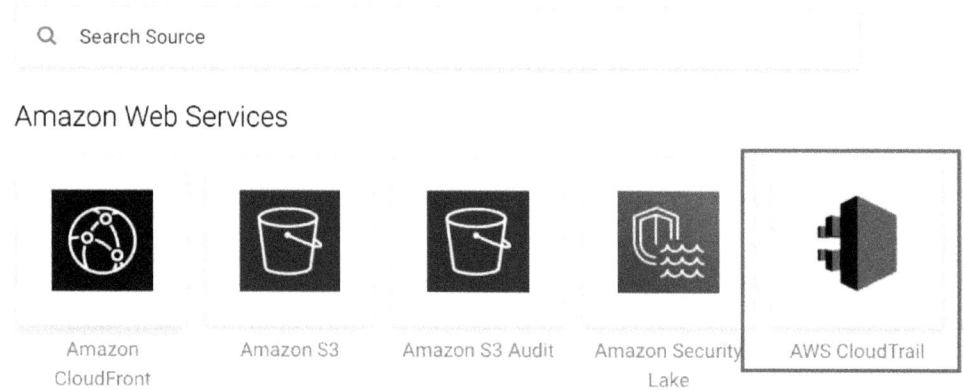

Figure 5.5 – Choosing AWS CloudTrail from the Hosted Collector sources list

This will bring up a source configuration window, shown in the following figure, where you must now enter all the necessary details to connect your CloudTrail data to the platform.

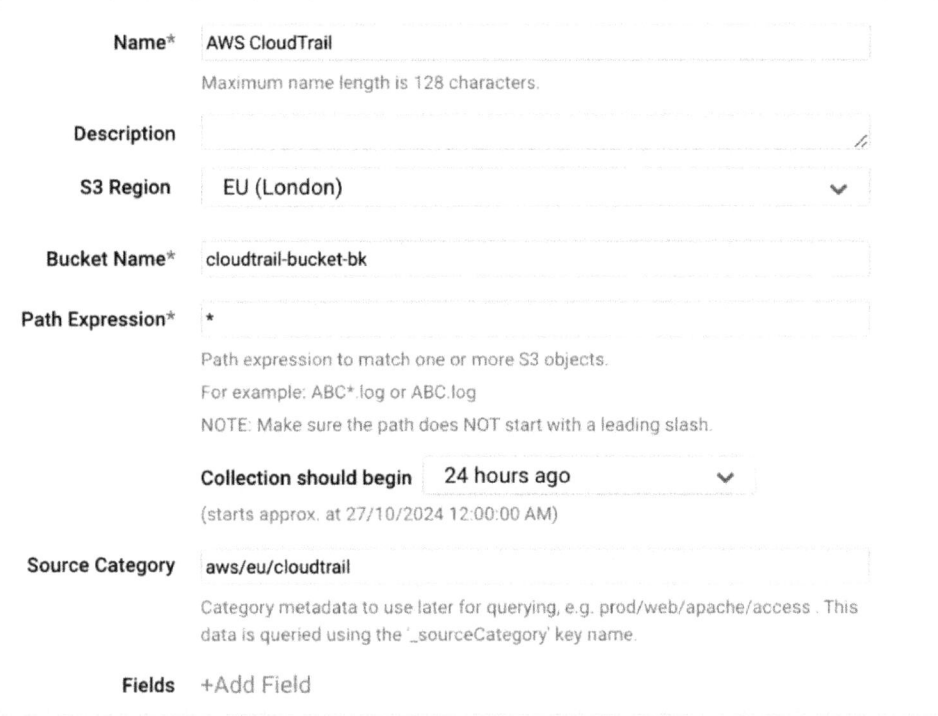

Figure 5.6 – The AWS CloudTrail source configuration

This is done via the S3 bucket, so you will need to set up the relevant role-based permissions as well. First, enter the basic details, such as the name of the source, the S3 region, the bucket name and expression, and the source category. Collection can begin any time from now, going back to the entire history of the bucket.

Scroll down and you will come to role permissions. Role permissions are important because, to extract data from the bucket, Sumo Logic must assume a role that can do this. Luckily, the template is provided for you; you just need to run it on CloudFormation. Click on **Generate role-based access template** and run it through CloudFormation. Then the role ARN will be generated, which you can then enter in the **Role ARN** field, as shown here:

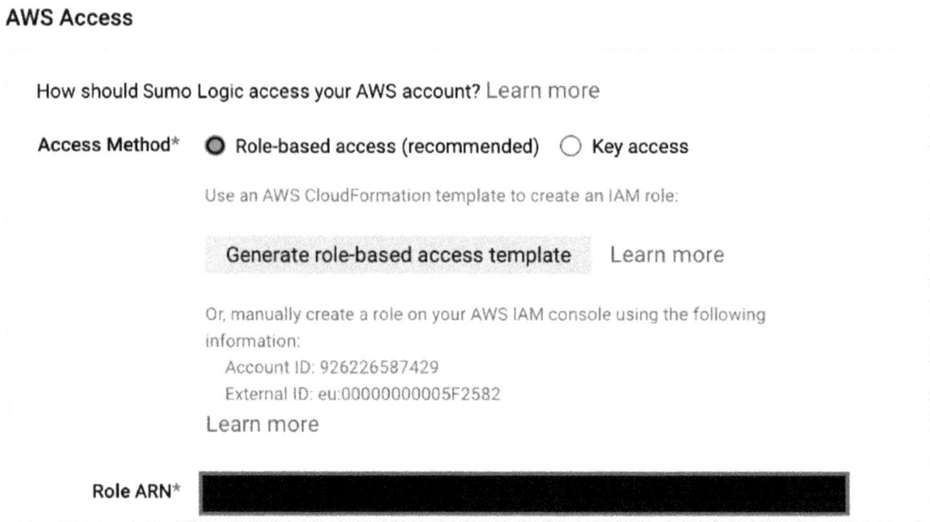

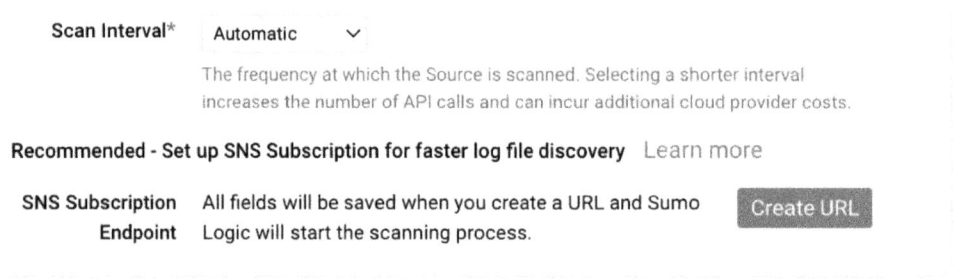

Figure 5.7 – Specifying the AWS role to help configure the source

That's it for the basic setup.

Additionally, there's a small section on SNS notifications below the **AWS Access** configuration, where you can set up a scan interval and an SNS endpoint to speed up detection and delivery of new events. This section is shown here:

Figure 5.8 – Setting up Log File Discovery to detect new files in AWS S3 more quickly

> **Note**
> Below the SNS section, you will find the advanced options for logs. These will be covered later in this chapter, in the *Best practices for data ingestion* section.

Hit **Save** and you will be taken back to the **Collection** screen. Now, just wait a few minutes until you see events start coming into Sumo Logic.

> **Note**
>
> With AWS data in particular, there is a more streamlined way of setting up AWS sources in bulk, using Terraform and CloudFormation. This is discussed in the next section, *Infrastructure as Code (IaC) collection*.

Here are our events!

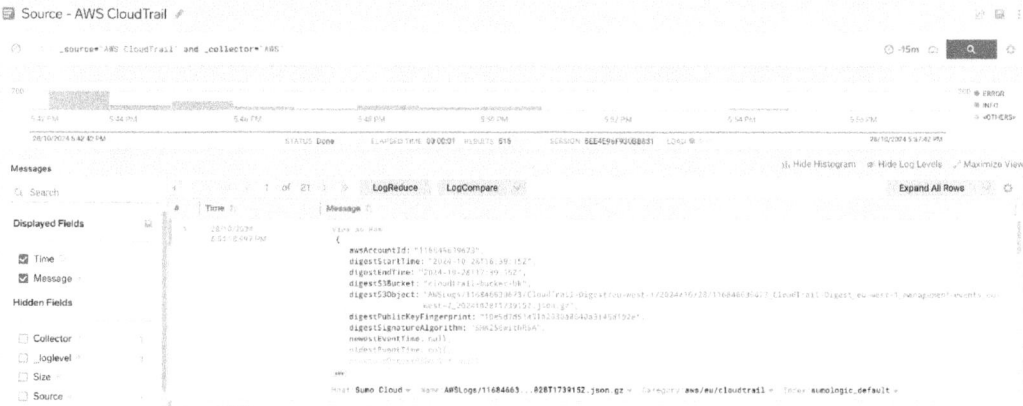

Figure 5.9 – Successfully returning events from the CloudTrail query

> **Tip**
>
> **Pro tip**
>
> Did you know you can view the logs flowing in like Neo from the Matrix? Click on **Live Tail** to see the logs flowing in real time. This is applicable to any source of data.

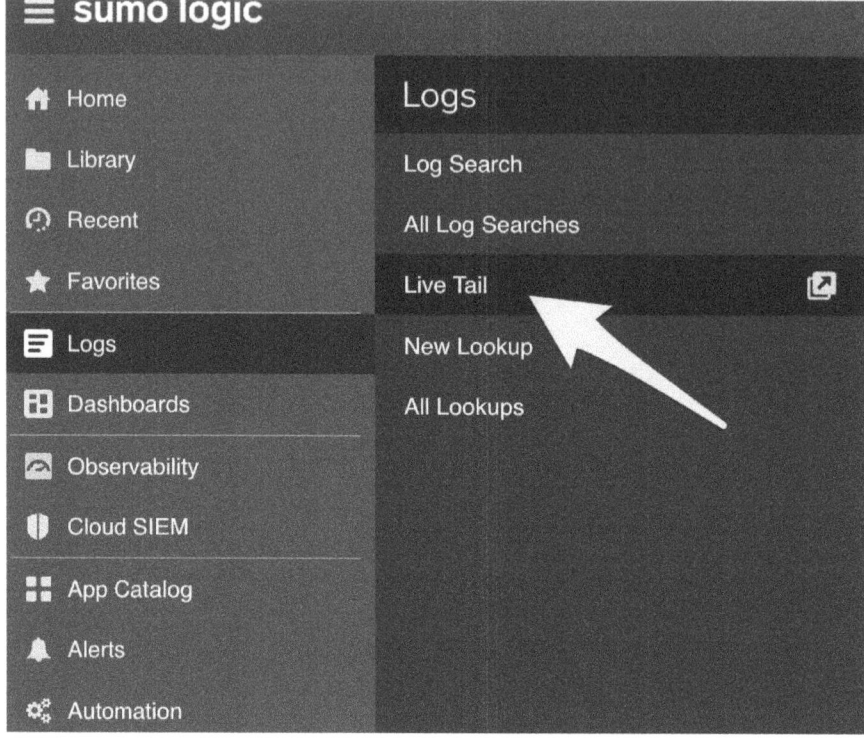

Figure 5.10 – Logs | Live Tail

Setting up Microsoft Office 365

Microsoft Office 365 is another popular source that tends to be one of the first ingested into Sumo Logic by a customer trialing the technology due to how widespread it is within a tech stack.

When you add a Hosted Collector and are asked to add a data source, choose **Office 365 Audit** from the list this time, as shown here:

Figure 5.11 – Choosing the Office 365 Audit source from the Hosted Collectors list

Once you select the source, you will be presented with the source configuration window. Fill it in once again, use **Single Sign On** (**SSO**) with Office 365 to connect the two:

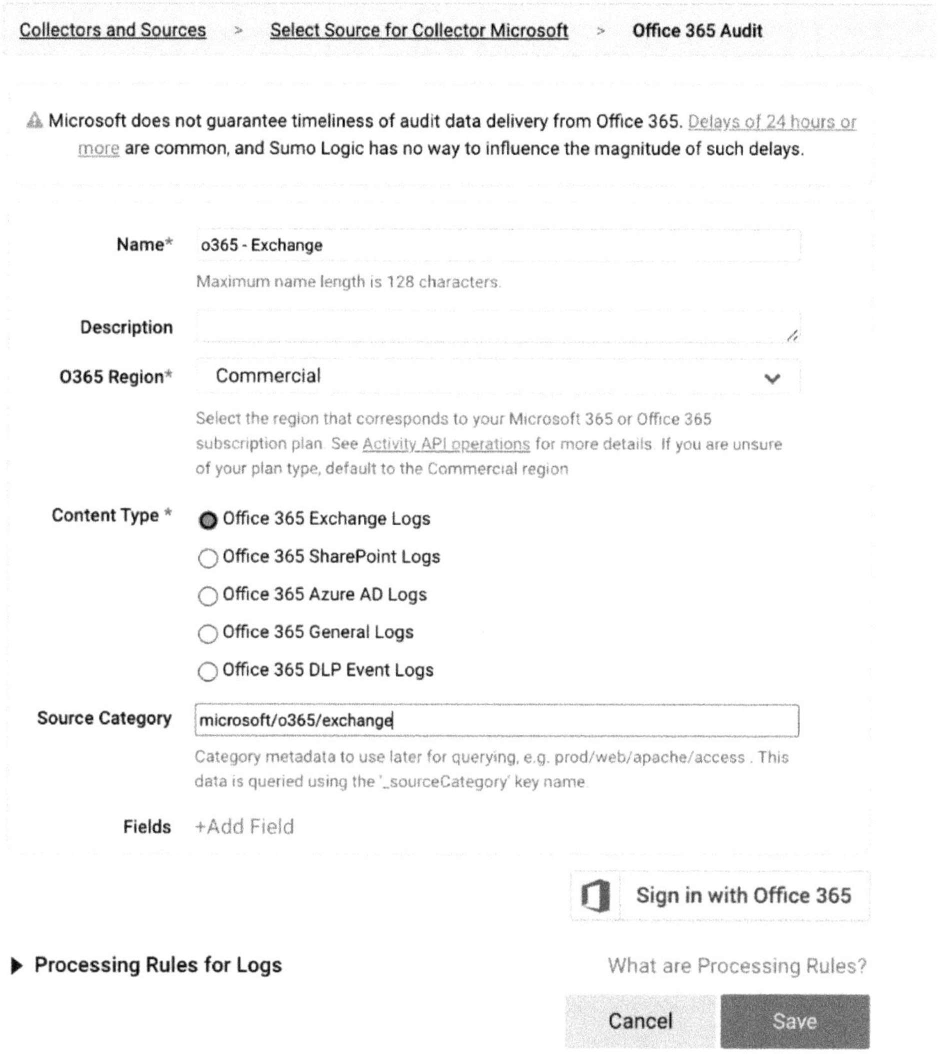

Figure 5.12 – The types of content that can be extracted from Office 365

You'll find that for a lot of these sources, the configuration is done via SSO or through an API to make it as straightforward as possible. If you've been a bit adventurous and looked through the rest of the Hosted Collector sources list, you might be wondering, "*Why don't I see my technology listed here?*" to which there is an answer. If the cloud source you'd like to ingest data from is not in the list, you can use Sumo Logic's generic sources to get it. We'll cover that next.

Setting up other sources

If you look at the cloud sources available, you'll see a **Generic** section. We're going to talk about three key sources over the next few sections to help send data from your cloud source to Sumo Logic:

- **HTTP Logs & Metrics**
- **OTLP/HTTP**
- **Universal Collector**
- **RUM HTTP Traces**

These sources are all visible in the **Generic** section shown here:

Figure 5.13 – Sources that help to ingest data from any cloud source

We will cover the **OTLP/HTTP** and **Rum HTTP Traces** sources in the *OpenTelemetry collection* section.

So, let's start with **HTTP Logs & Metrics**. This is an openly configurable source that allows you to have a generic endpoint that points to Sumo Logic from one of your sources. It's important to point out that the source in question should have data exporting or data streaming capabilities, where you can configure this endpoint in the first place. Sources that don't have data exporting capabilities will be covered at the end of this section.

It's a very basic configuration; you just have to add a name and a source category in most cases, as shown here:

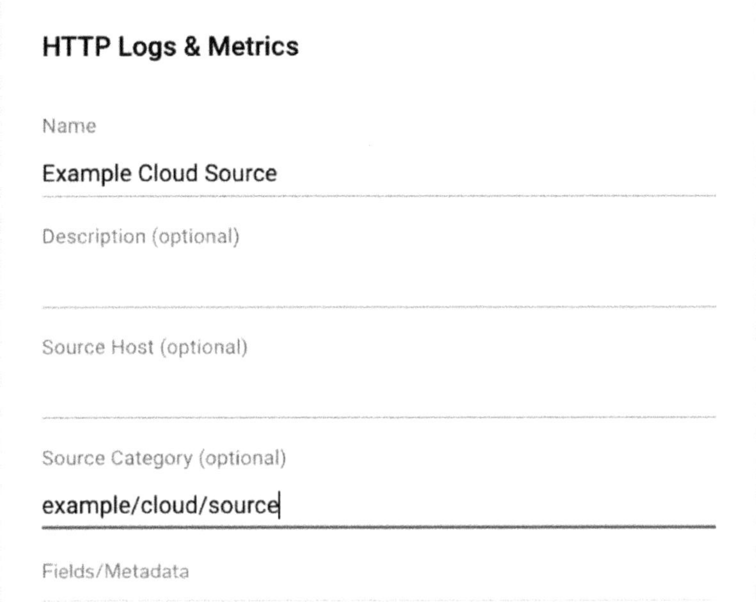

HTTP Logs & Metrics

Name
Example Cloud Source

Description (optional)

Source Host (optional)

Source Category (optional)
example/cloud/source

Fields/Metadata

Figure 5.14 – Looking at the HTTP Logs & Metrics source

Then click **Save**. This then gives you an endpoint that can act as your destination. The endpoint is given to you as a URL when you first save the source.

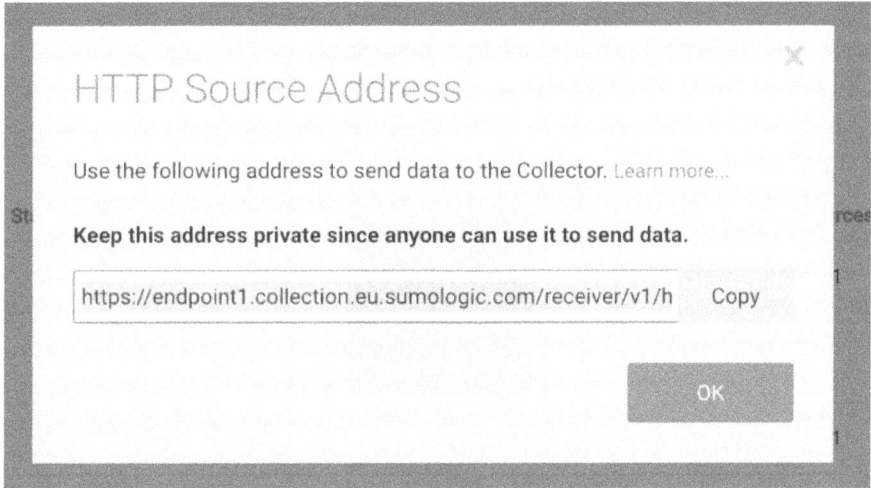

Figure 5.15 – When the configuration is saved, an endpoint is generated to help send data

You can access it at any time by looking at your source and, on the right side of the screen, choosing **Show URL**:

Regenerate URL | Show URL | Edit | Delete

Figure 5.16 – View the endpoint by clicking Show URL

For anyone eager to collect data from a cloud source that *doesn't* have any data exporting capability, Sumo Logic also has the option of using a source type called the **Universal Collector** to act as a REST API and interact with APIs to extract data from a source.

The Universal Collector

I know this sounds like something out of a Marvel movie, but the Sumo Logic Universal Collector was designed to be able to pull data from any source that has operational API endpoints. Just imagine, you have a proprietary logging tool. You haven't equipped it with data export capability, but there are APIs you can call. The problem is nothing has built-in integrations with it and you'd like to get that data into one centralized location. Typically, you'd have to write a Python script or something similar to call the endpoint, grab the data, and send it to Sumo Logic. Now, you can just use this **Universal Collector** instead.

It can help you make GET and POST requests to collect whatever data you need, and the focus here has very much been on versatility. Just a small caveat, the source requires an understanding of REST APIs and HTTP traffic to set up. There are a lot of options included that offer flexibility – request configuration (settings headers and parameters), setting parsing options and pagination configuration, and a few others that really let you interact in a comprehensive way with any API endpoints you have.

In the data sources, you can find it under the **Security & Compliance** section shown here:

Figure 5.17 – The Sumo Logic Universal Collector

The configuration available for the source is very detailed and gives you a lot of control when it comes to developing the integration. There are options to configure the authentication method, request details, choose the JSON response for logs, sort out pagination, and so on. I won't take up valuable real estate by screenshotting the whole thing. You can find the full documentation on the official website[1]. Once set up though, you can query any endpoint and get those JSON logs into Sumo Logic. Now that we've covered generic sources and those without a built-in source, let's move on to another way of collecting data, *Terraform* and IaC.

Infrastructure as Code (IaC) collection

Earlier in the book, I mentioned that Sumo Logic has a Terraform provider, and as a technology it is forward-looking and embraces automation and IaC. We will be looking at the provider in slightly more detail later in the chapter, but here I wanted to focus on data collection. Currently, there is one out-of-the-box data source that supports Terraform and that is **AWS Observability**. By following this ingestion method, our customers have ingested the entirety of their AWS ecosystem and gained access to full visibility via logs, metrics, and traces. Let's cover it next.

AWS Observability

Suppose you have an AWS environment with multiple accounts, multiple regions, and lots of different services in each. You want to have centralized visibility across *everything*. How do you accomplish this? You can use the AWS Observability suite built into Sumo Logic. The outcome of this approach is that you get over 100 dashboards, queries, and monitors that help get your teams up and running within 60 minutes.

Let's use the GUI to make the process as simple as possible. Search for **AWS Observability** in the App Catalog and make sure to select the Terraform dropdown. You'll notice two other options, **CLI** and **CloudFormation**. We're going to use Terraform in this example:

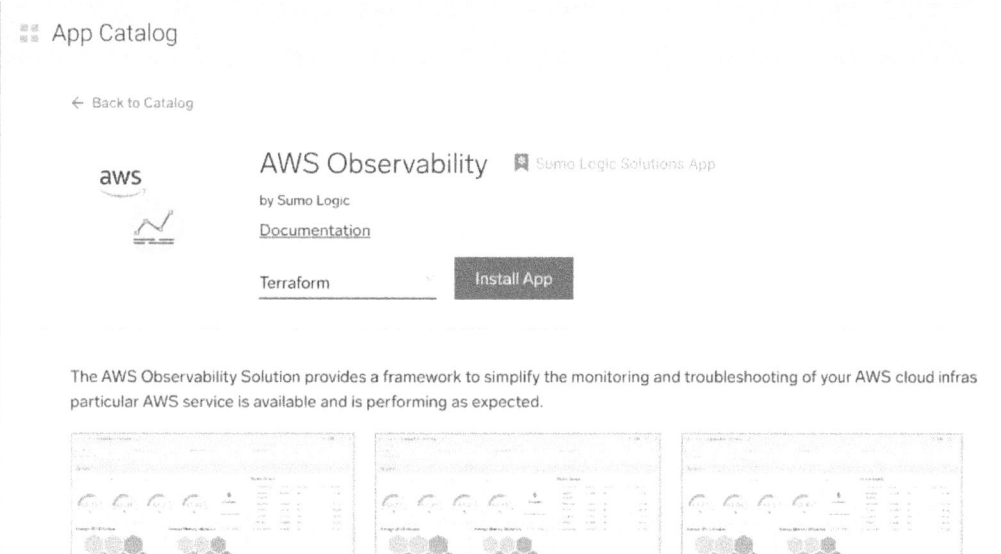

Figure 5.18 – Specifying the integration option we want with the AWS Observability app

Click **Install App** and you will be given a useful step-by-step guide to get everything up and running.

Then click on **Check AWS Role Permission**. This step is crucial because the setup and configuration on AWS' side must be done with a role that has the privileges to do so. By clicking on **Check AWS Role Permission**, you can spin up a quick template in your AWS environment to verify that the roles you used match the ones in the JSON file as part of the step. The documentation covers a list of useful troubleshooting steps if you bump into any issues[2].

The reason this solution is so useful is because it's easy to configure, as the process is agentless and the template and scripts have been provided to you. It's also straightforward to manage this setup and make any changes where necessary. Further, it comes packaged with a ton of content out of the box in the form of dashboards and monitors. In short, it's just easy to deploy, takes a short amount of time, and gives you very comprehensive visibility.

I thought it would be useful to share some of the out-of-the-box content available. For example, here is a dashboard showing us our AWS Lambda metrics and logs:

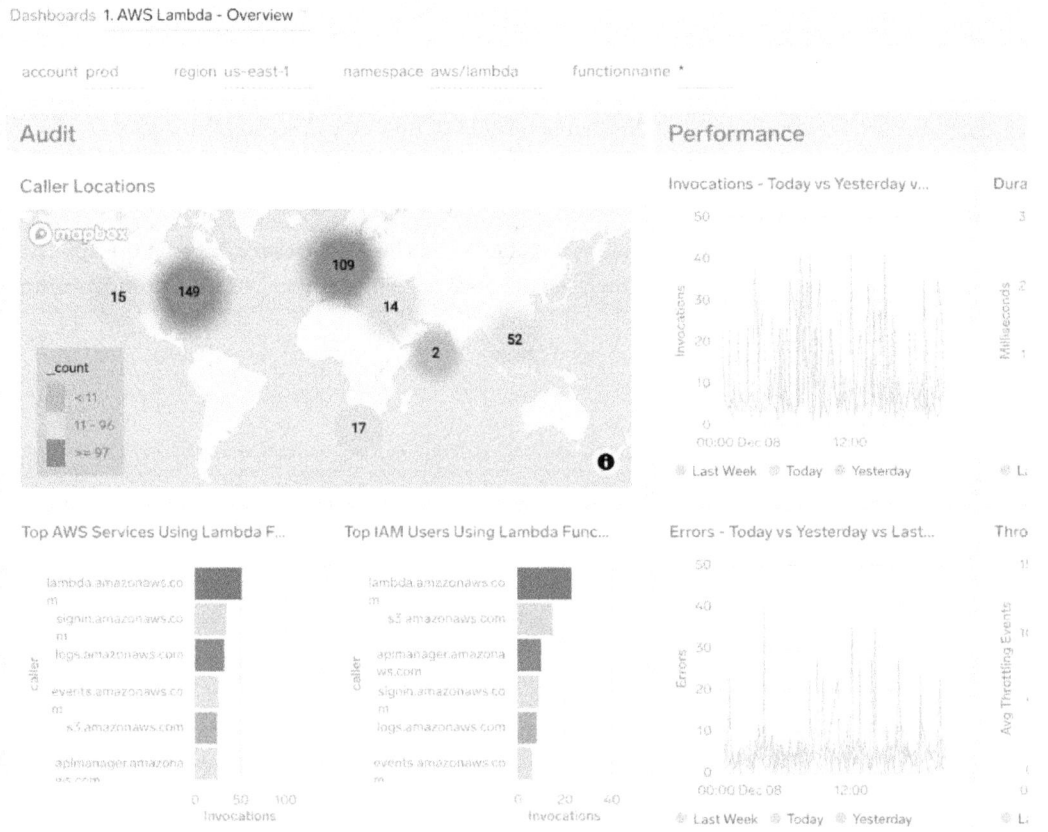

Figure 5.19 – AWS Lambda metrics and logs

Being able to monitor your AWS infrastructure efficiently is great, but you also get a selection of monitors that give you a good operational baseline level of coverage. Whether you have monitors in AWS or not, it's a great starting point that you can tweak in the future. Here's an example of an **AWS API Gateway – High Latency** monitor with outlier-based anomaly detection activated:

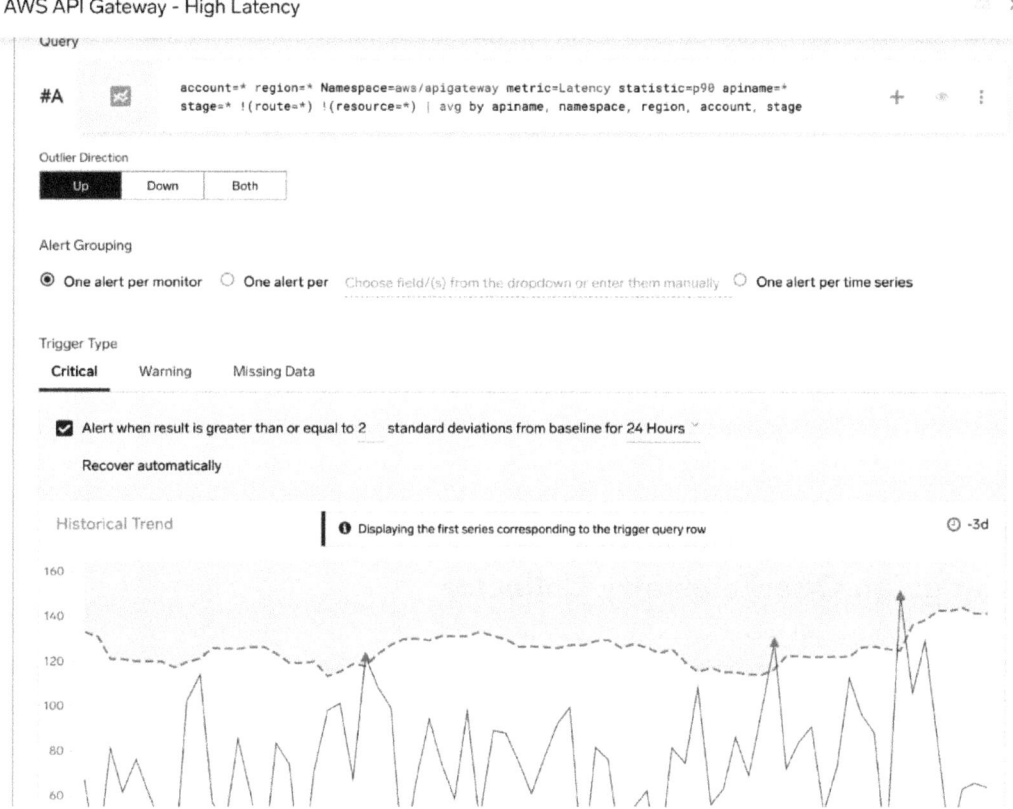

Figure 5.20 – A pre-created monitor looking at spikes in latency on API Gateway in AWS

This is only a fraction of the stuff you get with the app, so feel free to try it yourself and get some data in.

We've covered Hosted Collectors to facilitate cloud-to-cloud data collection and infrastructure as code methods to help streamline and ingest data at scale and in bulk, so let's now take a look at *OpenTelemetry*.

OpenTelemetry collection

OpenTelemetry, by the definition given on their website, is a "*framework and toolkit designed to create and manage telemetry data such as traces, metrics, and logs.*"[3]

Thus, OpenTelemetry Collectors, or agents, give organizations a vendor-neutral way to instrument a variety of systems and applications once and send observability data to platforms for monitoring, troubleshooting, and security analytics. The challenge that OpenTelemetry was brought into existence to solve is that there is no uniform standard for instrumenting code and telemetry to send to a backend. This was, and still is, an issue because modern environments have a vast number of applications, services, languages, libraries and infrastructure. Not only is it difficult to work with so many different formats, but it's also a full-time job to maintain. The great thing is it very much aligns with Sumo Logic's vision, which is to provide *complete visibility across your data islands and assets.* Sumo Logic, in this case, is the backend in question and once the data and telemetry reside within the backend, we can enrich that data to solve observability and security-related problems, such as troubleshooting applications and infrastructure, identifying malicious activity in one of your Kubernetes clusters. All of it powers the DevSecOps model.

Additionally, OpenTelemetry is open source. In a world with proprietary agents where you're tied into the capabilities of specific vendors, having an open variant that lets you customize things how you need is valued. By being open, and flexible (logs, metrics, traces, and a versatile schema), it takes out the pain of disjointed collection and allows for a universal collection architecture that can ingest practically all telemetry types.

Finally, it also synergizes well with Sumo Logic because the focus of OpenTelemetry is to make it *easy* to instrument applications, no matter the language, operating system, or infrastructure. So, what we're looking at is a way to unlock total visibility across your business – nice. Sumo Logic is committed to supporting OpenTelemetry and engineers contribute to OpenTelemetry every single day. There is a separate fork for Sumo Logic OpenTelemetry and we will cover what that entails as we get into the various methods of ingestion.

There are a few ways of getting OpenTelemetry to work with Sumo Logic. We'll cover what the main process looks like, how to run the setup through the App Catalog, and also how to set up the OpenTelemetry collection without using a Sumo Logic OpenTelemetry Collector but with any other flavor, including a vanilla OpenTelemetry Collector.

Setting up an OpenTelemetry Collector

Before we deploy the actual collector, it's worth dwelling a little bit on the fact that Sumo Logic has its own OpenTelemetry Collector. Since Sumo Logic has its own fork, it contains elements of Sumo Logic within the OpenTelemetry distribution to add some advantages when used together with the platform. They include the following:

- Platform-specific features
- Bypasses the OpenTelemetry release schedule for critical bug fixes
- Provides multiple installation methods
- Improved support when used together with Sumo Logic

The collector is still open source, and as we discussed, it's a strongpoint of OpenTelemetry. Whether using Sumo Logic's Collector, or the vanilla Collector directly from the OpenTelemetry repo, the way of working with your logs, metrics, and traces data is the same – you, the customer, just have more flexibility and fewer headaches.

With that small detail covered, let's begin by deploying an OpenTelemetry Collector. We are going to be using something called **source templates** in Sumo Logic. These are pre-defined collection templates for commonly used OpenTelemetry sources, and they come with several advantages:

- You can centrally manage your source templates in one place, meaning you get consistent collection across your sources
- You can create one template and deploy it on multiple collectors easily
- The configuration can be done in the GUI, making it easier than the traditional OpenTelemetry installation process (more on this later)

To start, head to **Collection** in the menu and go to the **OpenTelemetry Collection** tab:

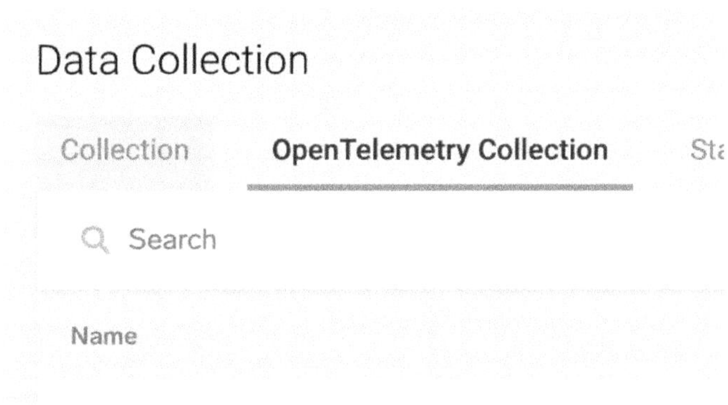

Figure 5.21 – The OpenTelemetry Collection option that lists all OpenTelemetry collectors

Click on **Add Collector** in the top right-hand corner of this panel:

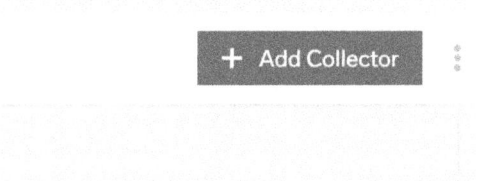

Figure 5.22 – The button that helps you to add a new collector

This will now show you the list of platforms where you can deploy an OpenTelemetry Collector. There are six options available here:

- **Windows**
- **Linux**
- **Mac**
- **Ansible**
- **Puppet**
- **Chef**

You are given four steps, culminating in a Bash, PowerShell, or configuration management script that will deploy and install the collector on the host and start sending data to Sumo Logic. Here, we have an example of the command used for a Linux OS, and that's the example we'll run with for the rest of this section:

Figure 5.23 – The Bash command that downloads and installs a collector onto your host

This will deploy a Sumo Logic OpenTelemetry Collector to your host machine, whatever that may be. All you'll have initially is a load of host metrics that capture anything from CPU utilization to disk space. Once the agent has been deployed and the service has started you'll see these messages in your terminal, as we're on Linux:

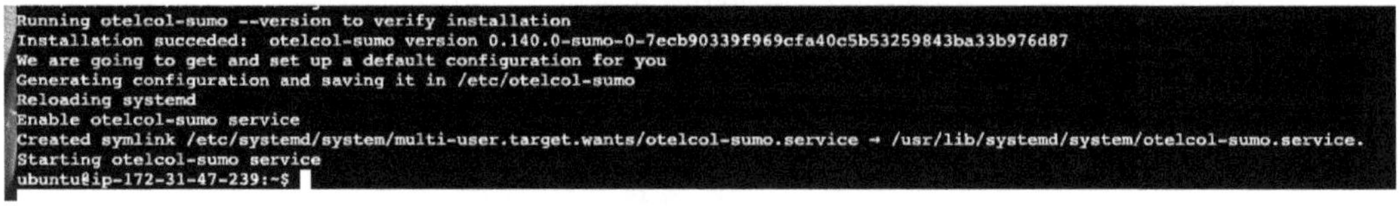

```
Running otelcol-sumo --version to verify installation
Installation succeded:  otelcol-sumo version 0.140.0-sumo-0-7ecb90339f969cfa40c5b53259843ba33b976d87
We are going to get and set up a default configuration for you
Generating configuration and saving it in /etc/otelcol-sumo
Reloading systemd
Enable otelcol-sumo service
Created symlink /etc/systemd/system/multi-user.target.wants/otelcol-sumo.service → /usr/lib/systemd/system/otelcol-sumo.service
Starting otelcol-sumo service
ubuntu@ip-172-31-47-239:~$
```

Figure 5.24 – Messages from the Linux terminal confirming successful deployment

You'll see a small checkbox under the command, which no longer says **Scanning for collector** but says **Detected collector**. **Detected collector** gets checked on the front end when it receives a ping from the Collector. This is shown here.

Figure 5.25 – The Detected collector status

You'll see the **Next** button has changed from gray to a dark blue, meaning you can proceed to the next step. What are we missing? Data! We need some logs, so let's get those in. On this page, you'll see a confirmation message that shows you've successfully deployed the collector, and, underneath, in the **Bring in data...** section, are the source templates that we can use to set up our collection in the GUI:

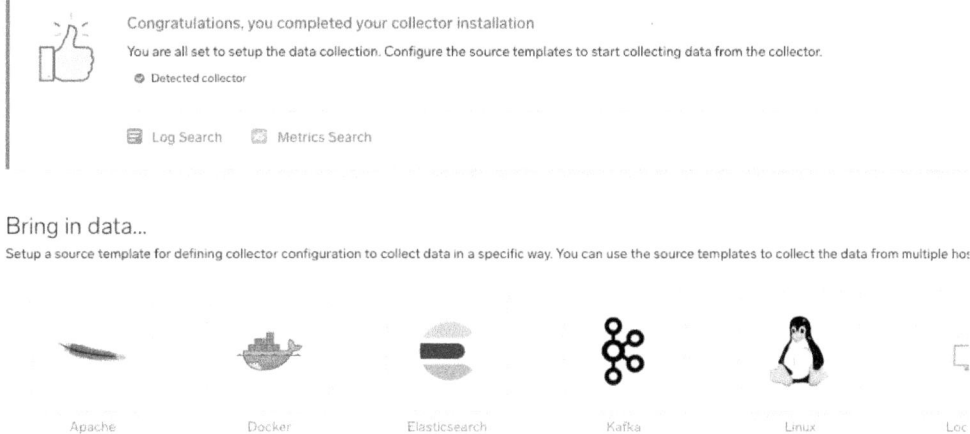

Figure 5.26 – Successful collector installation on Sumo Logic and source template options below

Let's choose the Linux source template, and we'll see the configuration. Previously, you had to put this configuration template together in a YAML file that you then dropped into a directory on the machine. We cover this process later in the chapter just so you know the ins and outs. It's useful if you ever need to ingest data that isn't covered by the pre-created source templates.

We give our collector a name and source category, adding any tags we feel are necessary. These tags could be anything—a network name, environment name, or part of an application stack.

Next up are the logs. This collection is already set up in terms of config; you just need to specify the file paths you want to collect logs from. As we've chosen Linux, there are file paths provided from a few different distros, so not all will be applicable, as we can see here.

# Logs Collection

The following fields are pre-populated with default paths for common log files that are used in different Linux distributions. Not all paths might be relevant for your operating system. Please modify the list of files as required or leave the default values.

Figure 5.27 – You have the option of choosing which log files you want to ingest

This also gives you the opportunity to add any file paths that you have that are custom; for example, if logs from a service go to a specific directory, you can retrieve them easily.

Finally, we have metrics. You can specify the metrics being scraped and the time interval:

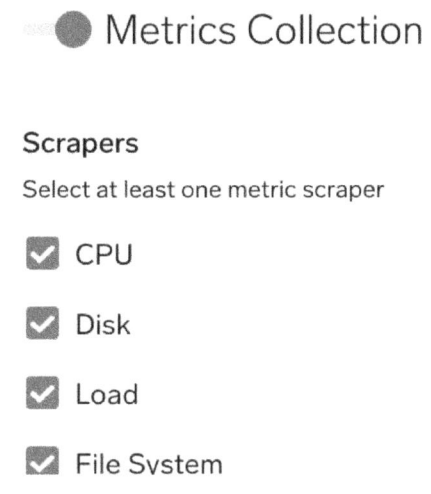

Figure 5.28 – You get to choose which metrics to scrape

You may have noticed that there are processing rules. What this lets you do is pre-process the data by choosing whether you want to include or exclude certain messages, as well as hashing and masking data to obfuscate it. Masking or hashing **Personally Identifiable Information (PII)**, whether it be addresses, emails, or credit card numbers, is a common talking point with customers. This capability lets you control what data is visible by using regular expressions to specify what you need. In the following screenshot, I've chosen to use a regular expression that will mask any Amex, Visa, or Mastercard cards:

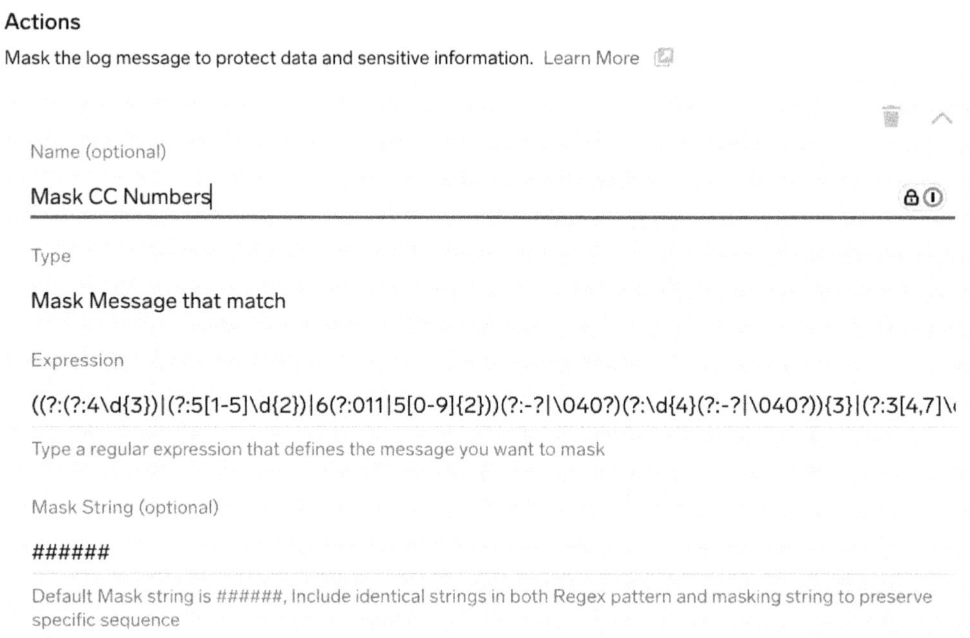

Actions

Mask the log message to protect data and sensitive information. Learn More

Name (optional)

Mask CC Numbers

Type

Mask Message that match

Expression

((?:(?:4\d{3})|(?:5[1-5]\d{2})|6(?:011|5[0-9]{2}))(?:-?|\040?)(?:\d{4}(?:-?|\040?)){3}|(?:3[4,7]

Type a regular expression that defines the message you want to mask

Mask String (optional)

######

Default Mask string is ######, Include identical strings in both Regex pattern and masking string to preserve specific sequence

Figure 5.29 – There are options to pre-process your data, such as excluding it and masking it

Once we are done with this step, we move on to the next step to link this source template to collectors. This is the step that lets you deploy the same source template to multiple collectors and scale this out. You can choose from a list of collector names to deploy to and deploy via tags, so deploying a specific source template to your pre-prod servers is easily done, as shown here.

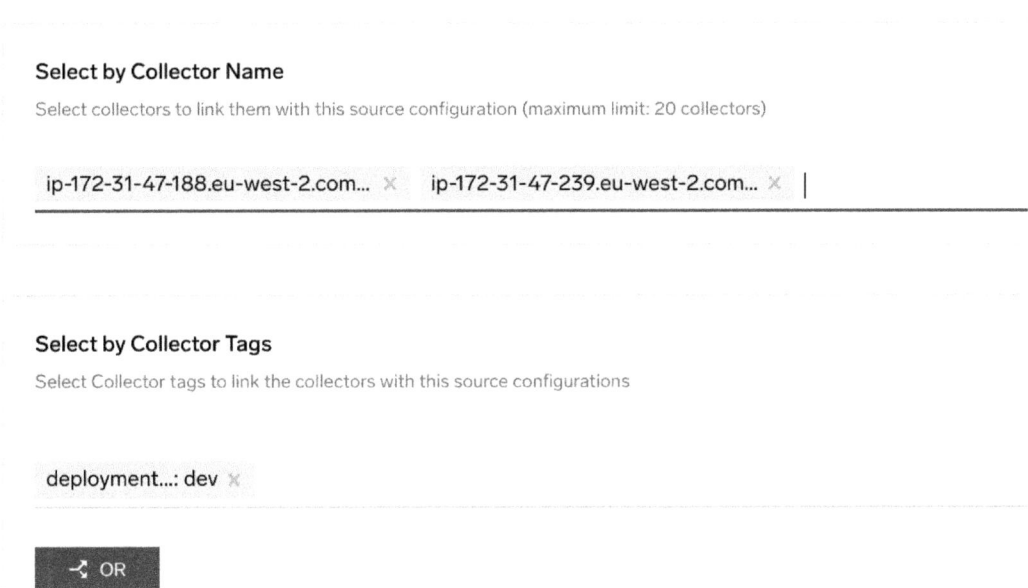

Figure 5.30 – Applying source templates to multiple collectors easily

Congratulations! The source template is deployed, and the data will be ingested in the next few minutes. Depending on the source template you've used, it recommends what app to install in the App Catalog to start visualizing the data too, making this process from zero to seeing useful information in your data as short and painless as possible. The confirmation screen is shown next.

Figure 5.31 – Confirmation that our source template is deployed, and we can install an app for visualization

Setting up an OpenTelemetry Collector through an app in the App Catalog

Let's look at OpenTelemetry setup through the App Catalog. As Sumo Logic has continued to adopt OpenTelemetry collection methods across the stack, the team has established app content to support these logging formats. While this is an ongoing process to build new and updated content, you can locate OpenTelemetry-related content in the App Catalog by searching for **OpenTelemetry**. The following figure shows **Next-Gen Apps**:

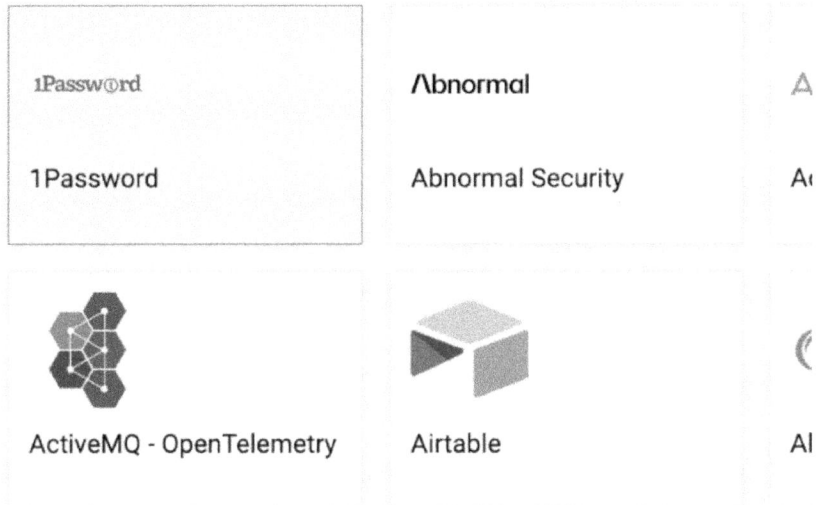

Figure 5.32 – A view of Next-Gen Apps and Classic Apps in the App Catalog

Let's take **Nginx** as an example. I've set up a basic Nginx server on the same EC2 instance I installed the Linux Collector on, and this will help me to explain how to go about adding additional sources on top of your existing collection, as well as how to add a brand-new collection.

Let's search for **Nginx** in the App Catalog and select the **OpenTelemetry** version as shown here:

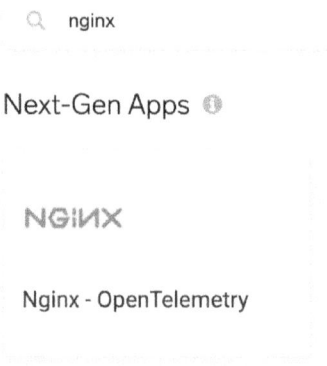

Figure 5.33 – The Nginx OpenTelemetry app

This takes you to the **Nginx** app screen that gives you a breakdown of the content you will be getting and some more information about the source. Click **Install App**:

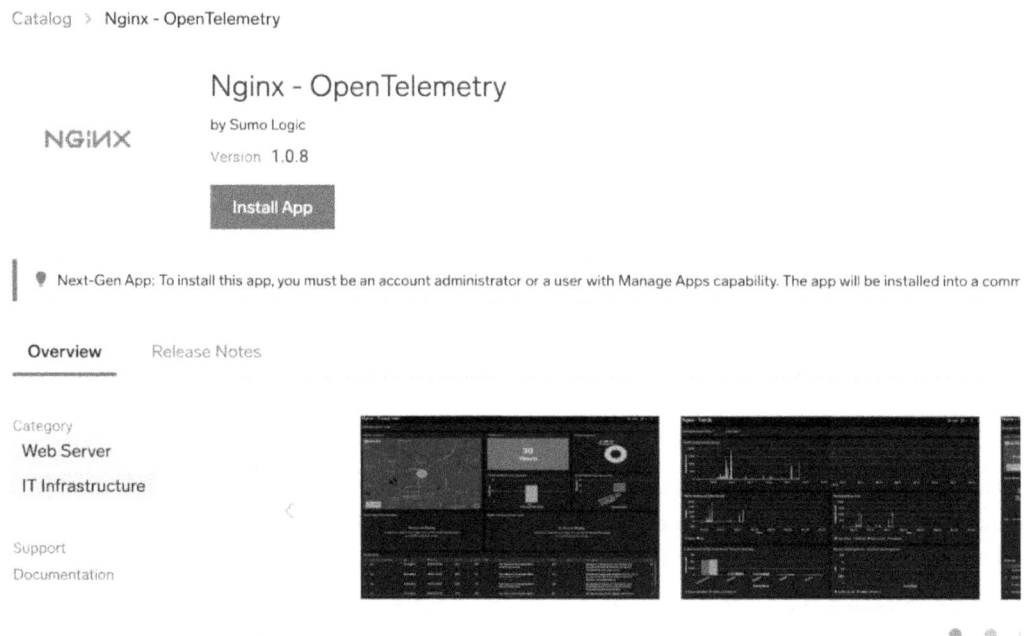

Figure 5.34 – An overview of what content to expect when you install the Nginx app

Let me explain the next screen that you will see in a bit more detail, as you get presented with a few options:

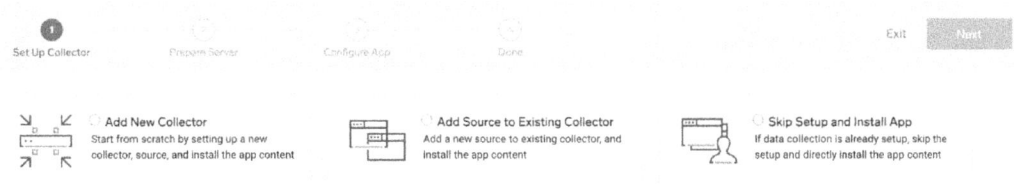

Figure 5.35 – Different options are available when you add OpenTelemetry apps

These options are as follows:

- **Add New Collector**
- **Add Source to Existing Collector**
- **Skip Setup and Install App**

If you *haven't yet* deployed an OpenTelemetry Collector at all, you choose the first option, as this helps to establish a collector on the endpoint that will collect OS logs and metrics *before* you add the source that you are looking at right now, which is Nginx.

The second option is what we'll go with now, as we already have a Linux OpenTelemetry Collector deployed on our EC2 instance, and we just need to add the Nginx source to this existing collector.

The third option is for when you have set the data collection up yourself but just need to install this app for the dashboards. You'd use this option when, for example, you have some content or dashboards and need to just reinstall the dashboards without messing around with the data itself.

Since we need to go with option 2 in this case, let's do it. When installing apps via the App Catalog in the GUI, there is a step-by-step process that gives you all the information you need. So, when you click **Next** and go to step 2, you get shown the prerequisites for data collection – any changes you need to make, any settings you must enable or disable, and so on.

Step 3 is where we get to do some configuration for things such as file paths. In this case, the collector needs to know the IP or **Fully Qualified Domain Name** (**FQDN**) of the Nginx server, as well as any file locations on the server. Access and error logs are very typical and required, but you have the option of including other files too. The **Create Configuration** screen is where you enter those details.

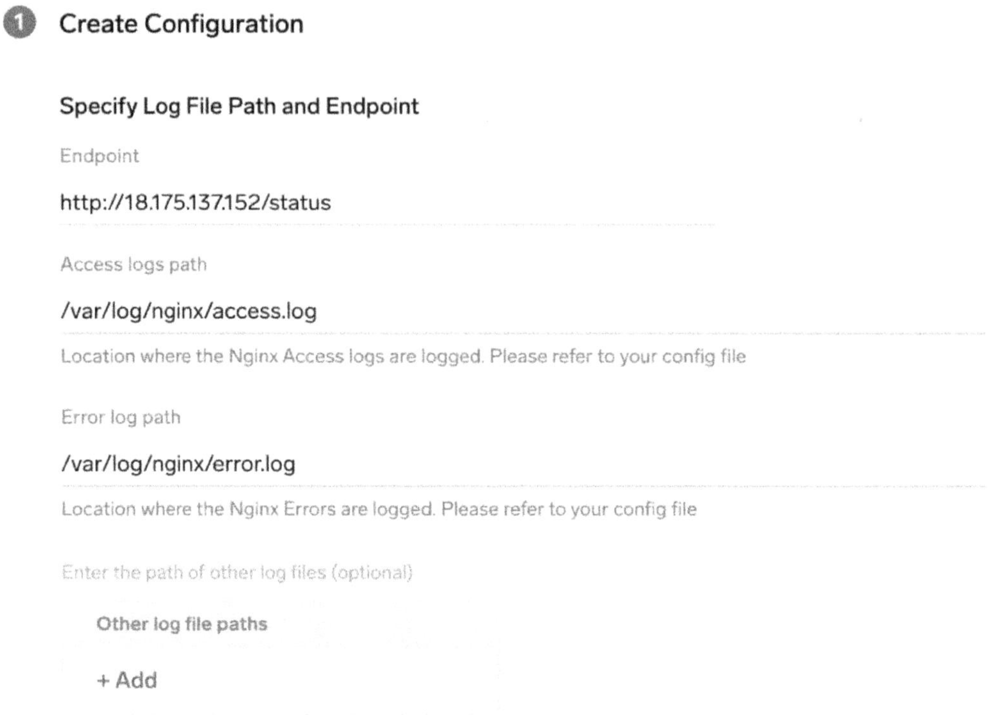

① Create Configuration

Specify Log File Path and Endpoint

Endpoint

http://18.175.137.152/status

Access logs path

/var/log/nginx/access.log

Location where the Nginx Access logs are logged. Please refer to your config file

Error log path

/var/log/nginx/error.log

Location where the Nginx Errors are logged. Please refer to your config file

Enter the path of other log files (optional)

　Other log file paths

　+ Add

Figure 5.36 – Populating variables that help to configure the OpenTelemetry YAML file

Whatever you populate here feeds into the bottom section (shown in *Figure 5.37*), where a YAML file is generated for you based on the Nginx service, along with instructions on where to deposit the file.

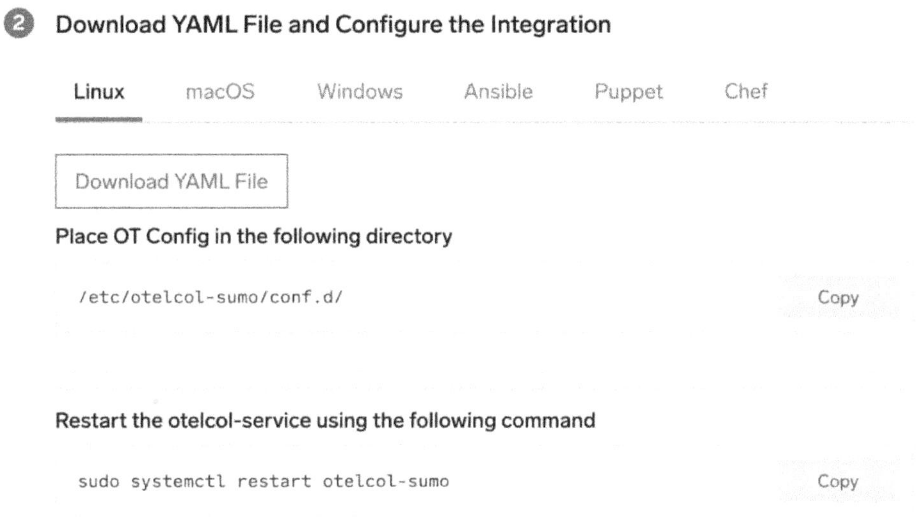

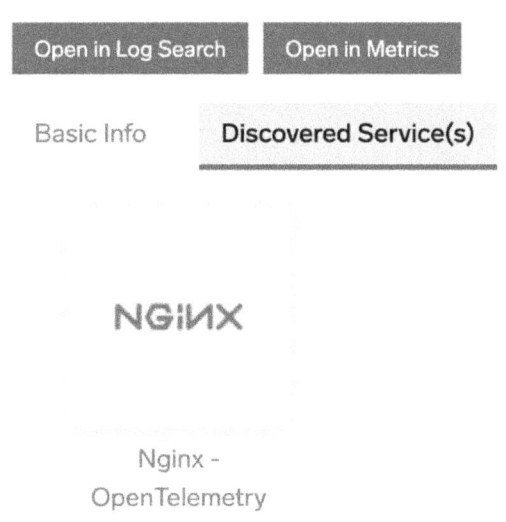

Figure 5.37 – The YAML file that contains the configuration you need to start ingesting

Click **Next** and go to the next step; it will sort everything out for you.

When you go back to your OpenTelemetry Collector, you'll see that it has discovered the Nginx service:

Figure 5.38 – OpenTelemetry service discovery within the Sumo Logic UI

When you open **Log Search**, you can see Nginx access records:

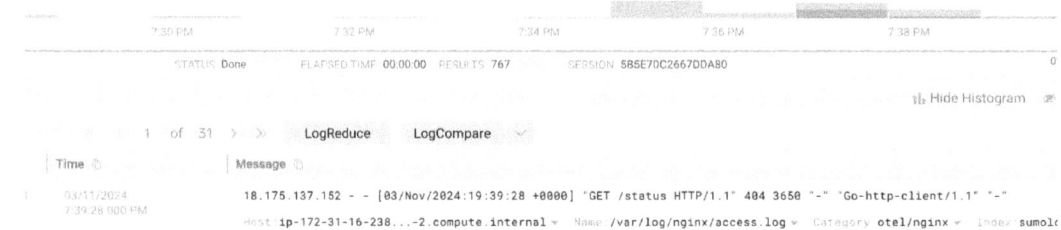

Figure 5.39 – Nginx log events queried after setting up the OpenTelemetry source

As we've installed the Nginx OpenTelemetry source through the App Catalog, we've not only set up the data collection but also the out-of-the-box content.

So far, we've covered the setup of an OpenTelemetry Collector on a Linux operating system, as well as for Nginx running on that same Linux machine. Other services and technologies work in exactly the same way.

What I want to cover next are the **Application Performance Management (APM)**, **Real User Monitoring (RUM)**, and the OTLP/HTTP source. I've saved these until the end because they all cover application-focused telemetry, and the OTLP/HTTP source covers logs, metrics, and traces, but is typically used for niche edge cases where you cannot send telemetry via an OTel Collector for any reason. Let's take a look.

Setting up Application Performance Management (APM) for a Python application

Let's build on the OpenTelemetry concept further and add traces to the mix to get this all working together. I want to explore why APM is so important anyway. We've got logs and metrics from our infrastructure, services, and other parts of our environment, so that's pretty good. What are traces all about?

Why do traces exist?

Traces are a way to follow the path of a request as it moves through various parts of an application or distributed system, giving insights into how different services and components interact to fulfill a user's request. I'm going to put it into more context by answering why we need them and what they're for, before explaining how it all comes together with logs and metrics.

Why do we need them? Well, picture this. You're working on a complex web application with many different moving parts. There are microservices in different languages, using two separate databases, and you have API calls here, there, and everywhere. You click a **Buy** button on your website, and the following series of actions begins:

1. A web server handles the request.
2. An authentication service checks your identity.
3. A product service is called to check whether the item is in stock.
4. A payment service processes the transaction.
5. A notification service is used to confirm the order and send you an email.

In many modern systems, these actions are performed by different technologies in different parts of the world – in other words, what is called a *distributed system*. Now, imagine something goes wrong with all of this. What's the easiest way of finding out quickly? You guessed it! Traces.

Now, we can look at what they're for and why they're helpful. In this scenario, traces can help to answer some key questions:

- *Where is the slowest performance?* If a request takes 5 seconds instead of the 1 second it usually takes, a trace can show this pretty quickly in a visual way.
- *Did something fail?* A trace can show whether a service is not communicating anymore.
- *How does data flow?* Traces and Service Maps can show how the data flows in an application between all the dependencies in an application, allowing engineers to identify isolated outages or downed chunks of an application.

Take a look at an example trace in the following screenshot, and you'll be able to see why traces happen to be such a useful tool:

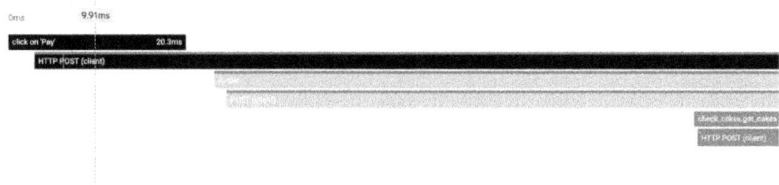

Figure 5.40 – The application traces view in Sumo Logic

You can clearly see how long each of these individual actions, or *spans*, as they are known, is taking to help us diagnose the activities in our application. Sumo Logic alerts you to any errors within these spans by labelling them red, and anomaly detection runs in the background to identify any abnormal activity.

So, now we know what traces and spans are for, let's look at getting some from an application ourselves. We'll be instrumenting a basic Python application to show how this is done.

Instrumentation

The application is going to consist of a Python and React.js microservice. The way we'll start is to have an OpenTelemetry Collector[4] deployed on our infrastructure. The great thing is, we've just done all of that! We've got a collector that we've deployed on our Linux machine, and we're ready to go.

To connect the app, we need to follow a process called **instrumentation**. Instrumentation is where you add code to an app, service, or technology to make that component *observable*. There are two methods of instrumentation – automatic and manual. **Automatic instrumentation** relies on instrumentation libraries that have been created and released for a particular language within the OpenTelemetry framework. Supported languages include Python or .NET, and it is definitely a more streamlined way of setting things up. I highly recommend it because a lot of the effort is taken away. It's quicker to set up and gives you broad visibility, so it's an ideal starting point. If you want deeper customization options – for example, coding in custom spans, objects, or unsupported libraries – you'll need the manual instrumentation option.

We're going to walk you through the auto-instrumentation process here.

For Python, all you need to do is install a couple of libraries and add some environment variables to make the whole thing work. Let me demonstrate. Let's install the two libraries we need here:

```
pip install opentelemetry-distro==0.47b0
```

And here:

```
pip install opentelemetry-exporter-otlp-proto-http==1.26.0
```

Before we set up the environment variables, let's run an important command. It's basically a command that speeds everything up by installing instrumented packages used by the application:

```
opentelemetry-bootstrap --action=install
```

This should set us up nicely. Now, what we need to do is create an environment file and set up some environment variables as shown here:

```
OTEL_METRICS_EXPORTER=none
OTEL_TRACES_EXPORTER=otlp
OTEL_EXPORTER_OTLP_PROTOCOL=http/protobuf
OTEL_EXPORTER_OTLP_ENDPOINT=http://OTLP_ENDPOINT:4318
OTEL_SERVICE_NAME=SERVICE_NAME
OTEL_RESOURCE_ATTRIBUTES=application=APPLICATION_NAME
```

Just a few points on these variables, the first three don't tend to change, but the rest are amended to be tailored to your app. The OTLP endpoint is the address where your OpenTelemetry Collector is located. In this case, it is on the same machine where we've hosted our application, so it would just be `localhost:4318`. Service and application names are designed to add some metadata labels to your trace data that comes through to Sumo Logic.

Finally, we run our app! Instead of running a typical python `<script.py>`, we instruct OpenTelemetry to instrument it instead, so the final command is as follows:

```
opentelemetry-instrument python3 app.py
```

If we visit our Service Map by going to **Observability | Services | Map**, we can see our new Python service in all its glory:

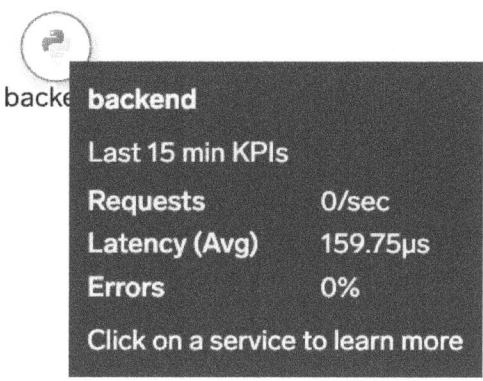

Figure 5.41 – Python service visible after instrumenting it with OpenTelemetry

When you do any actions on your app – for example, in this Python **Create, Remove, Update, Delete** (**CRUD**) app, when I visit an endpoint such as creating an item – it'll create a trace and a log that we can view in the traces and spans view:

Figure 5.42 – A list of traces and spans in Sumo Logic

So, now we've got some traces from our application, we're nearly done. Once you begin to instrument the other components of your application, your Service Map will begin to populate with your other distributed services. You'll be able to see the chain of events and calls being made for the lifecycle of the request. To add the cherry to the cake here, we're going to look at Real User Monitoring – what it is, what it does, and how we can set it up in Sumo Logic.

Setting up a Real User Monitoring (RUM) collection

Real User Monitoring (**RUM**) is a method for tracking and analyzing how real users experience a website or application in real time. It provides insights into how actual users interact with the app, identifying slowdowns, errors, and usability issues directly from users' perspectives.

Why does RUM exist?

When people use a website or app, they expect it to be fast, responsive, and error-free. However, different users have different experiences, depending on factors such as the following:

- **Their internet connection**: Some users may be on fast Wi-Fi, others on slow mobile data
- **Device and browser**: Different devices (desktop versus mobile) and browsers can lead to different load times or display issues
- **Geographic location**: Accessing a server from the other side of the world can slow things down

RUM exists to capture these real-world experiences as they happen, allowing companies to understand how real users see their applications. It takes telemetry from the front end of an application and delivers insights to engineers who then use that data to identify problems and correlate with other issues and events to get to the root cause. Examples of insights derived from RUM data could be the following:

- **Performance metrics**: How well is the application doing? How long is it taking to load the first byte, also known as **Time to First Byte** (**TTFB**), a great KPI that can be used for measuring performance. How long does it take for content to visually appear on the screen for the user? This is known as *contentful paint*, and once again can be an indicator of how good or bad the user experience is.
- **User engagement**: How are users exploring our application, and where do they keep visiting? Where is their attention drawn, and conversely, where do they stop exploring our content?
- **Error tracking**: We can get JavaScript errors and other client-side issues to help diagnose our application.
- **User environment**: We can see how users could have different experiences based on certain factors, such as where they're visiting from, what device they're using to visit the application, and so on.

So, RUM is great when it comes to the part of your application that users interact with. It might not be super clear at this point how RUM is different from APM. Let's do a quick comparison before we see how we can instrument RUM on our application.

The following table shows key differences between RUM and APM:

Aspect	Real User Monitoring (RUM)	Application Performance Monitoring (APM)
Focus	User experience (frontend)	Application health (backend)
Data Source	Client-side (browser/mobile app)	Server-side (infrastructure, application services)
Key Metrics	Page load times, first paint, TTFB, JavaScript errors, Core Web Vitals	Response times, error rates, latency, CPU/memory Usage
Environment	Captures device, browser, network, location	Captures infrastructure details (VM, container)
Primary Goal	Improve end-user experience	Ensure application stability and performance

Aspect	Real User Monitoring (RUM)	Application Performance Monitoring (APM)
Typical Issues Detected	Slow load times, client-side errors, UI responsiveness	Slow requests, server errors, infrastructure bottlenecks
Primary Users	Frontend, UI/UX teams	Backend devs, SREs, DevOps

Table 5.1 – The differences between RUM and APM

Instrumentation

We have our application with Python on the backend and a React.js implementation on the front end. Let's instrument RUM to start monitoring the user experience of the frontend portion of our application.

The first step is to set up a Hosted Collector, which we've done before. This time, from the sources list, we're going to select **RUM HTTP Traces**:

Figure 5.43 – RUM HTTP Traces data source

Fill in the name of the source and source category as a matter of course, but then swiftly move on to the **Advanced options for Browser RUM** section, which will look like this:

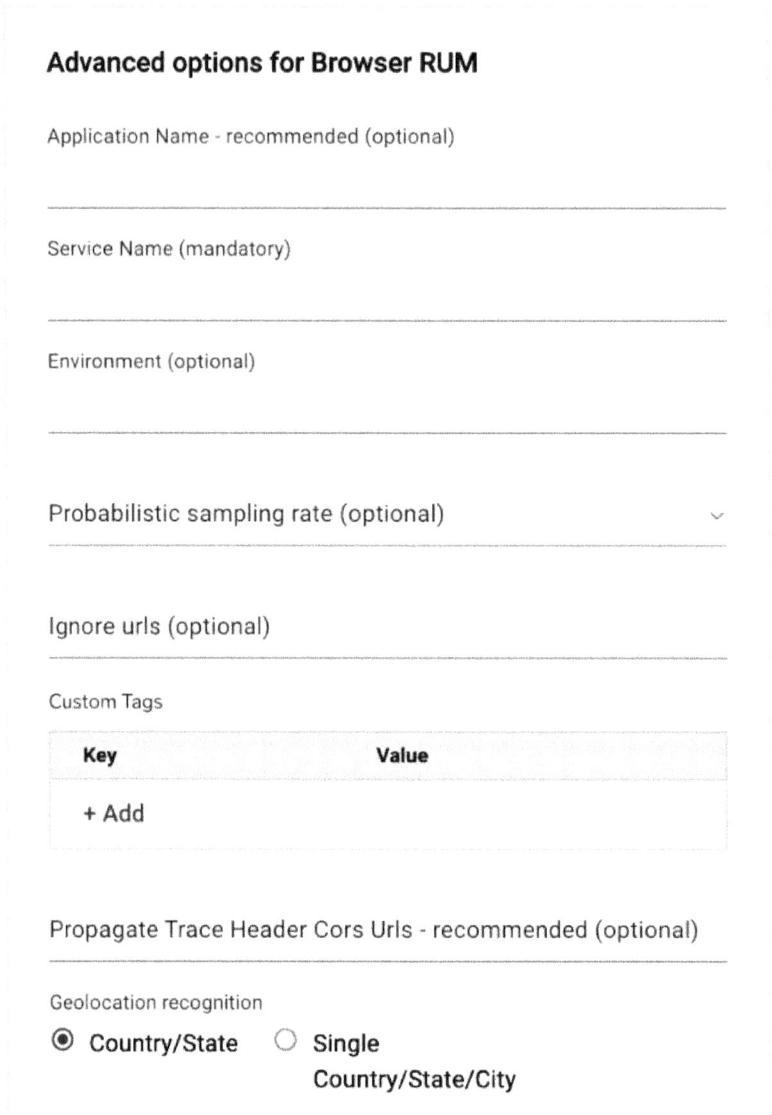

Figure 5.44 – A view of the advanced options, which help to configure the RUM source

These are all new, so let's walk through them briefly.

- **Application Name**: Link to your application name here to make it easier to correlate with spans and traces. This should match exactly what was in the **APPLICATION_NAME** environment variable from before, as it helps Sumo Logic work out whether this is part of the same app.
- **Service Name**: This is mandatory to help align it with the service.
- **Environment**: Another useful one to note down to help dev and DevOps troubleshoot.
- **Probabilistic sampling rate**: If you have a super noisy website, it might be a good idea to take a sample of all user traces. The percentage is entered as a decimal, so if you want to collect 50%, you'd enter 0.5.

- **Ignore urls**: This lets you leave out any URLs that you don't want any telemetry from.
- **Custom Tags**: Tagging of all types is very common in most operational teams, and this lets you bring that internal taxonomy into Sumo Logic.
- **Propagate Trace Header Cors Urls**: Add a list of URLs or URL patterns that pass tracing context to construct traces end to end (important as it helps to establish a complete trace in Sumo Logic and ties the frontend to the backend).
- **Geolocation recognition**: These options let you easily determine the geolocation of your visitors.

Finally, once you've configured this source and hit **Save**, you'll get a script. A few of the configuration options, such as **Service Name** and **Propagate Trace Header Cors Urls**, are taken and dynamically entered into this script. You then have to make a choice between three different types of scripts:

- Synchronous
- Asynchronous
- NPM

Depending on the makeup of your application and the tech stack, select the script most applicable to your frontend and then add it between the <head> and </head> tags in your JavaScript source code. With that, the process is complete, and you will get RUM data sent to Sumo Logic. The final result looks something like this, which I've taken from the RUM out-of-the-box dashboards:

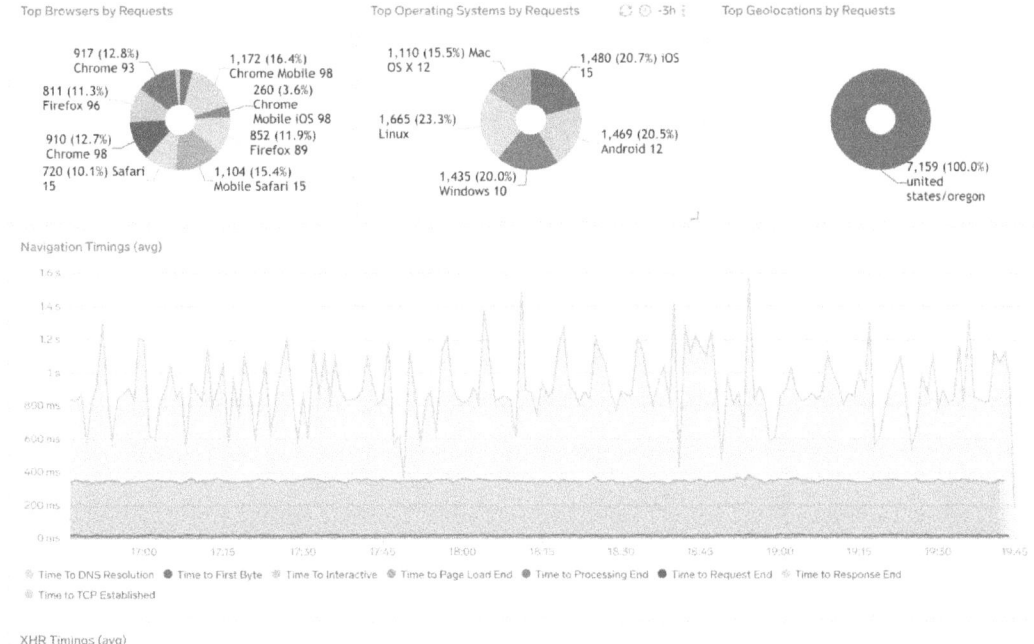

Figure 5.45 – A small snippet of the RUM dashboards that show frontend data

These dashboards can be found in the UI under **Observability** | **Real User Monitoring**:

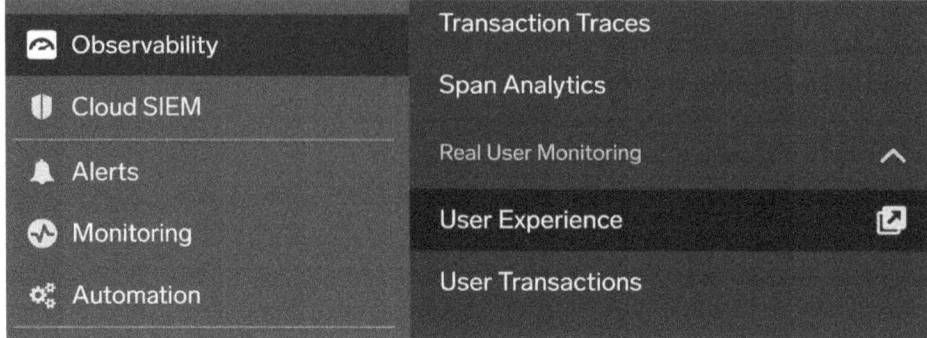

Figure 5.46 – Where the RUM dashboards are located

The **User Experience** dashboard shows metrics around frontend usage on your service or app, while the **User Transactions** dashboard shows traces from the apps. RUM is key to enhancing visibility across your applications, and we've seen how OpenTelemetry allows you to tap into this end-to-end view across your entire application and infrastructure landscape.

With RUM covered, let's talk about the last source available to us for data ingestion via OpenTelemetry, but in a *remote* way.

Setting up an OTLP/HTTP source

We've covered a lot of ground in this section by exploring all the different ways that OpenTelemetry helps you ingest data from across your entire business environment. Let's finish off with one more method of ingesting logs, metrics, and traces.

The OTLP/HTTP source provides a virtual endpoint where you can send logs, metrics, and traces *without* deploying a physical OpenTelemetry Collector. Customers use this in a lot of cases where deploying a collector might be tricky, or they just don't want to do it, and instead just want to shoot their logs, metrics, and traces over the OTLP protocol. This OTLP/HTTP source actually powers RUM under the hood, unless you specify you want to bring data in through a physical OpenTelemetry Collector.

For the last time, let's set up a Hosted Collector, and in the source list, choose the **OTLP/HTTP** source:

Figure 5.47 – What the OTLP/HTTP data source looks like

This source is very similar to an **HTTP Logs & Metrics** source, so give it a name and source category and click **Save**. This time, the endpoint generated will be one in line with the OpenTelemetry schema:

```
https://endpoint1.collection.eu.sumologic.com/receiver/v1/otlp/...
```

When you are editing the code in your application and adding environment variables to designate where the telemetry is going, you use this endpoint instead of the OpenTelemetry Collector endpoint. For example, from the examples we covered previously, the variable is usually this:

```
OTEL_EXPORTER_OTLP_ENDPOINT=http://OTLP_ENDPOINT:4318
```

In this case, the endpoint we see in the platform would be used as part of this variable.

Make sure to add /v1/logs, /v1/metrics, or /v1/traces to the Sumo Logic endpoint in order to comply with the OpenTelemetry schema and get the logs, metrics, or traces processed in the right way.

Bringing it all together

Up to this point in the book, we've covered a lot of different ingestion methods. We started with the Installed Collector for some quick wins, then progressed to Hosted Collectors to start sending in cloud data, and then really opened up the versatility of the OpenTelemetry Collector to get everything you want into Sumo Logic. We're slowly building our analytical bake by starting to add extra ingredients and textures above the base layer.

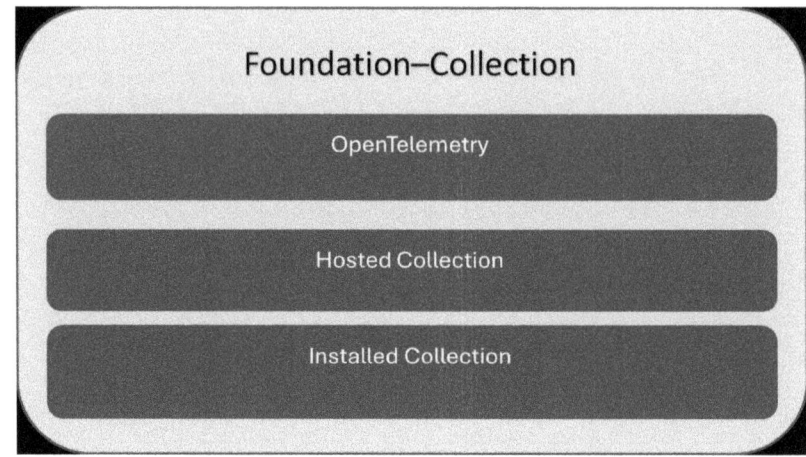

Figure 5.48 – The cake is growing, and we've added some crucial layers to it

This is incredibly important for everything we're going to cover in later chapters. When you have a strong foundation like this – scalable hybrid and multi-cloud ingestion covering logs, metrics, and traces, focusing on simplicity and cost-effectiveness – it unlocks operational efficiencies across your business and your teams because so much time is spent by teams on getting this base layer set up correctly. When it's easy to work with your data, teams can focus on actually delivering results and new innovative ways of doing things. This is the perfect combination for DevSecOps, which is what our objective is here.

Let's move on to an important topic, parsing. We've got the data in, and that's excellent. Most of it will be parsed automatically due to common formats and many out-of-the-box parsers available in Sumo Logic. What about when they don't get parsed, and those logs that are in a custom format or a custom application that you've designed? We need to show that data some love and get it analyzed too!

Parsing

Think of parsing this way: it's a way of understanding a sentence. When we humans see a sentence, we break down the nouns, verbs, and adjectives packaged inside to figure out the meaning. In the data world, it's the ability to turn a string into a structured format that can be understood and processed. Data in Sumo Logic is often, but not always, parsed in a *schema-on-demand* or *schema-on-read* way. Parsing data at runtime makes it easier to dynamically map and format without having to do that work in advance. This makes ingestion, parsing, and analysis easier for the user. However, sometimes you want to parse it at ingest time instead. Reasons include the following:

- Better query performance
- Not having to parse the same data for every query you do
- To normalize data across different data sources

When it comes to pre-parsing the data as it's streaming in, often called *schema-on-write*, you have two choices. For SIEM or security data, it's best to use the built-in parsing engine and library of parsers provided. However, for quick custom or ad-hoc parsers for log data, often the easiest choice is to build a **Field Extraction Rule (FER)**.

Field Extraction Rules (FERs)

FERs are tools that let you parse your data in multiple formats, including popular options such as JSON or regex format, and choose whether that parsing takes place at runtime or ingest time. Once set, these FERs can be used within queries, dashboards, monitors, and everywhere else on the platform. It's also worth noting that FERs are only active from the moment you set them, so if this will help you use your data more effectively, I recommend setting them up as soon as you can. Let's write an example FER to help you see the process.

When logged in, head to the left main menu and head to the **Data Management** menu, and under the **Logs** heading, select **Field Extraction Rules**:

Figure 5.49 – Field Extraction Rules is in the Logs section

Click **+ Add Rule** at the top right, and a panel will slide out. For this example, let's just use the AWS CloudTrail logs I ingested in the earlier section on Hosted Collectors. I want to parse this data at ingest time, so I give this rule a name, choose **Ingest Time**, and then select the source I want to target under **Scope**:

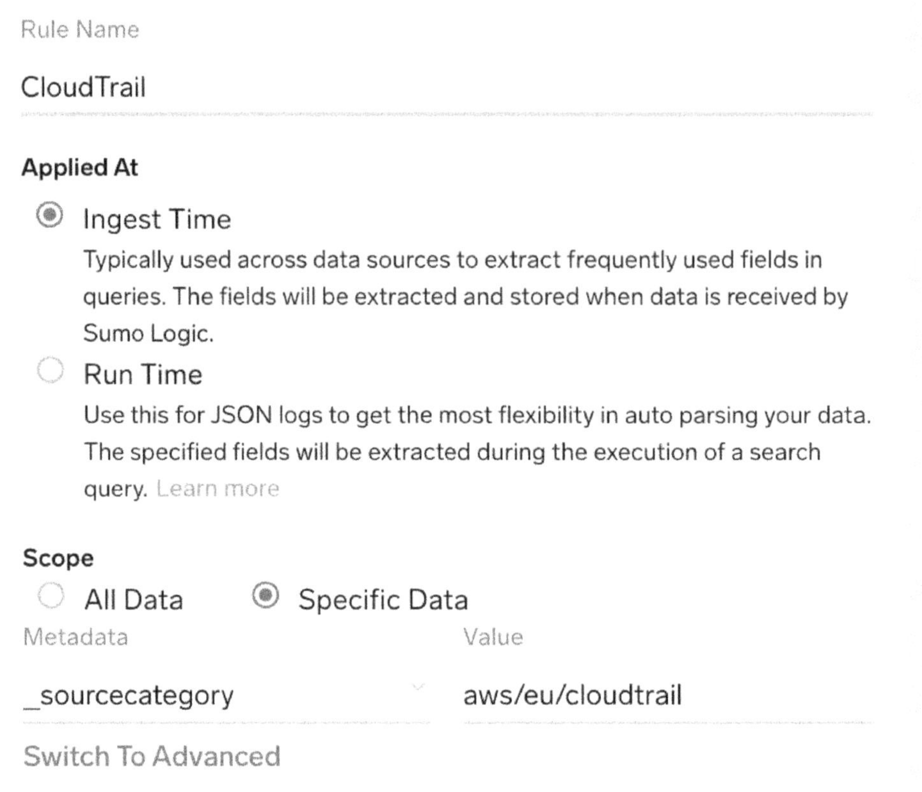

Rule Name

CloudTrail

Applied At

◉ Ingest Time
Typically used across data sources to extract frequently used fields in queries. The fields will be extracted and stored when data is received by Sumo Logic.

○ Run Time
Use this for JSON logs to get the most flexibility in auto parsing your data. The specified fields will be extracted during the execution of a search query. Learn more

Scope
○ All Data   ◉ Specific Data

Metadata   Value

_sourcecategory   aws/eu/cloudtrail

Switch To Advanced

Figure 5.50 – Defining the FER we're working on

It's worth mentioning that to help with the scope, it's best to use built-in metadata such as _sourceCategory or _sourceHost.

Partitions have become even more important after the rollout of the Flex pricing model, which means that customers pay for the data they scan, rather than just paying for ingesting it. A scan is where your data is queried for whatever purpose – a normal query, a dashboard panel loading up, or a monitor checking the data for any matches of its logic. If you scope more efficiently, it'll mean your queries will be both more performant and more cost-effective.

Back to the FER, once we've selected our scope, we can choose how we want to parse the data. In this case, I'm going to use the JSON parser as it's JSON data. Now, we haven't dived in depth into how the query language works yet, so we'll discuss this in the next chapter. I chose one of the fields I want to parse and rename it. If it successfully extracts, it appears in the **Extracted Fields** section, as we can see in the following screenshot.

Parse Expression *

```
1    json "eventVersion" as eventVersion
```

Extracted Fields (1)

- eventversion New

⚠ This rule will create 1 new field (currently 13 / 200)

Figure 5.51 – An example of parsing a field in JSON format for the FER

That's all there is to an FER. I wanted to cover some best practices to help make sure this tool is as easy as possible to work with.

FER best practices

The following are some best practices to follow when using FER:

- Target keywords that help to narrow down the scope as much as possible. This will ensure top performance, and if you're on Flex, it will be more cost-effective.
- Create a single rule per data source. This avoids any potential conflicts with the FER prioritization and keeps things clean and manageable over the long term.
- If you don't require any fields, don't extract them.
- Test the scope before creating the rule. You want to make sure that the fields you're extracting are searchable!
- Similarly, make sure all fields are available in the scope you define. If one field isn't found in a message, it won't get indexed.
- Use naming conventions that help you to apply FERs across your data effectively, making it easier to search through. A great source for naming conventions is in the documentation itself[5].

So, whether you have custom logs coming into Sumo or you just want to get the best performance possible, you can now use FERs to do so. There is one more way of parsing data, but it is specific to Cloud SIEM, so I will save it until we arrive at the right chapter to discuss it.

Best practices for data ingestion

As simple as data ingestion is in Sumo Logic, there are certain best practices that you should heed during the creation of these sources. Following these best practices will make your life a whole lot easier down the line!

Using source categories properly

A **source category** is arguably the most important bit of metadata in the Sumo Logic platform. It helps you categorize your data appropriately, and over the long term, it's much easier to manage and control it, as it (hopefully) grows after you embrace the complete power of the platform. Let's look at the naming convention, partitioning, and RBAC best practices.

Source categories help you to define the scope of your data for queries, dashboards, and so on, index and partition your data, and use **Role-Based Access Control** (**RBAC**) to control who can see and use the data.

In order to do this, you need a way to label your data effectively, so the naming convention we recommend for your source categories is as follows:

```
category1/category2/category3...
```

This pattern is useful at scale because it's possible to get more and more granular as you go through your data. For example, if we take an AWS WAF, I could do something like this:

```
aws/waf/eu
aws/waf/useast2
```

So, if I wanted to search through all my AWS WAF data, I could query for the following:

```
_sourceCategory=aws/waf/*
```

If I wanted to look at a particular region, I could do this:

```
_sourceCategory=aws/waf/eu
```

This gives the user more options and more flexibility when it comes to analyzing their data.

When and why to use partitions

When it comes to partitions, the source category comes in to help distinguish how you want your data to be indexed. Say you want to now create a separate partition for all your WAF data, you can do the following:

Go to **Data Management** | **Logs** | **Partitions**:

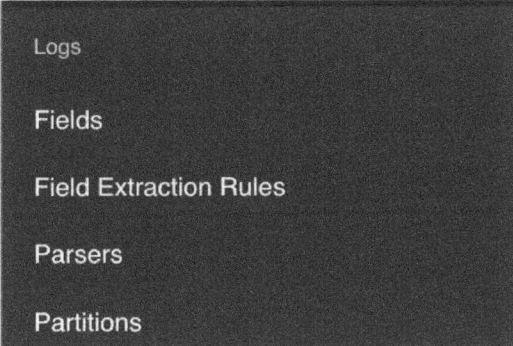

Figure 5.52 – The Partitions configuration is found in the Logs section

Then go to make a new partition with **+ Add Partition**, and a panel will swing open. Give it a name, define the scope or routing expression, and choose a retention period for the partition:

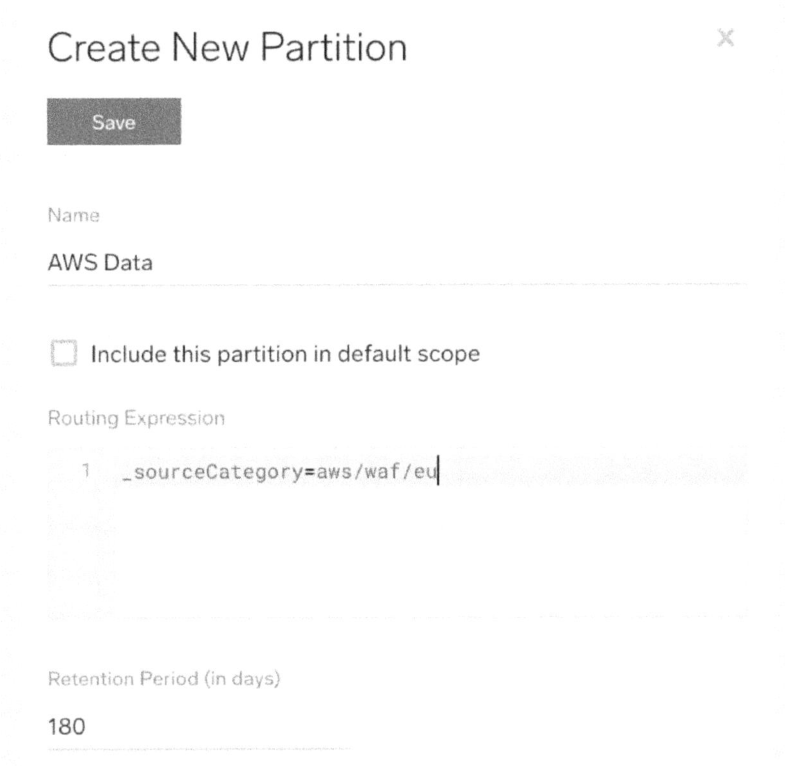

Figure 5.53 – The configuration options for a new partition

A routing expression is a normal keyword expression in the Sumo Query language that helps you narrow the scope of data. Any data that matches this expression will be forwarded and indexed separately in this new partition. So now, all the WAF data is going to a separate partition, where you can, for example, speed up the querying for a voluminous dataset.

How to use Role-Based Access Control (RBAC)

Another great use for source categories and partitions is to establish boundaries for your data. Follow me to the administrative part of the platform so we can dive into how this is done in a bit more detail.

To get there, head to **Administration** on the left menu and then **Roles**. You'll come to a list of roles – quite a short one to begin with, as it will only show the Administrator and Analyst roles. You can amend these or create your own, so click on **+ Add Role** to see what options we have:

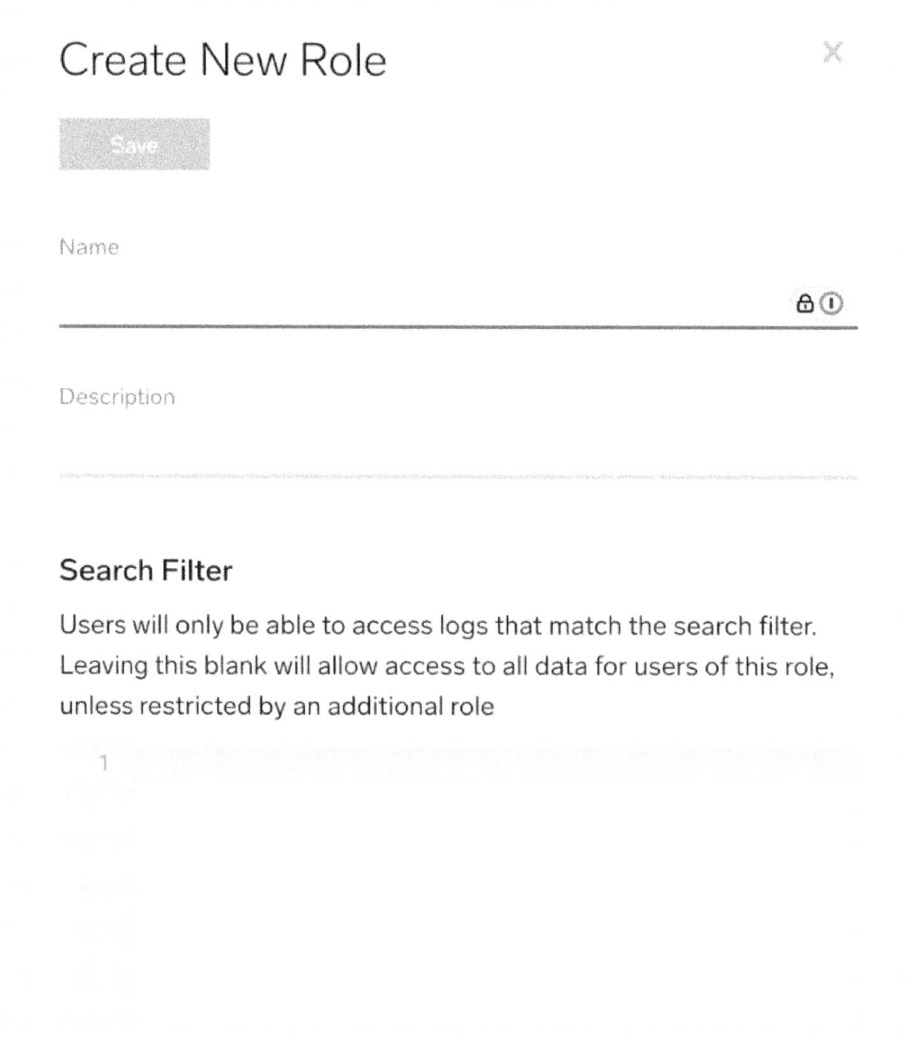

Figure 5.54 – Creating a search filter for a new role with Role-Based Access Control

You give the role a name and a description, but more importantly, **Search Filter** allows you to define what data this role can see and use. For example, if you only wanted your developers to access Kubernetes data and application logs, you could put something like this:

```
_sourceCategory=kubernetes/* OR _sourceCategory=funkyapp/java/prod
```

This will only let this role see and work with data from these two sources. Queries that use any other data from other sources won't return results, and only dashboards related to these two specified source categories will populate.

If you want to explicitly deny a role from viewing certain data, you can use this:

```
!_sourceCategory=audit/security
```

Other metadata tags can be used from within Sumo Logic's internal taxonomy. These include the following:

- _collector
- _source
- _sourcename
- _sourcehost

There are more options to manage what roles can be accessed. Under **Search Filter**, you will find a **Capabilities** section that allows you to specify what this role can do in the UI of the platform.

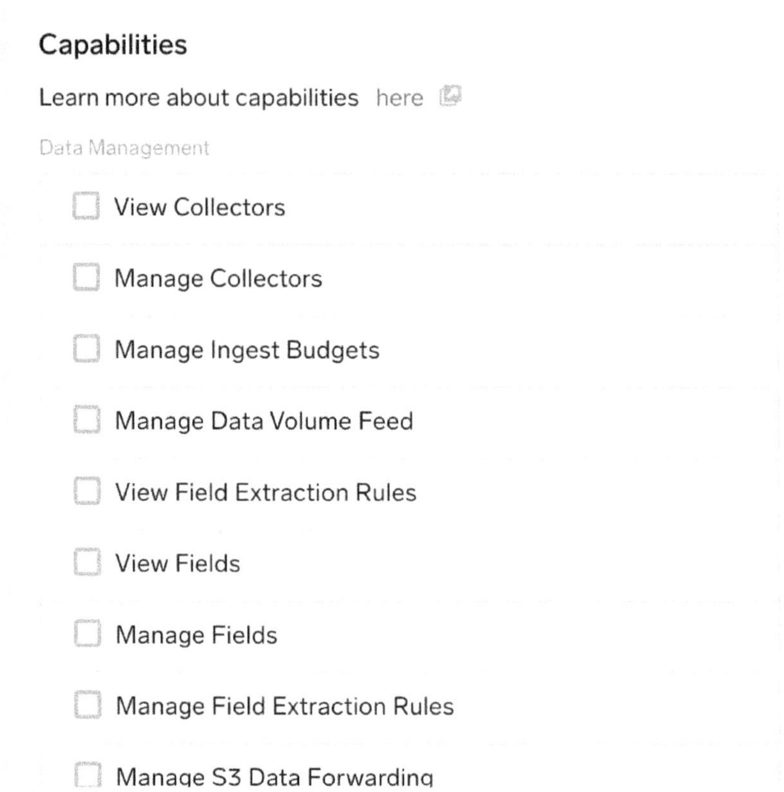

Capabilities

Learn more about capabilities here

Data Management

☐ View Collectors

☐ Manage Collectors

☐ Manage Ingest Budgets

☐ Manage Data Volume Feed

☐ View Field Extraction Rules

☐ View Fields

☐ Manage Fields

☐ Manage Field Extraction Rules

☐ Manage S3 Data Forwarding

Figure 5.55 – The capabilities that are defined for a role and that control what a role can do

The list is much longer, and I only took a short snippet, but there is a lot of granularity here with what your users and teams have access to. This includes creating and managing access keys and tokens, sharing dashboards, accessing the Cloud SIEM, and creating or editing playbooks, as examples.

> **Note**
>
> With the availability of Flex pricing, the possibility exists of users going rogue and querying massive datasets continuously, which would increase the costs of using Sumo Logic. To help alleviate this concern, Sumo Logic has implemented a feature called *Guardrails* that allows you to set organization-wide query budgets, as well as to control budgets at user and role levels.

How to pre-process your data

Quite commonly, teams need to "clean" their data or trim it or do something to it at source (the point of collection) before analyzing it. For example, before ingesting firewall data, the security team might only be interested in *allow* attempts, leaving the denies to be handled by the firewall logic. They would look to exclude all messages with *allow* in them so they can focus on the denies. This is called pre-processing (we covered this topic briefly back when setting up an OpenTelemetry Collector using source templates), and Sumo Logic has something called *processing rules* that allow users to do this. There are a few options available, all of which I'll cover here to highlight the possibilities. Customers have various levels of maturity when it comes to data processing, transformation, and any ETL tools and processes they may have.

This ability to process data prior to it being indexed in Sumo Logic allows you to have more control over what data actually lands inside the platform and what it looks like. There are four options here:

- Exclude messages that match
- Include messages that match
- Hash messages that match
- Mask messages that match

These processing rules all use regular expressions (regex) to specify data that you want to comply with the rules. The first two, *include* and *exclude* rules, basically act as an *allowlist* and a *denylist*. For example, to include or exclude messages from a Cisco ASA firewall, you can use the following regex:

```
.*%ASA-\d-\d{6}.*
```

Note that when putting these filters together, the *regex must match the entire message*. It doesn't work if you only specify a small subset of the message.

The third, hashing, lets you replace an expression with a hash code generated for that value. This is great for ensuring that certain data does not leave your premises. The fourth, *masking messages*, lets you hide irrelevant or sensitive information from the logs. A great example is credit card numbers. These can be masked easily with the following regex:

```
((?:(?:4\d{3})|(?:5[1-5]\d{2})|6(?:011|5[0-9]{2}))(?:-?|\040?)(?:\d{4}(?:-?|\040?)){3}|
(?:3[4,7]\d{2})(?:-?|\040?)\d{6}(?:-?|\040?)\d{5})
```

This takes into account any hyphens, dashes, or spaces, including solid strings of numbers in your data.

How to use ingest budgets

There may come a time when using Sumo Logic, when you decide you need to have a cap on your data ingest volume to control costs. It's not frequently used, due to the Flex pricing model and how much control customers have over their data, but it can be helpful in certain scenarios.

To get to the **Ingest Budgets** section, head to **Data Management**, then go to **Ingest Budgets** under **Logs**. Click on **+ Add Budget** and you'll see a panel to help you configure it.

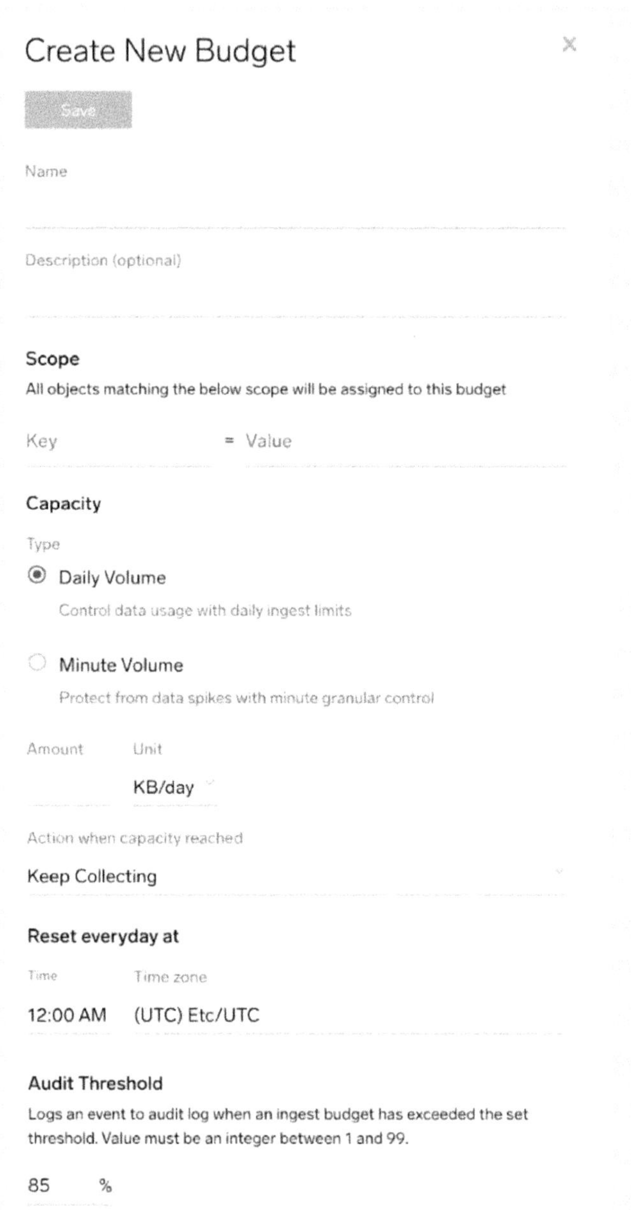

Figure 5.56 – Configuration for an ingest budget, which lets you create a cap for data ingest

You can give the budget a name, tell it the scope so that it knows what it's applying the cap to, and then choose **Daily Volume** or **Minute Volume**. Specify the amount of data per day and what to do when the capacity is reached. Most of the time, you stop collecting. That's about it!

Choosing your ingestion strategy

We've talked a lot about ingesting data, the different methods, and some best practices. Now you're looking at this and asking What do I do from here? I've got you covered. The next couple of pages will help you determine what the best way to implement all of this is *in your environment*. We'll look at a few different ingestion strategies that I've split up by the number of devices. It's the easiest way to categorize at this point.

Small organizations (1–50 devices)

In this bracket, the focus is on simplicity, low operational overhead, minimal infrastructure, and predictable cost. You don't need to create collection hierarchies and tiered ingestion. Let's keep it simple, because you probably don't have a platform team and you need visibility *now*, not after a 6-month architectural review. Here are the recommendations:

- **Locally installed collectors/agents** on each endpoint or server
- **Direct-to-cloud ingestion** (e.g., HTTP sources/cloud-native ingestion)
- **Minimal processing**: lightweight filtering or tagging, mostly push-based

Mid-sized organization (50–2,000 devices)

At this scale, you're more interested in consistency, automation, and basic security segmentation. You actually know what a change management process is, and spikes in data volume from observability and security sources cause a headache. 200+ agents sending data individually is a quick route to losing your sanity, and you appreciate the pre-processing and control of your data. Here are the recommendations:

- **Centralized collectors** per network segment or environment
- Agents/forwarders send data to these internal collectors, which then export to the cloud
- **Batching and filtering** are applied at the collector level
- **Config managed centrally** (GitOps, Ansible, Puppet, etc.)

Large enterprises (2,000–100,000+ devices)

In the big leagues, it's all about scale, compliance, segmentation, reliability, and governance. You have more security zones than some countries, and losing telemetry for 10 minutes triggers incident calls. With this big of an estate and this many devices, *everything* becomes a data pipeline problem, so you need structure, buffering, and multiple layers of control. Here are the recommendations:

- **Hierarchical ingestion tiers** (edge collectors → regional collectors → central collectors)
- **Local processing** near the source for PII scrubbing, enrichment, shaping, and dropping noise
- **Strict batching, retry, queuing, and failover configurations** to keep pipelines healthy
- **Segregated ingestion paths** for regulated workloads (PCI, healthcare, government)
- **Automated configuration management** across hundreds/thousands of collectors

Highly regulated or air-gapped environments

Here, it's all about security over practicality, and it's where federal, military, and finance environments live. Engineers need approval to open a port, and certain individuals in your company say "export controls" unironically. There is a focus on zero external dependencies, strong control, and auditability. A local ingestion pipeline with transparent YAML configuration (OpenTelemetry) beats any SaaS ingestion capability, as everything is reviewable and provable. Here are the recommendations:

- **Locally managed collectors only:** no SaaS-side pipelines
- **Strictly internal processing** with outbound traffic explicitly approved or disallowed
- **Heavy preprocessing before any data leaves the environment** (if it leaves at all)
- **Collector mesh architecture** with redundant paths

I hope this helps you identify which route and what level of ingestion architecture you need to have and how to best plan for it The basics are covered and you can ingest most things that you need to work around these ingestion strategies. As we've mentioned throughout this chapter, Sumo Logic's data ingestion capabilities will alleviate most struggles teams face and support you with reliable, usable technology, but you know your environment better than anywhere else.

Summary

In this chapter, we gave you all the knowledge you need to start ingesting data from across your environment, no matter where it sits – whether it's on your laptop or an on-premise server, or maybe it's in the cloud in AWS or GCP, and you need to monitor your cloud services and infrastructure. Have you got some applications? Awesome, we can get the traces from those into Sumo Logic as well. In addition to the Installed Collectors covered in the previous chapter, we looked at Hosted Collectors, **Infrastructure as Code** (**IaC**) collection, and OpenTelemetry collection, which we further split into logs and metrics, APM, and RUM.

We also covered parsing and explained the concept of **Field Extraction Rules** (**FERs**) to help you parse data that may not be covered by the dynamic parsing available with Sumo Logic out of the box. We also looked at best practices when it comes to data ingestion – how to use important built-in metadata such as source categories, how to partition your data, and how to implement RBAC to make sure that all the data you have in Sumo Logic is accessed properly and safely.

Finally, I shared some ingestion strategies that you can hopefully take away based on what type of organization you're working for and use Sumo Logic to help make the ingestion and centralization of data as straightforward as possible.

In the next chapter, we're going to be taking a detailed look at querying and analyzing your data. We've got it in the platform, now we can really do some cool stuff with it. While all this is fresh, let's go! Time is of the essence.

References

1. https://help.sumologic.com/docs/send-data/hosted-collectors/cloud-to-cloud-integration-framework/universal-connector-source/

2. https://www.sumologic.com/help/docs/observability/aws/deploy-use-aws-observability/deploy-with-terraform/#troubleshooting

3. https://opentelemetry.io/docs/what-is-opentelemetry/

4. https://github.com/SumoLogic/sumologic-otel-collector

5. https://help.sumologic.com/docs/manage/field-extractions/field-naming-convention/

Get this book's PDF version and more

Scan the QR code (or go to `packtpub.com/unlock`). Search for this book by name, confirm the edition, and then follow the steps on the page.

Note: Keep your invoice handy. Purchases made directly from Packt don't require an invoice.

6

Analyzing Data

This chapter dives into the analytical capabilities of Sumo Logic. Now that we've ingested some examples of different data in *Chapters 4 and 5*, the next step in our journey is extracting insights from it. At its core, Sumo Logic is a log analytics platform, so there is a comprehensive suite of tools when it comes to extracting value out of your data. It's time to look at querying and visualizing it. We're really peeling back the layers now!

In this chapter, we're going to be looking at everything from the query language to how to use it on your data, and the different types of analysis. Sumo Logic began its life as a log analytics technology, so the capabilities here are our bread and butter and cater to all levels of usage, from simple querying – for example, *show me which Windows machines have run a specific PowerShell command* – all the way to advanced and complex analytics. An example could be extracting network events, aggregating JA4 fingerprints, and then creating both a ratio of activity and a delta between events in the same query. You'll see cases for the entire spectrum and, more importantly, in the context of practical usage, so any developers, DevOps, and SecOps teams can begin implementing these straight away.

This chapter will cover the following key topics, both generally and in the context of what Sumo Logic is capable of:

- Querying logs deep dive
- Log search optimization

Querying logs deep dive

It's time to dive properly into log analytics. In this section, we're going to explore the UI to make sure you know where to go and how to navigate the tools at your disposal. Then, we'll identify the problems and difficulties with querying, historically and in the present. Finally, we'll discuss how Sumo Logic helps to alleviate these challenges and cover some examples for three different operation teams—developers, DevOps, and SecOps.

> **Note**
>
> If you're thinking, "wait, I thought AI can write queries for me," you're not wrong. In Sumo Logic, that capability shows up through tools like Mobot and the Query Agent. But relying on AI without understanding the fundamentals is a mistake. Learning how to write and interpret queries the traditional way gives you control, precision, and the ability to validate AI-generated results. Later in this chapter, we'll layer in natural-language querying once the core concepts are solid.

Navigating Log Search

So far, we've seen one way of accessing **Log Search**. When we were installing our collectors, we were on the **Collection** page under **Data Management**, where we could hover over our source and click the little blue document or metrics icon. That's the quickest way of seeing data coming in from the source you selected. There is another option that will be covered next.

First, head to **Logs | Log Search** in the menu to access a blank search from scratch, as shown in *Figure 6.1*.

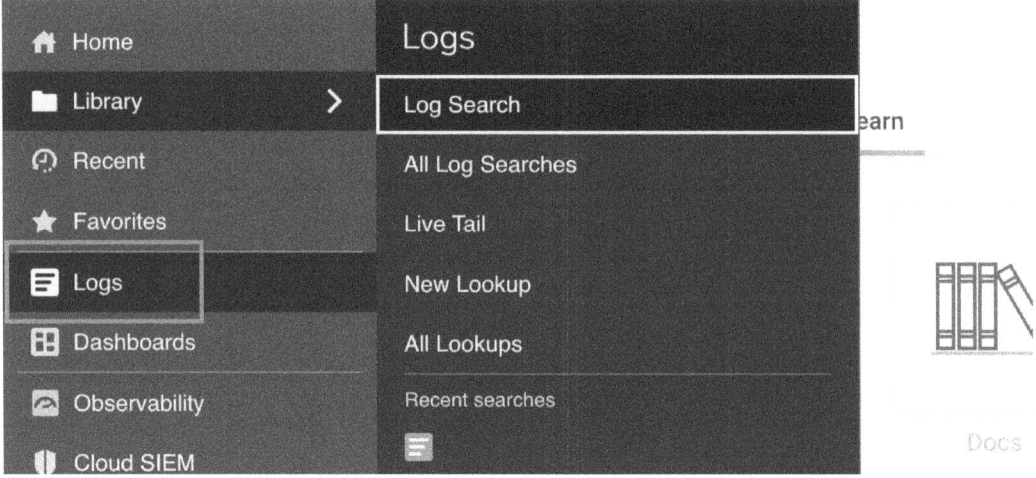

Figure 6.1 – Finding Log Search in the menu

You'll see on the **Logs** screen that there is a **Live Tail** option and lookup tables. We'll cover these later in the section, as they are useful to know about.

The first thing we see in the **Log Search** UI, shown in *Figure 6.2*, is a long query bar (top left):

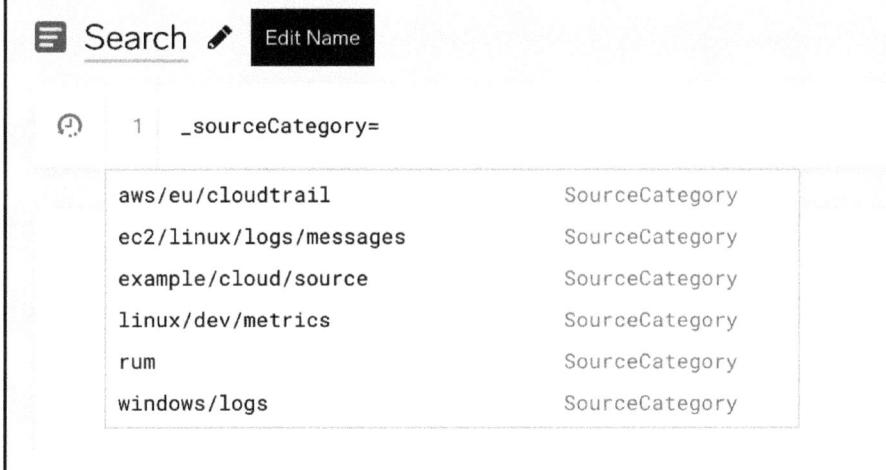

Figure 6.2 – Using _sourceCategory to start selecting what source we want to query

It is best practice to specify the source or sources you want to start querying your data from. If you remember from *Chapters 4 and 5*, we set the source category for our data when we set up the collection, and it's a great way to specify what data source you want to query. For example, we are using _sourceCategory= here in this query, and it's one of the most popular ways of specifying a source.

The top left of the query interface lets you give a name to the search if you intend to reuse it. Clicking the clock icon to the left of the **1** lets you see recent searches. Next to that is the actual query box, where a lot of the work is done.

It is crucial to specify what part of your data you're looking at the top of the query, even if it's all your data with _sourceCategory=*. Auto-completion exists within Sumo Logic on the default metadata, such as _sourceCategory and _source.

It's also worth looking at the right-hand corner of the search UI, shown in *Figure 6.3*:

Figure 6.3 – Focusing on share, save, and other options as part of the Log Search UI

Starting at the top, the first icon on the left is to open a new Log Search—pretty straightforward. The second icon with the **+** is to duplicate the current query, which is often used when you want to create a second query that shares the same foundation as your current one. The third icon is to share the query. It creates a link that allows you to share the results with anyone, as long as they have the right permissions. The fourth icon is to save the query, letting you choose a name, the time range of the search, and the query itself. *Figure 6.4* shows what that panel looks like:

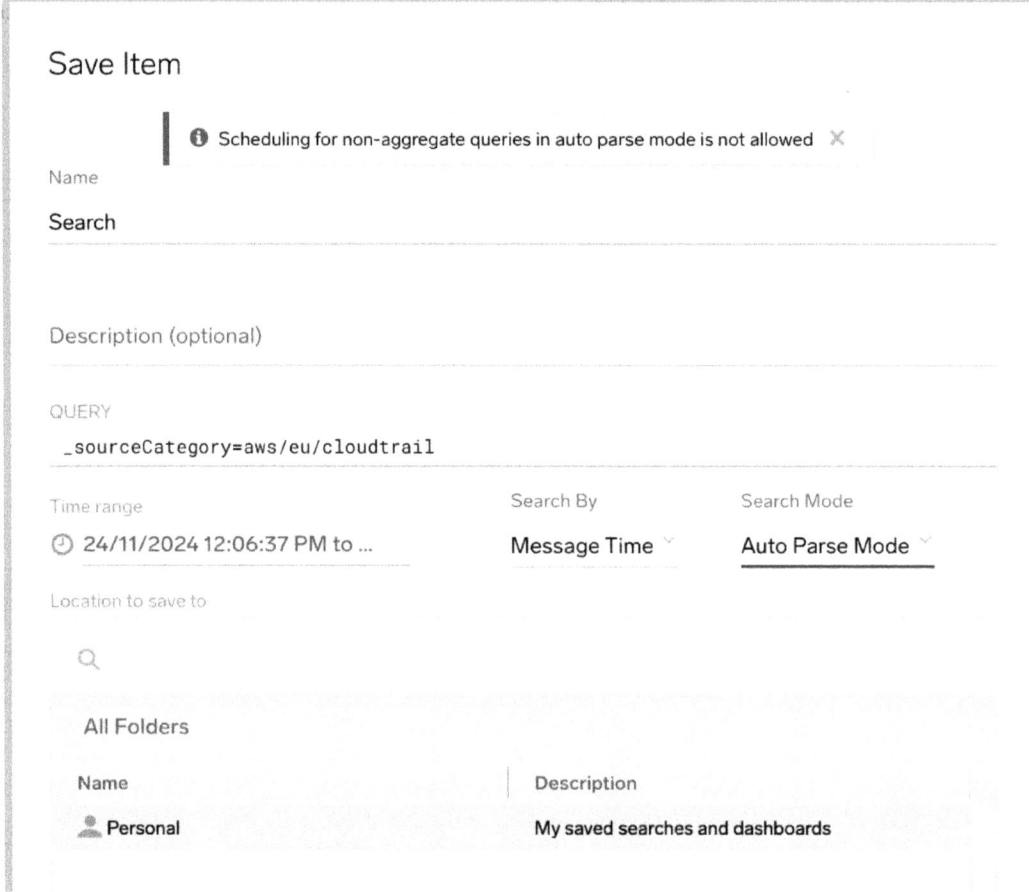

Figure 6.4 – The configuration box for saving a query and reusing it later

It contains different options to configure your saved search and has a way to schedule a search, but we'll discuss this later, in *Chapter 9*, *Cloud SIEM*. Going back to the buttons in the top-right corner, there are three dots that open a sub-menu with a few useful options, and this view is shown in *Figure 6.5*. Let's walk through some of them.

Figure 6.5 – Reviewing the additional options for our query

- **Basic Mode**: This lets you query with drop-down fields and select keywords you're interested in. You can see what this looks like in *Figure 6.6*.

Figure 6.6 – Basic Mode for querying, which lets you access data with drop-down fields

- **Cheat sheet**: This links you to the cheat sheet section in the Log Search documentation.
- **Save As...**: This lets you save the query as before.

- **Share…**: This lets you share the query.
- **Create a Monitor**: This lets you create a monitor for alerting purposes. We'll cover this *Chapter 8, Alerting, Monitoring, and Visualizing Data*.
- **Create an SLO**: This creates an SLO-based monitor.
- **Live Tail**: This streams your logs from a source in real time. We'll cover this in a later section.

Let's go back to the top-right corner of the search UI, shown in *Figure 6.7*.

Figure 6.7 – Shifting our focus to the timeframe, scan prediction, and query buttons

The first icon lets you set the timeframe for the query, **-15m** in this case, which looks at your log events from the past 15 minutes. This could be **-2h**, which would look back at 2 hours of logs, or it could be **-5d**, which is the last 5 days. Your queries can go back if your data is retained for, and you control this retention period; it can be up to 13 years for logs in Sumo Logic! The second icon, which is a gauge, shows you how many approximate megabytes or gigabytes of data will be scanned with this query, which helps you understand your scan volumes in relation to Flex-based pricing. We briefly noted in the last chapter that with the flex-pricing model, you pay for scans of your data, and this handy button will let you estimate that usage much more accurately. If you're on ingest-based pricing, however, the scan volumes won't be relevant for you. The third icon is the search button, with the magnifying glass, that triggers the search. Finally, the fourth icon, the cog, lets you configure the search parameters by choosing to use receipt time instead of message time, and choose whether JSON auto-parsing is enabled.

> **Note**
>
> JSON auto-parsing is a useful feature that helps you by taking away the need to write parse statements on all your JSON data in Sumo Logic. JSON is automatically parsed and extracted, no matter how nested it is, meaning you can search across it freely straight away.

Figure 6.8 shows what the options look like:

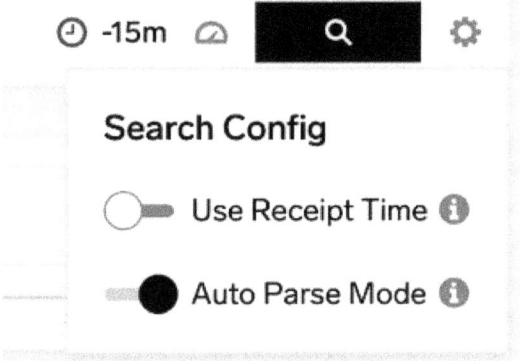

Figure 6.8 – Showing where Use Receipt Time and Auto Parse Mode are located

Using receipt time is sometimes useful when you want to ensure that logs aren't coming in under a different timestamp or if there is a delay in logs hitting the Sumo Logic receivers.

Once you've run a query, the UI changes to reflect the results received, as shown in *Figure 6.9*. Let's explore our new results, and as a side note, we have plenty of information about the UI and search basics in the official documentation [1].

Log results in the UI

The following is what the log results UI looks like:

Figure 6.9 – A view of the results from our first log query

The four key areas here are as follows:

- **Orange** (left panel): All the fields that have been extracted and parsed from your data.

- **Red** (top panel): A histogram of events on a timeline.
- **Green** (top middle): Pagination in the logs as well as easy access to the LogReduce and LogCompare operators. More on those shortly.
- **Blue** (center): The log events.

Color versions of the images can be found in this github repo: https://packt.link/gbp/9781835889763

Seeing results is great, but we can do more. Now that we can see them, we can do basic analysis. Basic analysis, and a very common starting point, is to do an **aggregation query**. An aggregation query is a way of grouping and structuring your data that is more easily digestible. Here's an example:

```
_sourceCategory=aws/eu/cloudtrail
| count by eventName
```

This basic query looks at the data in our AWS CloudTrail source (in the EU region – nice source category work!) and counts the number of messages by the eventName field. You will be presented with the aggregated results first. At the top of the aggregation, you'll see a **Messages** box and an **Aggregates** box. You can flip between a view of your aggregation and the raw results very easily in this way and it's helpful to see what raw data is part of the analysis. From here, we can apply different views to the aggregated data and start interacting with dashboards.

Aggregation results in the UI

Following on from the previous query, *Figure 6.10* shows the aggregated results:

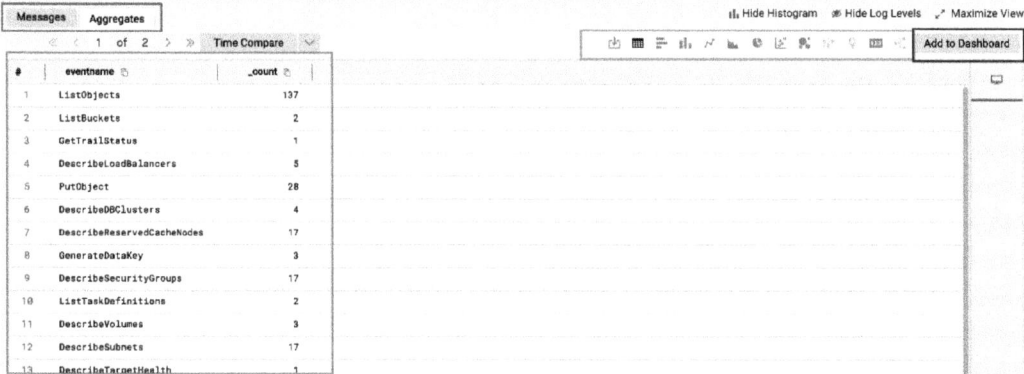

Figure 6.10 – An example of an aggregated result from our log query

Let's see the different ways we can process the data. This is a slightly different view from before, so let's look at it:

- **Red** (top left): This lets you choose between the aggregate view or the raw messages behind the aggregation
- **Orange** (left): The aggregation results
- **Green** (top right): Different visualization options for this data
- **Blue** (far top right): The button to add this view to a dashboard

This aggregation view is designed to extract analytical output from your data as quickly as possible, visualize it, and then add it to a dashboard. It's pretty intuitive, as when users interact with their data, the intention is to see something of value. For example, if you're looking at all the different IP addresses that a username has accessed for an investigation, you can build a table on that user on the fly as you do your research. No one sits around putting random queries in just for fun to see what kind of data comes out! If only we all had so much time on our hands.

Now that we can navigate around the UI, we want to put our first query together. There's one area I want to discuss before we do that – the historic and current problems with querying – to put some things into perspective.

Problems with querying

You might think, *What's so difficult about querying?* You're just asking some questions of your data – big deal. Well, there are a few problems that can arise when querying data – let's consider a few of them.

- **Reliance on schemas and formats**: The age-old problem of having to map your data to an exact schema for the technology you're using to read it effectively and return results.
- **Indexing difficulties**: Data that isn't indexed can't be searched effectively, and if possible, then expect a performance drop.
- **Query languages**: Most are derived from SQL; some are custom and proprietary. Each represents a learning curve and barrier to quick and easy usage.
- **Query performance**: Querying ineffectively or querying too large a dataset will mean slow processing times and waiting a long time for your data.
- **Complex data structures**: Data from all our varied systems and services is complex – nested and hierarchical, while containing many different attributes or properties that make it hard to search.
- **Distributed data**: If your data is spread around the business and across your data islands, perhaps contained in the cloud, on-premise, NoSQL databases, or various SQL databases, then it's going to be hard to find the answers you're looking for across these sources as they all use different syntax and languages.
- **Language limitations**: A lot of query languages cannot do more than do basic queries on log data. Without having a deep and comprehensive query language, you're unable to do things such as the following:
    - Transform and enrich data on the fly
    - Create advanced filters and searches

- Create complex aggregations across logs and metrics
- Correlate data across multiple sources
- Group, limit, or deduplicate results to help answer your questions
- Pattern matching and trend analysis
- Craft custom and personalized visualizations of your data
  - Custom alerting
  - Predictive analytics
- **Technical constraints**: Depending on the technology you're using to query your data, it's likely that there is a threshold above which it will struggle with limits on memory, CPU, or query complexity.

These are the problems that practitioners and power users face across any landscape where they have data and want to interact with it. The issue here is that we expect our ops teams to develop amazing applications, make internal processes and systems more efficient, and secure them at the same time. If these teams don't have the right tools to query any data source across their data islands, or if they can't get the right context from a particular **indicator of compromise** (**IOC**) quickly enough, it could have wider and more significant repercussions.

Covering these querying difficulties was important because in the next section, I want to start building some queries together with you, all while showcasing how Sumo Logic helps your operations teams to collaborate and respond to outages and threats in one place, where the preceding issues don't come into play with Sumo Logic.

Querying

Let's start with the first of many querying examples we'll find in this chapter. We'll keep it relatively simple, but before you know it, we'll progress to more advanced concepts such as search optimization. I'll be using Sumo Logic's sandbox environment for these examples, which you have access to after signing up for a free trial and accessing the learning and training environment containing terabytes and terabytes of data from a multitude of sources.

Query basics

Let's start by asking our AWS data a question around a certain IP address that we've seen floating around one of our dashboards. I've checked the **CrowdStrike** threat intelligence feed that's built into Sumo Logic, and we've got an IP address that has high malicious confidence and a lot of curated labels telling me that this indicator has been associated with several malware variants and is present within multiple stages of the Lockheed Martin Kill Chain. We covered this earlier in the book briefly, but it is under the **Threat Intel Quick Analysis** app in the App Catalog and is available for everyone using Sumo Logic from day one. We'll cover apps and integrations later in this chapter. The dashboard is shown in *Figure 6.11*.

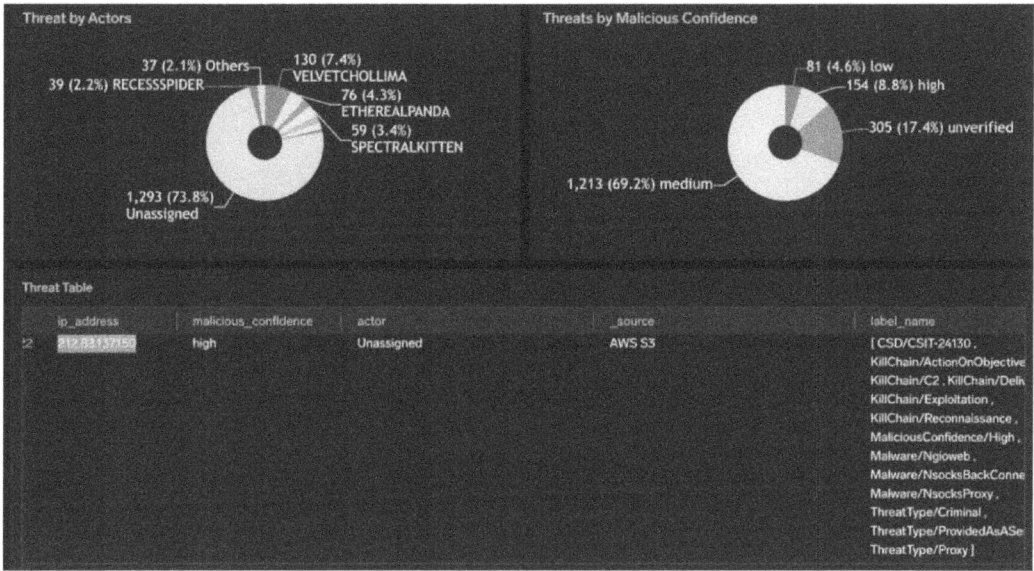

Figure 6.11 – The IP threat lookup dashboard in the CrowdStrike Quick Analysis app

In *Figure 6.11*, in the bottom table within the **_source** column, we're told that this IP address has been seen in our AWS S3 source of data, but I want to cast a wider net at this point, so let's put a query together. When deciding on how to phrase a query, in most cases it's formatted in the following order:

Keyword | parse | filter | grouping | sorting | limiting

Sumo Logic has pipe-based query language, so you start broad, and you get narrower through these pipes. Let's take that logic and write our query:

```
_sourceCategory=*AWS* 79.132.139.199
| count by _sourceCategory
| sort by _count desc
```

We begin by selecting our source category. I want to not only check the AWS S3 source but *all* our AWS data to make sure we don't miss anything. We also specify the IP address in question to do a full-text search on it. I then want to aggregate the data by running a count operator, which will show me all the different source categories it's been seen in, and then sort those results in descending order. The count operator counts all our log events and groups them by source in this case. This is the outcome:

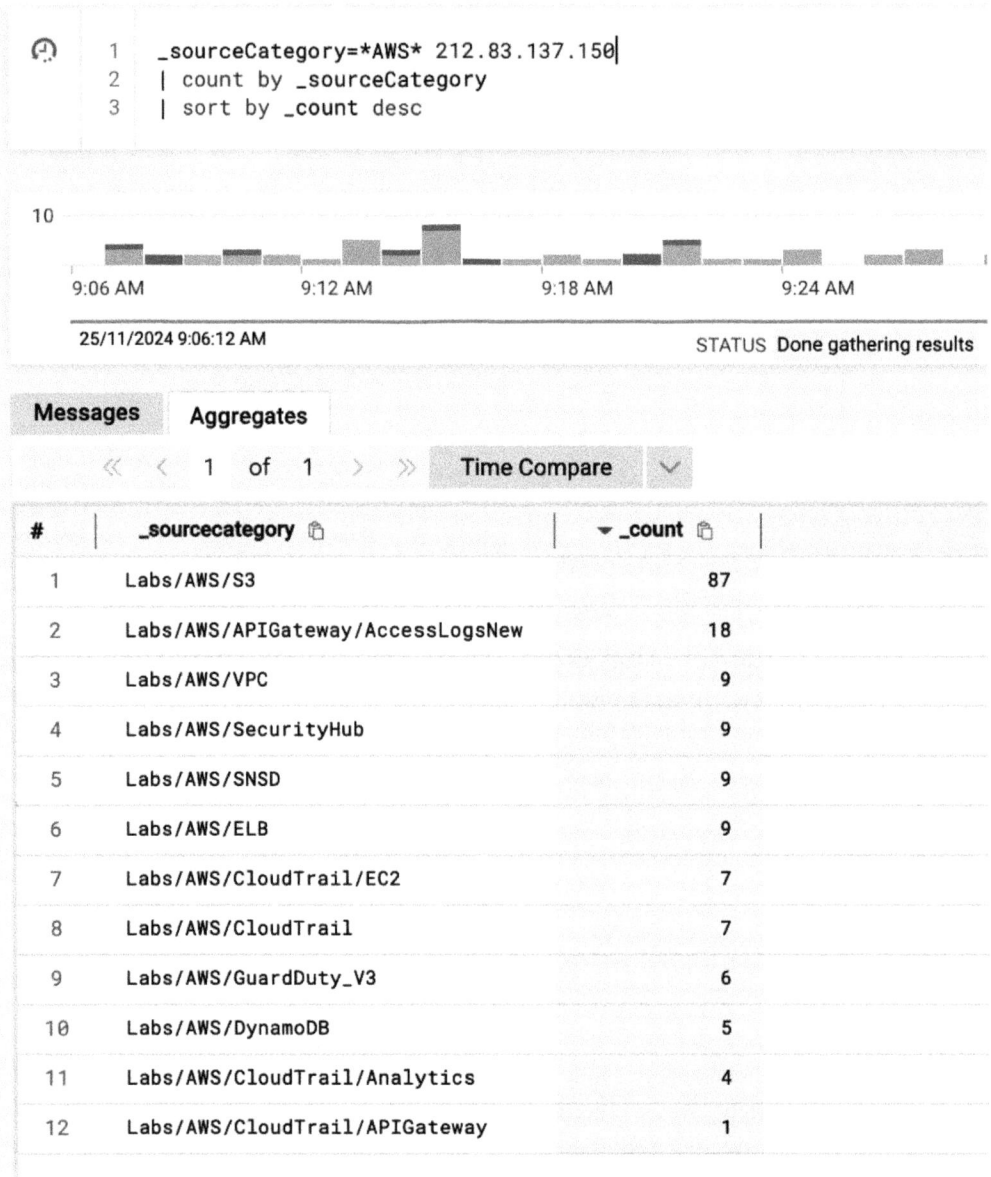

Figure 6.12 – Aggregated results showing all the sources of data where we've seen this IP

There have been numerous hits across a lot of different AWS sources. If we click on **Messages**, we can take a look at some of these log events to get a feel for this errant IP address. There are quite a few, actually, but we can see that in our AWS GuardDuty source, in *Figure 6.13*, this IP address seems to be linked to a development (dev) account that has demonstrated persistence capabilities:

Figure 6.13 – The IP address highlighted from our query in the AWS GuardDuty source

If you look at the above screenshot, I want to draw your attention to the data. Look at all that nesting...crazy! To see all your nested fields, right click on the white space in the event and choose **Expand Nested JSON**. One thing that Sumo Logic does with no difficulty is letting you query and use your data regardless of the nesting. This is not as easy as it seems and other log analytics technologies struggle to replicate it well. Nested data is more and more prevalent in our datasets now, with applications becoming more complex, filled with ever-growing metadata.

By the way, you're able to see which source of data the log event belongs to if you look under the log. Sumo Logic contains built-in metadata, which applies to all data. In this case, we have fields such as _sourceHost, _sourceName, and _index, which all appear by default under each event for your information. Looking at our S3 data, in *Figure 6.14*, we can see this IP address being involved with a GET request to an S3 bucket:

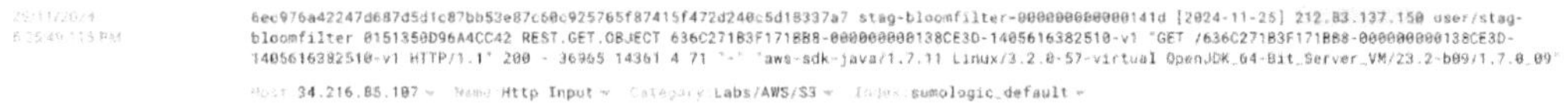

Figure 6.14 – We can see the same IP address in our AWS S3 data source

We're not feeling comfortable with this IP address, and it's starting to arouse some suspicion. Let's cast our net wider and cross-reference our other sources of data, such as Cisco Umbrella, Workday, and our Apache web server that our application sits on, as some examples. We can adapt our query to the following code:

```
212.83.137.150
| count by _sourceCategory
| sort by _count desc
```

Okay, but hold up, you might be asking why we have just started with an IP address instead of starting with a source category? Well, in this case, we don't need to specify anything, even _sourceCategory=*, because we just want a match on this IP address. The same could work for a username, domain, URL, and so on. You can see the new results in *Figure 6.15*:

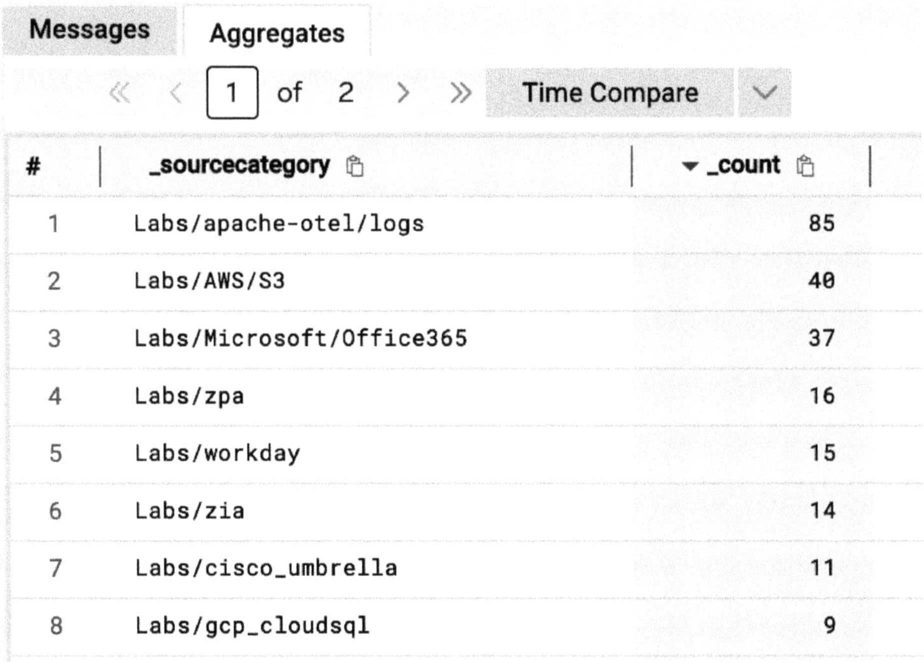

#	_sourcecategory	_count
1	Labs/apache-otel/logs	85
2	Labs/AWS/S3	40
3	Labs/Microsoft/Office365	37
4	Labs/zpa	16
5	Labs/workday	15
6	Labs/zia	14
7	Labs/cisco_umbrella	11
8	Labs/gcp_cloudsql	9

Figure 6.15 – All of the sources that have seen this IP address, excluding AWS sources

We're seeing this data across a whole range of sources. This is the power of visibility! Let's go into the messages to see what this IP has been up to. We've found the Workday log events, where this IP has started a new web service session, shown in *Figure 6.16*:

```
Time                    Message

25/11/2024              View as Raw
5:19:19.981 PM          {
                            sessionId: "6WLYuR",
                            userAgent: "Mozilla/5.0 (Windows NT 10.0; Win64; x64) AppleWebKit/5
                            ipAddress: "212.83.137.150",
                            requestTime: "2024-11-25T17:19:19.981Z",
                            deviceType: "Desktop",
                            systemAccount: "rick",
                            activityAction: "READ",
                            target: ▼ {



                            },
                            taskDisplayName: "Start New Session (Web Service)",
                            taskId: "5fH8zNfPH0f3taMM8YPS8tdsOK5w98EN",
                            tenant_name: "tenant1"
                        }


                                            ▼   Name:auditlogs ▼  Category:Labs/workday ▼  Index:
```

Figure 6.16 – Results from our Workday events showing the IP address starting a new web service session

In *Figure 6.17*, we can see it in our Apache logs, probing different endpoints in our web application:

Figure 6.17 – The same IP address is in our Apache logs

In *Figure 6.18*, Cisco Umbrella is showing us that this IP address has been linked to a shady-looking domain.

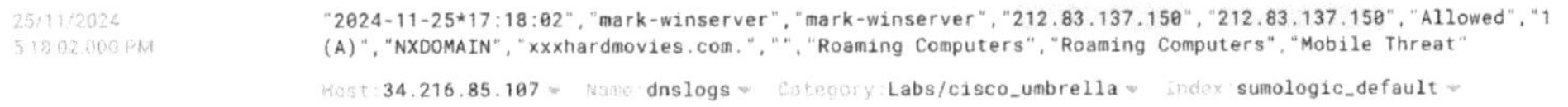

Figure 6.18 – Cisco Umbrella showing the IP address traffic linked to a shady domain

The point is this – giving operational teams this level of visibility across the environment and in one UI enables them to do a better job. Imagine not having a tool like Sumo Logic at this point. We'd have to log in to every source of data—our AWS console for GuardDuty, a separate view for S3, our threat intelligence tool for threat intel, and so on—and do the queries there, all which interface with you, the user, in different query languages and different UIs. Looking at log events from across these sources, we can easily start a threat hunt or begin an investigation. The IP address has apparently been seen making strange network requests from the dev account, but also prior to this, it has been hitting our application, and we have context from Cisco to confirm this IP address isn't here to give us any presents. Well, maybe one present – malware. Having data from all these different log sources and querying them all in the same way is a massive force multiplier. Teams will want to use Sumo Logic as their main source of truth for this reason, and this is why we have thousands of customers currently doing the same.

Having worked on this basic query, I wanted to tackle some of the earlier problems with querying that we encountered and bring them back into the conversation.

Querying problems resolved?...

...actually, it's nearly a resounding yes. We're on a good path, but we're not finished yet. We have already seen that some of the problems identified earlier in querying have been addressed in Sumo Logic.

- **Reliance on schemas and formats**: We've already encountered some different data types: JSON (AWS, Workday), plain text (Apache), and syslog (Cisco Umbrella). We didn't need to map any of this data to a schema; it's been sent to Sumo Logic, and we can analyze it straight away.
- **Query performance**: Even though I didn't capture the time taken to complete these queries, they are sub-10 seconds. To put this into context, some of these searches involved querying for an IP address across terabytes of data with no filters in place.
- **Complex data structures**: The JSON data that has been returned as a result of our queries has been deep and complex, with multiple hierarchies. It's all ready to be analyzed as soon as it's ingested and indexed, thanks to the JSON auto-parsing feature, allowing teams to navigate this type of data quickly and easily.
- **Distributed data**: In this example alone, we've seen over 10 different data sources that housed data that helped to provide context for this IP address. These sources included firewalls, web servers, APIs, edge access logs, audit logs, and others. Getting visibility of your distributed data is the key to thriving in the technological landscape that we find ourselves in.
- **Language limitations**: We've not covered this to its full extent; we'll have some more in-depth examples shortly, but already we've done some grouping and limiting on our dataset to help get some answers. The use cases coming up shortly for different operations teams will tap into the potential here in more detail.
- **Technical constraints**: The great thing about what we're doing here is that we're not limited by any technical bottlenecks. Sumo Logic is a cloud-native SaaS solution, so you run whatever queries you need, and the underlying infrastructure is there to support you by helping with performance or scaling to meet demand.

By getting the basics down, we've already displayed the versatility of the platform. What I really want to do is explore the power offered by the query language, so we'll build on this with some examples of how we can get your operations teams using Sumo Logic for more sophisticated investigations.

Different queries for different teams

A really useful way of demonstrating the versatility and power of the data analytics in Sumo Logic is to see how different teams would use it in different scenarios, so I have prepared three for you to look at. We'll look at scenarios involving SecOps, DevOps, and Developer teams during troubleshooting.

SecOps query

Let's take a look at an interesting example I helped a customer with recently. They wanted to be able to find command and control beaconing activity within their environment across their distributed datasets at any time. They were scarred by a previous incident where clear beaconing activity was overlooked from one of their hundreds of virtual machines residing in the cloud. This led to the exfiltration of sensitive data, and a breach was declared, costing the business millions of dollars and resulting in business impacts such as losses in revenue and customer trust. How do we go about doing something like this in Sumo Logic? Let's find out.

In this example, we're working with Cisco ASA data, and here is the query we're using:

```
_sourceCategory=Labs/Cisco built outbound
| parse regex "to .*?(?<dest_host>\d{1,3}\.\d{1,3}\.\d{1,3}\.\d{1,3})"
| parse regex "for .*?(?<src_host>\d{1,3}\.\d{1,3}\.\d{1,3}\.\d{1,3})"
| lookupContains (path://"/Library/Users/bkireeve+book@sumologic.com/Test table",
ip_address=internal_ip) as internal_ip | where internal_ip = false
| timeslice 1m
| count as event_count by dest_host, src_host, _timeslice
| stddev(event_count) as event_count_stdev by dest_host, src_host
// | where event_count_stdev < 0.5
// | order by event_count_stdev asc
```

We've got some operators in here I'd like to discuss and see how they've been used in this example.

Operators of interest – parse regex, lookupContains, stdev

The parse regex [2] operator is one of several parse operators that let you extract meaning from your data in different ways. Any unstructured or structured data in Sumo Logic can be parsed out with regular expressions, and this makes it very powerful, affording you, as the user, maximum versatility. In this example, we're extracting destination_ip and source_ip from the Cisco ASA data we're working with.

The lookupContains [3] instance lets us verify that a certain key or field exists within our lookup table. In this case, we have a lookup table with a list of internal IP addresses, which we ideally want to filter out because we are interested in traffic that doesn't concern our internal infrastructure. With Sumo Logic, you're able to apply filters even to this action to further drill down or cross-reference against a specific set of fields. We'll cover lookup tables in more detail in the next section.

Finally, stdev [4] stands for standard deviation, and it helps you to find a standard deviation for a distribution of numerical values within the time range analyzed. The smaller the standard deviation, the more precise and robotic the communication, which is what we want to find out in this dataset.

You can see I've commented on where event_count_stdev < 0.5 part, as well as the final line, because the results actually didn't bring back anything below 0.5, which is great, but I still wanted to use the example. So, to summarize, we've extracted the destination and source IPs, verified that they don't belong to internal IP addresses, bucketed the traffic into 1-minute buckets, and then applied standard deviation to find regular, consistent traffic between hosts. The results are shown in *Figure 6.19*.

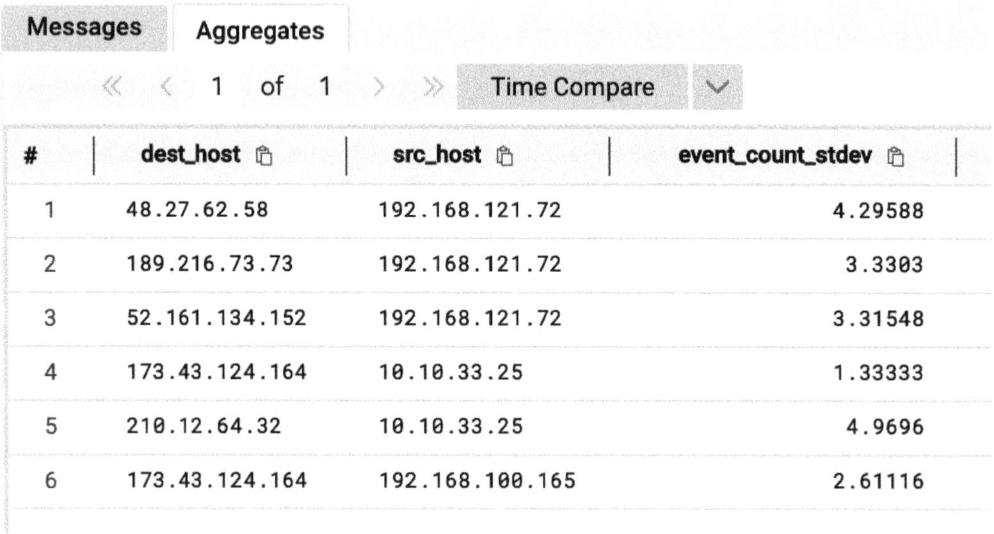

#	dest_host	src_host	event_count_stdev
1	48.27.62.58	192.168.121.72	4.29588
2	189.216.73.73	192.168.121.72	3.3303
3	52.161.134.152	192.168.121.72	3.31548
4	173.43.124.164	10.10.33.25	1.33333
5	210.12.64.32	10.10.33.25	4.9696
6	173.43.124.164	192.168.100.165	2.61116

Figure 6.19 – The standard deviation of source and destination IP pairings shows us how regular pings or traffic are across them

This is one of the handfuls of very interesting cybersecurity-related threat hunts or queries we can put together in the platform, and we'll be looking at a few more during the course of this chapter and this book. Let's move on to our friends in the DevOps team – we need to help them get the right answers from their data too.

DevOps query

We've covered an interesting security query, but let's not forget the DevOps side of things. These teams are prioritizing infrastructure, CI/CD pipelines, and cloud services to see how well they're running and that they're doing so as efficiently as possible. Let's take an example of a DevOps team that wants to make sure that no container ever runs for longer than a day. This could be for a few reasons – for example, if containers constantly get redeployed in relation to workload demand, or if containers need to be restarted for routine tasks or database syncing. Let's give it a shot:

```
_source="Kubernetes" and _collector="Labs - Kubernetes"
| json "status.containerStatuses[0].name" as container_name
| json "status.containerStatuses[0].state.running.startedAt" as start_time
| parseDate(start_time, "yyyy-MM-dd'T'HH:mm:ssX") as seconds
| timeslice 1h
| where _timeslice - seconds > 86400  // Running for over a day
| count by container_name
| order by _count desc
```

We've got a few new operators here to look at, so I've added the following explanations.

Operators of interest – timeslice, parseDate

Actually, I lied. Timeslice isn't new; it was in the previous query but luckily it's in this one too. The `timeslice` [5] operator aggregates data into time-based buckets, letting you bucket your data into fixed intervals – for example, 15 minutes or an hour. This operator helps primarily with grouping data for log aggregation analysis or time-based metric analysis. In the example, we're grouping our data into hourly buckets. It's very versatile and is also handy when putting together an outlier or anomaly detection query. We'll talk about this very soon.

The `parseDate`[6] operator lets you extract a date in many different common date formats and then do something with it. In this example, we're parsing out the date the Kubernetes container started running and doing a mathematical operation to check if it's up for longer than a day.

So, we're effectively parsing out the `json` fields related to container names and the start time of the containers, parsing the date to view it as seconds, and then seeing if the number of seconds the container has been up since it started exceeds 24 hours. We then aggregate the data by counting how many containers are worth investigating.

An alternate way of getting the current time, and another useful operator to know about, is the now operator. It gives you the current time and date down to the millisecond, which you can use in the comparison section of this query as well. In this example, these two lines can be replaced:

```
| json "status.containerStatuses[0].state.running.startedAt" as start_time
| parseDate(start_time, "yyyy-MM-dd'T'HH:mm:ssX") as seconds
```

We can use the following instead:

```
| now() as current_time
```

Then, for the comparison statement, we can use the following:

```
| where _timeslice - current_time > 86400    //
```

This is just another example of the flexibility afforded to you on the platform. The results when we run the query are shown in *Figure 6.20*.

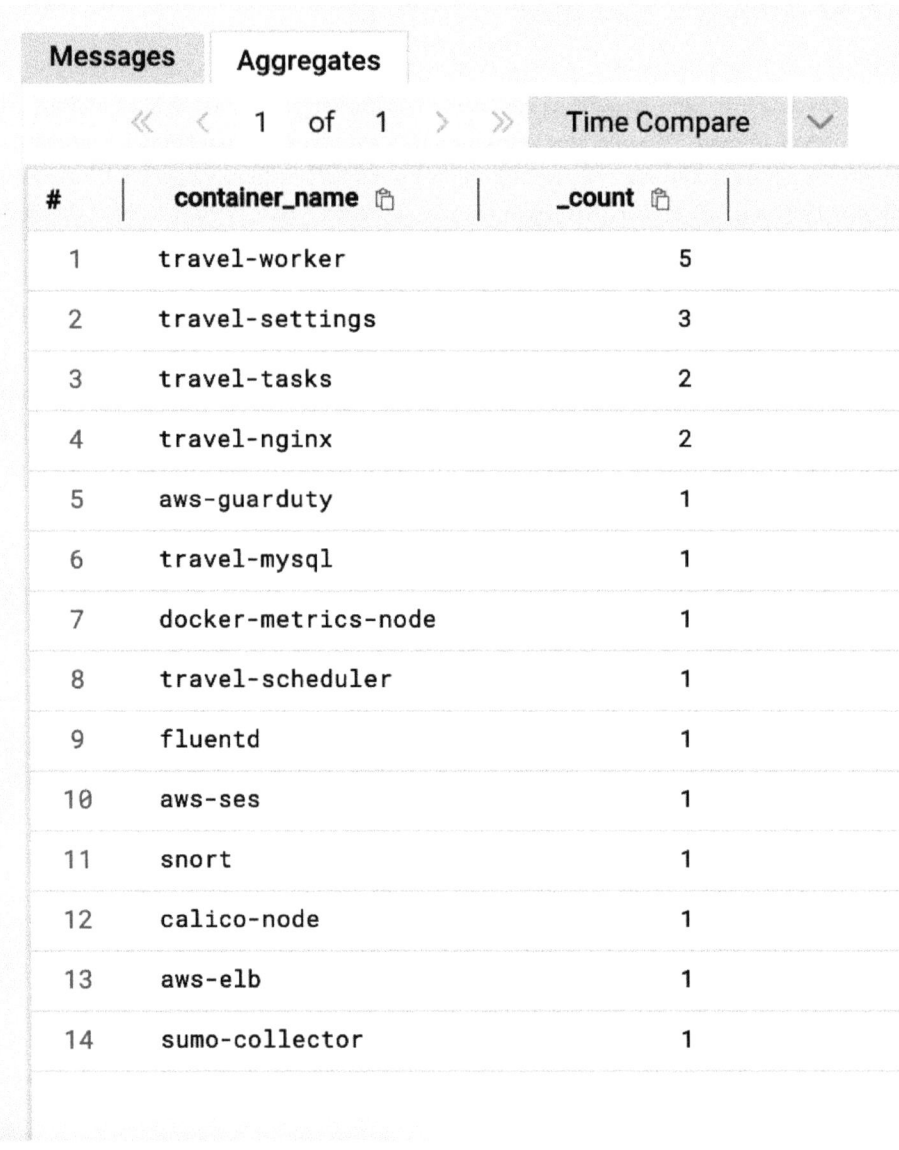

Figure 6.20 – An aggregated view of counted containers that have been running for a while

We can go into the logs to get a finer look at what these containers are, to help us decide our next course of action, or, if it helps, we can bring more data into the aggregated table view to help with the decision. Our next target is the Developer team. We want to look at a query from a developer's point of view and how they can run a query that helps make their job easier.

Dev query

Let's consider what's important for a developer. The focus for the Developer team is slightly different from DevOps, since they focus on the immediate problems that stop them from building or releasing code. However, they do get involved when there are outages or issues with their creations too, which brings us back to the importance of having complete visibility and the same dataset in one place for the teams. It makes working together easier and helps resolve these issues when they arise. Or, in other words, these teams can sing off the same hymn sheet.

Let's put ourselves in the shoes of a developer who has seen some problems with latency across their applications and APIs and wants to check how consistent or inconsistent latencies are across their ecosystem. Here's a query that we can use:

```
_index=astronomy_app_otel001
| timeslice by 5m
| avg(duration) as avg_duration by _timeslice, path
| rollingstd avg_duration as latency_stdev
| where latency_stdev > 3500
| sort by latency_stdev desc
| limit 5
```

As with the preceding queries, I've tried to include some advanced operators that can be quite useful in certain scenarios.

Operators of interest – avg, rollingstd, limit

The avg operator [7] lets you find the average in a set of numerical datapoints. In this example, we're looking at the average latency across our APIs while grouping the results across the timeslice and API path.

Next, we use rollingstd [8] to determine the rolling standard deviation for a given field over time, which helps to identify changes in the data over time. In this case, we're looking at how the average latency across our APIs has changed over 10 window time periods – 10 is the default, but this can be changed to anything between 1 and 1,000. We're also making sure that the latency across these rolling standard deviation windows is over 3,500.

We finish off by *limiting* [9] our results to the top 5 APIs. We don't want to get overwhelmed by too many results but just see the top APIs that need investigating.

The results, as shown in *Figure 6.21*, suggest that we need to investigate a specific API in more depth…

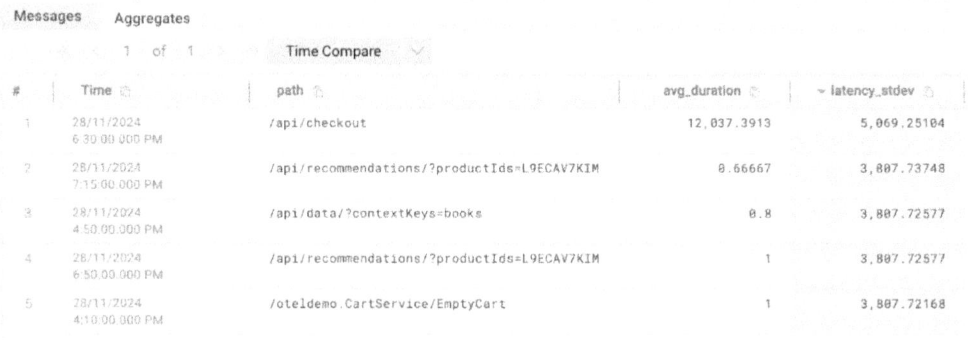

#	Time	path	avg_duration	latency_stdev
1	28/11/2024 6:30:00.000 PM	/api/checkout	12,037.3913	5,069.25104
2	28/11/2024 7:15:00.000 PM	/api/recommendations/?productIds=L9ECAV7KIM	0.66667	3,807.73748
3	28/11/2024 4:50:00.000 PM	/api/data/?contextKeys=books	0.8	3,807.72577
4	28/11/2024 6:50:00.000 PM	/api/recommendations/?productIds=L9ECAV7KIM	1	3,807.72577
5	28/11/2024 4:10:00.000 PM	/oteldemo.CartService/EmptyCart	1	3,807.72168

Figure 6.21 – An aggregation of the API paths that have the most erratic latency over time

Our **/api/checkout** API has a very high average latency, and it has a more erratic nature, as well as the standard deviation over time being so much higher than others.

This section has shown example queries that anyone from these teams can do and extract actionable insights from their data. These were only examples of single use cases, and there are thousands that Sumo Logic can help you to achieve across your teams. There are some core bits of functionality that it would be a sin not to include here, as they can elevate your querying to a new level. They include the following:

- Mobot
- `LogReduce/LogCompare`
- Live Tail
- Lookup tables
- Subqueries
- GeoIP

We'll cover them one by one to make sure we don't miss out on any details, but I'll leave Mobot until last.

LogReduce/LogCompare

These two operators are really interesting and most usually fit within the daily roles of devs and DevOps teams. I'll try to explain why here with a few examples. `LogReduce`[10] and `LogCompare`[11] are proprietary to Sumo Logic, with `LogReduce` using machine learning algorithms to find patterns in your log data to then group and cluster it, while `LogCompare` runs time-based analytics on your data to find major changes or anomalies in your dataset across different time periods. Let's go through `LogReduce` first.

LogReduce

Let's go straight into an example scenario, and I'll walk you through what's happening and where `LogReduce` comes into play.

Let's say we've received an alert on our Slack channel that one of our services is facing higher latency than normal. Pretty standard stuff – we'll cover alerting in more detail in the next chapter, but for now, let's go work through the flow. When clicking the link that takes us to the alert in Sumo Logic, we arrive at the **Alert Response Page** (lovingly named **ARP**). This can be seen in *Figure 6.22*.

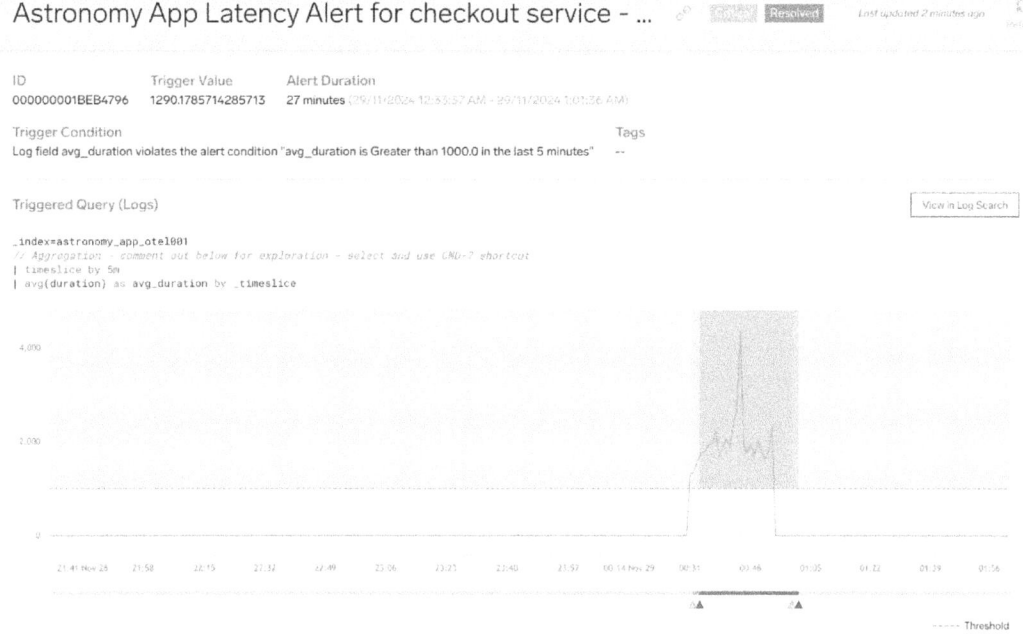

Figure 6.22 – A visualization of the parameters that triggered our application latency alert

Figure 6.22 shows that the threshold has been breached for a certain amount of time, and we now need to see what happened. Below this visualization, we've got that information. Without spoiling too much of the next chapter, let's just look at the logs that have been automatically correlated for us around this event of interest, in *Figure 6.23*.

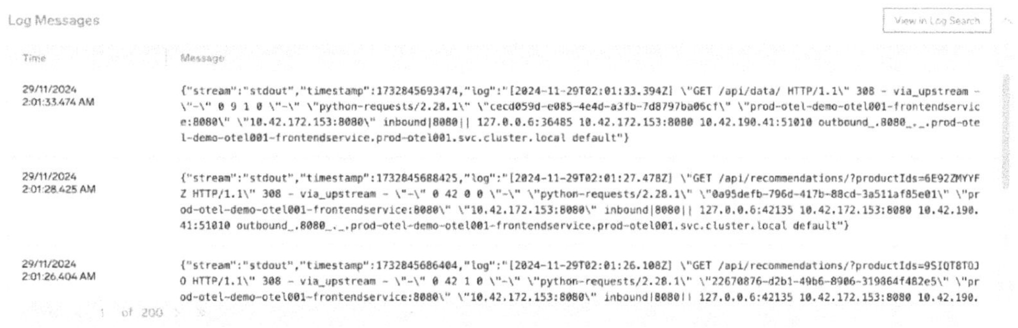

Figure 6.23 – All the log messages in our environment that have been correlated automatically

This isn't meant to be a needle-in-the-haystack approach at this point. Sumo Logic basically correlates everything that has happened in your environment around this time to help you get an understanding of events. The quickest way to demonstrate what LogReduce helps your teams with is to dive into the search here. So, we've got a view of *everything* that's happened in our environment, which is great, but even though it's still correlated around the time of interest, there's unfortunately still a ton of data to get through. At this point, teams have run into, or are going to run into, two main problems.

- Their data is distributed around their environment in various databases, systems, and services, and they must do additional work to even correlate events before we get to the point where we are now.
- Once they have all this data, or if they have a central repository, they need to query the data effectively enough to get an idea of where to go next. This means they need expertise and know-how around how to do this and apply it to hundreds, if not thousands of pages of log data.

In Sumo Logic, we can click on **View in Log Search** in the top-right corner and head to the logs to see how this process is made easier in the platform. *Figure 6.24* shows this view.

Figure 6.24 – 490 pages of logs is a lot to get through...

We have 490 pages of logs to look through. Uh-oh! Back-of-an-envelope math tells us we're looking at 490 x 25 events per page = 12,250 logs to work with. However, we have access to LogReduce, so we just add it to the query by replacing line 4, as seen in *Figure 6.25*.

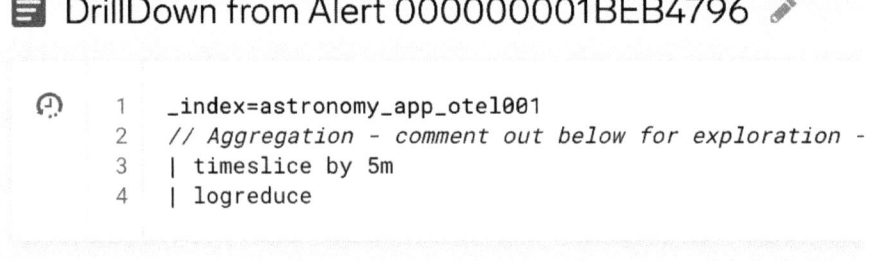

Figure 6.25 – Using the logreduce operator in the search

Figure 6.26 show us what we see when the `logreduce` function finishes its analysis.

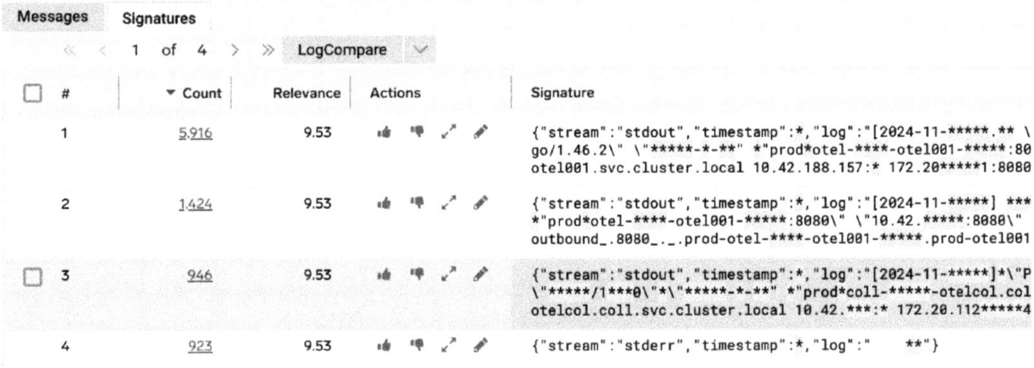

Figure 6.26 – The results of our logreduce analysis, showing pattern analysis

We can see that we now have 4 pages of results instead of 490, which is a good start. If we look at the first few log events, we can see how they've been grouped together. The `LogReduce` algorithm uses fuzzy logic to cluster messages based on string and pattern similarity. For example, the first log pattern appears 5,916 times. The logs at the top are normally healthy, regularly recurring logs, and the * symbols in the log reflect values that change, but overall, the structure of the log is intact. What's interesting here is that, because the regularly seen logs are grouped in this way, the opposite is true. `logreduce` identifies those logs that are *rarely* seen, the errors, bugs, and other typically problematic events that can easily be missed if we don't know what to look for.

Let's go to the penultimate page, as shown in *Figure 6.27*, to see these less frequently occurring events:

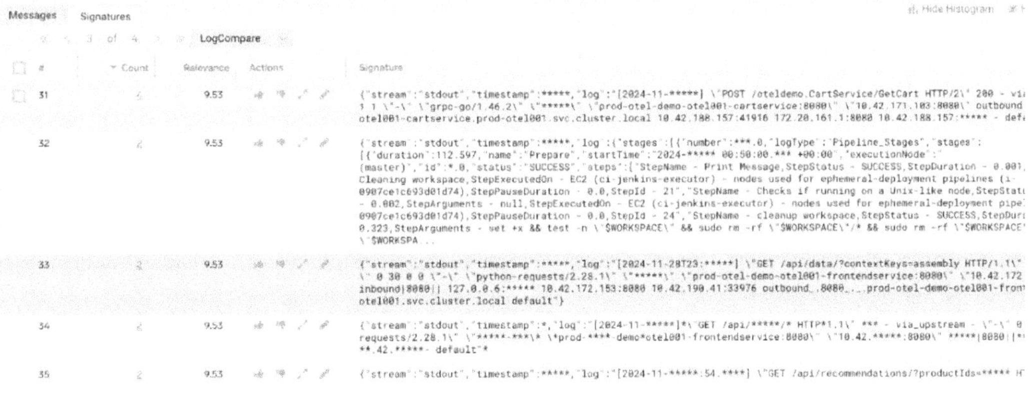

Figure 6.27 – We can see less frequently occurring events, typically filled with events of interest

We can see the count of these events is much lower – events that have been seen twice, three, or maybe four times, and these are usually the troublesome causes of the issue we are facing. In this particular set of events, we have an event that is related to a successful deployment of a new app version that is likely to be the root cause, which is the second event in *Figure 6.27*. We can see `StepStatus` has a `SUCCESS` value, and we can zoom in to see what service this was – if we click on the **2** in the **Count** column, it'll take us to where these log events were seen. At this point, we can click on the **Open Log Message Inspector** in the top-right of the event to open a detailed view of the log. The location of the Log Message Inspector is seen in *Figure 6.28*, and the field with the service name is seen in *Figure 6.29*:

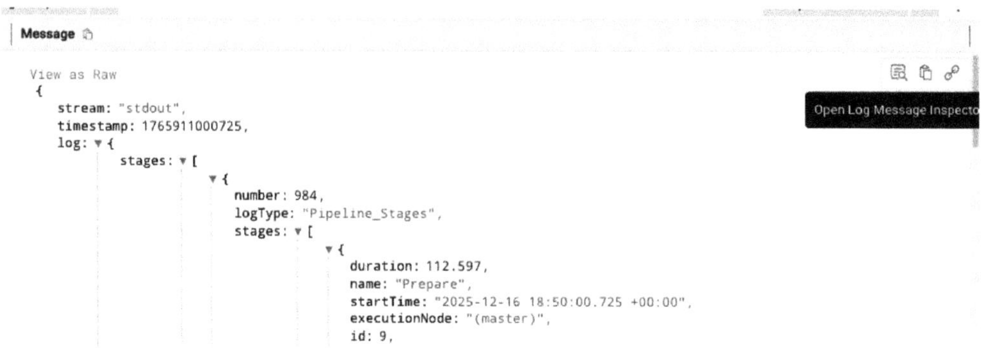

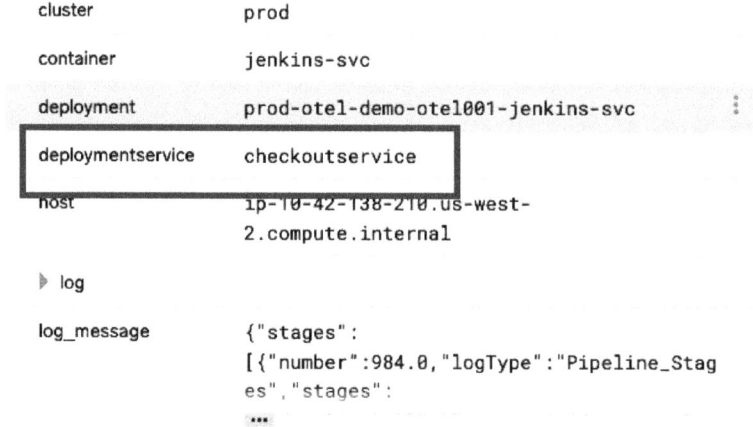

Figure 6.28 – The location of the Open Log Message Inspector button

Figure 6.29 – checkoutservice is clearly highlighted, and we know which service is the root cause

We just don't have to look through 490 pages to get there, but only through a handful of events. The time savings here help operational teams get to the bottom of problems within minutes, instead of hours of wading through logs, metrics, and traces.

We've looked at where `LogReduce` offers massive operational benefits. Let's take a look at `LogCompare`.

LogCompare

As briefly mentioned before, `LogCompare` uses time-based analysis of deltas between two time periods, set by the user. It creates a **baseline** query, which looks at the older timeframe and compares it to the **target** query, which looks at the current time.

Accessing it is very simple – above the search results, there's a handy **LogCompare** button to click, with a dropdown available that has pre-selected timeframes. Clicking on any one of them adds the following to your query:

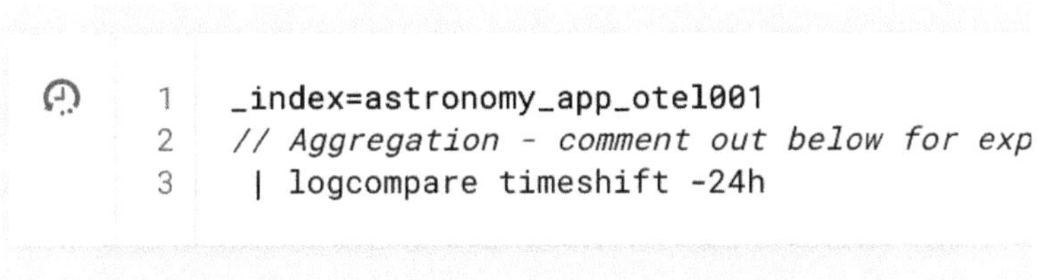

```
    1   _index=astronomy_app_otel001
    2   // Aggregation - comment out below for exp
    3   | logcompare timeshift -24h
```

Figure 6.30 – Using logcompare in our query with a 24-hour comparison

You're free to set the timeframe to whatever time range you need. If we just use the same example as before, but using LogCompare instead, you can see how the results change. This is shown in *Figure 6.31*.

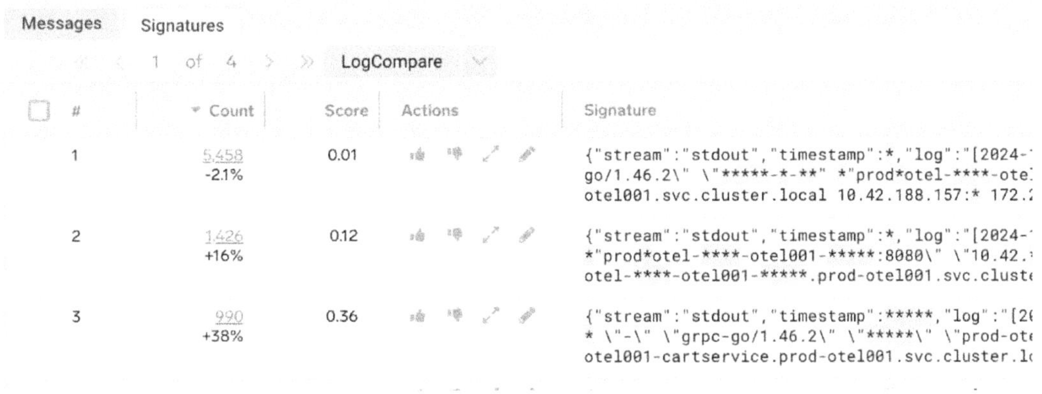

#	Count	Score	Actions	Signature
1	5,458 -2.1%	0.01		{"stream":"stdout","timestamp":*,"log":"[2024-" go/1.46.2\" \"*****-*-**" *"prod*otel-****-ote] otel001.svc.cluster.local 10.42.188.157:* 172.2
2	1,426 +16%	0.12		{"stream":"stdout","timestamp":*,"log":"[2024-" *"prod*otel-****-otel001-*****:8080\" \"10.42.1 otel-****-otel001-*****.prod-otel001.svc.cluste
3	990 +38%	0.36		{"stream":"stdout","timestamp":*****,"log":"[2(* \"-\" \"grpc-go/1.46.2\" \"*****\" \"prod-ote otel001-cartservice.prod-otel001.svc.cluster.l(

Figure 6.31 – The difference in results from LogCompare is in the historical comparison

Under **Count**, we can now see the difference between today's count and yesterday's for the same signature. There are other entries apart from +/-. If there are any **new** entries, that means the signature didn't exist in the original baseline. If there are any **gone** entries, then a signature that existed in the baseline query, the older one, isn't present in the target or current query.

Hopefully, you can see the power of these analytical tools. Sumo Logic customers place the platform into a central position within their organizations, so that different teams can make use of these capabilities and work together. Are the Security team and DevOps team working on something side by side to identify some suspicious activity in their environment? With this, they can group data together to find results more easily and quickly, and compare them to activity that took place yesterday, a few days ago, or a week ago to identify any anomalies or differences over time. This is what helps to lower the MTTD, MTTR, and so on as much as possible.

What if we want something more real-time while we're troubleshooting? Instead of SSH'ing into our machine and tailing our logs, we can do that in Sumo Logic. Let's look at how it's done.

Live Tail

Live tailing [12] logs perform the same function as running a `tail -f` command on a box and lets you see the logs being ingested in real time.

There are two different ways to access it. The first is to go to the **Logs** menu, as shown in *Figure 6.32*, and you'll find **Live Tail** at the top:

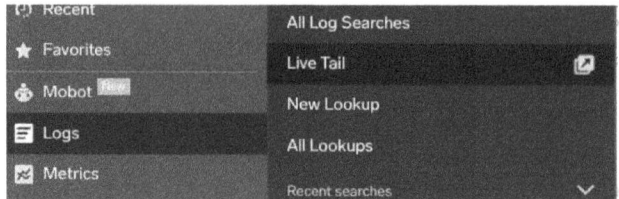

Figure 6.32 – Finding Live Tail in the main menu

Alternatively, when you're in the **Log Search** UI and looking at queries, you can go straight into **Live Tail** from the source you're querying by clicking on the three dots in the top-right corner and selecting **Live Tail**, as shown in *Figure 6.33*.

Figure 6.33 – How to enter Live Tail directly from a query

Live Tail only works with the following metadata in Sumo Logic:

- _sourceHost

- _sourceCategory
- _sourceName
- _source
- _collector

After specifying where the data is coming from, you should be able to see it streaming in real time, as can be seen in *Figure 6.34*.

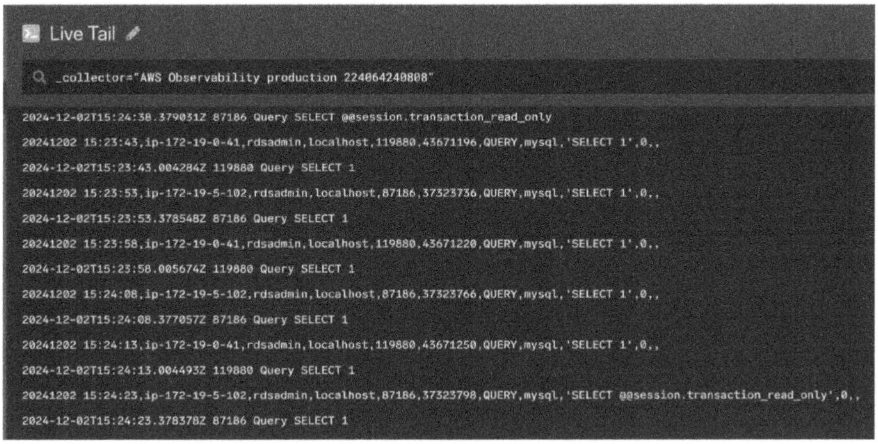

Figure 6.34 – Example Live Tail results from our AWS Collector

We can also use a couple of things to help our experience. For example, we can highlight key terms that will help us with troubleshooting. We access this in the top-right corner of the **Live Tail** screen, shown in *Figure 6.35*.

Figure 6.35 – How to highlight different terms for easier troubleshooting and debugging

We can enter multiple terms. Each is highlighted in a different color for clarity, and it makes it much easier on the eye. On top of that, we can even split **Live Tail** and have two screens side by side, where we can live tail two different sources that might be related or have similar errors. We access it in the same way, going to the top right and clicking on the dots, as shown in *Figure 6.36*.

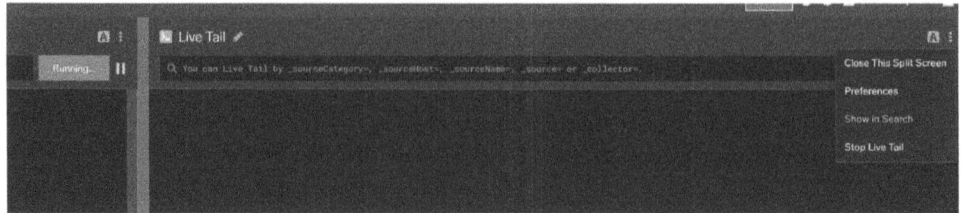

Figure 6.36 – We can have a split-screen view of our Live Tail from different sources

Every **site reliability engineer** (**SRE**), DevOps engineer, SysOps analyst, and IT analyst can attest to the power of tailing logs. Now you can do that in the same place as the rest of your data sits, instead of having multiple screens from multiple virtual machines or servers open, a great performance enhancer.

Live Tail is useful, but I wanted to come back to other tools that help you query your data more easily, such as lookup tables, as discussed in the next section.

Lookup tables

Lookup tables [13] exist to help you enrich your log data with some form of relational context. For example, you come across a workstation name in the logs and want to know which user it is associated with. You can then have another lookup table that tells you even more information about that user, such as location, reporting manager, Active Directory ID, email address, and more. They are incredibly versatile and help during both troubleshooting and investigation or remediation to speed up efforts.

My plan is to cover how to set up a lookup table quickly, before diving into some real-world examples for different operations teams, so your teams have as many tools as possible in their toolkit to fall back on when interacting with their data.

Creating a lookup table

Lookup tables can be created in a couple of different ways. The first way is to create it by manually creating a schema and then running a query to populate it. The second is to upload a CSV file with all the fields you need for your data. Let's look at both quickly.

Manual creation

To get to the lookup table section, we go to **Logs | New Lookup**, as shown in *Figure 6.37*.

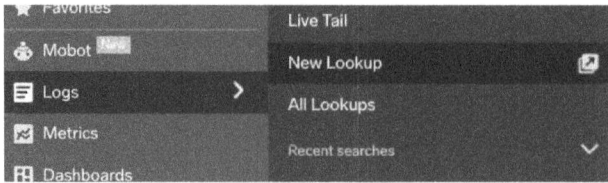

Figure 6.37 – Where to find lookup tables in the Logs section

When creating lookup tables manually, we set up the fields we want in the schema and choose a primary key. There must be at least one column marked as a primary key to help uniquely identify a row. In the following case, I chose the username as my primary key because that should be unique in the organization:

Figure 6.38 – Setting up a schema for our AWS Identity lookup table

When we click **Create** at the top right, we will have an empty lookup table. Now we need to populate this table with some data. The quickest way of doing it after a manual creation is to run a query. As this is an AWS Identity table with specific columns, I need to reference them in my query and have results returned from the query that then get entered as values. Here is what I have:

```
_sourcecategory=Labs/AWS/CloudTrail
| json "userIdentity.userName" as username
| json "userIdentity.arn" as arn
| json "userIdentity.accountId" as accountId
| json "userIdentity.accessKeyId" as accessKeyId
| where username != null
| save path://"/Library/Users/bkireeve@sumologic.com/AWS Identity"
```

You'll see the save[14] operator at the end, and that is what helps us save this data to the lookup table. It's important to parse out every individual field we want extracted from the dataset, which is what I've done from lines 2-6. I've filtered out all data that doesn't have a username to avoid any messy data or errors in the query. *Figure 6.39* shows what it looks like after the query.

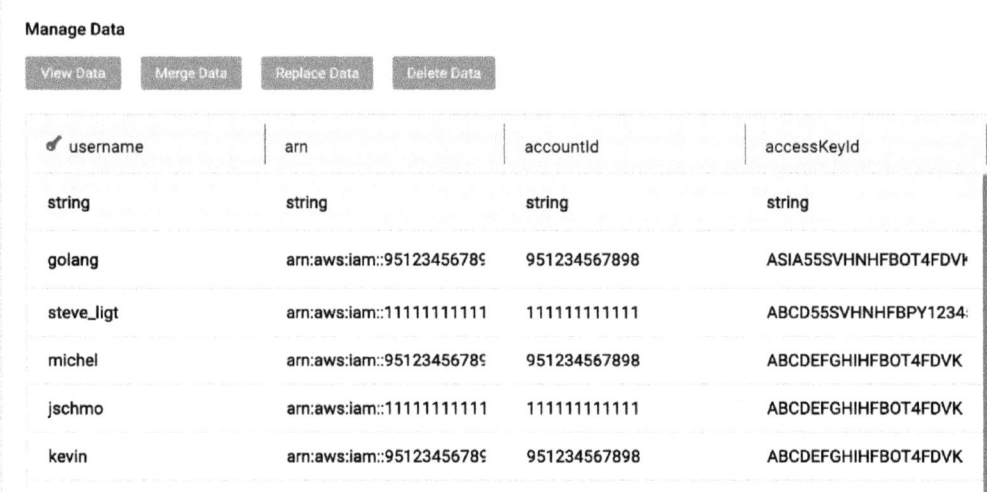

Figure 6.39 – Our lookup table has been populated with the query we ran

Now we can reference this lookup table when running a query – the most basic way of doing this is with a simple cat command, as shown in *Figure 6.40*.

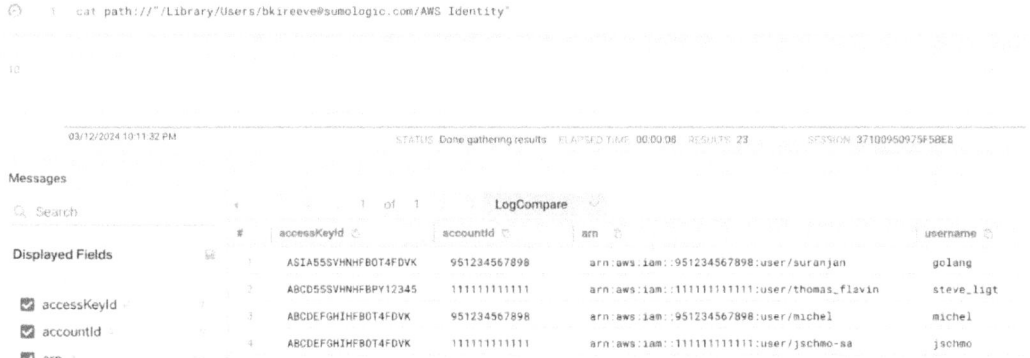

Figure 6.40 – Viewing our lookup table entries on the query screen

We won't look at queries yet, as we'll come to our examples shortly. Let's take a quick look at creating a lookup table with a CSV file.

CSV creation

The other method of creating a lookup table is to use a CSV file with all the columns and rows that you need already populated. In the **Create Lookup Table** config, select **Upload File** this time, and you'll be presented with a way to select a .csv file locally.

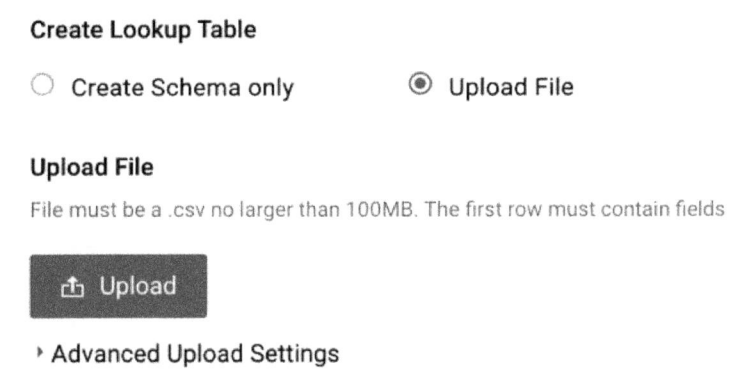

Figure 6.41 – The option to create and populate our lookup table using a CSV file

After you've uploaded your .csv file, it'll detect the rows and columns and present you with your lookup table, as shown in *Figure 6.42*.

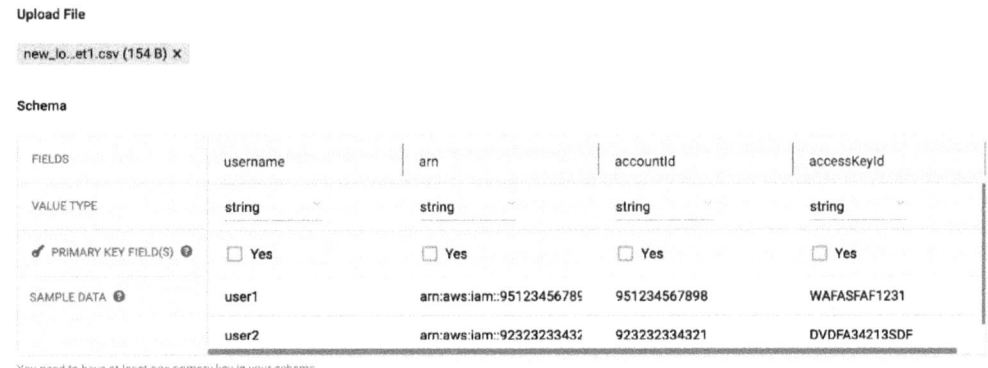

Figure 6.42 – The uploaded CSV file and entries in the lookup table

Don't forget to choose a primary key, otherwise you won't be able to create the table, but then you're all done. Now let's move on to some examples.

Lookup table examples

These tables are pretty powerful in different scenarios, and I want to try to outline some of these here, so you can get an idea of when to use them and get some inspiration for your own processes. We'll start with some SecOps examples before moving on to some DevOps scenarios.

Lookup tables – SecOps

This type of relational view into all the different data your organization owns is really useful to practitioners when doing a threat hunt or responding to an incident. They have the added advantage of all the data living in the same place with Sumo Logic, making these lookup tables as comprehensive and as accurate as needed.

Let's take an example of a scenario where an incident has been identified, and our defenders are trying to trace the adversaries' activity across their environment. They come across some servers that have been accessed by a foreign IP and now need to understand the overall impact and help with prioritizing their response efforts. With a lookup table, this becomes really easy. We could have a lookup table with the following entries:

Asset_name	Owner	Priority	Criticality
i-0211727c070f01719	SysOps Admins	High	Critical
i-042e2079345957b77	Dev Team - Test	Low	Non-critical
i-0823869eef76a957d	Dev Team - Prod	Medium	Important
i-0629a15566f7b20e4	Dev Team - Prod	High	Critical
i-063a532f4abe92c0c	IT Ops	Low	Non-critical

Table 6.1: The example lookup table we have uploaded to Sumo Logic for this scenario

During the team's queries, they can run the servers that have been accessed through the lookup table to determine how they need to respond, making the response effort communication clearer, more structured, and better aligned across teams.

When querying for this activity and trying to cross-reference it with our assets, we can run a query like this:

```
_source="CloudTrail Logs us-west-2" and _collector="AWS Observability production 224064240808" 52.88.8.29
| parse regex "(?<ip_address>\b\d{1,3}\.\d{1,3}\.\d{1,3}\.\d{1,3})"
| json "requestParameters.instanceId" as instanceId
| count as ip_count by ip_address, instanceId
| lookup * from path://"/Library/Users/bkireeve@sumologic.com/AWS assets" on asset_name = instanceId
```

You'll see we are specifying the foreign IP in the second line and doing a free-text search on it across our CloudTrail source. We're then parsing out several fields, including any IP addresses, as well as `instanceId`, which we want to correlate with. We're aggregating on `ip_address` and `instanceId` and doing a count of times we've seen this IP interacting with these machines. Finally, we want to enrich the results with the data from our lookup table – I'm bringing back all the fields from the lookup table and using the `instanceId` field, which we parsed out to align with the `asset_name` field in the table.

The results are concerning, to say the least, as can be seen in *Figure 6.43*.

#	ip_address	instanceId	ip_count	asset_name	owner	priority	criticality
1	52.88.8.29	i-0629a15566f7b20e4	19	i-0629a15566f7b20e4	Dev Team - Prod	High	Critical
2	52.88.8.29	i-063a532f4abe92c0c	18	i-063a532f4abe92c0c	IT Ops	Low	Non-critical

Figure 6.43 – We see the malicious IP address interacting with a critical asset

One of the assets this IP address has interacted with belongs to our Production environment and is owned by the Developer team. The asset itself is a high-priority asset as it is key to the operation of our main application, so it is critical for the business. Even though the event itself doesn't spell good news for us, we at least have the right tools to do the following:

- Find the issue
- Get relevant context quickly

This enables us to respond quickly and appropriately in line with the threat, escalate it to the right team quickly to get a response together quickly, helping communication, and most importantly, get the attacker out.

We can use the same principle in many other situations – for example, those that don't necessarily involve security data. DevOps teams could use the same method to cross-reference a malfunctioning Kubernetes Pod or microservices application to the team responsible, along with a criticality rating for that infrastructure, so they know whether it's a P1, P2, P3, or P4 when creating a ticket. Lookup tables are incredibly adaptable and come recommended for empowering your teams and their analytical capability.

There's one more area to cover before we wrap up the different ways we can query our data and focus on optimizing speed and performance. Sometimes, you want to be able to combine queries to ensure you're looking at the right data. For example, you might want to aggregate some data where you find all PowerShell scripts run between 13:00 and 14:00 today, but you then want to feed that output into another query. In this case, the list of PowerShell scripts could then be further refined by specifying one and seeing which computers have been exposed to that script. It's basically a cascading query, which brings me to subqueries.

Subqueries

Subqueries[15] are yet another asset that your operational teams have in extracting the right answers out of your data as accurately as possible. This will be the final type of query I'm going to cover in the book, and from an analytics perspective, we've covered a tremendous amount of ground, but let's see what subqueries are all about.

What is a subquery?

I'm going to compare subqueries to joins, just to make them relatable, but really, they're a way of doing a join on your data in Sumo Logic without the performance issues *in some cases*. That's the only caveat, and I'll explain why shortly. The way it works is that the results of one query are passed into another query to act as a better filter and narrow down the results, rather than uniting huge sets of data together that are then searched through.

Subqueries become useful and powerful when we apply them to specific variables – for example, looking for particular malicious behavior in our data or looking at the latency behavior across a certain Pod or a set of microservices. Don't worry, we'll definitely use an example later so you can see the specifics, but for now, let's start with the core concepts. Subqueries are made up of **a parent query** and **a child query**.

The child query is the main one in that it is used to do the initial filtering on the dataset. It runs first and provides output to the parent query, and even the time frame can be different from the parent query. The parent query runs with the child query results fed into it to get a much more refined result.

One of the main use cases I see is to use subqueries to filter out a really useful group of data to then compare with another relevant dataset. The syntax for a typical subquery is something like this:

Parent query:

```
[subquery [from=(<fromTime>)] [to=(<toTime>)] : <child query>
| compose <field1>[, <field2>, ...] [maxresults=<int>] [keywords]
]
```

Rest of parent query

We put the child query within square brackets, where the objective in most cases is to expose a set of fields that can be fed through into the parent query. These fields are surfaced with the compose operator. The compose operator is not standalone; it is only useful within the context of a subquery and controls the output by doing the following:

- Fields: More than one field can be output into a parent query
- Format: Tabular results are converted into a query format (example follows)

For example, say your child query returns the following results:

_sourceCategory	username	clientip
host_1	John_k	1.1.1.1
host_2	Freddy_p	2.2.2.2

It will be formatted into the following format, which can then be fed into the parent query:

```
(( _sourceCategory="host_1" AND username="John_k" AND clientip="1.1.1.1") OR
(_sourceCategory="host_2" AND username="Freddy_p" AND clientip="2.2.2.2"))
```

The results have AND operators between columns and OR operators between rows.

Sometimes, we don't need to bring back the field names in our query. This could be because we've already parsed them as part of the parent query, so we can use a keywords operator as part of the subquery to specify this. You can see it in the preceding syntax, after the compose operator is used, and we only get the *values* back, so using the preceding example, we would get the following results:

```
(("host_1" AND "John_k" AND "1.1.1.1") OR ("host_2" AND "Freddy_p" AND "2.2.2.2"))
```

With the syntax covered, I want to jump into an example. Mainly because this is a cool example I've witnessed where subqueries really gave the team the flexibility they needed, but also because it's a very practical example, which I hope you use within your instance of Sumo Logic.

Subquery example

Here's the requirement I came across. The security team wanted to know when a certain authentication event was made by a user from an IP address that hadn't been seen creating a valid session before. The goal was to catch this set of IP addresses and usernames to correlate them with valid IP addresses used for the usernames. If any IP addresses weren't valid for the usernames, it would most likely mean the users were compromised.

Let's run through the subquery process during the example.

Step 1 – Create the parent query

We want to use this parent query to correlate the results with the authentication events we've been seeing.

```
_sourceCategory=azure/ad/auth
| json "username", "client_ip" as username, client_ip
| fields username, client_ip, event_id
| lookup global_username as username, username_ip as username_ip from path://"/Library/Users/bkireeve@sumologic.com/Auth_IPs" on username, username_ip
| where client_ip != username_ip
| count by client_ip, username
```

Our parent query is done, and you'll notice we're referencing a lookup table here. This is intentional. I thought it would make sense to see how some of the elements we've covered previously can be mixed and matched to get the result we need. Let's move on to our child query.

Step 2 – Create the child query

Here, we need to create the logic that aggregates the types of authentication attempts we're interested in. The customer had these authentication attempts coming from the same source, so let's see what we did.

```
_sourceCategory=azure/ad/auth
| json "username", "client_ip" as username, client_ip
| where event_id = "1341"
| fields username, client_ip
| dedup username, client_ip
| format ("%s:%s", username, ip_address) as user_ip_pair
| count by user_ip_pair , username, client_ip
| save append path://"/Library/Users/bkireeve@sumologic.com/Auth_IPs"
```

Here is our child query, the one that initially gets the authentication results we're looking for by parsing out the username and `client_ip` fields and making sure we're filtering on the correct event_id. You'll notice there are a few operators here we haven't met before: `fields`, `dedup`, and `format`. The `fields` operator visualizes the fields in the tabular view, and we've also opted to deduplicate username and `client_ip` fields because we want unique pairings, instead of seeing each and every event. Another reason for doing this is that we want to be able to save these to a lookup table, so that we can build a knowledge base of this activity over time and can refer to it later, and we do this on the final line. Finally, the `format` field – this one helps you to format a string in any way you like. In this case, we paired the username with all IPs it has used, making it slightly easier to process.

Now that we have our parent query and our child query, let's combine them!

Step 3 – Create the subquery

Let's combine these queries together into a subquery using the syntax we looked at previously. This is what the outcome looks like:

```
_sourceCategory=azure/ad/auth
[subquery: _sourceCategory=azure/ad/auth
| json "username", "client_ip" as username, client_ip
| where event_id = "1341"
| fields username, client_ip
| dedup username, client_ip
| format ("%s:%s", username, ip_address) as user_ip_pair
| count by user_ip_pair , username, client_ip
| save append path://"/Library/Users/bkireeve@sumologic.com/Auth_IPs"
| compose username, client_ip keywords
]
| json "username", "client_ip" as username, client_ip
| fields username, client_ip, event_id
| lookup global_username as username, username_ip as username_ip from path://"/Library/Users/bkireeve@sumologic.com/Auth_IPs" on username, username_ip
| where client_ip != username_ip
| count by client_ip, username
```

That's the complete subquery we used to accomplish this. It looks big and mean, but really, when you break it down into individual steps, it becomes manageable. What's more important here is that you have the a universal query language that can accomplish this, which is what operational teams need to stay on top of the increasingly crazy amounts of data they have to work through on a daily basis. The enabling tools are here. The customer that we helped and put the query together with ended up using this method to identify suspicious activity that was then stopped and contained, even without the insight engine in the SIEM.

So, that brings us to a close on the analytical tools users have at their disposal. I would like to stress that this is far from an exhaustive list. We have even more comprehensive coverage of operators and other analytical nuances in the documentation[16]. For now, though, your teams have a great head start, and this is the glue that will bring your developers, DevOps, and SecOps teams together in the platform to get your security intelligence program working smoothly.

We've done a lot of work on querying so far, and in a complete 180-degree turn, I want to show you how you might not always need to apply a lot of what we've learned in this chapter. Counterintuitive, I know, but hear me out. Operational teams are already spending precious time managing their infrastructure, threat hunting, and committing code; sometimes writing queries is what slows us down when it comes to investigations and troubleshooting. What if there were a way to have Sumo Logic help you write queries with a natural language prompt? That's what Mobot is all about. We'll cover all the interesting details in the next section.

Mobot

So far, we've covered writing queries by hand. Sometimes, the job is easier if we use some out-of-the-box queries from dashboards found in the App Catalog, but otherwise it's manual. Historically, there has been a significant learning curve and a chasm that users had to cross to really get some deep analytical capability from Sumo Logic. So many users cried out to the heavens, "What if I could just ask my question in English instead of putting together a whole query by myself?!", and that cry has now been answered. In November 2025, Sumo Logic released Mobot (named after the Sumo wrestler mascot, Mo), an AI-powered agentic framework with the aim of helping users in key parts of the platform. The agents currently released as part of Mobot are the **query agent** and the **knowledge agent**, with the SOC Analyst Agent close to release. More are on the way in 2026.

Think of Mobot as a unified conversational interface that sits between you and the platform, and the agents as the workers who go about helping to get the result. The query agent in this case is a translator that converts your question, asked in natural language, to the exact technical language you need to use in the platform. Instead of learning a new syntax, remembering field names, or writing complex expressions, you rely on the translator to bridge the gap. Let's see what it looks like before we jump into a few examples of how to use it.

Mobot UI

Mobot is quite easy to navigate and steer to your desired result. Let's look at the important bits. First of all, we get into **Mobot** by accessing it directly from the left-hand menu:

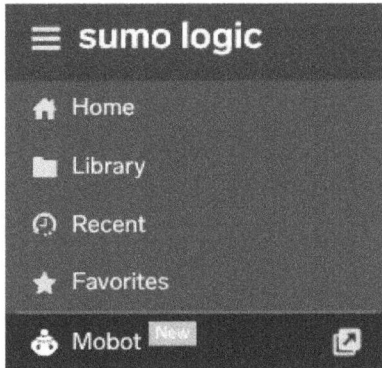

Figure 6.44 – The Mobot section in the main menu

You'll be presented with Mobot and the option to choose whatever agent is going to help you the most (if you haven't guessed already, we'll be using the Query Agent instead of the Knowledge Agent):

At the bottom is the prompt bar and a time range selector, the same as the one we've used in our queries so far. Now, you still need to define your timeframe with this time selector. However, for the sources, you have a choice. You can specify a particular source of your choice, or Mobot will try its best to infer the source you need to query.

Mobot usage

It's best if we approach our first forays into AI-generated querying by putting ourselves into the shoes of someone who's never used Sumo Logic before. How can they get insights from the initial data they've ingested into the platform as quickly as possible? A quick threat hunt is a great way to demonstrate. Let's go with something straightforward. We want to see login failure behavior from our Windows machines to see if anything fishy is going on. We type `Show all events with event code 4625 across Windows data`, and instantly the Query Agent chooses the right source and writes the following query:

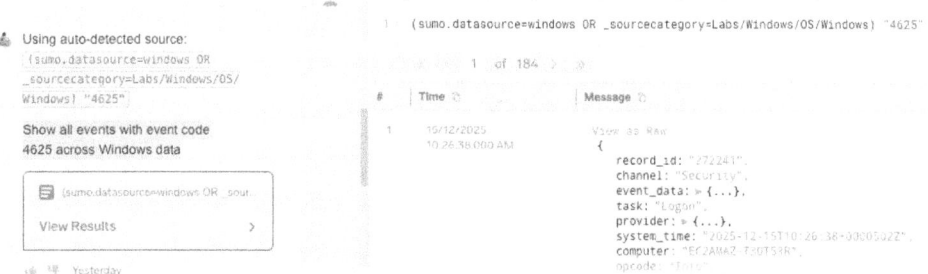

Let's focus on a few key areas here. On the left, you'll find a growing conversation with the Query Agent, as you continually refine your queries. The Query Agent has multi-turn refinement built in, meaning that it can retain context over the course of your conversation, and it's a much more natural way of investigating and feels like you're speaking to another analyst.

At the top right is the query that the Query Agent writes as a response to your prompt, while underneath are the results from the query.

Now, we've just got a bunch of login failure results from Windows machines. Let's break it down with this: `Count events with event code 4625 by username`. We see the result in *Figure 6.47*:

```
1   (sumo.datasource=windows OR _sourcecategory=Labs/Windows/OS/Windows) "4625"
2   | count by %"event_data.targetusername"
```

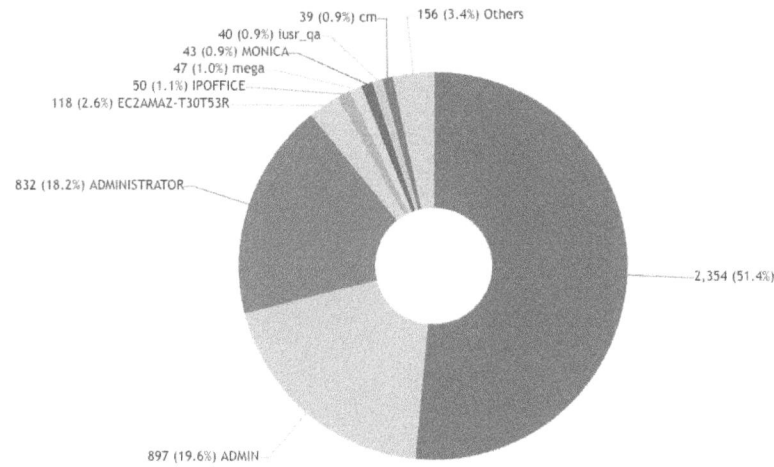

Figure 6.47 – The aggregation result from the query done by the Query Agent

We've got a breakdown of usernames now, which is good. An additional point of interest has appeared in our results! In the top-right corner, we can choose which visualization best represents the data. A pie chart was given to us here, but we can change that to a bar graph if we want.

We need to go a bit deeper. Let's ask the following: `Analyze the hourly trends of failed login attempts by target username and transpose the result with timeslice as rows and target username as columns`. To this, we get the result shown in *Figure 6.48*:

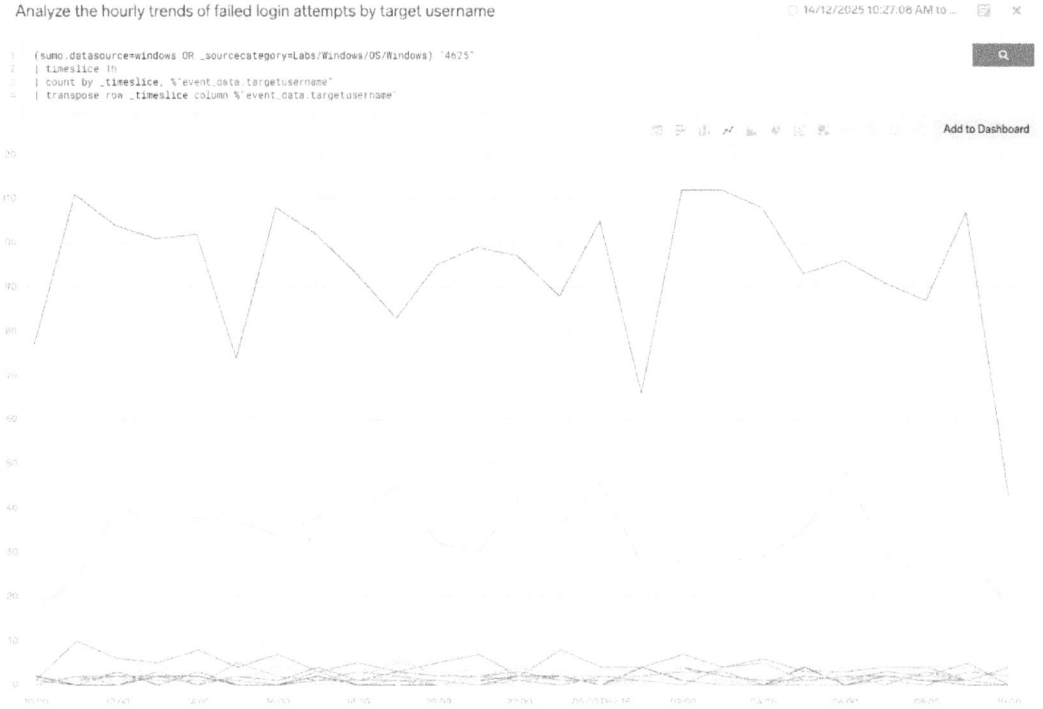

Figure 6.48 – An hourly trend view that has been put together for us

This is great, but the big line at the top is generated by log events with an empty username field. We don't want that, so let's refine further with `Remove log events with an empty username`, and we get a much better picture. It's filtered out the null username events with this line:

```
| where !isNull(%"event_data.targetusername")
```

This is perfect, and we can see a cleaner breakdown of the actual usernames. The `ADMINISTRATOR` user appears quite often. Let's run it through an anomaly detection query to see if anything strange is happening. We can write something like this:

`Create an outlier query for the ADMINISTRATOR username with the upper standard deviation band set to 3 to detect spikes in failed logins.`

This has successfully filtered on the ADMINISTRATOR users and given us an outlier-based view of failed login activity in *Figure 6.49*:

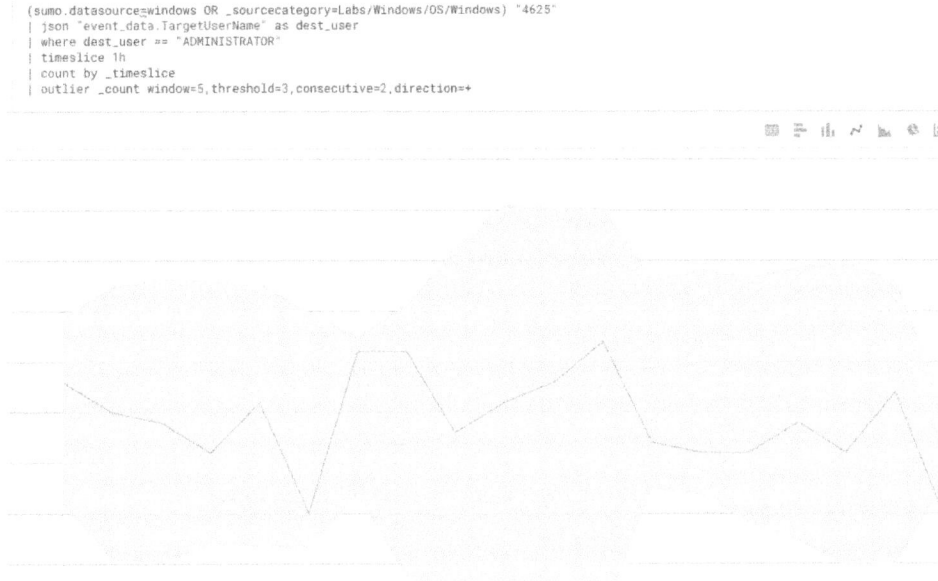

Figure 6.49 – The correctly filtered query and the outlier failed login activity

This process didn't involve me writing any queries but just asking questions of my data and leading the Query Agent down the route I wanted to go. Another useful thing is that the Query Agent tries to align itself with your way of thinking and provides suggestions for interesting refinements. For example, after running this last query, I can see a few useful suggestions, which I might want to run next, in *Figure 6.50*:

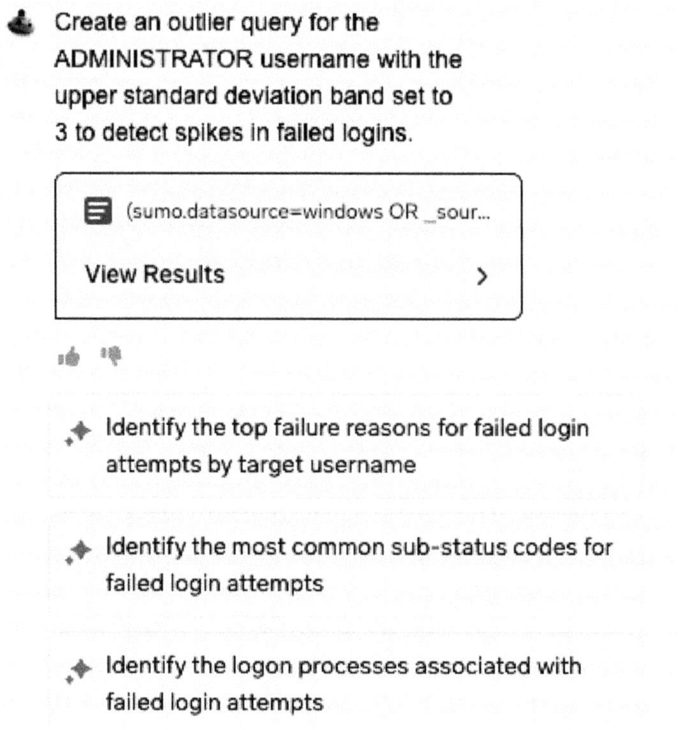

> Create an outlier query for the ADMINISTRATOR username with the upper standard deviation band set to 3 to detect spikes in failed logins.
>
> (sumo.datasource=windows OR _sour…
>
> View Results >

> Identify the top failure reasons for failed login attempts by target username

> Identify the most common sub-status codes for failed login attempts

> Identify the logon processes associated with failed login attempts

Figure 6.50 – A few interesting suggestions I can use to explore my data further

It's important to note that the Query Agent can also help you to try and fix broken queries or to optimize your query to make it run faster or improve the scoping – whatever you're aiming to do. We'll see an example in the *Log search optimization* section of the chapter coming up.

The way the Query Agent has been designed makes navigating your data very intuitive, even for someone who might be new to Sumo Logic, new to data, or new to log analytics in general. It's also useful for hardened veterans who just want to get to the root cause as soon as possible.

The objective of this book is to help you build a security intelligence program around the use of Sumo Logic. Mobot will let you harness machine learning and advanced analytics to tackle the deluge of data your operations teams have to deal with on a daily basis. I think it would help carry the point home to see some examples where this saving in both time and simplicity is tangible. Let's take some queries from different ops teams and see how we can get the same data much more rapidly.

Mobot SecOps

We're in the security team and we want to see all the rule IDs that have been triggered by our blocked traffic in our AWS WAF source. Here's a query that does this:

```
_sourceCategory = Labs/AWS/WAF  BLOCK
| where action="BLOCK"
| lookup country_name from geo://location on ip = clientip
| where country_name matches "*"
| where httpMethod matches "*"
| where clientIP matches "*"
| count as count by terminatingRuleId
| sort count
```

In this query, we're looking at blocked traffic, geolocating the IP address, specifying filters on some of the fields, and then aggregating on the terminating rule ID. Finally, we sort the results. Awesome. Here's what we type into Mobot:

```
Show me all blocked traffic, enrich source IP with geoip and count by terminating rule, sort by count
```

That's saved about 15-20 minutes *at least*. Let's show another query!

Mobot dev

We're a developer and we need to quickly see our environment deployment statistics, the results, and compare them to last week. This is a query that shows this:

```
event_type=deploy status=*  environment_name=* team=* service =*
| count as count  by status, environment_name
| compare with timeshift 7d
| fields environment_name, status, count, count_7d
| sort by _count desc
```

With Mobot, we don't need to know the operators or syntax here, or how to use `compare with timeshift`. We can just write the following:

```
Show me all environments, their current status, and compare with the count 7 days ago
```

This query is quick, concise, and elegant, and will help your developers get to the heart of any issues faster.

Mobot, as well as the Query Agent, is a crucial part of the platform, and we've only scratched the surface of the amount of efficiency it can deliver. You might be wondering about the Knowledge Agent at this point. I'm not going to spend too much time on it here, but it is a great way of getting answers to questions like the following:

- How do I set up an OpenTelemetry collector on Linux?
- How do I create a machine learning monitor?

It'll provide clear answers sourced from the official Sumo Logic documentation, so you spend less time looking through docs and more time actually implementing what you need or overcoming a hurdle with a concept.

Information on Mobot, the Query Agent, and the Knowledge Agent can be found here: `https://www.sumologic.com/help/docs/search/mobot/`

Rounding out the different querying mechanisms, hopefully, you have seen the amount of power and versatility at your disposal. Now that we have had some experience with writing queries and using the output, the natural follow-on discussion is how do we improve them? What does a good query look like versus a bad one? This is what search optimization is all about.

Even though Sumo Logic is a cloud-native, fully scalable data platform that can ingest petabytes of data and query quickly in a lot of cases, sometimes users and teams want to make it even quicker and more performant. There are many ways to go about this, and so I'd like to offer some best practices to help with this. You've got the sports car; let's show you how to eke out the best performance.

Log search optimization

Sumo Logic is a powerful technology, and sometimes, depending on what we need, with power, there is complexity. When there is an incident, an outage, or some other problem we need to resolve quickly, we must be able to call upon Sumo Logic's analytics capability to get us the answers we need. In this section, we'll look at the following points:

- Key optimization concepts within the search pipeline, such as scan, retrieval, and search time compute
- Using keywords and fields in the search scope
- Taking advantage of built-in optimization features such as FERs and scheduled views
- Tips and best practices around search speed

Optimization seems to be unnecessary for teams who might not use Sumo Logic often, or are on the smaller side, maybe, if the platform is so capable. However, there are some key reasons why it's important.

Why is search optimization important?

I have noticed that users of Sumo Logic who are able to work its data analytics capabilities to their fullest discover key insights in their data very quickly, and their teams, managers, and senior executives are happy about that because it has beneficial side effects on operations: quicker response times, easier pivoting between datasets to find vulnerabilities, bad actors, root cause issues, and more. Search optimization is key to how these Sumo Logic users are doing this, but let's cover why search optimization is useful to know about.

- **Security**: If we look at it from a security perspective, search optimization is important because it allows for faster incident response and threat mitigation, as we can navigate our data more quickly.
- **Observability**: From an observability angle, the **Mean time to Identify** (**MTTI**) metric, for example, is valuable and measures how long it takes to identify the cause of an issue after it's found. By searching your data quickly and easily, this becomes more achievable.

- **Scale**: Search optimization means you're able to search across larger datasets more efficiently and quickly. As our customers scale to meet the demands of their businesses across teams, we find that it unlocks the ability to meet more advanced use cases that rely on multiple teams, data islands, and complex architecture.
- **Cost**: By following best practices and embracing search optimization, we can control scanning activity across our data with better precision. This all reduces costs because you can manufacture queries that are incisive and get back the data you need to answer your question as efficiently as possible.
- **Speed**: Optimization ensures that queries are as fast as they can possibly be, and in so doing, helps to extract value from key business drivers:
  - Security posture
  - Deeper business insights
  - Protecting revenue
  - Improving customer experience
  - Faster application build and release cycles
  - Improved audit and compliance

So, having covered these areas, we know that taking search optimization seriously means more happy operations people, and that's really the main point, isn't it? Let's be honest, happy teams mean better performance and more problems solved overall. The other benefits are great, though. Let's start looking into the concepts and how to apply them.

Key concepts

In Sumo Logic, search optimization is driven by three core concepts: **scan**, **retrieval**, and **compute**. Each of these represents a different stage in how data is accessed and analyzed during a search, and inefficiencies at any stage can significantly impact query speed and resource consumption. These key concepts are discussed in detail in the following subsections:

Scan

The crux of this one is that if we scan less data, we're going to have a quicker, more cost-effective search. The goal is to know your data so that you can more easily specify the target area, instead of searching across the entirety of your data and praying there's something there. This is where partitioning becomes incredibly important. By setting up partitions of key operational segments in Sumo Logic, we can access these with a scoped query such as the following:

```
_index = astronomy_app_otel001 _sourcecategory = kubernetes/*
```

Retrieval

The premise here is that if less data is retrieved, we're going to have a quicker search. To optimize retrieval, we need to use keywords where possible, behind the first pipe (|) of the search, and to make abundant use of **Field Extraction Rules** (**FERs**). An example could be the use of the following keywords and fields that were extracted at ingest time:

```
error foo* container=*bar*
```

Compute

The less runtime compute we use, the quicker the search is going to be. This factor impacts search speed less than scan and retrieval, but it is nevertheless useful to make note of it. Items such as runtime parsing, aggregations, and formatting all add up to additional compute that can slow down the execution of a search.

Having covered the three key pillars of search optimization, I wanted to put them into the context of an actual end-to-end search, so let me introduce the *Search Pipeline Performance stack*:

Concept	Example
metadata	_index=astronomy_app_otel001
keywords	stdout error
Index fields	container=the_cashdesk
Search time parsing	| json "identity.username" as username
Search operators	| where level = "Error"
Filter	| sort failed_transactions
Aggregate	| count by source_ip

These are the components that make up the performance of a query. The first three – metadata, keywords, and index fields – are critical because they happen before the first pipe in the search. They effectively dictate what is scanned and retrieved before it gets processed with compute, and they are the key to unlocking performance and speed across your searches. As scan and retrieval have a greater impact than compute on a search, this is why. As we go through the three key pillars, bear these elements in mind, as we'll make plenty of references to them all.

Using scopes to reduce scan

The first key area is to cover scoping. Looking at the *Search Pipeline Performance stack*, metadata is the first entry point for the query. *Always make sure to specify the data that you need during the search.* This is the quickest and easiest way of obtaining better performance. In the preceding example, when talking about *scan*, we gave an example of an index, astronomy_app_otel001. *Figure 6.51* shows how scoping helps.

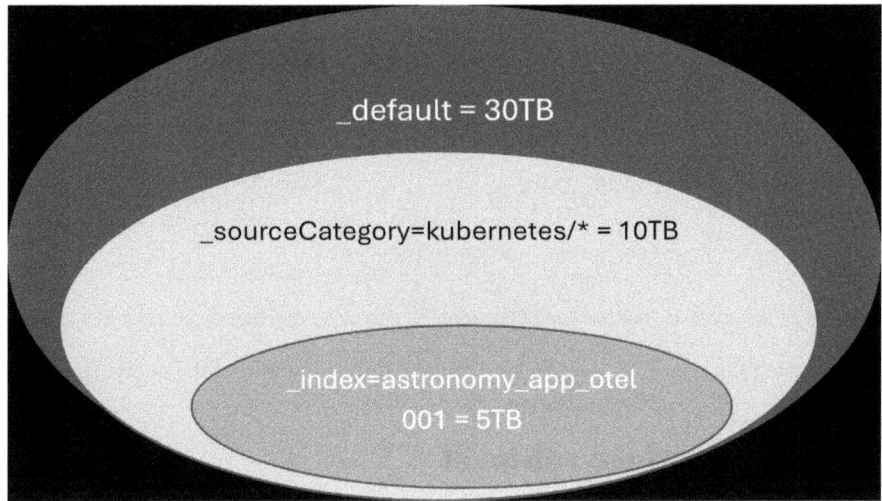

Figure 6.51 – Reducing the scan surface area of our search speeds it up

In the preceding diagram, if we query all our data every single time, we're querying data we might not need, and because we're talking about terabytes of data in this instance, we could be slowing down our query. If we scope down into our Kubernetes source categories, defined by kubernetes/*, we are only looking through a third of our data and saving compute cycles there. By focusing on the data linked to the app in question, the astronomy app, we are querying 5 terabytes of data and can get a quicker and more accurate result. The key here is that the less data we're scanning and feeding into the query, the quicker it will be. To check what index, _sourceCategory, or _source your data is in, we can refer to it in the logs within the metadata at the bottom of the event, this can be seen in *Figure 6.52*.

Figure 6.52 – Finding _sourceCategory and _index in your log event

If you're interested in knowing how much data will be scanned in line with Flex pricing, you can select the gauge icon to the left of the search button in the query UI, where it will tell you the size of the data scanned in **kilobytes (KB)**, **megabytes (MB)**, **gigabytes (GB)**, or **terabytes (TB)**, as shown in *Figure 6.53*.

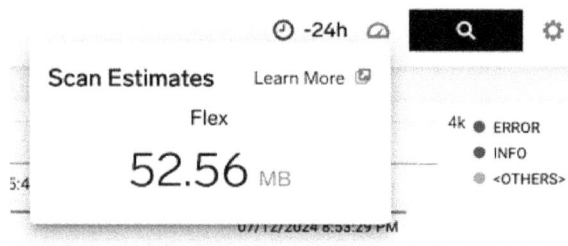

Figure 6.53 – We can estimate the size of our scan for Flex and have better control of our querying

Scan is all about reducing the size of the data we're scanning at the very start of the query. Let's take a look at reducing retrieval in line with search optimization.

Using keywords to reduce retrieval

So, we've reduced our scope to only target the exact data we're looking for. It's a good start! Let's see how we can manipulate our query to start reducing the overall compute required for the search and improve its performance.

Going back to the **Search Pipeline Performance** table, we have keywords and index fields marked in green, as these are all added to the scope of the query. Basically, anything before the first |. With keywords, the main point to be made is that *retrieving all data and using parsing or filtering* (for example, | where eventid = "1000") *is slow*. We can reduce data retrieved by adding a keyword such as cart 500 or *.php, or even an IP address, to reduce the data retrieved from within your original scope further. So far, we have something like this:

```
_index=astronomy_app_otel001 frontendservice
```

It might help to explain *why* this is better than using | where service="frontendservice". The answer is something called a **bloom filter**. As is explained on Dev.to by Shadid Haque[2], *"a bloom filter is a space-efficient probabilistic data structure used to test whether an element is a member of a set. It is very fast and consumes minimal memory, making it ideal for applications where quick membership checks are needed"*. This is an optimization at the platform level, built into Sumo Logic, where all logs are full-text indexed. This lets the keywords within the scope reduce retrieved data much quicker than other methods and is engineered for speed.

Here's a little cheat sheet of ways in which you can write keywords that can make this process straightforward:

- Case sensitivity: error and Error will both capture eRRor, for instance.
- Spaces: AND and OR statements use brackets, and ! And NOT can be used too – for example, (abc* AND (error or fatal)) not foo !bar.
- Keyword tokens: Each keyword token is alphanumeric, delimited by a space or punctuation – for example, 10.2.3.4 user@abc.com abc.com.

- Wildcards * and ?: These are very flexible due to free-text indexing; we can use *bar*, *b?r*, or bar/index*.
- String literals and escaping: If you want to use a string as a keyword, use "" – for example, "this is a string", and you have to escape certain characters with a backslash (\): "\"foo\"":\"bar\"".

The great thing about keywords is that they're really easy to use and also increase the performance of your query – win-win. Let's move on to the next trick we have up our sleeve, extracted fields.

Using extracted fields to reduce retrieval

FERs were discussed previously, in *Chapter 5, Ingesting Data*, and we talked about how we can parse our data at ingest time, instead of having to parse it at runtime every single time, and some best practices when it comes to creating them. I mentioned how they also help with performance, and that's exactly why they're part of our three pillars here, as they massively help with search optimization. There are some crazy performance gains here if FERs are used properly, and we'll cover them in some examples.

As we're here to discuss the nuances of using FERs for search optimization, we can let you in on a few tips:

- Define FERs on hard-to-parse or high-value logs and fields
- The x-sumo-fields header can post HTTPS index fields from external push sources
- Define FERs to pre-compute expensive fields such as response-time bands and URL strings

Let's look at an example of an FER and how easy it is for an end user to operate. As FERs are typically done by admins, the users don't even need to know what they look like. They can just query on typical fields but have much better performance.

Here's the FER on some Nginx access logs:

```
_sourceName=/var/log/nginx/access.log
| parse "* * * * \"* * HTTP/1.1\" * * \"*\" " as srcIP, foo, bar, dateTime,
method,url,status_code,size,referrer
```

And here are the query comparisons:

Extremely Fast	**Slow**

`_index=nginx`
 	
`_sourceName=/var/log/nginx/access.log`
 	
`url=*cart* status_code=5*`
	`_sourceName=/var/log/nginx/access.log`
	
	`| parse "* * * * \"* * HTTP/1.1\" * * \"*\" " as srcIP, foo, bar, dateTime, method,url,status_code,size,referrer`
	
	`| where url matches "*/cart/*" and status_code >= 500`

Table 6.2 – Query comparison

The reason there is such a big disparity in speed is that, in the fast query, no search time parsing is required, and only events matching the indexed fields, url and status_code, are retrieved. This is all in line with the search optimization concepts we've discussed so far.

Let's look at two examples where FERs show massive performance gains.

FER example 1

A user, Mo, wants to count the number of 500 or greater HTTP responses by URL and has this query:

```
_collector=Apache Nginx and _source=Apache Access
| parse regex "^(?<src_ip>\d{1,3}\.\d{1,3}\.\d{1,3}\.\d{1,3})"
| parse regex "(?<method>[A-Z]+)\s(?<url>\S+)\sHTTP/[\d\.]+"\s(?<status_code>\d+)\s(?<size>[\d-]+)\s\"(?<referrer>.*?)\"\s\"(?<user_agent>.+?)\".*"
| where status_code >= 500
| count by status_code,url | sort _count
```

Running this search on the last 7 days takes 54 seconds to complete, and he got the results shown in *Figure 6.54*.

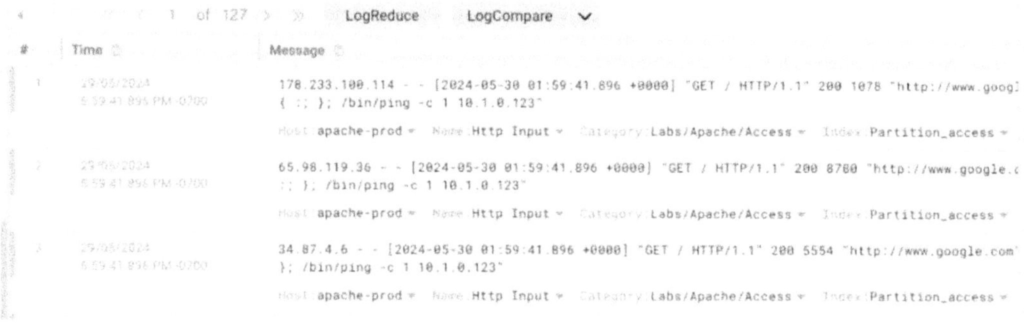

Figure 6.54 – The results from the initial, non-optimized query

How can we speed this up? Here are a couple of suggestions based on the data we have:

- Specify the index in the query by reducing the scan surface area – you can see the index for all the events is Partition_access.
- There is already an FER for status_code, so it's extracted and ready to use. We don't need to waste valuable search time compute parsing a field that's already parsed.

This is what Mo's enhanced query looks like:

```
_sourceCategory = "Labs/Apache/Access"
AND _index=Partition_access
status_code=5*
| count by status_code,url
| sort _count
```

We've included the index and the status_code keyword, and this took 13 seconds to finish, a gain of 4x on our previous attempt, as shown in *Figure 6.55*:

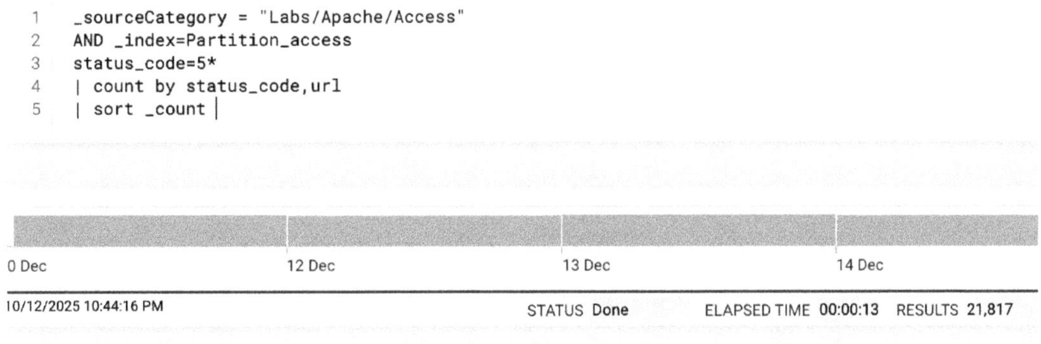

```
1    _sourceCategory = "Labs/Apache/Access"
2    AND _index=Partition_access
3    status_code=5*
4    | count by status_code,url
5    | sort _count |
```

Figure 6.55 – The optimized query, returning, in 13 seconds, a 4x reduction

It was also much easier to type! Let's look at another example, this time with a huge performance gain and some interesting tips on creative FER usage.

FER example 2

As mentioned already, running search operators such as where is actually quite computationally intensive and should be avoided where possible. Let's work with this example:

```
| where time_taken > 30000
```

This query was part of a case study where a customer wanted to identify IIS web servers that had a latency of over 30,000 milliseconds. The problem was that this data set was massive, and running this query:

```
_sourceCategory=prod/web/iis | where time_taken > 30000
```

This query took 5 minutes and 42 seconds when looking back over only 60 minutes. In this case, each log had to be retrieved, and the field value computed at runtime, but the main issue here is that numeric comparisons aren't possible, even with an FER field. So, what do we do? Here's a creative solution that solved the problem.

An FER was created where the time comparisons were hardcoded into separate fields. Here it is so you can appreciate it for yourself:

```
| "" as stripe
| if(time_taken>=5000,"Jgt5000",stripe) as stripe
| if(time_taken>=2000 and time_taken<5000,"Ilt5000",stripe) as stripe
| if(time_taken>=1000 and time_taken<2000,"Hlt2000",stripe) as stripe
| if(time_taken>=500 and time_taken<1000,"Glt1000",stripe) as stripe
| if(time_taken>=200 and time_taken<500,"Flt500",stripe) as stripe
| if(time_taken>=100 and time_taken<200,"Elt200",stripe) as stripe
| if(time_taken>=50 and time_taken<100,"Dlt100",stripe) as stripe
```

```
   | if(time_taken>=20 and time_taken<50,"Clt50",stripe) as stripe
   | if(time_taken>=10 and time_taken<20,"Blt20",stripe) as stripe
   | if(time_taken>=0 and time_taken<10,"Alt10",stripe) as stripe
```

Figure 6.56 shows some example results.

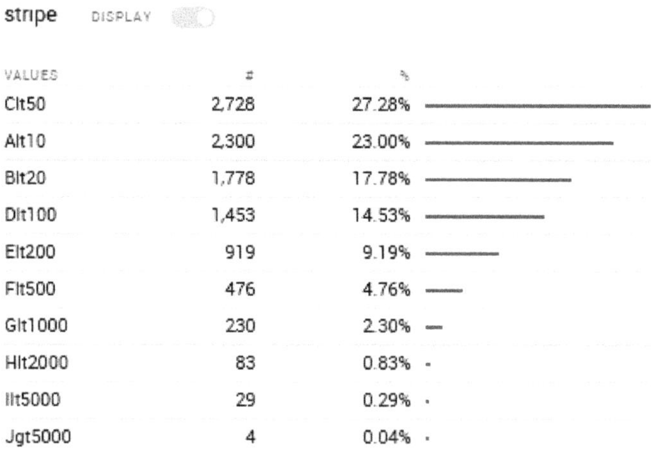

stripe		
VALUES	#	%
Clt50	2,728	27.28%
Alt10	2,300	23.00%
Blt20	1,778	17.78%
Dlt100	1,453	14.53%
Elt200	919	9.19%
Flt500	476	4.76%
Glt1000	230	2.30%
Hlt2000	83	0.83%
Ilt5000	29	0.29%
Jgt5000	4	0.04%

Figure 6.56 – The numerical comparisons are categories within the new indexed field

The results are all using the `stripe` indexed field and the numerical comparison is built into the parsing, so we have the logic we need, and to add to that, it's an FER! So, we get increased performance. How much is the increase in this case, for the following updated query?

```
_sourceCategory=prod/web/iis stripe=jgt5000 | where time_taken > 30000
```

Instead of taking 5 minutes and 42 seconds, it took *one second* – the same massive dataset, the same result. That's an improvement of 342x, which is awesome. The technology at your disposal is fast; sometimes it just needs to be tweaked and adjusted a little to get it working how you need it, and that's a testament to the platform's ability to be pliable and customizable to your use cases.

What we've learned here is that learning about FERs and making the most of them in Sumo Logic is worth your while. There's one more element to cover to wrap up our journey through search optimization—scheduled views.

Using scheduled views to speed up searches

Scheduled views[17] are a type of pre-compute or pre-aggregated index for small and historical subsets of data. Results are pre-aggregated over each successive time window – for example, every minute – and these views can execute 100 times faster than a normal search. Due to how scheduled views work, it's not always necessary to use a view. Let's cover when views might be best.

When to use a scheduled view

There are certain scenarios where using a scheduled view can unlock big performance gains. Here are a few of them:

- Repeated searches target days'/weeks'/months' worth of data, and your data scans go into terabytes
- You need to search back into extended periods of time – for example, a year or longer
- Your use case relates to aggregated data with a clearly defined use case
- Dashboards with panels that take longer than 30 seconds to load
- Your searches don't scale; for example, you're getting memory errors or operator max limits
- There is a lot of overlap between searches; for example, a search that looks back -7d every 15 minutes

Basically, we are taking queries and searches that are high-load and are done frequently, and pre-aggregating the data instead of doing all that computation on the fly. So, let's see how we go about setting a scheduled view up.

Setting up a scheduled view

To set up a scheduled view, we go to **Logs** in the configuration menu and choose **Scheduled Views**, as shown in *Figure 6.57*.

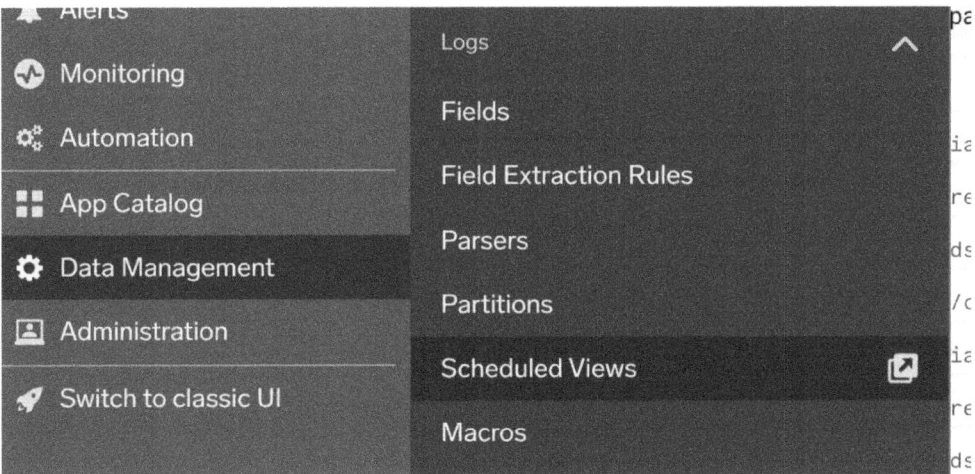

Figure 6.57 – Finding Scheduled Views in the Data Management menu

Then choose **+ Add Scheduled View** at the top right to open up the configuration. Here, the main parts are as follows:

- **Name**: Give the view a name, to then refer to in a query with _view
- **Query**: The query that populates the scheduled view
- **Start Date**: Choose when data starts populating from the query
- **Retention Period**: Select how long data will live in the scheduled view

That is pretty much it. Remember, a scheduled view reduces data down to the bare minimum, so they only contain the results you need for your query, so make sure the query highlights this. Aggregations and timeslices should *always* be included as part of the scheduled view query to facilitate this. Let's use an example to help you understand what the process is.

Scheduled view aggregation example

Let's use the use case of aggregate reporting as an example. This is the most common use case that I see among customers, so it's worth covering, as you will most likely benefit from this type of scheduled view. Typically, it's used for web servers, services such as load balancers, gateways, and so on, where there is a count by a status code over time, and this is then used in dashboards or outlier functions for analytics.

The query we're going to use for our scheduled view, called apache_status, is as follows:

```
_sourceCategory=Labs/Apache/Access
| parse "HTTP/1.1" * " as status_code
| timeslice 1m
| count status_code,_timeslice
```

Now, when we want to run a query on our status codes, or have dashboard panels that are visualizing data for these Apache servers, we can use the following query to get the result back in seconds, as it's pre-aggregated.

```
_view=apache_status
| timeslice 1m
| sum(_count) as requests by status_code,_timeslice
| transpose row _timeslice column status_code
```

Using sum(_count), the count will now return row counts, not the sum of the original count. This is what lets us view thousands of pre-aggregated rows instead of tens of millions of events. As mentioned, this is a very common use case for Sumo Logic users. I want to focus on another common use case, this time from a security point of view.

Scheduled view security example

One of the other main uses of scheduled views is to deal with expensive, highly computational queries by caching them for reuse. The example we're going to see here is storing positive threat intel lookup matches to help with quicker long-term threat reporting, while preserving a lot of useful metadata we can operate with to drill down to the raw data.

Here's the query that we add to the scheduled view, which is called threat_geo_asn_aws_waf_v1.

```
_sourcecategory = "Labs/AWS/WAF"
| json field=_raw "httpRequest.clientIp" as src_ip
| where (ispublicip(src_ip))
| json field=_raw "action"
| threatip src_ip
| where !(isempty(malicious_confidence))
| timeslice 1m
| "AWS" as vendor
```

```
  | "WAF" as product
  | malicious_confidence as threat
  | json field=raw_threat "threat_types"
  | count by
_timeslice,vendor,product,_sourcecategory,_source,src_ip,action,threat,actor,threat_types
  | lookup asn,organization from asn://default on ip=src_ip
  | geoip src_ip
  | fields -latitude,longitude,country_name,state
```

We search through our AWS WAF source for HTTP requests and the correlated IP addresses, checking if the IP addresses are public, before running them through the CrowdStrike Falcon Threat Intelligence feed built into Sumo Logic. We aggregate on several fields and then geographically enrich the data, and at the end, we remove unnecessary fields that add no value here.

When it comes to querying this pre-aggregated data, we can do something like this:

```
_view=threat_geo_asn_aws_waf_v1
  | timeslice 1d
  | sum(_count) as events by actor,_timeslice
  | transpose row _Timeslice column actor
```

We can search through our cached results historically. By doing what we've done through scheduled views, we've opened up some interesting use cases:

- Extremely fast searches across long-term time horizons
- Using this scheduled view query as part of a subquery
- Conducting more tailored forensic searches and threat hunts on the data, as the historical threat lookup and GeoIP enrichment are preserved

That covers the key concepts of search optimization, from the **Search Pipeline Performance** breakdown all the way to a discussion and examples of how you can start implementing these optimizations with your own data. Before we wrap up this section, I want to cover the tail end of the **Search Pipeline Performance** table – the very bottom, where we have no choice but to use compute. There are certain tips that we can use to help speed up compute-heavy operations as much as we can.

Compute time: best practices

In this last section, let's cover some best practices that can help when we've reduced the scan surface area and lowered retrieval as much as we can.

- Filter events as early as possible in the search.
- Don't parse unnecessary fields that are not required or that are already parsed by an FER.
- Sort at the end of your query. Sometimes multiple sorts are unavoidable, but keep them towards the end.
- Sorting by _messagetime is a massive burden on compute; try to sort on another field.
- Perform lookups on lookup tables *after* aggregating data to reduce the number of lookups required.

- Some operators are faster than others at similar tasks. For example, topk is faster than top.
- Use built-in fields for time: _messagetime, _receipttime, _timeslice. Don't waste compute parsing out date and time formats unless absolutely necessary. Here's an example:

```
formatdate(tolong(_messagetime),"yyyy-MM-dd HH:mm:ss ZZZ") as time
```

Including the preceding tips, the official Sumo documentation sums it all up[18]. I wanted to leave you with a final bit of help regarding search optimization. Within Sumo Logic, there is an app called Enterprise Search Audit[19]. *Figure 6.58* shows the App Catalog:

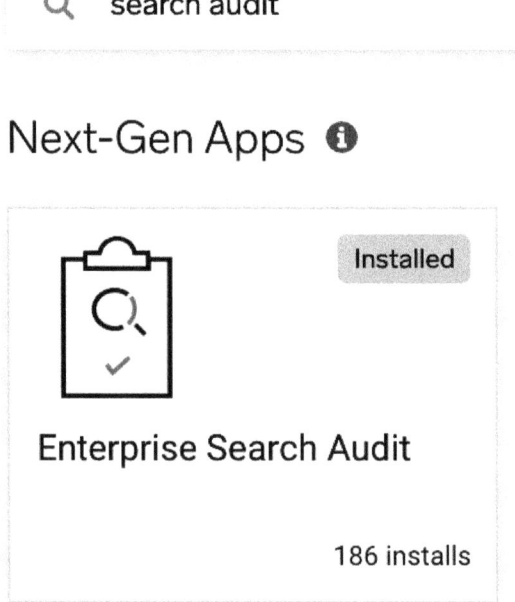

Figure 6.58 – The Enterprise Search Audit app in the App Catalog

Within are five dashboards with a treasure trove of information about how your users are querying data across the platform:

- **Commonly Referenced Data Sources**
- **Data Tier Usage Over Time** (less useful with the Flex pricing model)
- **Queries Characteristics and Opportunities**
- **Search Overview**
- **User Insights**

These views will help you discern things such as the top slowest queries by user, what data sources are being referenced, which partitions, and how to potentially improve your queries. We'll cover visualization and dashboards in the next chapter, but for now, I wanted to let you know what to look for in addition to using the preceding views.

When looking at all this search data, focus on four key areas to work on. This will help you prioritize and keep you on track to troubleshoot and improve querying for users:

- \> 1 TB scan on any query
- A query runtime of greater than 5 minutes
- Scanning more than 3 partitions at a time
- Scanning *all* data

With these four areas, you can apply any context to what you see in the dashboards and hopefully arrive at queries that are problematic.

Up to this point, we've been on a bit of a journey, and the focus has very much been on logs: how to query logs, different operators, and examples for your teams, and then, most recently, a section on optimizing your performance and efficiency when it comes to those logs. Don't you think it's time to bring in another friend to the conversation? Metrics have been sitting in a corner, waiting patiently for us to invite them to the discussion, and now is the time. In the next chapter, I'd like to cover metrics data, how we navigate the UI, how we conduct metrics searches, and at the same time cover span analytics and traces, as these querying UIs are ever so slightly different. While we're on the topic of metrics, we'll also cover visualization and alerting.

It's been a long chapter, and I bet you're hungry – let's revisit the analytical cake that we're baking! We've had two solid slabs of tasty, spongy foundation for our cake, and now we've covered a big chunk of the filling – imagine chocolate, jam, biscuit...mmm. Let's not get too distracted. We've covered a key functional layer in the architectural makeup of this cake, so here is what our creation looks like so far:

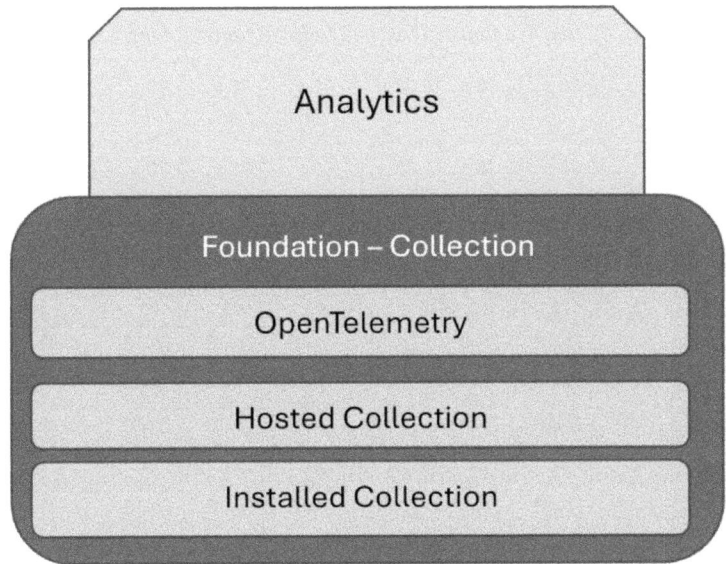

Figure 6.59 – We are adding a lot of tasty filling to the middle of our analytical cake!

Our analytics are part-baked because we have yet to cover the metrics side of the house, as well as some of the APM analytics we can achieve in Sumo Logic, plus the visualization, but we are well on our way!

Summary

This was a pretty meaty chapter; we covered everything your operational teams need to start to query and analyze all the data sources being ingested into Sumo Logic. We covered the UI and discussed historic challenges with querying, which made it difficult to master without an in-depth knowledge of querying languages. We then covered how Sumo Logic starts to tackle these problems by providing features such as Mobot, Sumo Logic's generative AI querying capability.

We covered querying in many different forms and gave plenty of examples for SecOps, DevOps, and Developer teams so that everyone can use the platform as a single source of truth and work off the same data to resolve issues more quickly. This was done while covering the top analytical tools at your team's disposal, such as LogReduce, lookup tables, and subqueries, to add to a growing arsenal of versatile tools to get the right data at the right time.

Finally, we ended on log search optimization, how to get the best performance and efficiency out of your queries, looking at the key reasons for wanting to do so and then providing actionable steps and methods to help your teams achieve a lightning-fast pace when running your analytics. We covered some best practices to make sure your teams are covered on the compute side of the house, too.

Data analytics is key to improving your security intelligence with Sumo Logic. What improves your security posture and your SecOps capability is complete visibility of all your data sources, no matter the data island, and having the power and flexibility to access and analyze this data at a moment's notice, with no technical limitations. That's what Sumo Logic provides.

As we'll see in the next chapter, there's even more that we can layer on top of log analytics – we have metrics, dashboards, and alerting coming in next.

References

1. https://help.sumologic.com/docs/search/get-started-with-search/search-basics/
2. https://help.sumologic.com/docs/search/search-query-language/parse-operators/parse-variable-patterns-using-regex/
3. https://help.sumologic.com/docs/search/search-query-language/search-operators/lookupcontains/
4. https://help.sumologic.com/docs/search/search-query-language/group-aggregate-operators/stddev/
5. https://help.sumologic.com/docs/search/search-query-language/search-operators/timeslice/
6. https://help.sumologic.com/docs/search/search-query-language/parse-operators/parsedate/
7. https://help.sumologic.com/docs/search/search-query-language/group-aggregate-operators/avg/
8. https://help.sumologic.com/docs/search/search-query-language/search-operators/rollingstd/
9. https://help.sumologic.com/docs/search/search-query-language/search-operators/limit/
10. https://help.sumologic.com/docs/search/logreduce/logreduce-operator/
11. https://help.sumologic.com/docs/search/logcompare/
12. https://help.sumologic.com/docs/search/live-tail/about-live-tail/
13. https://help.sumologic.com/docs/search/lookup-tables/
14. https://help.sumologic.com/docs/search/search-query-language/search-operators/save/
15. https://help.sumologic.com/docs/search/subqueries/
16. https://help.sumologic.com/docs/search/search-query-language/search-operators/
17. https://help.sumologic.com/docs/manage/scheduled-views/
18. https://help.sumologic.com/docs/search/get-started-with-search/build-search/best-practices-search/
19. https://help.sumologic.com/docs/integrations/sumo-apps/enterprise-search-audit/

Get this book's PDF version and more

Scan the QR code (or go to `packtpub.com/unlock`). Search for this book by name, confirm the edition, and then follow the steps on the page.

Note: Keep your invoice handy. Purchases made directly from Packt don't require an invoice.

7

Metrics

At this point in the book, I'd like to say we've only scratched the surface. Or should I say, we've only begun to *MELT* the tip of the iceberg?! Okay, bad jokes aside, thus far we've focused on the *L* part of MELT by learning how to query and analyze logs. What about the mysterious "M" of metrics? Sumo Logic is a very versatile, Swiss Army knife-type tool. The primary function is log analytics, but wrapped around it are some other very useful features that are worth exploring. Finding different ways to leverage the telemetry coming into the platform increases the value of the tool and means that when it comes time to consider cost-cutting, your team won't get the proverbial rug pulled out from under them. Sumo Logic's most mature customers are on a mission to *democratize data* by using Sumo Logic for continuous monitoring of applications, alerting, and visualization of their data, ingesting not just logs but also metrics such as CPU and memory usage, and maybe even inventory data, all adding extra dimensions to the value they're getting with logs. We're going to be covering some of these elements in this chapter, with complete explanations of how things work and, most importantly, real use cases that have solved problems.

The following topics will be discussed in this chapter:

- What are metrics and how do you collect them?
- Querying metrics deep dive

What are metrics and how do you collect them?

Metrics and logs are both essential components of observability, but they serve distinct purposes and operate differently. At a fundamental level, both metrics and logs are forms of time-series data; they are tied to a specific point in time. However, while logs are often verbose, unstructured records of events with detailed context, metrics are structured, numerical measurements aggregated over time. For example, logs might capture every transaction or event in an application, while metrics would summarize those transactions by providing aggregated time-series data such as CPU utilization, memory usage, requests per second, request latency, error rates, throughput, and disk I/O. Metrics are optimized for trend analysis, alerting on thresholds, and understanding system behavior at a high level rather than investigating individual events. This distinction makes metrics lightweight, easy to query, and highly efficient for monitoring trends over time.

Metrics and logs are complementary to each other in observability. Metrics provide fast, high-level overviews and are excellent for detecting anomalies, spotting trends, and monitoring system health over time. Logs, on the other hand, provide the detailed, granular context needed to investigate why a particular metric spiked or dipped. For example, if a metric reveals that CPU utilization suddenly jumped, logs can uncover the exact processes or errors that caused the spike. Together, they create a comprehensive view of system behavior; metrics guide you to the problem and logs help you diagnose it. I occasionally get asked "*Can't I just stream metric data in as logs?*" The answer is yes. It is just textual data. However, the structure of the data is different, and to maximize efficiency, the two types of data should be treated differently.

A key concept that differentiates metrics is cardinality. Cardinality refers to the number of unique values a particular attribute or field can have. For example, the cardinality of a metric label such as server_name could be low if there are only a few servers, but a field such as user_id could have extremely high cardinality if millions of users interact with a system. Cardinality is important because it directly impacts the performance and cost of storing and querying data. High-cardinality metrics, while offering deep insights, can become expensive to handle at scale, which is why careful design and aggregation are essential. Logs, by nature, often carry high-cardinality data since they record granular, event-level information, whereas metrics are designed to abstract and summarize those details.

Collecting metrics has traditionally been messy, usually with multiple tools or plugins being used across an environment, such as the following:

- **Nagios**, with lots of built-in plugins
- **Telegraf**, with some extensive plugins to cover a wide range of technologies
- **collectd**, an agent-based way of ingesting server metrics
- **StatsD**, which aggregates metrics and forwards them to backends
- **Fluentd**, a log collector that can also extract metrics
- **Prometheus**, a very popular pull-based system that collects metrics from exporting technologies

The nature of operations teams—dev teams in particular—is that people like to experiment with and test new tools to see how they can help them do their jobs better. Also, we all like a shiny new bit of tech. However, sometimes you'll find that a lot of these technologies are being used to monitor different parts of our ecosystem, and over time, they become entrenched. Collecting metrics in Sumo Logic is more streamlined. They can be collected from on-premise environments with agents and OpenTelemetry collectors, and from the cloud with cloud-based metrics collection typically using the native services themselves. Here is a diagram illustrating what this looks like:

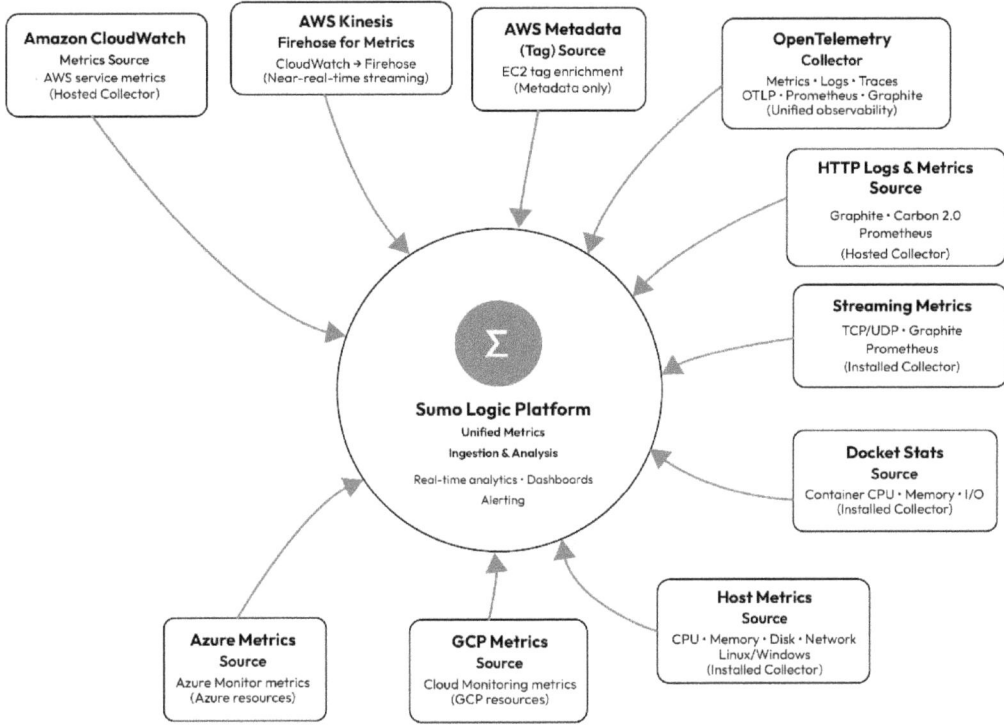

Figure 7.1 – The various methods of ingesting metrics into Sumo Logic

You'll notice, in the preceding diagram, that the main formats we use are cloud services, **OpenTelemetry**, **Carbon 2.0**, **Graphite**, and **Prometheus**.

In Sumo Logic, the end goal is to derive *actionable* insights from logs and metrics data. This is usually done by querying the data to discover the root cause of an issue, or through Sumo Logic alert monitors, which can immediately alert you when things go off the rails. Querying is discussed next.

Querying metrics deep dive

Again, Sumo Logic is a log analytics platform at its core, but as we discussed at the beginning of the book, the platform exists to create a multi-factor view of data, and that doesn't always mean logs. It also means using the metrics and traces data generated by your hardware, services, and applications to have visibility over all of this data and make sense of it, as well as to effectively troubleshoot across multiple layers of activity.

Of course, monitoring the health of critical servers is vital to keep systems running and operating efficiently. But to keep things interesting, and to stick with the theme of the book, let's also relate monitoring metrics to some unique security use cases. Then we can look at the Metrics Search UI and the process of extracting insights from our metrics. There are some nuances and interesting capabilities available as part of metrics collection and analytics too, so we'll cover these.

Are metrics that important for security?

It's well known that cybersecurity analysts and SOC teams are often busy looking at logs and security events. They may feel like Neo from *The Matrix* staring at streams of data and trying to make sense of it. Even with tools such as Sumo Logic, there's just no way of sugar-coating the tough and relentless battle faced by today's defenders.

But there are good days where your actions have prevented an attack or a patient and sophisticated adversary and you have a victory. You somehow pulled the needle out of the haystack to discover the indicator of compromise you were looking for. While logs are the best source of historical data, as part of this monitoring, if we solely look at logs we miss some context and information. We're seeing the actions, the behavior, and the root cause, but there may be some vital signs that security teams don't track and end up missing—metrics. Remember, metrics offer a real-time view of infrastructure, services, and applications that, when paired with logs, create an environment with unparalleled visibility into the business, deeper insights from the events, faster detection, and pre-emptive mitigation of threats. Let's explore these a bit more with some examples.

Benefits to a security team and examples

When we take a real-time view of our ecosystem, together with logs and metrics, we can do anything from articulating the logic we want to see and use for threat detection to applying multi-level views to incident data to understand root cause, entities at risk, and next steps.

Metrics provide near-instant updates, enabling faster detection of anomalies. For example, CPU spikes on an otherwise stable system might indicate cryptojacking.

> **Note**
>
> **Cryptojacking** is the unauthorized use of a computer, server, or device to mine cryptocurrency. Cybercriminals compromise systems, usually without the owner's knowledge, and install malware or scripts that utilize system resources (such as CPU, GPU, and memory) to perform cryptocurrency mining. This activity drains resources, slows down systems, and increases power consumption, often leading to higher operational costs.

Likewise, observing a sudden increase in network traffic might be indicative of a DDoS attack, or a spike in bytes leaving the network might indicate data exfiltration, for example. Metrics provide fast, aggregate views of things happening in your environment, and you can set threshold-based alerts to detect spikes within seconds.

Here are a few real-world examples of detections that can be accomplished through log monitoring and metric monitoring, but ideally, in a complementary way where both support each other's findings.

Network traffic analytics

A sudden spike in outbound traffic (*bytes sent*) to external IPs or destinations can signal data exfiltration. A prolonged session to an external destination may indicate large data transfers. An increase in DNS lookups to unknown domains could indicate exfiltration via DNS tunneling. Sometimes monitoring aggregate traffic and session patterns enables faster detection of anomalies without parsing entire logs.

Metric	Log
Unusual outbound traffic volume	Matching connection logs to external IPs for malicious activity

Correlating performance with security events

Metrics can highlight how infrastructure or application performance changes during an attack. Can the business sustain different attacks? The answer lies in the metrics!

Metric	Log
High memory usage on a web server	Application error logs indicating injection attempts

Anomaly detection

Metrics enable baseline behavior modeling and anomaly detection for proactive security measures. Metrics that monitor file I/O rates can highlight suspicious read or write activity on sensitive directories. An increase in active processes or unusual processes running can be tracked via metrics tied to **process IDs** (**PIDs**).

Metric	Log
A huge spike in request rates for an API endpoint	Network traffic logs indicating brute force or scraping activity

Incident impact assessment

Metrics quantify the impact of incidents on infrastructure and applications, helping prioritize response. Stress testing and cyber resilience are best achieved when you have hard numbers to analyze.

Metric	Log
Number of affected users during a phishing attack	Email logs and file access logs to identify suspicious file and directory interactions

Proactive defense with metrics thresholds

Define thresholds to trigger alerts before logs even register the issue. A simple alert on HTTP 4xx error rates spiking by 300% might precede any log-based alert showing repeated login attempts from a single IP address, revealing a potential brute-force attack.

Metric	Log
File transfer operations and size in time intervals	Firewall logs, file share logs to determine potential data exfiltration

Unified context for investigation

Correlating metrics with logs provides a full stack view of an incident, reducing the time to identify the root cause. While a metric might alert on outbound network traffic volume suddenly spiking by 10x, a log would show that, for example, the confidential_data.zip file is being sent to an external IP.

Metric	Log
Abnormality in network traffic from a **Virtual Machine** (**VM**)	Actual filenames of what files are being sent and by which user and system

These are only a handful of examples of methods that a security team empowered by having logs and metrics in the same place can use to make their lives easier.

Next, let's take a look at some best practices for combining metrics, because we'll be seeing how we can apply these best practices as we go through metrics in more detail.

Best practices for combining metrics and logs

Sumo Logic enables operational teams to get better at what they do by not only combining logs and metrics in the same place but also making it easy. Let's take a look at four key best practices.

Baselines of activity

Create baselines of activity across your environment to establish normal behavior patterns for traffic, performance, resource usage, and behavioral events. Lean heavily on the machine learning capabilities available in the platform, such as with the *outlier* operator. Outlier operators were discussed in the last chapter when covering log queries, and they can be applied in exactly the same way to your metrics queries.

Consistent metadata

If you use the same metadata schemas across your metrics and logs, it allows you to easily search across all of your data within combined queries and dashboards. For example, if you have the same fields and metrics labels across your Kubernetes containers, it's easy to search them all for certain actions or behavior to help with correlation.

Unified dashboards for logs and metrics

Create unified dashboards that have the metrics from your services along with the log events from the same services side by side. *Stop context switching*. Context switching kills productivity and adds to mental load when it counts the most. We've got some nice examples coming up later in *Chapter 8, Alerting, Monitoring, and Visualizing Data* in the *Visualizing data* section, where we build a small unified dashboard from scratch.

Pre-empt with metrics

Use metrics for predictive analytics by using not only anomaly detection and trend analysis but also forecasting tools, such as using the *predict* operator[1] with other useful correlation points to identify thresholds or areas where events are happening that shouldn't be. This is next-level pre-emptive capability in an easily accessible way.

To summarize, metrics provide fantastic context that enables your security and DevOps teams to fortify your defenses and reduce risk to the business. We've covered some very powerful points here already, and in the next section, we'll take a look at how to put metrics together which can help you to directly achieve these best practices and gain an edge over attackers.

Navigating Metrics Search

Before we look at putting those metrics queries together, let's learn how to navigate the metrics interface so that we know where to go and what the key functionality does. In the Sumo Logic menu on the left-hand side, under **Observability**, you will see **Metrics Search** at the top:

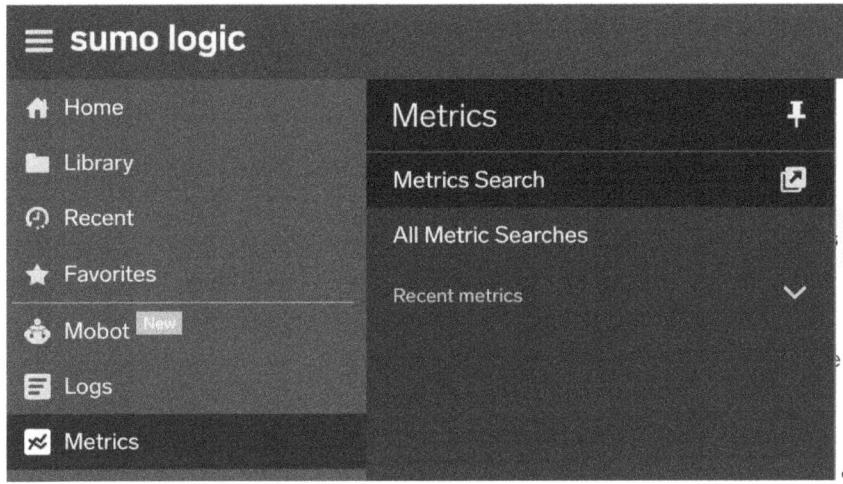

Figure 7.2 – Locating Metrics Search in the Observability section of the menu

You will be presented with the **Metrics Explorer** view, which is the main UI for querying metrics. The querying capability is slightly different here as the querying starts out in basic mode, which is the reverse of the log search. You start with the advanced view. Right out of the gates, you are presented with drop-down fields that you can use to access your data:

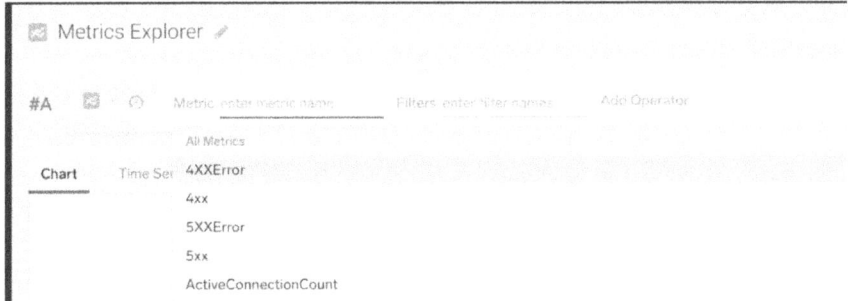

Figure 7.3 – Choosing your metrics, filters, and operators in the basic query mode

You can begin building your metrics query simply by clicking into the **Metric** field, which gives you a drop-down list of *all* the metrics you have across Sumo Logic. You can start typing to narrow down the list, or choose a metric and add a filter, such as `_sourceCategory` or a metric dimension. Finally, you then add an operator into the mix, such as avg or topk. Depending on what you need to achieve, Sumo Logic has you covered when it comes to analyzing numeric data. If you need to create a top 50, 75, or 99 percentile view, you can with the pct operator. If you need to work out how much a metric value has changed over time, you can use the delta operator. You can choose from all the operators in the dropdown, as in *Figure 7.4*:

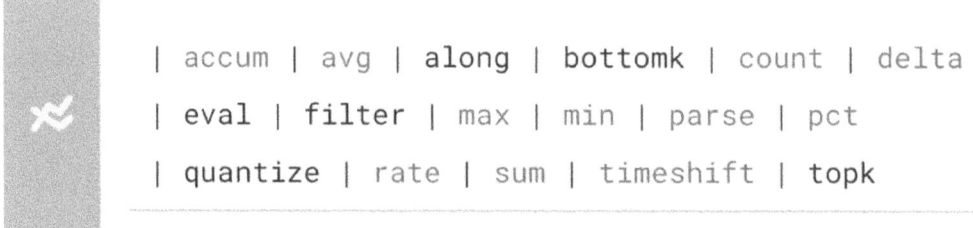

Figure 7.4 – The metrics operators that can be used to transform your data in different ways

On the right side of the screen, there are two sections to cover—the top and bottom halves. The top half consists of options that we've seen in log search:

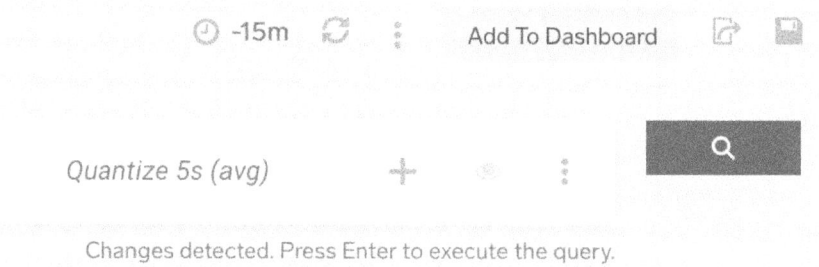

Figure 7.5 – The query options, including time range, refresh, and advanced search

We have a time range selector, an option to refresh our query, and the **Add To Dashboard** button, which does what it says and adds the result of your metrics query to a dashboard. The reason this happens is that the metrics that you query are aggregated by default. Even though the raw time-series data is stored in Sumo Logic as raw data points, visualized metrics data is presented as the aggregated value of the data points received during an interval[2].

We can also see the *share* and *save* buttons in the top-right corner, which let you share these views with other members or teams and save the metrics query. Within the query box to the left of the blue search button, we have the **+** symbol, which lets us add another query to our existing query (or queries), and a three-dotted menu that lets us choose from the following options, including specifying advanced mode and creating monitors and SLOs from the query:

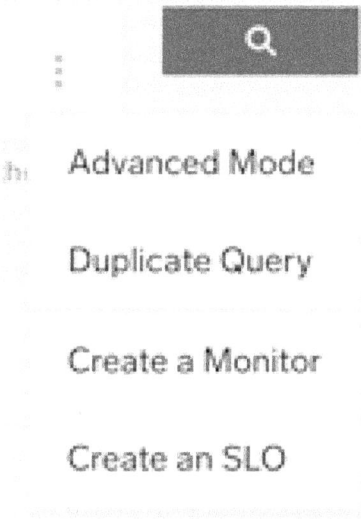

Figure 7.6 – Additional options

Advanced Mode lets you convert your query from basic to advanced mode, where you are no longer limited to selecting from the drop-down fields. **Duplicate Query** lets you duplicate the existing query so that changes across queries can be made more easily. **Create a Monitor** lets you create a monitor from your query directly instead of going through the Monitor UI, just like we can in the log search UI. **Create an SLO** lets you create a **Service-Level Objective** (**SLO**) monitor from your data, where you can monitor the performance of your services, applications, and processes.

Underneath this, we have the bottom half of the UI, which is all about configuring your visualization. We'll cover visualization in more depth in the next section of this chapter, but for now, I want to walk you through what to look out for within the metrics. As metrics are aggregated in Sumo Logic, visualizations are the main method of output.

The bottom half of the UI is split into the left side, which contains a visual and has a **Time Series** section, and the right side, which covers a range of configuration options. Let's start with the left. You can see the **Chart** section selected in the following figure:

Figure 7.7 – The Chart selection draws the visualization option specified in the configuration

If you click on **Time Series** next to **Chart**, you will see the raw data points that comprise this aggregated view:

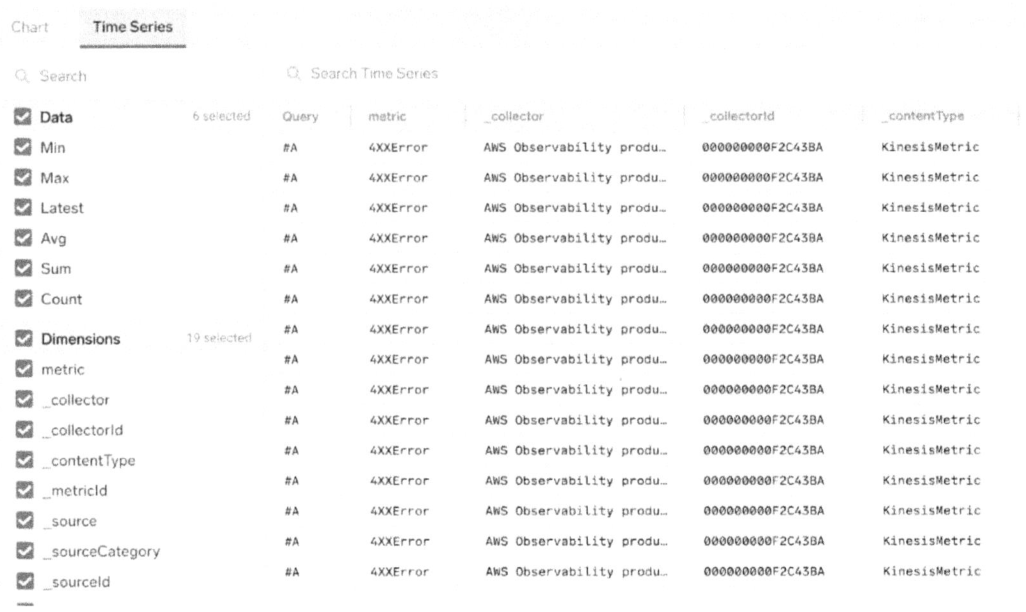

Figure 7.8 – The Time Series view shows all the dimensions the data offers

Now, on the right-hand side, you will see the configuration options, starting with the type of visual you're after. There are multiple types to choose from, including the following:

- **Time Series**
- **Categorical**
- **Single Value**
- **Honeycomb**
- **Map**

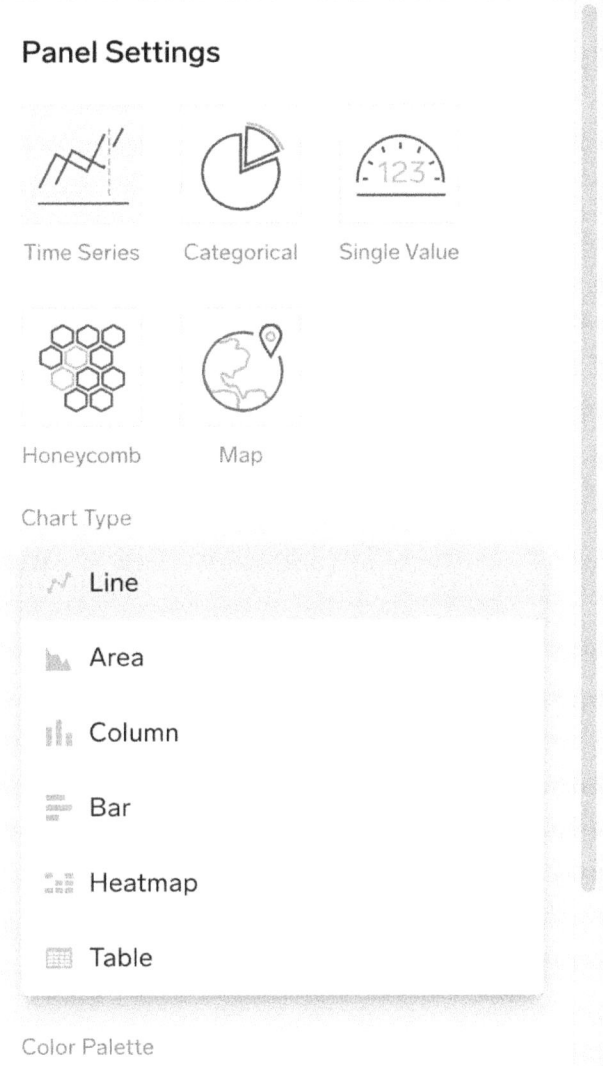

Figure 7.9 – Visualization options

On selecting a category, more granular choices within that type are available. For example, in *Figure 7.9*, you can see that the **Time Series** type has these options:

- **Line**
- **Area**
- **Column**
- **Bar**
- **Heatmap**
- **Table**

For now, I think that gives you enough information to get comfortable with the Metrics Search UI. Now, I want to move on to actual examples of metrics queries that are useful from a DevSecOps perspective.

Querying metrics

It's not often that someone starts an investigation from a metrics query, especially in the security team. I can count on one hand the number of times I've started with anything resembling a metrics query. This highlights the important dynamic and the difference between metrics and logs, mainly that logs have information about an event that has happened, which acts as the starting point, whereas metrics track things happening in the environment and, *in most cases*, are visualized. When something strange happens from a metrics perspective, that's what actually triggers some sort of investigation or question into events. This section won't go as deep as log querying, but I did want to run through a couple of examples where we query some metrics so you can see what the process looks like.

Example 1 – server CPU spike

In this example, I wanted to cover metrics around some VM activity and use them to contextualize suspicious events. Now, usually, you'd have dashboards that display information such as outbound and inbound requests, abnormalities in this behavior, and other useful metadata. However, say, for instance, that we want to find any strange behavior in our outgoing packets from Linux machines. We would go to **Metrics Explorer** and start putting the query together in the query bar.

With the default basic mode, we can select the following options from the drop-down boxes:

- **Metric**: **system.network.packets**
- **Filters**:
    - **sumo.datasource = linux**
    - **deployment.environment = ***
    - **host.group = ***
    - **host.name = ***
    - **direction = transmit**
- **Operators**:
    - **sum**[1] **by host.name**
    - **rate**[1] **all 10s**

The **Metric** field lets us specify which metric(s) we are interested in. The **Filters** section lets us add anything that can narrow the scope of the query; in this case, we want to look across our Linux machines and at the amount of bytes sent outbound. **Operators** let you apply analytics to the metrics data; in this case, we want to add together the number of packets *per hostname* with the sum operator, and the rate operator will help us calculate the increase or decrease in this metric over time. The whole query looks like this in the UI:

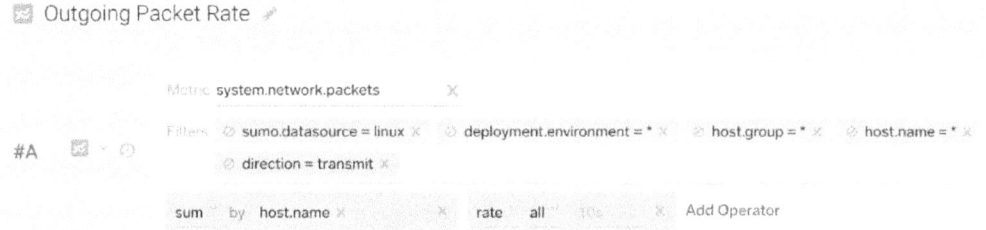

Figure 7.10 – The basic mode metrics query to view packets of data sent by our VM

> **Note**
>
> Information about the sum metrics operator can be found here: `https://www.sumologic.com/help/docs/metrics/metrics-operators/sum/`.
>
> Information about the rate metrics operator can be found here: `https://www.sumologic.com/help/docs/metrics/metrics-operators/rate/`.

With the advanced mode, we can write the same query like so:

```
sumo.datasource=linux deployment.environment=* host.group=* host.name=*
metric=system.network.packets direction=transmit | sum by host.name | rate
```

The results are displayed in a visual format, with the default being a line chart:

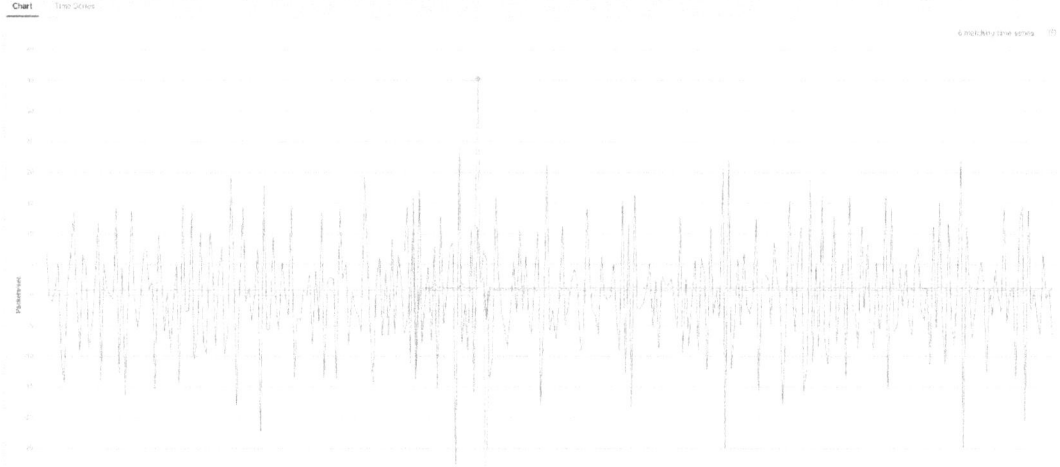

Figure 7.11 – The results from our metrics search, viewing outbound packet activity

Now, as I mentioned earlier, you have a dashboard showing you this information anyway, but let's review this as well. There's a very obvious spike in the middle of the graphic, so we can click on it to get some information on the right, letting you pivot to other related datasets as shown here:

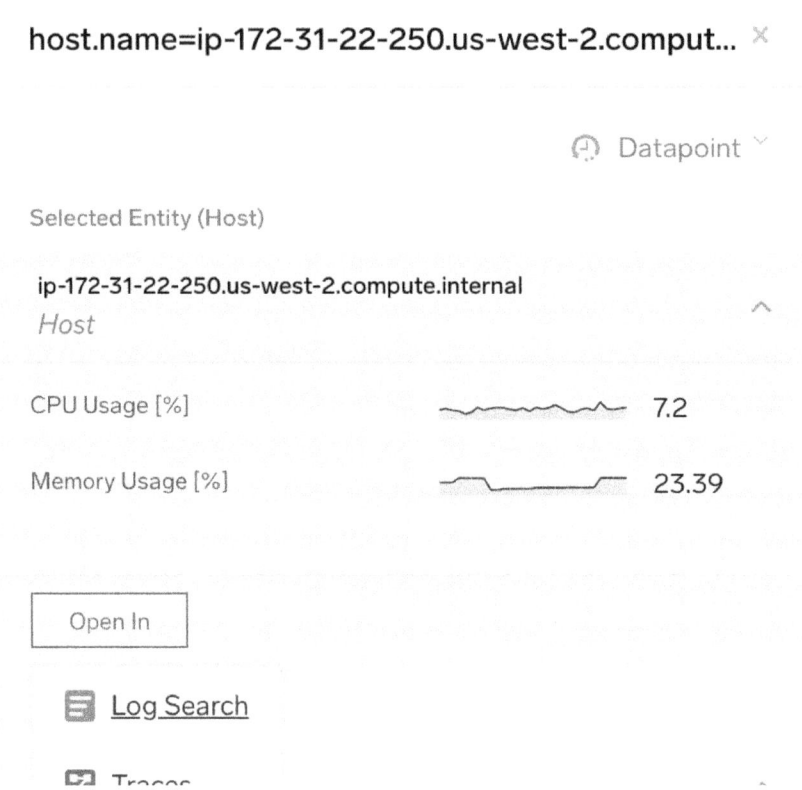

Figure 7.12 – Information about the VM in question

Select **Open In** and then **Log Search** to see what's been happening on this machine within this timeframe. It will open a search that is correlated to the timeframe of this spike automatically, so we just need to see what's been going on:

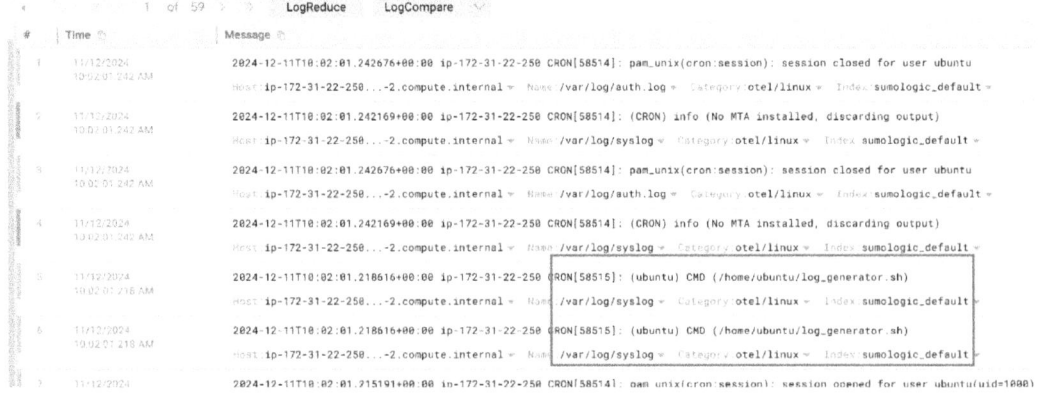

Figure 7.13 – Log results from the machine that we identified in the metrics search

Uh oh, dodgy script identified! Pivoting from metrics to logs helps you in this manner; you have the surrounding log events to put information into context. This is the advantage of having a centralized repository for your logs, metrics, and traces. Speaking of traces, let's take a look at a more detailed example where we start with metrics and make our way through spans and traces to finally land in the logs.

Example 2 – application spans and traces

Let's take a detour into the application level. We haven't done that too much, but I wanted to show you how you can query the metrics around your spans as well; it's a slightly different process. I'm in my application, and I can see that **frontendservice**, a JavaScript component, has a big red ring around it:

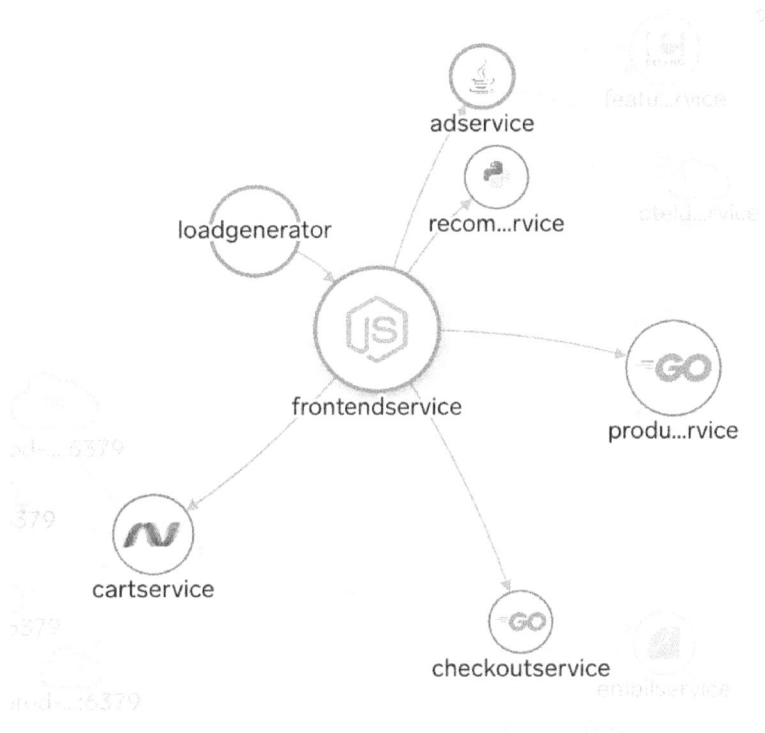

Figure 7.14 – My JavaScript-based frontendservice is not looking good!

I want to query some of the metrics to understand what might be happening. I click on one, then on **Open In**, and then on **Spans**:

Figure 7.15 – We can go to the spans of the microservice to see some metrics

I am taken to a page where I can see all the operations happening inside my application. At the top is a basic mode querying ability for spans in particular that lets me experiment with the *facets* that are extracted from my spans and traces. Facets could include the following:

- Duration
- HTTP method
- HTTP status
- URL
- Kubernetes container ID

Let's take an example just for demonstration. I want to see all of the operations my frontend service is performing and visualize the average duration of each. My filter is **frontendservice**, I'm visualizing the average duration, and I'm grouping by each operation, as seen in the following screenshot:

Figure 7.16 – The querying here is similar to the basic mode of metrics queries

As you select options, it provides facets that can be used with these aggregations. The key observation here is how easy it is to experiment with your metrics in this way. With a few clicks, you can change how it's sliced and diced and whether you get more granular or broader views of different segments of your data. The result I get for this example is shown here:

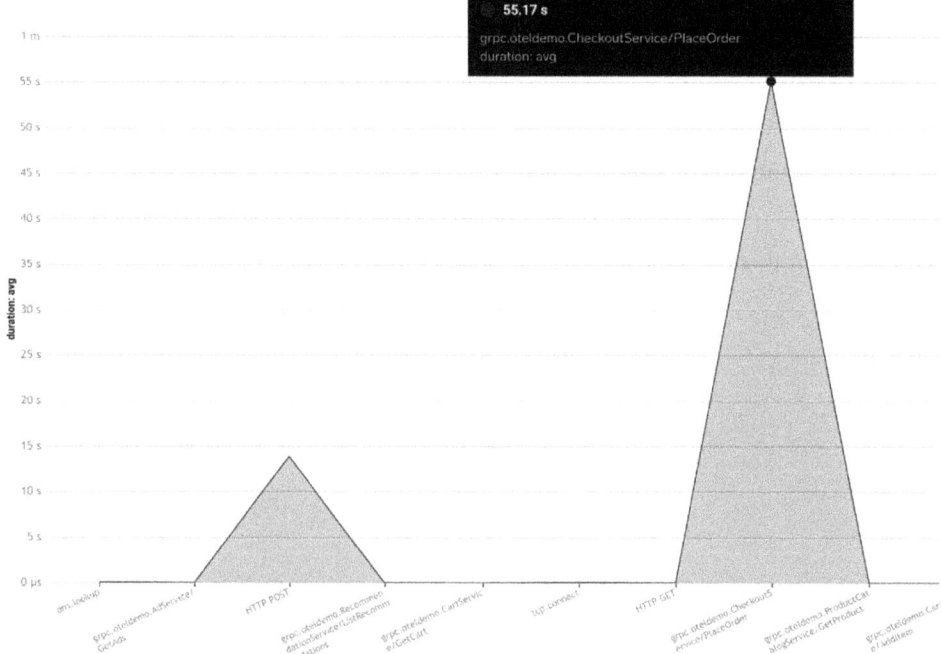

Figure 7.17 – The huge difference in behavior with the PlaceOrder API is very clear

We're able to see that our **PlaceOrder** API call is taking **55 s** on average compared to our other operations, and we can start to drill down further by searching for this operation in our logs, maybe by looking at traces to understand any bottlenecks, such as slow requests to databases or slower-than-average calls to dependent APIs.

Metrics in such cases are very useful for sifting through aggregated data in a visual way to identify operational issues like this. In most cases, a team would be alerted by Sumo Logic that this was happening much earlier, thanks to machine learning, but I hope that this example helped to highlight how you would begin with metrics in a similar scenario.

As I mentioned, we won't go too deep into the querying around metrics because the finer differences don't take long to explain. The key with metrics is playing around with aggregated views to create valuable insight into your data. We've covered enough metrics-related ground to open up the door to alerts and monitors. Now that we've looked at both logs and metrics as data types, we can more easily cover everything that monitors have to offer, which we will cover in the next chapter.

Summary

In this chapter, we looked at how we can work with metrics telemetry in Sumo Logic. This is a key pillar of DevSecOps as it is one of the four telemetry types of **MELT** (which stands for **metrics, events, logs, and traces**), and within the platform, there are numerous ways in which to apply this data to enhance your observability, security, and operations.

We started by looking at how to query metrics to extract value out of the data, and by doing so, considered the utility to not only operational teams but also security teams. Within Sumo Logic, it's possible to correlate logs across not only multiple sources but also logs and metrics, so we covered best practices to make sure you and your teams have total visibility.

We explained how we collect metrics, what their purpose is within DevSecOps philosophy, and a couple of example scenarios on how we can use metrics queries to find interesting insights in our data by discussing the types of operators available for metrics analysis.

In *Chapter 8, Alerting, Monitoring, and Visualizing Data* we'll take a look at additional tools that will help you to stretch the efficiency you're receiving from Sumo Logic. We'll be covering monitoring, alerting, and visualization, which add more ways to use your data.

References

1. https://www.sumologic.com/help/docs/search/search-query-language/search-operators/predict/#syntax-for-the-auto-regressive-model
2. https://www.sumologic.com/help/docs/metrics/introduction/metric-quantization/

Get this book's PDF version and more

Scan the QR code (or go to `packtpub.com/unlock`). Search for this book by name, confirm the edition, and then follow the steps on the page.

Note: Keep your invoice handy. Purchases made directly from Packt don't require an invoice.

8

Alerting, Monitoring, and Visualizing Data

Collecting telemetry is easy. Doing something useful with it is where most organizations fall over.

By this point in the book, we've covered how to ingest and structure logs, metrics, and supporting telemetry into Sumo Logic. That data now lives in a centralized, highly scalable data lake, queryable in real time, enriched, and ready to work. This chapter concerns the moment when observability stops being passive and starts earning its keep.

Monitors, alerts, and dashboards are how raw telemetry becomes operational awareness. In Sumo Logic, monitoring is not bolted onto a single data type or locked into rigid, pre-defined thresholds. Instead, monitors can be created across logs, metrics, and **Service-Level Objectives** (**SLOs**) using the same unified query language. Whether you're watching CPU saturation, error rates in application logs, authentication failures, or an SLO budget quietly bleeding out at 3 a.m., the mechanics are consistent and deliberately flexible.

This matters because modern systems don't fail politely, and failures rarely show up as a single metric crossing a clean red line. They manifest as subtle log patterns, compounding latency, or "everything looks fine" dashboards right up until customers start tweeting. Sumo Logic's monitoring model is designed for this reality:

- Log-based monitors detect behavioral changes, anomalies, and known bad patterns long before metrics catch up
- Metric-based monitors provide fast, lightweight signals for infrastructure and application health
- SLO-based monitors shift the conversation from "is something broken?" to "are users actually suffering?" and how much error budget remains

Because all of this telemetry lives in one platform, monitors are not constrained by data silos. You can alert on a metric and confirm it with logs. You can detect an error pattern in logs and trend it over time like a metric. You can visualize all of it together on a single dashboard without stitching tools together like a desperate arts-and-crafts project.

This chapter will cover the following topics:

- Monitor overview
- Visualizing Data

By the end of this chapter, you should be able to move from data collection to decision-making: building monitors that surface meaningful signals, alerts that people trust, and dashboards that actually get looked at.

In Sumo Logic, the word *alert* can mean different things depending on the context. For example, alerts generated from monitors or SLOs are typically operational in nature, focused on performance, availability, or reliability thresholds. These are very different from security alerts produced by the SIEM, which are based on correlated events and detection logic. In later chapters, we will cover security-specific alerting in detail, including the rules engine and the concept of Signals, which is Sumo's term for security detections. For now, when we refer to alerts in this section, we mean general platform alerts, not security signals.

Monitor overview

If you want to be alerted to a log event, metric event, or an SLO, you can create a monitor to do just that. Think of a monitor as a security guard watching for activity about which to raise an alarm. They leverage alerting policies to notify you about critical changes or issues affecting your production applications or services. A monitor can operate from three perspectives: metrics, logs, or SLOs. If you were to select the type of metric, you'd then be able to create the conditions on which to trigger an alert, as shown in *Figure 8.1*:

Figure 8.1 – Selecting how the alert will be triggered

Once an alert fires, two basic things happen. First, any actions that are configured for that alert are triggered. For example, maybe a simple notification via email or Slack is sent. Or, perhaps a more involved multi-step automated playbook is triggered. The second thing that occurs is that the alerts generated populate the **Alert Response** queue, which you can find by clicking on the **Alerts** button in the left-hand side menu. The most valuable part of these alerts is that each of the items on the **Alert Response** page has a link to drill down to a dynamic **Alert Response** page that curates and correlates all activity surrounding a particular alert. This page becomes like an analyst's workbench, where they can work to resolve or investigate the alert. It contains the following:

- Details about the alert, such as when it was fired and what triggered it
- Charts to visualize the alerting KPI before and during the alert
- Tables with the raw data that triggered the alert
- Related alerts firing in the system around the same time
- The history of the given alert being fired in the past

Before we get into building an alert monitor step by step and see the **Alert Response Page** (**ARP**) in detail, there is another concept to be familiar with, and that is the detection method the monitor uses. There are two options within the monitor creation pane: **Static** and **Anomaly**. These two options can be seen at the top of the screenshot in *Figure 8.1*. **Static** is, as you would expect, triggered when a static threshold is reached. **Anomaly** actually comes in two flavors:

- AI-driven alerting
- Outlier-driven alerting

If you opt for the **Anomaly** detection method and leave the outlier slider unchecked, the monitor will leverage machine learning to identify unusual behavior and suspicious patterns by establishing baselines for normal activity. This AI-driven alerting system uses historical data to minimize false positives and quickly detect deviations. Machine learning models drive detection by creating accurate baselines, removing guesswork and noise. The system also incorporates **AutoML** to self-tune, with seasonality detection that adjusts for recurring patterns to further reduce false positives while requiring minimal user intervention.

The outlier-driven option allows you to create monitors where seasonality doesn't really affect the data, and you just need something more straightforward to identify deviations in the data.

Here's an example: you are in the Ops team for an e-commerce business, and you want to create a monitor that will detect when your network traffic experiences a spike that you need to address. However, every Friday there is a surge in traffic because of items going on sale. An AI-driven alert will be able to take this seasonality element into consideration to better detect a genuine spike in traffic compared to one that is in line with business activity. On the other hand, an outlier-based monitor won't be able to do this and will ping you on Fridays when the network activity spikes, when it's not an anomaly!

Users can customize alert sensitivity and thresholds to provide context and filter out noise effectively. Monitors seamlessly integrate with the Sumo Logic Automation Service through one-click playbook assignments, expediting incident response by automating diagnosis and resolution, ensuring a closed-loop process from alert to recovery. Additionally, advanced detection rules, such as **cluster anomalies**, allow for precise monitoring by identifying multiple data points exceeding thresholds within a defined timeframe.

> **Note**
>
> Before Sumo Logic introduced the monitor feature, many of the same use cases were solved using **scheduled searches**. This feature still exists and is quite valuable, but for alerting on anomalies, monitors are the way to go. To see the difference between scheduled searches and monitors, visit this link: https://www.sumologic.com/help/docs/alerts/difference-from-scheduled-searches/.
>
> In short, a scheduled search is a standard log search that you save and run on a schedule, much like a cron job. Once configured, scheduled searches run continuously or on a defined interval, making them a great tool for continuously monitoring your stack by sending you query results or notifications (I know, it sounds a lot like a monitor, albeit simpler by design).

In this section, we will look at how to build a monitor from scratch and use it to monitor security logs. We will then look at what happens *after* an alert is triggered and the view that is accessible when responding to an alert, aptly named the **ARP**.

Building an alert monitor

We're going to create a monitor in this section, as well as look at the output when an alert is triggered based on our parameters. Let's start at the very beginning—putting a query together that finds suspicious activity in our security logs.

Monitoring security logs

Let's take an example of an activity we'd like to monitor from a security perspective. We're a FinTech company, and our code and financial documents are extremely sensitive, so data exfiltration is a top priority. We want to monitor any suspicious byte traffic in our environment to help detect entire patterns of traffic that are suspicious and could potentially lead to a threat. Our network data sources, grouped together in our `network_data` partition, are going to help us with this, so let's put a query together to focus on our `netflow` data, extract the total sum of bytes, and bucket it by time. Our query is as follows:

```
_index=network_data
| json "firewall_name", "availability_zone", "event" nodrop
| json field=event "event_type", "src_ip", "src_port", "dest_ip", "dest_port", "proto",
"app_proto", "netflow" nodrop
| json field=netflow "bytes", "pkts" nodrop
| where event_type="netflow"
| timeslice by 5m
| sum(bytes) as total_bytes by _timeslice
```

We can see some results, which show us an aggregated view of our bytes grouped into buckets of 5 minutes each:

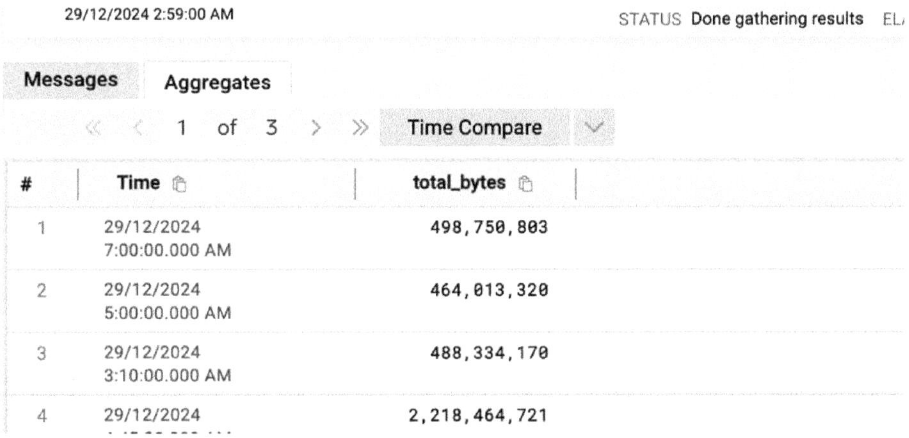
29/12/2024 2:59:00 AM
STATUS Done gathering results
Messages
Aggregates
1 of 3
Time Compare
#
Time
total_bytes
1
29/12/2024 7:00:00.000 AM
498,750,803
2
29/12/2024 5:00:00.000 AM
464,013,320
3
29/12/2024 3:10:00.000 AM
488,334,170
4
29/12/2024
2,218,464,721

Figure 8.2 – The logs monitor query, which we are going to turn into a monitor

If you remember from the *Navigating log search* section in *Chapter 6, Analyzing Data*, we can turn this logic into a monitor easily by clicking on the three dots in the top-right corner and selecting **Create a Monitor**:

Figure 8.3 – Option to create a monitor directly from the log query

This brings us to the monitor configuration panel, where we can now specify exactly how and when we would like to be alerted to events similar to this, as shown here:

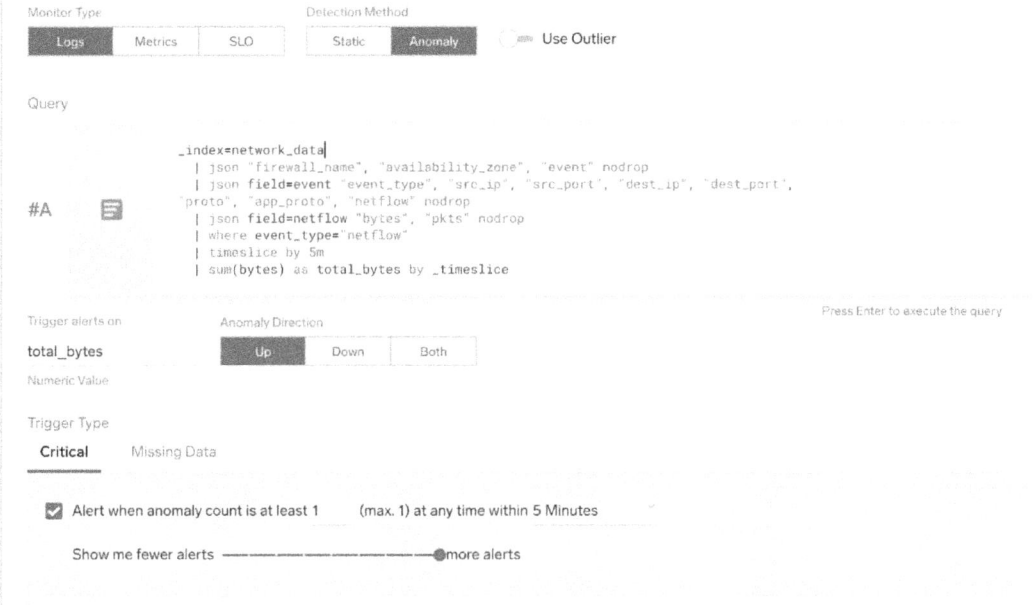

Figure 8.4 – Selecting what your monitor looks for and how an alert will trigger

Note that we added a `timeslice` operator to bucket our results. This is useful for alert creation because you can control how you want the alert to analyze your data.

Triggering the alert

One thing to bear in mind is the variable, `total_bytes`, to trigger alerts on, under the preceding query in the **Trigger alerts on** section: *Only numerical values can be used here; it's not possible to trigger alerts on strings*. So in this case, we're monitoring the `total_bytes` field within a 5-minute bucket.

> **Tip**
>
> Keep the **Alert Grouping** section from *Figure 8.1* in mind; we'll revisit it in a second, after we talk about detection methods.

As mentioned earlier, there are two main detection methods in Sumo Logic: *static* and *anomaly*. Static detection methods are the old-school way of monitoring. Choose a threshold that is concerning, and any results breaching the threshold will fire the alert. Anomaly-based detection is split into two types: *outlier* and *AI-driven anomalies*.

I find myself talking about, and recommending, anomaly-based detection to all the teams I speak to because it is so easy to use, and secondly, it alerts you in a way that reduces false positives by learning from your data in real time. For the scenario we're looking at here, it's a perfect use case for getting Sumo Logic to tell us when there is some anomalous behavior within our data.

We choose from the three trigger types:

- Critical

- Warning
- Missing Data

This will then allow us to set the thresholds and time evaluation. These different types allow you to categorize your monitors; you might not want all your alerts to be critical. For the time evaluation, here is what happens based on the window you choose:

Detection Window	Trigger Evaluation
< 15 min	Every minute
15 min to 1h	Every 2 minutes
1h to 6h	Every 10 minutes
> 6h	Every 20 minutes

Table 8.1 – A table showing how quickly the monitor evaluates based on the detection window

So, in the following example, we have selected a time window of **5 Minutes** for the alert, and we want to capture any new logs that match this query:

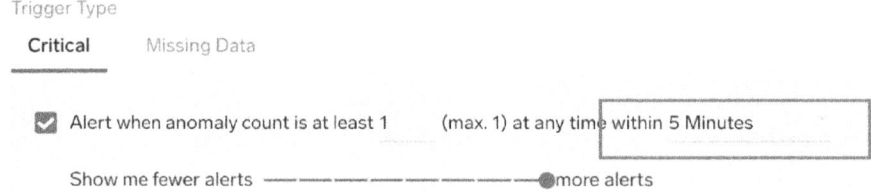

Figure 8.5 – Highlighting where the detection window is in the Trigger Type section

As we have selected **5 Minutes** as our detection window, the alert will re-evaluate every minute, effectively running a scan on our data all the time to detect this activity.

While we're here, let's run through a quick difference between outliers and AI-driven anomalies. Outliers are useful for running on data where you don't know what the thresholds are for good or bad KPI behavior. When choosing the outlier option, you can specify the top and bottom thresholds based on how far they deviate from a norm. Here's an example of some CPU time series data from our Amazon RDS instance using an outlier query:

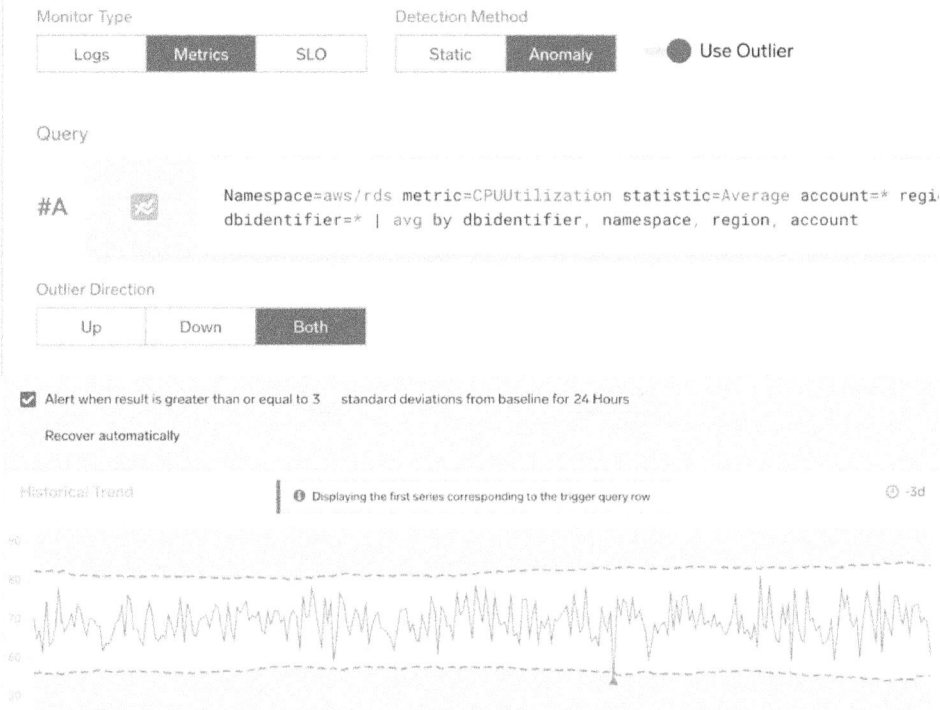

Figure 8.6 – The outlier method that looks at spikes of CPU in either direction

You can see the options: changing the number of standard deviations over a timeframe. The difference between this outlier method and the AI-driven anomaly detection that we are using for our scenario is that the AI-driven method automagically generates a model based on your *real* data and learns about it more accurately to give you a better baseline. Most importantly of all, *all of this is done automatically with no additional configuration*. Let's go back to *Figure 8.4*, so we can take a look at the options more closely:

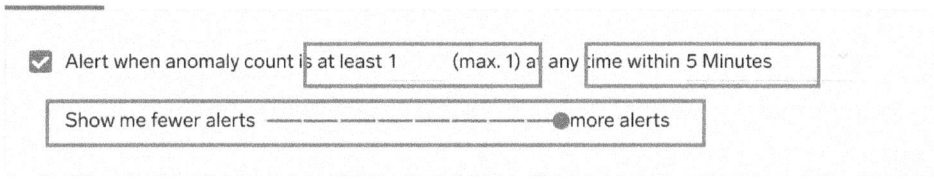

Figure 8.7 – The options available when setting up an anomaly-based monitor

From the top-left to the bottom:

- Choose the count of anomalies for the model to take into consideration. For example, if you know there is a lot of noise around your dataset, you can increase the anomaly count to account for this.
- It's worth experimenting with the detection window. Typically, it's recommended for the detection window to be 4-5x the timeslice you've set.
- Finally, you can tune your model by showing how strict you want it to be.

Now that we've talked about detection, I want to cover alert grouping. It becomes really useful when you have multiple instances of something in your environment:

- Multiple Kubernetes nodes in a microservice that need monitoring
- Multiple SQS queues in an AWS Region
- Multiple database instances supporting your applications

Alert grouping

The problem that Sumo Logic had before alert grouping existed was this: you had to make multiple monitors to cover different parts of the same service, account, or environment. For example, for each microservice in your app, you had to have separate monitors for each node that backed it. From an admin perspective, this was really cumbersome. Alert grouping was created thanks to customer feedback (the 'customer' is now a Technical Account Engineer at Sumo Logic, helping other customers do cool things. Go, Andy!), which brought it to life. Let's go back to the same RDS example we used in *Figure 8.6*, the high CPU monitor. If we had multiple RDS instances, we would need to create a separate monitor for each if we really wanted to monitor each one. However, with alert grouping, all we need to do is select how we want to group our alerts, in this case by **dbidentifier**:

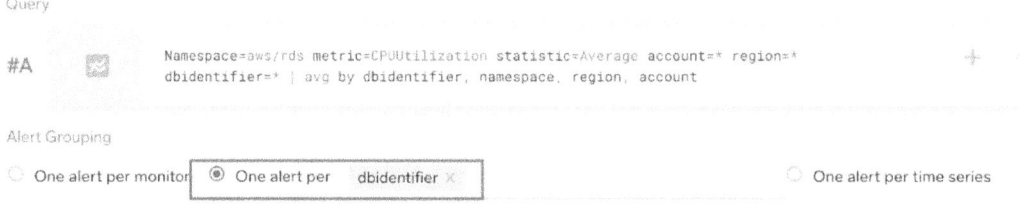

Figure 8.8 – Specifying we want the alert to group on each instance of RDS

Recovery

In this section, you can choose for the alert to auto-recover based on certain conditions. For example, if there is latency in an application that's over 2 seconds for a certain period of time, the alert will trigger. If the latency then drops below 2 seconds for a period, the monitor will auto-resolve, but you can still receive notifications for both the trigger and the resolution. We'll see examples of this later, but in security use cases, you don't want an automatic recovery to the alert, which is why we don't need the **Edit recovery settings** toggle enabled.

Notifications

When the alert triggers, we want the message to go somewhere. A lot of teams use tools such as Slack and Microsoft Teams, as well as IT Service Management (ITSM) and ticketing platforms such as Jira Opsgenie and PagerDuty. When you first select the dropdown, the only option is email. Emails are good at testing output from an alert to determine whether you're getting the correct payload. I want to run through two options with you—one where we send an email and the other where we configure an integration with Slack and send a message that way instead.

Sending an email

Let's send an email. During this process, we'll encounter alert variables[5], which let you filter through any variables you like from your data into the alert itself. For example, you might want to specify the URL that a particular user has visited, along with their IP address and the time of day. We're going to use another example here, though.

In the **Notifications** section, we select **Create New Email** before filling in any recipients.

Now, we have the subject and body sections. For the subject, let's make it clear what this alert is all about: a spike in cloud data transfer, as shown here:

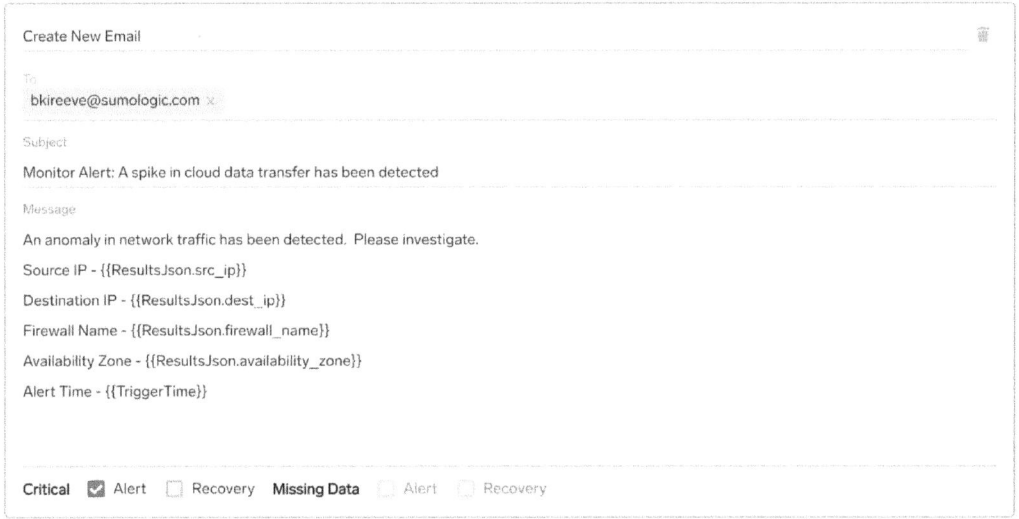

Figure 8.9 – Creating the subject line and contents of an email alert

In the message, we've got a breakdown of the Source IP, Destination IP, Firewall Name, and Availability Zone, along with the time of the trigger.

I'm accessing the variables I want with **{{ResultsJson.[x]}} - [x]** being the field of interest, so if I'm accessing the Source IP, I use **{{ResultsJson.src_ip}}**, as that is the name of the field. **ResultsJson** is an alert variable, and the most commonly used one, due to the need for customers to specify exact information from the data comprising the alert. For a full list of alert variables, you can either check the official documentation[5] or click on **Show available variables** in section **2** of the alert, **Advanced Settings**, as shown here:

Figure 8.10 – Showing the list of available variables in section 2, Advanced Settings

In *Figure 8.9*, you can see we also used another alert variable, **{{TriggerTime}}**, which shows the time the alert was triggered. You can also use this same formatting for any other type of alert destination, not only email.

Finally, importantly, at the bottom of the notification window are checkboxes with **Critical**, **Alert**, **Recovery**, **Missing data**, and so on. You have to specify what type of notification this is by checking the **Alert** or **Recovery** box for each trigger type. The reason this is done is to allow different types of notifications for the same alert based on certain parameters.

Let's look at how we can set up a connector for a particular notification technology, such as Slack or ServiceNow.

Sending a Slack message

What if we don't want to send an email, but instead we have a dedicated Slack channel where all of our teams are monitoring the latest happenings? In order to set this up, we need to create a "connector" first. Let's go to the configuration menu and select **Connections** from the **Monitoring** section:

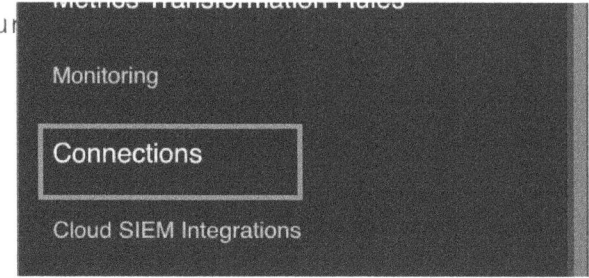

Figure 8.11 – Finding Connections under the Monitoring section of the configuration menu

This will bring us to a list of connections. Yours will be empty if this is your first time visiting, so you need to click on the **+** button in the top-right corner to arrive at a selection of technologies:

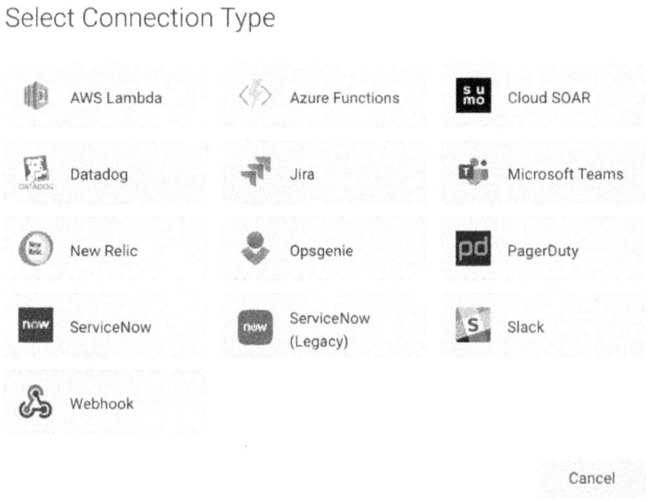

Figure 8.12 – All the different connection types available for monitors

We select **Slack** and get taken to a page where we can configure the connector as shown:

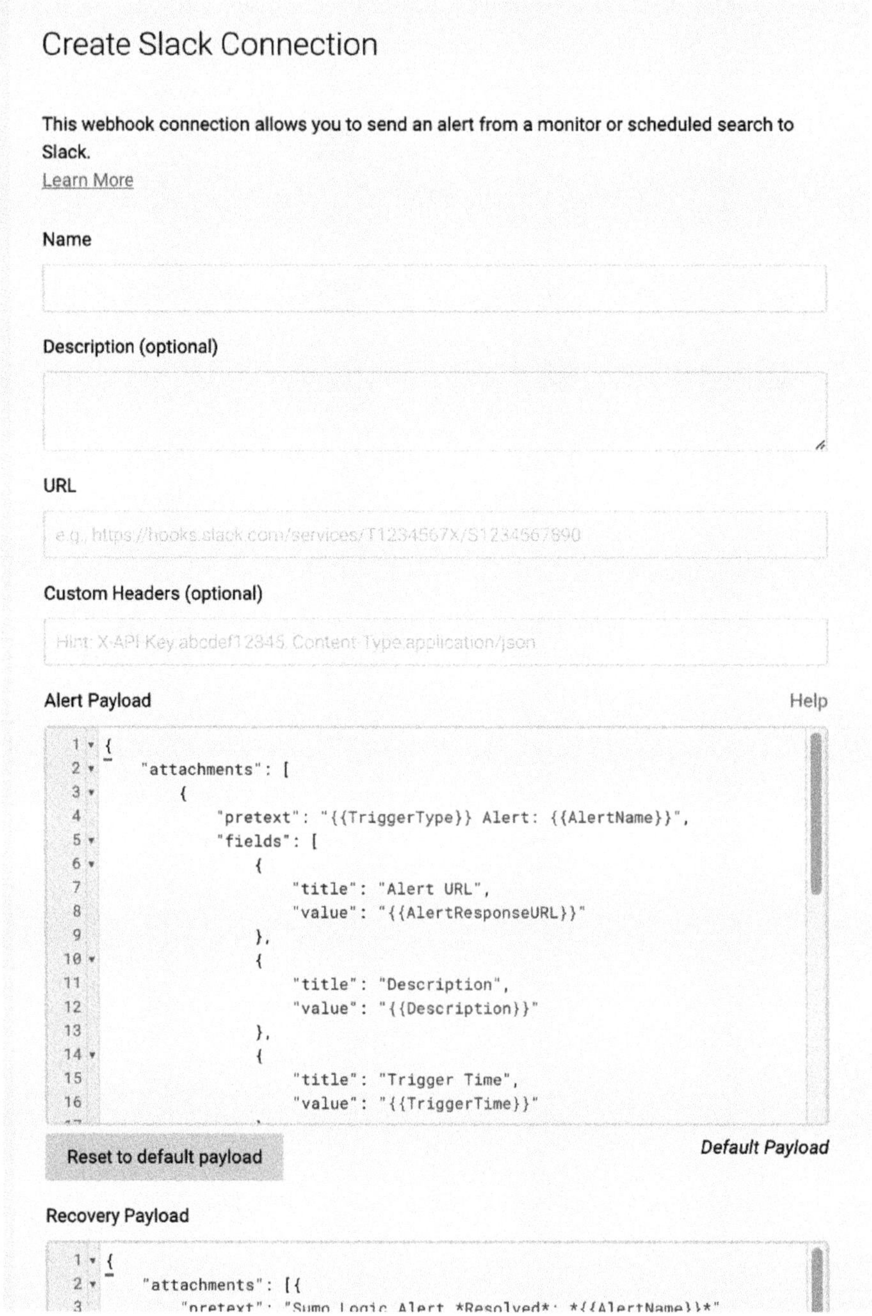

Figure 8.13 – The configuration of a Slack connector

We need to input a name for the connector, along with a URL. You'll see that an **Alert Payload** and a **Recovery Payload** already exist, and they both take various generic information to help populate the alert in the channel.

You can edit these payloads as much as you like in order to extract more useful information from your monitor. Right at the bottom is an option to test the alert and recovery payloads to see if everything is working fine, along with an option to save the connection, which means it can be referenced in the monitor creation pane. These connections are straightforward, so the whole process shouldn't take longer than a few minutes. In our case, I've amended the payload and added extra markdown; we'll see the result at the end.

Once this is set up, you'll be able to see the **Slack** channel you've set up in the **Notifications** list, like this:

Figure 8.14 – Specifying the Slack channel

Now that we know how to send notifications, there's only one last section to cover for monitoring—automation.

Automation

The conversation around automation has been growing steadily over the past few years as I have been helping customers get the most out of their data platforms. Sumo Logic not only lets you set up normal and anomaly-based alerting but also lets you automate the response. We might want to automate the escalation of an alert based on the severity or criticality of an asset involved. Maybe we want to automate the ticket management process? We will discuss the automation service in detail in *Chapter 12, Bringing a Security Intelligence Program to Life with Sumo Logic* but let's take a look at how it integrates with the monitor creation process.

This is what section 4, **Playbooks** looks like:

Figure 8.15 – An example of a text playbook, as well as specifying an automated playbook

There are two types of playbooks in the monitor configuration, which are discussed next.

Text playbooks

Text playbooks are for teams that might not be fully ready for automation yet, but just want to start standardizing processes and making them more uniform. There's a markdown field that lets you create a step-by-step response guide. For example, we could write something like this:

```
### Step 1
Visit this dashboard to confirm machines are up: https://eu.sumologic.com/dashboards/314521k35b2kj...
### Step 2
Contact Operations Team run by Joe Blogs–joe.blogs@company.com
```

And so on. A lot of operations teams have a lot of knowledge in their heads and sometimes don't have all of it down on paper, which can impact their ability to respond well and efficiently, especially when experienced team members are away from duty. Also, imagine life as a new starter to a team. So many people to meet, so much documentation to read and learn, and then a P1 strikes. Uh oh! What do we do? That's panic that no one needs in their life, so having a guided process in such cases is great for both onboarding and general resolution.

Automated playbooks

Then we have automated playbooks. These are processes that are automated with the help of low-code, no-code playbooks that automate hundreds of actions from hundreds of different technologies. When you are using one of the hundreds of ready-to-go templates or one of your own playbooks, it appears in the drop-down list in this section.

We will be covering automation in much greater detail in *Chapter 11, The Automation Service and Playbooks*.

Final details

To end the monitor creation experience, we have a few details to fill in, such as the name of the monitor, any tags you want to give your monitor, as well as a description for internal purposes, as shown:

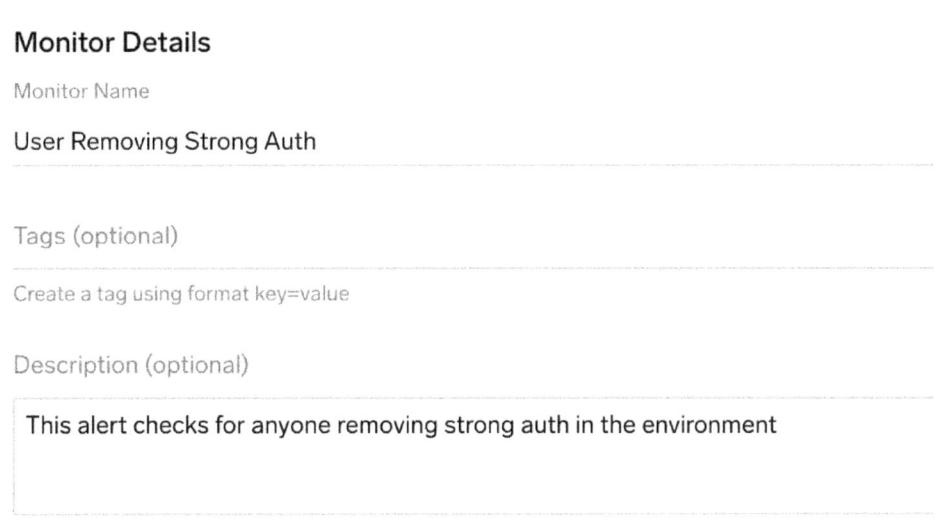

Figure 8.16 – Providing a name, tags, and a description for our monitor at the end

When we've finished our first monitor, and the activity we're looking for happens, we should get an email like this:

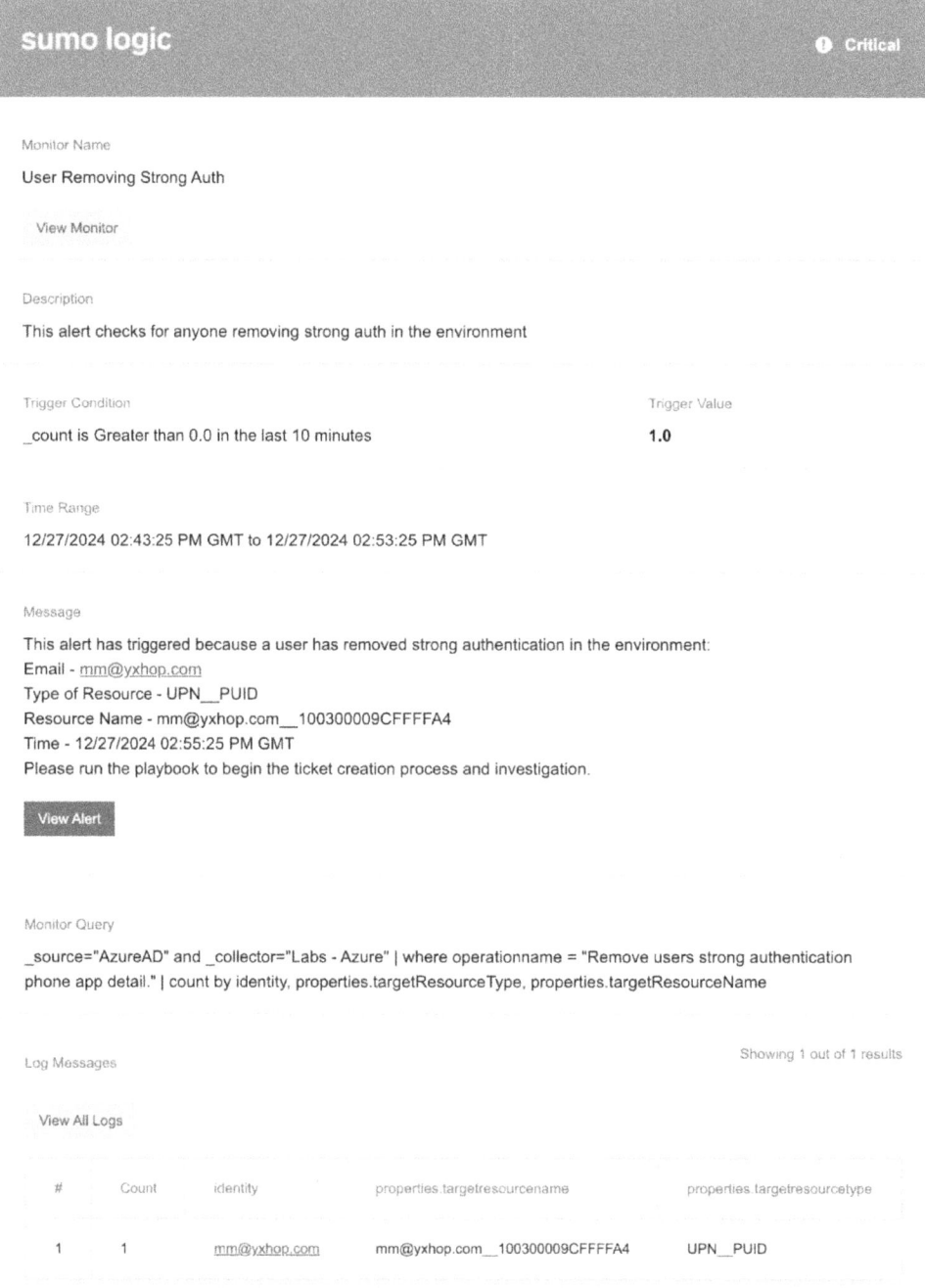

Figure 8.17 – The email we received when the alert was triggered

All the data that we specified in the **ResultsJson** variable has come through, and we have a **View Alert** option, which will take us to the ARP. We can take a look at an example of that with our DevOps monitor example, coming up next.

Before that, let's take a look at what our Slack alert looks like as well:

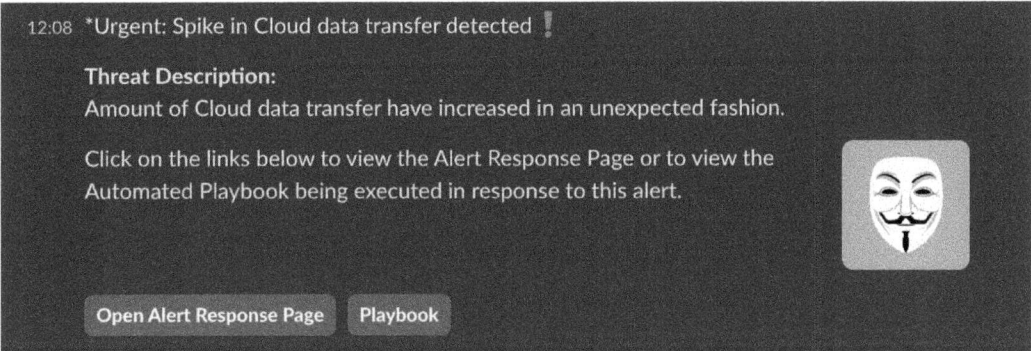

Figure 8.18 – What our alert looks like in Slack—it's completely customizable!

The ARP

The ARP is a place where useful contextual information is condensed together around a common time frame to help you work out the following:

- What the issue is
- How and where to resolve it

There is a mix of log-based and machine-learning-driven context to tap into, so let's see what this looks like during a real alert.

Visualization

At the top of the ARP, we've got a visualization of what occurred:

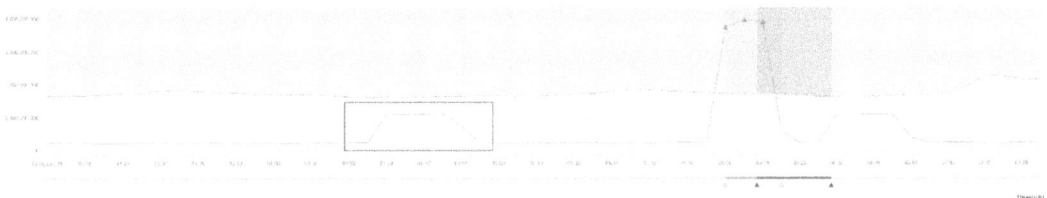

Figure 8.19 – The visualization of the event

There isn't anything fancy about the visualization, but note that due to the way the model is generated on your data and with the high-level config we enter during monitor creation, the model can find anomalies accurately. For instance, the spike you see prior to the actual anomaly on the right, in the box, is a false positive. It was ignored due to the historic learning it was able to apply when putting together the baseline. *That's fancy*.

There's more to the ARP, though, with plenty more context to discover from the surrounding data and environment.

Log context

If we scroll down, we get to all the logs that have been observed during the timeframe of the alert. This is useful because it correlates all the logs you need to help determine the root cause without having to manually query across the right time and data. It's like getting to a crime scene, and everyone's gathered all the forensic data and given it to you in a nice bundle. Bear in mind that this view is not meant to be a needle-in-the-haystack approach at this point:

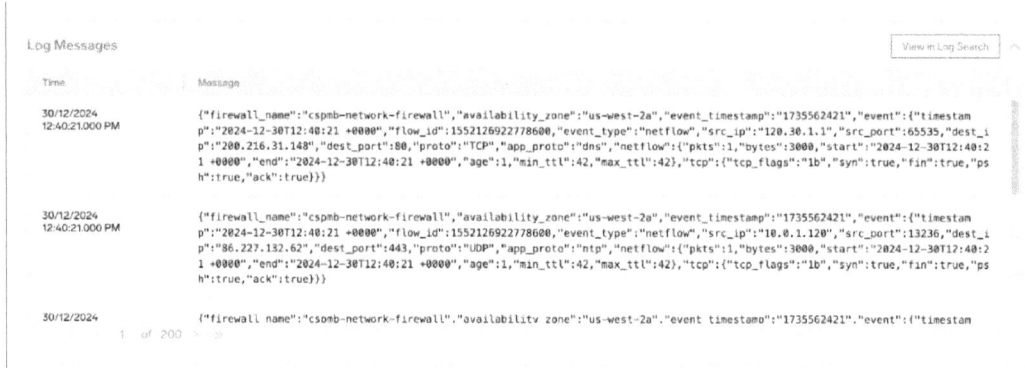

Figure 8.20 – A view of all the logs automatically correlated to the alert timeframe

As we explored in the previous chapter, when looking at LogReduce, we can easily pivot into all the logs from here and analyze the logs further. As we've already covered this previously, let's look at some other parts of the ARP UI, such as the related alerts.

Related alerts

On the right side of the UI, we can see other related alerts that have taken place at the same time. Sometimes, two separate alerts are part of the same incident; in the following screenshot, we can see two interesting events that happened at roughly the same time:

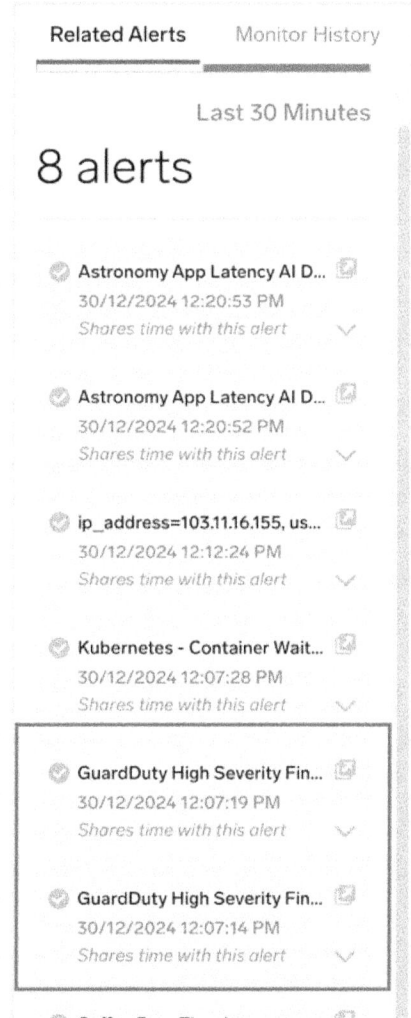

Figure 8.21 – Two interesting GuardDuty alerts

Clicking on one of these GuardDuty alerts will take you to the relevant alert, so you can see the visualization, logs, and other context:

Figure 8.22 – The GuardDuty High Severity Findings alert we have pivoted into

If we click on **View in Log Search** above the log entries, we get to an aggregated view that shows us the content of the logs. Apparently, a data exfiltration threat has been identified, and we can see the instance ID of an EC2 instance, as well as a destination IP address, as shown:

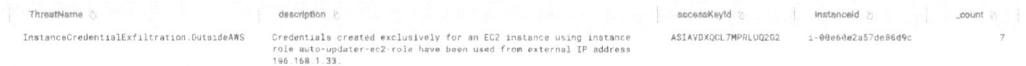

Figure 8.23 – The logs from GuardDuty are telling us about potential data exfiltration

Let's take note of the instance ID and the destination IP, which is 196.168.1.33. Going back to the ARP, let's look at another bit of context we haven't covered properly yet—alert context.

Alert context

This is context driven by machine learning using a few methods, but the two you will most commonly encounter are as follows:

- Log fluctuations
- Dimensional explanations

Log fluctuations are based on LogReduce and LogCompare. They monitor changes in signatures over a time period to show you how these correlated logs might be noteworthy. There are three categories within these changes in signature:

- New
- Changed
- Missing

Based on how the signature has changed over time, one of these labels will be applied. When an event takes place, there is usually an influx of logs, and one of the hardest things to do is identify the exact influx and what it consisted of with manual querying. That's exactly where log fluctuations are useful; they show you what that influx consisted of and how it compares to events before this alert. If you can see some incoming logs that are correlated with the alert taking place on the same timeline, that's going to help speed up your response to the problem.

Dimensional Explanations, part of **Alert Context**, uses analytics to identify which data points and key value pairs most likely caused the alert we're looking at. We have an example in our GuardDuty alert—let's take a look:

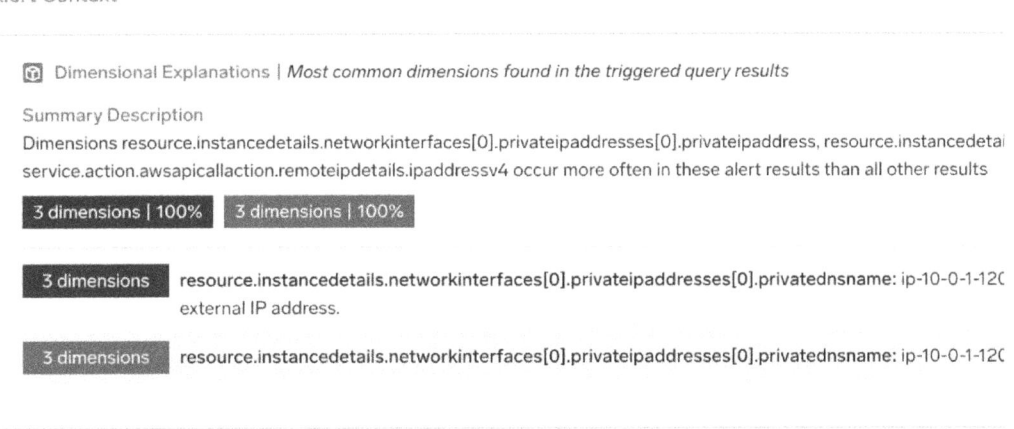

Figure 8.24 – Dimensional Explanations tells us what most likely caused this alert

We've had to zoom in a bit here, so you can't see the full entry, but the IP address 10.0.1.120, which is linked to a specific network interface, has been seen consistently within the data behind this alert. It looks like an internal IP address, so let's save it along with the instance ID and destination IP we came across earlier and head back to the original alert from the spike in transferred bytes and to the **Playbooks** button at the top of the screen.

Playbooks

The playbooks available to us in the alert are configured when setting up the monitor. At the top of the ARP, we have a **Playbooks** button. Click on it to see the text-based playbooks and automated playbooks linked to the alert:

Figure 8.25 – A text playbook and an automated playbook attached

Our playbook is telling us to visit our **AWS Network Firewall** dashboard, which we will do in a second. We also have an **Automated Playbooks** option at the bottom.

> We're going to leave the automated playbook until *Chapter 12*, where we will revisit it and bring this alert response to its conclusion.

As mentioned previously, the **AWS Network Firewall** dashboard is a great way to centralize knowledge in your teams to make it easy to aid response efforts across your teams. If we visit the dashboard, we see the following:

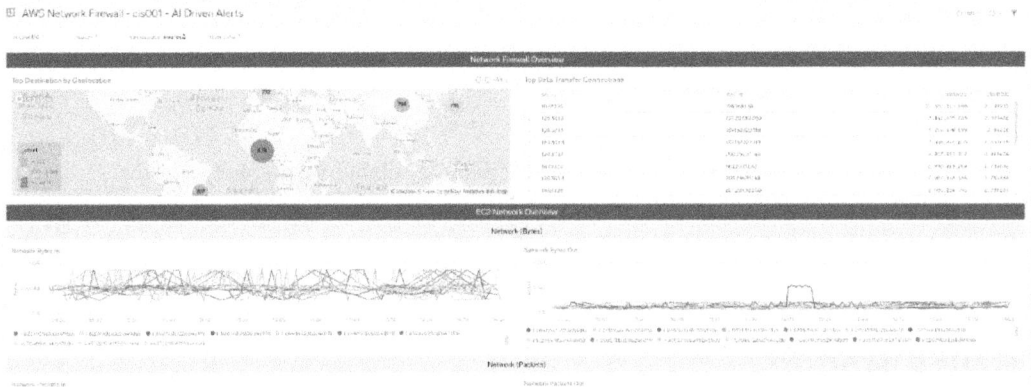

Figure 8.26 – The AWS Network Firewall dashboard, which is linked to our cloud spike alert

This is a bit hard to see, so let me zoom in on two of the most important panels here. The first is **Top Data Transfer Connections**, which lists the top data transfer connections by total size and inbound and outbound IP addresses:

src_ip	dest_ip	sizeBytes	sizeInGiB
10.0.1.120	196.168.1.33	22,655,115,000	21.09922
120.30.1.1	221.207.32.250	3,145,479,025	2.929456
120.30.1.1	139.162.122.110	3,056,470,599	2.84656
120.30.1.3	139.162.122.110	3,046,944,016	2.837688
120.30.1.1	200.216.31.148	3,017,895,312	2.810654
10.0.1.120	86.227.132.62	2,990,029,289	2.784682
120.30.1.3	200.216.31.148	2,989,843,188	2.784508
10.0.1.120	221.207.32.250	2,985,224,796	2.780207

Figure 8.27 – Top data transfer connections

Our source IP and destination IP addresses sit at the top, with a huge data transfer size between them in the last 5 hours. Further, the panel below shows us network bytes out by instance ID. Let's see if the instance ID we saw in the logs, **i-00e60e2a57de86d9c**, is on here:

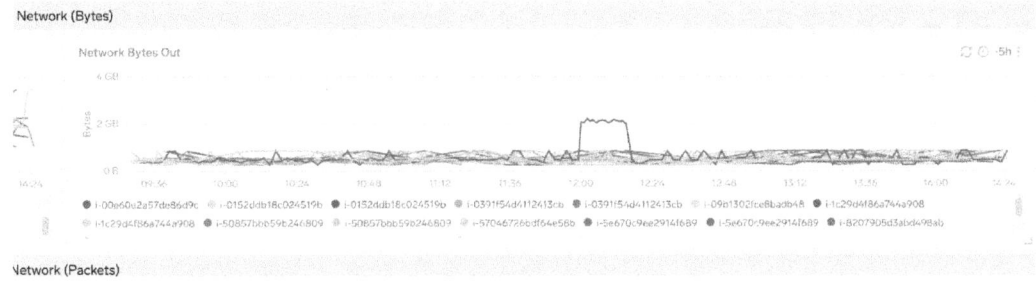

Figure 8.28 – Network bytes out

Our instance ID from the log search is clearly showing signs of increased outbound bytes activity.

Just by clicking through the data we've seen in the ARP and the context provided, we've been able to confirm that data exfiltration took place, and also isolate the following key variables:

- The instance ID of the EC2 machine
- The source and destination IP addresses
- The surrounding information around the account name, availability zone, and so forth

All of this serves to help our teams understand what happened to cause an alert and quickly find out how to deal with it, setting us up for better detection and response capabilities. Now, as we're on a dashboard, let's do a deep dive into the visualization available in Sumo Logic.

Visualizing data

One of the benefits of having a powerful query language is that you can dissect the data any way you like, which opens up the door to visualizing that data in myriad ways. Within Sumo Logic, you can create any view that you want from your data, as well as take advantage of a wide range of ready-made content for a lot of different technologies, which takes the strain away from having to create your own. There are many use cases for having useful visualizations of your data; these three are the main ones I encounter:

- A consolidated view of multiple clouds, services, and applications
- Compliance reporting
- Security and observability monitoring

In this section, we'll build a dashboard from scratch and explain key concepts as we go so you can create your own in any situation. Then we'll look at the App Catalog and some great examples of pre-made dashboards for your use.

Building our first dashboard

The first thing to note about dashboards is that they *only work with aggregated data*. Metrics are already aggregated when we do any form of metrics query; however, with logs, we need to use operators such as count by in order to create aggregations. With this in mind, let's see how we can spin up a few panels for ourselves to start getting a consolidated view of events across our AWS and Azure cloud environments.

Panel #1 – top 10 users

With AWS, we'll be focusing on CloudTrail data to understand login patterns of our users and layer some threat intelligence on top. I want to get a list of the top 10 users who have been logging into AWS. It's a pretty straightforward query.

For a lot of these examples, I'll try to use Mobot wherever possible, in order to show how streamlined the whole visualization process is. This is my Mobot query:

```
Give me a list of top 10 users that have logged in, ignore those logs with no username
```

We get the following result in a table by default as the data has been aggregated with the count by operator by Mobot:

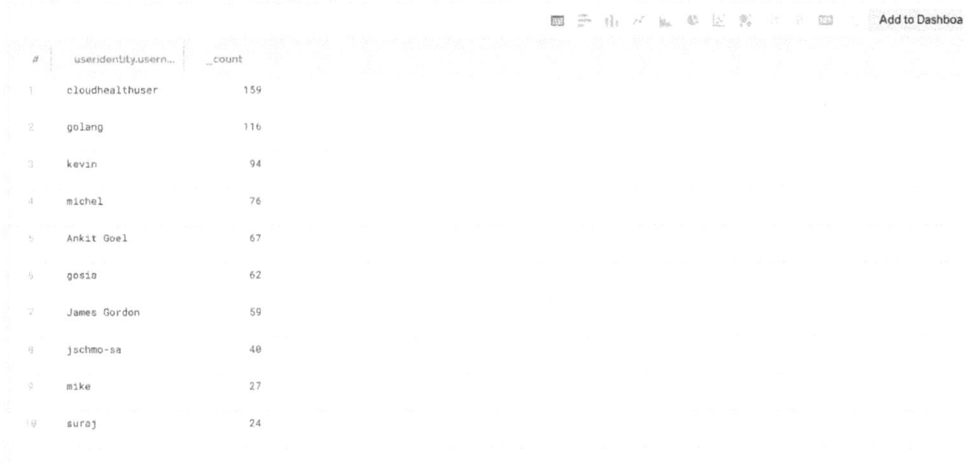

Add to Dashboa
#
useridentity.usern...
_count
1 cloudhealthuser 159
2 golang 116
3 kevin 94
4 michel 76
5 Ankit Goel 67
6 gosia 62
7 James Gordon 59
8 jschmo-sa 40
9 mike 27
10 suraj 24

Figure 8.29 – Top 10 list of users logging in the most on AWS

We can use the icons at the top of this table to have different views of the same data—for example, a bar chart:

Add to Dashboard
_count

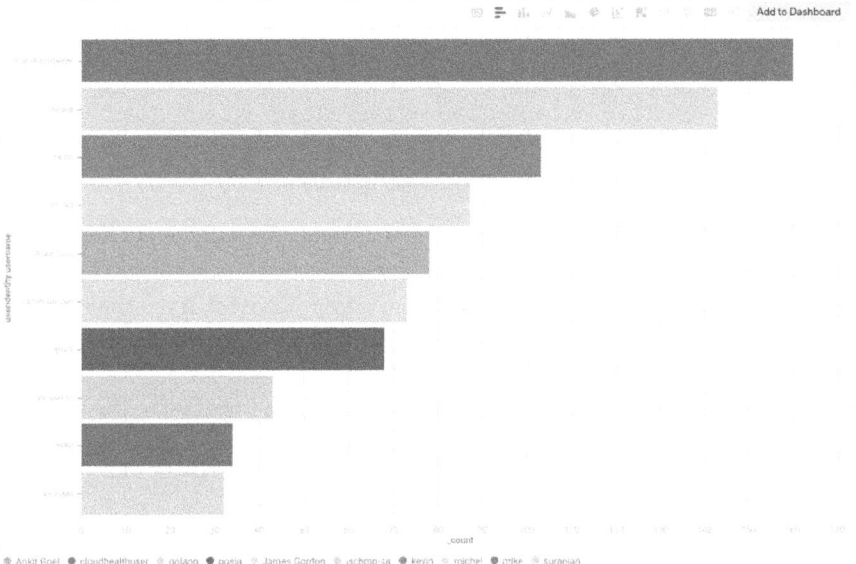

Figure 8.30 – A bar chart depicting our top 10 most frequently logged-in users

Whatever we choose, we can just click the **Add to Dashboard** button in the top right corner to add it to a dashboard of our choice or even create one from scratch. If we click it, we see the following:

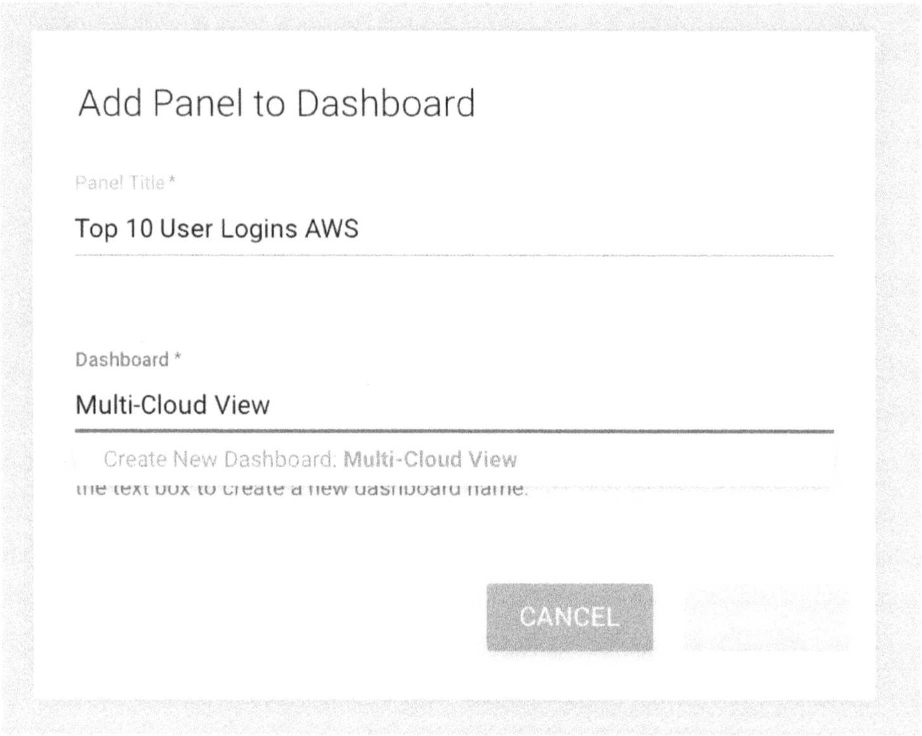

Figure 8.31 – Add panel to dashboard

As you can see, you have the option of naming the panel and choosing the dashboard before creating the visualization. In this example, I want to create a new dashboard, so I just give it a name and get given the option to create it. You can also choose any existing dashboard from a drop-down list. If you choose to create a dashboard, you'll be asked where to save it. Choose **Personal** or a team folder and you'll see the beginnings of your dashboard:

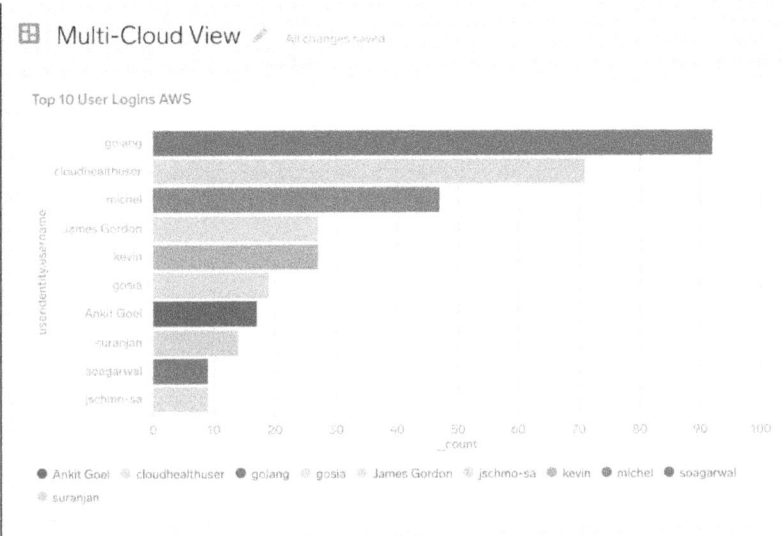

Figure 8.32 – Our first dashboard panel, looking at the top 10 user logins

Let's keep adding some more panels to get a useful dashboard.

Panel #2 – outliers in failed logins

We want to look at login *failures* now and try to identify anomalies in this behavior. Let's go back to Mobot and rephrase our request:

```
Show me all login failures. Count by timeslice of 5 minutes and find outliers
```

This is the result we see:

Figure 8.33 – A dashboard panel showing outliers in login activity

If we add this to our existing dashboard, here is our updated view:

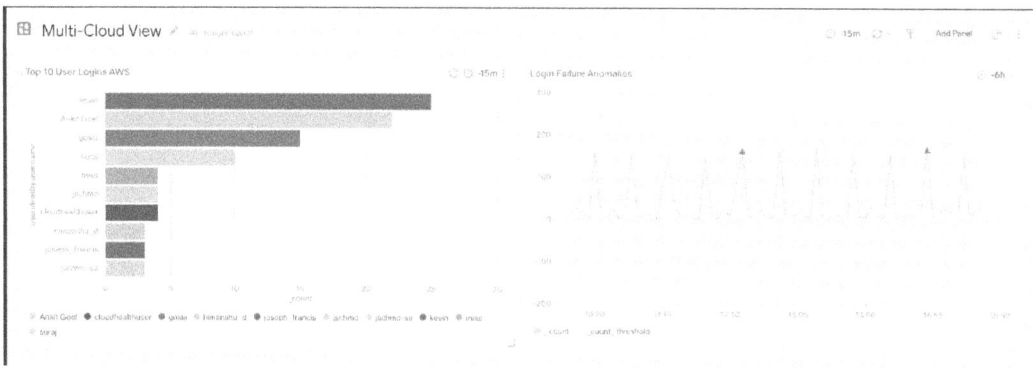

Figure 8.34 – Another panel added to our multi-cloud dashboard

Azure data and text

I'm going to speed things up a bit now and add some Azure panels to the dashboard. These queries will be the same as for the AWS source, top 10 logged-in users, but using an Azure Active Directory source instead.

Here is our dashboard with that Azure data added:

Chapter 8

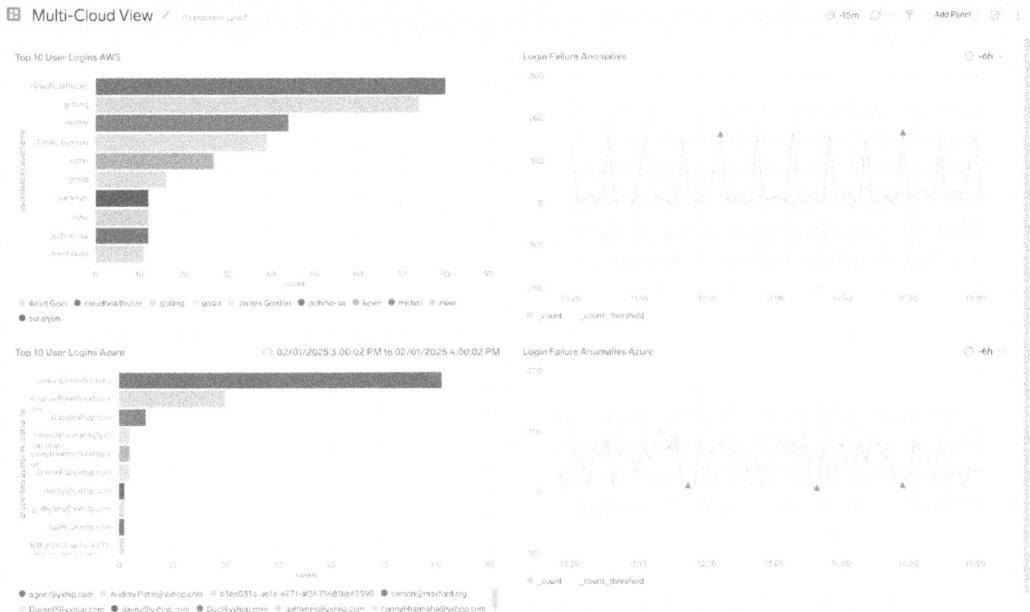

Figure 8.35 – AWS and Azure login activity consolidated view

Apart from the panel names, it still might not be completely clear what the view is here. Let's make it a bit more organized and add some helpful text. In the top right corner of your dashboard, you'll be able to see a button called **Add Panel**. This lets you add a blank visualization *before* you write a query and also allows you to do things such as add plaintext elements to your visuals. Let's click on it and select **Text**:

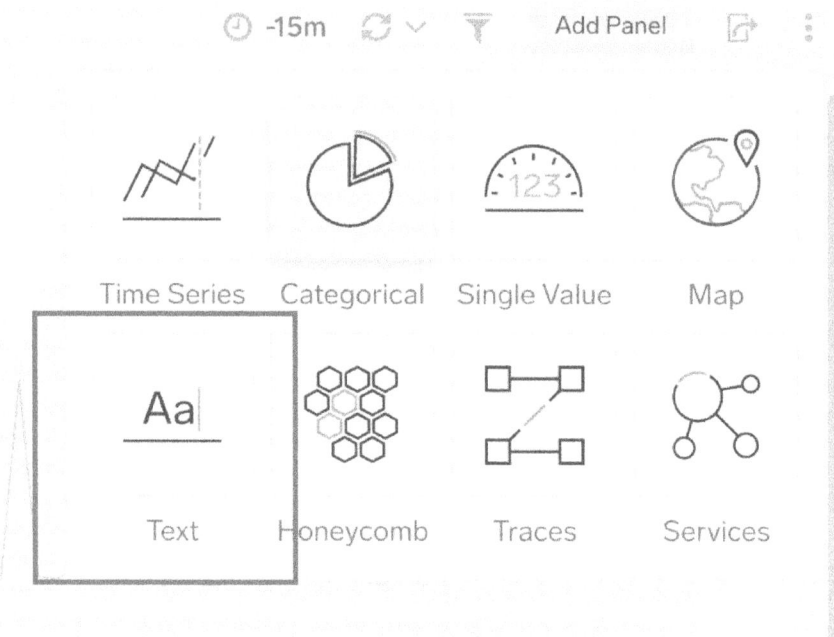

Figure 8.36 – Add text option

A configuration page opens up that lets you create a title, write any text messages you like, and choose sizes, colors of text, and a few other things. I've added **AWS Login Activity** as the heading and gone for a bright color, so we can easily read it:

Figure 8.37 – Adding text to the dashboard lets you customize it

We can add another one for the Azure data, and we'll have a complete dashboard:

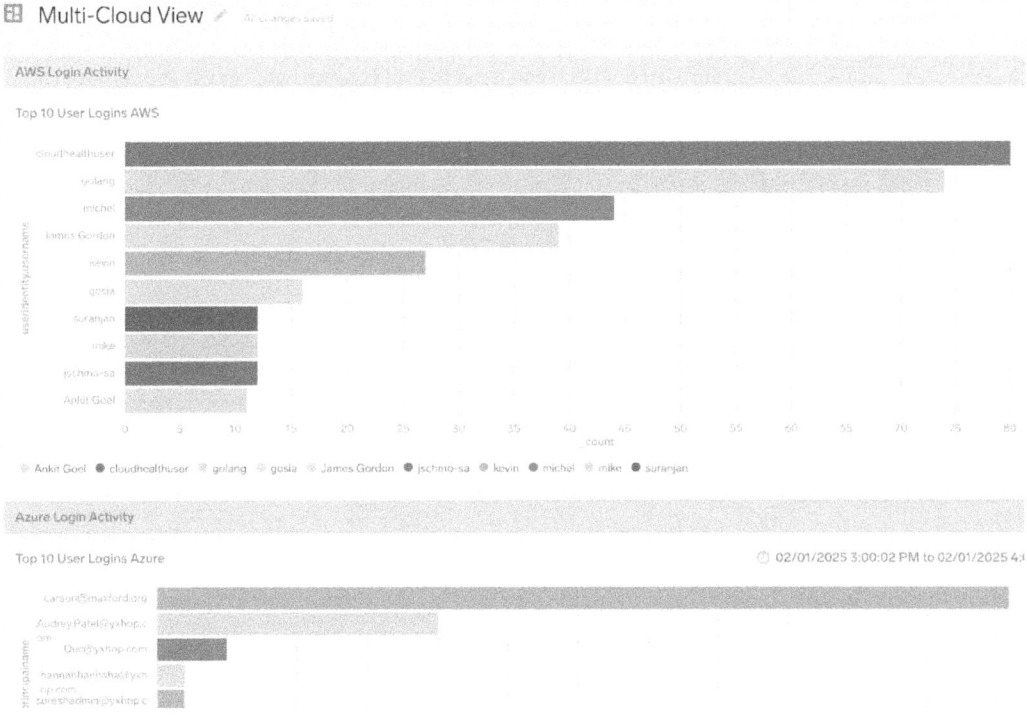

Figure 8.38 – AWS and Azure data split view for clarity

In only a few minutes, we've put together a functional multi-cloud dashboard. We can add GCP panels, and we can add more flavor around some of the AWS and Azure services in this consolidated view; whatever helps us get the context and insight we need, we can add. As we'll see, there are plenty of interesting and useful dashboards that come ready to go. Next, we'll cover some of the configuration options within the dashboard itself that I think are worth knowing about.

Dashboard configuration

Once you have a dashboard, apart from looking at it with your eyes, there are plenty of other things you can do with it. It might be pretty, but let's not get complacent! You can do things such as the following:

- Set the global or panel timeframes to have multiple time lenses
- Tell it how often to auto-refresh
- Turn it into a report
- Share it
- And more...

I thought it would be worth covering the capabilities in this section.

Timeframes

Changing timeframes within the dashboards is like being a surgeon and having a scalpel to precisely carve the data you're seeing into whatever granularity of time you need to find your answer. At the top right of the dashboard, you'll see options for the global time:

Figure 8.39 – The global time picker for the entire dashboard and all of the individual panels

We'll explore the other options there in a bit. While we're on the topic of time, let's look at the individual panels. In the top-right corner of each panel, you'll find a time picker as well. This is where you can change the time on a panel *separately from* the global dashboard time:

Figure 8.40 – The time picker on an individual pane

Let's revisit the top section next, and we'll look at auto-refresh, template variables, sharing, and other options.

Auto-refresh

If you have an operational need to view data in near-real time and have visualizations that stay up to date for either security or observability requirements, you can set auto-refresh on your dashboards. Imagine the CIA or MI6 cyber teams in films surrounded by displays showing triangulation points, personnel, and location markers. It allows you to monitor your assets and environment, and the whole room can monitor and respond more quickly. When you click on the dropdown on the auto-refresh icon, it will let you select how often you want to auto-refresh your dashboard, as shown here:

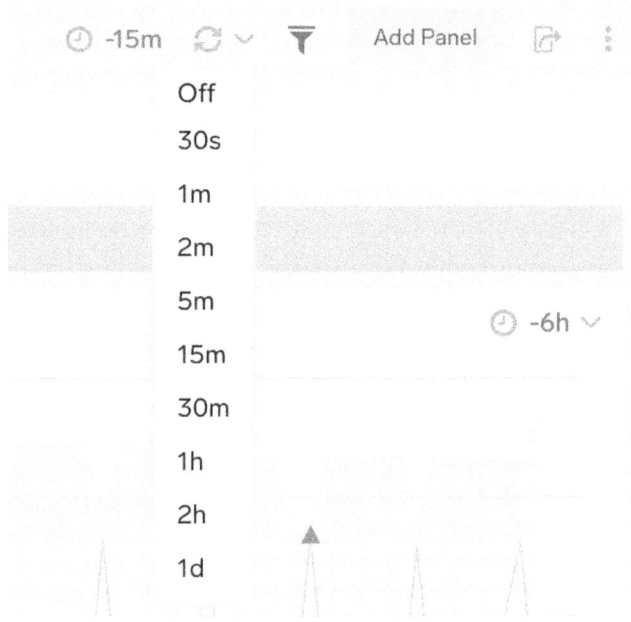

Figure 8.41 – The auto-refresh options available for dashboards

Note that you can even set the auto-refresh interval with the Sumo Logic API[6] or the Sumo Logic Terraform Provider[7]. Use these if you want to automate any part of your visualization capabilities.

Editing panels

We're going to look at editing panels after creation, and this is useful for several reasons. For instance, changing visual types might be required, adding thresholds, and linking to other contextually tied dashboards. Let's see how we can do that. The three dots at the end of the menu in the top right corner let us access some additional options, such as **Save** and **Export**:

Figure 8.42 – Additional options

We'll have the option to do things such as export the dashboard in various formats, save it somewhere, and of course choose between light and dark modes. Any self-respecting operations team can't be having light view dashboards.

Every single panel that we see inside a dashboard lets us zoom in to have a closer look at the data behind it; this can be done by viewing that data with the appropriate option. For example, if it's a log-based panel, like our top 10 users logging in on AWS, we can go directly to the logs making up that panel by clicking on the three dots in the top-right corner of the panel and selecting **Open in Log Search**:

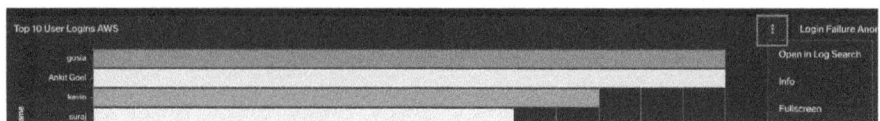

Figure 8.43 – Each panel has three dots for deeper query options or editing

The same applies to the metrics panels and even traces and service maps. I've gone to **Add Panel** for the dashboard and added a service map view of some application data I have in the instance to create this panel:

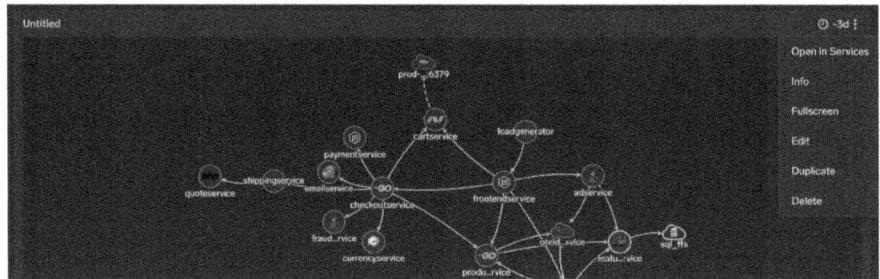

Figure 8.44 – A service map view of my applications and services for a specific application

When clicking on the three dots, I can see it takes me straight to the services part of the **Observability** view, which can give me a finer view of these different services.

Let's go back to our first panel and go to **Edit**, just to see what control we have over the data and visuals of the panel.

You'll be able to see the query at the top of the screen, the visual from the panel, and along the right, you'll see the configuration. I'm going to give you a whistle-stop tour of the most visited places rather than hanging out around every nook and cranny here. The headings on the right are in numbered order:

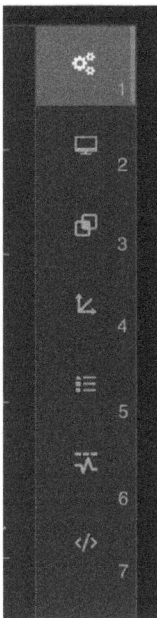

Figure 8.45 – The seven sections available to you when editing your dashboard

The options are briefly explained here:

1. **General**: Change the title font size and link dashboards. To add a link, select **Add Dashboard Link**, choose the dashboard, and it'll be linked. See *Figure 8.45*.
2. **Display**: Lets you change the visual style and color palettes.
3. **Display Overrides**: Override data types to tell more of a story by customizing the data to a form that makes the most sense to you. An example is shown in *Figure 8.46*.
4. **Axes**: Re-label axes on the chart.
5. **Legend**: Sets font sizes and positions of legends.
6. **Thresholds**: Sets visual thresholds on the chart (shown later in *Figure 8.57*).
7. **JSON**: View JSON code for the dashboard to export or use elsewhere.

Display Overrides

Sometimes you need to have more direct control over your visual information—highlighting a metric in a specific color, renaming an axis, stuff like that. You can use the **Display Overrides** panel to do that. Here's a super quick showcase. I have a username in my data called **SumoIntegrationRole**, whoever that is. Anyway, I want to change that name to **Testing** and also make their bar appear purple in my panel. *Figure 8.46* shows these options I've selected, but there's lots more to tinker around with here if need be:

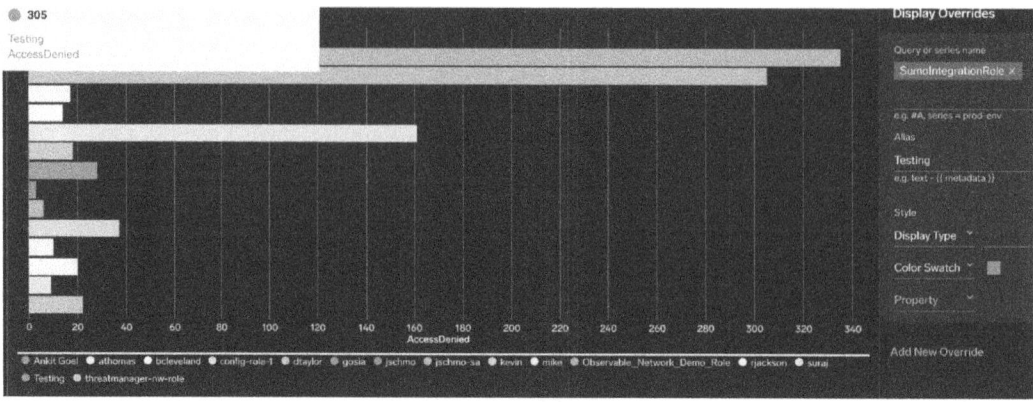

Figure 8.46 – Overriding some of the visual elements in our dashboard panel

Template variables

You can set variables within your dashboards that will filter the panels based on your selection. For example, if you want to quickly filter down your EC2 CPU usage by machine to a particular machine, you can select it from a list. If you see a Linux host behaving strangely, you can filter it quickly. Let's go over this process, as it's very useful to know.

Clicking on the funnel-shaped icon presents the template variables and lets you create a new one if you have none on the dashboard:

Figure 8.47 – The icon to show or hide the template variables in the dashboard

Some out-of-the-box dashboards already come with template variables, but if there are none, you should see the option to create one, as shown here:

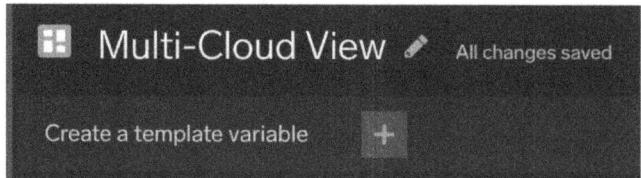

Figure 8.48 – The option to add a template variable from scratch

You can create template variables by building a query and then extracting the fields you want out of it. For example, we want to create a filter that looks at usernames and filters them out for us so we can see their logins in the dashboards. There are three types of variables we can choose from:

- Logs

- Metrics
- Custom

The first two are self-explanatory, and the third lets you create custom variables for your dashboards. Here is what our example looks like—we've chosen the variable type, named our variable, entered our query, and then pulled out the field we want, which is the **Key**:

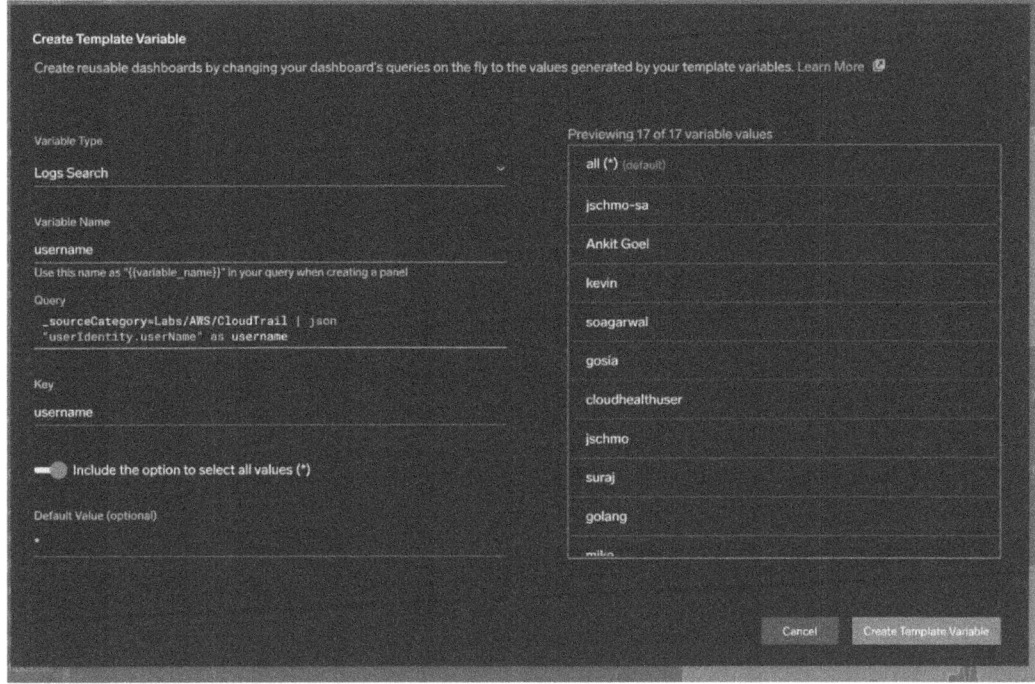

Figure 8.49 – Our example template variable for the dashboard

After you've created the template variable, you'll be able to filter on all the values the key brings back by selecting them from a list:

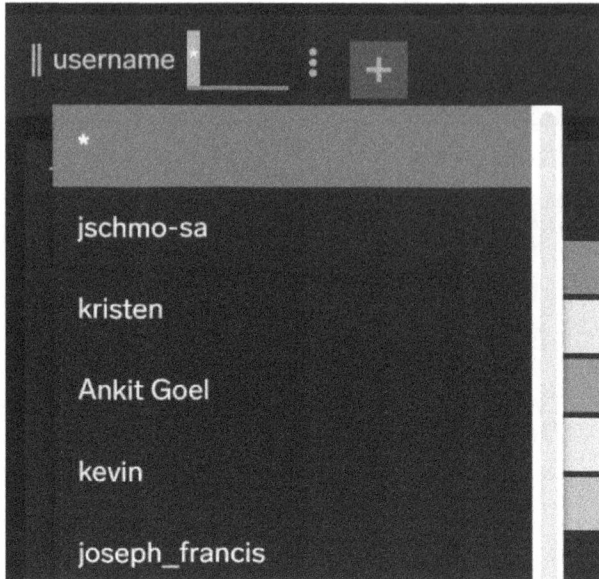

Figure 8.50 – The list of values from our template variable

Let's not forget the final step, which is to modify or create queries in your dashboard panels that actually use these template variables. To follow the example from *Figures 8.49 and 8.50*, let's create a query that will let you filter on the usernames present within the AWS CloudTrail dataset we've been working with. The query is shown in *Figure 8.51*:

Figure 8.51 – A query that uses the template variable filter

In Sumo Logic, you use mustache syntax in order to choose which variables in a query are affected by the template variables you have set, similar to what we've done in *Figure 8.51*, so now you know how to get your panels to respond to the filters in the dashboard!

Template variables help with ease of use when it comes to dashboards and helping users select the right data they need. One of the things that tends to happen with dashboards is that they get shared—internally, externally, it could be anywhere. In this next bit on sharing dashboards, I'll also talk about how content such as a dashboard actually lives in Sumo Logic.

Sharing a dashboard

So, we want to share a dashboard. It could be with an executive, with your team, or with another part of your business. It helps to have a flexible way of doing this, but before we start with sharing, let's look at dashboard content in general. This will also set us up nicely for the next section about the App Catalog and out-of-the-box content.

Every single user has a mini-tenant within their Sumo Logic instance for content. This allows users to experiment with dashboards before releasing them to their team, for example, or create content that's useful for them. Someone in the team might have a way of improving a query or, like previously, incorporating some template variables, but they don't want to play around with the main dashboard because, well, it's up on a massive monitor, looking at our microservices' health. The user can replicate it to their personal folder, amend it, and if it works, share it with the rest of the team. We can see this when we visit the **Library**, which we get to from the top of the main menu on the left:

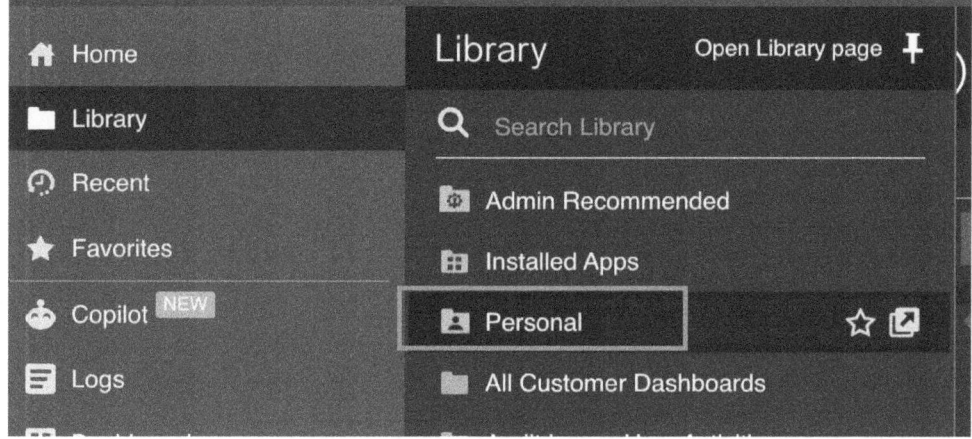

Figure 8.52 – Opening the Library tab shows all the content in Sumo Logic

Looking at *Figure 8.52*, you can see there are three folders at the top:

- **Admin Recommended**: **Admin Recommended** content is content created by an Administrator role and is shared with the rest of the organization. This is useful when an admin wants users to only see things they should be working with.
- **Installed Apps**: **Installed Apps** is for any apps that have been installed directly from the App Catalog. If you can see items in here, you've either installed them yourself or they've been shared with you.
- **Personal**: Finally, the **Personal** folder houses all the content you have installed from the App Catalog or created yourself.

When we share dashboards, based on user roles, it will be visible here.

We have covered content in Sumo Logic and how it is categorized. Now, let's see how to share a dashboard. We use this icon here, next to the **Add Panel** button:

Figure 8.53 – The icon that shares the dashboard with selected roles and users

Once you click this icon, you will be given several options for sharing. You can choose roles and users that will be able to see this dashboard, or the whole organization, before setting access rights. At the bottom is an option to create a shareable URL; the current time range and variables are retained in this URL. If you want to share this dashboard with anyone outside of Sumo Logic, there is also an option to do that. In this screenshot, I've opted to share my dashboard with the entire organization and admins, given them **View** access rights, and also made it publicly shareable, generating a few URLs:

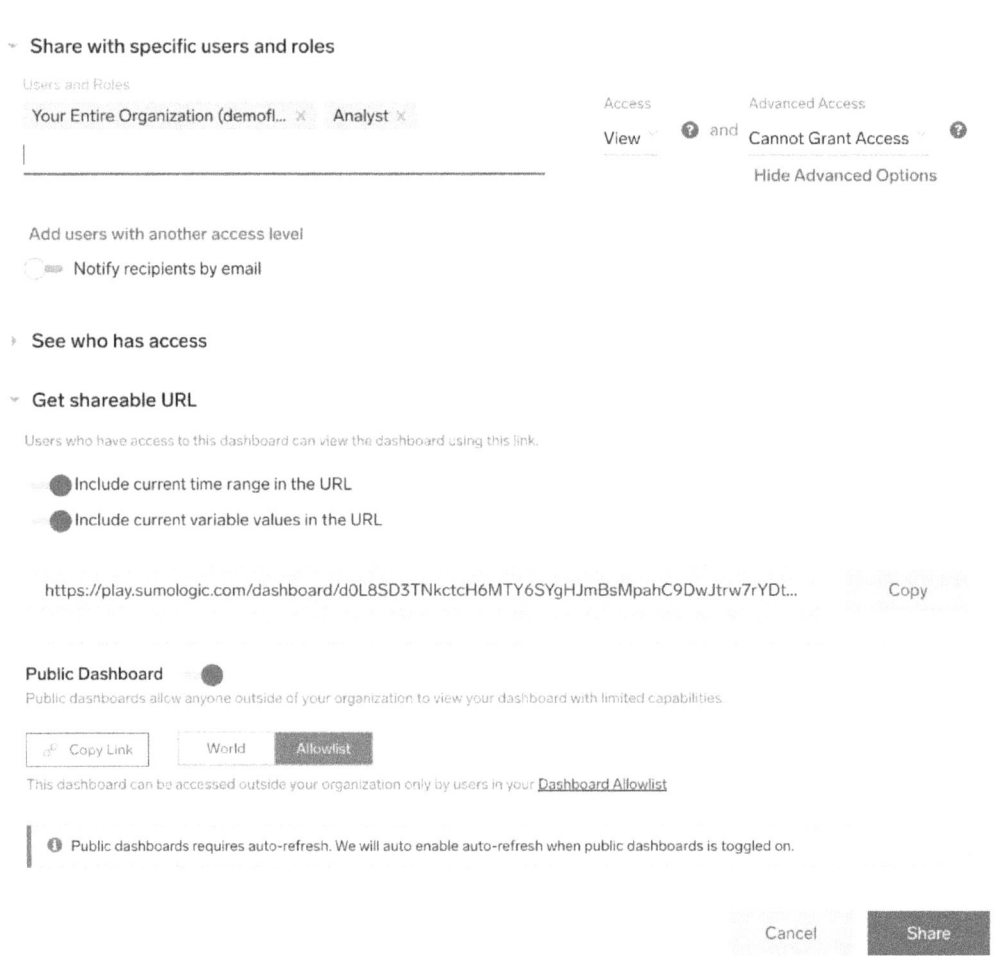

Figure 8.54 – What our sharing configuration looks like for the dashboard

You may have noticed the **Advanced Access** field. This just lets you specify whether these users and roles you've shared with can in turn grant access to other people. Let's now wrap up the dashboard creation overview by going over a few final things.

Linking dashboards

If you have dashboards connected with context that you'd like to tap into during an investigation or for more information, *link them*. Maybe you have a consolidated dashboard that you can't fit *everything in*; with this capability, you'll be able to have smaller datasets that can link to larger datasets. I'll give you an example. I've linked the AWS CloudTrail Console Logins dashboard (that comes with the AWS CloudTrail app in the App Catalog) to my top 10 user logins on the AWS panel. When I click on the entries in the panel, a pop-up on the right comes up that lets me pivot into log search or see the linked dashboard:

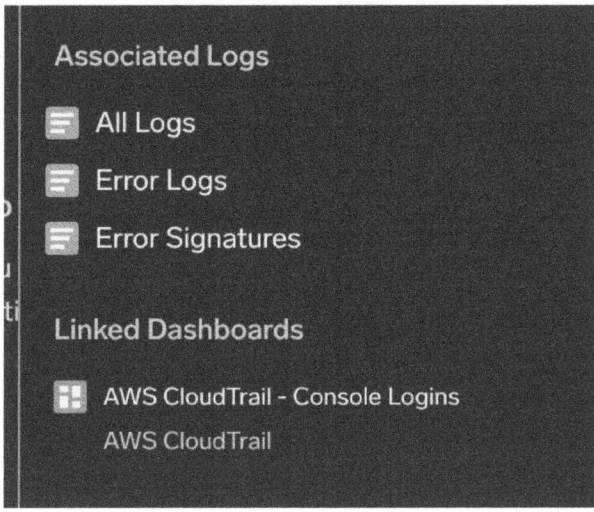

Figure 8.55 – The linked dashboard we applied in the panel configuration

When we visit the linked dashboard, we get to see a ton more visual information on specific login activity on AWS:

Figure 8.56 – The AWS CloudTrail dashboard we are linked to for further information

> **Tip**
> Remember, linking applies to logs, metrics, traces, and service dashboards. You can pivot between any and all of these data types. If there is synergy between them, we recommend linking them.

Visual thresholds

For dashboards that are typically monitored by eye or up on a big screen, you could just have visual thresholds that will alert you to things going wrong. You enable the threshold, enter your values from the dataset, and define the critical and warning zones, and it ends up looking something like this graph:

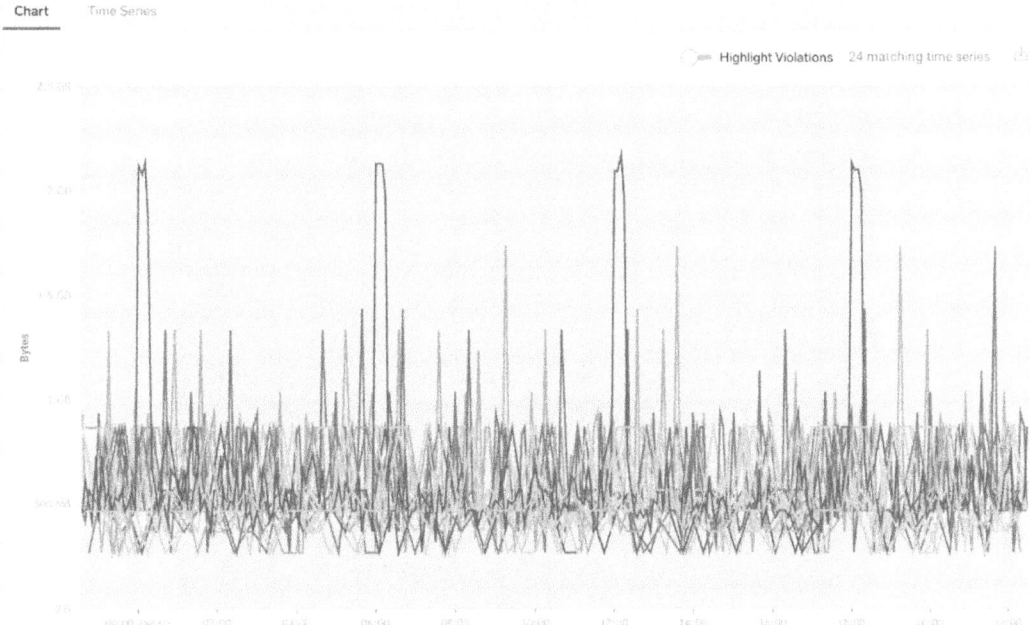

Figure 8.57 – Visual red, amber, and green thresholds on the chart to signify zones of interest

So far, we've created our own dashboard from scratch, using some fairly straightforward examples to bring some panels together and look at some other parts of the dashboard UI to help with fine-tuning some details around presentation. We then looked at a range of configuration options when dashboarding to give you as much control as you need to have these visualized datasets doing the job you need them to do, that is, help you and your teams make sense of your data quickly and easily, no matter the data.

We've covered a staggering amount of information on how to work with your data. This is because the options are so extensive, and there are a lot of things to discuss and a lot of examples of where those capabilities come into play.

If you haven't forgotten, the oven's on and we're baking. The layers of our analytical cake are growing taller and becoming ever more colorful and flavorsome. The previous layer we were working on, *Analytics*, is now complete, and so is our visualization layer:

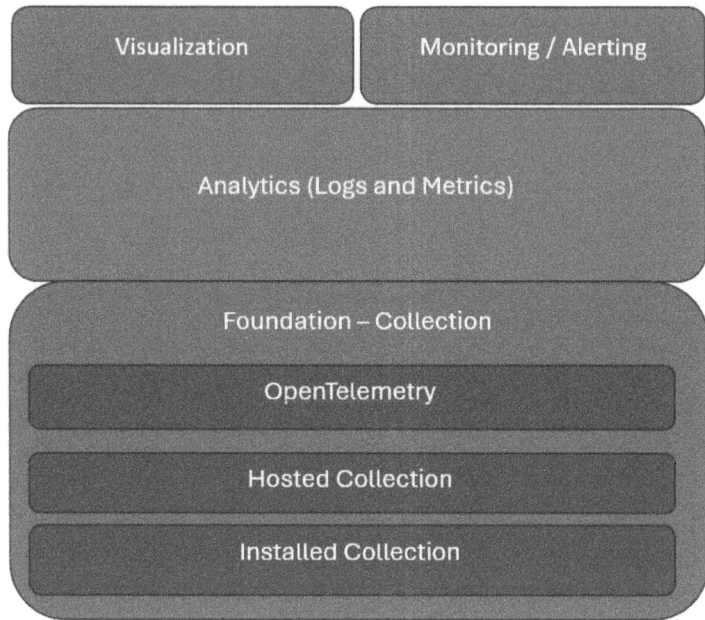

Figure 8.58 – Our analytical cake is stacking up pretty tall!

The next couple of chapters are very significant, as we'll be breaching the topic of the Cloud SIEM and all the amazing technical capabilities it offers. Just in time, too, as we're going to be using it as a sugary glaze on the outside of our entire cake. Pick your flavor.

Summary

In this chapter, we showed additional ways to use the data you have ingested into Sumo Logic by covering monitoring, alerting, and visualization. These concepts are incredibly important to apply to your data because they maximize the utility you get out of it and bring you a few steps closer to achieving total observability from a DevSecOps perspective.

We built a monitor together while covering the key details and nuances during the process, as well as the key differences between the types of options your team will face when creating monitors or using out-of-the-box content. As part of this section, we also covered the **Alert Response Page** (**ARP**), a really useful tool to help you understand why an alert happened and how to resolve it as quickly as possible.

Finally, we looked at visualizing data and dashboards. As with monitors, we built a dashboard from scratch while taking a tour of some of the more useful options that will help you quickly and easily work with dashboards in Sumo Logic.

The next chapter will introduce you to the Cloud SIEM—what it is, why I don't agree with the name, and why you need it as part of your cybersecurity arsenal. See you there!

References

1. https://help.sumologic.com/docs/search/search-query-language/search-operators/predict/#syntax-for-the-auto-regressive-model
2. https://help.sumologic.com/docs/metrics/introduction/metric-quantization/
3. https://help.sumologic.com/docs/metrics/metrics-operators/sum/
4. https://help.sumologic.com/docs/metrics/metrics-operators/rate/
5. https://help.sumologic.com/docs/alerts/monitors/alert-variables/
6. https://api.eu.sumologic.com/docs/#operation/updateDashboard
7. https://registry.terraform.io/providers/SumoLogic/sumologic/latest/docs/resources/dashboard

Get this book's PDF version and more

Scan the QR code (or go to `packtpub.com/unlock`). Search for this book by name, confirm the edition, and then follow the steps on the page.

Note: Keep your invoice handy. Purchases made directly from Packt don't require an invoice.

Part 3

Cloud SIEM and the Security Ecosystem

In Part 3, we'll be diving into Cloud SIEM, the powerful engine wrapped around Sumo Logic, in order to identify threats happening across all your data sources simultaneously. We'll cover the nuances of this engine and how to feed it properly in order to get the best results possible. Finally, we'll take a look at the automation layer available in the platform that can help you with automating basic or complex sequences of events as part of incident response and investigation.

This part of the book includes the following chapters:

- *Chapter 9, Cloud SIEM*
- *Chapter 10, The Insight Engine*
- *Chapter 11, The Automation Service and Playbooks*

9

Cloud SIEM

Thank you for sticking with us! Hopefully, up to this point, you've managed to start building Sumo Logic up with other data sources covering **Metrics, Events, Logs, and Traces** (**MELT**) to power the underlying engine as much as possible.

So far in this book, we've focused on using the core platform and its analytics for logs, metrics, and traces to gain valuable insights from our data. While we've touched on some security scenarios, everything covered up to this point has been more about collecting the logs and not actually being proactive to achieve better detection and response. That's about to change! Now, we'll dive deeper into how Sumo Logic Cloud SIEM can significantly enhance an organization's security posture, elevating it to what we'll refer to as an "intelligent SOC." Modern SIEM solutions don't just collect data at cloud scale; they also offer advanced detection, correlation, and behavioral analytics across all ingested log telemetry. Ultimately, our goal isn't to stockpile logs for their own sake, but to build a highly efficient security operations program capable of detecting and mitigating adversarial behavior before it puts the organization at risk.

Having full visibility over all of that data is immensely powerful, but visibility on its own isn't going to help you detect malicious events and respond to them as effectively as possible. The next two chapters are designed to arm you with information about how Cloud SIEM works and how you can get the most out of it, like a mechanic that can look under the bonnet or under the car and know how to tune, maximize performance, and fix issues. By the end of this chapter, you will have a grasp of what Cloud SIEM does and its intended purpose, how you can start forwarding your data to Cloud SIEM, how this forwarded data gets normalized automatically for you (yes, really!), and how it then gets processed and makes its way through the analytical funnel. You will also learn how the underlying data model works and what **records**, **signals**, and **insights** are, including how entities help with detection. In addition, you will learn how to use out-of-the-box security rules and write your own with some walk-through examples.

Remember, everything that we discuss in this chapter will lead us to the heart of the insight engine, the real power and brains behind Cloud SIEM and the advanced security capability that the platform has. However, before we get there, we need to cover a substantial bit of ground and the fundamental concepts of Cloud SIEM. We will cover the following topics:

- What does Cloud SIEM do?
- Getting data into Cloud SIEM

- Records, signals, and insights
- SIEM rules – configuration and usage
- The MITRE ATT&CK coverage matrix

What does Cloud SIEM do?

Before diving into what makes Cloud SIEM so good at detecting threats across your organization, I wanted to spend some time explaining what Cloud SIEM does and why it's important and also provide brief coverage of modern threat detection.

Cloud SIEM exists in order to *automatically* (emphasis on "automatically"; I'll explain shortly) normalize, enrich, and correlate data across all your different data sources to detect incidents within your business that are worth investigating. It is designed to minimize the amount of noise produced by data and signals and, consequently, reduce the number of false positives that a security team faces. This automatic correlation runs entirely in real time across any number of data sources and data going into Sumo Logic, handling any scale you throw at it.

But what makes these capabilities so important? It will help if we look at some key challenges that security teams face in this day and age to understand where this technology really helps. There are three key challenges that security teams have always faced (and still face)—**visibility**, **context**, and **noise**. These are covered in detail next.

Visibility

Security and DevSecOps teams at the moment are faced with a bewildering array of data sources: **Identity and Access Management** (**IAM**) technologies, applications, containerized infrastructure, firewalls, endpoints, and some kettle somewhere that is connected to a network. These data sources have their own data formats; they usually live in different places, and seeing the bigger picture across all of this data is becoming more difficult by the day. Blind spots are everywhere, and they are ruthlessly used by adversaries in our networks.

As we've covered in great detail in prior chapters, Sumo Logic is a centralized data lake that lets you bring all these data sources into one place. This helps with visibility because we can normalize these various sources and formats and search through them all as if they were the same source of data. I'd like to say no more blind spots, but that would be a lie (thanks, Shadow IT).

Context

A follow-on challenge is context. When your data is so siloed across the business, when an event of interest occurs, it's not easy to answer key questions around what this event is. Where did it come from? Why did it happen? Who did it? When did it happen? To answer all these questions, you need supporting data from other sources of data to confirm facts and intent.

What Cloud SIEM helps with is surrounding your events of interest with context that instantly shows the true sequence of events that an entity has performed across your business infrastructure and assets, resulting in a quicker time to understand and respond.

Noise

The bane of every security analyst's life that is the dreaded alert barrage. Ping, ping...ping. There is no shortage of events of interest in a modern-day business. Which ones are important? Which ones do you spend your precious time investigating? This is the challenge that leaves most security events completely uninvestigated by human analysts.

Cloud SIEM is designed to minimize the amount of noise that security teams face by only correlating those events that are tied to entities and a certain severity threshold, allowing them to identify false positives and also use built-in capabilities such as signal suppression, which is discussed a bit later in the *Records, signals, and insights* section.

One way of addressing these challenges is to solve what is effectively a data problem. How do we get the data to live harmoniously in the same place and be processed in the same way to create links between all these data sources? The answer to that is with the right architecture and the right data model, both of which exist in Sumo Logic.

Next-gen SIEM architecture

The way a technology is architected is crucial to it being performant, reliable, and a useful asset. When it comes to security, I would argue that it becomes even more important, especially as SIEM tools tend to be an important part of a business's defenses. SIEM solutions historically tended to struggle architecturally because the main limitation was coupled storage and processing, *often built using on-prem solutions that don't dynamically scale*. The more data that teams ingested into their SIEM solutions, the bigger impact it had on the performance of the tool, affecting scalability, query times, investigations, and threat-hunting sessions. The fragility and brittleness of SIEM solutions are now a thing of the past, as are the days of running a query across your environment and coming back the next day to see the results! Also gone are the days of someone shouting, "Who wrote this rule that brought the SIEM down?!" or "No one run any searches for the next hour, I'm waiting for my queries to finish!"

When you decouple the storage and processing layers and move them to elastically scalable cloud compute resources, you create a new architecture where your data is stored in a data lake, searchable such that it can scale to many simultaneous users. Many people are shocked to hear that Sumo Logic, at its core, is a multi-tenant system sharing many microservices and resources across thousands of customers simultaneously with virtually zero downtime. I remember consulting a team recently that still had to manage multiple data tiers and needing to know the storage limits of their nodes, how quickly they would consume compute resources, and whether data for a particular investigation needed to be rehydrated. Juggling all of this in a big data, cloud-enabled world should not be necessary. The beauty of cloud SaaS solutions is that you can get back to dealing with threats in real-time and adversaries that are growing in sophistication without worrying about whether your tools will be up to the task.

Does it matter if the SIEM is in the cloud far away from many of your data sources? Absolutely not! At a high level, all of the security sources, from across on-premises environments, multiple cloud environments, third-party tools, and solutions, contribute to the growing knowledge base of activities in your business:

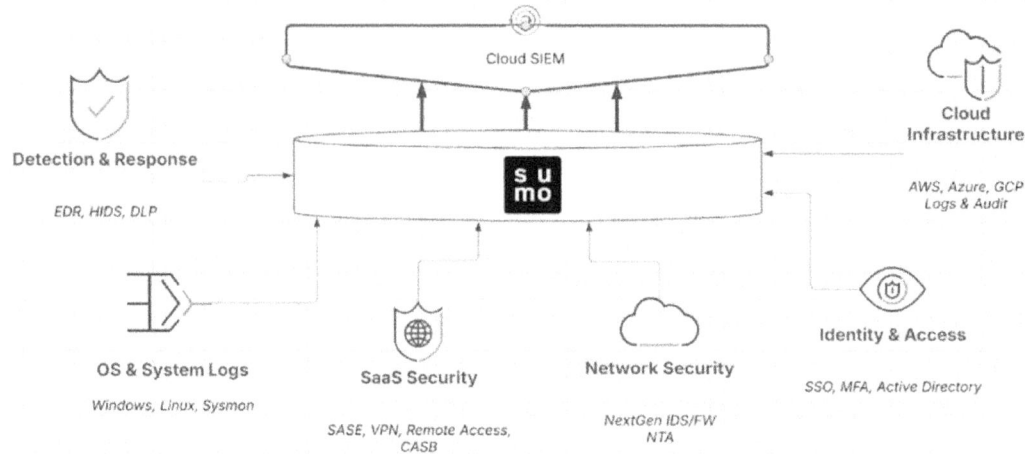

Figure 9.1 – The data flow behind Cloud SIEM

All your data lives in the cloud data lake, ready to be searched at will; no need to thaw or rehydrate. The resource-intensive detection work, including the real-time rules and powerful machine learning algorithms, is handled above the data lake in the Cloud SIEM layer, where it's actively analyzing, correlating, and clustering events of interest that happen across all of these data sources. How can it correlate and cluster so effectively across these sources? Because they all live in the same data lake (and Sumo Logic can bear super powerful compute). It's that simple, and this is the key point we've been making all along. Having data stored in one centralized data lake opens up massive performance and operational gains with the correct supporting elements.

The architecture forms the robust foundation that can then help us to discuss the second part of the data problem, which is the data model.

The data model

If you've ever tried to make sense of logs from 50 different applications after your third cup of coffee, you know the score: log data is a wild menagerie of competing formats and chaotic field names. Every vendor has a habit of labeling fields in weird ways (looking at you, *SRC_IP*, *sourceIp*, *ip_source*, *192.168.0.1-ish*, and that's just the IP address).

A data model (or log schema) is an overarching structure that dictates how logs should be represented, what fields exist, how they are named, and what type of data each field holds. Think of it like a well-labeled filing system in a library: each piece of data (or "book") has its place on the shelf according to topic, author, and publication date.

A robust data model does the following:

- Eliminates the confusion of differing field names ("Wait, do we call it *sourceUser* or *SrcUser*?")
- Makes cross-application searching and analytics easier
- Speeds up threat detection because you can rely on the same field names being used across all sources

The following are examples of common data models:

- **Elastic Common Schema (ECS)**: A generic schema for logs, metrics, and security data, widely used in the Elastic ecosystem
- **Open Cybersecurity Schema Framework (OCSF)**: An emerging open-source standard that aims to unify and standardize security telemetries (currently popular among multiple vendors)
- **Common Event Format (CEF)**: A syslog-based format from ArcSight, widely recognized for its security-related logs
- **Sumo Logic schema**: A schema specifically designed and maintained by Sumo Logic to handle a wide variety of security and operational data (see Sumo's `full_schema.md` on GitHub for reference)

One of the key strengths of Sumo Logic's SIEM solution is its ability to leverage a common data model for detection and response. Out of the box, Sumo Logic provides roughly 1,000 rules; this is prebuilt detection logic that is designed to be vendor-agnostic and over 2,000 log mappings for common security technologies that help to normalize that data to a single schema.

Why is this important? Consider a common security use case: network port scanning or port sweeps. Whether an attacker is probing an environment protected by Cisco, Fortinet, or Palo Alto firewalls, the rule should trigger. However, each of these vendors has drastically different log formats. Some label source IP addresses as *src_ip*, others as *sourceIP*, and some as *IPAddress*. Even worse, some vendors, such as Palo Alto, provide raw logs as **Comma-Separated Values** (**CSV**) with no field labels at all.

Without normalization, a SIEM solution would need vendor-specific rules, making threat detection brittle and hard to maintain because it is harder to do when you're working with different schemas and syntaxes. A Palo Alto rule would be completely different from a Cisco rule, which would differ from a Fortinet rule, and that's just for one detection type. Extrapolate that across every detection use case, and the complexity becomes unmanageable.

The solution would be to parse and map every log message into a common data model, and this is what the Sumo Logic Cloud SIEM data pipeline does (see *Figure 9.15* for a diagram). By structuring logs into a consistent schema, Sumo Logic ensures that rules always know where to find key data fields, such as source IP, destination IP, usernames, and other critical attributes, regardless of the vendor.

This means that a port scan detection rule doesn't need to care whether the log came from Cisco, Palo Alto, or Fortinet. Instead, it simply looks for repeated connection attempts from the same normalized source IP to multiple destination IPs or destination ports, making the logic simpler, more scalable, and easier to manage.

I'm going to stop talking about data models and architecture now. There is one other part of the data model that is crucial to the whole automated correlation capability, and that is entities. However, we won't delve into entities now, as they will make more sense later when we talk about signals. For now, the logical next step is to get your data into Cloud SIEM. This way, you'll be able to see for yourself how the data model comes to life with your sources, and the concepts we discuss will be easier to apply.

Getting data into Cloud SIEM

Let's get our hands dirty! Here, we're going to walk through how to forward AWS CloudTrail data to Cloud SIEM. The concept will apply to any data source that you have sending data to Sumo Logic, whether cloud or non-cloud.

All of it is being indexed and stored in the centralized data lake. I'll let you in on a little secret; there is a huge benefit to having Cloud SIEM connected to your central data lake from an architectural perspective and part of the same *data model* that was outlined previously. This data synergy means that a lot of the out-of-the-box parsing, married with the range of out-of-the-box parsers in the platform, plus a couple of thousand log mappings, ensures that getting started with Cloud SIEM is a piece of cake. We're talking minutes to go from raw data ingestion to powerful analytics. Boom.

Here's how it works. You go to the data that you want to forward to Cloud SIEM; you have complete control over this. For example, here I'm taking my AWS CloudTrail source and forwarding it to Cloud SIEM:

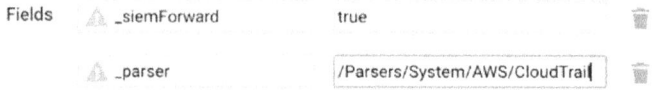

Figure 9.2 – Entering the two fields required to forward data to Cloud SIEM

When forwarding data, there are two fields we need to add to a data source:

- _siemForward
- _parser

> **Note**
>
> Some sources have a **Forward to SIEM** checkbox in the source configuration, which basically does the same job as the _siemForward field in *Figure 9.2*. It looks like this:
>
>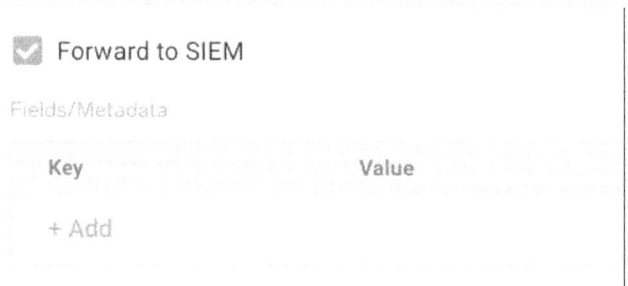

Figure 9.3 – The checkbox on some sources that lets you forward to SIEM without manually having to enter the _siemForward key

The value of _siemForward is always true in this case. For _parser, it's dependent on the parser your data source relates to. Within Sumo Logic, there is quite an extensive list of parsers for varied security-specific sources. These can be accessed by going to **Data Management** and then **Parsers**:

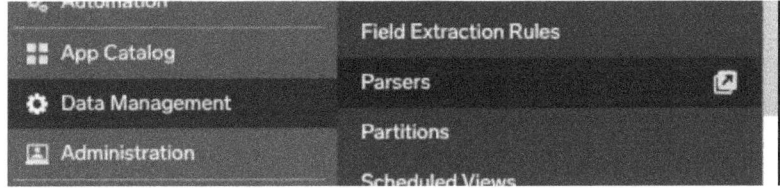

Figure 9.4 – The Parsers option in the Data Management menu

You'll find all of the readily available parsers in the **System** folder. If I go to the **AWS** folder, we can see the **CloudTrail** parser I'm looking for:

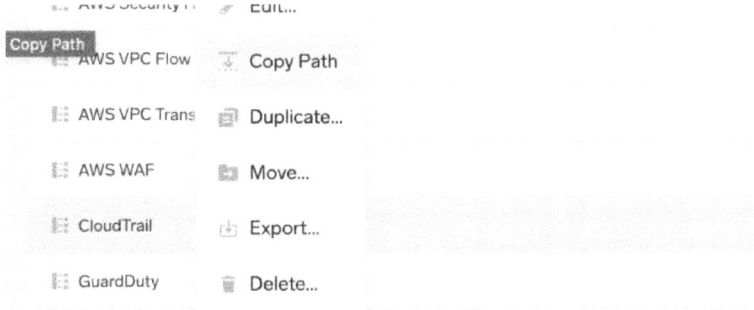

Figure 9.5 – AWS CloudTrail out-of-the-box parser

When we right-click these parsers, we can copy the path, which we can then use for the value when we fill in the

Back in the source configuration, as soon as we hit **Save** at the bottom of our source configuration, that's it. The data will get forwarded to Cloud SIEM. Note that this isn't data duplication; it's taking the original data, enriching it, and then forwarding it, as shown in *Figure 9.3*. For most sources, your work is done by following these steps. In the space of one or two minutes, you've set up everything you need. The reason for this is that part of the enrichment process involves mapping that raw data to fields and *normalizing* it automatically. Let me restate that. Normalization is done automatically across a vast range of security technologies, and this alone will save you and your team countless hours having to do this across your dataset.

Let's walk through an example, so you're aware of the following:

- Where to find these log mappings
- How to modify them if necessary

Let's head to the **Cloud SIEM** menu, scroll down, and choose **Log Mappings**:

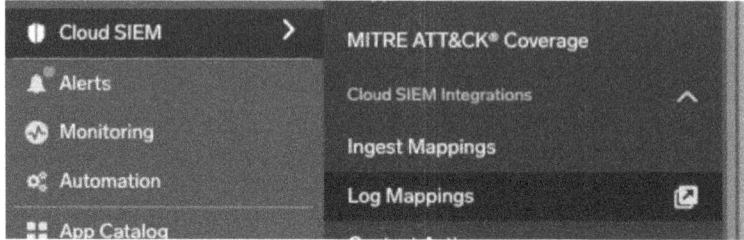

Figure 9.6 – The Log Mappings option in the menu, which takes you to the list of mappings

This will bring you to a screen showing you the extensive list of log mappings that exist in Cloud SIEM out of the box. Let's stick to our example and search for `cloudtrail`. We'll see a good few log mappings for the default mapping and other variations that can be used during certain events and scenarios. Let's click on the default mapping. We are now in the log mapping. It's very convenient because everything is already mapped for you and Cloud SIEM knows where this data has come from. The metadata is linked to the out-of-the-box parser, which helps the log mapping enrichment process take place as shown here:

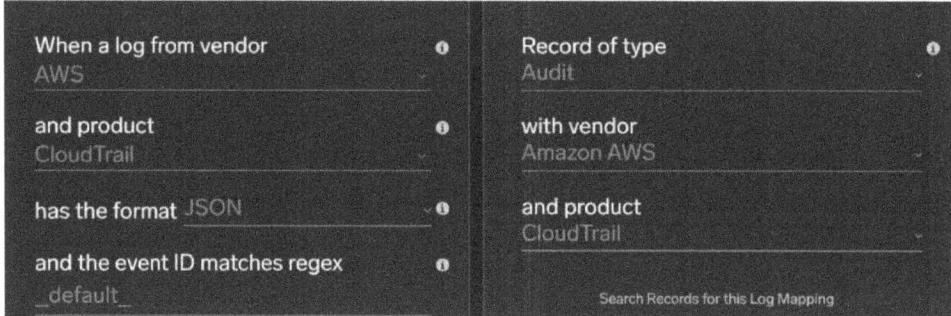

Figure 9.7 – The parser configuration shows up here in the log mapping to link them together and successfully parse and map the raw data

This becomes helpful when it comes to some of the rule syntax that we'll cover later in the *SIEM rules – configuration and usage* section, as there are some intelligent things we can do based on which source the data has come from. If we scroll down, we can see the raw fields that have come from CloudTrail and the normalized fields they are being mapped to:

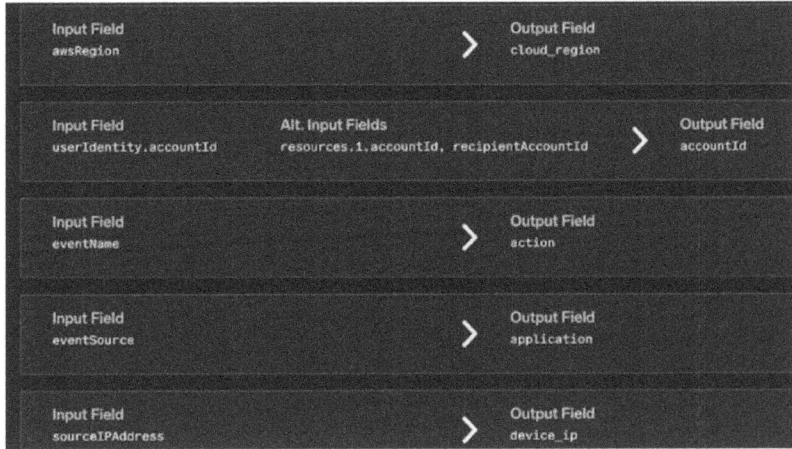

Figure 9.8 – The list of raw fields that are being normalized to a set of 135 fields

This list of 135 normalized fields is what helps Cloud SIEM cluster and correlate data across multiple data sources simultaneously in real time. Therefore, a lot of this heavy lifting is already done for you.

If you want to modify a log mapper, all you need to do is duplicate it first in order to change anything. This applies to most things in Sumo Logic, including rules. Next to the log mapper, you can see three vertical dots. Click that and you will get the option to duplicate the log mapping.

Once this is done, you'll be able to add new fields or change existing ones. For example, if you want to add a new test_field to map to something in the Cloud SIEM schema, scroll down to the fields and add one in. Reference the field name in **Input Field** and choose what field to map to, as shown here:

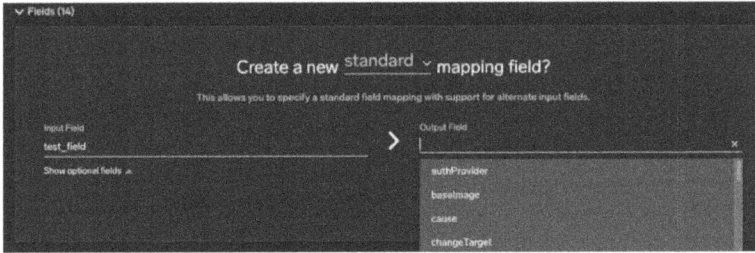

Figure 9.9 – Adding a new test_field map

In *Figure 9.9*, you'll notice that **standard** is highlighted in blue in the sentence at the top. This is because you can select from a range of mappings, including splitting data or joining data before mapping. Even though standard mappings are used most frequently, there are times when you need some flexibility. The following full list of field mapping options appears when you click on **standard**:

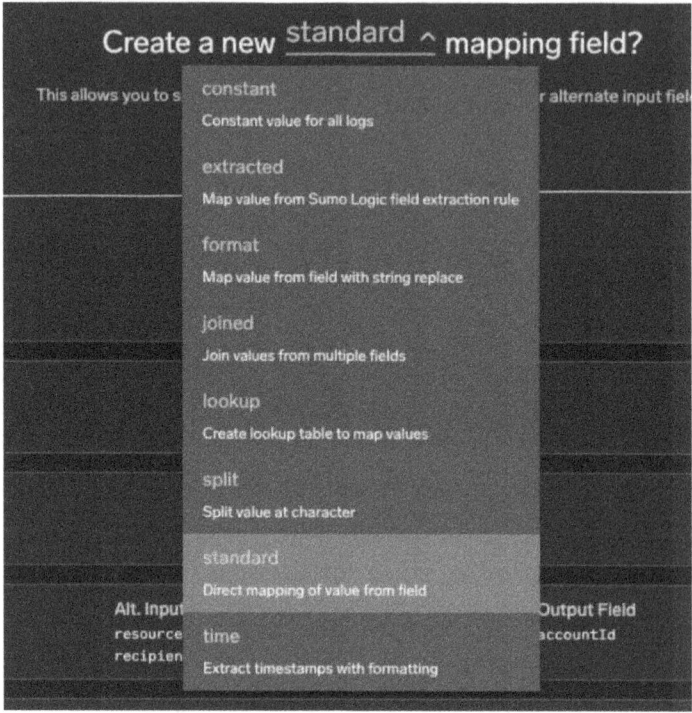

Figure 9.10 – The list of mapping field types available to you

For example, if we have two separate fields that we want to combine into one mapped and normalized field, we can use the **joined** mapping field type. We could have two fields in our data, one that carries the first name of a user and a separate field that carries the surname. We can join them and map them together so they create a normalized username field, like this:

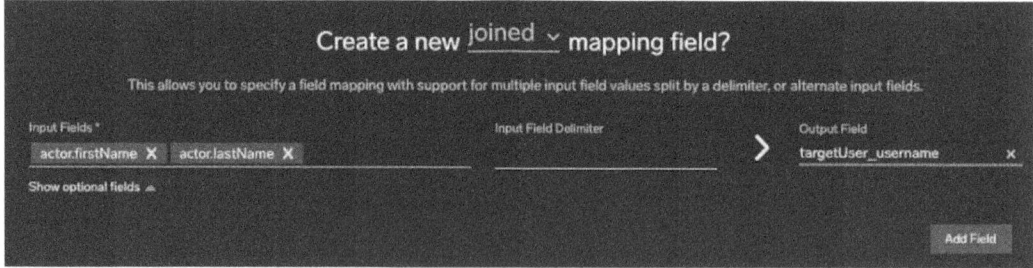

Figure 9.11 – We're using a joined mapping type to combine multiple fields into one

As we go down to the fields in the log mapping, we can click on the icons to the right of each field to edit or remove them:

Figure 9.12 – We can edit individual mappings or delete them

The output of these log mappings is normalized *records* that contain all the metadata that Cloud SIEM needs for rule expression logic to create signals. This is shown here:

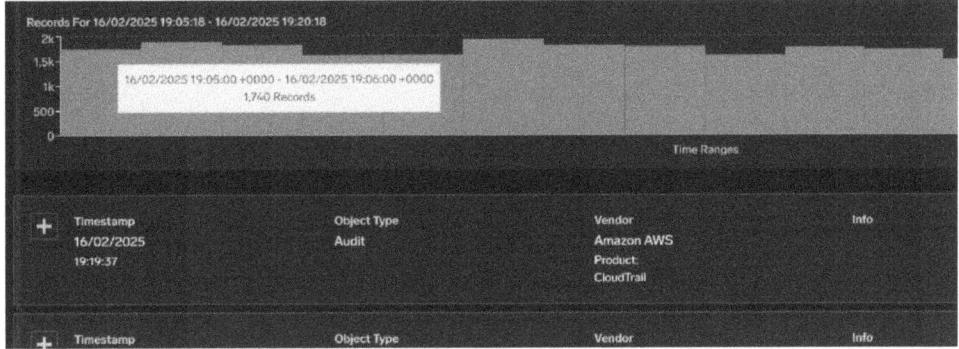

Figure 9.13 – An example record for an audit event from AWS CloudTrail

We discussed the data model in the previous section, so let's now see how everything gets processed under the hood. We will start by looking at the data pipeline.

The data pipeline

The flow of data from an initial raw log message through the pipeline looks like this:

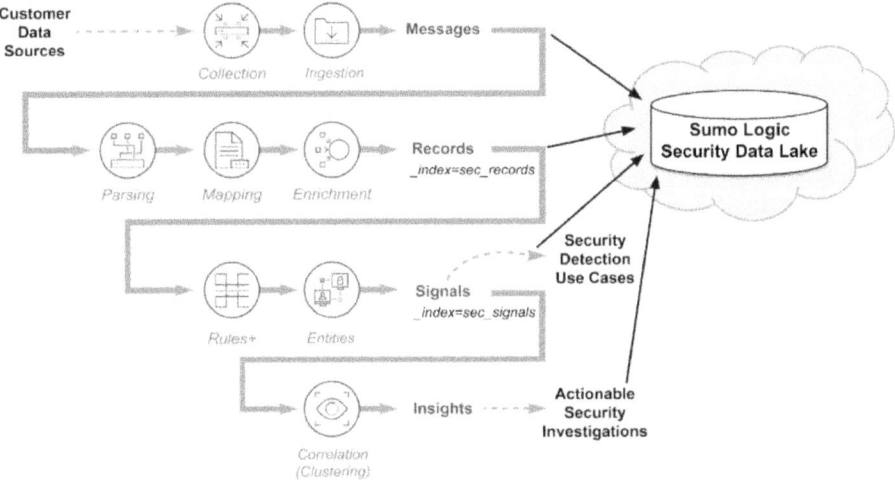

Figure 9.14 – The full data pipeline

We've covered collection and ingestion in *Chapters 4* and *5*, and now we are at the second level after we forwarded some of our data to Cloud SIEM. From this point on, there are three levels of processing that happen to a raw log before it turns into a normalized record: parsing, mapping, and enrichment. We'll cover them here before we jump into a breakdown of what a record, signal, and insight are.

Parsing versus mapping

I think it's worth clearing up the difference between parsing and mapping for those of you who may not have worked with these concepts before[5]. **Parsing** identifies key fields (key-value pairs) that get extracted from your data, such as time/date, and headers and the format they are using.

Once you've identified these key-value pairs, **mapping** aligns these fields to a canonical schema. For example, you might have the following:

- user → srcUserName
- source_ip → srcIp
- action → activityType

After mapping, everything lines up with a standard name (and data type) as per the Sumo Logic schema.

The astute reader may look at the many Sumo schema fields and wonder, "What happens when a log has an obscure value that is not represented in the Sumo Logic data model or list of fields? As a rule, we do not drop data as messages get transformed into normalized records. So, what Sumo Logic does to solve that issue is to simply create a JSON field called fields and have that be the catch-all dumping ground for the one-off data values that don't quite fit into our out-of-the-box fields. The name of the field, when referenced, simply uses the fields ["key"] = value syntax.

For example, Proofpoint email security logs have a field called **Threat Status**. While there are fields that cover aspects of threats, there isn't one for status. When present, this value gets labeled under the field's parent and can be referenced in a rule like this: AND fields['threatStatus'] = 'active'.

Finally, if you are ever in doubt as to how a record was parsed, you can always go back to the unaltered raw message. Thus, one reason Sumo Logic stands out is because it *collects and indexes raw log messages* in their entirety and simultaneously parses and maps data into a schema[4]. In other words, you get the original logs *plus* a consistent data model. While it takes more storage to provide both raw messages and normalized logs, there are critical reasons to take this approach. It enables effective threat detection, rapid response, and robust compliance across a variety of use cases and industries because you always have access to your original data.

Enrichment

Enrichment in Sumo Logic is the third critical step in the data processing pipeline, where parsed and mapped logs are enhanced with additional information not originally present in the vendor's data. This helps analysts gain deeper insights and improve detection capabilities. According to Sumo's *Record Processing Pipeline* documentation (https://www.sumologic.com/help/docs/cse/schema/record-processing-pipeline/#overview-of-processing-steps), there are several forms of enrichment:

- **Lookup table mapping**: Dynamically appends auxiliary fields such as threat intelligence, user department data, or device details from external tables.
- **IP address enrichment**: When a record contains an IP address, whether it's a source IP, destination IP, NAT IP, or any other network-related field, Sumo Logic automatically enriches the record with

additional metadata. This enrichment includes attributes such as ASN, organization name, and geolocation details such as city and country. Each individual IP address within a record is processed separately to ensure complete enrichment across all relevant fields. Enriched attributes follow a structured naming convention by appending an underscore and a descriptor to the original field name. For example, if a record contains

- **Match list enrichment**: Compares specific fields in an event (e.g., IP, domain, or username) against a configured list of known or suspicious entities (referred to as match lists). When a match is found, Sumo tags or appends a designated field to the record, enabling more targeted alerts and streamlined incident triage. Note that match lists are one of the most under-utilized features I see in Sumo implementations. New users don't realize that many of Cloud SIEM's built-in rules rely on predefined standard match lists. These are lists that users must create and populate to enable Cloud SIEM to effectively utilize them in its rule logic. For example, the

These enrichment options give teams the flexibility to merge real-time data with contextual knowledge, ensuring logs are not only structured and mapped but also enriched with critical intelligence to power more effective analytics and threat detection.

After these steps, the data is no longer just a raw message; it's transformed into a record. This record is now normalized, enriched, and ready for deeper security analytics as it feeds into the Sumo Logic correlation engine included with Sumo Logic's Cloud SIEM.

We've just covered the initial stages of the pipeline leading up to the key data concepts within Cloud SIEM: records, signals, and insights. The next section will build upon everything we've analyzed so far and give you a greater understanding of how it all ties together.

Records, signals, and insights

The entity model and rules tied together act as the foundation for Cloud SIEM, and records, signals, and insights are the data pillars on top of this foundation. We're going to cover the Insight Engine in the next chapter, but we're still going to cover how all of these elements layer on top of one another in this section.

What's a record?

As we've been discussing, a **record** is a normalized event that has been parsed, mapped, and enriched automatically with the help of the data model in Sumo Logic. Here is a zoom of the pipeline we saw in the previous section to provide you with a better idea:

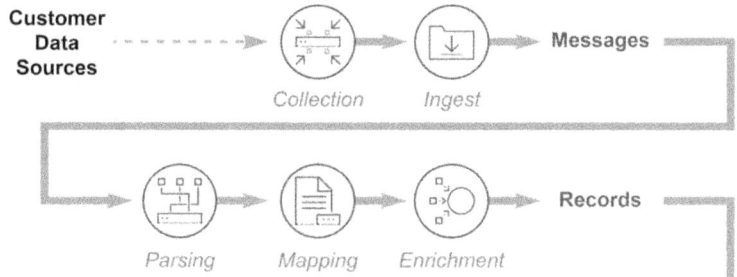

Figure 9.15 – The transformation a single log message goes through to become a record

There are different types of records in Cloud SIEM, and they categorize the behavior that each activity falls into. These record types can be used for querying and for use in rule expressions, as we'll see later in the *SIEM rules – configuration and usage* section. Let's look at some of these record types, and then we'll look at an example record.

Record types

When looking at records, it's best to understand them in terms of types[3]. After the enrichment and mapping process takes place, each record is labeled with a certain type such as **Authentication**, **Network**, **Audit**, and so on.

If you go to **Cloud SIEM | Records**, you can search through them. You have to use a filter to get some results; the ones most frequently used are **Object Type** and **Metadata Source Category**. For example, a nice and easy way to see all of your most recent records is to click into the filter, type in Metadata Source Category (it should auto-suggest it pretty quickly), and then type in your source category from the collector page. If you know the object type of the record—for example, AWS CloudTrail, which we covered earlier, is an **Audit** record type—you can go to **Object Type** and then select the type. The **Metadata Source Category** filter is shown here:

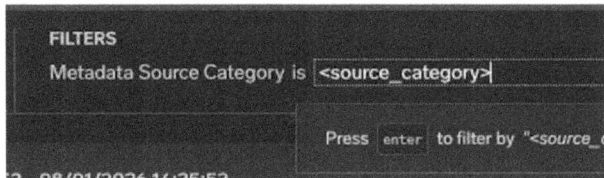

Figure 9.16 – Seeing the latest successful records using <source_category>

Continuing with our example, now that we have forwarded AWS CloudTrail data to Cloud SIEM, we're going to explore a record. The following screenshot shows four major parts of a record:

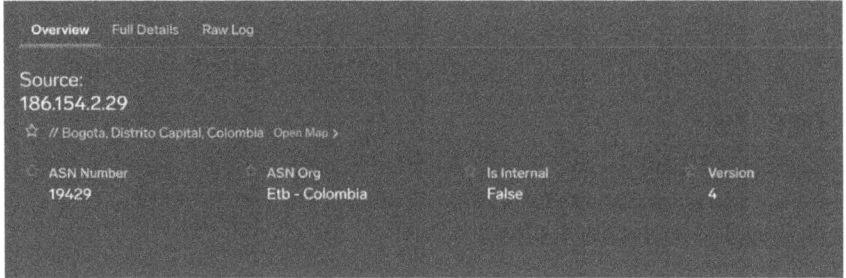

Figure 9.17 – The top part of the record, showing the initial source and some enrichment metadata

You'll see that the top section shows the **Source** of the event, such as an IP address or a hostname. If it is an IP address, it will be enriched by the data pipeline, and you'll see an **ASN Number** and **ASN Org** as well. As mentioned in the *Enrichment* section, there is also internal enrichment that happens; for example, the **Is Internal** label tells us whether this is an IP address that belongs to our environment or whether it is from an external source.

The middle of the record contains those fields that have been normalized to the Cloud SIEM schema, as shown here:

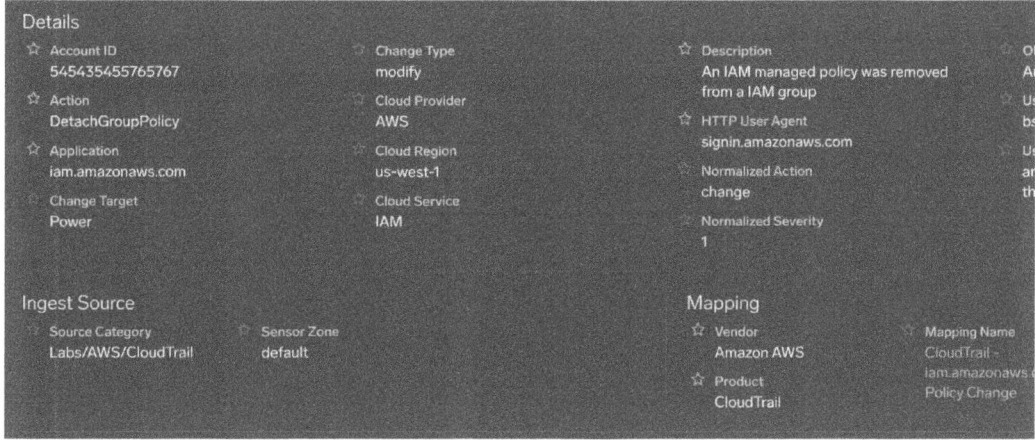

Figure 9.18 – These fields have been mapped from the raw log to normalized fields

Those fields you can see on the left—**Account ID**, **Action**, and **Application**—are the normalized fields that data from a source is mapped to. This differs from source to source, but because it's normalized, it's easier to correlate across your data. You'll see other metadata, such as the **Ingest Source** and the mapping used as part of the data pipeline for this particular record, at the bottom.

Finally, at the bottom, we have a list of all other extracted fields from the data, which can freely be used in rule expressions, as shown here:

Figure 9.19 – The rest of the fields extracted in the record

You can choose to map these extracted fields to normalized fields by amending the mapper being used to create the record; or, as mentioned previously, you can use any of these fields within a security rule's logic.

There's one more thing. As shown at the top of *Figure 9.20*, by clicking on **Full Details** and **Raw Log**, you can access the raw data that was used to create the record:

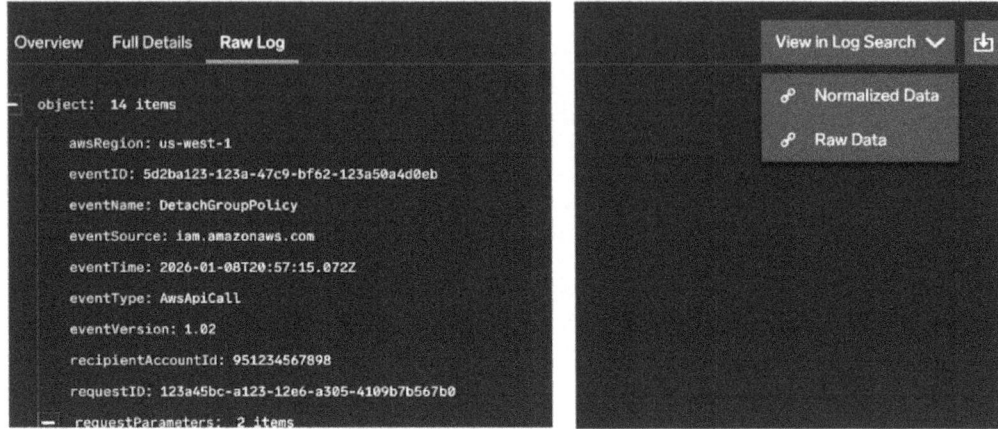

Figure 9.20 – The raw log is also accessible from within the record

You can also then view both the normalized data and the raw event directly in Sumo Logic's Log Search by clicking on **View in Log Search** on the right. The benefit of this was discussed previously, as it lets you always have access to the original data, which means detections can be trusted and verified. Analysts can pivot from a high-level signal straight back to the original log to validate intent, investigate edge cases, support forensics, or satisfy audit and legal requirements, all without leaving the platform.

Records are fundamental to the automated correlation capability within Sumo Logic because records turn into signals when the security logic from a rule is matched to that record. So, let's move on to signals.

What's a signal?

Records are normalized events that are ready for correlation. Signals are the output of our rules and detection logic. When a rule expression matches that of a record, a signal is created. Let's look at the flow for the next level below:

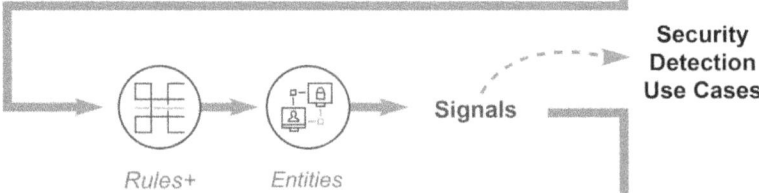

Figure 9.21 – Rules and entities come together at this stage during signal creation

When a signal is created, the entity-centric model that we have in Sumo Logic gets to work. I'll try to break the activity down into a few key areas where you can see this tracking taking place. The first place we can start is the signals themselves. Let's take a look at our signals by going to **Cloud SIEM | Signals**:

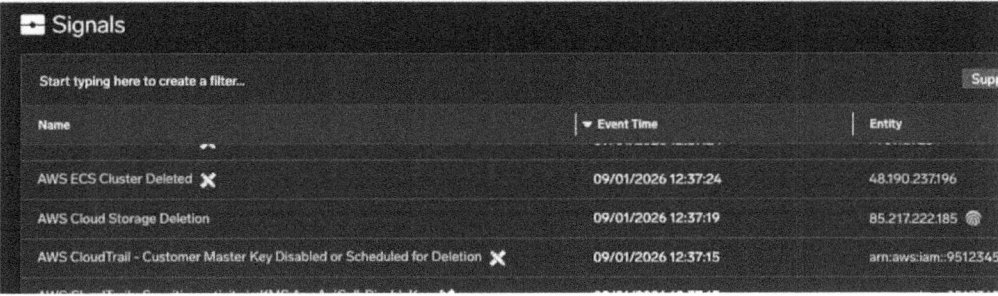

Figure 9.22 – Our list of signals in Cloud SIEM

I haven't shown the full view as it's quite wide, but after the **Entity** column, there are **Severity** and **Rule Type** columns. Let's take a look at an example signal from the list, **AWS Cloud Storage Deletion**. If you click on it in the list, you'll see a tab pop up on the right side of the screen to give you a quick, high-level view of the signal, including the **Description**, **Severity**, MITRE ATT&CK tags, the rule name, and expression:

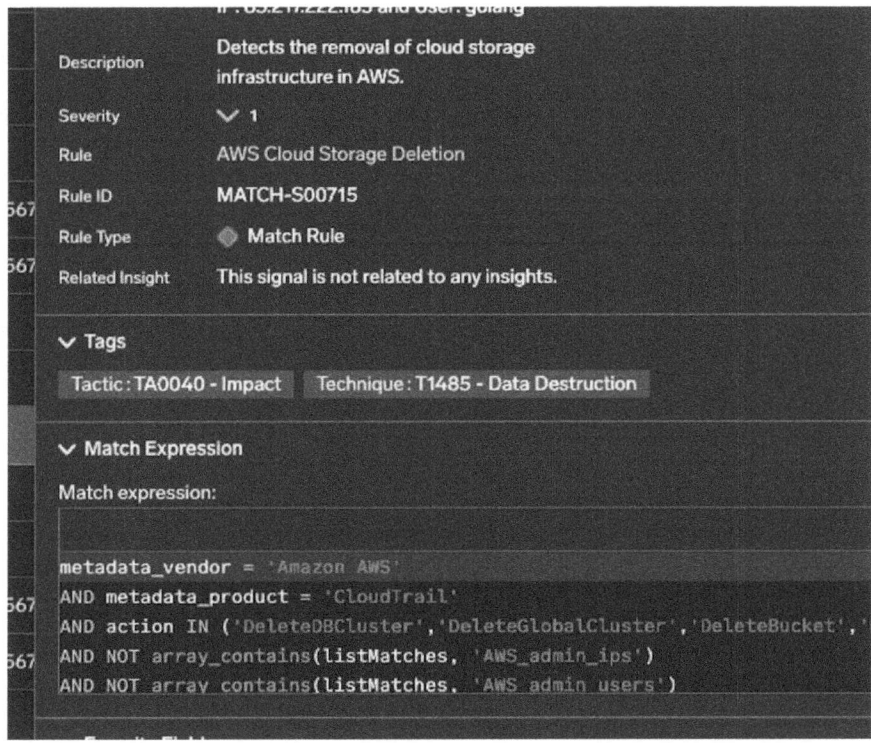

Figure 9.23 – A quick view of a signal with a lot of useful information about what it represents

If we open the signal, we can see the records that have matched a security rule in Cloud SIEM to create that signal, giving us a complete view of what log events were seen. The expression is based on the rule configuration for the **AWS Cloud Storage Deletion** rule. We'll explore rule expressions, including how to use the out-of-the-box rules and how to create your own, in the next section.

At the end of the *The data models* section, I briefly stated that there is another key part to the data model, which is entities. This is a perfect time to examine them in greater depth.

The importance of entities and tracking "Bob"

The reason why you see entities in the signal view and signal information is that entities are created during signal creation. An entity could be anything, such as a username, email address, domain name, or serverless function, essentially anything that has caused the behavior specified in the rule. When this happens, Cloud SIEM starts tracking this entity for up to 45 days to see what other signals they trigger. We've locked onto the target and we can now start to cluster any other actions they undertake.

Sumo Logic is described as an *entity-centric solution*. That means extra effort goes into normalizing and correlating entities so you can easily follow the breadcrumbs.

Apart from this ability to create entities and use them as a correlator, there are useful views we can explore. Let's click on the entity in our signal; mine is this IP address: **85.217.222.185**. By clicking on the entity, we get taken to the entity-specific view, where we can then see what signals that entity has triggered on a timeline, as shown here:

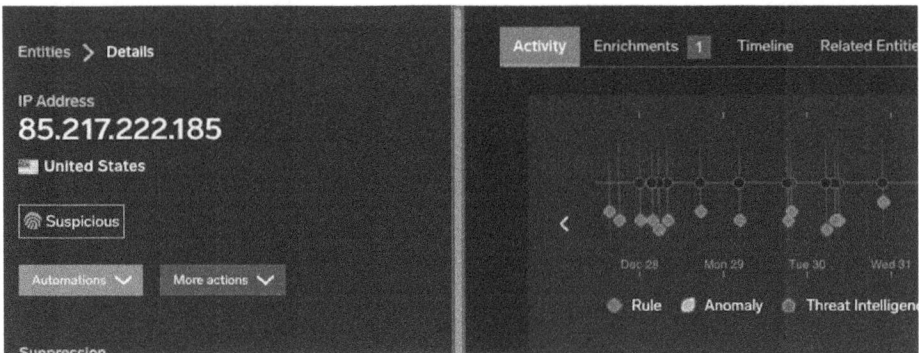

Figure 9.24 – The base timeline view of activity for an entity

> **Tip**
>
> You can see all the entities in your Cloud SIEM by going to **Cloud SIEM | Entities**.

Underneath the timeline, you're able to see the exact signals triggered by this entity. This gives you a pretty accurate picture of what this entity has been up to in the past 45 days, and correlation and clustering around this entity can take place over a few minutes, hours, days, or weeks! When we dive into the insight engine in *Chapter 10, The Insight Engine*, we will cover the nuances of how this is done.

There are two more useful things to cover here. At the top, you'll see five tabs: **Activity**, **Enrichments**, **Timeline**, **Related Entities**, and **Automations**. The **Timeline** view is great because if you have audit and network data sources being forwarded to Cloud SIEM, you're able to see how this entity has been authenticating and how they've been moving on the network. For this IP address, we can see AWS CloudTrail data around this IP address's activity:

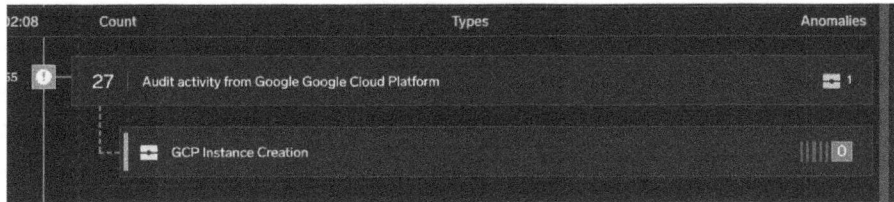

Figure 9.25 – Pattern of login attempts visible on AWS. Any suspicious events get flagged

Finally, from here, you can also automate the enrichment of an entity with Sumo Logic's automation service playbooks. This allows you to very quickly assess the important characteristics of an entity in an automated way, getting the context delivered to you so that a response can be made quicker. If you click **Automations**, you can run a playbook that enriches this IP address with **VirusTotal**:

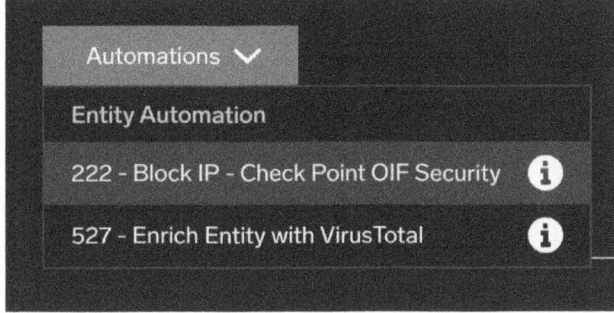

Figure 9.26 – Running automated playbooks from within the entities UI

We'll cover the Automation Service in depth in *Chapter 11*, *The Automation Service and Playbooks*, so hopefully that whets the appetite, but once the playbook runs, we can see the results in the **Enrichment** tab above the timeline:

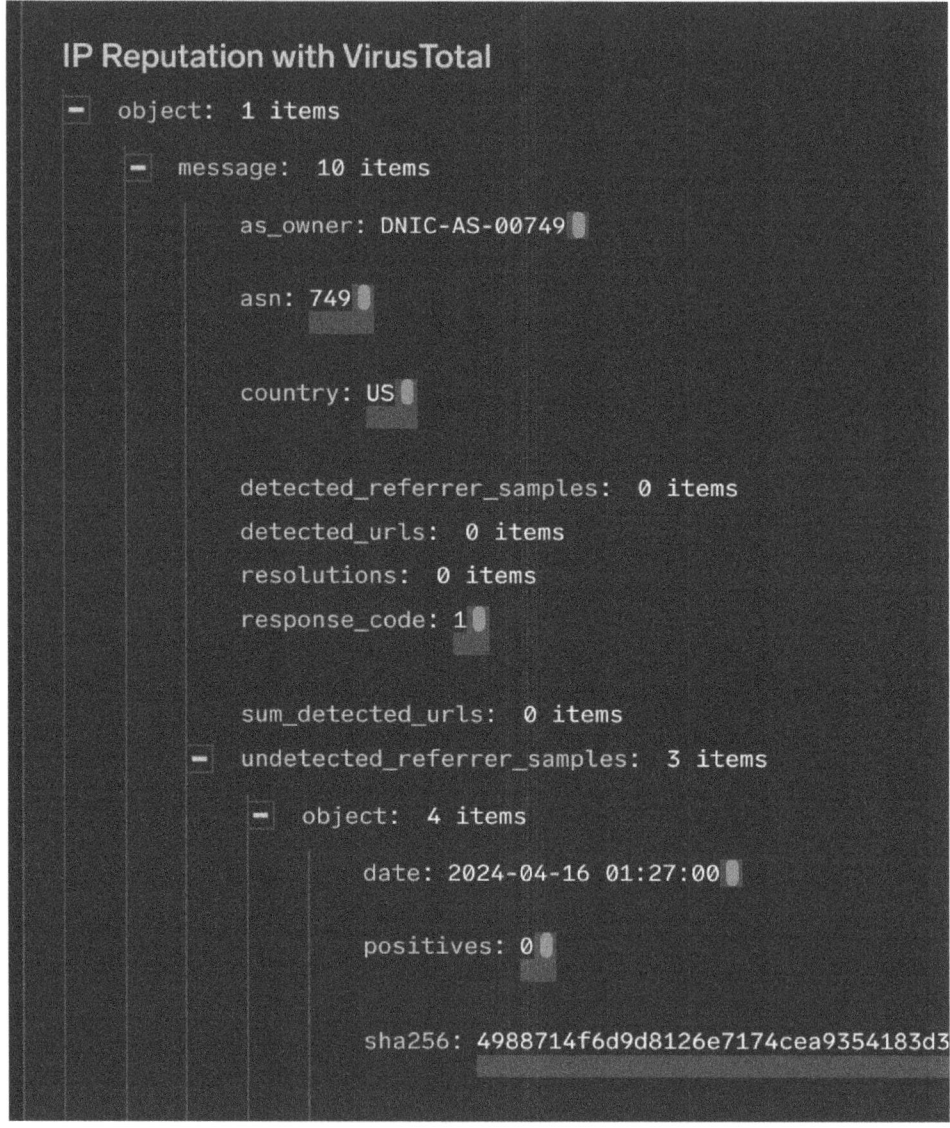

Figure 9.27 – Results from VirusTotal using our automated playbook

Remember, all this is being done in real time and at scale across your entire business. There are hundreds, if not thousands, of entities moving across your business at all times. Imagine how much easier your life would be if, among all the noise, you could see what these entities are doing, before picking out the ones that deserve your attention without being overcome with anxiety when looking at the sheer volume of data you must work through. That's the beauty of an entity-centric model, especially when it feeds the insight engine.

You might have a question at this point. What if we're working with an entity that is a username, but they have different domain names, or their username looks different across internal sources? What a pain that would be…unless there were a way to normalize them. In Cloud SIEM, you're able to do exactly this.

Imagine a user called "Bob". Bob logs in as *bob@company.com* one day and simply *bob* the next. Sumo Logic's entity normalization[6] can automatically recognize that these refer to the *same person*. This is called **username normalization**. If you're investigating suspicious activity on user accounts or servers, it's incredibly powerful to unify all references to a single entity.

Similarly, machines can have fully qualified domain names (e.g., `server1.prod.company.com`) as well as short hostnames (e.g., `server1`). Sumo will unify these; this is **hostname normalization**. The process is outlined in the *Username and Hostname Normalization* documentation (`https://help.sumologic.com/docs/cse/schema/username-and-hostname-normalization/`).

In short, lookup tables are created manually or programmatically to map one entity name to another when, in fact, they are referring to the same person or system. By systematically tracking all aliases, Sumo Logic keeps a consistent thread of data that belongs to the same user or host, even if the raw logs use different formats or naming conventions.

But why does that matter? Because the everyday chaos of your environment and disparate systems doesn't always adhere to a single naming convention. They might have multiple accounts, or your environment might refer to the same server under two different names. Without normalization, your threat detection rules or user activity searches could easily miss half the data. With entity normalization, you can see *all* activity for Bob across *bob@company.com*, *BobbyS*, and *bob.smith*.

Next, we'll cover suppression, which is a built-in mechanism that tries to reduce noise and redundancy in your signals to feed the insight engine with cleaner, higher-fidelity signals.

Suppression

If a rule is triggering frequently on a certain entity and the signal is too *spammy*, the suppression mechanism will stop it from producing insights and flooding your security team with unnecessary results. It does this very well thanks to the entity model, as the suppression kicks in when a signal is seen together with an entity multiple times. Consider the following scenario.

John from IT forgets his password, tries a few times, and then manages to log in on the fourth try. This will create a brute-force or password attack signal on John's entity and most likely his IP address. He ends up resetting his password to a more memorable one and logs out. At the end of the day, he tries to log back in again, forgets he changed his password, and remembers it again on the fourth try and gains access. The second time this signal occurs on John's entity, it will be suppressed.

There is a 12-hour window for signals (you can change this to go up to 72 hours) that monitors how often signals are firing on the same entities. There's a simple reason for this: it stops the creation of multiple identical insights, reducing the burden on the security team to go through the same stuff over and over again. Also, there's a way to override this suppression window *per rule* at a more granular level if necessary. This is important because, for example, I've worked on scenarios where the activity only ever has the same name and is tied to the same entity, such as a critical asset that runs an important script, but it is important for wider context and correlation, so instead of being suppressed, it can contribute to insights.

As we'll see briefly now and in much more detail in the next chapter, insights are the secret sauce in Sumo Logic Cloud SIEM and your main weapon against cyberattacks.

What's an insight?

An insight is created when an entity has created a chain of activity, consisting of multiple signals (there are exceptions) that breach a severity threshold. The activity score is based on the signals they've triggered, correlated over a time window (minutes, hours, days, or weeks) and *automatically* clustered together. All the previous concepts we've covered around the data model data pipeline culminate in an insight. Let's go back to the key advantage Sumo Logic provides—visibility. When you have visibility over how an entity navigates your environment *across data islands*, you are empowered because you see the behavioral chain, which the attacker *may not know that you can see*. If you've ever played the card game *Uno* before, this is like playing the reverse card. Let's take a look at the final section of the data flow in Cloud SIEM. It culminates with an insight, as shown here:

Figure 9.28 – All the prior data structures and elements are correlated and clustered together to provide insights

The following figure visualizes a chain of events that have different severity levels, correlated against a single entity (an admin carrying out unauthorized actions) and then turned into an insight (beaconing activity) automatically:

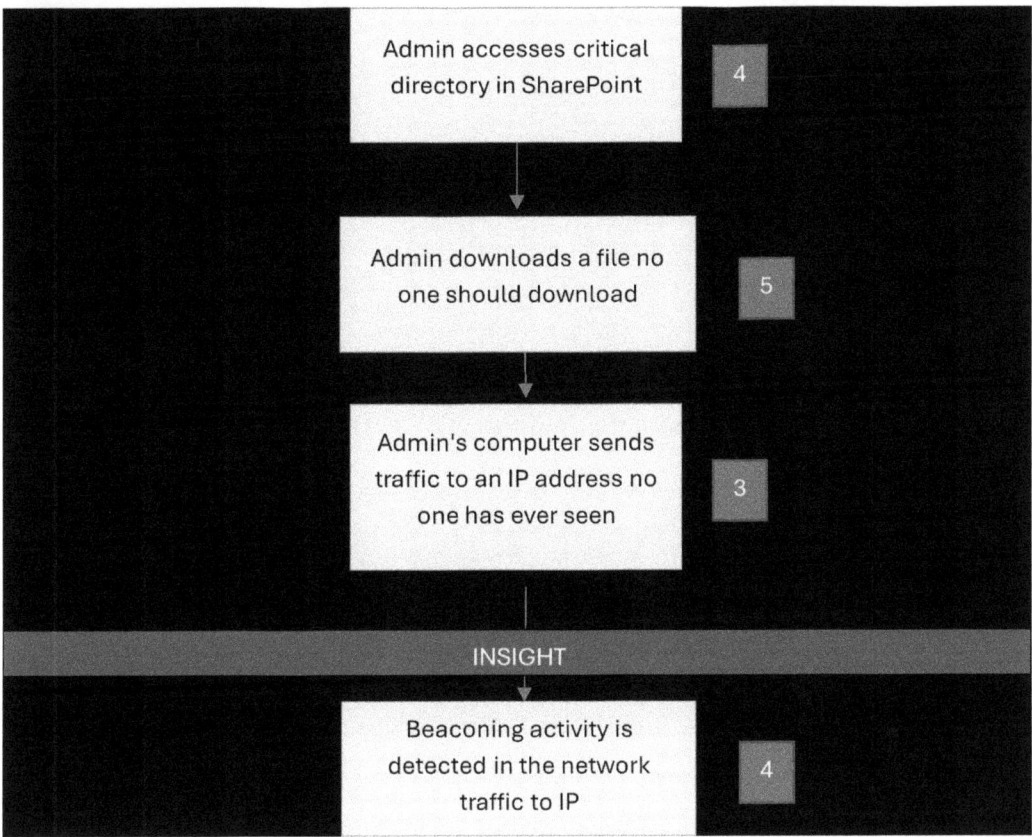

Figure 9.29 – How a chain of events becomes an insight

By default, the severity threshold for an insight is 12, so when signal severity adds up to 12, as shown in the preceding figure, an insight is created. This can be changed, however, as can most things in Cloud SIEM, to better suit your environment and the type of adversaries and threats you deal with most.

At the start of this sub-section, I said that multiple signals are correlated and create an insight. This isn't always the case. There are some situations where a signal proves to be so critical that it needs investigating immediately. This is where the ability to create custom insights is really helpful. By going to **Cloud SIEM | Security Detection | Custom Insights**, you can create logic that will let you specify combinations of rule names or signal names to generate an insight for you.

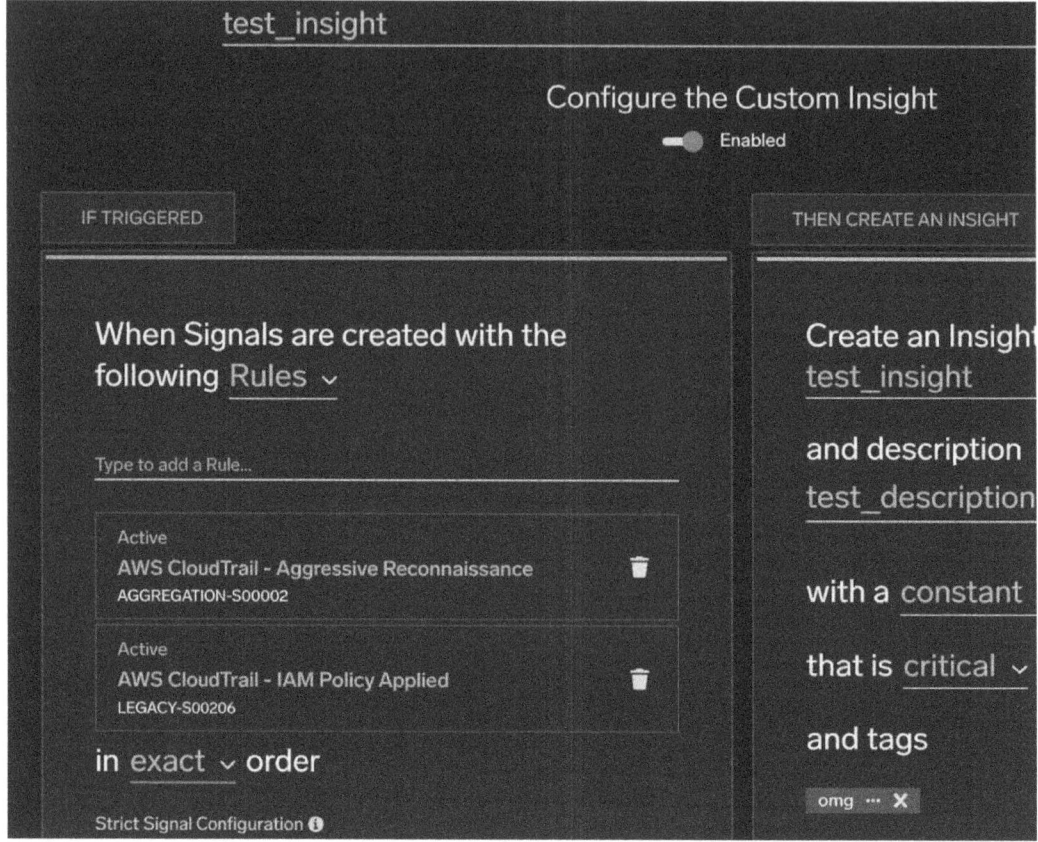

Figure 9.30 – Choosing exactly how high-criticality insights are generated

This gives you more control over what insights are generated in addition to the ones that are automatically brought to life by automatic correlation, giving you the best of both worlds and, once again, making it tailored to your environment and business. We'll explore some other uses of this in the next chapter when we dive into the insight engine properly.

It's safe to say that a key driver of the advanced capabilities in Cloud SIEM is the rules. They help to create the signals that get transformed into insights, helping you to identify key threats across your data.

In the next section, we'll look at rules in all their glory, including how to configure and use them and all the different options available to you.

SIEM rules – configuration and usage

In the previous sections, we covered how the data pipeline in Cloud SIEM works to take you from a raw log event to a normalized record, to a signal that is triggered based on behavior and, finally, to an insight. Rules are key to the record -> signal transition. An effective rules-based security syntax is more powerful than a query-based syntax, and in this section, we're going to cover the nuances of why that is, as well as providing you with some different real-world use cases of security rules. You can use these examples for your own security team and build on them to create unique rules that are tailored to your business.

Let's begin by viewing the rules already available and then dive into the nuances of rules and creating them yourself.

Rules ready to go

If you go to **Cloud SIEM** | **Security Detection** | **Rules**, you'll be presented with over 1,000 rules:

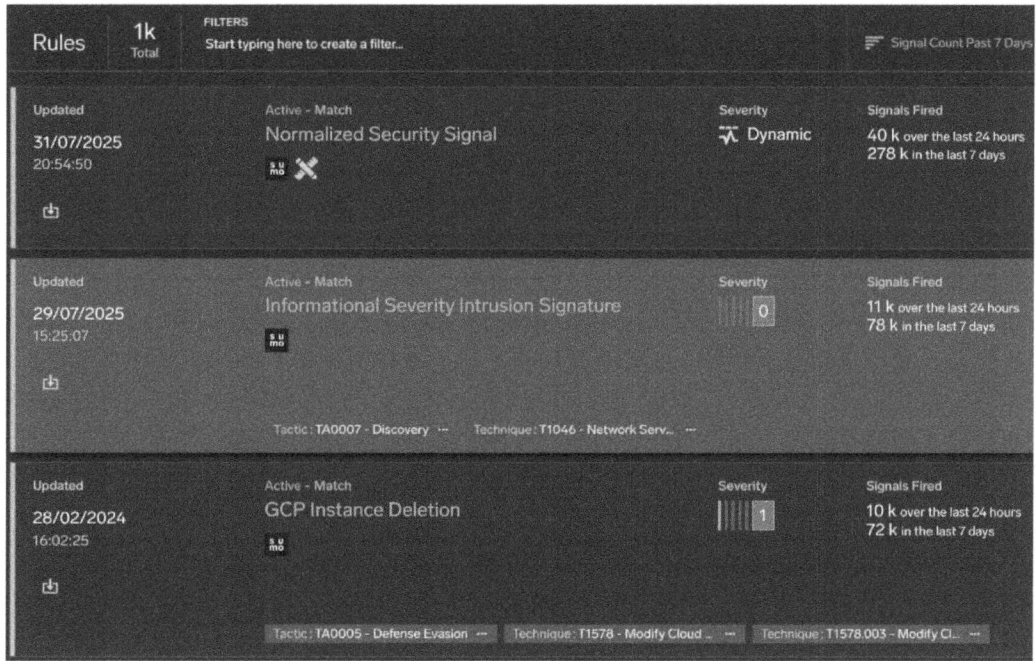

Figure 9.31 – There are over 1,000 rules ready to use across different technologies and scenarios

There are rules covering Windows, Linux, AWS, Azure, GCP, and more technologies as well as use cases. They are all enabled by default, and examples include catching Mimikatz, commands for data exfiltration, and many, many more.

Each rule has a rule expression, which is the logic that a record needs to match in order to create a signal, along with other useful metadata, including what entities you want the rule to track and what severity it will be. In the out-of-the-box rules, if you want to amend any part of the existing configuration, you just need to duplicate the rule (similar to the log mappings). As a quick example, we want to amend the severity of the **GCP Instance**

Creation rule. Let's open it up; from the top, we need to choose **Duplicate** or **Duplicate and Disable Original**, and then we can change the severity from 1 to 5, as shown here:

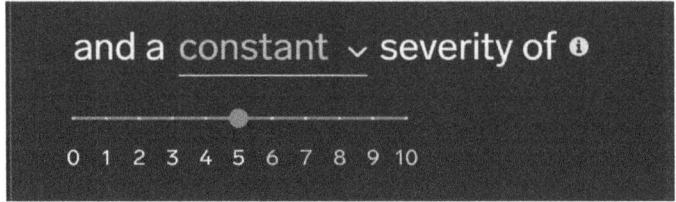

Figure 9.32 – We can change the severity as well as any of the other configurations in a rule

When we look at creating our own rules later, we'll cover all of the rule configuration as it always becomes a bit clearer when you join in with some hands-on work. There are six rule types in the platform that cover pretty much any security logic you might need to work with:

- **Match rules**: Simple match conditions
- **Threshold rules**: Adding numerical boundaries for our data
- **Chain rules**: Looking at sequential events
- **Aggregation rules**: Grouping data from several sources together
- **Outlier rules, based on machine learning**: Numerical machine learning-based deviations from a baseline
- **First-seen rules, based on machine learning**: Identifying behavior done for the first time with machine learning

In the list of out-of-the-box rules, you can see what rule type that particular rule is above the name. In *Figure 9.31*, you can see that the first rule is a match rule because it says **Active - Match**. If the out-of-the-box rules don't capture your requirements well enough, you'll want to create your own rules! When you click on **Create** in the top-right corner, you see all six rule types, namely **Match**, **Threshold**, **Chain**, **Aggregation**, **Outlier**, and **First Seen**:

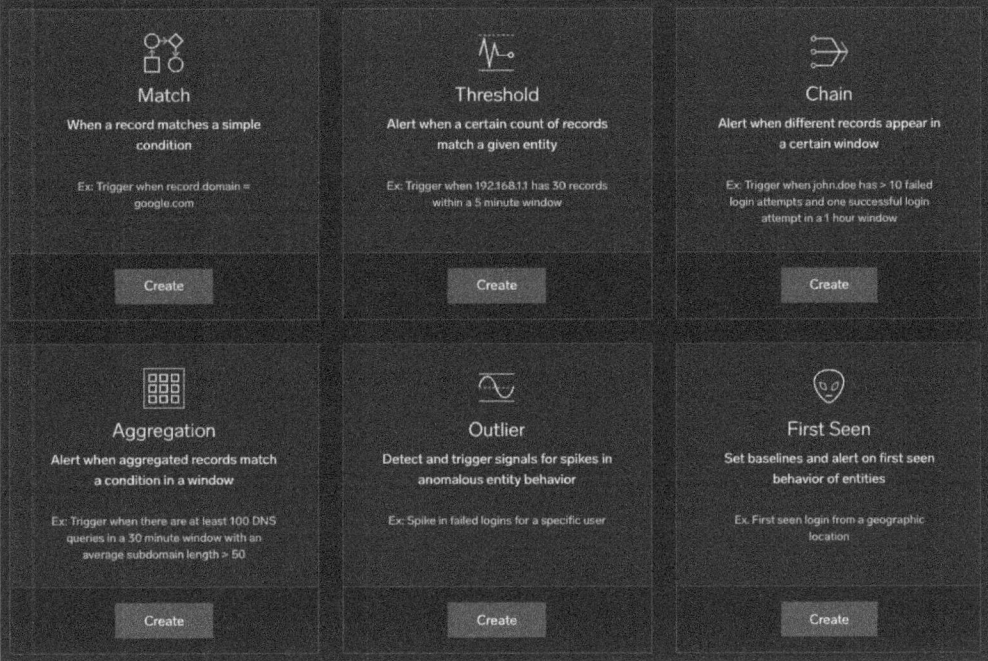

Figure 9.33 – The six different rule types we can use to express our security logic

The rules in Cloud SIEM are rules-based, not query-based, which gives you more power at your fingertips. Let's dive in.

Search versus rule

One common question I hear is, "What is the difference between a scheduled search-based detection and a real-time rule?" Or, even more pointed, "How do I know when to use a search versus a rule?" The answer to these questions is very nuanced and ties back to the use case or purpose of the detection or alert. More generally, however, I would say try to use a real-time rule first and fall back to a scheduled search if needed. Why? The biggest advantage of real-time rules is that they operate on data that has already been normalized into a common schema. This makes detection logic more resilient and eliminates the need for vendor-specific parsing in each query. Additionally, during the normalization process, new metadata fields can be added to enrich and categorize the log events, providing even more valuable context than what existed in the original message. Now that is cool!

This is best illustrated with a real-world use case.

Let's say we want to author a detection that identifies a successful brute-force login event. This detection must first identify a series of failed logins (the brute-force part), followed by a single successful login attempt. We could choose to write this as a search targeting Windows events, or we could write this as a rule that is agnostic of the originating data source.

Looking at the following two examples, which do you find most intuitive and efficient?

The following is query-based:

```
_sourceCategory=Labs/windows-jsonformat ("4625" OR "4624")
| where EventID=4625
| json "Computer",
       "EventData.SubjectUserName",
       "EventData.TargetUserName" as computer, src_user, dst_user
| where
  [subquery:_sourceCategory=Labs/windows-jsonformat
    | where EventID=4624
    | json "Computer",
           "EventData.SubjectUserName",
           "EventData.TargetUserName" as computer, src_user, dst_user
    | count by src, computer, dst_user
    | where _count > 5
    | compose src, computer, dst_user]
| count by src, computer, dst_user
```

The following is rule-based:

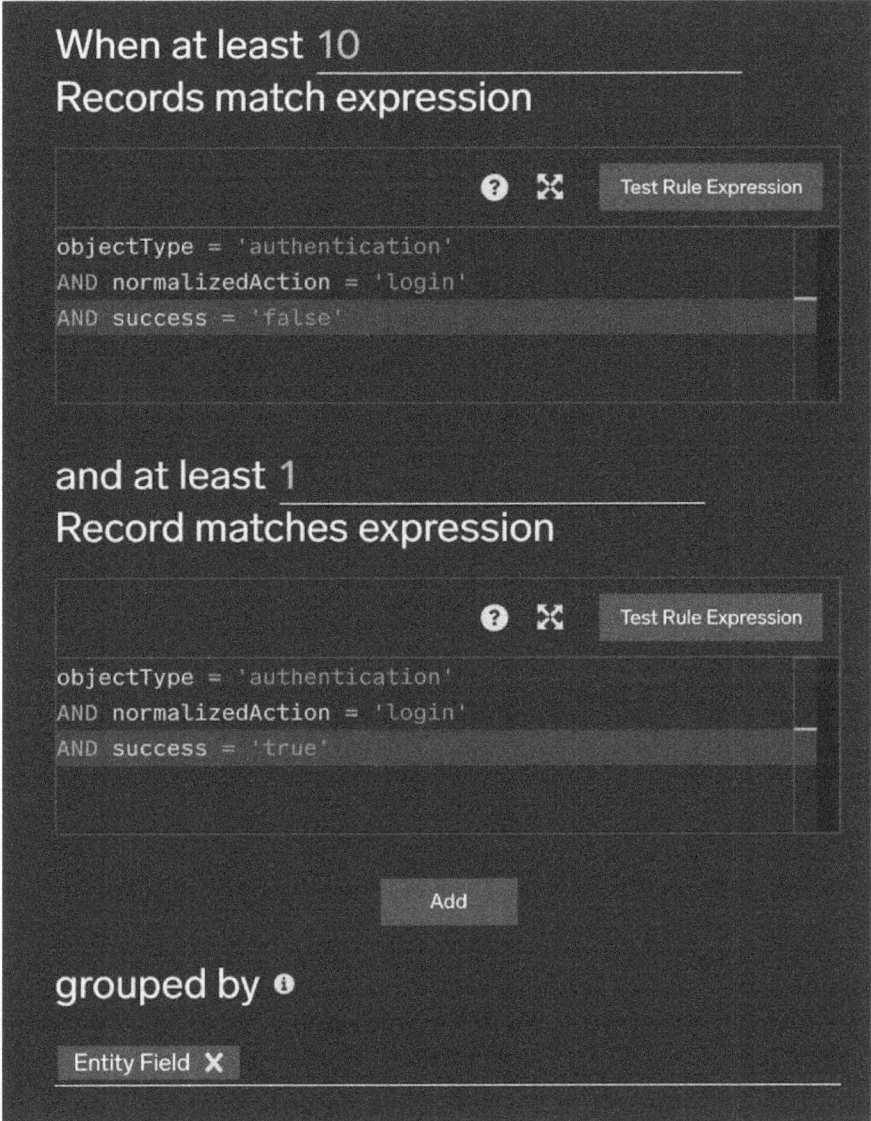

Figure 9.34 – Rule-based detection

With the search-based approach, you must account for vendor-specific log formats. This means manually handling how usernames and hostnames are labeled in different log sources (

In contrast, the rule-based approach benefits from a normalized schema. It condenses the detection logic to just three lines, relying on metadata that wasn't even in the original log message.

Rules operate on records, allowing them to take advantage of additional context and enriched metadata. Here's an important point, and I'm going to be frank and set some expectations. There is no technology out there that is going to magically know the ins and outs of your business and catch every malicious attempt at exploiting your business processes, people, and technology. You have to put in the work to make sure that the technology you're working with is as capable as possible when stopping threats. What's handy is that Sumo Logic gives you the power to create any versatile rule you need to ensure this is the case.

Enough theory! Let's get hands-on with this stuff. Together, we will create a few different rules that encompass some interesting real-world security use cases so you can see how adaptable the language and syntax are and, more importantly, how these rules then play a part in the creation of insights. When constructing rules, you specify the conditions to trigger the rule and then what happens when a signal is created. This is shown in the following screenshot with the **IF TRIGGERED** and **THEN CREATE A SIGNAL** sections:

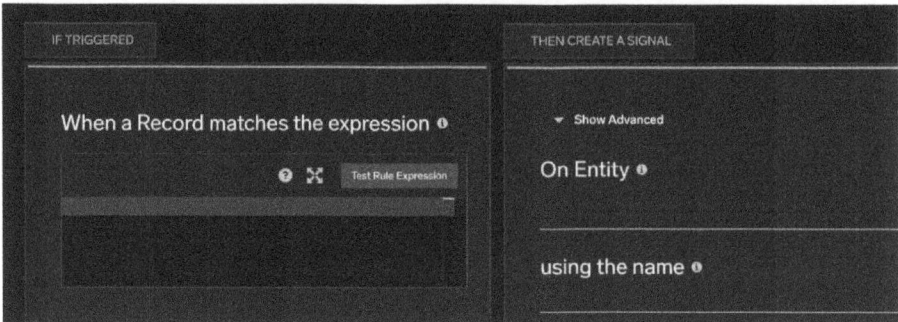

Figure 9.35 – The expression box to write your rule logic

The difference between all the different rule types is reflected in the rule expression; it changes based on the rule type you're working with. We'll get experience with all of them; we'll cover how to work with the section that creates the signal later on. Let's begin with match rules!

Match rules

The logic behind a match rule is the simplest: every time a *single* record matches the rule expression, a signal is triggered. So, with that in mind, let's go through a simple yet powerful example for a rule like this.

Authentication with MFA

We're going to look at a very common scenario. Someone logs in to a service without MFA. MFA is an integral part of identity security within the enterprise in consideration, and any login attempts made without it are treated with suspicion.

There are many ways we can approach this, but we wanted to use an example that highlights how easily this can be achieved with Sumo Logic syntax. This is the "authentication without MFA" rule that comes out of the box in Cloud SIEM.

Let's deconstruct the logic, as shown here:

Figure 9.36 – Rule logic to catch any login attempts that have been made without MFA

Here is the syntax:

```
ObjectType = 'Authentication'
AND normalizedAction IN ('logon', 'domainLogon')
AND success = true
AND mfa = false
```

It's a beautiful thing when all the data you need can be captured in four lines. What we're doing here is looking across *all* of our **authentication** data from sources that have authentication attempts. Examples include AWS CloudTrail, Microsoft Entra ID, Okta, and Windows Event Logs.

If we were to do this using a search-based method, this would entail specifying all of the authentication data sources that we have one by one while bearing in mind any source-specific log formats and fields. This would result in an insanely bloated query and the detection wouldn't work in real time.

The normalization and smart syntax (terms such as objectType and threat_category) give you the flexibility to capture what you need to bring that logic to life. The normalizedAction variable in *line 2* lets you command Cloud SIEM to look at the actions that are involved in logins and domain logins, instead of specifying the syntax involved with each of those actions. This, once again, really underlines the advantage of normalization in Sumo Logic, as normalization is done for you across dozens of sources. You can define all this breadth of activity in two lines! You can find all the normalized actions here: https://help.sumologic.com/docs/cse/schema/cse-normalized-classification/#normalizedaction.

Finally, *lines 3 and 4* are binary outcomes that we want to specify in the expression, so we're looking for all successful login attempts where MFA has not been used.

A match rule is the most commonly used type of rule because it's the easiest way of focusing on a clear definition of suspicious or malicious behavior; it's very black and white. When it comes down to it, we know when something's bad. "These users shouldn't be logging in without MFA, let me know when anyone doesn't use MFA" is easy to articulate with this syntax. Four lines, to be precise!

Alerting on traffic to certain countries

While match rules are simple, they are also very versatile, and most rules within a customer environment are match-based for this reason. Before moving on to the next rule type, I wanted to show another match rule example. Let's take a look at a scenario where traffic ends up going to a country that you definitely don't want it to go to; we'll be using the **Traffic to Embargoed Countries** rule that comes out of the box:

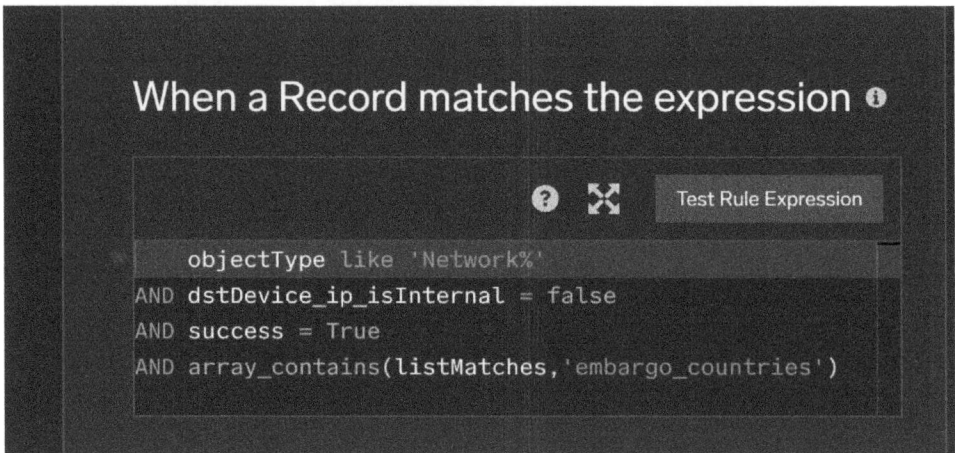

Figure 9.37 – The logic for a rule to catch traffic going to unauthorized countries

Here is the syntax:

```
ObjectType like 'Network%'
AND dstDevice_ip_isInternal = false
AND success = True
AND array_contains(listMatches, 'embargo_countries')
```

The reason I wanted to show you this rule is that there are a couple of different options that were used here. The first is a different objectType. As you can see, this one is Network% instead of Authentication. This means we're looking across all of our network sources of data, such as firewalls, IDS and IPS tools, and proxies.

The two new elements we can see here are dstDevice_ip_isInternal and array_contains. The first one relates to the built-in metadata regarding *network blocks*[1]. Network blocks let you define and categorize your internal environments, which helps with investigations. You enter CIDR ranges of your internal assets, and it marks these as internal. You can then mention these network blocks in rule logic. For example, if you know that certain actions are taken in an isolated internal network, you can elect to ignore those actions by specifying the dstDevice_ip_isInternal flag.

array_contains is part of the Cloud SIEM rule syntax. It lets you specify what arrays you'd like Cloud SIEM to cross-reference against if a matching record is found. To use the array_contains operator, we need an array, right? We can create one with **match lists**[2]. Match lists help you organize and categorize your assets, whether it's a list of admin email addresses, a list of critical server IPs, and so on. Any list you create can be used in a rule expression with the help of the `array_contains` syntax. In this example, we're looking at a list of embargoed countries we've put together. Any successful packets going through to a network that meet the following criteria will create a signal:

- If it is not an internal network
- If it is a country identified as an embargoed country in our match list

GeoIP and ASN enrichment happens automatically when raw events turn into a record (more on that later in this chapter), so this is very straightforward to achieve.

Identifying a phishing email

You might be thinking at this point, "OK, this makes sense, but there are surely cases that aren't covered by normalized actions, or custom bits of metadata from my source that I want to look out for?"

Perfectly valid question. It's a good time to talk about record fields. When putting together a rule, I advise looking at a record from the source of data you're trying to build logic for. For instance, one of the rules that tries to identify a phishing email from Proofpoint has this logic:

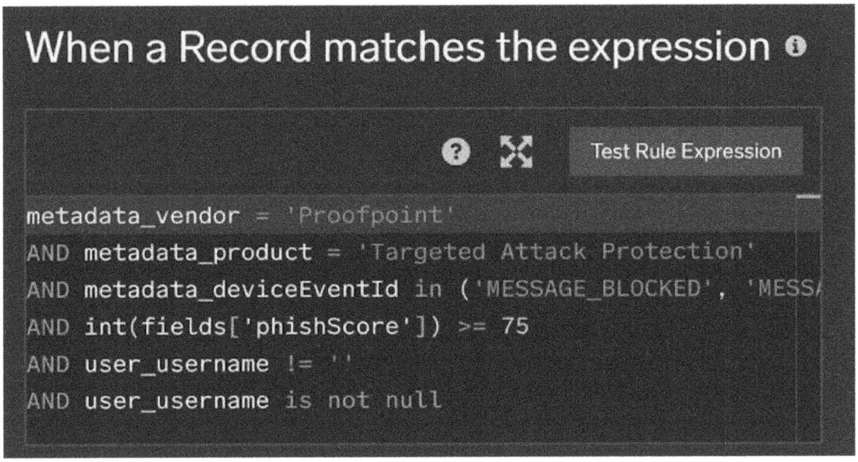

```
metadata_vendor = 'Proofpoint'
AND metadata_product = 'Targeted Attack Protection'
AND metadata_deviceEventId in ('MESSAGE_BLOCKED', 'MESS
AND int(fields['phishScore']) >= 75
AND user_username != ''
AND user_username is not null
```

Figure 9.38 – Starting to add a few more bits of logic to our match rules

Here is the syntax:

```
Metadata_vendor = 'Proofpoint'
AND metadata_product = 'Targeted Attack Protection'
AND metadata_deviceEventId in ('MESSAGE_BLOCKED', 'MESSAGE_PERMITTED', 'MESSAGE_DELIVERED')
AND int(fields['phishScore']) >= 75
AND user_username != ''
AND user_username is not null
```

This is monitoring the Proofpoint data source and some event IDs that relate to phishing. The field we're interested in here is on *line 4*, where we have `int(fields['phishScore']) >= 75`. There are a lot of alerts coming in from Proofpoint, and we want to narrow down to those events for which the phishing score is worth reviewing. Basically, we can use this `fields` operator to extract a field from a record and use it in our logic! Here is what the `phishScore` field looks like in our record data:

Figure 9.39 – The phishScore field among all our Proofpoint metadata

The `int` before `fields` in *line 4* from our example is basically telling Cloud SIEM to address the value as an integer so that we can correctly apply the comparison logic of ***if greater than or equal to 75***. This applies to any record and field you have in your data.

There is an even quicker way of adding this to our rule expression logic. We can just click on the `phishScore` text and then choose **copy expression**. This will just copy this exact field into the expression of the rule and we're good to go. Using this method, we can start to easily tailor our rules to what we need them to find.

We've got some match rules under our belt—that's great. It's a core part of rule-building. But what if we want to introduce a number after which we want to be alerted? This is where threshold rules come into play.

Threshold rules

Threshold rules build upon match rules nicely because the two are practically the same, apart from one small difference: with threshold rules, you can specify how many records of a certain type occur within a period of time. Let's run through a quick example, once again using a ready-made rule in the Sumo Logic Cloud SIEM, **Multiple Windows Account Lockouts on Endpoint**:

Figure 9.40 – A threshold rule lets you specify the number of records and the timeframe

Here is the syntax:

```
Metadata_vendor = 'Microsoft'
AND metadata_product = 'Windows'
AND metadata_deviceEventId = 'Security-4740'
```

Here, we are matching all Windows event codes that equal **Security-4740**, which relates to all Windows lockout events happening on Windows devices. What we add to the expression is a temporal and numeric condition. Here we want to just turn this rule into a signal when there are at least **5** records that match this expression *within* 10 minutes.

That's all there is to it! You'll find that threshold rules are being replaced by **outlier** rules more frequently, mainly because you don't have to manually set the thresholds of anomalous behavior and instead can rely on the built-in anomaly detection models in Cloud SIEM. We'll talk about this a bit more in a short while when we cover outlier rules.

Next, let's up the complexity slightly and consider an example where you need not only one but additional conditions to trigger a rule, within a particular time window, as part of your security logic. These types of rules are called aggregation rules.

Aggregation rules

In many security scenarios, looking at single events in isolation isn't enough. You need to piece together multiple indicators over a window of time to see the bigger picture. This is precisely where aggregation rules in Sumo Logic come into play. An aggregation rule monitors event volume or patterns over a specified timeframe and fires when a certain threshold is met.

While general-purpose query languages are flexible, as defenders, it's easy to get bogged down with writing complex queries that keep track of time windows, user identities, IP addresses, or other dynamic fields. Aggregation rules remove much of that complexity by letting you define grouping fields (e.g., user, IP address, or even a custom dimension) so that multiple events tied to that entity are gathered automatically. You don't have to manually craft the logic to group events or maintain the counts; the rule type handles it inherently.

>
>
> A single aggregation rule can do what might otherwise require a sophisticated sequence of join, group by, and time bucket operations in a standard query-based system.

As a defender, it's important that we cover as much ground as possible and take different scenarios into account. We might want to monitor individual events that are odd, such as downloading a particular file that shouldn't be downloaded, for example, but sometimes we need to keep an eye on more activity taking place within a certain timeframe. This is the premise of the aggregation rule. As data stored on cloud storage continually grows in volume, whether it be AWS S3, Azure Blob Storage, or other solutions, such as Dropbox, there is a higher risk of exfiltration that comes with this.

Some of these services have inbuilt mechanisms to catch data exfiltration, but sometimes they cannot stop someone sneaky enough. We want to monitor our S3 infrastructure, in particular when there is lots of data being exfiltrated from our buckets.

Consider the following aggregation rule that captures actions done on AWS S3:

```
metadata_vendor = 'Amazon AWS'
AND metadata_product = 'CloudTrail'
AND fields["userIdentity.type"] != "AWSService"
AND application = "s3.amazonaws.com"
```

Figure 9.41 – Example aggregation rule

Here is the syntax:

```
Metadata_vendor = 'Amazon AWS'
AND metadata_product = 'CloudTrail'
AND fields["userIdentity.type"] != "AWSService"
AND application = "s3.amazonaws.com"
```

We are looking at CloudTrail data, as this data contains the interactions we are looking for with our buckets. We exclude any service roles that are interacting with the bucket and, of course, we are only looking at S3 events.

Unlike with a match rule, there are additional behavioral parameters we can set to define the actions that will trigger this:

- Which entities to group on
- The timeframe
- The aggregation

In our expression, we choose how the data is going to be grouped. We want it to be grouped by the username and device IP doing the interactions, because we want to track what else these entities are doing, so we specify this *as well as* a time window of five minutes. But wait! There's more! We can also choose the specific action to aggregate with these grouped entities, and in this case, it's `GetObject`. Here's what it looks like:

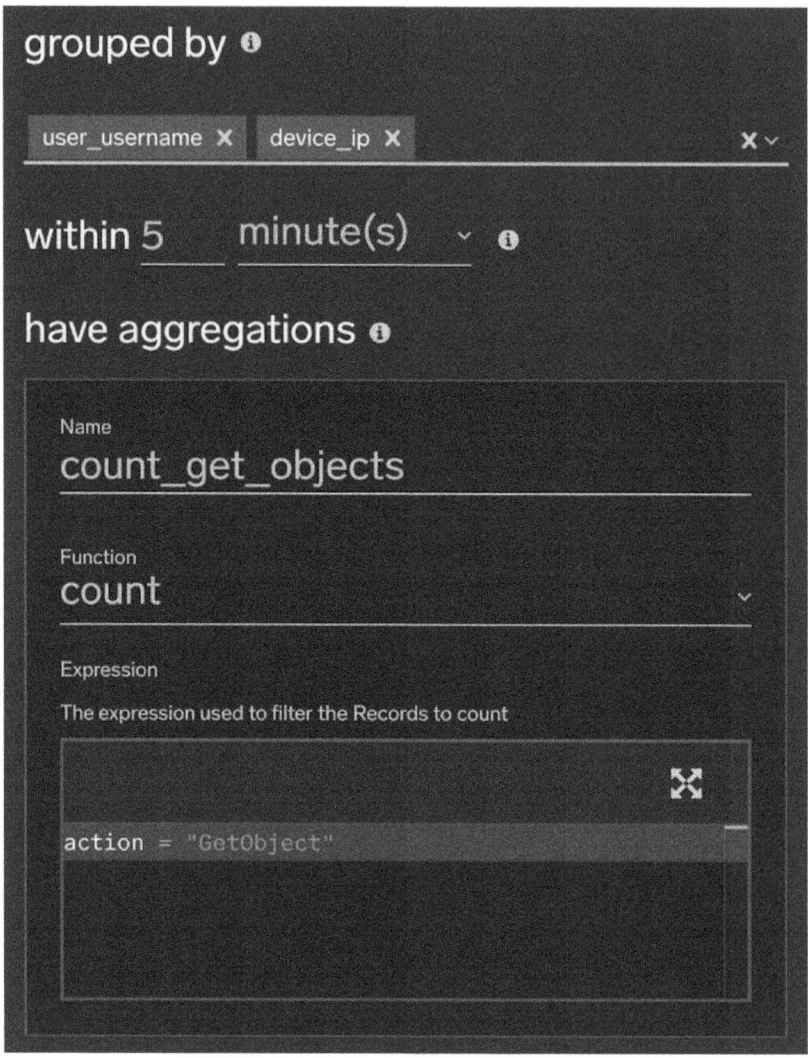

Figure 9.42 – For an aggregation rule, we need to define the exact behavior we're monitoring

So, in summary, we're looking at all GetObject API calls made to S3 buckets by a non-service user and counting the number of those calls that happen within five minutes. It's worth mentioning that you can add more aggregations to this rule as well, but the best practice is to keep the rules modular in nature and not to make them too monolithic or cluttered. This makes it easier for the insight engine to automatically cluster and correlate these events when they happen. More on that soon.

There's one thing missing from the rule so far, though. We have our expression, we have the grouped entities, and we have the action, but how do we know when to trigger the signal? Does it trigger when one object is downloaded? Or does it trigger when 100 are downloaded? We can set this in the final part of the rule by getting everything we've done so far to match a condition. In this example, we want this rule to get curious when *more than 20* objects are downloaded *within 5 minutes* by a user:

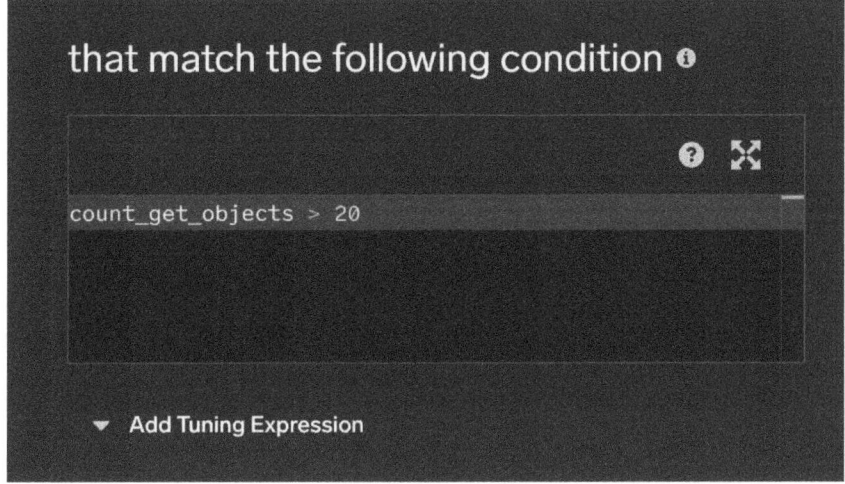

Figure 9.43 – A condition applied to the behavior in an aggregation rule

This here is the beauty of the aggregation rule. You're able to group data across windows of time to better sculpt when malicious or suspicious events take place.

From here, I want to get into the machine learning rules. We're going to cover the outlier rule type by revisiting this aggregation rule so that you can see the difference and how to implement it. I also made a comment earlier about threshold rules being replaced by outlier rules; you will see an example of both in the next section.

Outlier rules

Finding outliers in your data is a tricky business. Usually, it's a complex process where you configure dozens of variables, or it comes out of the box, but you have no idea what is being input or how accurate the data is. In the machine learning rules available to use in Cloud SIEM (outlier and first-seen), you dictate to the platform how it should learn about the different behaviors that you're interested in. We'll explore this now.

If we take a look at the previous example, we were interested in finding any events where a user downloads *more than 20 objects* from an AWS S3 bucket in the space of *5 minutes*. As we saw, there were a few variables we needed to configure in order to get there. Let's take a look at how an outlier rule can help. I've decided to split the outlier configuration into three sections so it's easier to explain as we go. The first section is the expression, which we are already well acquainted with. To enhance the aggregation rule, we need to tweak the expression very slightly; here it is:

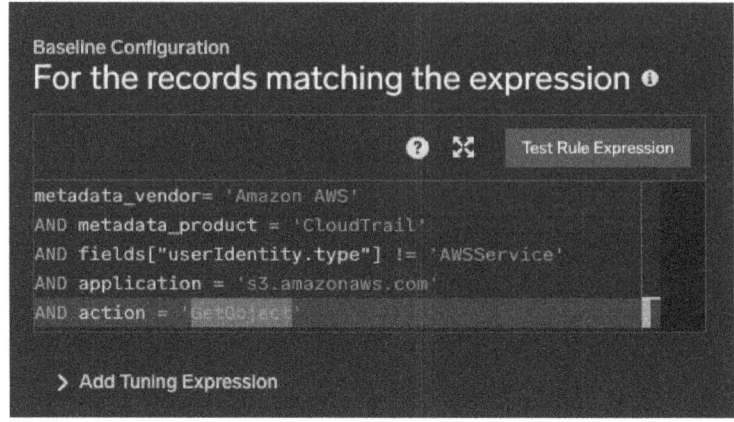

Figure 9.44 – Setting up an outlier rule. Not many variables compared to typical matching learning methods

Here is the syntax:

```
Metadata_vendor = 'Amazon AWS'
AND metadata_product = 'CloudTrail'
AND fields["userIdentity.type"] != "AWSService"
AND application = "s3.amazonaws.com"
AND action = 'GetObject'
```

As you can see, we add the action of GetObject into the expression itself instead of relying on the aggregation operator. By doing this, we specify the exact action that we want to build a baseline of behavior for. You'll see the reason why in a minute.

The next section of the configuration is the baseline area:

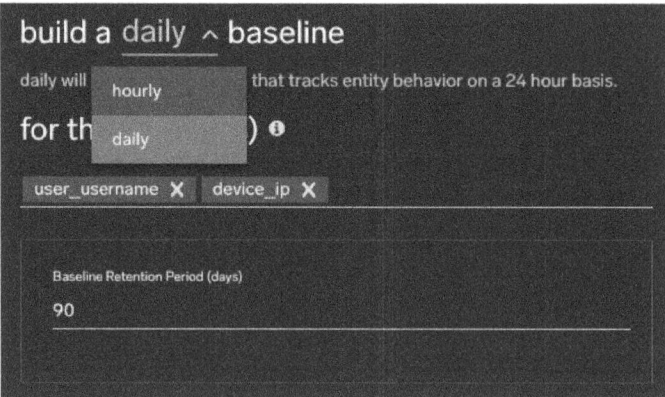

Figure 9.45 – You can set an hourly or daily baseline and choose how much data is used for learning for the entities of interest

We build a daily or hourly baseline based on the *entities* with this behavior. As Cloud SIEM is built on top of this entity model, it needs to know exactly how to correlate any linked activity to the entities we've listed here—the username and IP of the account doing this exfiltration. Underneath the entities, we also get to choose a baseline retention. What this refers to is the amount of training data that will be used for this rule. If we set a 90-day baseline retention period, Cloud SIEM will look back at the last 90 days of data in your data lake and build the model on top of that. If you're just getting started with using Sumo Logic, Cloud SIEM will need at least seven days of data to build a baseline model for these rules.

Finally, we configure the model in the third section, which looks like this:

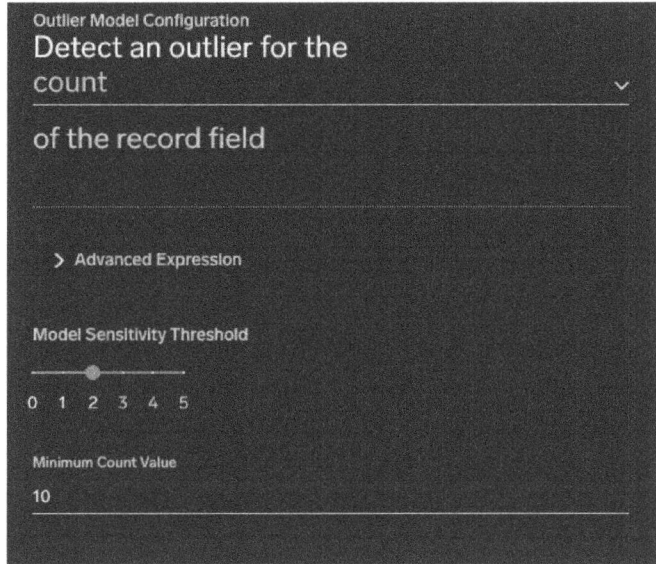

Figure 9.46 – We're able to tweak the sensitivity of the model in this section

You might look at this and think, "Is this it?" The answer is a resounding "Yes!" Within Sumo Logic, you'll find that in most cases, configuring machine learning models is very straightforward as a lot of the complexity has been abstracted away, but you can still define and push the model to the outcome you need. Here, we want to look at the count of events that match our expression at the top. Note that if we didn't specify the action of GetObject in the expression, it would consider every S3 event that is executed by a username and/or IP address, which would be nuts.

To tweak the model, you can change the sensitivity using the slider. All this does is widen or narrow the deviation from the mean, or normal, behavior, but you can temper this with the minimum count value at the bottom. For example, I'm only interested in at least 10 events, but from there, it'll factor in the baseline behavior.

Now, this was a longer explanation due to the fact that we encountered some new UI elements, but if you compare the two ways of setting up the same rule, you'll find it takes less time to spin up the machine learning rule *and* it's more powerful.

We've covered the detection of outliers in our security event data. Let's take a look at the *first-seen* rules and what they have to offer.

First-seen rules

When analyzing security events, it's often critical to detect anything "new" in your environment because what's new could be suspicious. First-seen rules in Sumo Logic CSE serve exactly this purpose: they watch for entities, attributes, or behaviors that appear *for the first time* in a given dataset. While these rules may sound simple, they can be incredibly powerful in detecting anomalies or potential threats before they become ongoing problems. First-seen rules are interesting in that the signals generated are not considered to be malicious straight away when they are created. As a security practitioner, you can identify the context surrounding this first-seen event very quickly to help you understand whether it is malicious or benign.

You no longer have to wade through mountains of data to verify that an admin who has run a command on the terminal for the first time is a threat actor or whether they're just trying out a funky new admin tool. A first-seen rule triggers when a unique value (or combination of values) has never been observed before, or at least not within a defined timeframe or dataset. In other words, it captures the very first instance of something new in your logs or events.

The following are some examples of *first-seen* triggers:

- New IP address accessing your network
- New user logging in to a sensitive system
- New user agent making a request to your application
- New process or filename in your endpoint logs

Because these are first-time occurrences, they often stand out as potential early indicators of suspicious activity, ranging from new infiltration methods to brand-new user accounts that may or may not be legitimate.

We'll see some examples of great first-seen rules when we look at the insight engine in greater detail, but for now, let's put a first-seen rule together.

Let's use this moment to shift to a more traditional DevOps/dev topic, which is code repositories. They are packed with sensitive and business-critical information, so having security oversight of these repositories is pretty high up there in terms of priority. There are a lot of people who can technically do pull requests across our repos, and some might even bypass some policies that can hinder them…so we'd like to stay on top of that. Let's write a first-seen rule to capture pull request policy abuse:

Figure 9.47 – Our rule logic to capture pull request policy abuse in our first-seen rule

Here is the syntax:

```
Metadata_vendor = "Microsoft"
AND metadata_product = "Azure DevOps Auditing"
AND metadata_deviceEventId = "AzureDevOpsAuditEvent"
AND action = "Get.RefUpdatePoliciesBypassed"
```

Using the Azure DevOps tooling, we can easily pick out this type of activity via an action. First-seen rules are straightforward in that the main variable you specify, apart from the expression, is to tell the machine learning model what new entity you're interested in seeing this activity from. In this case, we want to know the username (**user_username** in *Figure 9.48*) that bypasses our pull request policy:

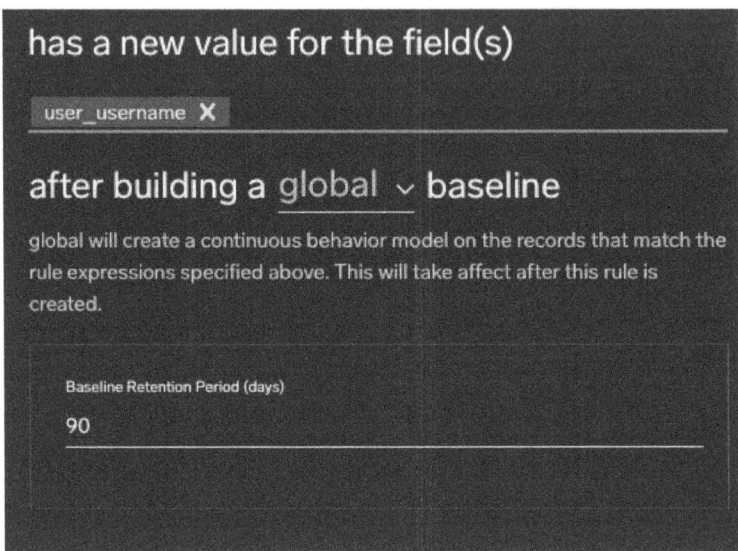

Figure 9.48 – The simple way to define the entity that we're monitoring

It's still necessary to specify a baseline retention to make use of the historical baselining to build the model.

At this point, we've covered five out of six of the different rule types available—we're on fire! Hopefully, you're still with me because there's one final rule type to cover, the *chain* rule. I've left it until last because this is the least common rule type in Cloud SIEM, but it has its uses.

Chain rules

Chain rules let you specify two or more activities that are done over a particular time window *in exact order*. You have the option of creating chain rules where the records aren't in order, but that is rarely required due to the nature of the insight engine, which we will cover in the next chapter.

There are times when you want to make sure that a particular behavior pattern is caught in the exact steps you need, rather than having that behavior as individual signals. For instance, someone changing their MFA isn't the worst crime in the world, but what if that same user then has a higher-than-normal login event following this? Uh-oh! To help us with this scenario, we'll call on the help of another ready-to-use rule—**Change of Azure MFA Method**—followed by **Risky SignIn**:

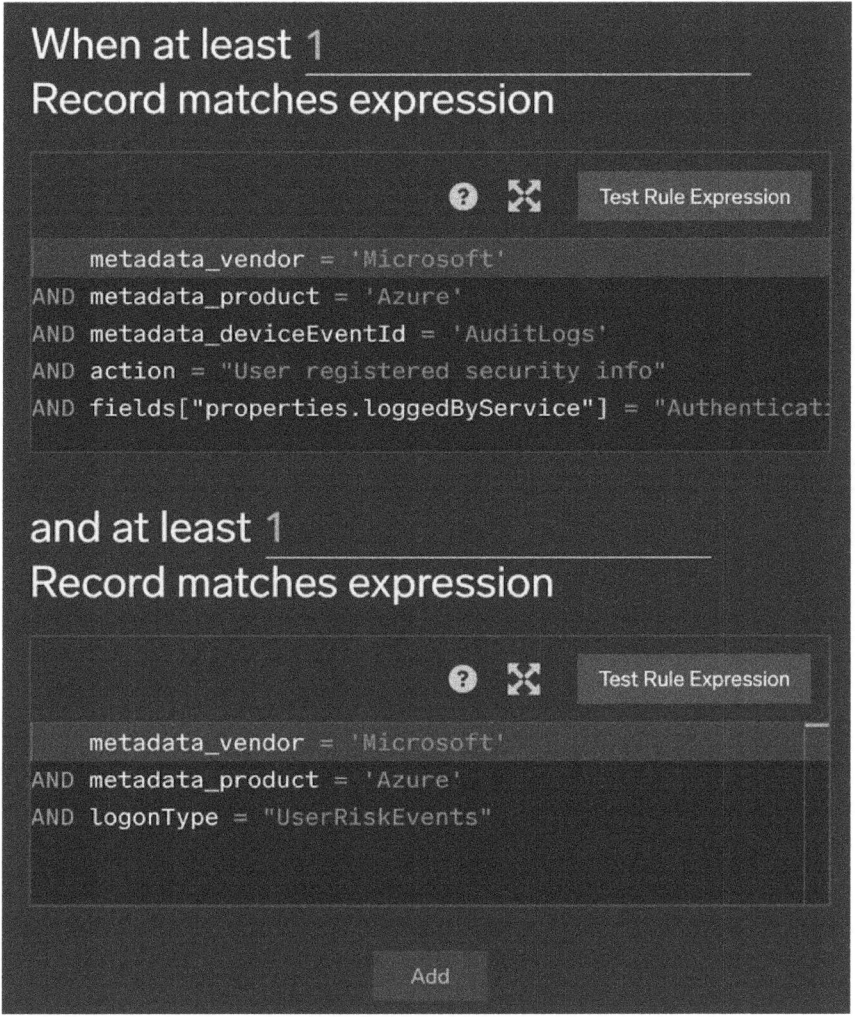

Figure 9.49 – Example chain rule

Here is the syntax:

```
Metadata_vendor = 'Microsoft'
AND metadata_product = 'Azure'
AND metadata_deviceEventId = 'AuditLogs'
AND action = "User registered security info"
AND fields["properties.loggedByService"] = "Authentication Methods"

Metadata_vendor = 'Microsoft'
AND metadata_product = 'Azure'
AND logonType = "UserRiskEvents"
```

The chain rule lets you specify multiple expressions, with threshold logic over the top. As you can see, we're looking at two separate records: the first is where a user changes their MFA details on Azure at least once. This is followed by a record where the login type of that user is labeled as "high risk" by Azure. This order isn't implied; you have to tell Cloud SIEM that you'd like to capture this pairing of activity together:

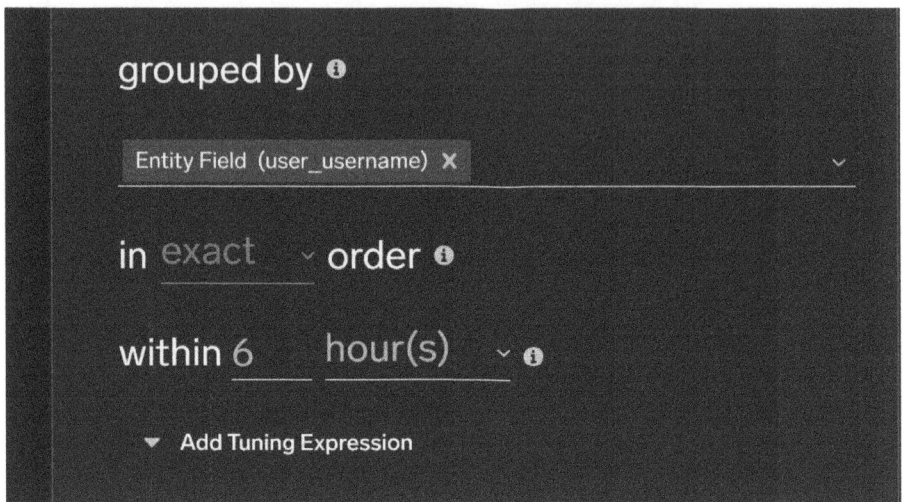

Figure 9.50 – Choosing how to order the records and setting the timeframe

Similar to the aggregation rule, you can group this combined behavior on an entity, which is useful because in this case, we want to monitor the username involved and see whether they get up to more shady business. You also get to choose the order that these records are seen in Cloud SIEM, whether they follow each other in *exact order* or they happen in *any order*.

Even though you have the Insight Engine at your disposal, pairing events like this together is still particularly useful when investigating this behavior. By the way, if you want *exact* ordering between two records, you can only chain on a maximum of two records. You'll see that most out-of-the-box chain rules in Cloud SIEM are chained on two records in exact order, for example, this **Successful Brute Force** rule. A rule like the following is really easy to put together in Cloud SIEM (it's actually done for you):

Figure 9.51 – Brute-force rule example

Here is the syntax:

```
ObjectType = 'Authentication'
AND normalizedAction = 'logon'
AND success = false
AND NOT metadata_deviceEventId = 'Security-4776'

ObjectType = 'Authentication'
AND normalizedAction = 'logon'
AND success = true
AND NOT array_contains(listMatches, 'vuln_scanners')
```

Finally, going back to *Figure 9.50*, you specify the timeframe over which you want these records to happen one after the other. Hey presto, you have a chain rule!

We've put in all this effort to define what will trigger the rule, but what about turning it into a signal? Let's take a look at the right (or bottom, depending on your screen resolution) part of the rule creation screen.

Creating the signal

Once we've told Cloud SIEM what behavior we're looking for, we want to tell Cloud SIEM how we want to derive the most benefit out of the signal. We do that by filling in this section on the right. I'll walk through it step by step to try and cover the six most important parts:

- Entity
- Signal name
- Signal summary
- Signal description
- Severity
- Tags

I will cover the ones that need elaboration. We'll be using the **AWS CloudTrail – Public S3 Bucket Exposed** rule as an example.

On Entity

The **On Entity** field is all about specifying the entity types that Cloud SIEM will correlate and cluster on:

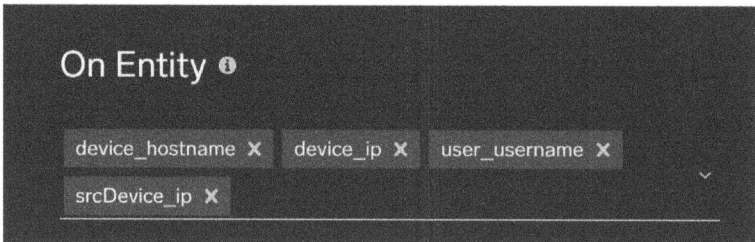

Figure 9.52 – The entities we want Cloud SIEM to cluster this activity on

There is a big reason for this. While it's great to have a machine decide these entities for you when signals are generated, that could be fraught with inaccuracies and mistakes. *You know your environment better than a machine.* You have the opportunity to use the entity model and specify to Cloud SIEM what entities are important when certain scenarios are encountered to assist the advanced machine learning algorithms under the hood. In this day and age, everyone wants a machine to do everything for them, but that is currently a level of intelligence not available right now, so the best alternative is to help you steer the models and the capabilities in the best and most accurate way.

Severity

Severity can be constant or dynamic in Cloud SIEM. If you choose a constant severity, you choose a number from 1 to 10, and that's it. The dynamic option provides you with the option of changing the severity based on the value of a field. For example, you can have two domain controllers, one more critical than the other. If the **server** field is equal to **DC1**, then the severity is **8**, and if the **server** field is equal to **DC2**, then the severity is **5**. You get the gist. The following figure shows this:

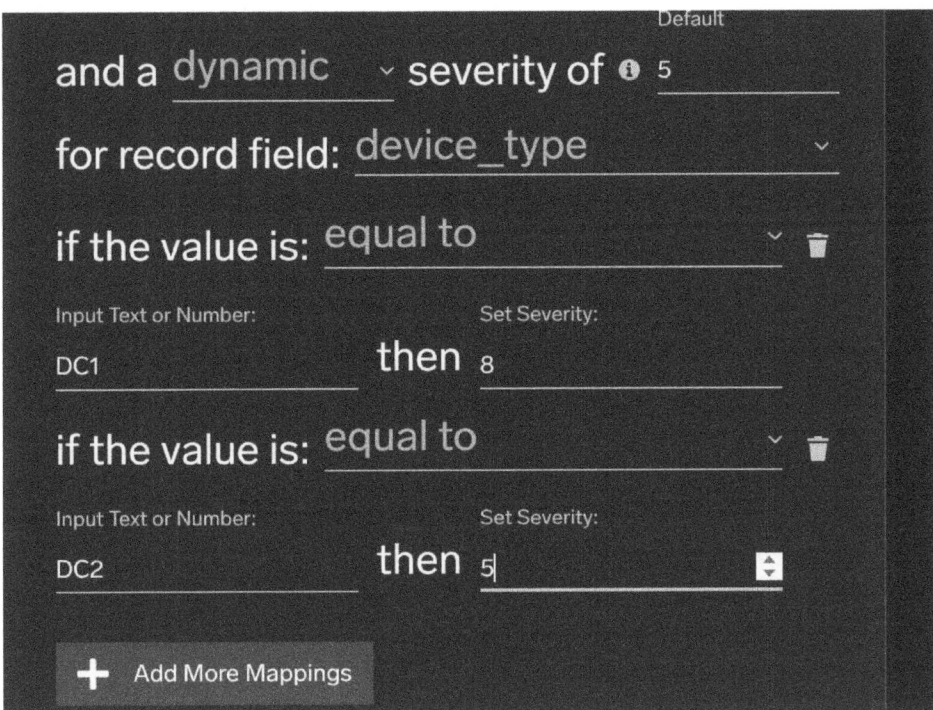

Figure 9.53 – Setting a dynamic severity depending on fields and values

These severity values feed into how the insight engine decides when to create an insight, so it's important to tailor them appropriately.

Tags

Tags are vital to rule creation because they help you to map any rules to the MITRE ATT&CK framework. There is a tool in Cloud SIEM called the **MITRE ATT&CK coverage matrix**, and it's populated with a built-in schema that's ready to use in Sumo Logic that maps to each technique and sub-technique within the MITRE framework. The coverage matrix will be covered later in this chapter, but it's a great way for you to do your security analytics work with the MITRE framework in mind.

You can also add any custom tags to these rules, for example, particular threat intelligence tags or internal taxonomy, as well. Example tags include dev_machine or contractor, if you have contractors operating in your environment and activity from these external third parties should be under more scrutiny.

Signal Name, **Signal Summary**, and **Signal Description** are all self-explanatory. The added point is that you can use some of the entities as variables within the signal name; for example, here the signal will tell us the name of the changed S3 bucket:

Figure 9.54 – Dynamically specifying what variables you want to appear in the signal names

Now that we have some great, practical, and everyday examples of rules under our belt, we can move on to some of the pro tips for using rules. These are going to come in handy after you've been running for a while with the rules you have, and you want to improve some things after getting some experience.

Rule tuning

As you use Cloud SIEM more, you'll naturally notice areas that need to be improved, changed, or tweaked. Much like a car or computer enthusiast who is constantly looking at the best way of improving their parts and specs, you can make sure your rules are as good as they can be to help you locate cyber risks. I personally prefer cars and/or computers, but there are people who are *very* keen on having the best security rules.

What rule tuning allows you to do is add logic to an existing rule or rules without having to replicate or modify that rule, even when it comes to updating rules in bulk.

There are two ways of accessing rule tuning. The first is by going to the **Cloud SIEM** menu on the left and then going into **Rule Tuning**:

Figure 9.55 – Accessing the Rule Tuning section from the main menu

Alternatively, you can access rule tuning from the rule UI. Underneath your rule expression, there should be an option to tune the rule by selecting **Add Tuning Expression**:

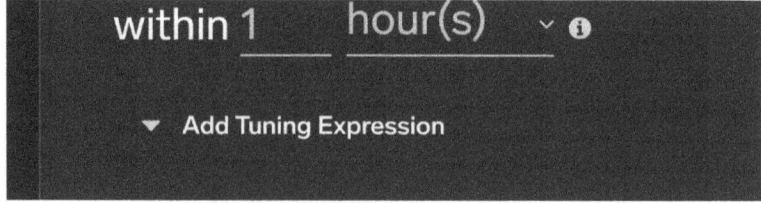

Figure 9.56 – Where to access rule tuning in the rules UI

Once you click that, you'll be able to select from a list of existing tuning expressions or create a new one. Now, let's get our hands dirty and see what this looks like in practice. Let's use the last rule we worked with, the chain rule looking at brute-force success. We want to keep the existing brute-force logic we have in place; it works great! All we need to do is add a couple of existing conditions because lately we've been seeing quite a few false positives on a new server.

Let's create a new tuning expression. When tuning, you get to select whether this tuning applies to specific rules or to **all** of your rules, so you get that flexibility. You then select the rules you want to apply it to and, finally, include your expression. In this instance, let's update not only the brute-force success rule but also the initial MFA rule that we looked at in the *Match rules* section.

We then specify whether we want to **include** or **exclude** the expression we're tuning with. In our case, we want to trigger a signal only when this new server isn't in the records and also want to ignore how the dev team is authenticating to this server because they keep failing to log in properly. This is what the picture looks like so far:

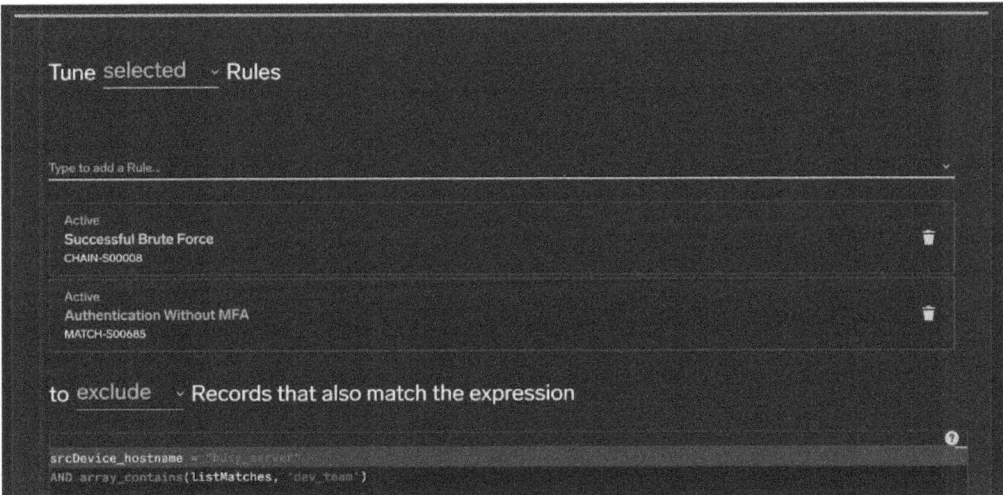

Figure 9.57 – Our tuning rule that is adding additional logic to specific rules

The power this affords you is clear. You can selectively apply extra logic to certain rules with two main benefits in mind:

- No need to change existing rules
- Can tune rules in bulk without having to do it one by one

Both of these benefits mean it's easier and quicker for you to make sure your rules are as accurate as they can be without the usual hassle involved with this process.

Tuning your rules is great when you actually take the time to review how Cloud SIEM is operating and how you are responding to events and incidents. It's a manual process.

I hope this deep dive into the wide array of rule types and options available to you gives you the confidence to maximize security coverage of your environment. The combination of rules and tags feed into an important part of growing that coverage, which is the MITRE ATT&CK Coverage Matrix. Let's check it out now.

The MITRE ATT&CK coverage matrix

MITRE ATT&CK is a framework dedicated to mapping out the tactics and techniques of threat actors. It is a detailed guide on how the bad guys do their thing. It's become a staple in cybersecurity teams worldwide, and for good reason. The more teams use it and contribute to it, the better it gets. It's a virtuous cycle of detection, defense, and maybe a few less stressful incident response meetings.

Once upon a time, threat analysis meant juggling a dozen browser tabs like some kind of digital circus act, jumping from logs to vendor docs to threat intel feeds, trying to piece together the puzzle. How much time has been lost in the Tab Abyss? Probably enough to finish watching *The Matrix*, twice!

Sumo Logic recognized the value of MITRE ATT&CK early on, which is why it's tightly integrated into the platform. When events of interest pop up, you want to move fast, ideally faster than Agent Smith dodging accountability. Within an insight, multiple TTPs are often condensed into a single, correlated incident, making it easy to identify what techniques are at play and what actions to take next. No trench coat required.

The foundation — rules

When we covered rule creation, we covered the foundation of how the MITRE ATT&CK matrix comes together. The rules that come out of the box have TTPs from MITRE that relate to the activity they were created to monitor. When creating your own rules, as we discussed earlier, it's easy to specify the TTPs that are important for that rule. These TTPs are passed on to the signals that are generated based on these rules, and this feeds the coverage matrix. For example, here is a signal that was generated recently, and we can see the TTPs associated with it as tags underneath:

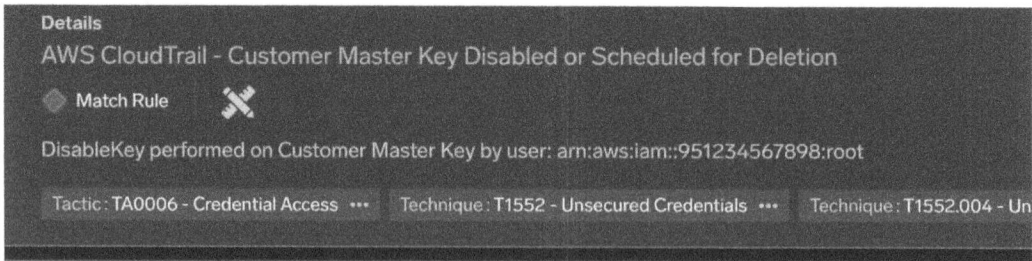

Figure 9.58 – MITRE ATT&CK TTPs appear underneath signals for quick reference

The coverage matrix tells you how well you are protected against a particular attack vector, with thresholds as follows:

- **High**: 7+ rules
- **Medium**: 4–6 rules
- **Low**: 1–3 rules
- **None**: No rules

As you use Cloud SIEM, the goal is to naturally grow your coverage and cover as much ground as possible over time, mitigating as much risk to the business as possible and staying ahead of threats. Let's take a look at the matrix itself.

The matrix

"Mr. Anderson, we've been expecting your logs" is something you *don't* want to hear your laptop tell you, but like in *The Matrix*, Agent Smith wanted control. In your world, so do attackers. The MITRE ATT&CK matrix is your blueprint to understanding their methods. Think of it as the *red pill* version of threat detection, only less kung fu and more JSON. Here is the Sumo Logic version:

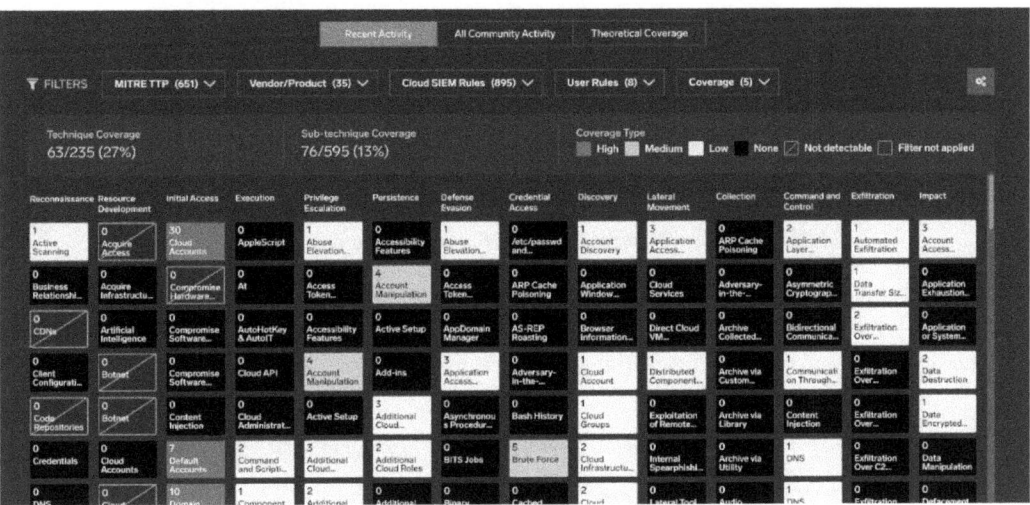

Figure 9.59 – The MITRE ATT&CK coverage matrix in all its glory

It helps if you've mapped your most vulnerable areas to the MITRE ATT&CK framework, but even if you haven't, the goal is to start small and choose broader areas that are common, such as phishing or cloud services. Out-of-the-box rules help with this because what's the point in reinventing the wheel, right? The framework also helps you by automatically mapping a lot of this behavior for you.

The crux of the main value that Sumo Logic adds is that it makes the framework way more approachable. As part of normal, day-to-day operations, you get help in understanding where you are covered based on signals and insights that are generated and also see where you may need to improve that coverage. Let's walk through an example section of the coverage matrix to show how everything is made easier. The one I'm interested in is **T1556.002 - Spearphishing Link**. When you click on it, you get to see a description of the TTP, as shown here:

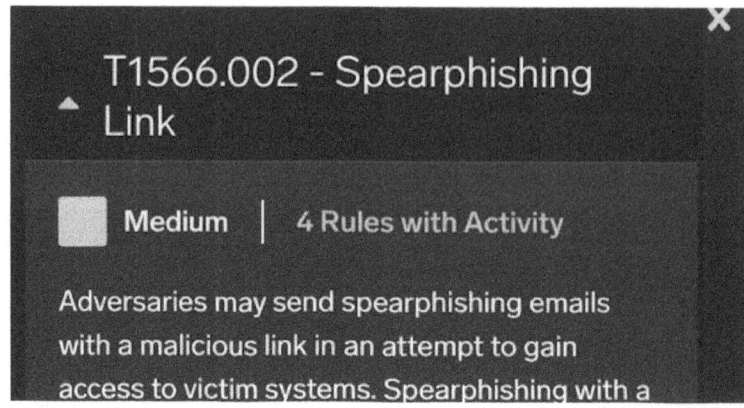

Figure 9.60 – Having a description of the TTP is always useful as a reference point

The really useful bits of information, and how they relate directly to your security posture, are the fact that you're able to see what signals have triggered in the past 180 days with this TTP, as well as what rules are covering you. You can see that for this particular attack vector, we have four rules covering us. Let's take a look at them:

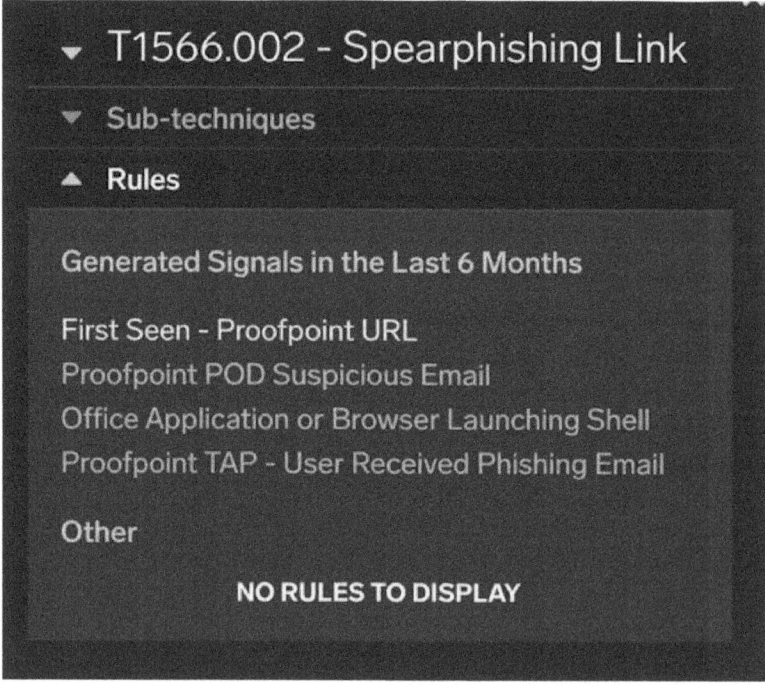

Figure 9.61 – The rules that are covering us for the Spearphishing Link attack vector

This is where the out-of-the-box rules come in useful, for example, the Proofpoint ones, because they already cover you across a lot of different parts of the attack chain, depending on what sources you're ingesting, of course. When you add your own rules, you've got a head start and can cover yourself based on the *specific exposure areas your business faces*. Who said that using SIEM technologies was difficult?

We'll revisit the MITRE ATT&CK coverage matrix briefly when we look at insights in the next chapter, but for now you can step out of the virtual world and enjoy some coffee before we reconvene to cover the secret sauce of Cloud SIEM.

Summary

This was a pretty beefy chapter. We dove quite deep into Cloud SIEM and what makes it tick, as well as its most important capabilities. The goal of the chapter was not only to share with you the powerful capabilities of Cloud SIEM but also to give you insight into what makes it so special under the hood. We learned that a combination of the following is extremely powerful for security detection, analysis, and response:

- A cloud-native architecture
- A powerful data model grounded in log analytics
- Out-of-the-box normalization and enrichment on any data source
- Built-in sophisticated machine learning and baselining models
- Over 1,000 security rules ready to go
- Flexible and versatile query language to create any security rule logic needed
- Automated correlation of signals to create security stories

We discussed the pipeline that makes the data model tick and transforms data into usable data structures in the form of records, signals, and insights to progressively analyze important data and piece it together like a jigsaw.

You also explored how to write security rules and how to make use of each type of security rule as well, so you can be prepared and ready for any situation if the 1,000 out-of-the-box rules aren't up to your requirements.

Finally, we explored the MITRE ATT&CK coverage matrix and the benefits it can provide to your team and the wider organization, as you can dynamically map your security posture and improve it over time. These components are the bedrock that powers the insight engine, the automated clustering and correlation capability that is able to group events of interest into an insight.

In the next chapter, we're going to home in on what the insight engine is and does. We'll look at example insights with best practices on how to use both Cloud SIEM and Sumo Logic for investigations and analysis.

References

1. https://help.sumologic.com/docs/cse/administration/create-use-network-blocks/
2. https://help.sumologic.com/docs/cse/match-lists-suppressed-lists/create-match-list/
3. https://github.com/SumoLogic/cloud-siem-content-catalog/blob/master/schema/record_types.md
4. https://github.com/SumoLogic/cloud-siem-content-catalog/blob/master/schema/full_schema.md

5. https://help.sumologic.com/docs/cse/schema/parsing-language-reference-guide/

6. https://help.sumologic.com/docs/cse/schema/username-and-hostname-normalization/

Get this book's PDF version and more

Scan the QR code (or go to

Note: Keep your invoice handy. Purchases made directly from Packt don't require an invoice.

10
The Insight Engine

So far in our discussions, we've covered a lot of the problem areas that security teams face—lack of visibility and context and too much noise. In a modern environment, there are *a lot* of accounts, APIs, endpoints, and identities to keep an eye on. In the previous chapter, we looked at why a solid data foundation is imperative to creating an environment where your data can be processed and normalized to give you a single environment in which you have as few blind spots as possible. The cherry on top of this cake is the Insight Engine.

Across the security industry, vendors use different terms to describe the same core concept. Alert, detection, correlation event, rule fire, and signal are often used interchangeably. In Sumo Logic, it's important to understand the specific meaning behind the terminology. A signal is the output of the real-time rules engine, generated by rule types such as correlation, aggregation, threshold, first seen, and outlier. While signals can be loosely thought of as security alerts, they are not always actionable on their own. Instead, Sumo groups related Signals together into an Insight, which provides the broader context needed to understand an attack, assess impact, and drive response.

An insight is a packaged incident that automatically clusters signals and entities across all your data sources that are being forwarded to Cloud SIEM. It walks a security team through all the events of interest that have occurred over time related to these entities. These events could span minutes, hours, or weeks; an insight bundles it all into a coherent narrative. The result is reduced cognitive load, a clearer picture of your data, and better prioritization and response.

In this chapter, you'll learn how signals and entities are clustered into a single insight, how to quickly triage, pivot, and investigate using the Insights UI, what an insight investigation looks like from start to finish with two scenarios, best practices for insights, and making the most of the Cloud SIEM app in the App Catalog for even more useful metadata.

The following topics will be covered in this chapter:

- From signals to insights
- Navigating an insight: Deep dive
- Cloud SIEM audit app: Deep-dive analytics on your SIEM solution's DNA
- Real insights and use cases

- Custom insights
- Cloud SIEM best practices

From signals to insights

Insights are designed to help teams prioritize and understand threats. Signals are rarely actionable on their own, and most security environments and SIEM tools are misconfigured or not fed with the right data, which impacts the effectiveness of the tools serving defenders. The situation is so bad that we have terms such as alert fatigue, swivel-chair syndrome, and analyst burnout to describe the situation.

In this section, we're going to be exploring the final stage of the data pipeline—how a collection of signals turns into an insight.

We'll stay with the baking metaphor that we introduced in the last chapter. The ingredients to whip up the foundation for the Insight Engine were the following:

- Out-of-the-box parsers and log mappings to help normalize security data
- Records, which are normalized security events
- Signals, which fire when a record matches a security rule
- Entities, which are tracked by Cloud SIEM and are used to cluster signals based on activity across data sources
- A centralized data lake, which allows the data to live in the same place and be processed by the same data model and data schema, as well as opening the floor up to the analytical and clustering algorithms that tie the signals together

For easier reference, here is the data pipeline overview that we first saw in the previous chapter. It shows how raw data goes through an enrichment and normalization process to turn into records, signals, and then insights:

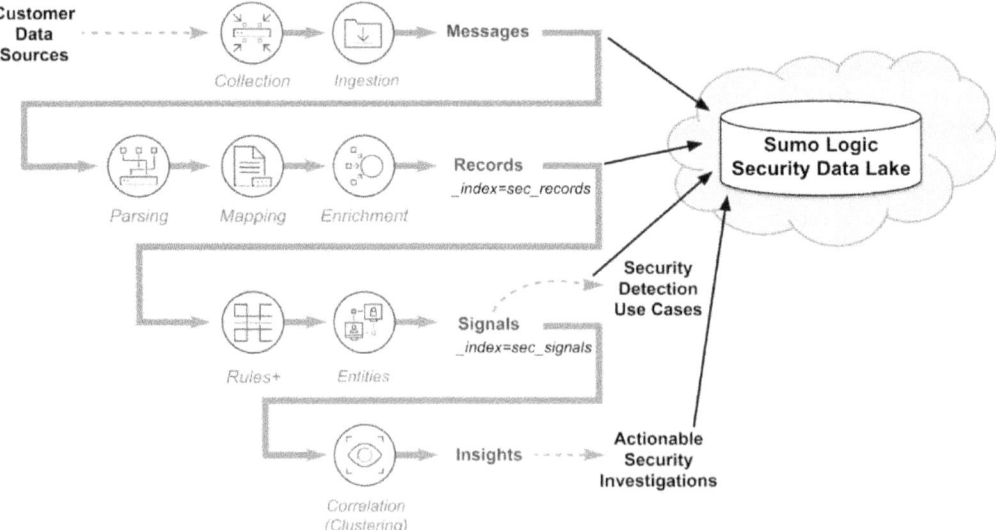

Let's begin this section by introducing Jasmin, a tier 1 security analyst in a **Security Operations Center** (**SOC**). She has an eight-hour shift where she gets bombarded with alerts and doesn't have enough time to investigate all of them. She has to prioritize the alerts she can work on and is also under pressure to justify any escalations. We'll follow her throughout to see how insights can elevate her ability to identify threats using Sumo Logic.

One day, Jasmin starts with 350 alerts in the queue. Most are duplicates or irrelevant. She spends 70% of her shift just closing alerts without any real triage. One alert that was missed because it looked like the others actually signified lateral movement from a compromised endpoint.

This scenario underscores a critical issue in modern security operations: alert fatigue. Attackers exploit the overwhelming volume of alerts, taking advantage of the fact that genuine threats can be lost in the noise. Even when an analyst senses something amiss, investigating requires sifting through vast amounts of data, correlating events across timeframes, and manually piecing together the narrative, which can be a daunting task.

Sumo Logic's Cloud SIEM addresses this challenge through advanced correlation and deduplication mechanisms, notably the clustering algorithm and entity activity scoring.

Deduplication and suppression

To combat alert duplication, Cloud SIEM employs suppression techniques. Signal suppression can occur for a variety of reasons, including entity suppression, network blocks, suppression lists, and identifying redundant signals by the rules correlation engine. Redundant signal suppression is the most common reason. Examples of suppressed signals are shown here:

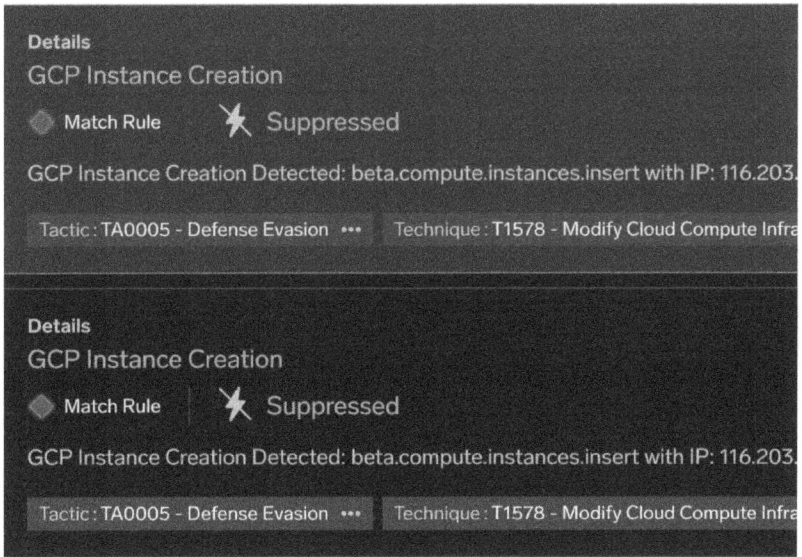

Figure 10.2 – Examples of suppressed signals

When multiple identical signals are detected, only the first counts toward the insight threshold. This threshold dictates whether an insight is generated. More on this in a bit. Subsequent duplicates are tagged as *suppressed*. In order for a signal to be suppressed, the *signal name* and *entity name* have to be the same. They also have to have occurred within the same configurable time window, typically 72 hours, but you can also reduce suppression down to 0 if you wanted to. I've encountered a few examples of this while working with customers when they had events linked to the same entity and behavior. Such events were frequent enough to cause suppression by default but this behavior was necessary to create a link between other events of interest if an adversary were to pivot from this asset type to another. This approach can dramatically reduce the number of alerts analysts must review. For instance, Jasmin's 350 alerts could be consolidated into a manageable set of insights, each representing a unique security event.

Importantly, suppressed signals aren't discarded. They are stored in the **signal index**, complete with metadata indicating their suppressed status. Depending on the reason, the suppressedReasons field will be populated in the sec_signal index. This data allows for comprehensive reporting, rule tuning, and analysis of signal-to-noise ratios.

> Note
>
> The sec_signal index/partition is a set of SIEM-focused indexes that is created when you start using Cloud SIEM. The full list of eight partitions is as follows:
>
> - sec_record_audit
> - sec_record_authentication
> - sec_record_email
> - sec_record_endpoint
> - sec_record_failure
> - sec_record_network
> - sec_record_notification
> - sec_signal
>
> They can be found in **Data Management** | **Logs** | **Partitions** and contain useful metadata that feeds into some of the Cloud SIEM enterprise dashboards, which we'll cover toward the end of the chapter.

Keeping the signals is useful because the security team retains the data for any audit or forensic activity, but it is worth highlighting that *a suppressed signal does not contribute to the activity score of an insight*. This means that insights aren't created from very high-volume noise that you may be being bombarded with; this keeps the insights as high-fidelity as possible.

In Jasmin's case, she won't be faced with those 350 alerts in the first place; some of them might be repeat activity, such as a few users accidentally inputting their passwords incorrectly too many times. This already helps a great deal. If Jasmin can focus on unsuppressed activity, she can use her time better to find true positives, that is, actual suspicious activity, instead.

Suppressed lists: Fine-tuning signal suppression

Beyond duplicate suppression, Cloud SIEM offers suppressed lists—a feature that allows analysts to define specific indicators (such as IP addresses, domains, or usernames) whose associated signals should be suppressed. Unlike match lists, which are referenced in rule expressions to influence signal generation, suppressed lists operate independently, automatically suppressing any signal containing a listed indicator.

For example, if a known vulnerability scanner's IP address is added to a suppressed list, any signal involving that IP will be suppressed, regardless of the rule that would have generated it. This ensures that routine, non-threatening activities don't clutter the alert queue.

Each suppressed list is defined by a target column (such as **IP Address**, **Domain**, or **Username**). When a record matches an entry in a suppressed list, specific fields are populated, providing transparency and aiding in downstream analysis. Often, the default suppression behavior is satisfactory, but all of the different ways to tune and customize suppression are well documented for those who would like to get deep under the hood. See *about-signal-suppression and redundant-signal-suppression* in the help docs[2].

By leveraging clustering, activity scoring, and suppression mechanisms, including suppressed lists, Sumo Logic's Cloud SIEM empowers analysts such as Jasmin to focus on genuine threats, reducing alert fatigue and enhancing the overall security posture.

Signal clustering

Now that we've cleared out the duplicates and reduced the noise through suppression, let's look at the mechanism behind insight creation. Each signal has a severity score, which is defined in the rule that creates that signal. There are three main contributors to the severity score:

- A flat severity score set in the rule
- A dynamic severity score, which changes the score based on fields
- Criticality, which adapts the severity based on perceived risk

Setting the severity

When you set the severity in a Cloud SIEM rule, you can choose from **constant** or **dynamic**, as shown here:

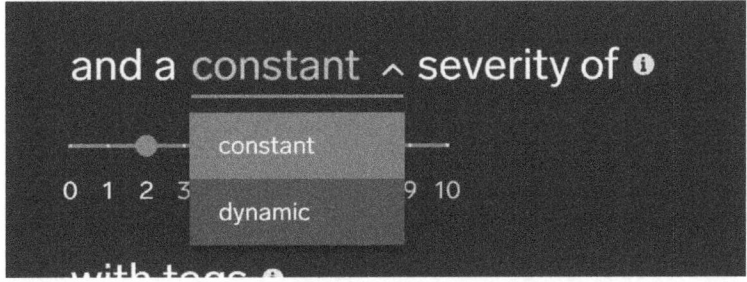

Figure 10.3 – Choosing whether the severity will be constant or change based on field values

constant is self-explanatory, but when you choose **dynamic**, you get to choose how severe the occurrence is based on any field that is mapped to the Cloud SIEM schema. This is shown here:

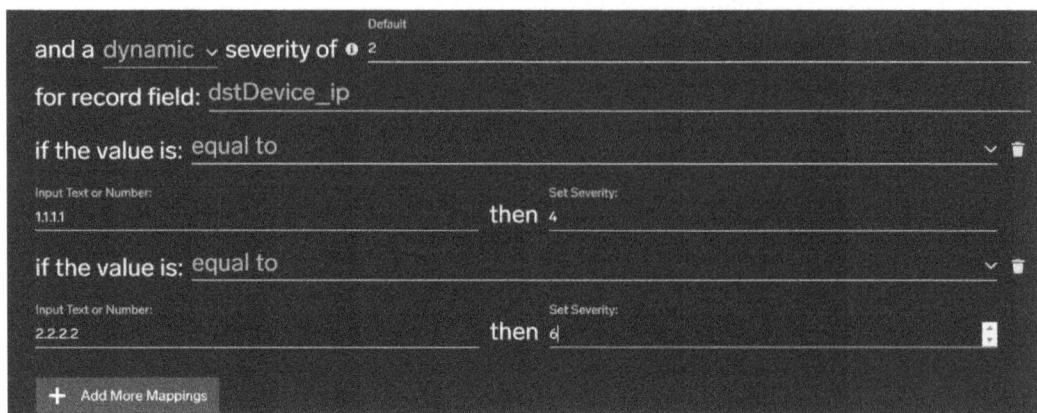

Figure 10.4 – You can specify how the severity changes based on fields and values

In the preceding example, the severity of this signal will be **2** if it triggers. However, if the IP address **1.1.1.1** is seen, the severity will go up to **4**, and if **2.2.2.2** is seen in the results from the rule expression, the severity will go up to **6**.

Criticality

Another concept is criticality—this is a separate list of entities that Sumo Logic customers use to highlight key assets of interest (crown jewels), individuals of interest, important admin accounts, or directories that will cause a change in the severity when they are present.

To get to the criticality menu, go to **Cloud SIEM | Cloud SIEM Entities | Criticality**, as shown here:

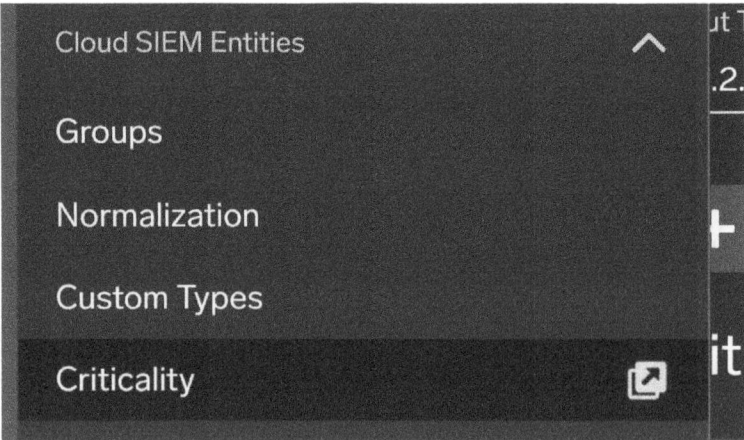

Figure 10.5 – The Criticality area of Cloud SIEM, which lets you apply expression changes based on the entity

To add a criticality, we click on **Add Criticality** in the top-right corner and then give it a name and a severity expression. In the following screenshot, we've called our criticality list Important Servers and specified that when one of these servers is seen in a rule (any rule), it will multiply the severity score in that rule by 3:

Figure 10.6 – Adding a criticality list and defining the change in expression

The main benefit of doing it this way is that it is more scalable. You don't have to set a dynamic severity for each rule that is related to a set of entities, meaning less work. Jasmin will want to know whether a critical server is seen in a signal, no matter what the behavior is, and this will immediately draw her attention to any scenario like this. By using criticality in this way, Jasmin ensures that she can rely on the score accurately reflecting the situational context.

When your critical list gets created, you have to click on it and go to **Import Metadata** in the top-right corner. This will tell you to import a CSV with specific headers so that the entity metadata aligns nicely with the Cloud SIEM schema, which makes the severity expression work, as shown here:

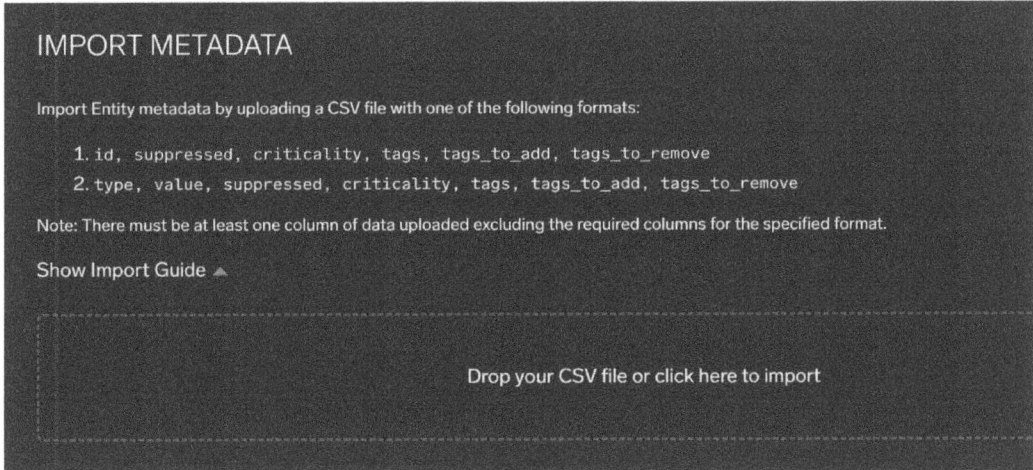

Figure 10.7 – The area where you upload your CSV with entity metadata

Severity is crucial to insights because, as we briefly covered in *Chapter 9, Cloud SIEM* in the *What's an insight?* section, the combined score of *unique* signals that an *entity* triggers is used to check whether the insight threshold is breached. By default, this threshold is 12. So, for example, if three signals with a severity of 5 are linked to a common entity over a period of time, Cloud SIEM will generate an insight.

This threshold can, of course, be changed by navigating to **Cloud SIEM | Cloud SIEM Workflow | Insight Detection**, as shown here:

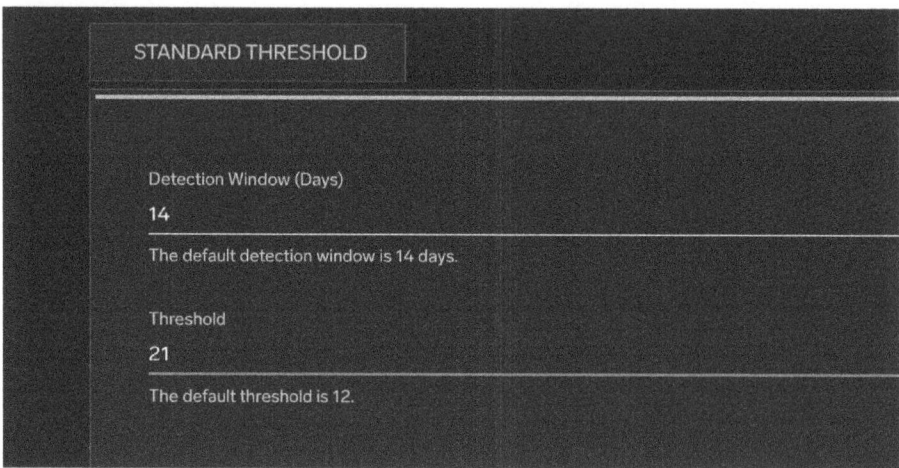

Figure 10.8 – You have the ability to change the severity threshold as well as the detection window

In the preceding example, I've set a threshold of 21 instead of 12. This flexibility is important; you may have an environment where you need an entity to trigger a longer sequence of signals before an insight is generated. If you're unsure, keep the threshold set to **12**. What you also undoubtedly noticed is the **Detection Window** setting, which is in days. This is set to **14** by default, but you can expand this. What **Detection Window** basically means is *if an entity's activity score goes from 0 to 13 within a 14-day period, create an insight*. By making the window larger, you can cover a longer period of time.

An advantage that you are afforded here is the ability to detect advanced adversary behavior. More and more adversaries are improving their sophistication when attacking and can last in an environment longer without being detected, by conducting what are known as **low-and-slow** attacks. They do some activities, then go to sleep for a few days, maybe a couple of weeks, and then do something else. With the way Cloud SIEM tracks entities and takes this contextual information into account, you will be able to catch attackers that rely on these techniques. This is because an attacker only has certain options at their disposal—accounts, services, and endpoints. If these entities behave differently, it will get picked up and correlated automatically by the Insight Engine, no matter how the attacker pivots or moves.

If Jasmin encounters a signal that is linked to something a user has done in the environment two weeks ago, she will know straight away. She won't have to dig deep into the logs with complex queries to identify this, which massively reduces the time for her to come to a conclusion about whether the behavior is malicious or not.

Let's now look at some signals. You might have several alerts that happen, say, over the span of a few hours, as shown here:

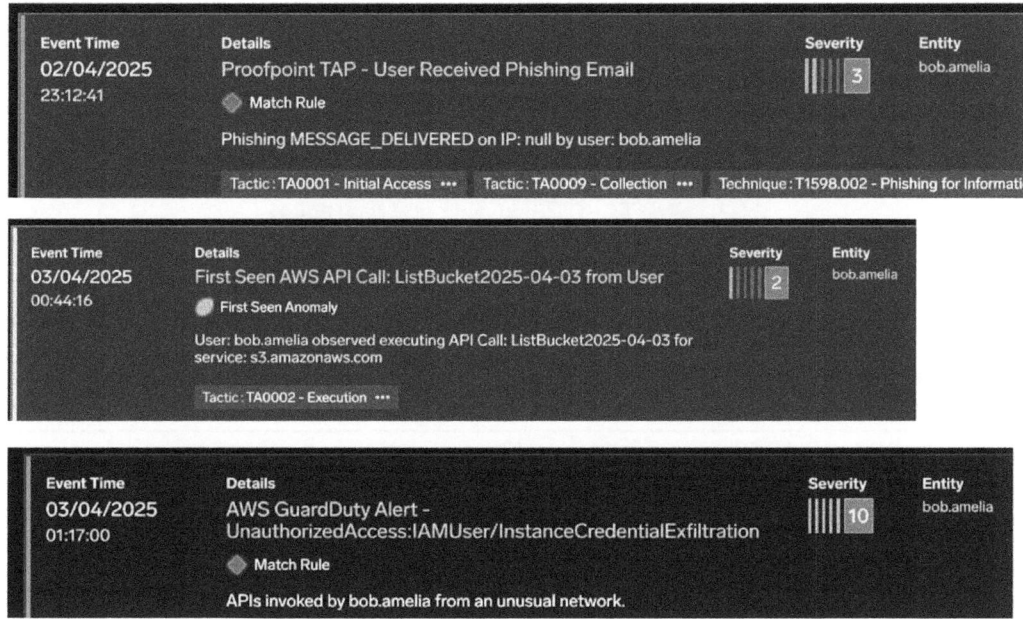

Figure 10.9 – Typical signals that a SOC analyst sees on a daily basis

Notice that each of these signals is anchored to the same entity, in this case, Bob. Investigating alerts together in the form of insights, all in the context of the same entity, changes the game. This doesn't mean that signals are useless—far from it. Signals produce needed data; the problem is that there can be an avalanche of that data, and many security technologies use signals as the main method of working out what is a threat and what isn't. One of the main problems compounding this is the fact that there are dozens of security tools being used in any medium-sized organization and larger, which creates not just noise but an avalanche of signals, like trying to listen to different songs all at the same time. That's chaos. You have your **Endpoint Detection and Response** (**EDR**) tools, email security tools, any **Network Intrusion Detection System** (**NIDS**) or **Host Intrusion Detection System** (**HIDS**) tools, plus stuff in the cloud! Think about AWS—there's GuardDuty and Security Hub, and it gets hard to work with, fast. There is an additional score that's calculated to help with insight prioritization—the entity activity score.

Entity activity score

Each entity, be it a user, IP address, host, serverless function, and so on, is assigned an activity score, calculated as the sum of the severities of unique signals associated with that entity over a customizable time window. The emphasis on *unique* ensures that repeated signals don't inflate the score, maintaining the integrity of the alerting system, which is why the suppression concept we just looked at is so important for both reducing noise and making sure that scores are accurate and represent real, suspicious, or malicious behavior.

The entity activity score can be found within the **Entities** page. We covered how to get there in the last chapter. Either click on the entity in a signal or go to **Cloud SIEM | Entities**. You'll see the activity score under the timeline, as shown here:

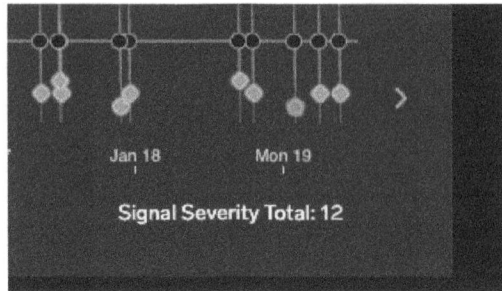

Figure 10.10 – The signal severity total dictates the risk level of the insight

Based on this activity score, the severity of the insight is changed. Here's a table so you can see the thresholds:

Entity Activity Score	Insight Severity
13	Low
14–15	Medium
16+	High

Table 10.1 – How the insight severity thresholds are defined by the entity activity score

It's important to clarify that this entity score is not an alert but a way of *prioritizing the insight* by using the entity score and signal scores together. Based on the score, the severity of an insight changes to reflect how potentially risky the combination of *unique* signals is.

So, now we know the following:

- How records turn into signals, and signals turn into insights
- How signals are deduplicated and suppressed
- How signals are clustered
- How entities and insights are scored

Let's jump into the Insights UI, which we'll walk you through before covering a full insight investigation.

Navigating an insight: Deep dive

We've got an insight—what happens now? In this section, we're going to be covering the **Heads-Up Display (HUD)** within an insight so you know exactly where the key information is, how to get it as quickly as possible, and how to respond to any insight regardless of the situation. Remember, for security teams, the *most important* thing is speed; the quicker we can understand the situation and the quicker we can respond, the better the outcome. Plus, by ensuring such optimal outcomes, you'll come to be known as a cybersecurity ninja, which is a nice bonus.

First, let us go through the Insights UI and its components. Where are our insights? We find them on the main SIEM overview page after clicking on **Insights**, or by going to **Cloud SIEM | Insights**:

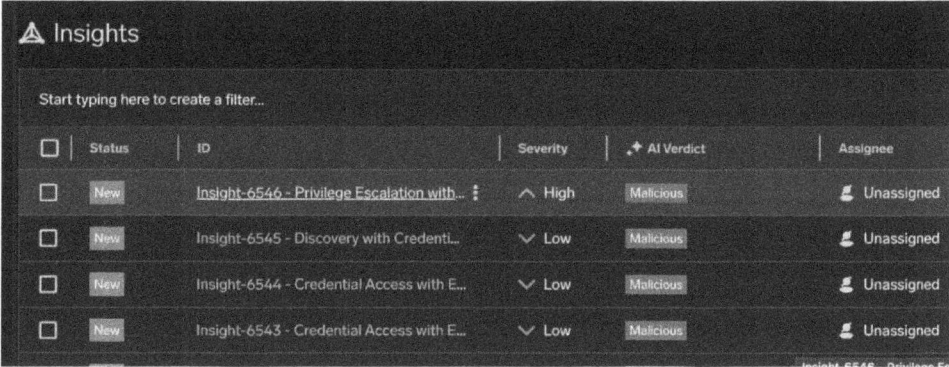

Figure 10.11 – A list of our insights, which can be ranked by Severity, AI Verdict, and other variables

When clicking on an insight, you get a slide-out panel on the right that contains most of the information you need about the insight without seeing the full story. It has the scores, entities, assignees, and key findings, as well as a button to take you to Mobot, the agentic framework that will let you investigate this insight with generative AI. If you choose to dive in, just click the insight name and you can see the full picture.

The Insights UI

The **Insights** page is split into the following key areas, which can be seen in *Figure 10.12*:

- The metadata of the incident
- The AI-centered investigation
- The incident timeline, as well as extra context and automation
- The story of the incident, including the signals clustered, entities seen, enrichments performed and automations run

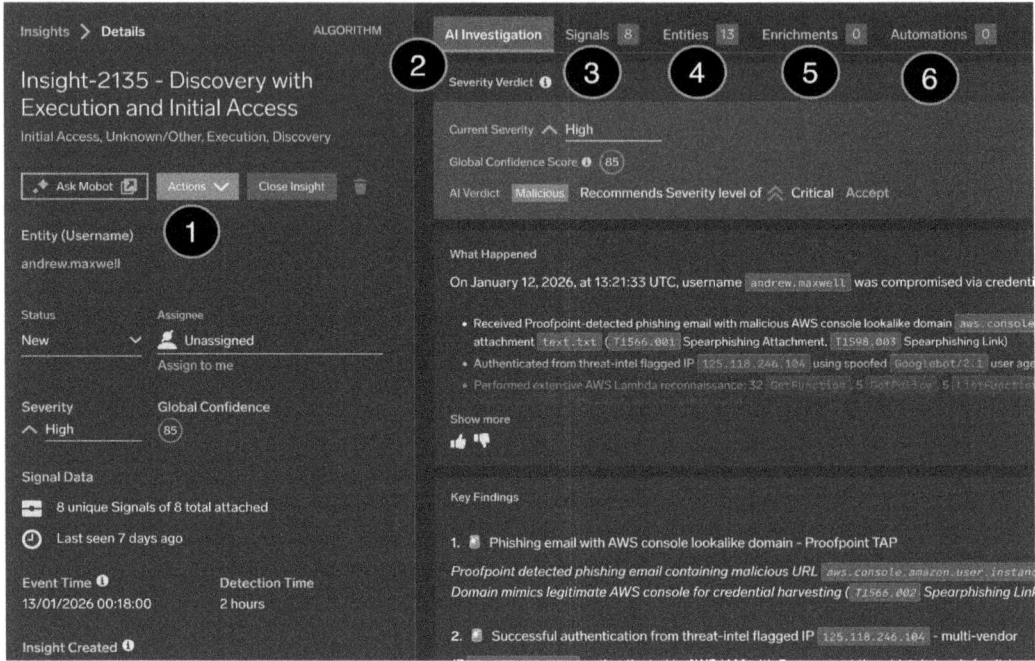

Figure 10.12 – The main parts of the Insights page – metadata, AI investigation, and the story

Let's start with the first part and introduce you to the metadata of the incident.

Metadata

In the metadata section, you'll find things such as the name of the insight, who the insight has been assigned to, and what MITRE ATT&CK tags are linked to this insight.

Let's start with the naming. Every insight is given a number followed by a very high-level summary of what kind of activity took place. In this case, it's **Discovery with Execution and Initial Access**, so you can understand straight away what has roughly happened. Underneath this, you'll see a button for **Actions**, which we'll cover later, as this is tightly linked to the automation capabilities in the platform. The option **Close Insight**, lets you resolve this insight and select *how* you want to resolve it. There's a range of useful metadata that you can tap into on this left-side panel, from a summary of the insight to the MITRE ATT&CK tags linked to the insight. We'll cover them all before we cover the timeline.

Resolution

Cybersecurity incidents can take on many shapes and forms, and being able to label them appropriately is crucial for internal reporting and incident response processes. You can do that in Cloud SIEM. Let's take a look at what that looks like.

When deciding how you want to respond to an incident, on selecting the **Close Insight** option, you are provided with four options initially: **Duplicate**, **False Positive**, **No Action**, and **Resolved**.

These are great starting points, since many teams don't need any more ways of resolving an incident. When incidents are marked with one of these options, they not only get categorized into groups that help you keep track of what insights are new versus which ones have been seen, but they also actively contribute to Insight Trainer, which is a set of dashboards in Sumo Logic that helps you to tune your rules. We'll cover this later in the *Cloud SIEM audit app: Deep-dive analytics on your SIEM's DNA* section.

Entity

Underneath the insight summary, we can see the entity that is at the nucleus of this whole event. This is the entity whose actions have triggered the insight, and we will be finding out more about what it did in the timeline and story. If you're using inventory sources such as Active Directory or Okta, you can see additional information when you hover over the entity, as shown here:

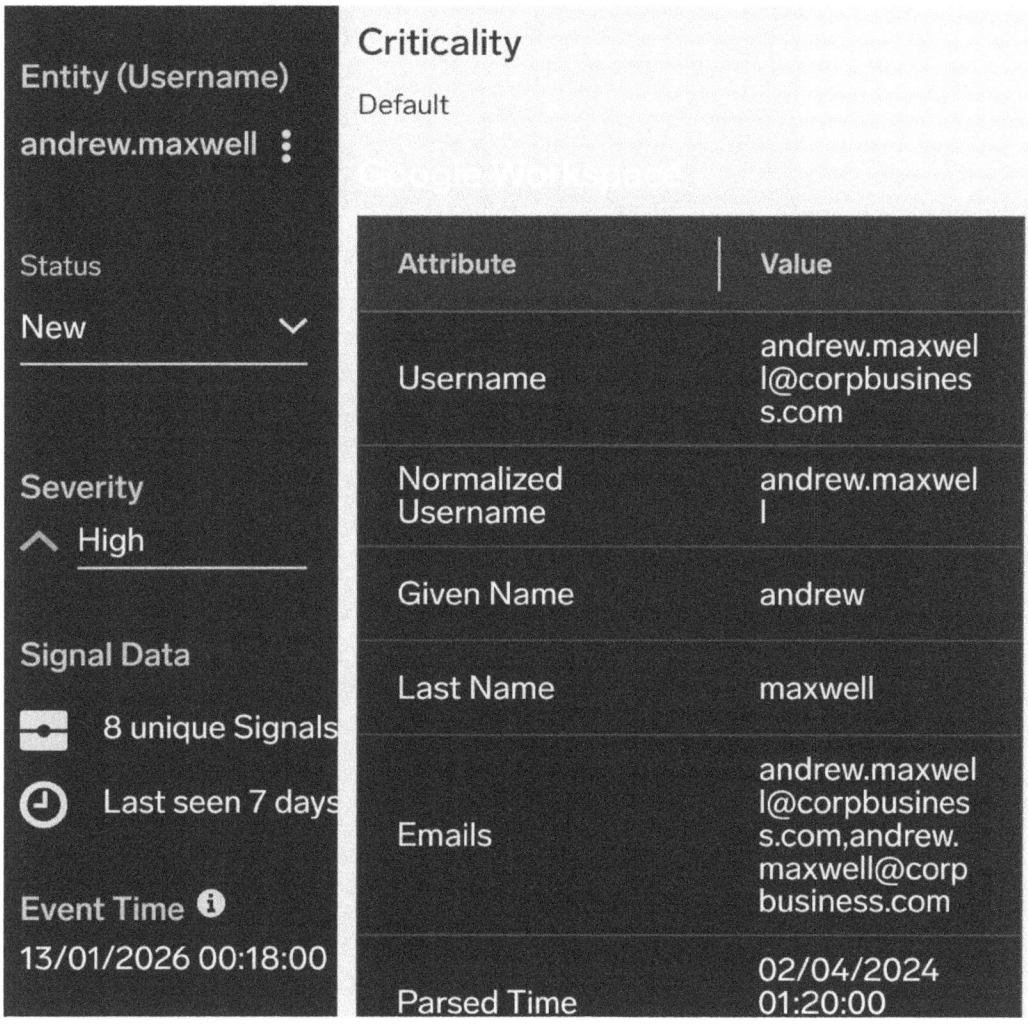

Figure 10.13 – High-level information about the entity at the heart of this insight

Case management elements

Underneath the entity, you'll find a field for status and assignments. This lets you choose what stage this insight is at. Statuses are completely custom to fit your incident response process. You can also assign the insight to individuals or teams, manually or in an automated way.

If you're looking to change the default insight resolutions or insight statuses, then head over to **Cloud SIEM Workflow** in the **Configuration** menu and you will see the options shown here:

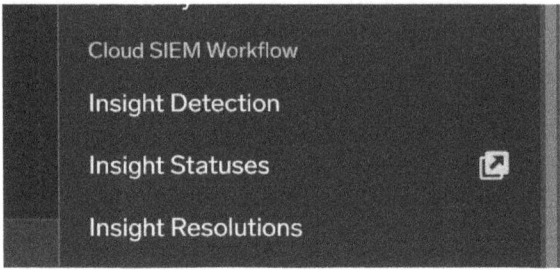

Figure 10.14 – Some of the Cloud SIEM workflow configuration options

When adding a resolution in the **Add Insight Resolution** field, all you need to do is specify a name for the resolution, a *parent*, which sits under a default resolution, and then a description, if necessary, as shown here:

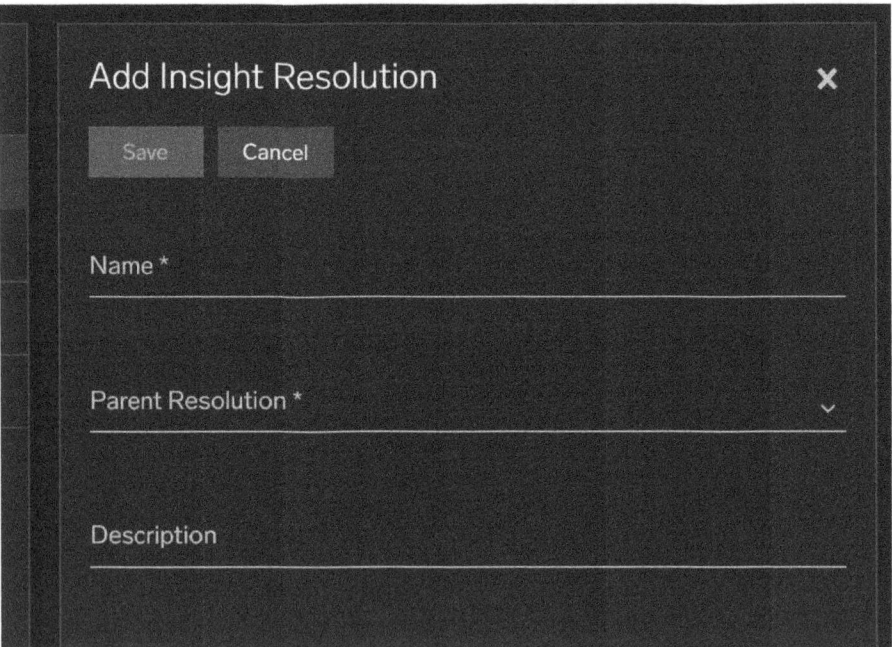

Figure 10.15 – Adding a custom insight resolution type is easy

The process is similar for adding the insight status. You can add a status by giving it a name and a description, and the game-changer—you can give it a color. Sweet!

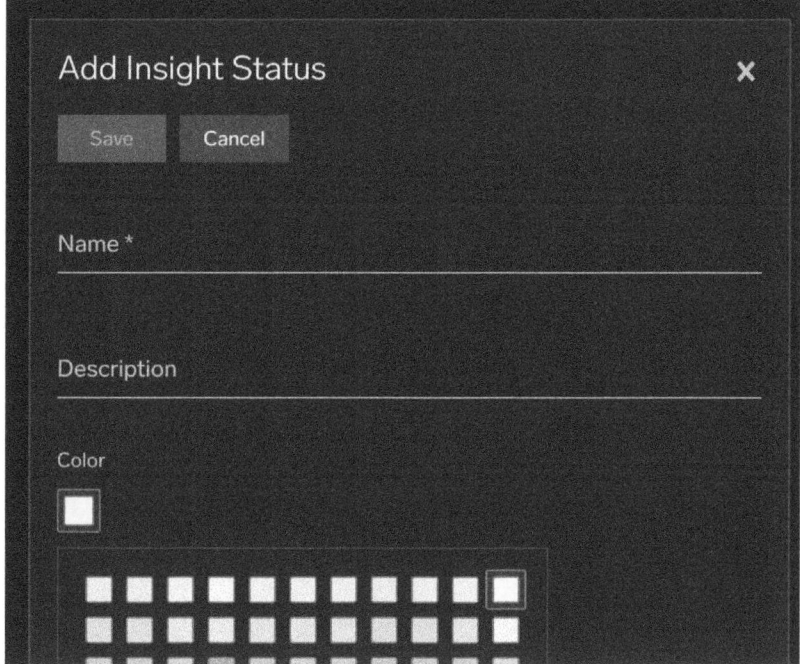

Figure 10.16 – Adding custom insight statuses is also straightforward

These bits of metadata, such as the severity, status, assignees, and global confidence (covered next), can all be interacted with in an automated way.

The Automation Service will be covered in the next chapter, but you're able to achieve full incident response automation within Sumo Logic itself without having to use third-party tools. Processes that many people are used to, for example, performing *X* action if the severity is high, compared to *Y* action if the severity is low, can all be achieved, but we'll save this riveting discussion for *Chapter 11*.

Severity and global confidence

Say you log in to Sumo Logic and see that a few insights have been created overnight—not good, but how do you determine which one should get your attention first? The first element is severity, and the second is global confidence, both of which I'll elaborate on now.

Insight severity is a sum of the entity's activity score that led up to the insight being created. As you now know, when signals are created due to entity activity, they have a severity value. As an entity causes these signals to trigger one after the other, these signals get clustered together, and the severity scores add up for that entity (we covered this in the *Entity activity score* section. Once the threshold of 12 is reached, an insight is created, and that score is turned into an insight severity rating. This is just a way of showing you the concerning stuff that an entity has been doing, and naturally, if there is a more elaborate chain of events that have higher criticality ratings, you should probably pay more attention to that!

There is, however, another wingman that'll help you obtain a bit of context about the situation—**Global Confidence** (**GC**). The way it works is you're given a score from 0 to 100 based on the *pattern of signals within the insight*.

This is a capability that uses AI to apply a score based on the pattern of signals that has been seen within this insight. For example, a user failing their password a few times, gaining access, then running a file that *seems* malicious might get a GC score of 35–40. A user who has done the same but clicked on a phishing email followed by Mimikatz activity on their machine will have a GC score of 90–100. This value is meant to be actionable—the higher the score, the more likely that it is a threat.

MITRE ATT&CK tags

As discussed in previous chapters, the MITRE ATT&CK schema is hard-wired into Sumo Logic's tag database. When you scroll down, you'll see all the MITRE ATT&CK tags that have been added to the insight from all the correlated signals. You can use the **Create a tag...** space at the bottom to add additional tags to the insight if necessary, as shown here:

Figure 10.17 – Adding tags is simple

It's unlikely you'll need to add a MITRE ATT&CK tag here as those are usually set up during rule creation. However, this is a perfect example of being able to add custom tags to insights. You could use your own internal taxonomy to tag the insight with a specific network that has been targeted, or maybe an asset. Here's a quick how-to on how to set up any custom tags. Go to **Cloud SIEM | Cloud SIEM Workflow | Tag Schemas**:

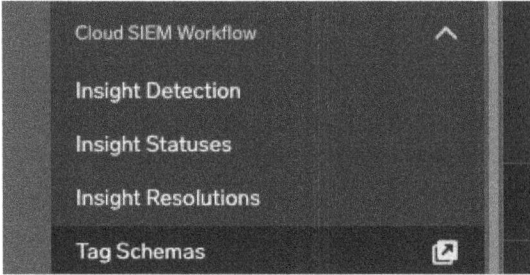

Figure 10.18 – The Tag Schemas section in the menu

You'll get to a page where you see the ready-made tag schemas for you to use, but we can, of course, add our own. Click on **+ Add Tag Schema** in the top right and fill in the fields. It needs to have a key and a label. Then you select where you want the tag to be applied. Do you want the tag to be applied when you create a rule or in an entity? Both? You get to choose, as shown here:

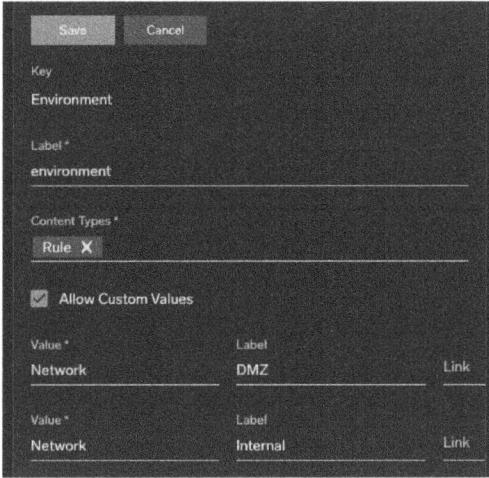

Figure 10.19 – We get to define our custom tags to be merged with the Cloud SIEM tag schema for use anywhere in Cloud SIEM

You get to create links externally in this way. For example, if a critical asset has certain information that users need to know, they could link to an internal Confluence page or something like that to get some info. As I've selected **Rule** under **Content Types** in this example, when I'm creating or editing a rule, I can now specify this tag and choose the options:

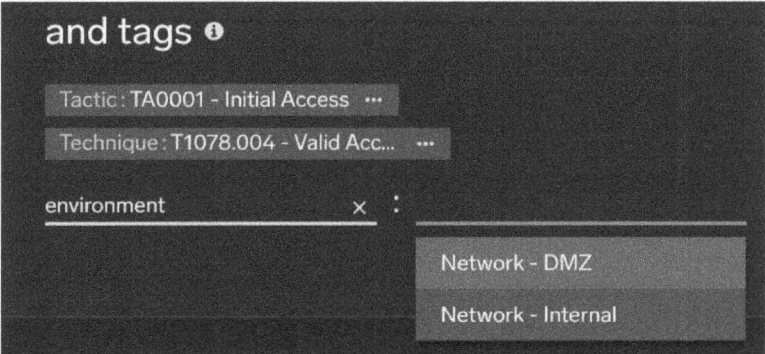

Figure 10.20 – Adding custom tags to a rule

The custom tags you specify then appear as part of the insight metadata in Cloud SIEM. This means you can start to do things such as visually break down your insights by these tags in a dashboard and create a report of the insights that took place in the past seven days, for example, but using your *own internal language*. We'll cover more interesting reporting examples in *Chapter 13, Compliance and Reporting*.

AI investigation

The first view you're presented with is the output of the SOC Analyst Agent and intelligent analytical work combined with AI-driven information from your data and from the platform. This section houses three key bits of information:

- Severity verdict
- What happened
- Key findings

Let's go back to Jasmin. She's working her shift, and she finds some interesting signals and has to do the work to not only understand how these events are connected but also verify that nothing is missing and her story is "complete." That takes ages. But AI investigation comes to the rescue. It looks at all the signals that make up this insight and not only assesses them to give them a score (GC) but also runs analytics queries on the data sources and data involved to work out whether this is truly a malicious scenario or just a benign set of events. All without Jasmin lifting a finger. This is what a streamlined workflow looks like; it lets Jasmin do what she is really there to do and apply her human intelligence, knowledge, and craft to the situation.

We first see the severity verdict, which is comprised of the entity score that the signals are linked to, as discussed previously. However, below that, we have a combination of the GC and results from the analytics queries done automatically, which allows the AI to take the severity into context but also *include its own analysis and understanding of the situation* to give you another opinion:

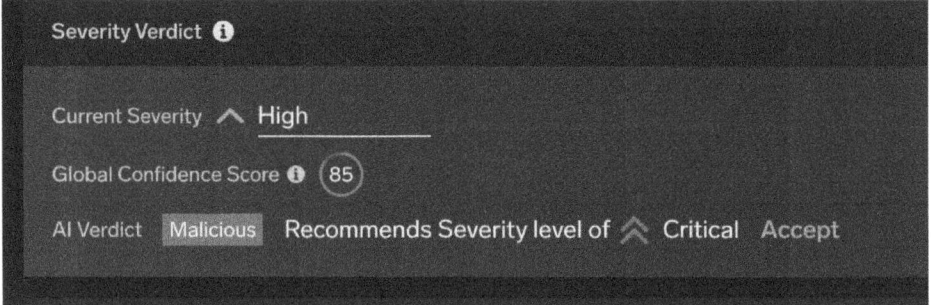

Figure 10.21 – The severity verdict here was High initially, but the AI verdict is Malicious, and it also recommends a severity

You can see that it started out as **High**, but after reviewing the insight, the AI recommended bumping the severity up and also gave its own verdict. Most importantly, you have the option of accepting or denying this verdict. This gives you the best of both worlds—you have an automated analyst sidekick telling you what they think, but you can override that if necessary. Why is this useful? Because you get to control and feed the models that are conducting the analysis and come to a decision by drawing your own conclusions.

Below this, we see the **What Happened** section. This is basically a summary of the insight but in a nicely formatted style that highlights the key events and how they're linked over time:

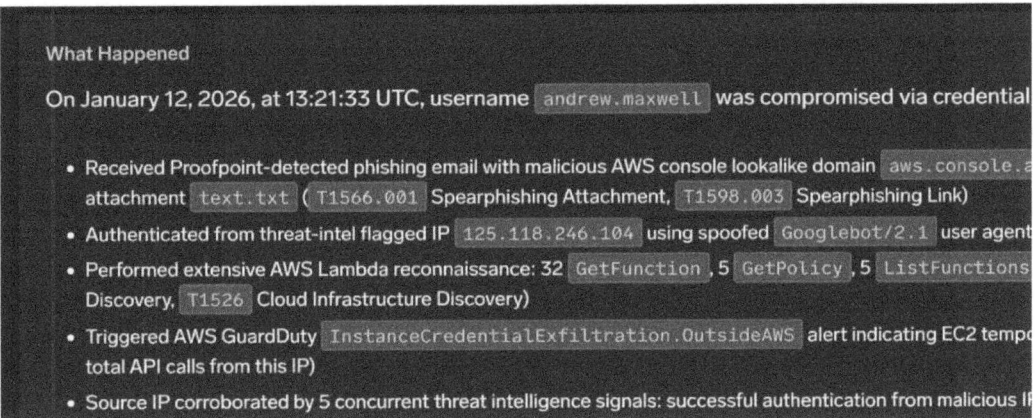

Figure 10.22 – An overview of the key events and how the story has progressed in a readable way

The key entities are identified in the text and highlighted for the analyst to easily be able to pick them out and investigate them further if necessary. At the bottom, there is a "verdict" that gives you an idea of how the AI got to its conclusion:

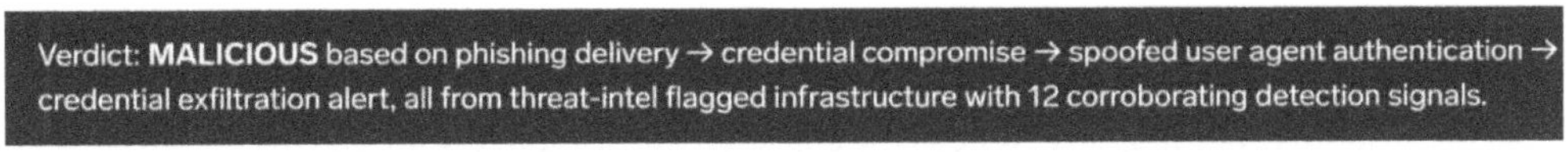

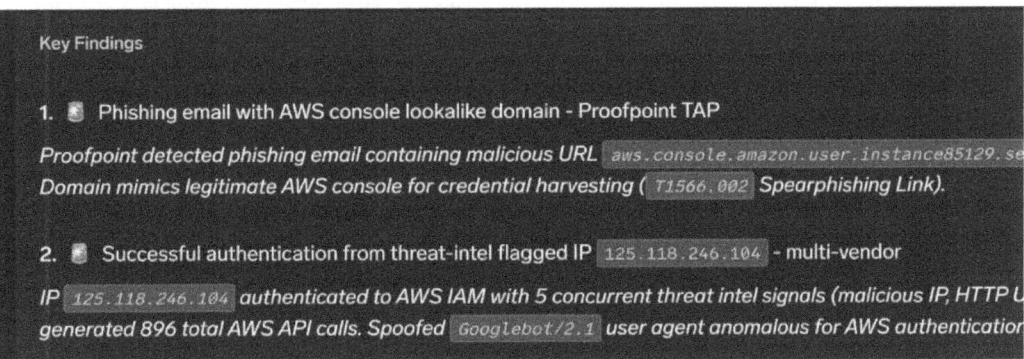

Figure 10.23 – The verdict that the AI investigation has reached

If you put yourself in the position of Jasmin, our SOC analyst, who typically has had to understand this series of events across all of her data sources and data islands manually, this is a total game-changer. In a data-agnostic way, across her business (as long as it's ingested into Sumo Logic), she can see these incidents in complete detail over time.

To help her further, there is the **Key Findings** section:

Figure 10.24 – The key findings from the investigation are listed, which help to pinpoint malicious areas of activity

With these key findings, Jasmin has support in knowing what to look for, confirm, and evaluate instead of starting from scratch. A truly sentient AI defender is still a way away, but with this ability to empower your investigations by automating a lot of the footwork an analyst needs to do, Jasmin has the luxury of knowing where to focus her time and energy.

Both in the top right of the **Key Findings** section and in the top left, under the insight name, is an **Ask Mobot** button. This lets you open up Mobot, pull in the context from the investigation, and explore the findings further. We will look at this later in this chapter in the *Real insights and use cases* section, where we will look at an end-to-end investigation.

Insight timeline

The second part of the UI is the insight timeline, marked as area **3** in *Figure 10.12*, under the **Signals** tab. This shows you a chronological view of all the signals that are part of the insight and when they happened. If you've been in the game long enough, you'll know how problematic this process is. You know what I'm talking about: it's a Friday, and you're looking forward to the weekend. You're glancing through some work emails and web-related stuff, and none of the alerts you're seeing are anything major.

Then bam! There it is, you see it—a .kirbi file has been created on a Windows machine, which is when Kerberos tickets have just been extracted from memory and saved to a file. Tools such as Mimikatz and Rubeus can then be used to get access to these **Ticket-Granting Tickets** (**TGTs**) in order to gain access to other systems on a network.

Basically, you have a problem.

You then begin the journey of using this event as the epicenter and scrambling around, trying to query all the commands on that machine to localize the issue and try to get as much evidence of wrongdoing as possible. Don't forget, you're only human. You can easily miss things as you're rushing to understand the issue before it becomes something much worse.

Also, you are faced with questions such as, *How do I know where the attacker gained access? How do I know their lateral escalation methods? Could they have gained a foothold in the cloud, or on some other internal network?*

Frankly, I'm exhausted just reading those few paragraphs. Imagine searching your entire business for these crumbs, across all the different sources that modern enterprises use. Then, when you think you've found enough, you have to put it in an order that makes sense, and you've not even begun forensic investigations yet.

That's why the timeline within insights is so important. These events of interest are clustered together and put on a timeline straight away, saving you hours, if not days, of work. It lets you focus on responding to the situation with more context, rather than spending valuable time clutching at straws.

Above the timeline, you can see some tabs, namely **Signals**, **Entities**, **Enrichments**, and **Automations**:

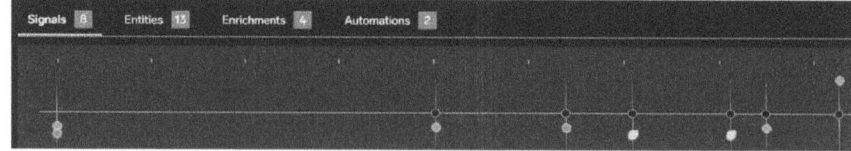

Figure 10.25 – The tabs above the timeline found at the top of every Cloud SIEM insight

Signals is the default and shows the signals that make up the insight. Let's dive into the others.

Entities

This view shows the visual relationships between the entities that are found within the signals in the form of entity maps. An entity map shows how the entities in the insight are potentially linked together. This information can be expanded further by clicking on the **+** icon under individual nodes, as shown here:

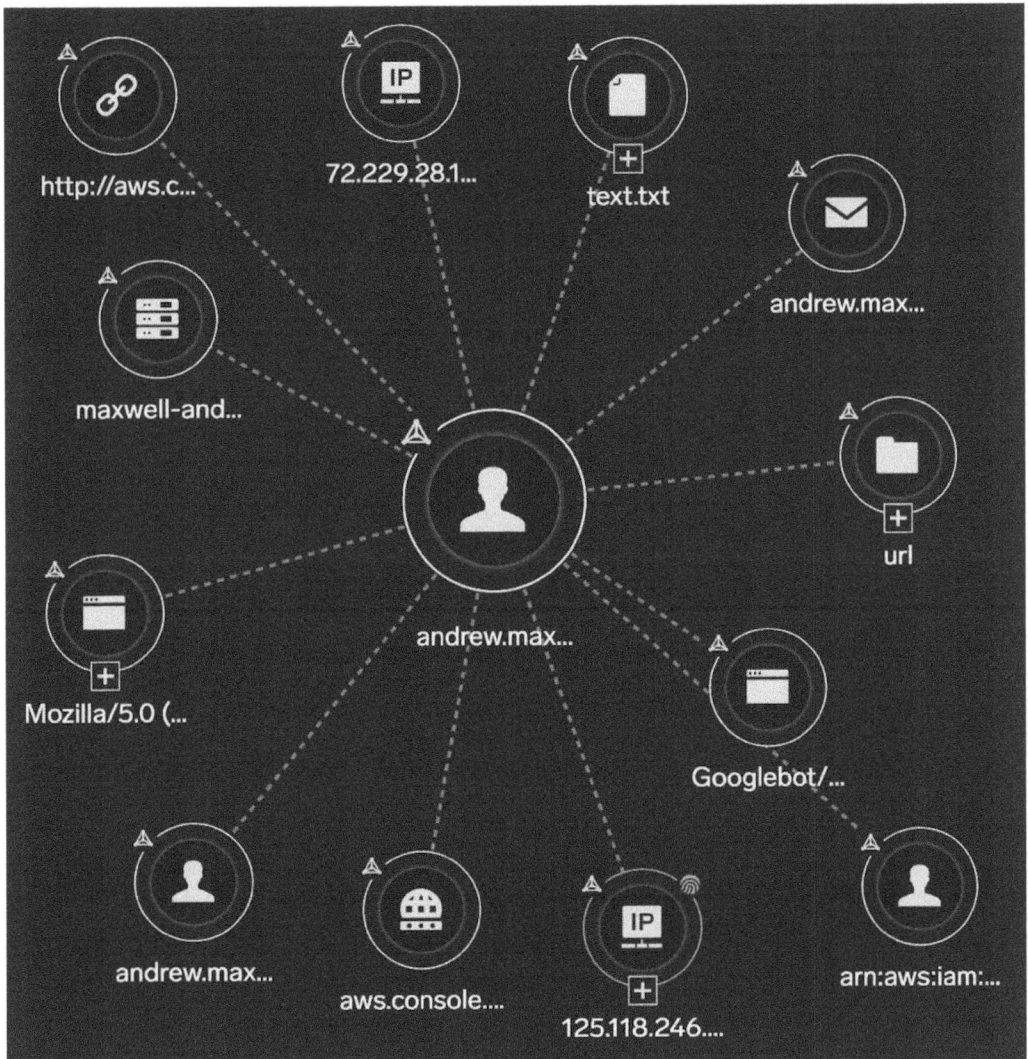

Figure 10.26 – An entity map

This graph view helps defenders by giving a quick birds-eye view of who, or what, is important as part of this insight. In this example, two of the entities are ringed in red with a fingerprint icon—the AWS entity starting with **aws.console...** as well as the IP address **125.118.246....**.

This happens when the threat intelligence feeds in Sumo Logic identify a match on the feed. These threat intelligence feeds could be the ones that Sumo Logic comes with—**CrowdStrike Falcon** and **Intel 471**—but could also be any custom threat intel feeds that you bring in yourself. This process is covered in *Chapter 12, Bringing a Security Intelligence Program to Life with Sumo Logic*, in the *Implementation* section, where we look at how to bring a custom feed into the platform.

To create these rings of amber or red, Cloud SIEM automatically enriches signals, which have data on the entity in question, an IP address, a domain name, and so on. This is due to the threat intelligence match rules that exist already, whose names typically start with *Threat Intel*. Here's one that looks at any matches with suspicious file hashes:

Figure 10.27 – An example of a ready-to-use threat intelligence rule in Cloud SIEM

Cloud SIEM decides whether the ring is amber or red based on the labels associated with that entity from the source. To visualize this, let's take an example from an insight I have with an IP address:

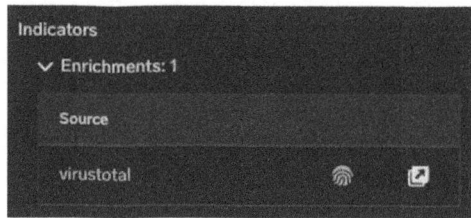

Figure 10.28 – The severity label of suspicious or malicious is dictated by the enrichment

This is telling us that VirusTotal has enriched this IP address and a rating of **Malicious** has been seen with this IOC. It gets flagged with a red ring. Sources of intel such as this have labeling built in, making it easy to enrich for the data pipeline in Sumo Logic.

Back to the entity graph. On its own, this graph can get quite large on some insights, and it might not always be clear what the key relationships are. If you could just get a steer on what the key or critical ones are, that's going to make your comprehension and response faster.

When you click on these entities, you get a sidebar that gives you additional details about the entity, including some geo and ASN enrichment, notes, and what signals this entity has been seen in, as shown here:

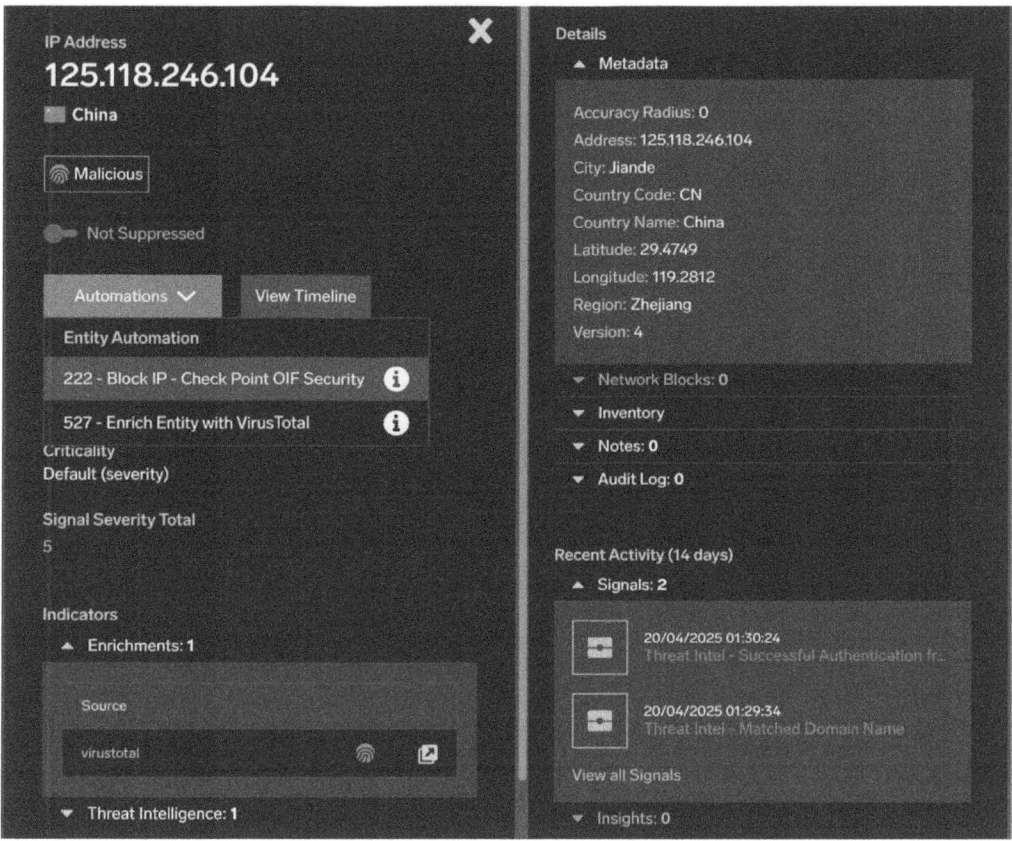

Figure 10.29 – A deeper dive into an entity on the map, giving access to automation and valuable metadata

This is practically an all-you-can-eat entity buffet. This is where you can get all the information on an entity that you need. You can run automations from here, for example, enriching with certain sources, doing internal Sumo Logic queries (we'll see a good few examples in the next chapter, *Chapter 11, The Automation Service and Playbooks*). You can also see the geo-enriched data, as well as any recent signals that this entity has been seen in. By clicking on **View Timeline**, you can jump straight into the entity record for this entity.

Enrichment

When you enrich any data about an insight, whether it's around the signals, the entities, or anything in between, that enrichment will be dumped into the **Enrichments** tab. We covered this in the previous chapter; basically, it takes the JSON-formatted results from that enrichment, whether they've come from VirusTotal, abuse.ch, or any other threat intelligence feed or vendor, and deposits them in this tab.

This tab allows quick contextualization and helps you understand more about a given entity. Say we use abush.ch (an open threat intel source); we can enrich our insight automatically by looking through our entities, and that information appears in the **Enrichment** tab:

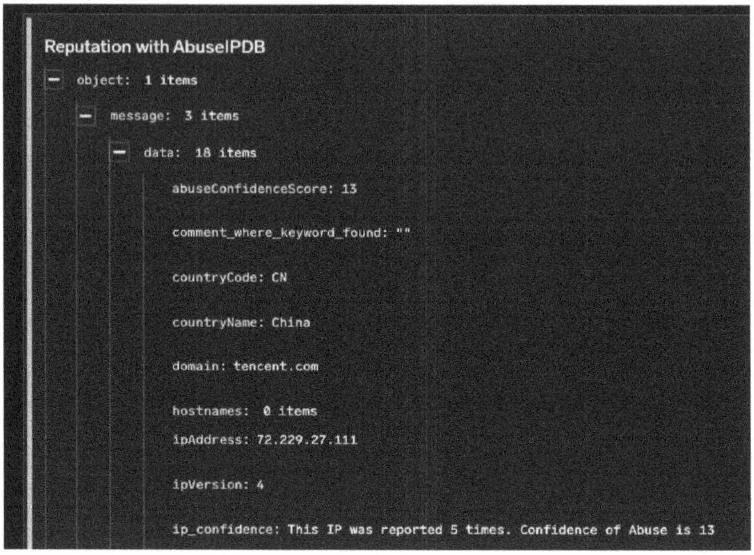

Figure 10.30 – Automated enrichment can be viewed in this way on any insight or entity

Even better, you can use the automation service to put some results in there before a human has even looked at it.

Just picture it—no more manually enriching an IOC with a source. It's a win!

Automation

This section is the focus of the next chapter, *Chapter 11, The Automation Service and Playbooks*. Briefly, this tab shows you all the playbooks and automated actions that have taken place within the insight. We won't dive too deeply into this section here.

Instead, now let's move on to *the story* behind an incident.

The story

Cybersecurity teams around the world share a dream. A dream in which everything about an incident is cleanly and neatly broken down, step by step, *chronologically*, to help them answer a simple question—what happened here?

This is the primary goal of the Insight Engine, as we discussed earlier in this chapter.

In this part of the Insights UI, you will find all the signals that have been automatically clustered and correlated together in order to give you and your team an actionable insight. Going through the signals one by one lets you see the events that took place around the activities of *one central entity*. It doesn't matter if this activity took place across different data sources, such as an email security solution, then on a host operating system, then Active Directory.

Here you're able to jump into each individual signal for extra context. You're able to see all the individual records that comprise that signal and the full extent of the metadata that comes through with each of those records.

When investigating, you need as much information as possible, right? So, at every point, you're able to zoom in and see key details at each step.

Seeing as an insight is where you'll be aggregating all the incident information, you can add signals here that you think are pertinent to the "case." There is a convenient **+ Add Signals** button to help you do this:

Figure 10.31 – You have the option to add other signals to the insight

When you click this, you'll be presented with a list of signals that have been seen recently, as shown here:

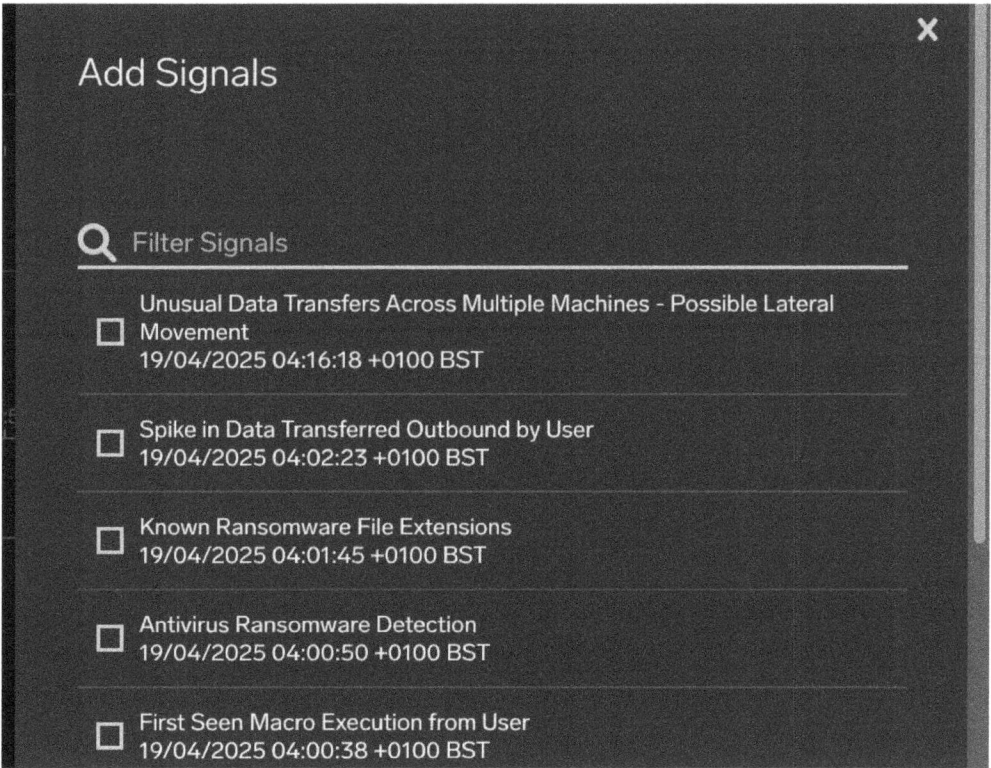

Figure 10.32 – The list of recent signals

You can search for some of the signals you found during your investigation as well, and even remove signals from the insight that you think don't add anything to it and are just noise. The **Remove** button can be found on the right-hand side of every signal:

Figure 10.33 – Remove signals from the list that aren't helpful

Before we approach some real-life use cases and insights that we've compiled to share with you, let's talk about a really useful app in the App Catalog to help you stay on top of everything happening in Cloud SIEM: **Enterprise Audit - Cloud SIEM**.

Cloud SIEM audit app: Deep-dive analytics on your SIEM solution's DNA

Most security platforms stop at spitting out alerts. Sumo Logic goes several steps further by funneling every piece of Cloud SIEM activity—**records**, **signals**, **insights**, **parser diagnostics**, **rule evaluations**, **UI clicks**, and **analyst actions**—straight back into the core analytics platform as richly structured JSON. Because Sumo Logic began life as a log analytics solution, it can apply the same powerful search and dashboarding capabilities to the internal workings of the SIEM solution itself. It provides this out of the box in the Enterprise

This can be found in the App Catalog just by searching from `siem`, as shown here:

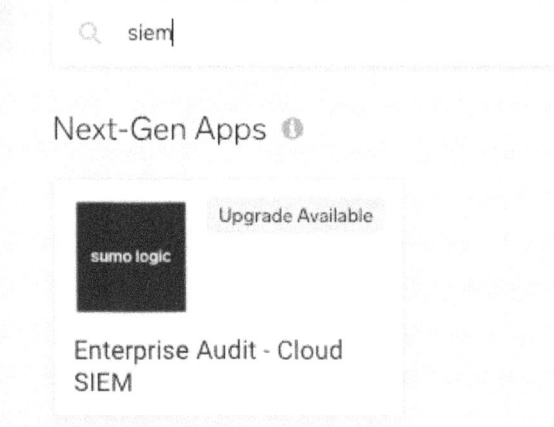

Figure 10.34 – Finding the Enterprise Audit – Cloud SIEM app in the App Catalog

Once installed from the App Catalog, it auto-populates dashboards that deliver both high-level and deep-dive views, split into the following sections:

- **Overview**: Total records, signals, and insights over time with drilldowns by source category and severity
- **Signals & Insights**: Ratios of suppressed versus active signals, top-firing rules, noisy entities, and insight escalation trends
- **Rule Management Activity**: Who created, edited, enabled, or disabled rules; before/after severity deltas; change history heatmaps

- **Analyst Operations**: Queue size, acknowledgment lag, dismissal reasons, and workload distribution
- **Insight Trainer**: Data-driven recommendations to right-size rule severities, backed by historical false positive statistics (`help.sumologic.com`)

Next, you will see a couple of examples of dashboards from this app. This one, **Cloud SIEM - Insights Closed**, is a dashboard that allows you to visually analyze and dissect the insights your team has closed, allowing you to categorize them in any way to identify trends:

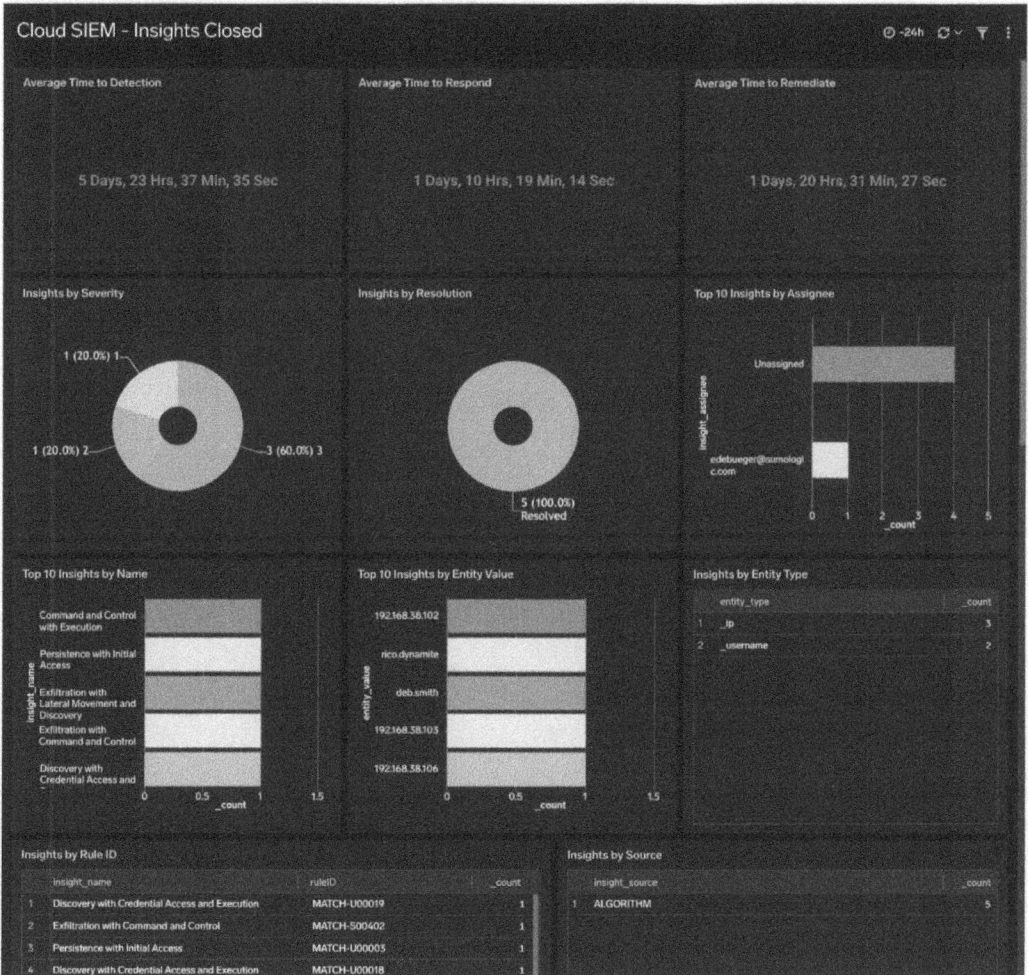

Figure 10.35 – A visual analysis of insights that have been resolved

Are most of our insights coming in regularly from the same IP address or endpoint? How long does it take to remediate an insight on average? These questions, which can help to drive the efficiency of any SOC team, can be used to enhance your processes in a practical way, as well as supplying management with really useful metrics.

Next we have a similar dashboard, but instead showing us **Insights Created**:

Figure 10.36 – A visual analysis of new insights created, sometimes much easier to distill and understand in this format

This metadata can further drive decisions internally. If insights keep getting created from a certain rule over and over again, maybe we need to investigate it and tweak it to avoid so many insights being generated from it. Data like this is king, because it informs you as to why things are happening the way they are in the platform, and you can make the tool more aligned to your team's needs.

All visualizations query the dedicated **Audit Event** and **System Event** indexes, which capture Cloud SIEM internals by default. And if it's not obvious, every dashboard and panel can be customized or modified by simply changing the query on which it is based. What's also great is that all this comes at no cost. The data is already in your account, so you gain immediate observability into the health, effectiveness, and ROI of your detection program.

Now, you might be wondering how this impacts DevSecOps in the real world. Think about how many times teams have to tinker around with parsers, work out which ones aren't working, and why. These are real problems when it comes to large environments. With this app, we've seen that teams are regularly able to spot misparsed logs within the first hour of deployment. Further, noise is massively reduced. In conjunction with the Insight Engine, you're covering as much ground as possible but not getting swamped in alerts and signals.

If we go back to what we discussed in *Chapter 3, Measuring Security Outcomes and Performance* Sumo Logic helps with measuring our security outcomes. MTTR and MITRE coverage visuals translate technical performance into business risk language.

By turning the SIEM solution back on itself, Sumo Logic closes the feedback loop between detection engineering, SOC operations, and executive reporting. This ensures continuous improvement informed by hard data rather than hunches and is exactly what the DevSecOps philosophy is all about.

Let's summarize this section with a brief overview of why having embedded analytics like this is crucial to your usage of security technology:

Challenge	How Embedded Analytics Helps
Alert fatigue and tuning: Noise overwhelms analysts and obscures genuine threats.	Identify the noisiest rules, signals, and entities at a glance. Track suppression versus active firing rates to fine-tune thresholds. Spot gaps where rules *never* fire and may be misconfigured.
Parser coverage: Raw logs sometimes fail to map cleanly onto records.	Dashboards surface parsing errors and "unmapped" log volume so engineers can expand or correct parsers before blind spots form.
Analyst KPIs and workflow health	Visualize queue depth, **Mean Time to Detection (MTTD)**, **Mean Time to Acknowledge (MTTA)**, and **Mean Time to Resolve (MTTR)** by analyst, shift, or severity. Demonstrate SOC efficiency improvements to leadership.
MITRE ATT&CK coverage	Correlate fired signals to ATT&CK techniques to reveal detection gaps and over-represented tactics.
Audit and compliance	Full history of rule edits, suppression list changes, user logins, and permission changes satisfies auditors without extra tooling.

Table 10.2 – Why embedded analytics is helpful

Now that we've walked through some theory on the Insight Engine and acquainted ourselves with the UI, let's step forward and take a look at this thing in action. We've got some interesting use cases lined up for you in the next section.

Real insights and use cases

In this section, I plan to show you how Cloud SIEM handles realistic security events. This isn't just theory and hypotheticals; these are examples of insights that have actually taken place and have been preserved to show how it all comes together.

We've got two of these insights to get through, so let's begin.

A phishing scenario

Phishing is a threat to the mental well-being of every cybersecurity practitioner. You could say that security teams get DDoSed by phishing-related alerts all the time! Historically, teams have lacked the context and information they need to definitely say whether the suspicious email that hit the finance guy's inbox, and that was clicked on, has caused mayhem or not.

The reason that Sumo Logic is so useful in detecting and responding to phishing threats is that phishing is only an initial vector of attack into the business. If the initial phishing step is successful, the attacker tries expanding out from there, and that requires visibility over at least a few sources of data, such as the following:

- Email/inbox
- Host machine (VM or otherwise)
- File shares
- Network
- Firewalls
- EDR

The attacker, in most cases, tries to expand by running commands or scripts on the victim's machine, tries to enumerate the network to see where they are and where they can go, and starts to establish a foothold in the environment. All of these actions aim to develop some persistence in the environment and spread laterally, so we need to have eyes across all these potential routes.

In our real use case, Jasmin identifies a user, Andrew Maxwell, who has been targeted by a phishing attack, and looks at the whole story before diving into the interesting details. In the initial stages of this incident, we can see the first three events:

- **Threat Intel - Matched Domain Name**
- **Proofpoint TAP - User Received Phishing Email**
- **Phishing Link Then Proxy Allow**

These details appear as shown here:

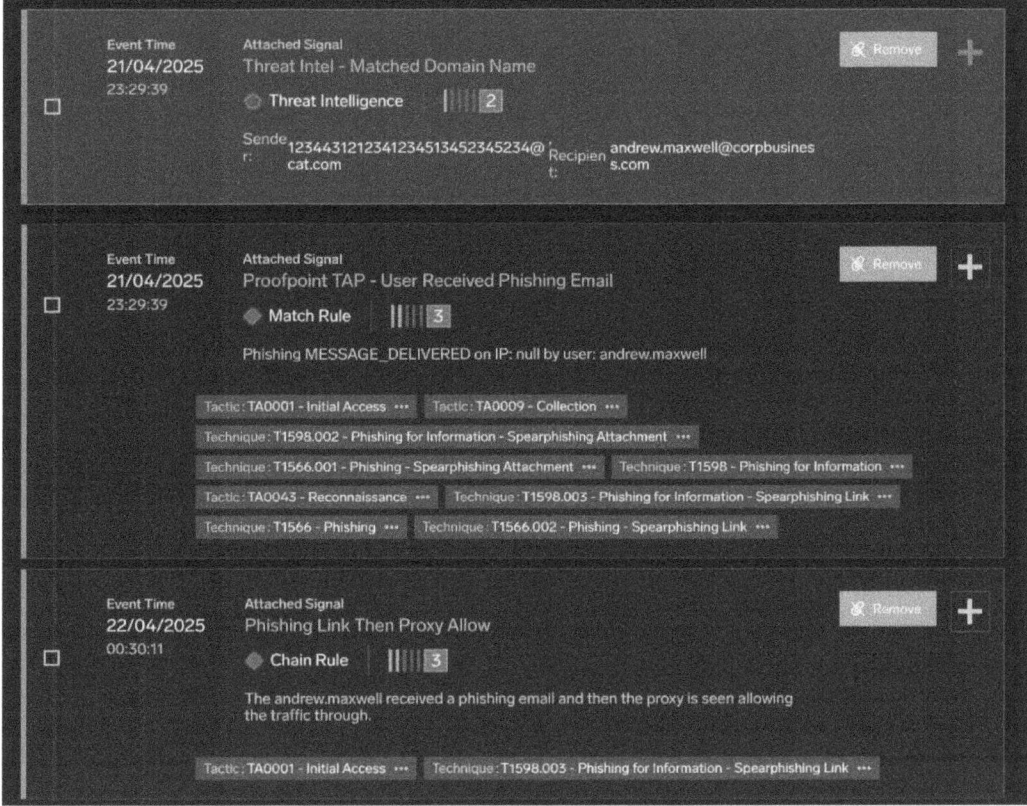

Figure 10.37 – The first three signals of this phishing insight, a very typical start to an incident

Let's address threat intelligence here. Threat intelligence is meant to be actionable; it's the whole point of using all of those nice feeds. However, in its base form, it's really hard to use. Whenever a match happens, you can get a signal easily. Great! The issue then becomes, *what do I do with this*? You have a threat intelligence signal, and then you have to work out exactly why, where, and how this is related to anything, and most importantly, whether it's important enough to even bother looking into!

This dance that cybersecurity defenders have to do all the time gets tedious and saps the willpower of even the hardiest professional.

Looking at this example insight here, we don't have to do the merry dance anymore. The clustering and context aggregation that happens within the Insight Engine does it for us. Here, we can see that, yes, we have a threat intel match on the domain name—but so what? Well, looking below the threat intelligence signal, we can see that the domain has been seen within the context of a phishing email. Now that's useful context that can steer us in the right direction.

Following on from that, not only has there been a potential phishing email, but the link within it has been clicked, and our proxy has allowed traffic from this user/endpoint to the domain. Another helpful point to know is that this activity is taking place *outside of working hours*. If we unfurl the first signal, we can see some useful metadata, as shown here:

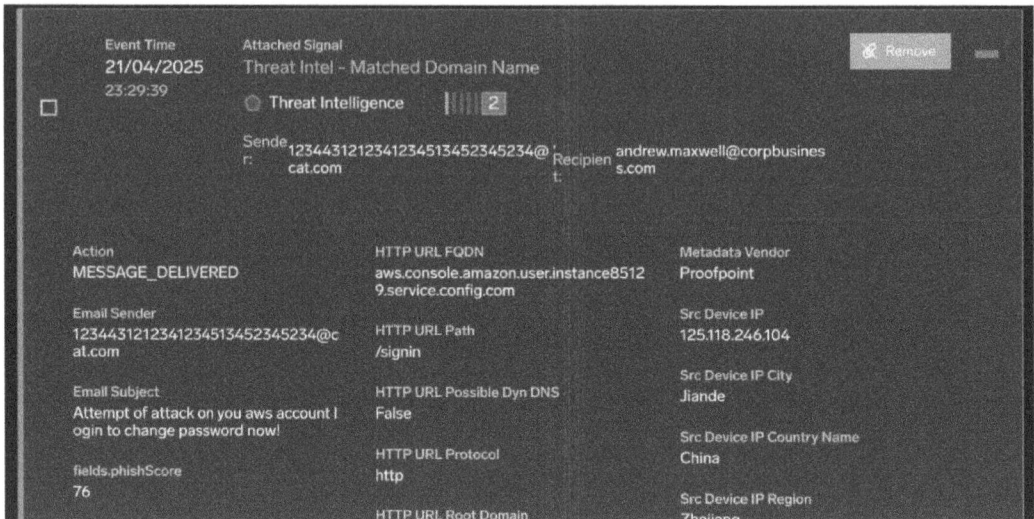

Figure 10.38 – Accessing all the metadata that comes through with a signal, in this case, looking at the threat intelligence match

We can see that the source device IP, along with the geoIP and ASN enrichment built into Sumo Logic, shows us that this domain and IP are based in China. This is not a region we have presence in. It also shows activity outside of our working hours. Threat intelligence confirmation? Phishing activity? I can already hear the alarm bells ringing!

Already, with the help of the first three signals, we've built a picture of what's happening. We've only scratched the surface, though.

Up to this point, though, even though these events are correlated and there's a strange IP involved, we're not convinced this is big news. I mean, we're a large enterprise, we get all kinds of weird traffic all the time! Right? Well, the next few signals, as shown, really underline that some pretty strange things happened:

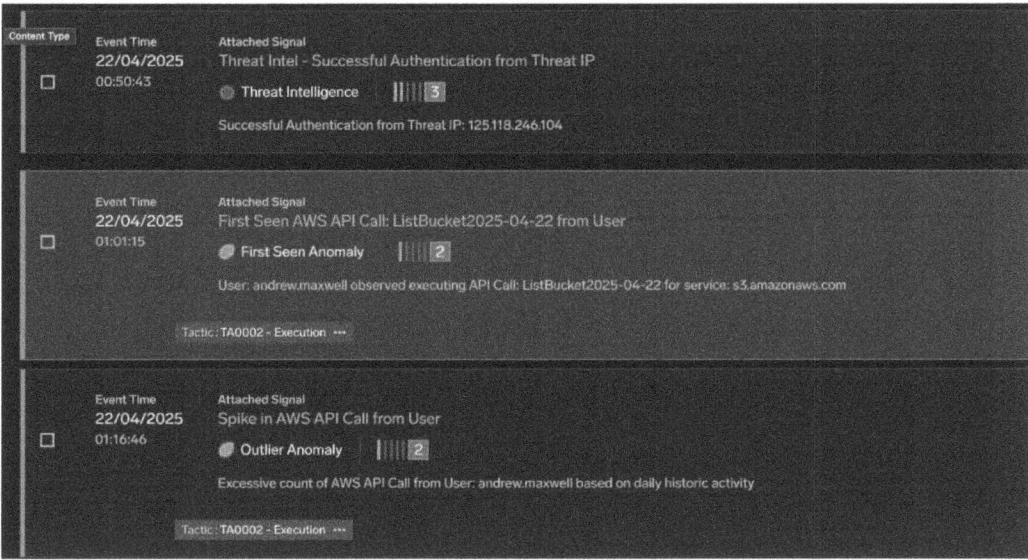

Figure 10.39 – We start to see some UEBA signals that tell us of anomalies in behavior

The first signal following the first three we looked at, **First Seen AWS API Call**, is yet another confirmation from the high-fidelity threat intel feeds built into Sumo Logic that these entities are not good. The following two signals, from **01:01:15**, indicate anomalies in the behavior of our main entity.

> Note
>
> We covered outlier and first-seen rules in the previous chapter, so you should be up to speed on what the goal of these rules is and how to define them. Feel free to brush up on the concepts if needed!

This is a prime example of where their appearance is incredibly useful to the security team, *given the right context*.

The first-seen signal is telling us that this entity has engaged in behavior that has not been seen before in the history of our log data, in this case, doing an AWS API call to list a specific S3 bucket. Let's pause here for a second. Think back to a time when you came across something like this, usually with a very complicated alert that you configured, or maybe you have a resident data science team who put some of these anomaly detection models together. Let's go back to Jasmin.

Jasmin is going to be clocking off for the day soon but comes across an interesting alert. Apparently, a certain user has made an AWS API call to list an S3 bucket that they don't seem to have accessed before. "Hmm, that seems to be someone from the DevOps team," Jasmin thinks. Her curiosity gets the best of her, and she tries to take a closer look. She filters her alerts on this type of alert and all of a sudden is bombarded by a lot of other users doing similar things across their vast estate! Where to even begin?

She starts sifting through some of the other alerts, but that's all they are: individual events that tell her what has happened and not much else. She wants to see all the other activity by this user. She goes to CloudTrail and searches for the username Andrew Maxwell. She does come across some logs to see that he's accessed that particular bucket, but he's also accessed a bunch of other buckets too—is that suspicious? This investigation is going to take *hours*!

Jasmin, in this case, lacks context and can't discern suspicious behavior from non-suspicious behavior. She also has no clue that the activity that took place prior to this particular signal, the phishing activity, even happened. She is effectively blind. She sighs, closes her laptop lid, and heads home for the night.

Jasmin's situation is one experienced by thousands of cybersecurity analysts around the world. When you come across these individual signals, it's hard to know the full picture ***quickly***. Speed is paramount in security because it means a quicker time to comprehend and respond to an attack or breach. However, with our insight, we have context from across the rest of the business on our side. Let's move on to the next signal—**Spike in AWS API Call from User**, presented here:

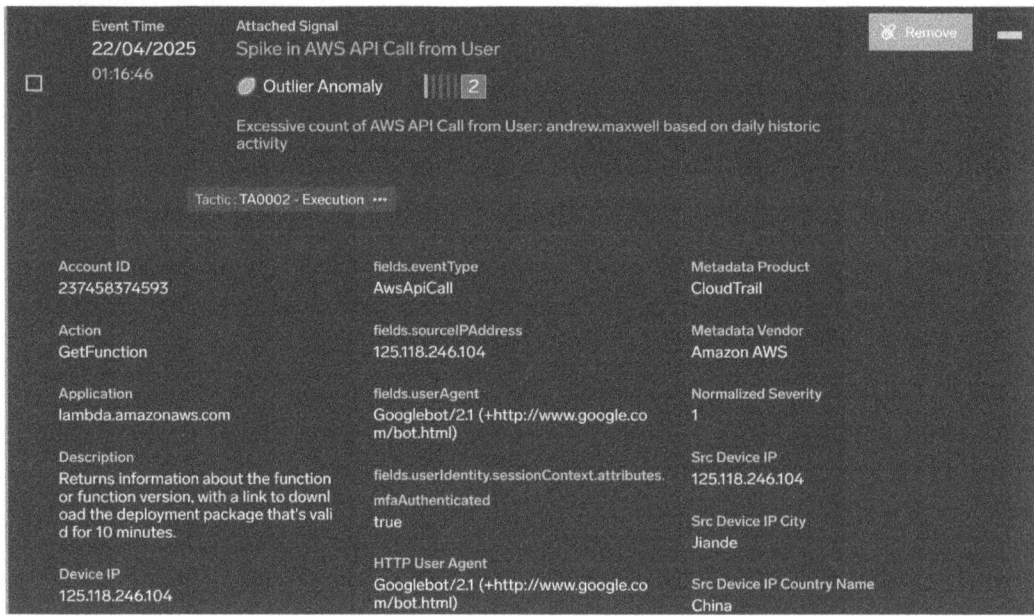

Figure 10.40 – Opening up the metadata for the spike in API calls lets us see more info

This is telling us that a user has been doing more API calls on AWS than usual. It is based on an **Outlier Anomaly** rule that looks at deviations in API calls done by users and learns from this behavior. It's looking at anomalies in counter-based behavior and finding statistical deviations from a baseline. On the face of it, it's quite a general signal, but let's click into it to see what happened. Here is what we see:

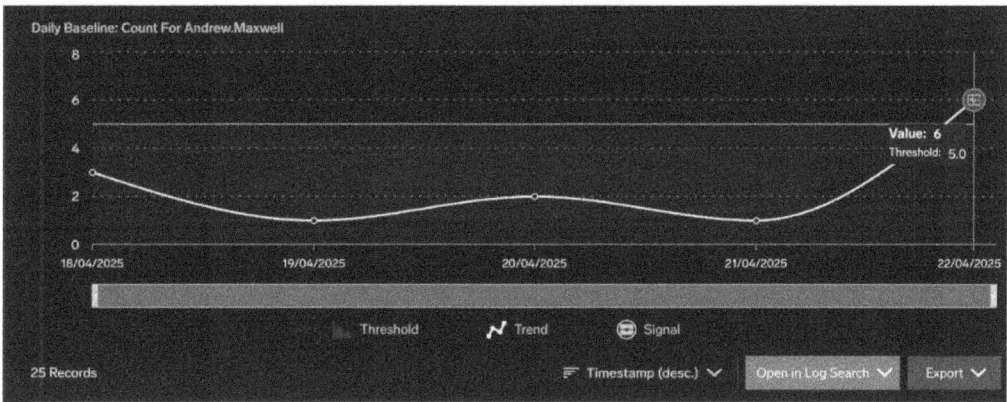

Figure 10.41 – If we pivot into the signal, we can see why it was triggered

What we're seeing here is the number of API calls done every day by our user, Andrew Maxwell. The activity is tracked over a longer timeframe, however, which explains why we see **Threshold** as **5.0** on the right side of the graph. You'll notice straight away that this signal was seemingly triggered as soon as that threshold was broken, by *one*!

"This is going to cause too many false positives!" I hear you cry. "It makes no sense!" I would agree with you *if* I were an L2/L3 security engineer in the SOC who would never write a rule like this in the traditional sense.

Let me break this down. When you write a security rule, you have this mystical vacuum that you're trying to estimate and preempt. It looks something like this:

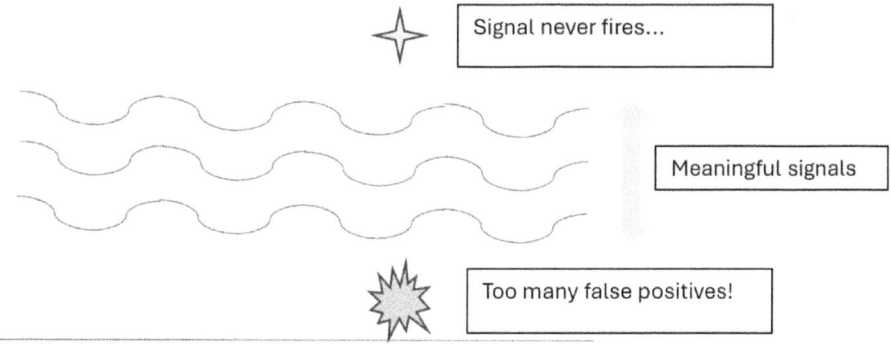

Figure 10.42 – My interpretation of how hard it is to create security rules

The battle is a never-ending one. You have some sort of behavior you need to capture, but to what extent? If you create a rule that triggers too frequently or is too vague, you get loads of false positives; that's not great. If you narrow down the logic too much or have a threshold that's too high, you're not going to see the signal frequently and may, in fact, miss true positives.

What's the answer to this predicament? **Context**. When looking at the graph for the signal, the threshold has only *just* been broken, and usually, this rule would be perceived as very noisy. But we need to consider that we have the Insight Engine on our side. There are two things helping us:

- We don't really care about signals overall—yes, they're great and point to interesting behavior, but we can't focus on each one. With Cloud SIEM, you can ingest your data and not have to worry about tuning these thresholds for every rule.
- The automated clustering and correlation that happen under the hood help to surround this signal with the events that help give this signal *significance*, and it's much easier to commit to identifying the issue.

So, the fact that this threshold (which was dynamically learned by Cloud SIEM) has been breached in the first place is important, but we are only convinced of its importance when there is a genuine sequence or pattern of activity that surrounds it. *This is the sweet spot that Cloud SIEM is able to fill.*

We have these anomalies in behavior that have happened *after* a successful phishing attempt on this user. With this immediate context from email security and the threat intelligence feed, we can conclude that something is very wrong. There are a few extra key signals, **Suspicious AWS Lambda Enumeration** and **AWS GuardDuty Alert**, as shown next:

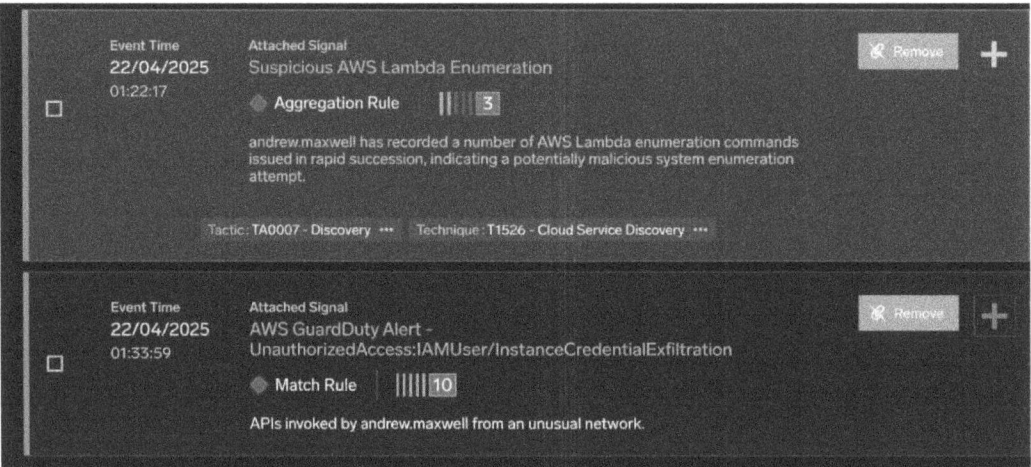

Figure 10.43 – The final two signals, which tell us that our AWS environment is being impacted

These signals indicate additional actions on AWS that have been taken by this entity. By opening these signals individually, we're able to see what types of actions are being executed with the Lambda functions, and we ultimately see that a remote host is running API operations using temporary AWS credentials that an external entity, in this case, the attacker, gained.

Before we wrap up this example, let's jump into the **Entities** tab to see a visual representation of the entities that make up this insight (take note of the red-ringed entities with the fingerprint icon that show a match with our built-in threat intelligence feeds):

Figure 10.44 – The entities involved in this insight

We covered this particular view earlier in this chapter, but now you can see that it's actually a part of this phishing incident. Visually, we can quickly grasp the behavior between our main entity, Andrew Maxwell, and the other entities that have been seen in the surrounding signals. This looks at *immediate* links between these entities based on the signals in the insight. For example, if the IP address in question (**125.118.246...**), highlighted in red and originating from China, had communicated with some of these other entities within some of these signals, that association would be clear.

We can look at deeper links, though. Remember, Sumo Logic is one big data lake where all of your logs, metrics, and traces live, right? So, you have all the data you need to check whether this suspicious IP address has actually touched other parts of your environment.

Below each entity is a **+** button that lets you see any other connections across your *entire* dataset. This is huge because it lets you glean context from data *outside of this insight*. We're effectively doing a quick form of enrichment on this IP address on our internal data. So, let's click the button and see what we get:

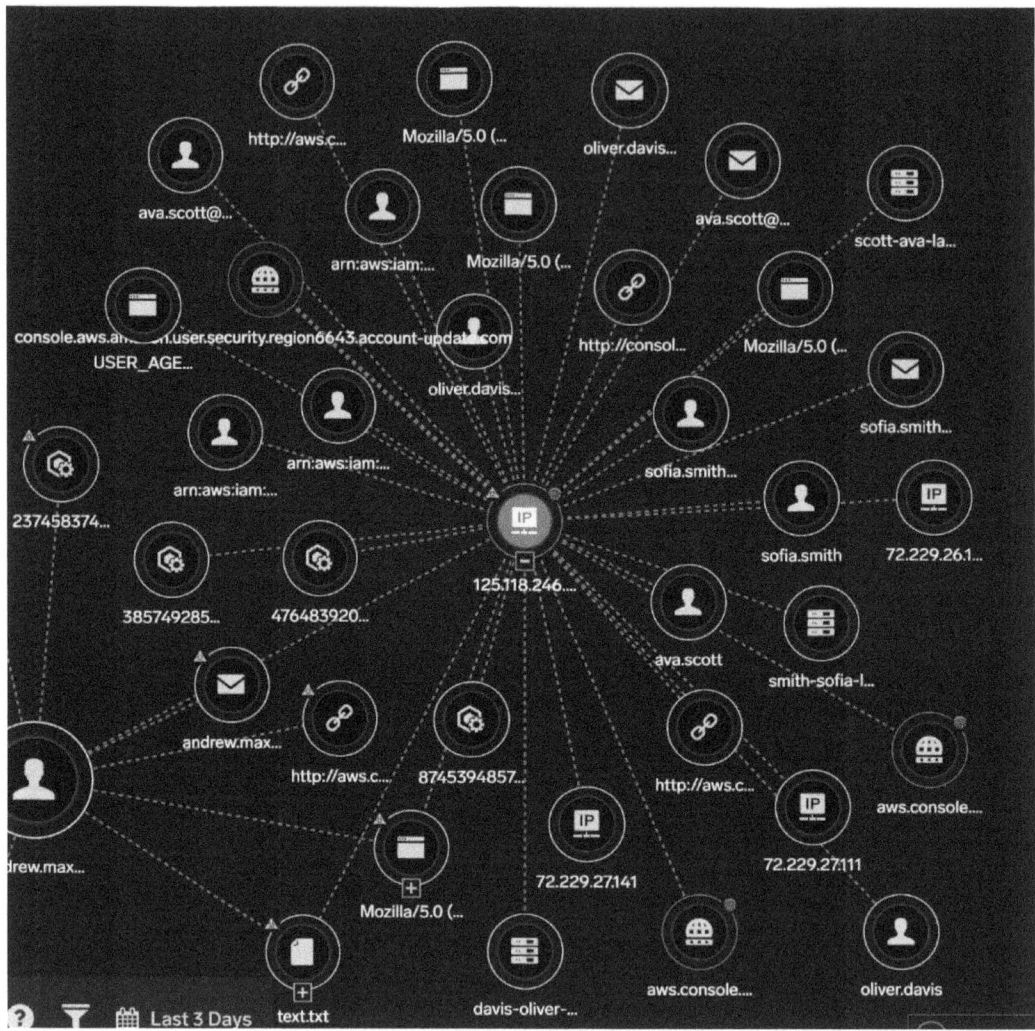

Figure 10.45 – Expanding the IP address entity

Hmm, OK. That doesn't look as good. We can immediately notice that this IP address has, in fact, interacted with other entities in our business—usernames, other IP addresses, workstations, and files. This visual way of looking at our data across our sources means it's much easier to understand the scale of a threat and also what components of the threat we need to contain or isolate first. The result? Quicker time to comprehend and resolve the incident! (In most cases...)

We have unraveled a range of useful avenues to cover—IP addresses and usernames that need to be contacted and their machines isolated for further inspection. Jasmin's role is escalating more important incidents to levels 2 and 3 of the SOC, so she can write her report and be done. Or is it? I think it's time to look at the AI investigation and Mobot, because this is going to elevate Jasmin's response to the next level. Let's click on the **Ask Mobot** button under the insight name and we'll get taken to the chat interface in Mobot with the prepopulated information from the insight and the key findings:

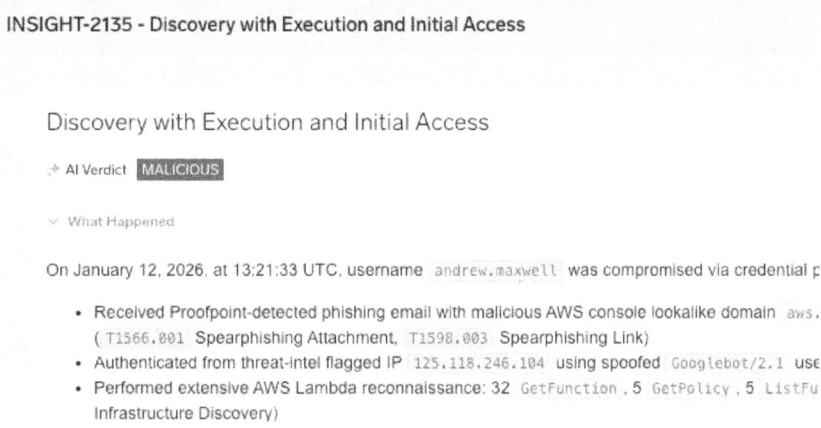

Figure 10.46 – The overview of the insight populated in Mobot

Underneath this are the key findings. You'll notice that under each key finding, you are recommended an automatic query to run to investigate this further:

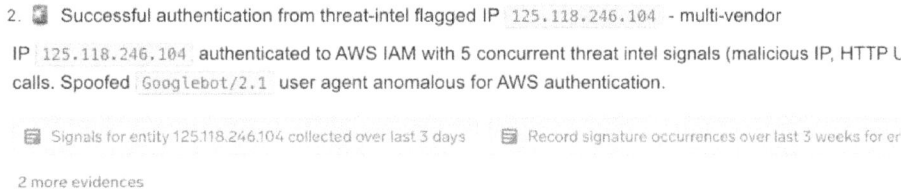

Figure 10.47 – Key finding number 2 highlights the IP address entity and useful queries to run to explore

Remember, though, Jasmin is low on time. Every minute counts! Let's just tell the SOC analyst agent, which is the one that will be used in this context automatically, to investigate everything for us:

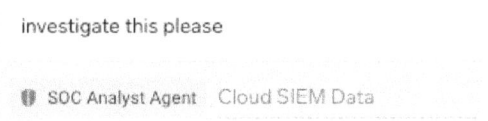

Figure 10.48 – We can ask any questions we want regarding this incident and it will be processed with that context in mind

Remember, people, be nice to our AI overlords. Asking this will generate a complete report, full of analytical queries that break down the signals and records of the insight further:

Now let me display my investigation plan and then query the relevant datasets:

Investigation Overview

I'm analyzing a **HIGH severity** security incident involving user **andrew.maxwell** with the following attack chain:

1. **Initial Access** - Phishing email with AWS console lookalike domain
2. **Credential Compromise** - Authentication from threat-intel flagged IP `125.118.246.104` (China)
3. **Discovery/Reconnaissance** - AWS Lambda enumeration and cloud service discovery
4. **Credential Exfiltration** - GuardDuty alert for EC2 credentials accessed externally

Key Timeline:

- Jan 12, 22:14 UTC - Phishing email delivered
- Jan 12, 23:35 UTC - Successful console login from threat IP

Figure 10.49 – The SOC analyst agent breaks the attack chain into discrete steps based on the MITRE ATT&CK framework

As it goes through this process, the SOC analyst agent explains what everything means and why it's important. In this case, it runs an aggregation query on the API calls to work out exactly what calls were made with the compromised credentials and breaks the pattern down:

AWS API Activity - Reconnaissance Pattern

API Calls from Threat IP (125.118.246.104):

API Action	Service	Count
GetFunction	Lambda	200
GetPolicy	Lambda	40
ListFunctions	Lambda	40
GetFunctionConcurrency	Lambda	40
ListBucket2026-01-13	S3	8
PutObject	S3	8

Total: 336 API calls from the compromised credentials

This pattern indicates:

- **Systematic Lambda reconnaissance** - 320 calls to enumerate Lambda functions, policies, and concurrency settings
- **S3 bucket enumeration** - 8 ListBucket calls to discover bucket contents
- **Data exfiltration attempt** - 8 PutObject calls to S3 (potential data staging)

This aligns with **T1580 (Cloud Service Discovery)** and **T1526 (Cloud Infrastructure Discovery)** MITRE ATT&CK techniques.

Figure 10.50 – Another example of an automatic aggregated query to understand the context and assess it

The SOC analyst agent runs whatever query is required to understand the threat, and the underlying models are able to assess, dynamically, what the threat represents, surrounded by the context that the other correlated signals provide.

At the end, Jasmin will get a report that specifies the verdict and how the SOC analyst agent reached it, with its own hypothesis, followed by a remediation plan. This is gold, because it outlines what steps Jasmin, or the team that Jasmin escalates to, should take to mitigate the situation *based on the data sources, attack techniques, and entities observed.*

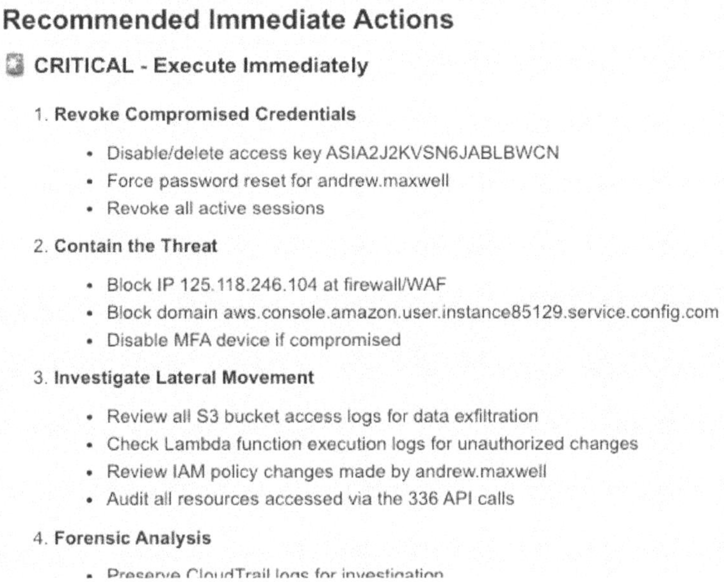

Recommended Immediate Actions

🟥 **CRITICAL - Execute Immediately**

1. **Revoke Compromised Credentials**
   - Disable/delete access key ASIA2J2KVSN6JABLBWCN
   - Force password reset for andrew.maxwell
   - Revoke all active sessions

2. **Contain the Threat**
   - Block IP 125.118.246.104 at firewall/WAF
   - Block domain aws.console.amazon.user.instance85129.service.config.com
   - Disable MFA device if compromised

3. **Investigate Lateral Movement**
   - Review all S3 bucket access logs for data exfiltration
   - Check Lambda function execution logs for unauthorized changes
   - Review IAM policy changes made by andrew.maxwell
   - Audit all resources accessed via the 336 API calls

4. **Forensic Analysis**
   - Preserve CloudTrail logs for investigation

Figure 10.51 – The recommended remediation actions for defenders to undertake

With this in mind, these actions would have to be taken manually. However, in the next chapter, we'll cover the Automation Service in detail, where we'll be able to create playbooks that can run these actions with a click of a button, or automatically (based on certain criteria) from our insights.

Having looked at one use case, phishing, let's move on to our second use case, ransomware detection.

A ransomware scenario

We've covered a pretty common scenario in our initial use case, phishing, and I wanted to carry on the real-world practicality of these insights. Let's look at an organization that experienced a ransomware event that was captured by the Insight Engine.

Ransomware is the bane of organizations globally. It is as adaptable and has as many forms as standard malware, but it has far more devastating consequences. Think pure destruction—destruction of intellectual property, destruction of customer and supplier trust, destruction of business processes. It is the stuff of business owner nightmares. I'm sure you know what ransomware is, but for anyone who doesn't know much about this particular malware, it encrypts files, to which only attackers have the key. The attackers then ask for a ransom. If it's not paid, say goodbye to your data. Fortunately, a lot of cybersecurity teams are aware of this threat, and there are steps that can be taken to mitigate the effects of this destructive strain of malware.

We all hear it—prevention is better than a cure—and ransomware is no exception. We want to always make sure we can catch the type of behavior that leads to a ransomware attack before the *Actions on Objectives* step of the Cyber Kill Chain[2].

> **Note**
>
> The Cyber Kill Chain is a cybersecurity model developed by Lockheed Martin that defines seven separate steps that attackers go through when attacking organizations. The earlier these steps are identified, the better.

In our case, our chain begins with, surprise surprise, a phishing attack! However, it developed in a way that is different from our previous example. Let's take a look at the first two signals in this insight:

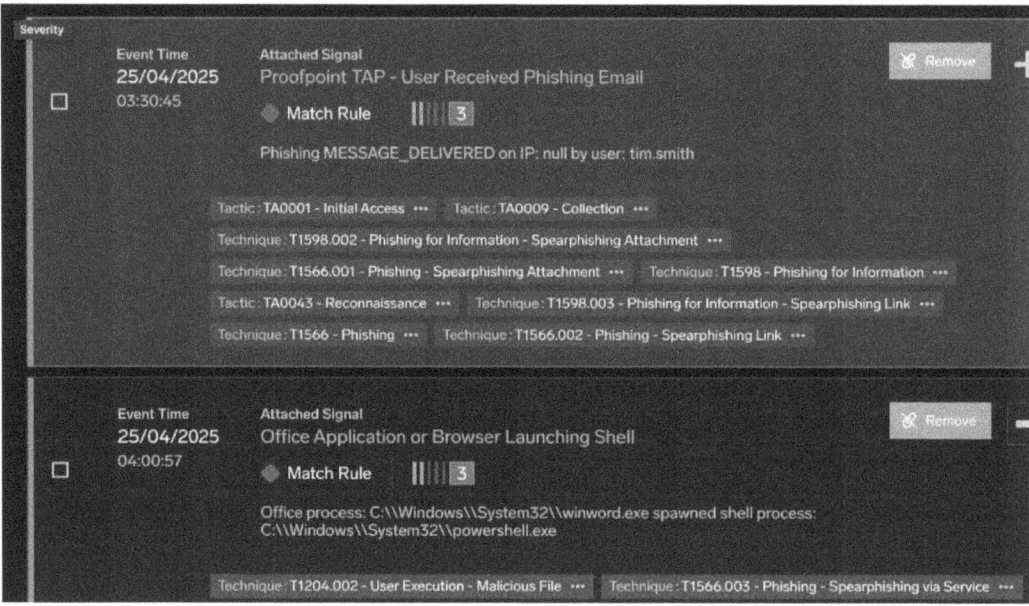

Figure 10.52 – Similar to the previous insight, we can see that this one starts off in the same way

Half an hour after the initial alert from Proofpoint warning of an email with a high phishing score, we get a follow-up signal telling us that this user's laptop has had a shell launched from an office product or browser that should not be creating shell processes. These two signals together are usually enough to pique any security analyst's interest, and any analyst worth their salt will be saying, "I bet there's a macro execution somewhere here." And they'd be correct! As shown in the following screenshot, the anomaly in user behavior is clear, and we have proof from our antivirus solution that the events are being flagged:

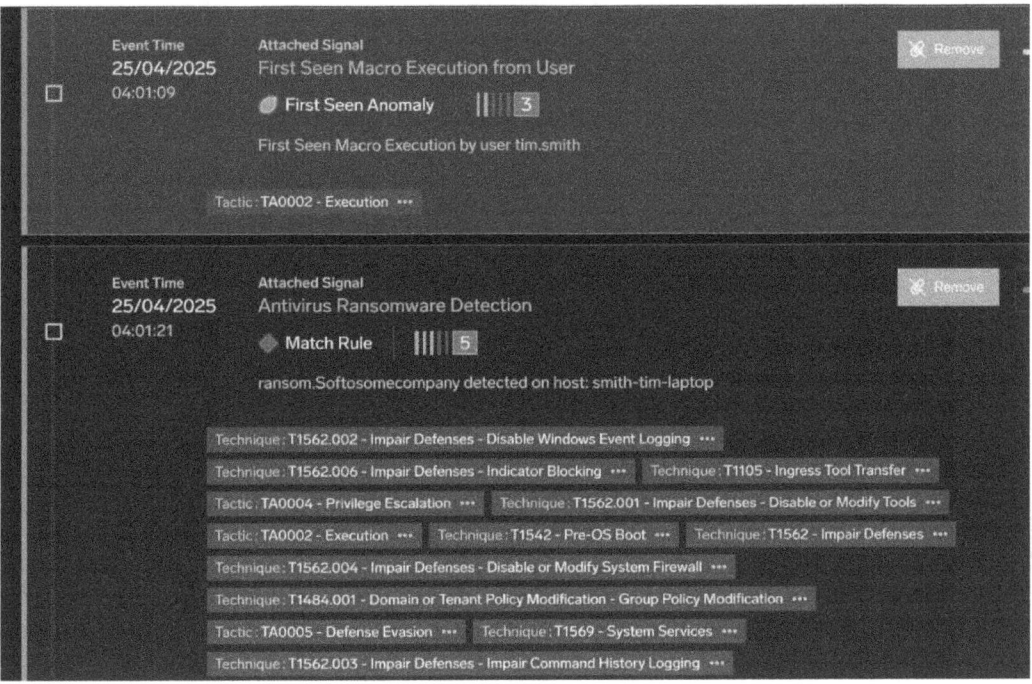

Figure 10.53 – Insight context

We have the context that we need.

Office applications running macros are still very prevalent in today's landscape and constantly pose a threat. In this case, this user has never run a macro in the history of our log data, and now they have, so we instantly get a signal. However, that signal is up for correlation and clustering due to the surrounding events taking place. Being able to surface correlations in this way makes your life 10x easier. If we take a look at this macro, we see some useful details, such as **Device Hostname** and **File path**, as shown in the following screenshot:

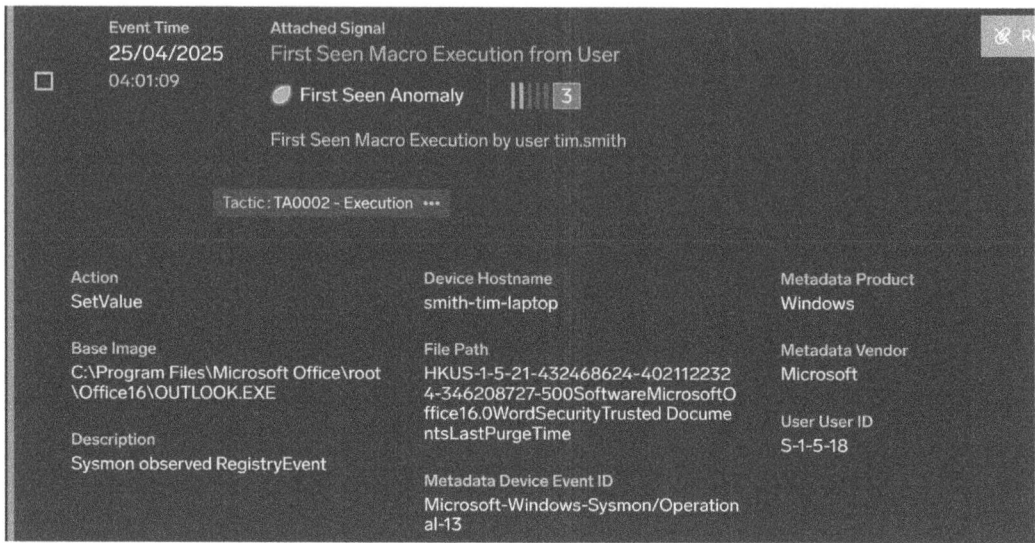

Figure 10.54 – Diving deeper into the macro execution from the user

Macros are still the typical method of choice for an attacker after gaining entry into a network because they help attackers establish persistence and/or escalate privileges; macros still work because they are still successful.

This is why the file path in *Figure 10.54*, `HKUS-1-5-21-432468624-4021122324-346208727-500SoftwareMicrosoftOffice16.0WordSecurityTrusted DocumentsLastPurgeTime`, is so relevant. It's part of the *Trusted Documents* feature of Microsoft Office, and **LastPurgeTime** can suggest Office is updating when it last cleared its trust cache. However, when paired with the highlighted macro activity, it can signal escalation privilege taking place. The registry is being amended by something that shouldn't be there and, therefore, we know that something shady is most likely going on.

This particular chain of events has ultimately led to our antivirus perking up and detecting this macro as a malicious event, which further confirms the severity of what's taking place on this machine.

To finalize the intrusion, we now review these signals:

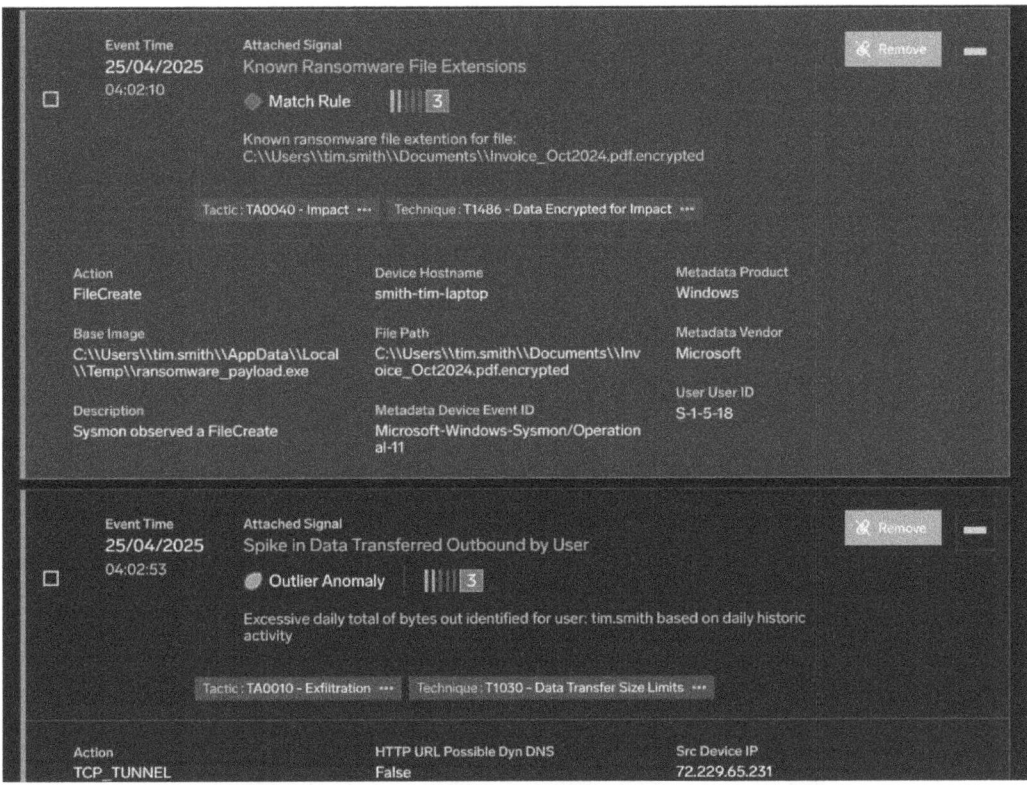

Figure 10.55 – Explicit ransomware signals combined with anomalies in data transfer

We're being told that ransomware file extensions have been seen in our environment, followed by a spike in outbound packets from our user's device.

>
>
> Note that the last few signals have been detected within minutes of each other; however, the Insight Engine would've correlated these events even if they were hours, or even days, apart.

The spike in data transferred is a great example of the **outlier** rule type because you can use it to monitor unusual network activity across any part of your estate. The benefit of this is two-fold:

- You don't have to create thresholds manually across different servers, devices, and virtualized infrastructure, which massively reduces management and tuning overheads
- It delegates the detection to the engine so that it can automatically cluster these anomalies with surrounding behavior, reducing the time it takes for you to understand what's going on

Let's check out something really useful that we can do to investigate a particular entity here. You've seen a wide range of signals so far, including how to expand them to see the full picture and also how you can add new ones.

In this ransomware attempt, when the spike of outbound network traffic was detected, it went to a particular IP address. This IP address hasn't been flagged by any threat intelligence feed, but it certainly is still worth investigating, and we have two options:

- Use a playbook to enrich the IP with a few sources of data
- Do an internal Sumo Logic search to see what else we know about this entity from our own data

When working in an SOC environment, in most cases, the first question you ask when you see a new IP, or in fact any new IOC, is: "What do we know about this IOC and have we seen it before?"

All the signal metadata in insights is clickable, so you can interact with any of the values. In this case, we want to click on the IP address, and we get presented with the following contextual menu:

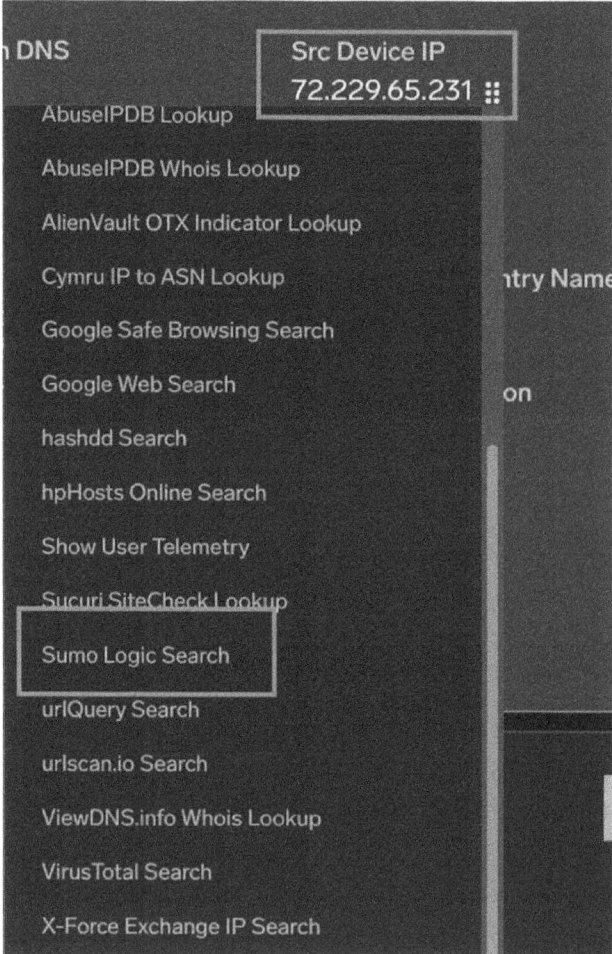

Figure 10.56 – The contextual menu

As you can see from the list, you can create a lot of useful links based on the value in question. In this case, there are a lot of external threat intelligence lookups that will take us to the source, and then we can see what these sources tell us about this IP. That's pretty standard stuff, though, and you can get a playbook to do it. We want to go to the **Sumo Logic Search** menu item to see how we approach this type of scenario in the platform. This item takes us to the Log Search UI and prepopulates the value into the query field for us. Let's just say that we want to go back one week and see everything that this IP address has been up to. We go to the right of the query bar and select the timeframe we want, or just type in -1h and hit *Enter*. The results will look like the following:

Figure 10.57 – Searching for an entity of interest across all our data sources and across any timeframe to find more information

We can see that the IP address has been seen across our load balancer logs and our Kubernetes proxy logs to begin with, and there are more results below this. Let's just dwell on this for a second:

- We have searched across the entirety of our centralized data lake
- We have seen all activity in the raw logs tied to this IP address
- We didn't need to write a query
- We searched 4–5 TB of data in four seconds

Nothing complicated, nothing requiring any waiting around—just fast and easy threat investigation.

I am often asked whether Sumo Logic can find zero-day attacks.

If you don't know what *zero-day* means, it simply refers to attacks or threats that have never been seen "in the wild" before, such as a new strain of malware or a new method of conducting an attack (TTP) that does damage to a business.

It's an interesting question, because cybersecurity teams and CISOs aren't asking this from the right perspective, in my opinion.

The main bugbear for me is the amount of marketing that certain cybersecurity vendors push to users (*Use us to stop the apocalyptic zero-day attacks!!!*) when in fact you'll never have any signatures, hashes, or scripts that match a database out there to tell you: "*Yep, it's a zero-day, you better start praying.*"

A zero-day attack is all about behavior. We need a way not to *find* zero-day attacks, but to have full, unfettered visibility into our entire environment. We also need a way of knowing when entities within our business have shown strange activity, maybe for the first time, maybe more often than usual, and also where, when, and how. This kind of visibility and entity information should be the rock-solid foundation that our monitoring and threat detection sits upon. An incident, especially a zero-day, *never takes place in isolation in a single event*. There is always a sequence of events executed by someone, or something, to get to the point where the explosive stuff happens—encrypting files, exfiltrating data, destroying IP, and so on.

What anyone should be asking for is a way of detecting chains of behavior that are unusual and could be highly malicious among all the noise they see on a daily basis. The behavior is the key, and we've shown that in these two use cases alone. The Insight Engine is designed and primed to identify such behavior for you. Central to this is machine learning, which can detect abnormal changes in behavior compared to other behavior of the same type and find novel attacks or events of interest. The ability to have this machine learning apply in a data-agnostic way across your data estate is also important. Bringing all your business data together into the same place will let you see patterns across these sources that you otherwise may not be able to, allowing you to find behavior that would have gone unseen with blind spots.

Letting the Insight Engine find threats for you is great, but sometimes you just need to be able to tell Cloud SIEM, "In this particular situation, I don't care about waiting to group signals together; all hell will break loose." In the platform, you're able to specify this so that when some crucial criteria (to you) are met, Cloud SIEM has your back. Let's review custom insights.

Custom insights

Even though we've been talking about insights and how important an insight is compared to a signal because of the fact that it's a single event without much context, *some* signals are still major events. Here are some examples:

- Authentication attempts out of hours to a particularly important "crown jewel" server
- A PowerShell script that highlights the use of a particular tool, such as Mimikatz or Empire
- A pull request initiated on a repo that should not be pulled

Whatever it is, there are plenty of situations where an individual event is actually really bad. You can create custom insights in Cloud SIEM that let you define these signals and then turn them into insights when they happen. The key thing to note here is that it doesn't necessarily have to be one signal either; it can be multiple.

You know your environment best, and Cloud SIEM provides all the tools you need to personalize the cybersecurity experience, including the ability to make custom insights. This can help with incident management, as you'll then have an insight that you can respond to with a playbook, do an investigation in, and so on. The way to do this is to head on over to the **Custom Insights** menu under **Cloud SIEM**:

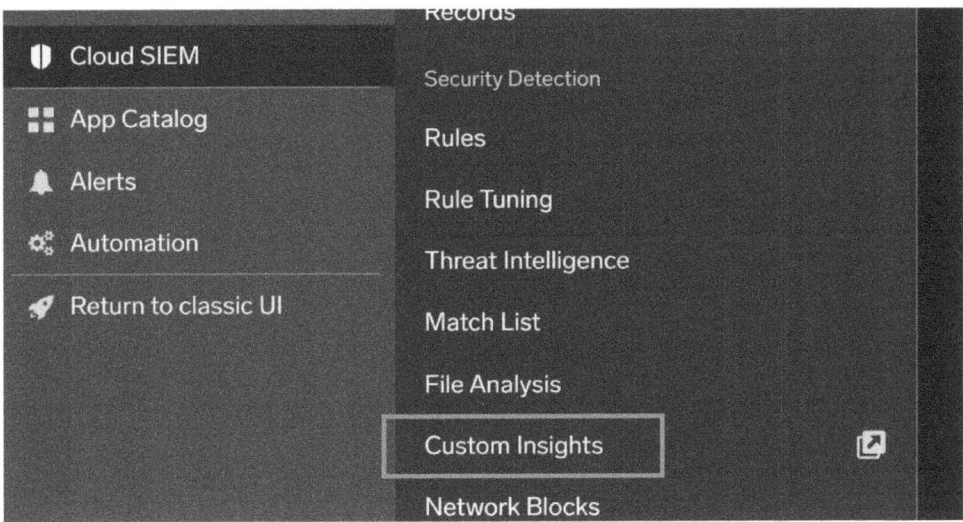

Figure 10.58 – The Custom Insights menu

Then you can create your custom insight by either defining particular rules that get triggered or signal names, as shown here:

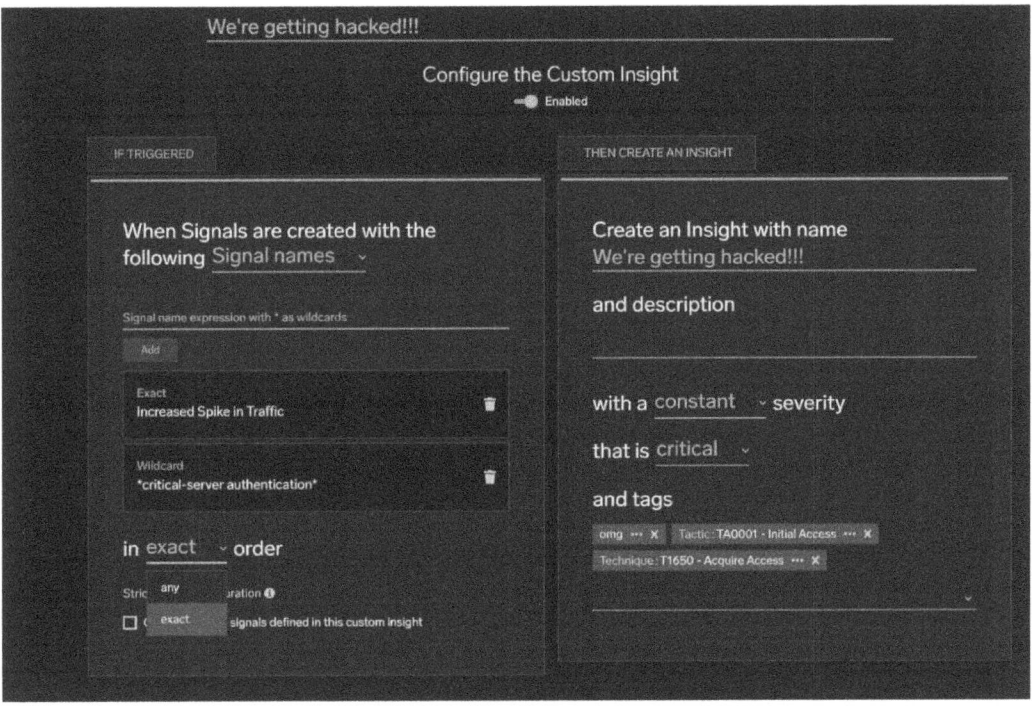

Figure 10.59 – Configuring a custom insight

Let's break a few things down here. First of all, you can choose either rules or signal names; you can't choose both. Then you specify what those are, either in the **Exact** field or with wildcards in the **Wildcard** field, because we're working with expressions here.

Second, you can choose for these signals/rules to occur in a specific order to trigger the insight. It's kind of like a *chain* rule in that sense, but this is specifically designed to ensure that you can respond in line to whatever threat causes these events to happen.

Finally, you can specify the name, description, and severity of this insight along with any tags.

The whole point is that even though it's similar to a chain rule, and the Insight Engine already exists to automatically correlate and cluster events, you and your team can effectively guide and direct Cloud SIEM to ensure that you know when something really blows up.

Cloud SIEM best practices

The following are some Cloud SIEM best practices based on everything we have discussed so far:

- **Normalize everything up front**: Make normalization non-negotiable. By forcing every log, whether it comes from a SaaS API, a Windows host, or a cloud workload, into a common schema, you ensure that a single query or rule reliably captures every variant of username, commandLine, or source IP, laying the groundwork for consistent detection engineering and threat hunting across the estate. Parser configuration and log mapping are day 0 tasks, so that fields such as commandLine and user_username mean the same thing everywhere. A consistent schema accelerates detection engineering, threat hunting, and dashboarding.

- **Follow the onboarding checklist religiously**: Solid hygiene that includes user RBAC roles, data source routing and retention, parser validation, threat intel feeds, match and suppressed lists, and realistic insight thresholds sets up the SIEM solution and its insight algorithm for success and prevents noisy or silent failures later. The official checklist walks you through each prerequisite and retains audit data for a full year, covering KPIs and compliance needs out of the box: https://help.sumologic.com/docs/cse/get-started-with-cloud-siem/onboarding-checklist-cse/.

- **Start with built-in content and tune before you build**: Begin with the fundamentals: map out the behaviors you want to detect and check whether an existing built-in rule already covers them, then *tune rather than reinvent*. This preserves the benefit of Sumo Logic's continuously updated core logic and its crowd-sourced machine learning models while sparing you the overhead of writing and maintaining custom code.

- **Instrument the feedback loop**: Because every record, signal, and insight re-enters Sumo Logic as structured JSON, you can layer the platform's analytics on top of the SIEM solution itself. Install the Enterprise Audit - Cloud SIEM app and Insight Trainer dashboards to surface parser gaps, noisy rules, dormant content, analyst MTTR, and MITRE ATT&CK coverage, then iterate with data-driven confidence.

Summary

In this chapter, we covered the Insight Engine in more depth and illustrated, with the help of some key use cases and examples, how automatic clustering and correlation happen under the hood. We discussed the Insight Engine UI elements to get you acquainted with what you can expect to see when looking at an insight and how you can use it to start running your investigations and dive into the details of an incident.

We then covered some of the tools that are invaluable to working with all the data that you send to Sumo Logic and that is analyzed by Cloud SIEM. We covered tools such as the Cloud SIEM audit app in the App Catalog, pivoting to log analytics queries from a signal or insight and how to conduct threat-hunting investigations on the data.

We covered two use cases, phishing and ransomware attacks, and showed how insights are crucial to detecting attacks such as this in real life across your environment. Finally, we covered some best practices to keep in mind when starting to use the Cloud SIEM capabilities.

Most importantly, we covered the new battlefield, where security analysts and AI work hand in hand to solve tougher and tougher investigations, all with minimal effort, using Sumo Logic's Mobot.

In the next chapter, we're going to dive into the final piece of the puzzle, the *Automation Service*, where we bring our incident response to life.

References

1. https://help.sumologic.com/docs/cse/records-signals-entities-insights/about-signal-suppression/

Get this book's PDF version and more

Scan the QR code (or go to `packtpub.com/unlock`). Search for this book by name, confirm the edition, and then follow the steps on the page.

Note: Keep your invoice handy. Purchases made directly from Packt don't require an invoice.

11

The Automation Service and Playbooks

SOAR, no-code/low-code automation, AIOps, agentic SecOps; there's no shortage of automation buzzwords in this industry, and most of us are desensitized to them by now. However, let's bring it back to its core purpose: automation is about helping you do manual, repetitive work faster and smarter, so you can focus your human brainpower on what actually matters.

Despite what flashy product videos and investor decks might imply, no one in cybersecurity, DevOps, or SecOps is being replaced by AI-powered robots (yet). Not in 2026, and probably not for a while. Yes, our roles will change as our IT systems become more intelligent. Yes, the market's obsessed with plugging generative AI into everything, but it still can't do the most important thing: apply human judgment and reasoning to complex, ever-changing situations.

Fundamentally, humans created computers to do low-level tasks so we can level up where we focus. The *low level* is getting higher, no doubt. What is exciting to watch is the evolution from systems *knowing* things and helping us with analytics to systems *doing* things on our behalf. This is the evolution of practical, well-designed automation. Scripts, playbooks, decision trees, and smart workflows—these are the tools that make life bearable in modern security teams. Whether you're responding to threats, managing alerts, or coordinating with IT and Dev teams under pressure, these tools are what we have to make our jobs easier.

However, let's not fool ourselves into thinking automation solves *everything*. We're still plagued with the old garbage-in, garbage-out problems, and the fidelity of our alerts is still mostly lacking. For these reasons, nobody's running full, autonomous playbooks for every security incident. We're also not yet in the era of AI-powered SOC copilots who understand your environment better than your own team does. That dream is still on the horizon.

What *is* clear, and widely agreed upon, is that modern security automation needs to be the following:

- **More intelligent**: beyond static rules and brittle scripts
- **Easily accessible**: not limited to people who can code Python in their sleep
- **Affordable and low-friction**: no $500k consulting engagements just to create a ticket

In this chapter, we'll walk through how Sumo Logic addresses these needs with its Dojo AI framework and its *Automation Service*, a fully integrated, low-code orchestration engine built into the platform. We'll cover the following topics:

- Why automation matters
- Creating and managing playbooks
- Real-world examples of automated responses

Whether you're a lean, under-resourced team or part of a large enterprise, this chapter will show you how to design, manage, and trigger automation with ease without needing to become a software engineer in the process.

Why automation matters

Let's go back to our SOC analyst, Jasmin. With help from the Insight Engine, she's just identified a threat. A compromised laptop, suspicious user activity, shady attachments, and potential data exfiltration. Great detection. But now what?

In many teams, what comes next is painful: manually digging through logs, cross-referencing events, opening tickets manually, pinging teams in Slack or via email, writing reports, waiting for replies, and, ultimately, losing time.

Doing it all manually is pretty bleak. It's slow, repetitive, and error-prone in a lot of cases, *especially* when under pressure during an incident. Some teams have already started scripting these tasks. Python is a favorite for a reason: it's flexible, powerful, and widely adopted. As security environments scaled and threats grew more complex, a new class of tooling emerged, **SOAR,** which stands for **Security Orchestration, Automation, and Response**.

SOAR tools promised what everyone needed:

- **Speed** in handling complex, multi-step incidents
- **Consistency** to reduce human error
- **Scale** to process huge volumes of alerts
- **Relief** from the grind of endless ticketing and coordination

For the most part, SOAR delivered. But it also came with baggage such as steep learning curves, brittle integrations, and a tendency to require heavy customization to make them truly useful.

Through my discussions with many security teams every single day, the following emerged as the most valued aspects of automation on a daily basis:

- Automation that's easy to adopt
- Playbooks that don't require engineers to build them
- Systems that integrate cleanly into existing workflows
- Tools that help, not hinder, already overstretched defenders
- Automation integrations that are extensible and customizable

That's exactly what the **Sumo Logic Automation Service**, and in many ways, Dojo AI is designed to provide.

Automation in Sumo Logic

So how does Sumo Logic actually deliver automation that's useful, usable, and built for modern teams? Meet the Automation Service, a fully integrated orchestration layer within the Sumo Logic platform. It's enterprise-grade, scalable, and ready to run actions across hundreds of technologies. More importantly, it's built for people who don't have time to wrestle with overly complex tooling.

Much like the App Catalog provides plug-and-play dashboards, monitors, and queries, the Automation Service offers out-of-the-box playbooks and prebuilt integrations that work from day one. There's no extra licensing layer, no bolt-on interface, and no steep learning curve. It's part of the platform by design.

> **Note**
>
> **Fun fact**: Sumo Logic didn't build its Automation Service from scratch. In 2019, they acquired a SOAR vendor, and instead of keeping it as a separate product, they gradually integrated its capabilities across the platform as a freely available feature. By late 2023, that work was complete. Now it's just part of how Sumo Logic works.

This native integration is important. It means that there is no context switching, no API glue code to pass data between different parts of your environment and tools, and there are no headaches when it comes to the syntax, normalization, and field mappings between all these different sources.

Automating some of the most time-consuming areas of your SecOps workflows is relatively painless with the automation service. This is because it runs on the same backbone as your analytics and SIEM workflows. It can respond to insights created in the SIEM, run a variety of enrichments against indicators (IPs, URLs, usernames, etc.), and append this gathered intelligence directly back into Insights. What's even more promising, and as you have seen in the previous chapter, many of the automation actions are included in the new Dojo AI agents, so that when you run the SOC Analyst Agent, for example, to help you investigate an alert, it will not only help you research the alert context, but it will close the loop with recommended remediations and response actions. AI is still new, but we expect the connective tissue between agents and automation to continue to expand until it has full integrations across your security stack and can do "all the things" via simple natural language prompts and without complex playbooks.

Don't forget **role-based access control** (**RBAC**). With automation, you can control access to automation, whether to view playbooks and integrations or being able to actively amend them, to ensure that playbooks aren't changed for no reason. With version control hard-wired into the Automation Service, it becomes impossible to make changes without anyone noticing.

Here's a final thought for you to ponder before we jump into the nitty-gritty. Unlike traditional SOAR tools that stop at security, Sumo Logic automation goes beyond that. With the **Open Integration Framework** (**OIF**), you can orchestrate actions across IT, DevOps, and observability domains too. Want to reboot a server? Roll back a container? Call a script in Jenkins or send a notification to ServiceNow? It's all possible from the same platform, with the same playbook editor.

In the sections ahead, we'll walk you through how to create playbooks using a visual, drag-and-drop interface, use triggers from Insights, signals, or external webhooks, chain together actions such as alerting, ticketing, enrichment, and remediation, and connect automation to both security and operational use cases. By the end, you'll be able to build powerful response flows that match your organization's needs without needing to write complex code or maintain brittle scripts.

Let's dive in.

Creating and managing playbooks

Before we actually create a playbook, we're going to look at what is ready for use for teams. Remember, we're trying to minimize the friction when it comes to embracing these capabilities, and we do that by making it easy.

App Central

Let's go and see where all of this is. In the left-hand side menu, we can go to **Automation | App Central**:

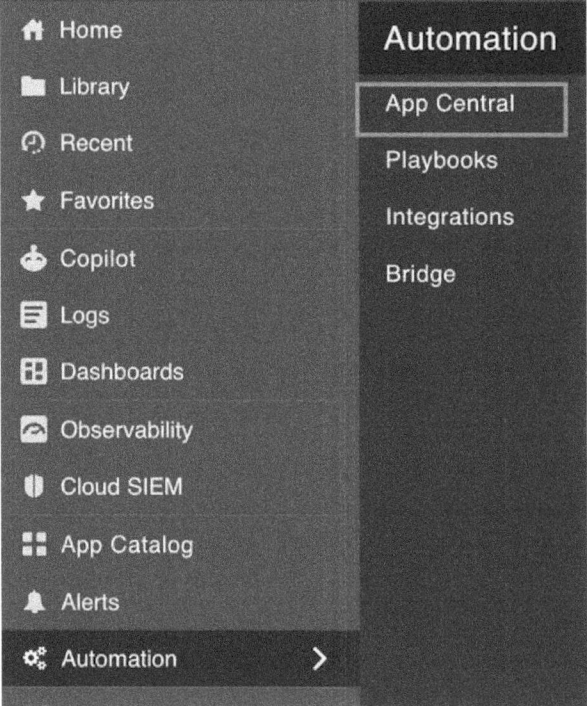

Figure 11.1 – App Central menu in the Automation section

App Central is the main hub where you can find all the playbook templates and out-of-the-box integrations, with over 300 data sources. Let's start with **Integrations**. When selecting it, you get a long list of integrations, and each integration carries a range of automated actions. The list is shown here:

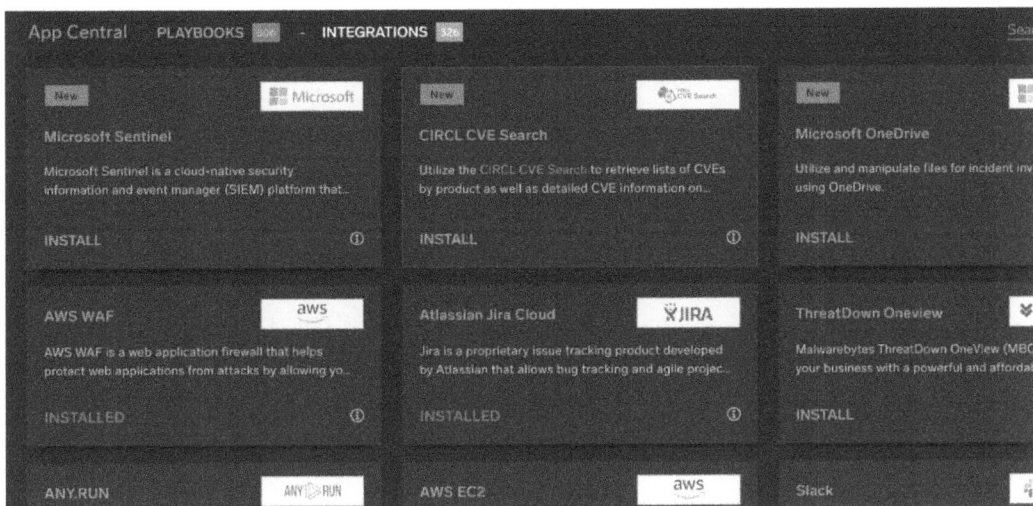

Figure 11.2 – The INTEGRATIONS screen

Each integration holds several actions that are accessible and usable without doing any complicated setup. For example, if we go into **Azure AD**, we can see actions such as **Delete User**, **List Users**, **Create Group**, and so on. These are shown in the next screenshot:

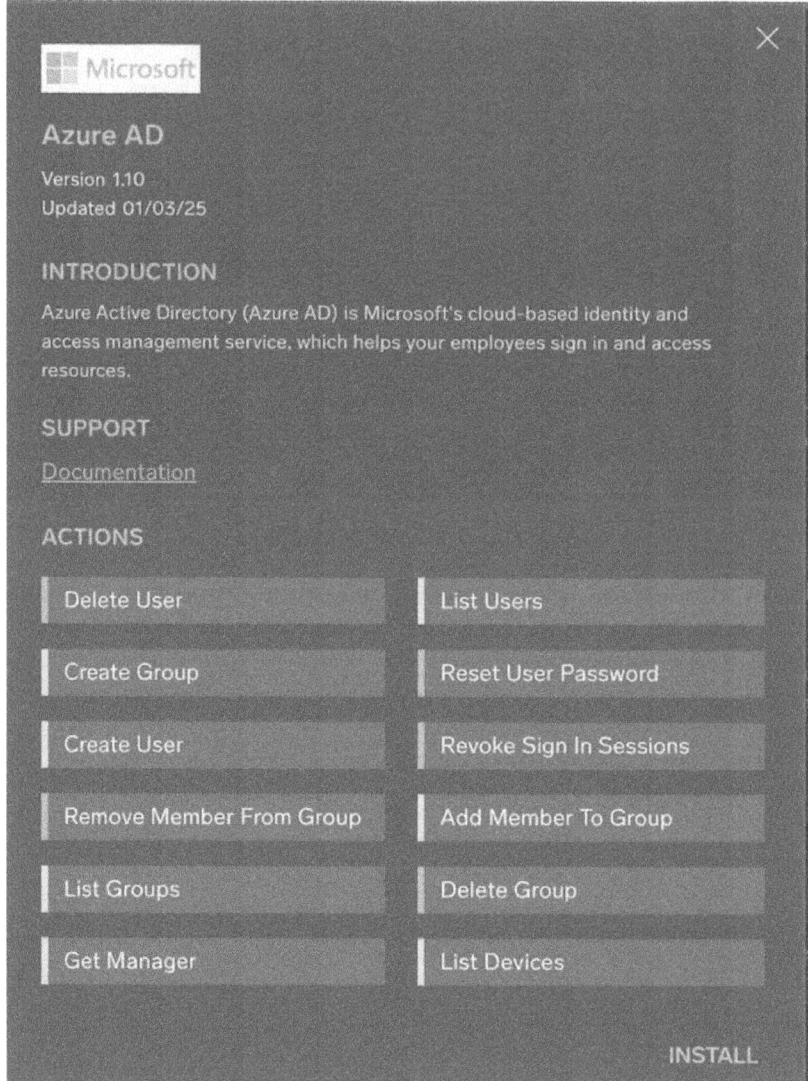

Figure 11.3 – The actions available with the Azure AD integration

For most integrations, there is an extensive list of actions that can be used within an automated process. Under the hood, these actions are written in Python, so if you want to roll up your sleeves and view the code driving these integrations, it's all available and even editable in the built-in IDE or coding interface. You'll see different colors next to the action names. This is because actions are categorized into the following groups:

- Green – **ENRICHMENT** actions
- Red – **CONTAINMENT** actions
- Blue – **NOTIFICATION** actions
- Purple – **CUSTOM** actions

Here are some example actions for **ENRICHMENT**, **CONTAINMENT**, and **NOTIFICATION** actions:

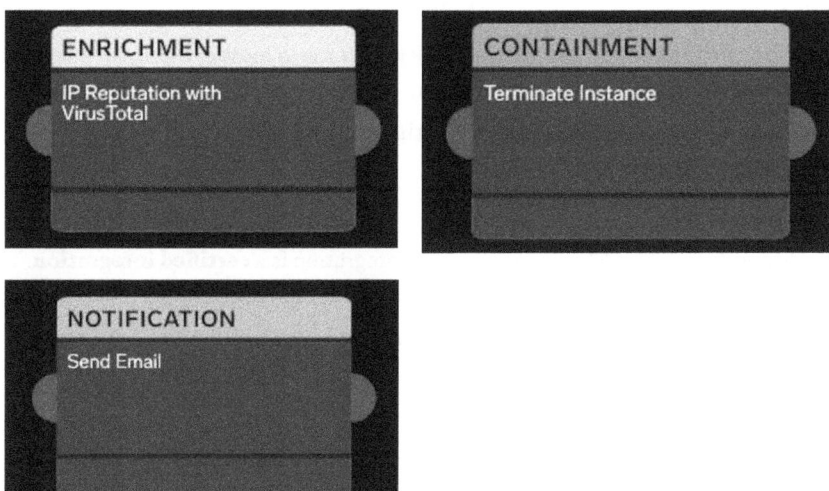

Figure 11.4 – Examples of various actions you can automate in Sumo Logic

We'll use some actions like these in the *Creating a playbook* section shortly, but for now, let's go back to the Azure AD integration shown in *Figure 11.3*. Clicking **INSTALL** at the bottom right sets up the main integration and then asks for authentication details to connect to the source. This usually requires an API key or token of some sort, but there are cases where basic authentication is the only way to authenticate.

Integrations

Once installed, you can see your integration in the **Automation | Integrations** menu:

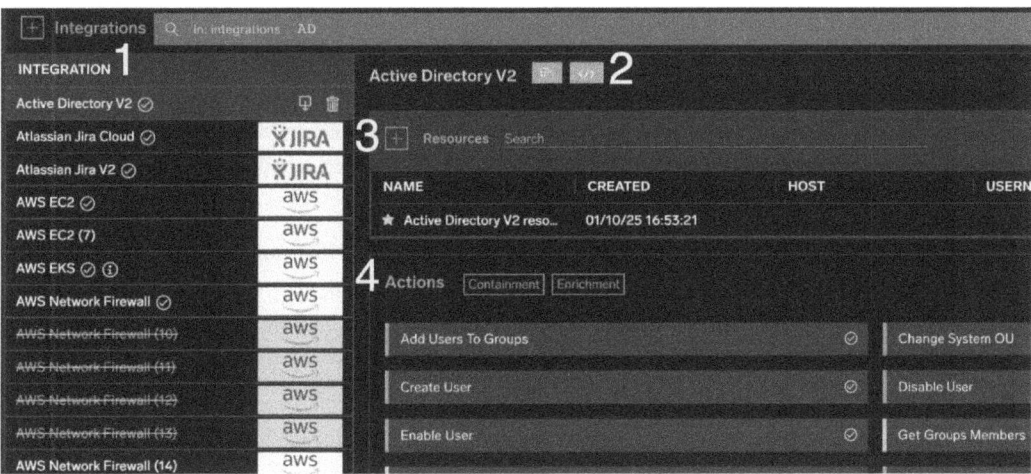

Figure 11.5 – Focusing on one integration in our installed integrations list

Here, you can see the actions that are usable in your playbooks. There are four key areas highlighted in yellow on the screen in *Figure 11.5*:

- 1: The list of integrations on the left, with a check mark next to most of them, such as the one next to **Active Directory V2** on the left side of the screen
- 2: The two icons next to **Active Directory V2** in the upper middle of the screen
- 3: The **Resources** section
- 4: The individual actions

The check mark indicates two things. The first is that this integration is a **certified integration**. This is an integration developed and maintained by the Sumo Logic integrations team. The second is that a certified integration doesn't need to use an *automation bridge*[1] to help communicate between the Sumo Logic platform and your data source. Wait, what? Automation bridge?

Let me clear up any confusion.

Automation bridge

Under the hood, all actions taken run through an automation bridge. It's the engine that wakes up and does things. Often, this bridge is transparent in the background because it's running within the Sumo Logic cloud platform. But because Sumo Logic is a SaaS solution hosted in the cloud outside of a customer environment, it may not have the ability to interact with all the solutions in a tech stack. In those cases, you will need to add an additional bridge that is installed or deployed by you where you need it. Because the customer is assuming some of the risk of this custom self-hosted bridge, it also unlocks the ability to run custom automations built and managed by the customer (for obvious reasons, Sumo wouldn't like the idea of its platform being used for nefarious purposes or doing bad things).

Thus, the automation bridge is used for two things: custom actions and automating actions within an on-premises environment.

The reason for this is that certified actions use the built-in API framework to communicate between the integrations; however, they don't apply when teams need to get Sumo Logic to communicate with their on-premise assets or custom actions with cloud-based sources. The bridge itself is just a Linux OS that needs to be deployed on a server or machine to perform this function. There are Ubuntu, CentOS, or RedHat options available, as well as Dockerized deployment options too.

There is a third bonus reason for anyone who has guessed it, reading this and thinking "Hold on...I can run any code?" Security. Custom actions, for example, allow users to run any code or scripts on the automation bridge. As this can take the form of anything, even malicious code, they can't run in Sumo Logic's infrastructure. That would be a bad idea. By running custom actions on your personal bridge, you can manage them and keep them inside your environment.

When you've deployed an automation bridge, you'll see it in a list where you can have more than one, as shown here:

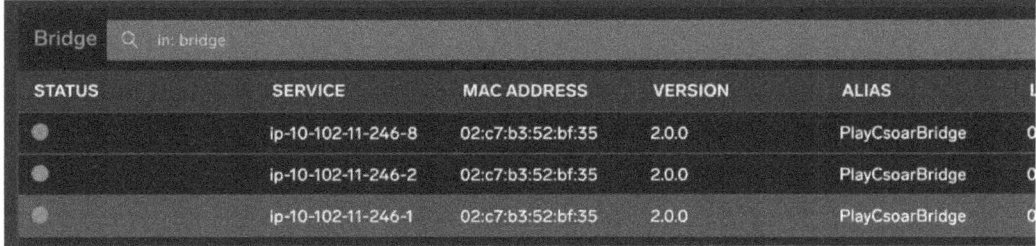

Figure 11.6 – The list of automation bridges currently being used

A lot of users deploy automation bridges with high availability in mind. So, when we have this bridge set up, and we have a custom action or an on-premise automation that is required, the traffic runs through this bridge. For that reason, the automation bridge *does need to connect to pre-defined public-facing API endpoints within Sumo Logic's infrastructure*. The information about these can be found in the documentation[1].

Within the Automation Service UI, however, there isn't anything fundamentally different for using these actions. For example, here we have a custom integration and a set of custom actions we've put together:

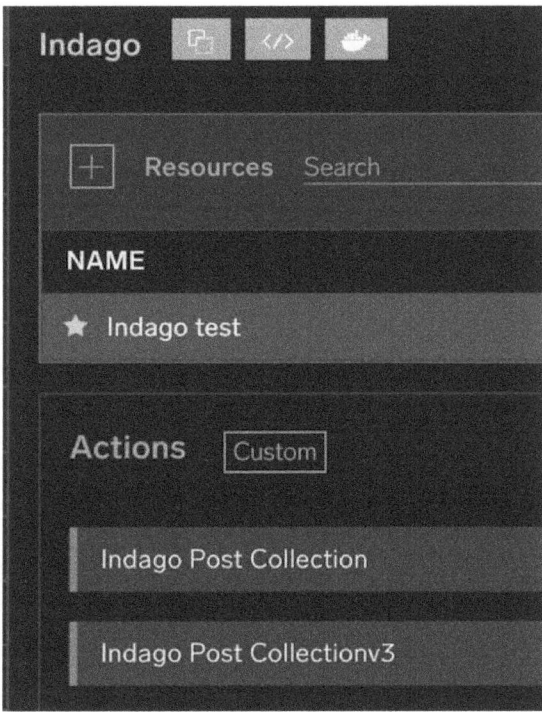

Figure 11.7 – Our custom integration with a couple of custom actions visible

When we specify these actions within a playbook, there is nothing we need to do apart from filling in some details for the action in question. The automation bridge handles the rest. Adding these actions to playbooks is a topic reserved for the *Creating playbooks* section coming up in a bit.

Editing code

Editing existing actions and creating your own isn't difficult in Sumo Logic. There is a development environment in the **Automation Services** area of the platform that lets you edit existing integrations and add your own. This is done with the edit button that you can see next to the name of the integration, as shown here for **Indago**:

Figure 11.8 – The clone, edit, and Docker configurations

There are three buttons here: **Clone**, **Edit**, and **Docker**.

Clone does exactly what you think it does, so let's skip that one. **Edit** lets you jump into the code for the integration. We won't explore this in detail in this book as The Open Integration Framework[2] deserves one or even two chapters to cover it, but here is a glimpse into what it looks like:

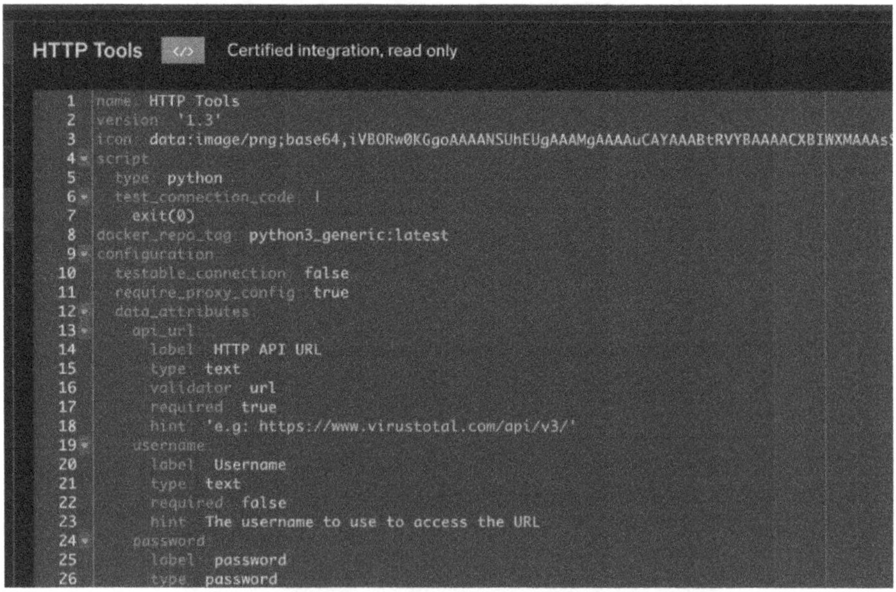

Figure 11.9 – An example of the coding environment to build and edit integrations and actions

Finally, if you have a Dockerized automation bridge, then you can customize the Dockerfile from within the Automation Service as shown here:

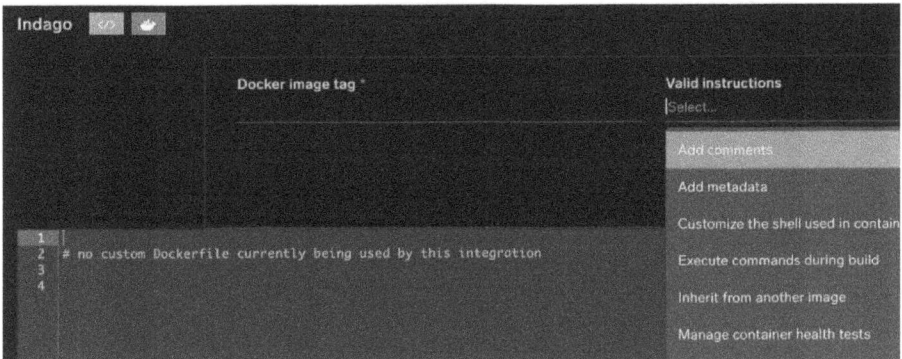

Figure 11.10 – Executable instructions and Dockerfiles can be added here

Going back to *Figure 11.5*, let's take a look at **Resources** next.

Resources

A resource is like a connector between the Automation Service and the technology you intend to automate. Usually, a resource has connection information such as API tokens, credentials, and any other parameters required to communicate. When looking at resources, there is always at least one. You can edit it by going to the pencil icon on the far right, or you can create a new resource by clicking on the **+** button next to **Resources**, as shown here.

Figure 11.11 – You can also add a new resource to the integration

For example, in the case of this **Indago** integration, we have fields such as **Label**, **API URL**, and **API Key** to populate, as shown here.

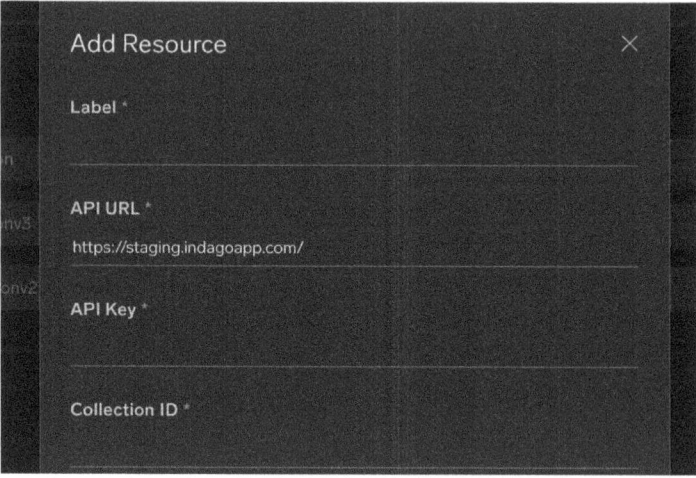

Figure 11.12 – The Add Resource fields to fill in

The fields are directly tied to the code in the integration and are set by you when you upload any code. Please refer to the *Open Integration Framework* documentation[2], which discusses some of these elements.

To finish up on resources, you can have more than one. This is handy if you have a central integration and multiple accounts or hierarchies in the data source. For example, with AWS IAM, we authenticate with one account at a time. If you'd like to automate activities across different accounts, you can do that and specify which account you'd like to use when specifying the resource in a playbook.

Actions

These are the programmable steps that you can use to help automate your response. As we've already seen, out-of-the-box integrations carry a variety of automated actions ready to use; you just need to authenticate with the resource and you're all set. However, you can edit each individual action, as well as creating your own if you want, downloading the YAML version of the action, or deleting the action altogether using the buttons shown below:

Figure 11.13 – Actions buttons

Editing actions lets you make amendments to any existing actions – for example, if the action goes to the source and does something, such as creating a user, you could add a bit of code to also add that user to a specific group (just an example, not necessarily practical). Downloading it lets you use the code in a text editor or IDE to work in if the development environment in Sumo Logic isn't sufficient for your needs. Often overlooked, you can also test the action in this view by clicking on the action name and inputting test parameters.

Playbook templates

Going back to App Central, the other view we have here is of the *playbook templates*. There are over 500 of these templates, and they are definitely an eclectic mix of use cases and technologies. I've personally rarely seen anyone use these templates in their out-of-the-box form, because environments are different and tweaks and customizations usually need to be made, but that's the great thing. The groundwork is there, and what I *have seen* is teams using the base template to tweak it and customize it to their hearts' content to get the results they need. It does save time and effort.

Here's a useful example. All security teams enrich their IOCs and data with sources, and one of the biggest sources out there is **VirusTotal**. There is already a template for this; all you need to do is install the playbook template, which will install the actions that are part of the flow, and follow this up by authenticating to VirusTotal. You are then ready to go! Here is what the playbook looks like:

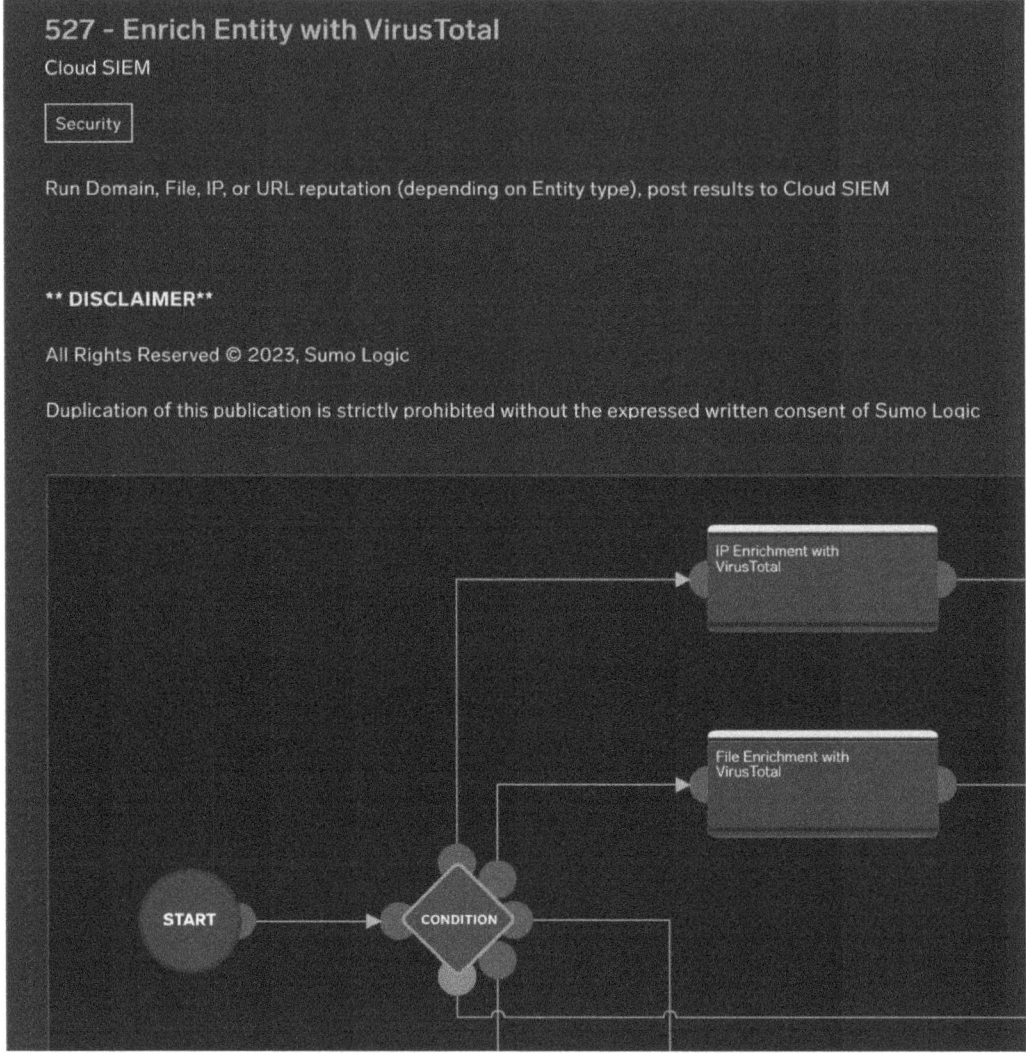

Figure 11.14 – A cropped snippet of the Enrich Entity with VirusTotal playbook

These templates have served as inspiration for countless teams, and even if not immediately useful, they can be a crucial crutch to lean on.

I covered App Central just to give you a quick welcome to the automation side of things. Now let's help you build your first playbook!

Creating a playbook

The Automation Service uses a low-code, no-code canvas to build playbooks with a drag-and-drop interface. This makes it very accessible and pretty quick to throw something together as the first version or iteration while you map out your process. Don't look at me like that, a bit of trial and error is one of the fun things about building out playbooks! Don't let anyone tell you any different.

Let's go back to Jasmin at the start of the chapter. She's got access to Sumo Logic, and up to this point, she's been relying mainly on manual effort when responding to an incident with a script here and there to try and save time. One of the processes she does *every single time*, when there is a significant event, is she enriches some IOCs with a few intelligence sources and then creates a ticket to open an investigation. This takes *a significant amount of time*, up to half an hour, so let's help her out.

Let's go to **Automation** | **Playbook** in the left-hand menu and then create a new playbook by clicking on the **+** button next to **Playbook**, shown here:

Figure 11.15 – Create a new playbook here

This will prompt us to enter some details about our new playbook:

- **Name**
- **Type**
- **Tags**
- **Description**

Once we've filled in the information, we're ready to go. Tags are useful for managing your playbooks once you have a few of them, but we'll cover that later. Here is a screenshot of the fields to fill in:

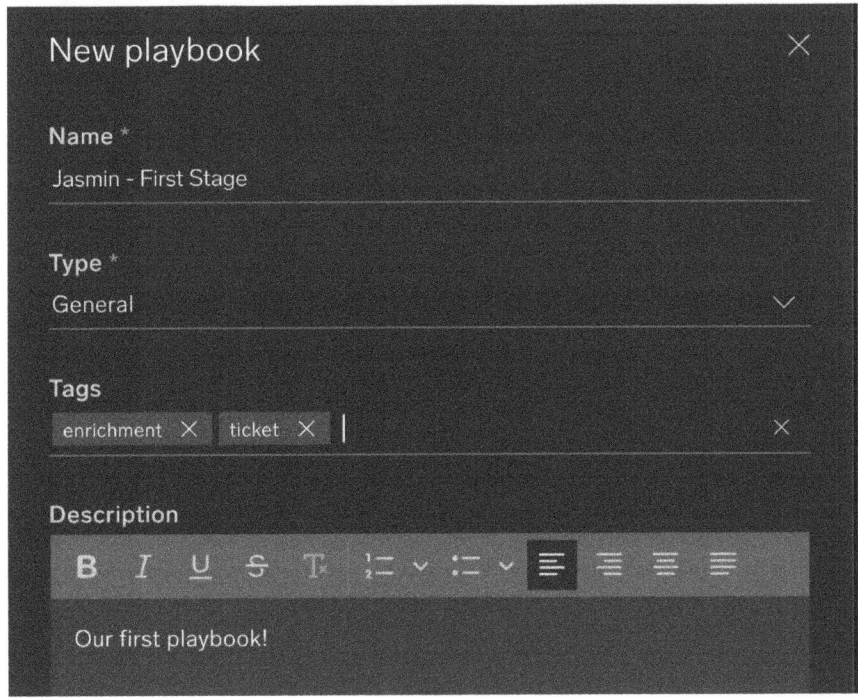

Figure 11.16 – We've entered some basic information about the playbook

We then arrive at the main playbook creation canvas. It has a few sections to it, but we'll cover them as we make our way through the process of making Jasmin's playbook. The first part is to start creating. Let's click on the pencil icon below our first two nodes, **START** and **END**, as shown in *Figure 11.17*:

Figure 11.17 – The edit button is just below the main canvas, highlighted here

Once we click on the edit button, we can add things. The first thing we do is tell the playbook how it's going to start. We can run playbooks manually from Cloud SIEM, of course, but we need to do this for every playbook anyway, as they usually run when something happens.

Our **START** node now has a **+** button and a pencil icon. We use the **+** button to add components to any node, not just a start node – for example, an action or a condition. We'll cover these in a minute, but we want to click on the pencil to edit the **START** node. When we do this, we can add parameters to the playbook input by selecting how it's going to be initiated. We can choose to launch the playbook from **Insight**, **Entity**, **Alert**, or **Parse from json**, as shown here.

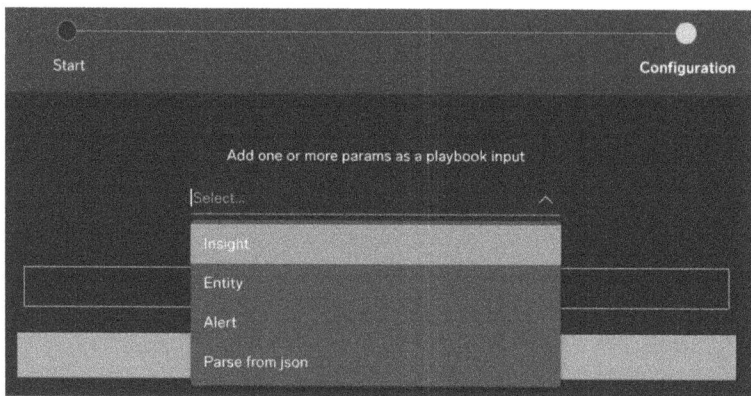

Figure 11.18 – Selecting parameters

Depending on what you select, the relevant parameters are created, and the playbook will populate these from wherever we have selected.

> Note
>
> Quick shout out to the **Parse from json** option. If you select this, you can paste JSON-formatted objects, which will extract the fields from the object, and they can be populated that way. Essentially, it's a way to customize the ready-made parameters from **Insight**, **Entity**, or **Alert**.

So, we choose **Insight**, and we can see the vast array of parameters (there are 56 that get pulled in!) that would get sent through to our playbook:

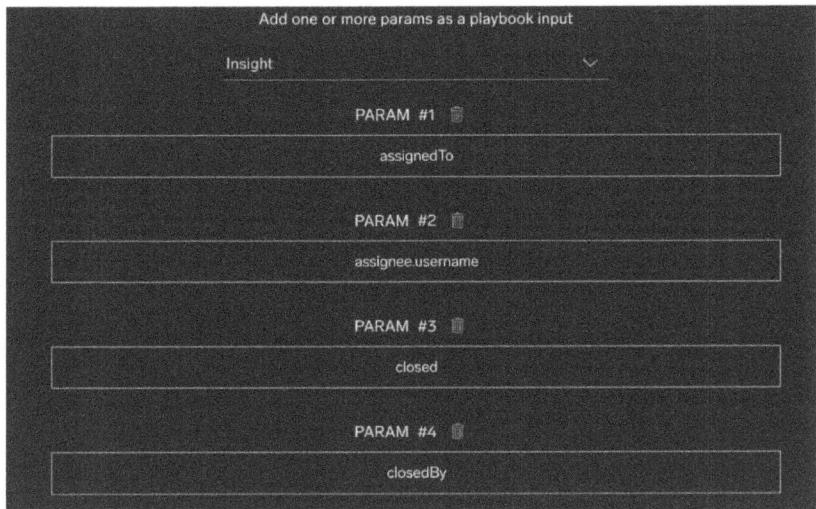

Figure 11.19 – The first four parameters of the Insight option

We can also add custom parameters to the end of this by clicking the **ADD NEW PARAM** button at the bottom, as shown here.

Figure 11.20 – Button for adding custom parameters even to existing templates

Click **Update**, and you'll see no changes at all. That's fine, the node is ready to go, and we can now start adding components to our playbook! When you choose the **+** button, you can select from a range of things to add. See *Figure 11.21*:

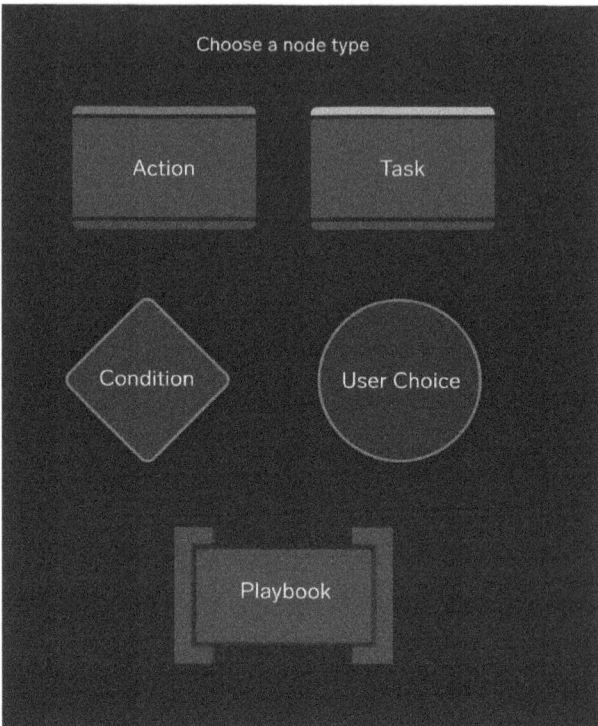

Figure 11.21 – The components/nodes you can add to your playbook

Let's run through them quickly:

- **Action**: This will be the most common node you create. This houses the individual actions from your integrations.
- **Task**: Tasks are used to assign individual actions to users, and these actions wait until the owner has completed and approved them before continuing.
- **Condition**: This node lets you create conditional statements that help the playbook decide how to proceed based on given variables.
- **User Choice**: Inject a user straight into the automated process, where they will have options to choose from before the playbook continues executing.
- **Playbook**: You can nest playbooks within other playbooks. It's great for being able to turn processes into modules that can be dropped into other sequences.

Now that we've caught up to what types of nodes we can create, let's add an **Action** node to our playbook. If we go back to our scenario, we want to get the entities we've seen in Insights and run them through some checks. Jasmin uses VirusTotal every day, so we'll use that. Even though there's a playbook template for VirusTotal enrichment, we're going to build our own here so you can see what that looks like. Click the **+** button and add an **Action** node. It asks us for some details, so let's fill them in. In the following screenshot, some important areas you need to know about are highlighted:

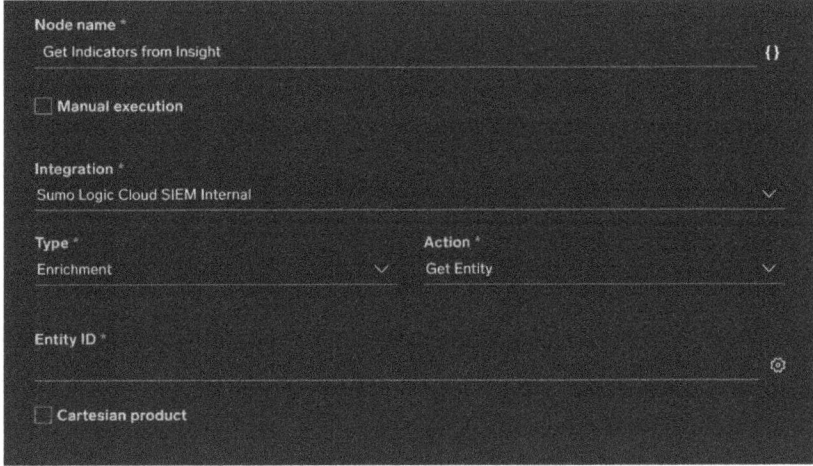

Figure 11.22 – The configuration options for our first Action node

We've given it a name, **Get Indicators from Insight**, to make it clear what this node is going to do. You should see a **Manual execution** checkbox. This lets you specify that you want this playbook executed manually *only*, and a dropdown with an **Authorizer** selection comes up, letting you choose who must approve it before it gets executed.

We then choose the integration we want to use; in this case, we're using the built-in **Sumo Logic Cloud SIEM Internal** one. This lets us extract useful information from **Insights**. We specify the type of action we want to do – in this case, **Enrichment** (**Notification** is the only other one available for this integration, and lets you update an existing insight with additional information). Other integrations – for example, those dealing with endpoints or authentication, have containment actions available too.

After selecting the type, we see a list of actions that correlate with that type. Here, we're interested in getting the entity values out of Insight, so we select the **Get Entity** action.

Now for the **Entity ID** field. It's worth mentioning that you don't need to hardcode your fields and values manually. You need to do this only in certain cases and where an integration asks for specific values, for example. There is a cog on the far right of your fields. You can click it to be able to select values from playbook actions we have previously seen. This is what we can see after selecting the cog:

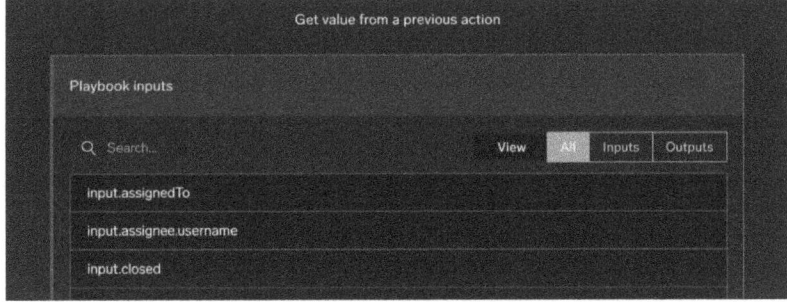

Figure 11.23 – Choose previous playbook actions and values dynamically

We want to select the value that has an array of entries, because it's very likely there will be *at least* one indicator to work with, so we need the input.involvedEntities[].id variable.

Click **Create** and you've got your first action. Your first enrichment action should look something like this:

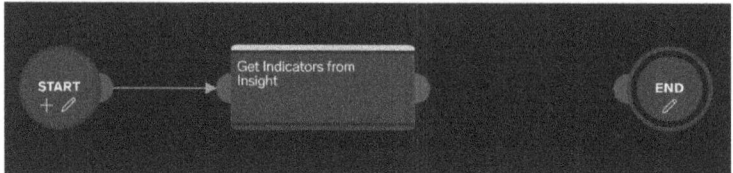

Figure 11.24 – Our first enrichment action, which is going to look at indicators in an insight

This action is going to iterate over all the entities identified in Insight, which is great, as the base format of the entity ID isn't very nice, in all honesty. The entity ID, by default, looks something like *ip_xxx.xxx.xxx.xxx*, if it's an IP address, for example. The output of this enrichment will produce the actual values, which are easier to feed into something else.

Before feeding VirusTotal with IOCs, we need to know which type of IOCs are in Insight. VirusTotal has a separate action for each IOC – for example, **IP Reputation**, **URL Reputation**, and so on.

When we add our next action, let's add a **Condition** node, as shown here:

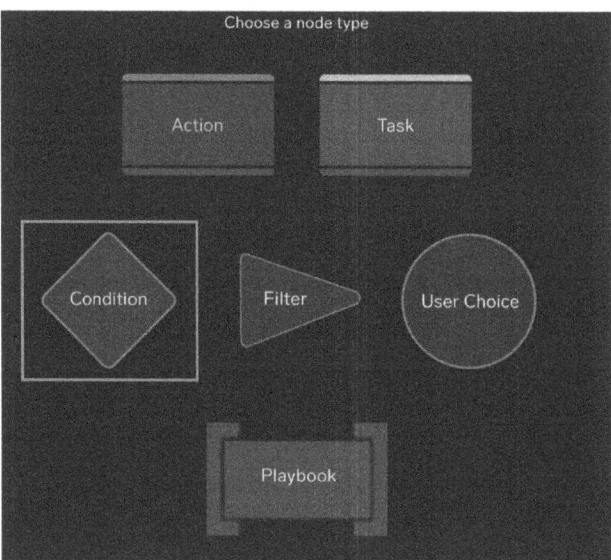

Figure 11.25 – Choosing the Condition node lets us start using decision-making

Condition statements require you to select a parameter and check whether it returns true or false. In this node, we're going to compare against **output.entityType** from the previous action, as shown here:

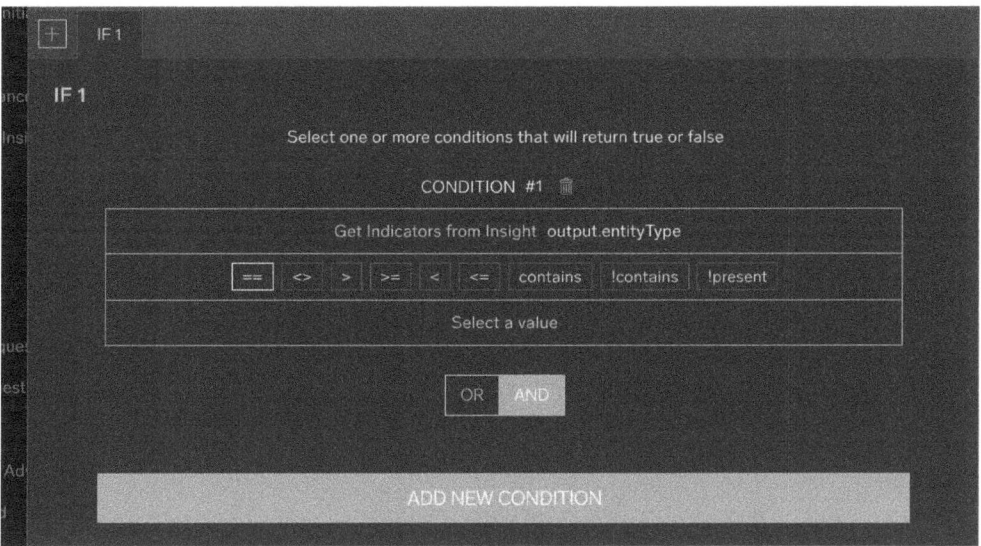

Figure 11.26 – We've selected our first parameter, and now we need to check

We then go to **Select a value** and specify our entity type. Entity types look like this in Sumo Logic:

- **_ip**
- **_hostname**
- **_url**
- **_domain**
- **_username**
- **_useragent**
- **_file**
- **_email**
- **_process**
- **_command**

So, we specify the correct entity type as follows – IP addresses in this case:

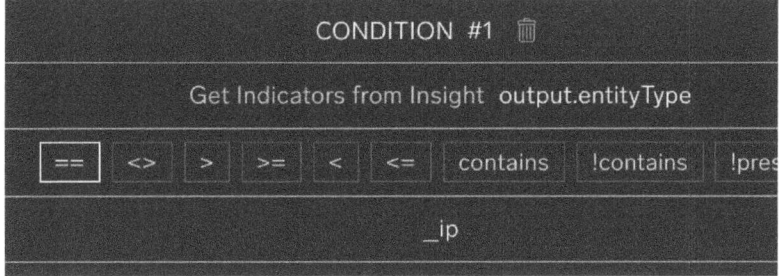

Figure 11.27 – Entering the correct entity type to compare against

Our first conditional statement is complete, and we can now add additional nodes to it. Let's add the **VirusTotal** action to enrich an IP. When adding an action, you'll see an option to create a node either from the **IF 1** side or the **Failure** side, so you can choose whether you're creating the success side of the condition or the failure.

Our next **VirusTotal** action looks like this:

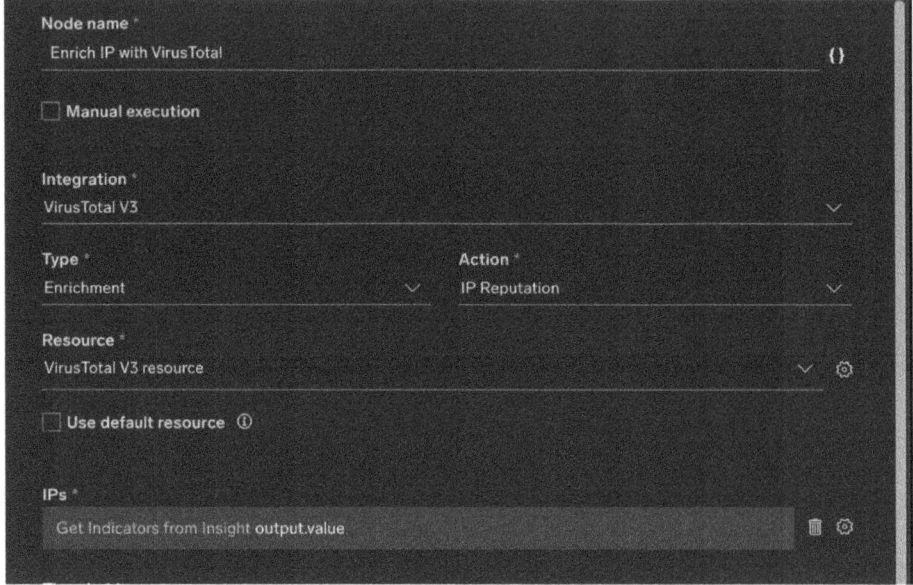

Figure 11.28 – The VirusTotal action to enrich an IP address

We should now have something like this:

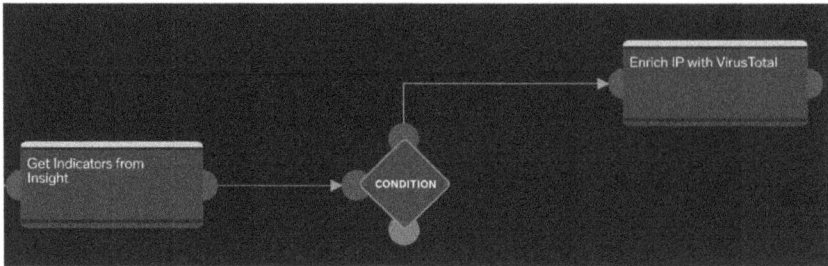

Figure 11.29 – Our progress so far in this playbook

> **Note**
> We're not going to go into every single entity type here. We're going to just build out some of the conditionals and carry on with the other logic.

Let's create a node with another exit. We'll leave the failure exit point empty for this test playbook, but basically, any conditions that aren't met by this condition node will go out via the failure route. In most cases, a failure route either skips to the end of the playbook or does some other action, such as a Slack message or email, to denote that something hasn't worked. We're going to add *another* **IF** condition to the existing condition node to check if we have a URL and do the exact same process for the VirusTotal action, except now we'll be using the **Scan URL** action. The way we do this is to hover over the condition node again, click the pencil icon to edit, and add another condition at the top with the **+** button:

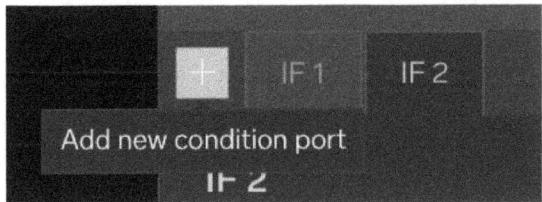

Figure 11.30 – Adding another conditional port to the condition node

We then specify our second condition to see if the entity type matches a URL:

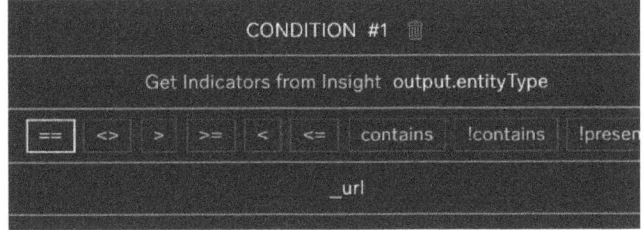

Figure 11.31 – Specifying our second condition – a URL entity type

This is what it should look like:

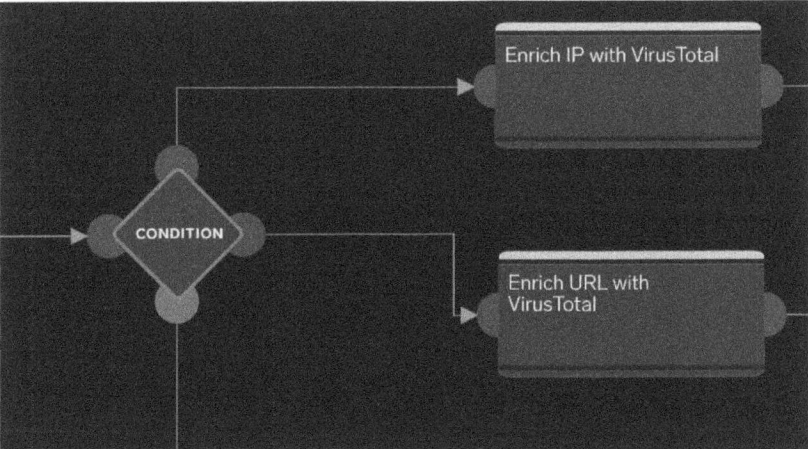

Figure 11.32 – Our next condition, which checks against URLs and then enriches with VirusTotal

When testing conditional statements like this, or any node for that matter, you can test individual nodes instead of the entire playbook. When you edit a node, you'll see a test slider at the top. Click on it to expand two panels, the left one with JSON and the one on the right with results:

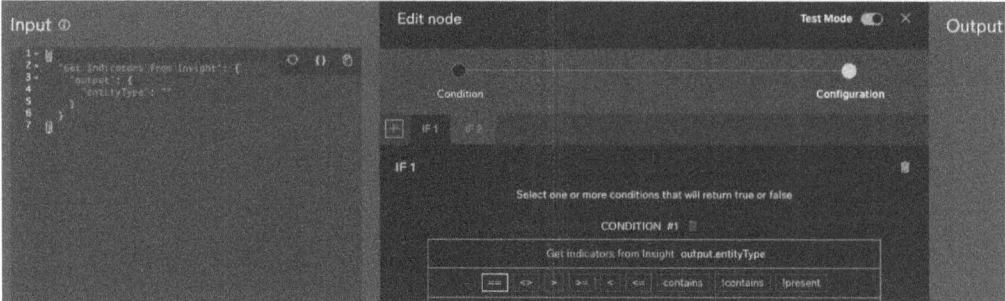

Figure 11.33 – The node test mode. You can see the Test Mode slider in the top-right corner

This testing mode gives you the ability to test the node with the input that this node would expect. In this case, because our condition revolves around an entity type, we can feed an entity type that would come from Cloud SIEM (the full list of entity types precedes *Figure 11.27*), and the output will confirm if it matches. Let's test this one to see if it works. I'll enter _ip into the entityType JSON and then see the following result:

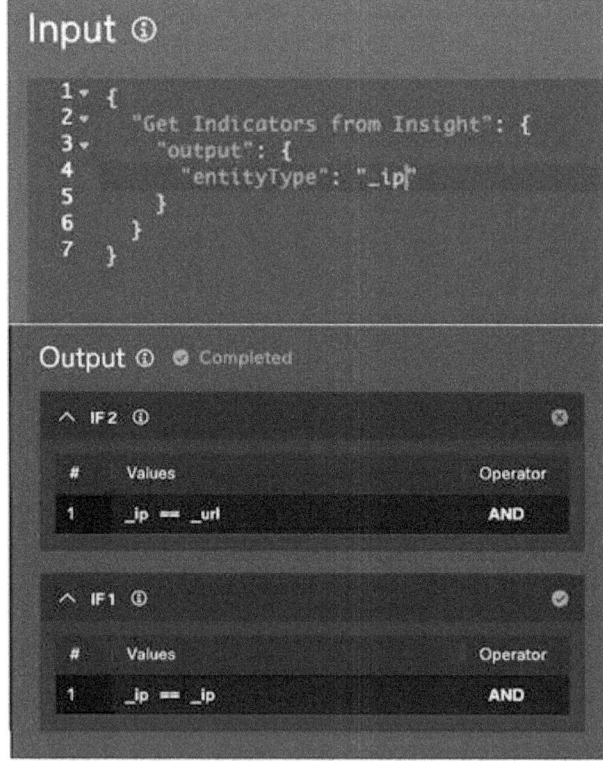

Figure 11.34 – We can see that the conditional check succeeded on the entity type it was expecting

You can apply this to any node! It stops you from having to run a whole playbook to test it, which is a great way to iteratively build your playbook as you go. Let's go back to the **Enrich IP with VirusTotal** action. We want to take the results of our enrichment and do a couple of things to it:

- Update the insight with the information
- Send an email with an update to the SOC team

Let's add our next node—**Update Insight**. We hover over the **Enrich IP with VirusTotal** action and choose the **+** button to add a new node, and select **Action** from the list:

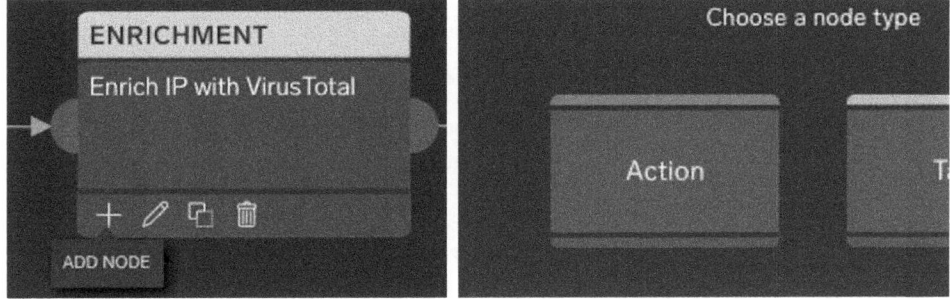

Figure 11.35 – We add a node and choose another action

We want to update the **ENRICHMENT** tab in any given Insight with this information. Here is the **Update Insight** action configuration:

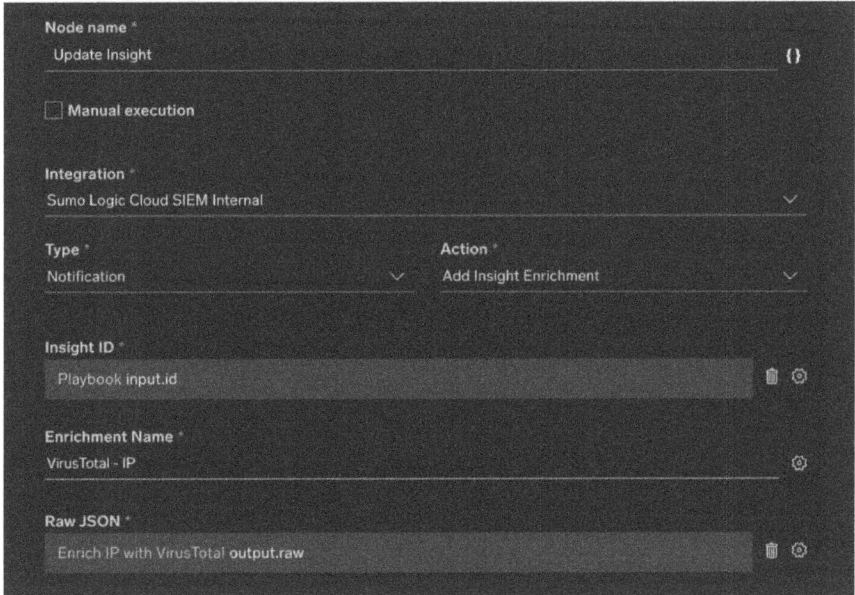

Figure 11.36 – Configuring the action that updates the insight that started the playbook

Hopefully, all the fields necessary make sense, and you can find them in the values provided by the previous **Enrich IP with VirusTotal** action. Now we have a new notification action that adds that information to our insight:

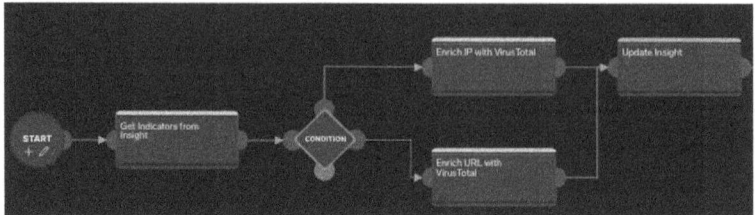

Figure 11.37 – Our current playbook ends with updating the insight

Let's do the same following that action. Now that we've updated our insight with any enriched IP information, we want to go to the next step, which is to see if any of these IOCs are actually malicious and start to factor in a response if so.

Let's add a conditional node after the **Update Insight** node and pick out the parameter called **output.response.[].total_votes.malicious**. I'm keeping it simple by keeping the comparison to at least 1 malicious vote, as shown here:

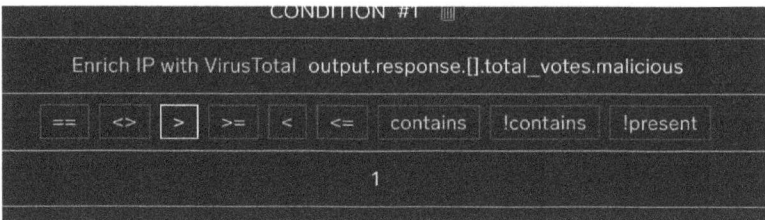

Figure 11.38 – Adding the conditional node

If any of the IP addresses have a malicious vote of at least 1, we want to send an email to track these malicious IOCs and start an incident report. This can be done as shown here:

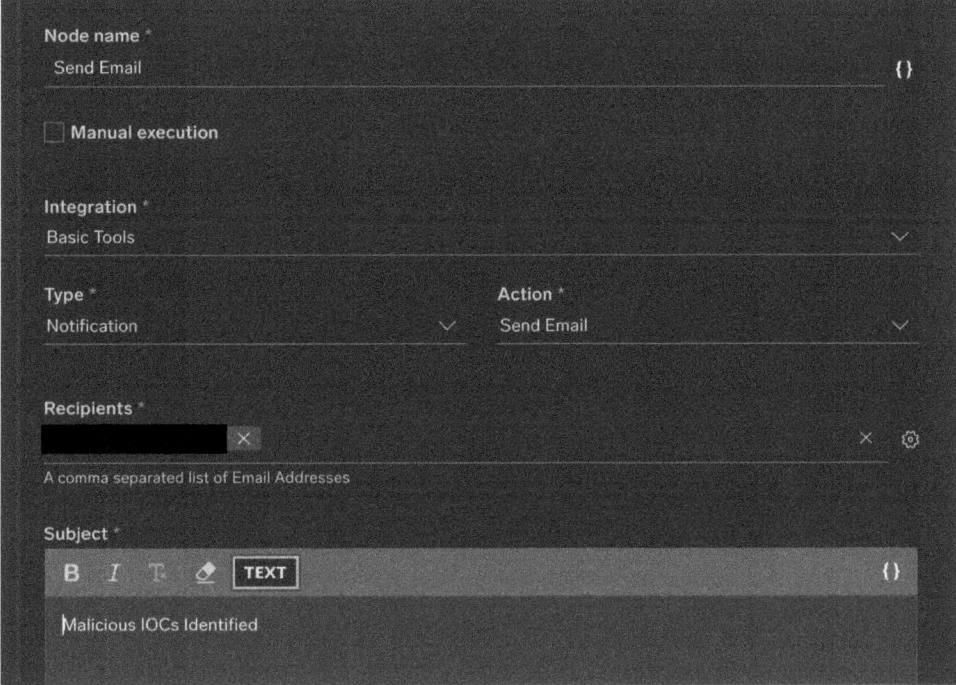

Figure 11.39 – Sending an email to track malicious IOCs

I wanted to show this type of action because we can walk through placeholders in our notifications and messages. If you scroll down in this action, you come across a **Summary** and a **Description** field. These are great opportunities to populate a ticket with dynamic variables, and we can find them towards the right side of a text-based panel, as shown here:

Figure 11.40 – Inserting a placeholder from the right-hand side of a text panel

Placeholders work in the same way as finding dynamic variables to use within actions. Just choose a variable from an existing action and pull it out. It'll appear in your text like this:

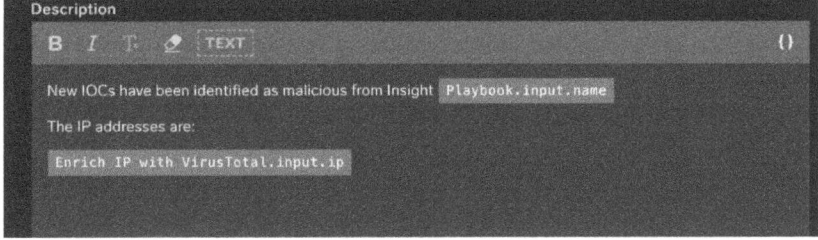

Figure 11.41 – The placeholder variables look like this in our description

We can start to test this playbook! Testing is a vital component of the whole process because sometimes you want to make sure that you're extracting the right values out of your data, or if you're feeding them into the right places, so let's see how we do that.

Our complete playbook looks like this:

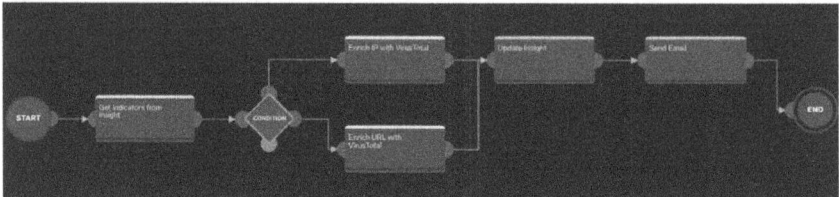

Figure 11.42 – We have finished the playbook off by adding the Send Email action and connecting it to the END node

Down at the bottom, after doing these additions, we can save and exit the **Edit** mode by clicking on this icon:

Figure 11.43 – Save and exit Edit mode, or just exit edit mode

Once this is done, you'll see three dots in the top-right corner of your canvas where a **Run Test** option appears, as shown here.

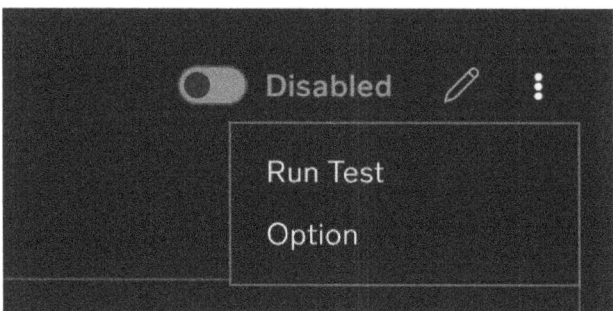

Figure 11.44 – The option to run a test, which is vital to playbook development

Let's talk about testing, because it'll really make your life easier once you get to grips with it.

Testing your playbooks

Once you choose to run a test, you can specify how you'd like to run the test by choosing either of the following:

- **Insight**
- **Custom JSON**

By choosing **Insight**, you get to run your playbook on an existing insight to see how it interacts with the data. If you choose **Custom JSON**, you can feed any JSON into the box to run the playbook from these parameters.

For example, let's test what we have so far. Based on what we've done, we expect our insight to be updated, and then get an email with some malicious IPs. Let's click on **Run Test** and choose an insight that we want to test on – for example, **INSIGHT-1920**, shown here:

Figure 11.45 – Specifying the insight we want to test on

A new tab will open, and you'll see your playbook executing, all the while being able to see what has happened at each step of the playbook to understand useful information such as the following:

- The fields and values that get picked up from the JSON data
- Any unintended successes or failures
- Any iterations or loops that aren't working properly

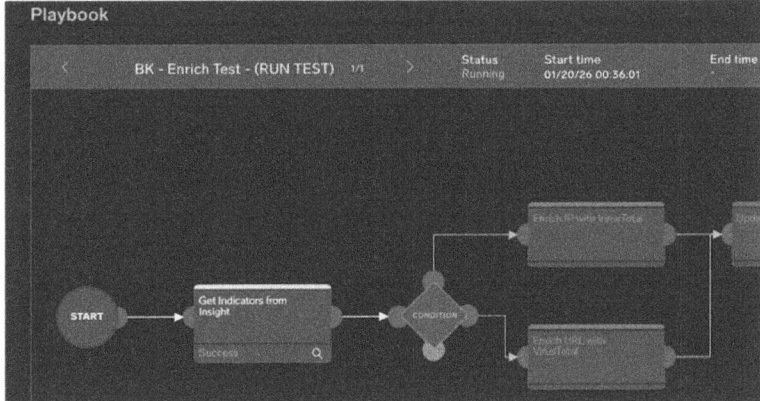

Figure 11.46 – The playbook test runs in real time and shows Success or Failed next to each action

The playbook runs through the paths you've set, and it is a great way of seeing how it responds to real data and scenarios. The grayed-out boxes, like the condition node in *Figure 11.46* and the two enrichment nodes, indicate that those actions are yet to run.

If we click on the **Enrich IP with VirusTotal** action, we can see all the entities that have been fed in and enriched with VirusTotal, as shown here:

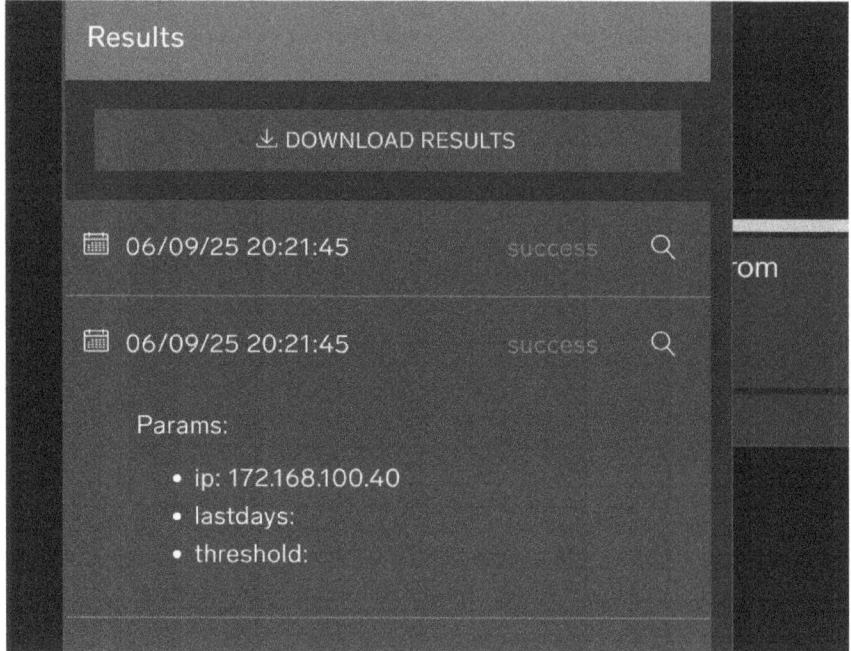

Figure 11.47 – Seeing each parameter that has been fed into the action

If you click on the magnifying glass, you open the full details of the JSON record that has come back for the API used – in this case, VirusTotal, but you'd always be able to see a response from any integration in this way.

The following **Action result** screen lets you dive into the details when you select the curly braces:

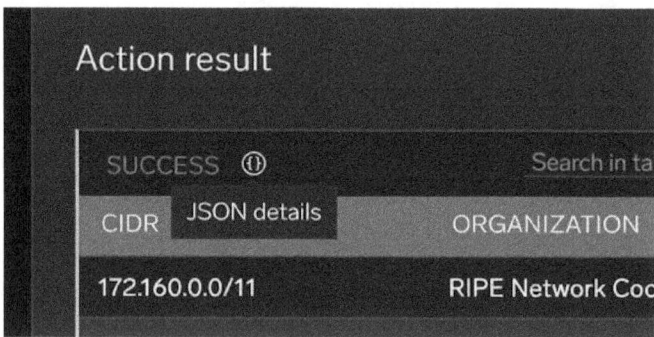

Figure 11.48 – The JSON details section, which lets you dive into the keys and values

This reveals all the information that has come back. This is very useful when building your playbooks because, as you can imagine, knowing the inputs and outputs of your playbook actions allows you to be specific with the actions you want to take.

After this execution is finished, we'll get an email to confirm the malicious IP addresses involved with **INSIGHT-1920**, as shown here:

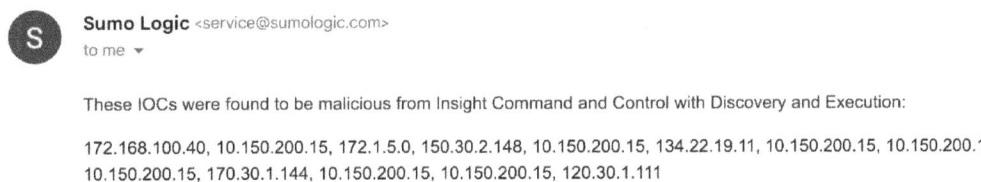

Figure 11.49 - The results of our enrichment have resulted in an email to the SOC team

There we have it – our first playbook!

If you're going to take this playbook further, you can try doing the following:

- Add additional entity types to the conditional node
- Add a user choice to take an action after receiving the email
- Create a JIRA ticket instead of an email, or use another ticketing or ITSM tool
- Block the IPs!

Building these automated processes in Sumo Logic is straightforward, intuitive, and fun, and really helps you become as efficient as possible.

How to Connect Playbooks

We aren't at the point where an Insight or an Alert know which playbook to run. This might happen sooner that we realize but for the time being it's something that you have to specify. There is a different process for Monitors and Cloud SIEM Insights which I'll quickly cover.

The first thing to do before we do any of the following steps is to publish the playbook. You can find this button next to the edit one on the completed playbook.

Figure 11.50 – The publish button to make the playbook seen within the instance

After this, the Sumo Logic platform can see the playbook and we can reference it.

Monitors

When creating your monitor, all you need to do is select the playbook under Section 4 of the monitor creation page shown below, which we ran through in *Chapter 8*.

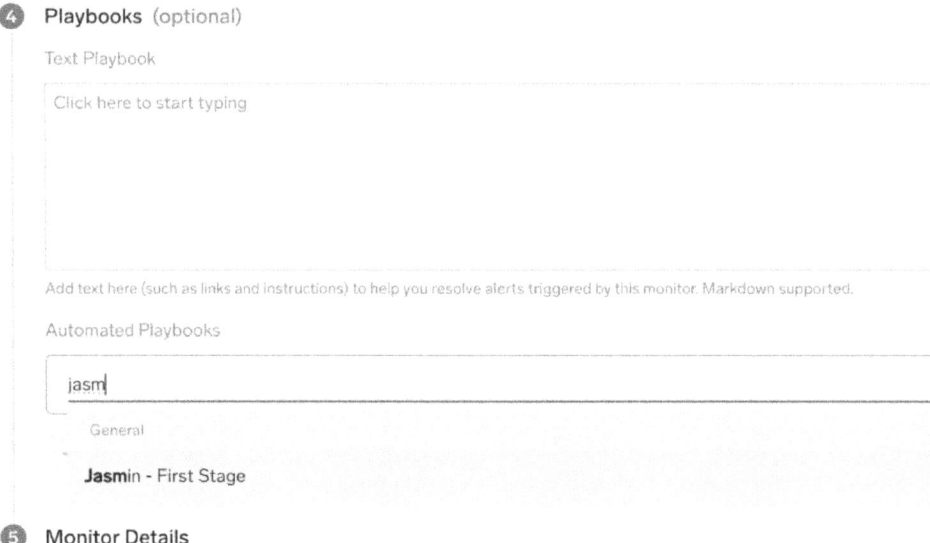

Figure 11.51 – Selecting the playbook to run when the monitor triggers

It's important to know that in this case, we created a playbook that leverages some of the Cloud SIEM data types, such as Insights. If you aren't on the enterprise version of Sumo Logic which gives you access to Cloud SIEM, this playbook will work. If you do, alerts can run across the SIEM interchangeably.

Cloud SIEM

When you want to reference a playbook for an Insight, the approach is different. You need to go to **Cloud SIEM | Cloud SIEM Integrations | Automation**

Figure 11.52 – The automation section, with options to add automation and go to your playbooks from here

When we add automation, we'll be presented with a side panel that will ask for certain criteria for when to use automation:

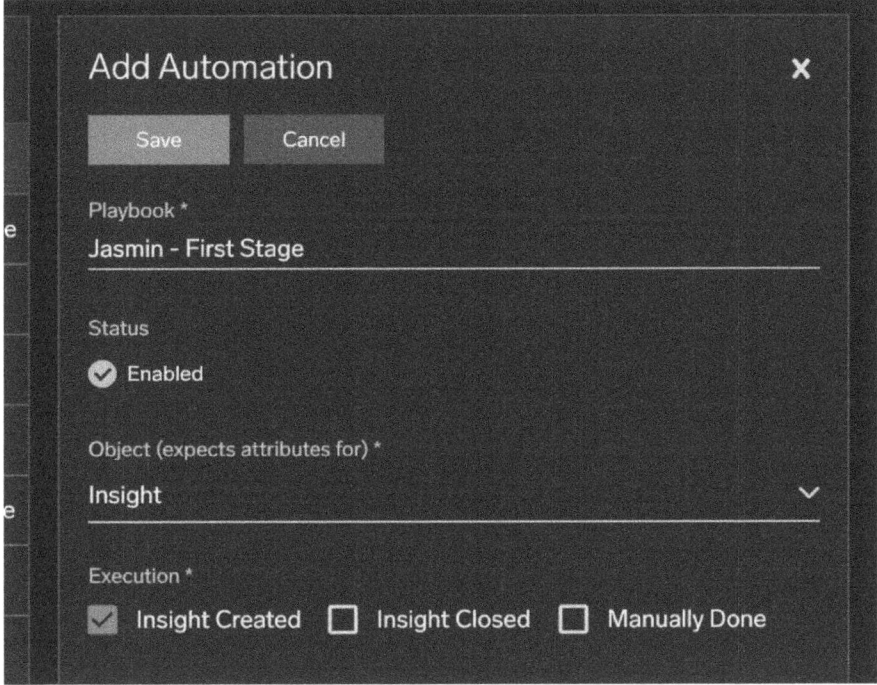

Figure 11.53 – Specifying when we want to run a playbook in the Cloud SIEM

As you can see, I've referenced the playbook, I've chosen as well as whether it's going to run on an **Entity** or **Insight** (the **Object** field) and then when it executes. You get to choose from when an Insight is first created, when it's closed and if you want to run it manually.

If you opt for manual launch, you'll see it under the Insight name when clicking the **Actions** button as shown here:

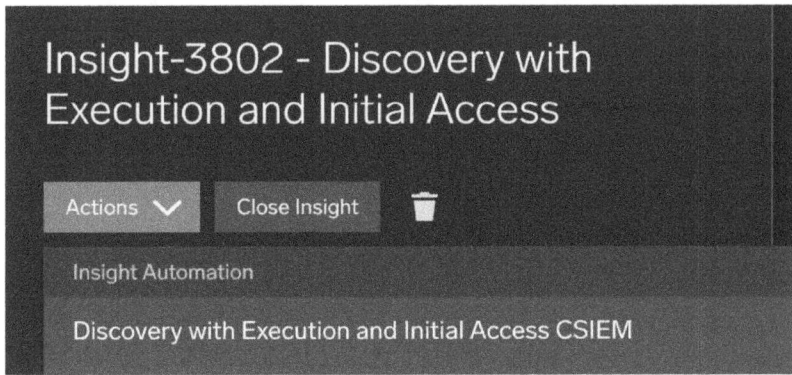

Figure 11.54 – Running a playbook manually can be done from the Insight UI

Next, we'll look at real world examples that customers have used and that are common enough to be used for pretty much all security teams.

Real-world examples of automated responses

Part of understanding how to best make use of automation is to be inspired by what other teams have automated to become as efficient and effective as possible when dealing with threats. I wanted to use this section to focus on a couple of examples where some existing Sumo Logic customers have put together interesting processes that solve real-world challenges.

Let's focus on two examples here: Gmail phishing and changing user accounts.

The first example is pretty clear. Phishing is so widespread and is such a lucrative angle for criminals that the more we harden ourselves from this angle, the better. The second is interesting and unconventional because it shows you what's possible with the metadata available within the platform.

Gmail phishing

This playbook lets you take any insights that are created from emails or that contain signals with email content and create an automated investigation into them. I'll split this playbook into two parts to accommodate the page width. The first stage is shown here:

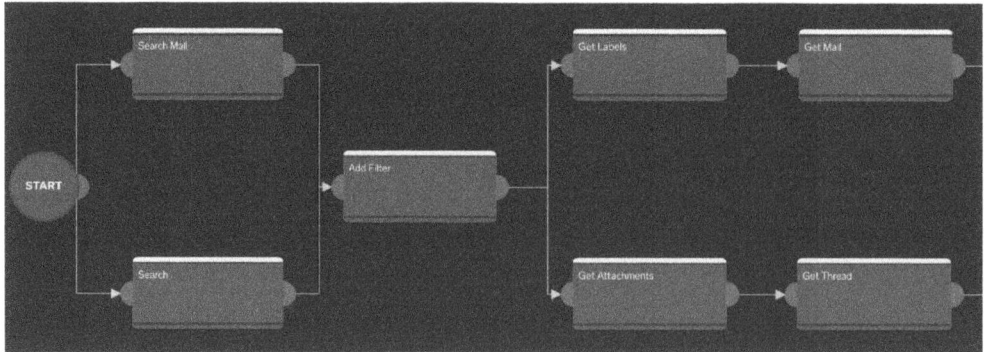

Figure 11.55 – The first stage of this playbook – lots of enrichment

All these actions are green (enrichment) actions. When the insight gets created, we take the following steps:

- Searching the email messages
- Searching filters
- Adding filters
- Getting labels
- Getting attachments
- Getting the individual email
- Getting the email thread

These individual actions compile all the usable material we would need at that point to assess whether something is awry or benign. However, this collection of data takes place over a few seconds. Doing this manually consumes so much more time than it's worth, and here we can set ourselves up with the information we need with minimal fuss.

The second stage of the playbook is where we begin to start taking some action, as shown here:

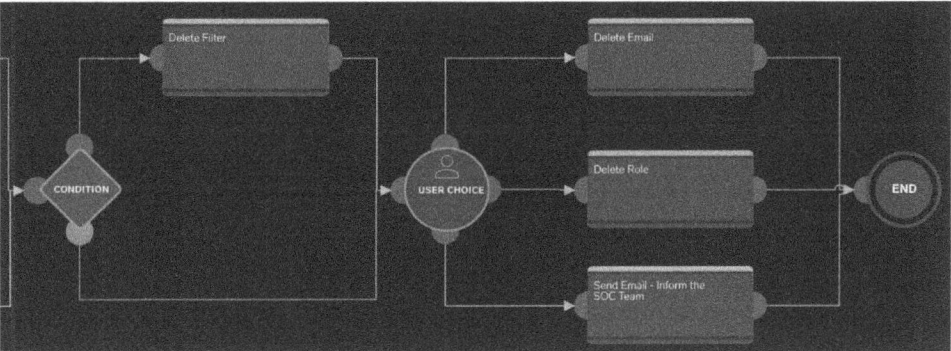

Figure 11.56 – The second stage of the Gmail phishing playbook, with containment actions

The action stage begins by checking whether filters exist that aren't in line with company policy or configuration and that could have been created by an external adversary as part of a phishing campaign. Deleting malicious filters in Gmail is a crucial step in limiting the impact of a phishing attack, renewing any healthy email flows, and preventing future attacks. This condition lets us delegate these actions to the machine to try and respond as quickly as possible.

The next step is a **USER CHOICE** node that can be added to our automated steps. This node lets us inject a human user into any part of our automated flow to make some key decisions. In this case, after reviewing the initial details gathered from the email and looking at any deleted filters, the user is presented with three questions:

- Should we delete the email(s)?
- Should we delete the role(s)?
- Should we inform the SOC about this event?

This user choice usually presents itself in the form of an email, Slack, or Teams message, but could also be sent to an **Information Technology Service Management** (**ITSM**) or ticketing tool. Whatever the case, when clicking on the choice, the relevant action gets executed, and the playbook ends.

With a playbook like this, we're taking advantage of two key areas. Firstly, we're automating the gathering of key information and delegating basic decisions to help speed up the response. Secondly, we're applying human intelligence at a key junction of the process to ensure we respond accordingly.

This particular playbook reduces the investigation time for customers from typically 30 minutes down to around 10 minutes.

The next real-world example we'll cover is from a case where a customer wanted to put an automation sequence together for when there were specific changes in user accounts, alerted via Active Directory.

Changes in user accounts

I wanted to use this example because it's triggered not from Cloud SIEM, but from a monitor, which opens a lot of opportunities for any of your teams that either don't or won't use Cloud SIEM, or just need a more versatile query to detect the behavior you need.

In this scenario, the customer is monitoring for any changes made to user accounts with a query, as seen here:

Figure 11.57 – A query that looks for usernames that are associated with event IDs 4725 and 4722

The query groups usernames that are correlated with user-change events that fall under event IDs **4725** and **4722**. Any results get passed to a playbook that either removes the active user tags and tags them as disabled or vice versa. The playbook that changes tags on users based on any changes made in the logs is shown here:

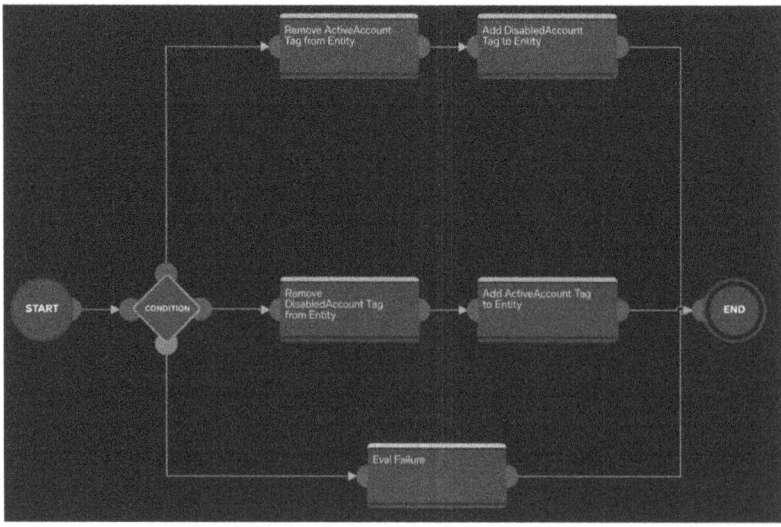

Figure 11.58 – The playbook that changes tags on users based on any changes made in the logs

Why do this? Well, automating this process means that user changes aren't missed by a human, where this type of event can slip through the cracks. Also, there is a benefit to using tags and labels in this way. This particular customer then takes those labels and tags, adds them to a *match list* in Cloud SIEM automatically, and uses those values in rule tuning expressions to make sure they always have an accurate list of active/inactive users when doing security investigations.

The following screenshot shows the rule tuning expression that makes use of these tagged accounts:

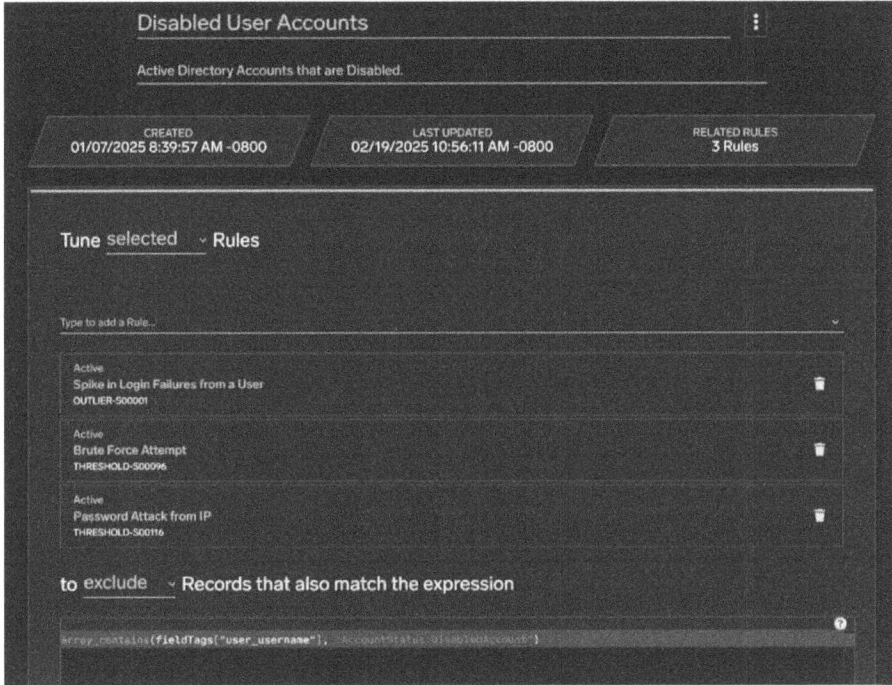

Figure 11.59 – The rule tuning expression that makes use of these tagged accounts

Summary

So, after seeing the capabilities, is the juice worth the squeeze? Or, in other words, is the effort of setting up automation worth it? Modern SOCs drown in repetitive, low-value tasks – context lookups, screenshot gathering, ticket creation – while the volume and velocity of alerts keep climbing. **Security orchestration and automated-response (SOAR)** and automations relieve that pressure by codifying those chores into playbooks the moment the alert lands.

Those micro-savings compound quickly.

Time isn't the only dividend. Automated playbooks ensure every incident follows the latest standard-operating procedure, draws context from the same authoritative sources, and documents actions in a single ecosystem. Analysts gain richer threat-hunting context from machine-learning-assisted enrichment, while leadership gets consistent metrics on mean-time-to-detect, respond, and resolve.

SOAR's open integration model means each new security tool, SaaS API, or home-grown tool can be wired into existing playbooks in days rather than quarters, so ROI accelerates as your stack evolves. Teams typically adopt a crawl-walk-run strategy: start by automating enrichment, notification, and escalation; layer in analyst-approved containment; then progress to fully autonomous triage and nested playbooks.

In the next chapter, it all comes together. We will cover threat intelligence from all sides – strategic, operational, and tactical, but most importantly, put a plan in place for how to place Sumo Logic at the heart of your business and bring your security program to life.

References

1. `https://help.sumologic.com/docs/platform-services/automation-service/automation-service-bridge/`
2. `https://www.sumologic.com/help/docs/platform-services/automation-service/integration-framework/`

Get this book's PDF version and more

Scan the QR code (or go to `packtpub.com/unlock`). Search for this book by name, confirm the edition, and then follow the steps on the page.

Note: Keep your invoice handy. Purchases made directly from Packt don't require an invoice.

Part 4
Advanced Topics and Future Trends

In this final part, we'll look at how to bring together everything we've covered in the book up to this point. We also introduce threat intelligence, a typically hidden layer that helps to create an enterprise-grade security program. We'll cover compliance and reporting, another requirement that is ever-present within security teams and auxiliary operational teams, and how this information can be used in Sumo Logic. Finally, we'll talk about the future. The rate of change in security is breakneck, and we've identified some areas to help prepare security teams for the future and what steps should be taken.

This part of the book covers the following chapters:

- *Chapter 12, Bringing a Security Intelligence Program to Life with Sumo Logic*
- *Chapter 13, Compliance and Reporting*
- *Chapter 14, The Future of Security Intelligence*

12
Bringing a Security Intelligence Program to Life with Sumo Logic

So far, we've shown you how to collect, analyze, monitor, detect, and even automate. You've got logs, metrics, insights, dashboards, playbooks... all the moving parts of a modern security capability. But there's an important layer to add here, and that is the ability to use external context to benefit your cybersecurity program, to bring this entire system to life: **intelligence**.

This chapter is where we start to move from reaction to *anticipation*, from alerts to *awareness*, and from *we saw it happen* to *we saw it coming*.

Cyber threat intelligence (**CTI**) is the glue that connects internal telemetry to global context. If you do it well, it transforms your SOC from a noisy alarm system into an informed, proactive defence engine. But it's often done poorly or, worse, not at all. Our goal in this chapter is to help you build an intelligence program that works, one that integrates natively into your Sumo Logic environment and amplifies everything else you've built.

We're going to cover the following topics in this chapter:

- Cyber threat intelligence: beyond feeds and PDFs
- Sumo Logic as the nucleus of actionable intelligence

Cyber threat intelligence: beyond feeds and PDFs

Let's get one thing out of the way: threat intelligence is not a PDF report you download once a quarter and forward to your SOC team with a shrug and an "FYI." It's also not a magical feed of bad IPs and malware hashes that you dump into your SIEM system and hope it makes your detections look smarter. CTI is about making better decisions with *context*. It's the layer that helps you say, "This alert actually matters because..." or "Let's prioritize this investigation because...".

At its core, CTI is the structured practice of collecting, analyzing, and applying knowledge about current or emerging threats. When used properly, it enhances visibility, accelerates investigations, and enables proactive defense. CTI builds on top of the craft of intelligence used during war and geopolitical conflict but adapts it to today's digital battlefield. Other forms of intelligence exist, such as **Open Source Intelligence** (**OSINT**), **Signals**

Intelligence (**SIGINT**), and other forms of intelligence, but CTI is primarily designed to handle the threat of adversaries with cyber capabilities and the devastating threat of malware.

Think of it like having a military-grade map during a conflict. It not only shows you where the enemy is but what kind of weaponry they're bringing, how they tend to behave, and whether they're targeting you specifically.

Types of threat intelligence

There are three main types of threat intelligence, all based on what level of granularity we're dealing with: **tactical**, **operational**, and **strategic** CTI. These are discussed in detail in the following subsections.

Tactical

When it comes to tactical CTI, think of **indicators of compromise** (**IOC**): file hashes, domains, IPs, user-agent strings, and so on. This provides short-lived data but is extremely actionable. You can match it against your logs and block it at the firewall or proxy level.

Essentially, tactical CTI is the level of intelligence we're working with on a daily basis. IOCs are seen everywhere and anywhere, and it's our job to identify which ones need to be prioritized. There's a very famous "intelligence ranking" of tactical intelligence. It's called the *Pyramid of Pain*[1] and defines how important certain IOCs are *to attackers*. David Bianco, who designed the concept, thought that the quicker we respond to IOCs, the less use adversaries can get out of them. But what impacts that is the *usefulness* of one type of IOC over another.

For example, an IP address is at the *easy* level. If we identify, respond, and remediate an issue involving an IP address, the attacker just shrugs and gets a new one, or uses another botnet, and so on. If we have identified the *tool* that the attacker uses, such as **Cobalt Strike**[2] or a specific phishing kit to target Facebook users, Gmail users, and so on, then attackers have to do more than just use another IP address. They might have to shift their strategy and use a different toolset. See? More pain for the attacker. Here is the Pyramid of Pain in all its glory:

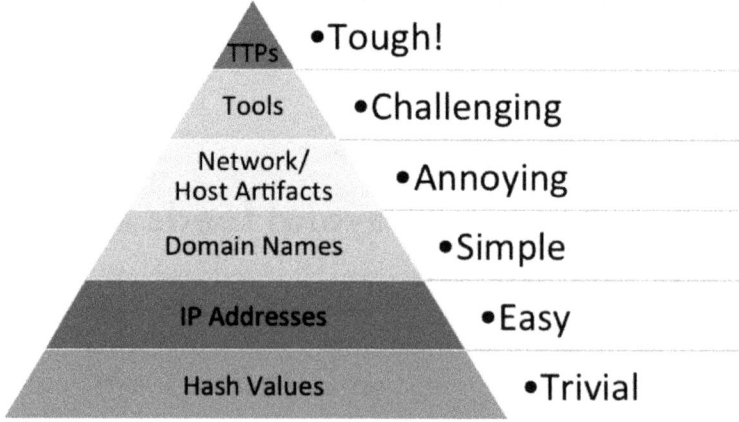

Figure 12.1 – The Pyramid of Pain (pain for the attacker)

Getting things right at the tactical level is important; it'll mean less wasted time and more focused effort when it comes to dealing with investigations.

Operational

The operational level of intelligence is all about adversary **Techniques, Tactics, and Procedures** (**TTPs**). We covered TTPs in *Chapter 9, Cloud SIEM* when we looked at the MITRE ATT&CK Coverage Matrix, which helps you to manage TTPs seen within Signals and Insights in the Cloud SIEM. Instead of seeing the raw data points from adversary actions, like in the tactical layer of intelligence, we try to understand *how* adversaries operate at this layer. An example is a phishing campaign that consistently uses the same Dropbox links or a known malware family using the same PowerShell obfuscation techniques.

These TTPs often map to the MITRE ATT&CK Matrix and provide the crucial bit of information that helps you tap into added context during your threat detection operations and security investigations.

Strategic

This layer of intelligence focuses on the high-level, executive-facing side of threat intelligence. We're talking threat reports that are designed to both summarize and delve into some detail about specific malware campaigns that are targeting your particular business vertical in a part of the world. This type of information should guide executive-level decision makers about how to set risk appetite, dictate budgets and investments into security and mitigation, as well as provide an understanding of what threats the business is facing.

You don't have to scramble to set up all these layers of intelligence on day one. That's too difficult and also not practical. While I don't know where you are on your security maturity journey, the good practice I recommend is to always start from the bottom up, in this case, from the tactical layer up. When doing so, the direct effects on your security team and program are felt much more significantly. A lot of value can be derived from doing things from this level, namely, more refined processes, quicker responses to threats, and more effective incident management.

So why are we talking about all this like it's difficult to implement? *Because it is*. In a lot of cases, I've worked with teams who encounter the three key problems described here:

- **Teams working in silos**: A team buys a threat intelligence feed, it's piped into a security platform or other tool that can ingest this data, but it's never properly linked to logs, alerts, or automation. Large enterprises might have multiple such teams overlapping in terms of coverage and using different feeds or intelligence that others can't see. Chaos.
- **Feeds not being actionable**: If you have too many feeds, too much noise, and no ability to filter or wrap context around this information, it will be difficult to actually use it when the time arises.
- **Reactive instead of predictive**: Good CTI should not just tell you what the threat was *after the fact*. It should help power your efforts before the real damage is done, and to predict and prepare.

When we take CTI and use some of the Sumo Logic tools we've already covered, such as detection logic, playbooks, dashboards, and entity models, we turn this intelligence into a force multiplier, not just a random security exercise. With Sumo Logic's capabilities combined with CTI, we can do the following:

- Automatically enrich logs with intel data (e.g., VirusTotal, AbuseIPDB, and commercial feeds)
- Detect and correlate IOCs across data sources in real time
- Tune detection rules based on actor TTPs (mapped to MITRE)

- Highlight recurring threat infrastructure across your estate
- Prioritize alerts with contextual risk scores

This tactical, operational, and strategic stuff doesn't just happen by itself. There's a level of awareness that needs to exist about what is important around the different teams. This brings us to **Priority Information Requirements** (**PIRs**), which guide the direction of intelligence collection.

Priority information requirements

When building security intelligence initiatives, we use PIRs. PIRs are high-priority intelligence questions that are gathered from different parts of the organization to help make decisions, reduce risk, and minimize threats. You can see where this can go wrong; PIRs tend to be nebulous, and when faced with the daunting prospect of finding out what is most important to different teams, it can get confusing very quickly.

That's why PIRs have three core criteria to make them *valuable*:

- They should be focused so they consider only *one* question
- The scope should be narrowed to *one* event or activity
- The intelligence should drive action for *one* decision

You'll notice that the criteria for these PIRs and the process are *exactly the same* as building KPIs for our DevSecOps teams. A target-driven approach to measuring your key outcomes is incredibly important for CTI, too!

For instance, let's consider a team that develops new AI or LLM-focused capabilities. These people are working with cutting-edge tech and pushing the frontier. That can't escape the eyes and ears of intelligence, though. The following will be our key PIR in this case:

Do we have an inventory of authorized and unauthorized LLM/AI models and services?

This primary PIR can further be broken down into intelligence levels as shown here:

- **Tactical**:
  - Do we have a list of these authorized AI/LLM systems (foundational models, vector stores, etc.)?
  - Who owns or maintains each asset?
- **Operational**:
  - What security tools are in place to detect compromise or leakage? Are **Endpoint Detection and Response** (**EDR**), **Cloud Security Posture Management** (**CSPM**), and **Data Loss Prevention** (**DLP**) tools used?
  - Where are these models being accessed from, or what are they integrated with?

Now, let's take a different example and look at a finance team. You might think there's not much to do here for an operational security team. However, what about the systems that hold payment data, vendor information, and PII? This is all vital to any attacker. Let's consider another important area of concern within this department for modern businesses, which is the supply chain. Remember SolarWinds? TeamCity? Everyone is at the mercy of supply chain attacks, so we need to be ready. The primary PIR would then be something like the following:

Are third-party vendors and financial services being monitored for risk?

This can be broken down into tactical and operational levels again:

- **Tactical**:
    - Do we maintain a list of key third-party vendors?
    - Are single sign-on or federated access portals being audited?
- **Operational**:
    - Are any vendor systems linked to public breaches or CTI feeds?
    - Are there login attempts to vendor sites from unauthorized IPs or geos?

> Note
>
> Going back to the centralized data lake concept in Sumo Logic, we can store the raw data behind all these PIRs and gather intelligence in one place. This allows for greater insight into this data and also visualization, examples of which we'll cover in a bit.

PIRs help because they form the groundwork for what is important to the business and the teams securing the business. In a world with so much data, such large and diverse environments, we have to make sense of it as much as we can. Even though uncertainty pervades the security space (*What is this command? Have we seen this tool before? Where has this user gone?*), we have to manage that uncertainty as best we can by using strong foundations. This leads us to decision-making. Intelligence on its own has no value apart from when it's operationalized, so it has to be actionable so it can help us with making the decisions around those actions.

> Note
>
> **Common failure pattern**
>
> Buying threat intelligence feeds without defined PIRs, clear telemetry ownership, or a central correlation layer results in alert fatigue, unused dashboards, and intelligence that never influences decisions.

Decision-making with threat intelligence

Let's talk about why use threat intelligence in the first place. It's crucial in modern teams because *good* threat intelligence allows us to make better decisions in the heat of the moment or when we're surrounded by noise. It could be said that threat intelligence *only* creates value when it improves decision-making. To do that consistently under pressure, security teams rely on structured mental models. Rather than introducing multiple competing frameworks, this chapter focuses on **how complementary models work together** to accelerate understanding, response, and learning.

At a high level, the following is determined:

- The **OODA loop**[3] explains *how decisions are made*
- **F3EAD** explains *how intelligence is operationalized*
- **Cyber Kill Chain** explains *how adversaries progress*

Used together, they help navigate the world of threat intelligence, and we'll start with arguably the most powerful one, the OODA loop.

OODA loop

The OODA loop was devised by Air Force Colonel John Boyd in the 1990s and has been embraced not only by the military but also in the business world. **OODA** stands for **Observe, Orient, Decide, Act**, and the main premise rests on a loop. Imagine a circle going round with these four areas. The *actual* diagram that Boyd drew is this:

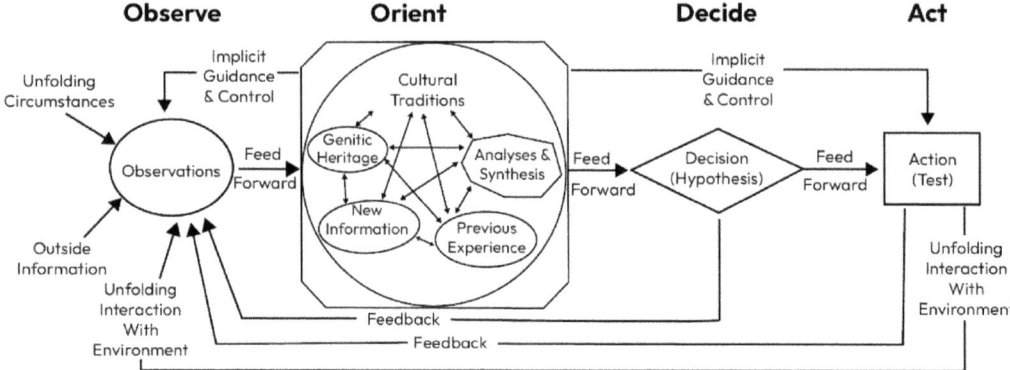

Figure 12.2 – The OODA loop as originally drawn by John Boyd

I want to put this loop into the context of security. The loop begins with **Observe**. We are collecting our telemetry from across our business and understanding the data, monitoring it to understand baselines.

The second stage is **Orient**. We start applying context to the telemetry through threat intelligence, criticality, and how historical behavior compares to current behavior across these vast datasets. The objective is to be armed and ready to deal with deviations from the norm that could lead to suspicious or malicious events.

The third stage is **Decide**. This is where we choose a remediation method that is appropriate based on risk and impact. With Sumo Logic, the amount of telemetry, analytical tools, and AI-driven capabilities means that knowing how to respond comes with the technology. A big responsibility for all the teams involved is to have communication paths open to facilitate this response effort.

The fourth and final stage is **Act**. Here, we take all the information gathered so far, known and unknown, as well as other contextual details, and execute the remediation. Whether it be containment, isolation, or suspension of accounts and services, we've seen how to both understand where to aim our response efforts and the tools we have at our disposal.

The most important thing to remember about OODA is that *the one who cycles through the loop quickest tends to win, whether it be the attacker or the defender*. Maneuverability and mobility are massive advantages that typically decide engagements, especially when you consider the rate at which malware can spread and propagate through an environment.

There are other frameworks to consider that I think are worth knowing about. The next one is the Cyber Kill Chain[4], a framework pioneered by Lockheed Martin.

Cyber Kill Chain

The Cyber Kill Chain was created to map key adversary touchpoints on their way to achieving their objectives. It consists of seven steps:

1. **Reconnaissance**: Harvesting information about the business, networks, and individuals
2. **Weaponization**: Crafting an exploit that can target vulnerabilities from a discovered weakness
3. **Delivery**: Sending this weaponized bundle to end users via email, hosted storage, and so on
4. **Exploitation**: Running the payload and exploiting target vulnerabilities
5. **Installation**: Installing malware on an asset
6. **Command and Control**: Setting up a beacon server to remotely gain and preserve access to the environment
7. **Actions on Objectives**: Achieve objectives with direct access into environment

The reason we're discussing the Cyber Kill Chain in this context is that if you think about it, it correlates very nicely with the OODA loop. I first saw this in a book by Wilson Bautista Jr. called *Practical Cyber Intelligence*[5]. I highly recommend reading this book if you want to delve into very nuanced detail about threat intelligence, but also about how to build an entire operational capability from scratch.

Coming back to the link between the Cyber Kill Chain and OODA loop, let's remember that the attackers have their own OODA loop, which they are trying to cycle through as quickly as possible. The following diagram from *Practical Cyber Intelligence* illustrates this:

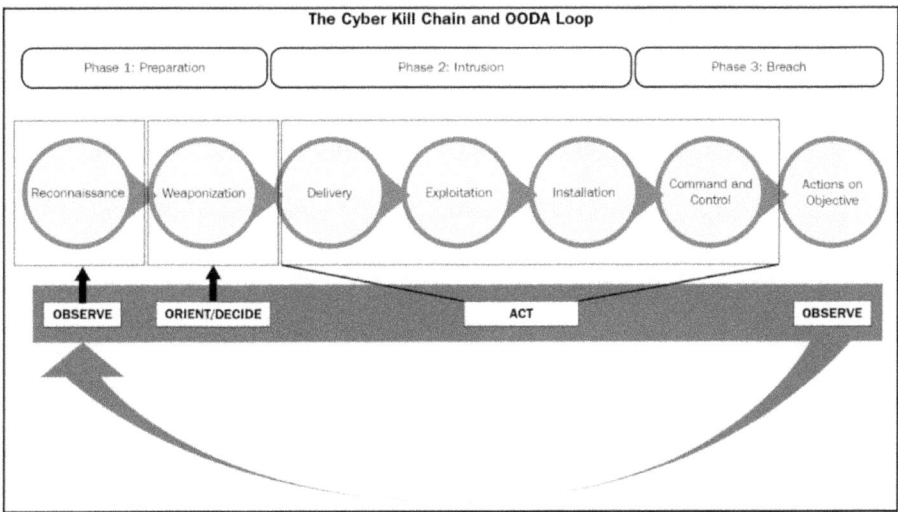

Figure 12.3 – The OODA loop and the Cyber Kill Chain working together

This is what an adversary is constantly trying to do: constantly looking, moving, and reassessing actions to help get them to their objectives.

In this chapter, however, the Cyber Kill Chain isn't really an operational model, but more of a lens that can be used for support during analysis. By knowing these stages and how attackers might approach them within our environment, we can do the following:

- Understand where an adversary currently is
- Identify which stages can be disrupted
- Map detections and gaps against attacker progress

This perspective is best utilized together with the MITRE ATT&CK framework, especially the way it works within the Sumo Logic MITRE ATT&CK Coverage Matrix.

Let's end this section on another loop! This one is called **F3EAD** (which stands for Find, **Fix, Finish, Exploit, Analyze, Disseminate**) and is discussed next.

F3EAD

The F3EAD model has a cool background. Originally, it's a military intelligence and targeting process that has been used heavily in Special Operations campaigns since around 2001. This model is and has been used for targeting key individuals, assets, or groups and bridges the gap between tactical intelligence and operations. It is, once again, a loop.

Figure 12.4 – A loops meme I couldn't resist adding to this section

Where OODA governs *decisions,* F3EAD governs intelligence-driven action. F3EAD helps us hunt, disrupt, and learn from adversaries. Whether we are doing reactive incident response or proactive threat hunting, there are benefits to using the F3EAD model to power our efforts.

Let's break down the elements of F3EAD, and while doing so, we'll cover the individual actions involved as part of these steps, as well as the tools you'd be using.

Find

This is the discovery phase, where we try to identify the adversary or threat activity. This could involve analyzing logs, looking at threat intelligence feeds, or threat hunting. The tools you might use are an SIEM system, such as Sumo Logic's Cloud SIEM, an EDR tool (e.g., CrowdStrike Falcon or MS Defender), or DNS/firewall logs.

An example is detecting a suspicious IP communicating with multiple endpoints using Palo Alto firewall data and CrowdStrike EDR data.

Fix

At this stage, something has been found, such as the suspicious IP in the previous example, or a string of events where a user has been seen exfiltrating data. We now need to track it. Triage and containment begin at this stage. At this point, we do things such as correlate indicators and related activity, identify infected or compromised assets, users, or credentials, and confirm whether lateral movement or privilege escalation has taken place.

We want to prepare a response without tipping off the attacker. If they know they are being tracked, they will change their approach. If they're good enough, that is. We can take further actions, such as correlating entities within the Cloud SIEM or with log queries, confirming the timeline of events with an insight, isolating endpoints, and segmenting networks.

An example is tracing an initial phishing login to follow-on access to finance documents via CloudTrail and Microsoft 365 logs.

Finish

We've identified the threat activity, and now we have to disrupt the operations of the adversary, with the objective of removing them from the environment.

At this stage, we're looking to undertake actions such as blocking IPs or domains, disabling or suspending compromised user accounts, revoking tokens/API keys, and quarantining endpoints.

We've talked about the automation capabilities within Sumo Logic, and this is the step where they are deployed. With playbooks, it's possible to take a range of actions, such as enriching IOCs with VirusTotal or suspending a user on Okta or Entra ID.

The end of this phase is typically used to update the existing detection logic in order to mitigate a similar attempt in the future.

Exploit/analyze

We want to structure our intelligence and assess it. This way, we get to better understand the adversary's capabilities and intent. The reason I've combined exploit and analyze in this context is that both these steps work together, because we also want to take what we've learned (the tools, logs, and tactics used by our adversary) and convert it into usable knowledge. This is where CTI shines. We get to turn a security event into an opportunity to learn.

For example, we could analyze malware for additional IOCs such as IPs, strings, or behavior, analyze logs post-incident to understand attacker techniques, interrogate adversary infrastructure (map C2s, GitHub repos, etc.), and identify stolen or exfiltrated data.

As the aim is to turn raw data into usable knowledge, we also want to be doing the following:

- Mapping actions to the MITRE ATT&CK framework
- Profiling the threat actor based on TTPs and infrastructure reuse
- Assessing impact and how our environment has held up
- Combining with existing intelligence to understand campaign evolution or other targets

We can use things such as the MITRE ATT&CK Coverage Matrix in the Cloud SIEM, CTI reports, or dashboards in Sumo Logic to help with visually assessing entities.

An example is recognizing behavior that is consistent with an **advanced persistent threat (APT)** group you have identified via research that has been targeting your industry with spear phishing emails about new regulation changes.

Disseminate

At this stage, we have quite a trove of information. Intelligence exists in order to be shared; otherwise, its benefit is limited. This is the step where the information we have gathered is *operationalized* across the organization. We send an executive summary to leadership, we share IOCs and TTPs with detection engineers and the SOC, we update the EDR and other detection tools with IOCs, and we share a report with an **Information Sharing and Analysis Center (ISAC)** or other intelligence sharing community.

An example is updating Cloud SIEM rules and any Sumo Logic dashboards, then publishing a *TLP: Amber* report to internal stakeholders, and then the industry intelligence sharing group.

> **Note**
>
> A **Traffic Light Protocol (TLP)** intelligence report is a way of telling recipients how widely this intelligence can be disseminated. Basically, who can I send this to without being fired?
>
> There are typically four levels to a TLP report: **White** denotes *free to share publicly*, **Green** denotes *share within organization or intel community*, **Amber** denotes *share internally, or on a need-to-know basis*, and **Red** denotes *only share with named individuals*.

We can take the phishing insight that we analyzed in *Chapter 10, The Insight Engine* with the SOC analyst agent and ask it to create a threat intelligence report for exactly these purposes, as shown here:

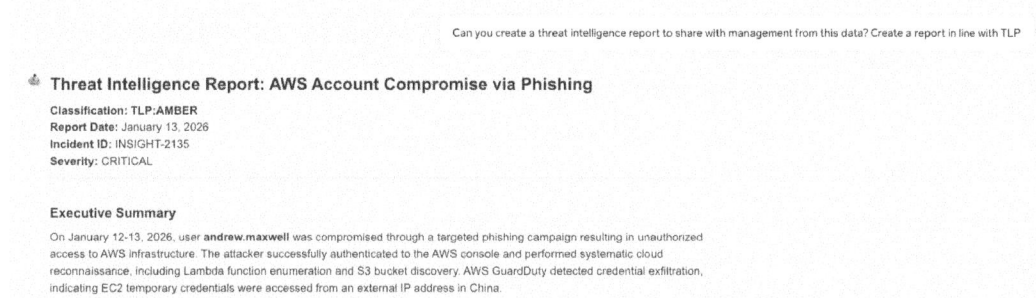

Figure 12.5 – We can ask the SOC Analyst Agent to create a TLP report for us based on the findings and remediation required

In the preceding figure, I asked, **Can you create a threat intelligence report to share with management from this data? Create a report in line with TLP**.

Within 60 seconds, I had a full report with incident details, a threat actor profile, and attack chain analysis, like this:

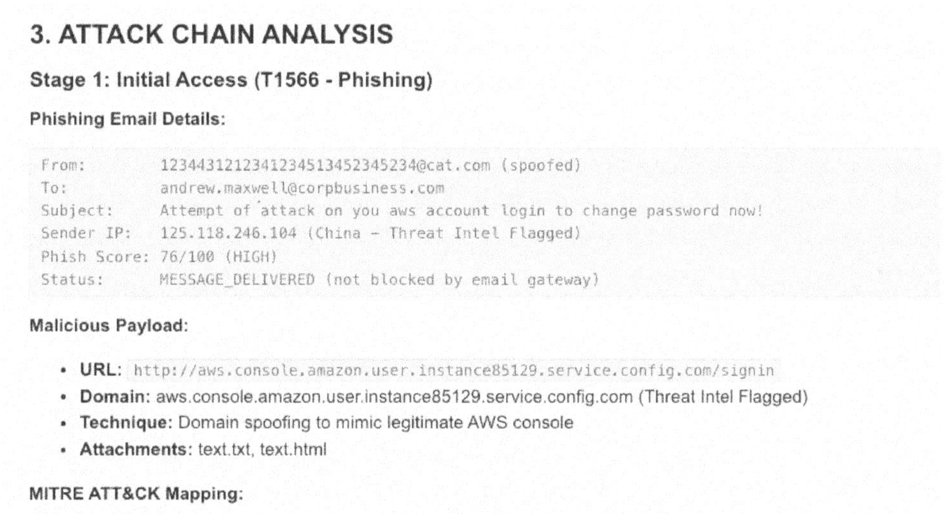

Figure 12.6 – Attack chain analysis as part of the TLP intel report

The days when I had to spend one or two days creating a nice report like this to present to customers post-incident, or as part of threat intelligence landscape reviews, are long behind us. This level of efficiency leads to better consumption and use of this intelligence, rather than spending valuable hours assembling and formatting it.

Threat intelligence exists in order to help make better decisions, and I hope an understanding of these models makes it easier for you to incorporate them into your own systems.

We've covered some of the basics of CTI and how it enhances decision-making. Let's look at the real point of this chapter: how to turn Sumo Logic into a central decision-making engine for the whole business.

Sumo Logic as the nucleus of actionable intelligence

By the time an organization starts talking seriously about threat intelligence, it has usually already made a critical mistake: it assumes intelligence is something you add to a security platform.

In reality, intelligence only becomes valuable when it sits at the center of how a business already operates.

Modern enterprises generate an overwhelming amount of telemetry in the form of logs, metrics, traces, identity events, cloud signals, SaaS activity, and network traffic. Each team sees only a fragment of the picture, optimized for their own priorities: uptime, velocity, compliance, or risk reduction. The result is not a lack of data, but a lack of shared understanding.

This is where Sumo Logic earns its place.

Rather than acting as yet another destination for security data, Sumo Logic functions as a common intelligence layer, a system where operational reality, business context, and external threat intelligence converge. Development teams contribute signals through application telemetry, CloudOps through infrastructure and control plane data, security through detections and investigations, and leadership through the questions they need answered to make decisions.

Threat intelligence, in this model, is not a static feed or a dashboard for analysts. It is a force multiplier that enriches existing telemetry, sharpening detections and turning raw events into evidence-backed answers to the business's most important questions.

This chapter focuses on how to position Sumo Logic at the heart of that ecosystem: not as a tool used by one team, but as the connective tissue that allows intelligence to flow across the organization, drive prioritization, and, ultimately, change outcomes. Let's visualize this, having learned what we have so far about the platform and its capabilities:

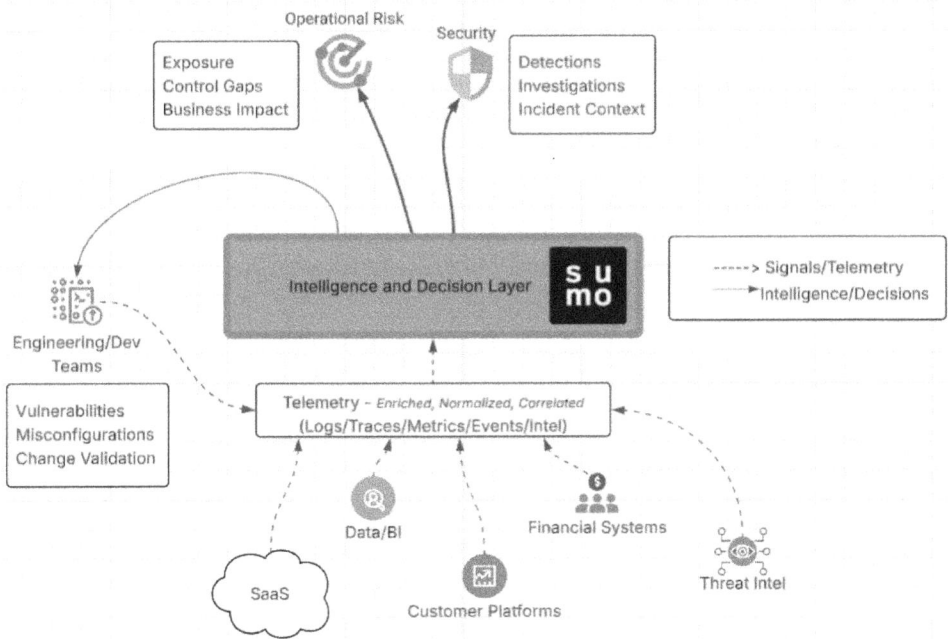

Figure 12.7 – How telemetry, threat intelligence, and teams converge through a centralized intelligence layer

The preceding diagram shows that Sumo Logic isn't just a "place that logs go." *It's a place where decisions are made across the business.* It reinforces security's role as a business enabler and also highlights the operational need and benefits that come from organizational units working together. These are key principles we covered back in *Chapter 2, The Role of DevSecOps in Modern Security*, and that set the foundation for everything we've discussed up to this point.

You'll notice that both engineering and dev teams contribute to Sumo Logic with telemetry from infrastructure, applications, and other services, but also benefit from the decisions and intelligence from this information, especially when coupled with a security view. This is how we work in a modern business; security teams don't actually implement the fixes. Engineering teams do. What engineering teams don't do is own risk, which is why the arrow going back to **Engineering** isn't as thick as the ones going to **Operational Risk** and **Security**.

From this point on, we'll focus less on what threat intelligence is and more on how it is operationalized across teams. The goal is not more data, more alerts, or more feeds; it is alignment between business priorities, technical telemetry, and security decision-making.

Building a security intelligence program with Sumo Logic: a cross-team model

You don't need a team of analysts in hoodies and war rooms filled with plasma screens to start building a security intelligence program with Sumo Logic. What you *do* need is a plan.

But before tools, you need intent. How do we orchestrate this across different teams and bring it together in your business? I want to help you answer one primary question after reading this far into the book, something that you can take back to your team and wider business and have practical outcomes:

How do I align teams, telemetry, and intelligence so Sumo Logic produces decisions instead of noise?

In the following sections, we will talk about how you can take practical steps to make Sumo Logic a focal point of your business-wide telemetry and ensure that it is able to support decision-making across teams.

Establishing intelligence flow

If you follow the basic stages of the intelligence cycle shown next, you will find yourself making some great progress:

1. **Planning and Direction**: What decisions need to be made? What threats do we care about?
2. **Collection**: Gather logs, telemetry, IOCs, and CTI reports.
3. **Processing**: Parse, normalize, and enrich data in Sumo Logic.
4. **Analysis**: Use queries, dashboards, and Cloud SIEM insights to find patterns.
5. **Dissemination**: Share alerts, reports, and dashboards, as well as playbook outputs, with the right teams.

Arguably, the hardest part here is the first step, planning. How do we understand what threats we care about? We need to understand that security doesn't live in isolation anymore. The real power of your intelligence program comes when you bring other teams into the loop, and this action alone really gets the ideas flowing and the plan. Effective security intelligence programs do not begin with feeds; they start with questions.

In the following table, to start you off, I have suggested some questions to consider when planning your security intelligence program. The questions are separated into the relevant team that would benefit, but also a quick telemetry mapping that can help to start adding context to them:

DevOps: Expose indicators or anomaly alerts tied to new builds or deployments	Are there IOCs or threat actors known to target CI/CD pipelines or software repositories?
	What tactics are being used to compromise containers, build agents, and so on?
	Are there any vulnerabilities surrounding some of the tools we use, for example, Jenkins, Jira, and so on?
	Have we seen any anomalous login events on our build systems?
	How could a supply chain compromise happen in our ecosystem?

Finance: Alert on suspicious access to payroll or invoice systems	Have any of our finance SaaS vendors been linked to any recent compromises?
	What are the most recent credential theft or session hijack techniques linked to financial fraud?
	Which IP addresses or domains are tied to known invoice or wire fraud infrastructure?
Product: Share threat reports that impact customer-facing features	Are there public vulnerabilities in our product stack, such as libraries, APIs, or plugins?
	Are threat actors targeting our brand or discussing vulnerabilities in our products online or on the dark web?
	Have similar companies in our vertical been compromised recently?
	Is our login/authentication process being abused or mimicked in phishing infrastructure or campaigns?
	How could an attacker create a path from public-facing product features to internal systems?
Vulnerability management: Identify, prioritize, and remediate vulnerabilities across systems	Are there newly disclosed CVEs (N-day) affecting our tech stack? Typically, public-facing tech is more of a concern, such as Apache, Exchange, and VPN gateways.
	Are any adversary groups exploiting CVEs that are applicable to us?
	Which assets in our estate are tied to internet-exposed or high-risk CVEs?
	Do we have intelligence on exploit toolkits, such as Metasploit Modules, GitHub **Proof of Concepts** (**PoCs**), or ransomware loaders?
	Can we correlate threat intel (TTPs, tools, and campaigns) with our current vulnerability backlog to help reprioritize?

Red Teams / SOC – Feed real-world behaviors back into detection logic	Are our detection rules aligned with the latest TTPs seen in active campaigns?
	What gaps exist between threat actor behaviors and our current coverage in the MITRE ATT&CK Coverage Matrix?
	Which infrastructure (IPs, C2s, and DGA domains) is actively being used in campaigns targeting our geographic region or industry?
	Can we build internal threat profiles or threat hunting hypotheses based on this intelligence?

Table 12.1 – Questions to consider when planning your security intelligence program

Telemetry is a shared responsibility. By contributing telemetry that helps to answer these PIRs, there will be clearer outcomes in terms of decisions feeding back to the business:

- Engineering owns the **application and pipeline telemetry**
- CloudOps owns the **infrastructure and control plane**
- Security owns **detections and response**
- Finance/product own **business-critical SaaS context**

Sumo Logic removes the burden of correlation from individual teams by centralizing normalization, enrichment, and intelligence mapping in a single query and detection layer.

Operationalizing intelligence across teams

You want a shared language across your teams for understanding threats. When we were discussing DevSecOps concepts throughout the first few chapters of the book, there was a big focus on communication and transparency. This is the exact same here. By speaking the same language, we can achieve more and react more quickly to potential problems.

The best and quickest way to start operationalizing data at the moment is with the MITRE ATT&CK framework, both due to its foundational status as well as the amount of shared intelligence that uses it. Running the following loop will let you mature from *indicator matching* to *behavior detection*:

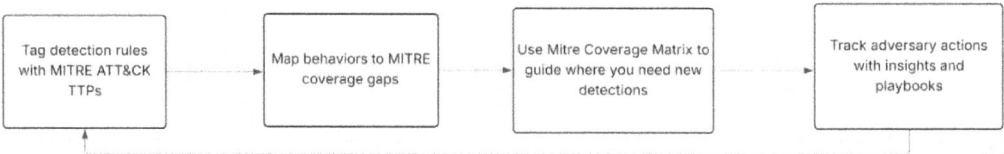

Figure 12.8 – Loop to let you mature from indicator matching to behavior detection

Embracing the MITRE ATT&CK model opens up the playing field to both wider and deeper analytics into surrounding events. You'll be able to make sense of the noise much more easily when the events are mapped based on what is important to you.

Further, as mentioned earlier, adopting the F3EAD model into your threat intelligence and Sumo Logic usage can slot perfectly into your tactical and operational processes.

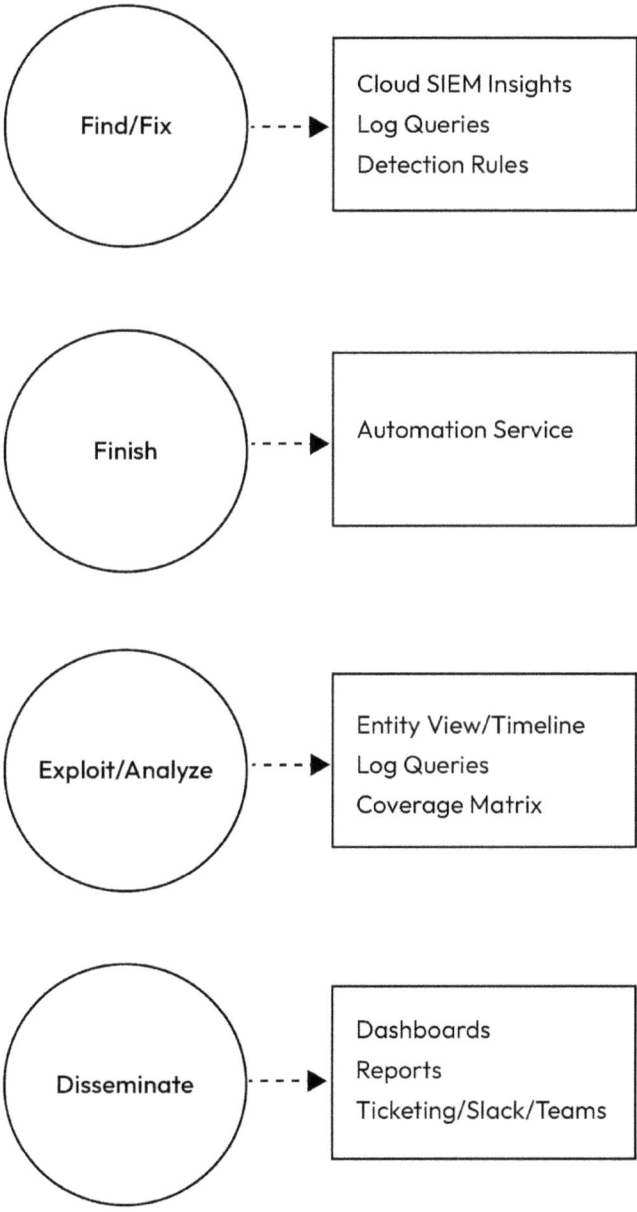

Figure 12.9 – Adopting the F3EAD model into your threat intelligence

The *find*, *fix*, *exploit*, and *analyze* steps can be consolidated because of the overlap in the capabilities provided by Sumo Logic. Even if you don't have, for example, a *disseminate* process ready to use internally, start with the first few steps.

Evolving intelligence maturity

No security program has ever started from a position where they have all their PIRs on day one, their team collaboration is through the roof, and their internal and external intelligence channels are working smoothly. Even if you have *none* of these things, let's see what the journey looks like from start to high maturity; I won't say "end" because I hate to break it to you, there is never an end (sorry). The following diagram aims to highlight how teams that are higher in maturity (especially those I've encountered and worked with) converge and work together more, compared to siloed and fractured teams who drown in noise all the way on the left side of the spectrum:

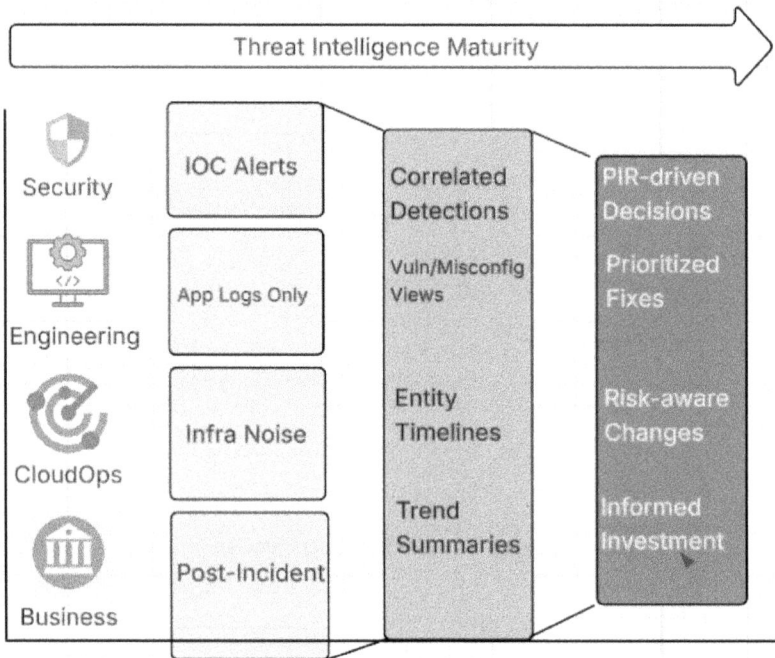

Figure 12.10 – Threat intelligence maturity across teams over time

As threat intelligence maturity increases, teams do not produce more data. They reach decisions faster, with shared context.

It's worth bearing in mind that the ability to interact with other teams and the rest of the business is an ongoing cycle in addition to successfully growing capability and understanding on each level.

At this point, we've aligned teams around shared intelligence questions, centralized telemetry, and a common decision framework. What remains is execution, that is bringing intelligence into Sumo Logic in a way that supports these goals. We'll cover the different ways to use threat intelligence in Sumo Logic in the next section.

Implementation

So, in effect, what we have is a phased system of filtering data to make it actionable. It looks like this:

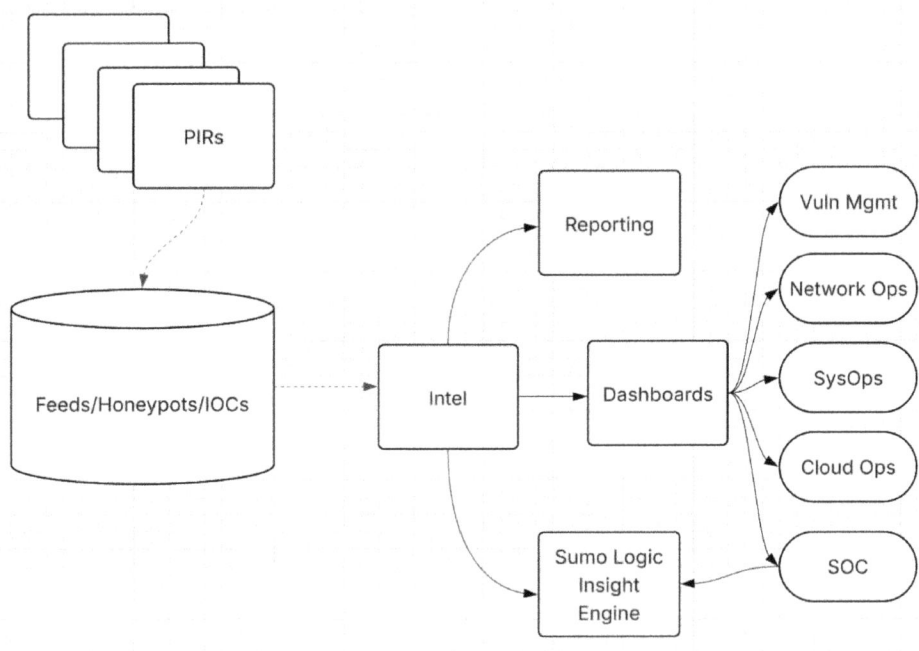

Figure 12.11 – System for filtering data

We've gone through a lot of theory up to this point, and if you're still with me, take a breath. We're getting into the practical side of things. How do we start to really use intelligence in Sumo Logic? Well, the PIRs, which we've already discussed the importance of, feed the whole intelligence process. This identifies what sources of information are the highest priority for you and your organization. We can start to put processes into place to gather those key sources of information and build the foundation of our intelligence.

You already know that you get two high-fidelity threat intelligence feeds in the platform that you can use from day one, which makes it a great starting point. These feeds are quite broad in terms of scope, so whether you're interested in malware types, industries, or phishing campaigns, they have you covered. Let's walk through these, and then we'll look at how to get your own feeds in.

Intelligence feeds ready to go

As Sumo Logic is designed to be a single source of truth, the way of using intelligence is quite centralized. What I mean by that is when you set up rules or do queries on your data, there is no need to specify each individual feed. Your data gets cross-referenced against everything you have all in one go. For example, the quickest way of getting started with the out-of-the-box content is by going to **App Catalog** and finding the **Threat Intel Quick Analysis** app, as shown here:

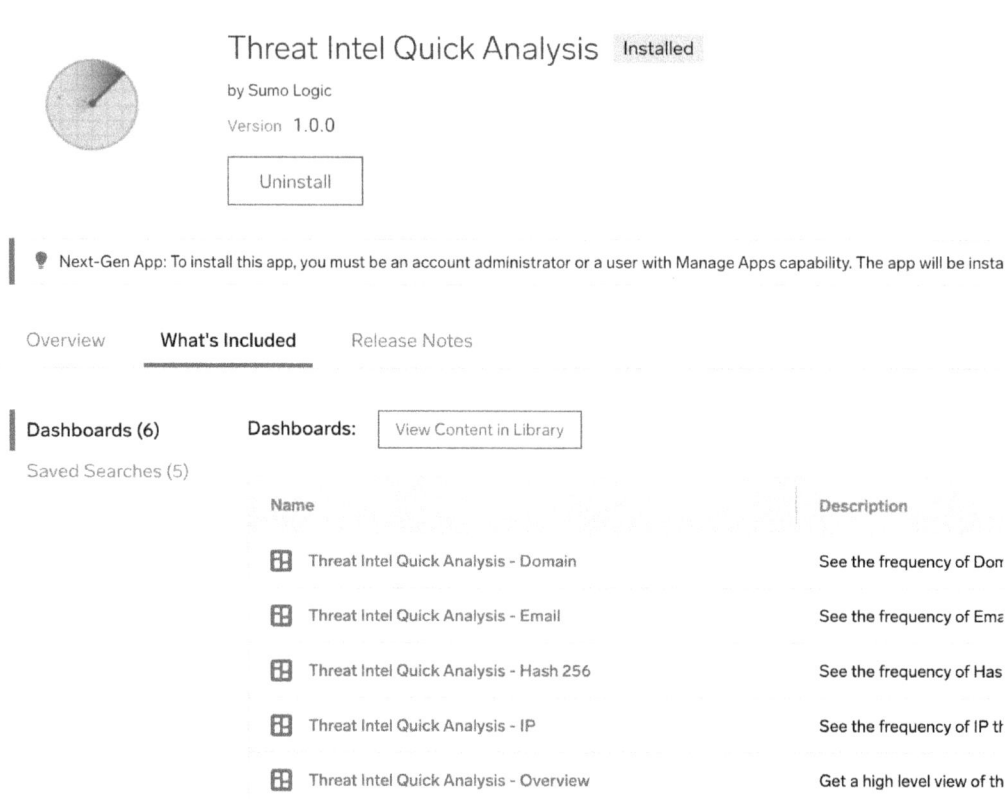

Figure 12.12 – This app is a really easy way of tapping into threat intelligence visually across your data sources

What this gives you access to is a set of dashboards that make it easier to visually identify trends and hits in the threat intelligence data. Furthermore, if we head over to the IP dashboard, we have something that looks like this:

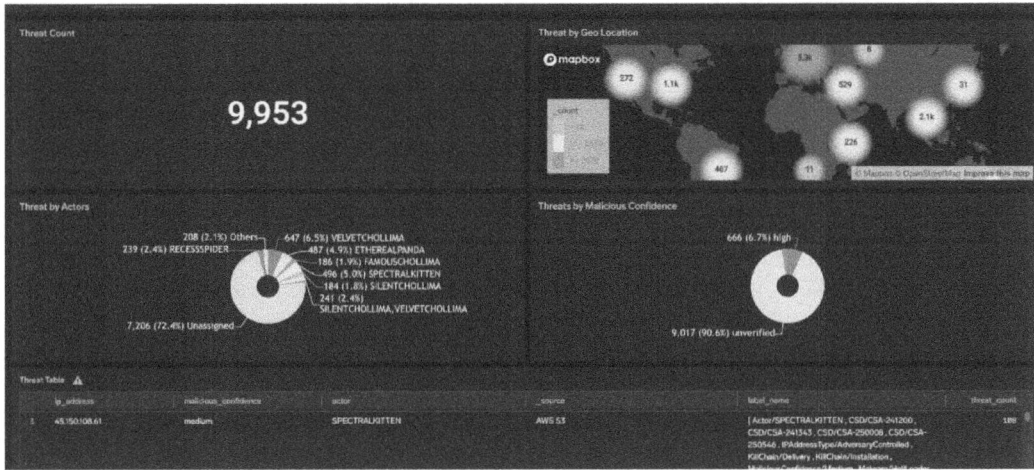

Figure 12.13 – One of the dashboards from the Threat Intel Quick Analysis app

Wherever you are in the intelligence maturity journey, this view makes it easy to digest. Let's set the scene.

Alex is looking through his Sumo Logic log events when he sees a spike in login attempts from an IP address on his 1Password source. He notes the IP address, 45.150.108.61. He opens up his threat intelligence IP dashboard and scans through the threat table. He can see the IP address popping up in the threat table, where it has been tagged with a medium confidence, an association with the *SPECTRALKITTEN* threat actor group, and the source of data is Amazon S3. A useful list of labels gives Alex an idea of what type of indicator this is and what it might be doing. As there is a high count of events, he opens the table in log search, drills deeper into the IP address in the logs, and identifies a range of failed login attempts, followed by successful ones, some triggering AWS Security Hub rules around policy changes and instance credential exfiltration. He launches an investigation at a critical level to try to stop the potential threat.

You can see that even if you have a small team, the fact that data is being constantly cross-referenced and analyzed, ready at a moment's notice, makes it easier to use and act with.

Bring your own feed

What about if we have some feeds that we've subscribed to? If we're further along the intelligence maturity journey and subscribe to other feeds? Great examples include industry-wide feeds called **Information Sharing and Analysis Centers** (**ISACS**), which provide feeds for member organizations. A wide range of industries are catered to, for example, **Financial Services Information Sharing and Analysis Center** (**FS-ISAC**), Maritime ISAC, Aviation ISAC, and Communications ISAC.

There are many more; I won't list them here, but they are worth taking a look at. There's a fantastic resource on GitHub with a collection of great threat intelligence resources[6]. Many useful free feeds exist, but here I'll mention five good ones that I've worked with before:

- **Abush.ch**: Very strong community, frequent updates
- **AlienVault OTX**: Huge community, great tagging for metadata
- **Malware Traffic Analysis**: Contains some great indicators for phishing and malware campaigns

- **Feodo Tracker**: Focused on financial services malware such as Dridex and Trickbot
- **CIRCL Passive DNS and MISP Feeds**: MISP Threat Intelligence is a massive source, publicly accessible and updated with MITRE ATT&CK-focused tags and attributes

The obvious thing to do with these, if you use some or find ones you think will help you, is to get them into Sumo Logic to start adding this enrichment to your data.

The primary method of collection used for threat intelligence is called STIX/TAXII. These are two standards that are used to send threat intelligence indicators from one system to another, and most threat intelligence vendors or feeds support them. STIX defines the format and structure of the data, and TAXII governs how API endpoints are served and accessed. Not all vendors support this, though, so we'll talk about how to get those in after.

STIX/TAXII collection

When adding a source to a **hosted collector**, we can use **TAXII 2 Client** available from the list, as shown here:

Figure 12.14 – What the STIX/TAXII source looks like when adding to a hosted collector

This lets you configure collection from a vendor's STIX/TAXII 2.x endpoints. Don't think I'll leave you to fend for yourself, sometimes all of this information about threat intelligence, formats, and API conventions can be a bit crazy! Let's walk through an installation of MISP, mainly because MISP is so popular and quite foundational to threat intelligence gathering.

Setting up MISP

Visit the download page of MISP[7] and follow the instructions in the **Requirements** section. If you're anything like me and spin up a cloud VM to test things, then I'm doing this on an Amazon EC2 instance. Just copy the install script and paste it into a text file called misp_install.sh or something similar. Because I've used MISP in the past, it usually needs a misp user to be created. In Linux, that takes five seconds using the following:

```
sudo adduser misp
```

Create a password for this user, and you're done. Then, you add the new user to a `misp` group, as shown here:

```
sudo usermod -aG sudo misp
```

Then, you change to the new user with the following:

```
su - misp
```

The reason it's best practice to use these commands in this order is that it keeps the installation isolated and prevents accidental changes as root.

Run the script, and you should see it complete with the following message:

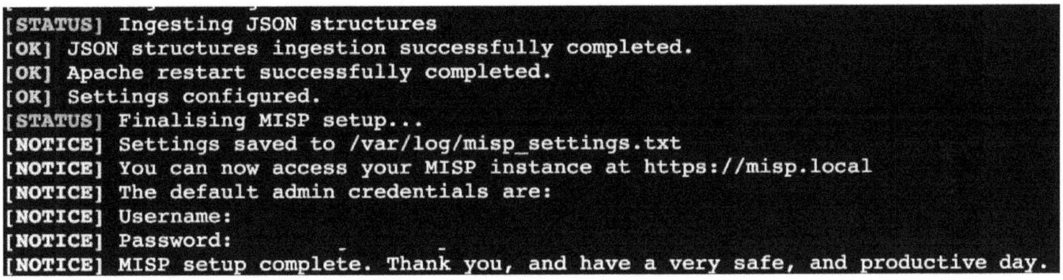

```
[STATUS] Ingesting JSON structures
[OK] JSON structures ingestion successfully completed.
[OK] Apache restart successfully completed.
[OK] Settings configured.
[STATUS] Finalising MISP setup...
[NOTICE] Settings saved to /var/log/misp_settings.txt
[NOTICE] You can now access your MISP instance at https://misp.local
[NOTICE] The default admin credentials are:
[NOTICE] Username:
[NOTICE] Password:
[NOTICE] MISP setup complete. Thank you, and have a very safe, and productive day.
```

Figure 12.15 – The messages that confirm the MISP setup is successful

Everything is set up, but there's one hitch – the default path of `https://misp.local` doesn't work as we are on a cloud VM, so let's change it. Open up the file at `/etc/apache2/sites-available/misp-ssl.conf` with nano or VIM and then change the two lines underneath `<VirtualHost *:443>`:

- `ServerName` (change to your public IP or public DNS name)
- `ServerAdmin` (change to admin@localhost)

Finally, change MISP's base URL, which is important as we don't want it redirecting or forwarding back to `misp.local`:

```
sudo -u www-data /var/www/MISP/app/Console/cake Admin setSetting "MISP.baseurl" "https://ec2-xx-xxx-xxx-xxx.compute-1.amazonaws.com"
```

> **Tip**
>
> I know you're all intelligent people reading this, but don't forget to add an inbound TCP 443 rule to your firewall if you're on a cloud VM. Trust me, if I told myself this every time I did some kind of setup, I'd have saved myself hours…

We're done! Browse to >, and we're ready to rock and roll. You will see the **Login** screen, as shown here:

Figure 12.16 – The Login screen of MISP when you visit the URL set during configuration

Here, we enter the **Email** and **Password** values found in the original message when the MISP setup was completed, and we can search across MISP. Now, to save you some time, because there's a bit of a learning curve here, I'm going to walk you through some initial steps. You can learn about the magical land of MISP with some great resources available on the MISP website[8].

At the top of the site, click on **Sync Actions** and then **Feeds**. This will show you a list of feeds that you can enable initially to start receiving a stream of IOCs. Let's enable some, so we have something to work with. I'm going to select **CIRCL** and **Botvrij** and enable them as shown here:

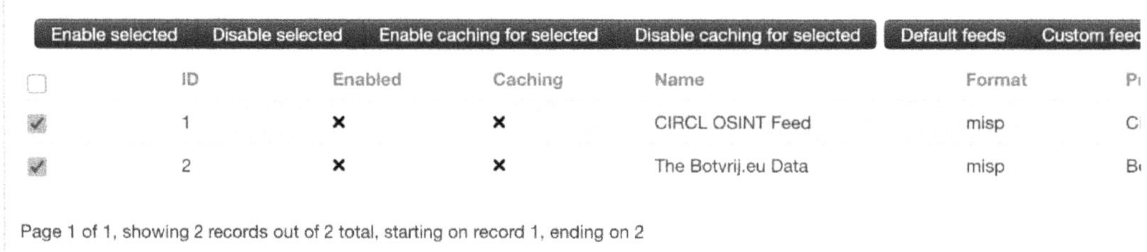

Figure 12.17 – Selecting the CIRCL and Botvrij feeds to test the intel ingestion into Sumo Logic

Next, there's a button above this view labeled **Fetch and store all feed data**. Click it and your MISP instance will pull the IOCs from these feeds. If you go to **Home** in the top-left corner, you get a list of IOCs as shown here:

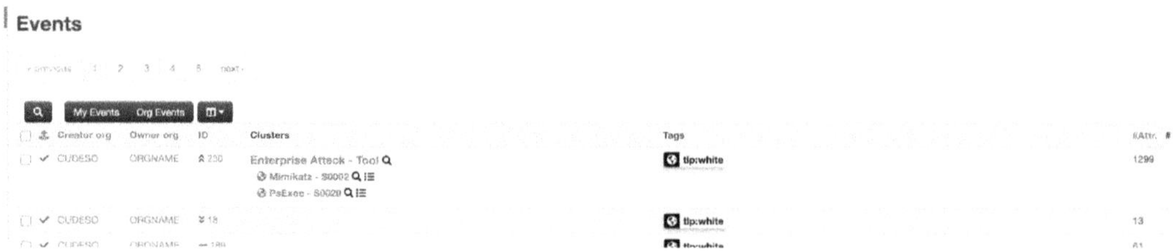

Figure 12.18 – Seeing the list of IOCs from our selected feeds!

That's all we need to do at this point. We now need a TAXII server for our Sumo Logic instance to pull from. MISP doesn't provide a TAXII server, so we can set one up on the same server we have MISP running, and luckily, this doesn't take too long, as MISP has some great libraries to help.

Setting up a TAXII server

We need to get active on the CLI again on our Linux machine. Rather than use the same server in this example, I'm going to have a separate VM to run as a separate server.

All credit for the following instructions goes to Dan Kaiser, one of my colleagues who is part of the Sumo Logic Threat Research team. This is one of the easiest guides I've ever seen, and I wanted to share it with you.

We're going to be using OpenCTI, which is an open-source threat intelligence platform that is capable of communicating via TAXII-compliant protocols and can push indicators to share them with, for example, Sumo Logic. Follow these steps:

1. Stand up a VM, and give it plenty of resources (I suggest 4 vCPUs and 16 GB RAM):

```
sudo apt install docker.io (to install Docker)
sudo apt install docker-compose (to install Docker Compose)
```

2. Set up OpenCTI with the following:

```
mkdir -p opencti && cd opencti
git clone https://github.com/OpenCTI-Platform/docker.git
cd docker
sudo apt install -y jq
```

3. Run the following command to create a .env file for OpenCTI. There is a sample one, but you can remove it:

```
(cat << EOF OPENCTI_ADMIN_EMAIL=admin@opencti.io
OPENCTI_ADMIN_PASSWORD=ChangeMePlease OPENCTI_ADMIN_TOKEN=$(cat /proc/sys/kernel/random/uuid) OPENCTI_BASE_URL=http://localhost:8080
OPENCTI_HEALTHCHECK_ACCESS_KEY=$(cat /proc/sys/kernel/random/uuid)
MINIO_ROOT_USER=$(cat /proc/sys/kernel/random/uuid) MINIO_ROOT_PASSWORD=$(cat /proc/sys/kernel/random/uuid) RABBITMQ_DEFAULT_USER=guest
RABBITMQ_DEFAULT_PASS=guest ELASTIC_MEMORY_SIZE=4G CONNECTOR_HISTORY_ID=$(cat /proc/sys/kernel/random/uuid) CONNECTOR_EXPORT_FILE_STIX_ID=$(cat /proc/sys/kernel/random/uuid) CONNECTOR_EXPORT_FILE_CSV_ID=$(cat /proc/sys/kernel/random/uuid) CONNECTOR_IMPORT_FILE_STIX_ID=$(cat /proc/sys/kernel/random/uuid)
CONNECTOR_EXPORT_FILE_TXT_ID=$(cat /proc/sys/kernel/random/uuid)
CONNECTOR_IMPORT_DOCUMENT_ID=$(cat /proc/sys/kernel/random/uuid)
```

```
CONNECTOR_ANALYSIS_ID=$(cat /proc/sys/kernel/random/uuid) SMTP_HOSTNAME=localhost
EOF ) > .env
```

4. Rename the OPENCTI_ADMIN_EMAIL and OPENCTI_ADMIN_PASSWORD fields with whatever credentials you want. Save and close the file

5. Run sudo sysctl -w vm.max_map_count=1048575 (to support running the Elasticsearch Docker containers).

6. In your /etc/sysctl.conf file, add the following at the end:

```
vm.max_map_count=1048575
sudo systemctl start docker.service
sudo systemctl enable docker.service
```

7. Start the Docker containers with sudo docker-compose up -d.

Open a browser on the IP or localhost over port 8080, for example, , and you'll be presented with the login screen to OpenCTI. If you're on a VM, use the public IP, http://<public_ip>:8080, and you'll see this:

Figure 12.19 – The login screen to OpenCTI, accessible with the URL we configured

Enter your username and password, and we've got our TAXII server set up. The OpenCTI platform is a full threat intelligence platform, so you're more than welcome to use it, but that is outside the scope of this chapter.

By setting up a TAXII server, we can now funnel our MISP collections to this server, where we can then extract IOCs to send to Sumo Logic.

There is a file that governs the entire setup of this OpenCTI Taxii server, which is in the same docker directory—the docker-compose.yml file. We need to add something to this file to complete the link in the chain between our MISP deployment and OpenCTI:

1. Execute the following:

```
sudo nano docker-compose.yml
```

(You can use vi if you want.)

2. Add this section to the bottom of the .yml file, indented in line with the other connectors:

```yaml
connector-misp:
    image: opencti/connector-misp:latest
    restart: unless-stopped
    depends_on: [opencti]
    environment:
        # OpenCTI (inside the compose network)
        OPENCTI_URL: http://opencti:8080
        OPENCTI_TOKEN: # real key string
        CONNECTOR_ID: "a0d8e9e6-5d75-4c2a-9f9f-1a2b3c4d5e6f" # any UUID
        CONNECTOR_TYPE: "EXTERNAL_IMPORT"
        CONNECTOR_NAME: "MISP (Prod)"
        CONNECTOR_SCOPE: "misp"
        CONNECTOR_LOG_LEVEL: "info"
        # MISP
        MISP_URL: https://<;your-misp-host>;/
        MISP_KEY: <;YOUR_MISP_API_KEY>;
        MISP_SSL_VERIFY: "true"          # or "false" if self-signed
        MISP_IMPORT_FROM_DATE: "2024-01-01"
        MISP_POLL_INTERVAL: "300"
        MISP_CREATE_REPORTS: "true"
        MISP_CREATE_INDICATORS: "true"
        MISP_CREATE_OBSERVABLES: "true"
        MISP_ADD_LABELS: "src:misp"
```

> **Tip**
>
> Your MISP API key is in **Profile** -> **Auth Keys**, where you can generate one.

When you log in to OpenCTI now, you'll see indicators and events populated in your instance, as shown here:

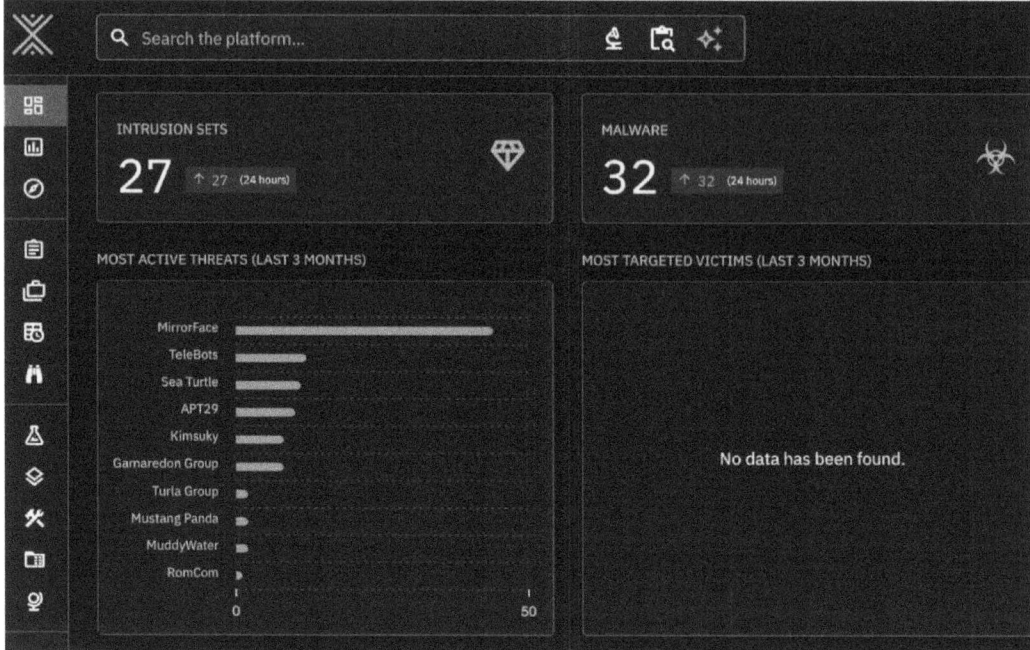

Figure 12.20 – The dashboard in OpenCTI, which contains threat intelligence that can be forwarded to Sumo Logic

Setting up the hosted collection

Let's head back to Sumo Logic and create a hosted collection, followed by the TAXII 2 client. When configuring it, use bearer authentication and enter your MISP API key, select **STIX/TAXII 2.1** in the TAXII configuration, and your discovery URL should be `https://<public_ip>/api/taxii2`.

Indicators should now be coming into Sumo Logic, where you can access them in the threat intelligence section of the platform and use the `hasThreatMatch` operator to create Cloud SIEM rules across your data sources.

Intelligence API

Sumo Logic also has a solid set of APIs when it comes to helping get your flashy IOCs into the platform. There are two different endpoints for ingestion. The first is `/v1/threatIntel/datastore/indicators/normalized`. This lets you ingest indicators in a Sumo normalized format that looks like this:

```
{
  - "indicators": [
    - {
        "id": "indicator--d81f86b9-975b-4c0b-875e-810c5ad45a4f",
        "indicator": "182.158.1.1",
        "type": "ipv4-addr",
        "source": "FreeTAXII",
        "updated": "2023-03-21T12:00:00.000Z",
        "validFrom": "2023-03-21T12:00:00.000Z",
        "validUntil": "2023-03-21T12:00:00.000Z",
        "confidence": 1,
        "threatType": "benign",
        "actors": "actor1,actor2",
        "killChain": "KC1,KC2",
      + "fields": { … }
      }
  ]
}
```

Figure 12.21 – Ingestion through normalized Sumo format

Alternatively, there is a STIX 2.x JSON format available as well: /v1/threatIntel/datastore/indicators/stix. This has a richer object structure to benefit from platforms such as MISP, as shown here:

```json
{
  "source": "FreeTAXII",
  "indicators": [
    {
      "type": "indicator",
      "spec_version": "2.1",
      "id": "acme:indicator-bf8bc5d5-c7e6-46b0-8d22-7500fea77196",
      "created": "2023-03-21T12:00:00.000Z",
      "modified": "2023-03-21T12:00:00.000Z",
      "created_by_ref": "identity--f431f809-377b-45e0-aa1c-6a4751cae5ff",
      "revoked": true,
      "labels": [ ... ],
      "confidence": 1,
      "lang": "en",
      "external_references": [ ... ],
      "object_marking_refs": [ ... ],
      "granular_markings": [ ... ],
      "extensions": { ... },
      "name": "string",
      "description": "string",
      "indicator_types": [ ... ],
      "pattern": "[ipv4-addr:value = '1.2.3.4']",
      "pattern_type": "stix",
      "pattern_version": "string",
      "valid_from": "2023-03-21T12:00:00.000Z",
      "valid_until": "2023-03-21T12:00:00.000Z",
      "kill_chain_phases": [ ... ]
    }
  ]
}
```

Figure 12.22 – Ingestion through STIX 2.x JSON format

These will also appear within your **Threat Intelligence** section of the platform.

Cloud SIEM rules

We've covered this before when looking at SIEM rules in *Chapter 9*, *Cloud SIEM*, but I thought I'd give a quick overview of how to interact with these threat intelligence feeds in Sumo Logic. Let's look at a brief example, where we want to check any IP address that we see that matches any record in our threat intelligence feeds:

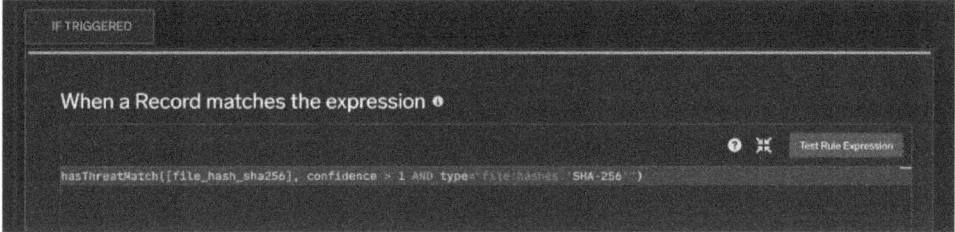

Figure 12.23 – How the hasThreatMatch operator is used in a Cloud SIEM rule expression

Nice and simple, and it lets you have complete coverage across all your data sources while overlaying your threat intelligence feeds.

Dashboards and dissemination

The final stage of the intelligence cycle is dissemination, which is the ability to get the hard-earned intel and share it with the right audience, whether it be another team or management.

You not only have the scope to centralize your threat intelligence in one place and have full visibility across the enrichment spectrum, but you can also disseminate this information in any way you like. The flexible language in the platform lets you create visualizations and reports that cater to the requirements of any team and for any objective. Here is a quick example of a consolidated **IAM and Network Threat Intelligence** dashboard:

Figure 12.24 – A dashboard showing multiple sources of data and threat intelligence combined

You can create roles for your users in the platform to help with managing who can see what data, but you can also just create links to dashboards for users that don't log in to the platform, as shown here:

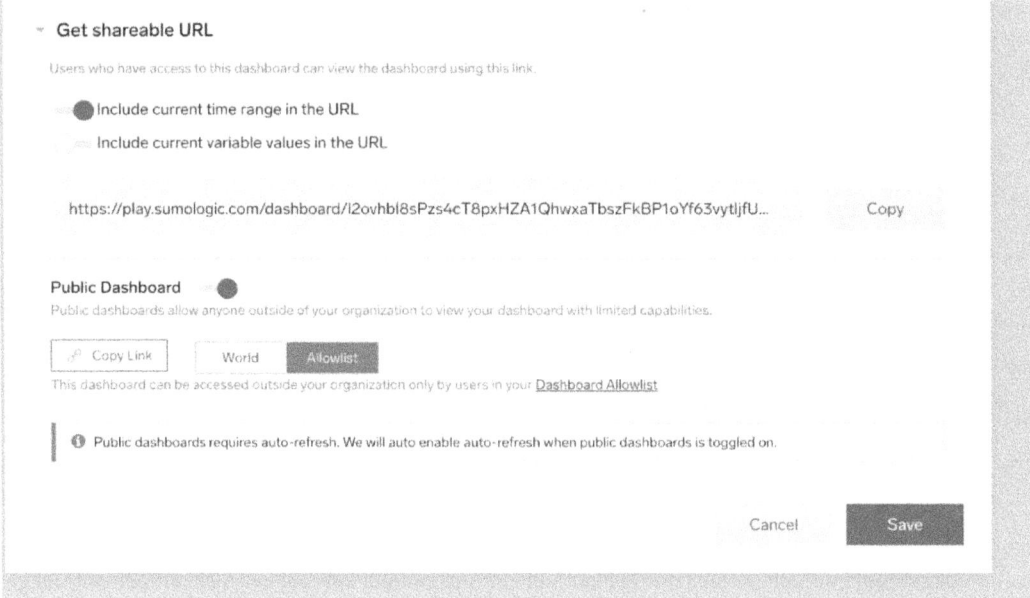

Figure 12.25 – Sharing dashboards lets you disseminate visual reports and views easily

This gives you flexibility and also control, because you can specify users in a dashboard allowlist. This means you can publicly expose a dashboard without worrying about someone viewing sensitive data, even if they have the link.

Whether the recipient is someone from the vulnerability management team or a CISO who wants to see how things are lining up after implementing additional controls and investing in security technologies, this is how you share that data.

With that, our journey into threat intelligence has come to an end, but we will revisit this important topic in the final chapter on the future of security intelligence, as there are many rapid developments that will impact the space and our ability as defenders to respond accordingly.

Summary

In this chapter, we focused on threat intelligence and the three different levels of intelligence: strategic, operational, and tactical. We discussed the different frameworks for intelligence analysis and how you can start using them within the context of Sumo Logic and the wider platform.

Finally, we walked you through how to place Sumo Logic at the heart of your business with a cross-team security intelligence program and ended with a guide on how to practically implement the theory that was covered in the first half of the chapter.

Let's head to our penultimate chapter, *Compliance and Reporting*, to see how Sumo Logic can help you to stay on top of compliance requirements.

References

1. https://detect-respond.blogspot.com/2013/03/the-pyramid-of-pain.html
2. https://www.cobaltstrike.com/
3. https://oodaloop.com/the-ooda-loop-explained-the-real-story-about-the-ultimate-model-for-decision-making-in-competitive-environments/
4. https://www.lockheedmartin.com/en-us/capabilities/cyber/cyber-kill-chain.html
5. Practical Cyber Intelligence, Wilson Bautista Jr., Packt Publishing
6. https://github.com/hslatman/awesome-threat-intelligence
7. https://www.misp-project.org/download/
8. https://www.misp-project.org/documentation/

Get this book's PDF version and more

Scan the QR code (or go to `packtpub.com/unlock`). Search for this book by name, confirm the edition, and then follow the steps on the page.

Note: Keep your invoice handy. Purchases made directly from Packt don't require an invoice.

13
Compliance and Reporting

Compliance. The word alone is enough to make security engineers roll their eyes and auditors get excited! To many, it feels like long queues of checkboxes, endless paperwork, and the gnawing suspicion that none of it really keeps attackers out. And yet, compliance is the part of security that executives lose sleep over, regulators demand, and customers quietly (or loudly) expect as proof that you're not winging it with their data.

The real trick, and the point of this chapter, is realizing that compliance doesn't have to be an afterthought or a once-a-year panic attack when the auditors show up. If you're already collecting logs, monitoring infrastructure, and alerting on threats, congratulations, you've already done 80% of the work. The challenge is turning that stream of raw data into structured evidence that proves you're in control. That's where Sumo Logic steps in, giving you a way to automate evidence gathering, monitor controls in real time, and feed compliance intelligence back into the rest of the business.

And here's the bit we don't talk about enough—compliance data is not just for auditors. Finance cares because fines and penalties cost money. Legal cares because contracts depend on it. Marketing cares because customers love to see shiny badges such as SOC 2 or ISO 27001. Security, of course, cares because half the "compliance violations" are just "things that attackers will exploit if we ignore them." In other words, compliance is a way to show every part of the business that risks are being managed and trust is being earned.

In the pages that follow, we'll explore how to use Sumo Logic to make compliance less about paperwork and more about automation by looking at the following sections:

- Using Sumo Logic for compliance management
- Generating reports and audit logs
- Ensuring regulatory compliance

Using Sumo Logic for compliance management

One of the great things about using a centralized data analytics platform like Sumo Logic is that you are most likely collecting data from all the important sources that auditors value—namely, authentication, network, IAM, cloud configuration, and many more.

By layering compliance requirements on top of your existing data, you're adding more purpose to that data, that is, protecting the organization and meeting compliance needs. Further, compliance is also tightly intertwined with security monitoring and threat detection.

Whether you're aligned to the PCI-DSS, NIST, or SOC 2 frameworks, as long as you have the logs coming into Sumo Logic, you're able to track and audit activity, as in these examples:

- Authentication logs can demonstrate control effectiveness for access restrictions
- CloudTrail events can prove that you are monitoring configuration changes
- Firewall and endpoint logs can show continuous monitoring of critical systems

On top of being able to have dual-purpose data, with Sumo Logic, there is the option to use some out-of-the-box content in the form of dashboards and queries that can help with setting up relevant views of your data.

Holding yourself and vendors accountable

Are *you* compliant, or is the *vendor* compliant? Trick question: ideally both, but in different ways. A vendor's attestations (think SOC 2 Type II, HIPAA-readiness/**Business Associate Agreement** (**BAA**), GDPR processor commitments, FedRAMP Moderate, etc.) prove that their house is in order. That's necessary for your compliance story, but it doesn't magically confer compliance on your environment.

For example, PCI-DSS requires you to vet and manage service providers. *Requirement 12.8/12.9* says you must contractually ensure that providers protect cardholder data and acknowledge their responsibilities. Using a PCI-compliant tool doesn't satisfy your *12.8* obligations; you still need the contracts, oversight, and evidence trail.

For HIPAA, a BAA with a vendor handling **electronic Protected Health Information** (**ePHI**) is mandatory. The vendor's safeguards matter, but you still need your own policies, minimum necessary access, and monitoring. Similarly, as per GDPR *Article 28*, as the controller, you must have processor contracts with specific clauses and ongoing oversight. The processor's certification helps, but you remain accountable.

Further, if you hold U.S. federal data, services generally must be FedRAMP-authorized. Sumo Logic offers a FedRAMP Moderate authorized environment, but you still have to implement your side of the controls and continuous monitoring.

>
>
> **Vendor attestations you can point to (but not hide behind)**
>
> Sumo Logic publishes its certifications/attestations (e.g., SOC 2 Type II) via its Trust Center and platform security pages[1]. These are great inputs to third-party risk management and your auditors' questionnaires; they're not a substitute for your own control design and operation, however.

'Show me' culture: turning promises into proof

Compliance conversations rarely fail because policies are missing. They usually fail because when someone finally asks, "*Show me*," there's nothing concrete to point to. Auditors don't want reassurance. They want *evidence*. Your SIEM system should be the system of record that produces it.

In practice, a *show me* culture means being able to demonstrate, on demand, that controls are not only defined, but operating, monitored, and reviewable. In Sumo Logic, that shows up in a few very specific ways.

First, you must be able to prove that sensitive activity is being monitored. Authentication events, administrative actions, configuration changes, and content modifications should all be observable through the audit index and audit event index. These indexes cover user actions, API calls, and scheduled job changes. When an auditor asks, "*Are you monitoring logins?*", the answer shouldn't be verbal. It should be a search or dashboard that shows exactly how, and how often, those events are reviewed.

Second, detection without response doesn't count. Alerting and escalation need to be visible and auditable. Monitors provide real-time detection, while scheduled searches act as recurring control checks and evidence snapshots. When someone asks, "*Do you alert on unusual activity?*", the proof is the monitor definition, its triggering conditions, and its incident history, not a policy document that says you intended to do so.

Retention is where a lot of compliance quietly falls apart. Auditors will ask how long evidence is retained and how quickly it can be retrieved. Frameworks such as PCI DSS 10.7 are explicit: at least one year of audit trail history, with three months immediately available for analysis. Your Sumo Logic retention settings and partition strategy must reflect those requirements and, crucially, you must be able to demonstrate that they do. Retention is not just a storage decision; it's part of the control itself. Fortunately, in Sumo Logic, you set any retention period that you need in the **Partitions** section of the platform. We covered this earlier in the book, but as a refresher, head to **Data Management** > **Logs** > **Partitions**, and you'll see the **Retention Period** column, as shown here:

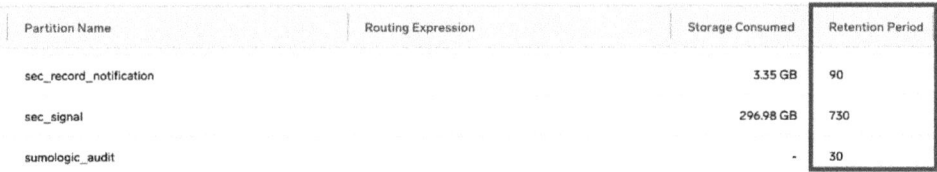

Figure 13.1 – These retention periods can be set to any time up to 13 years

Finally, evidence only works if the right people can see it. One of Sumo Logic's strengths is how easily read-only access can be shared. Dashboards can be exposed directly to control owners, risk teams, and auditors, allowing them to review evidence without waiting for exports or screenshots. With plan-dependent unlimited user licensing, broad visibility is practical, while RBAC ensures that least privilege is enforced. Auditors get transparency; you keep control.

We covered sharing dashboards in the previous chapter, where we looked at disseminating intelligence in this way. At the end of the day, the goal is simple; when someone asks, "*Show me,*" you give them a link instead of scheduling a meeting.

Practical accountability checklist

Here's a practical accountability checklist for you, which you can copy/paste into your runbook:

- **For vendors (prove they are compliant)**:
    - Current SOC 2 Type II report and bridge letter; list of in-scope controls[2]
    - HIPAA BAA (if handling ePHI); confirm breach notification timelines[3]

- GDPR Article 28 DPA with sub-processor transparency[4]
- FedRAMP authorization (if applicable), service boundary, and POA&M status[5]

- **For you (prove you are compliant)**:
  - **Monitoring**: Monitors and scheduled searches mapped to control statements (e.g., privileged access, change management, and malware detections)[6]
  - **Evidence**: Dashboards showing control coverage, exceptions, and MTTR/MTTD; scheduled exports or saved results to index/lookup[7]
  - **Auditability**: Searches and panels over the audit index/audit event index proving SIEM admin activity is tracked (who changed what, when)[8]
  - **Retention**: Documented settings that meet frameworks such as PCI 10.7; prove hot versus cold availability windows[9]
  - **Access control**: RBAC roles for auditors (read-only), control owners (edit-limited), and admins (least necessary)[9]

If any of these can't be demonstrated live, they're not controls—they're aspirations. We opened this chapter by jumping straight into ensuring your compliance posture is rock solid, referencing the relevant areas of Sumo Logic to start putting this into practice.

Next, let's look at how we can use all the telemetry that lives inside your Sumo Logic instance to create compliance reports any time you need.

Generating reports and audit logs

Trust but verify is what we are aiming for. Audits and compliance checks ultimately require evidence that your controls are working in practice, while reports and audit logs are the concrete evidence you need to prove that your monitoring, alerting, and data retention practices are functioning as expected.

You can use vendor attestations to clear the third-party risk bar and then use Sumo Logic to prove that *your* controls work, that your alerts are defined, dashboards are alive, audit trails are intact, and retention is aligned to the regulations you should abide by. For effective reporting and audit, you can borrow broadly from general SIEM best practices (prioritize use cases; centralize logging; protect data; and lean on analytics) while operationalizing them in Sumo with rules, monitors, scheduled searches, dashboards, and audit indexes. So, how do we actually do this? This section walks you through how to generate and use reports and audit logs in Sumo Logic.

Step 1: Don't reinvent the wheel, raid the App Catalog

Start with the App Catalog and install the content that already does 80% of the job. It's designed to drop in prebuilt dashboards and saved searches you can tune for your environment[10]. For example, here are some compliance-friendly apps to grab right away:

- **PCI Compliance for Linux** (and **Linux – OpenTelemetry** flavor): Dashboards for logins, privileged activity; covers PCI requirements such as 02, 07, 08, and 10
- **PCI Compliance for Windows JSON** (and **Windows JSON – OpenTelemetry**): Windows security/system events wired for PCI evidence
- **PCI for AWS CloudTrail**: Maps CloudTrail activity to PCI-relevant views (02/07/08/10)
- **CIS AWS Foundations Benchmark**: Opinionated dashboards aligned to CIS controls, great for posture & audit reviews
- **AWS Security Hub (CSPM/OCSF)**: Centralizes findings (policy/compliance violations) across AWS services
- **Azure Audit/Entra ID/graph reporting**: Sign-ins, role changes, directory activity—classic audit evidence
- **Sumo Logic Audit app** + **audit indexes** + **search audit index**: Prove who changed what in Sumo, which queries ran, and when (yes, auditors love this)
- **Tenable** and **Automox**: Vulnerability and patch compliance views, which round out your "security posture" reporting
- **ChatGPT compliance**: One of a growing library of LLM-focused auditing content

> **Note**
>
> Quick win: these install into your library with ready-to-use dashboards and example searches. You get instant evidence with your data.

The following screenshot shows the **App Catalog** screen with the **Compliance and Security** filter selected. You'll find lots of other great apps that cover more technologies in addition to the ones listed previously as starting points:

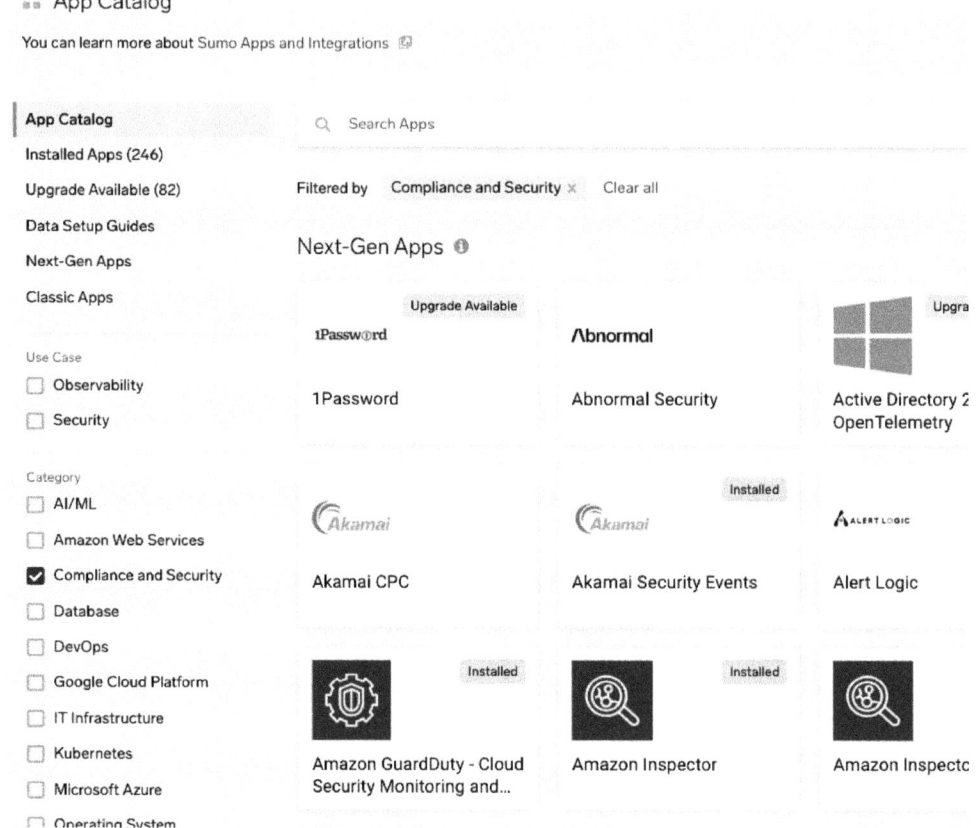

Figure 13.2 – The Compliance and Security section in the App Catalog

Let's run through a quick example to set up some compliance dashboards for Microsoft 365.

Deploying a hosted collector

Go to **Data Management** > **Collection** > **Add Collector**, and select **Hosted Collector**:

Figure 13.3 – Deploying a hosted collector to set up a cloud-to-cloud connection

Adding a Microsoft Office 365 source

On your hosted collector, click on **Add Source**:

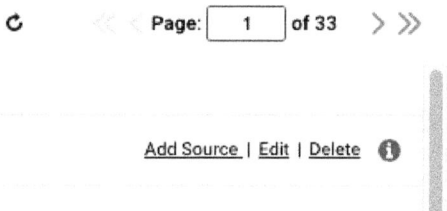

Figure 13.4 –Add Source is located in the collection page (right side of the screen)

Then, select **Office 365 Audit** from the list of integrations:

Figure 13.5 – The Office 365 Audit integration, ready for deployment

In the configuration, select each content type (in this example, Azure AD), and sign in to Office 365 via SSO:

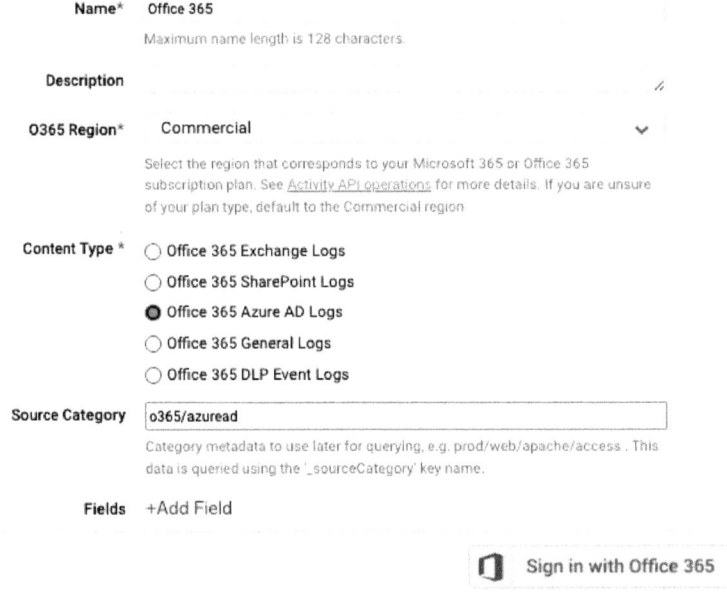

Figure 13.6 – Choosing the Azure AD content type to collect the Azure AD logs

Repeat the same process for the other sources.

Checking that logs are coming in

Next, we go to our collector, hover over the Azure AD source, and click on the blue document icon:

Figure 13.7 – Quickly accessing the logs landing in Sumo Logic

And they're in! You'll see your logs from Azure AD:

Figure 13.8 – We can see our logs in the Log Query screen

Installing the app

Finally, we head to the App Catalog, search for `Office 365`, and install the app by pointing it at our source. This is usually done by specifying the source category or the collector name. For this particular app, specify the collector name as the app incorporates multiple content types within Office 365. Then, we can go to our content and see a compliance dashboard that has evidence of us monitoring login activity on Azure AD, as shown here:

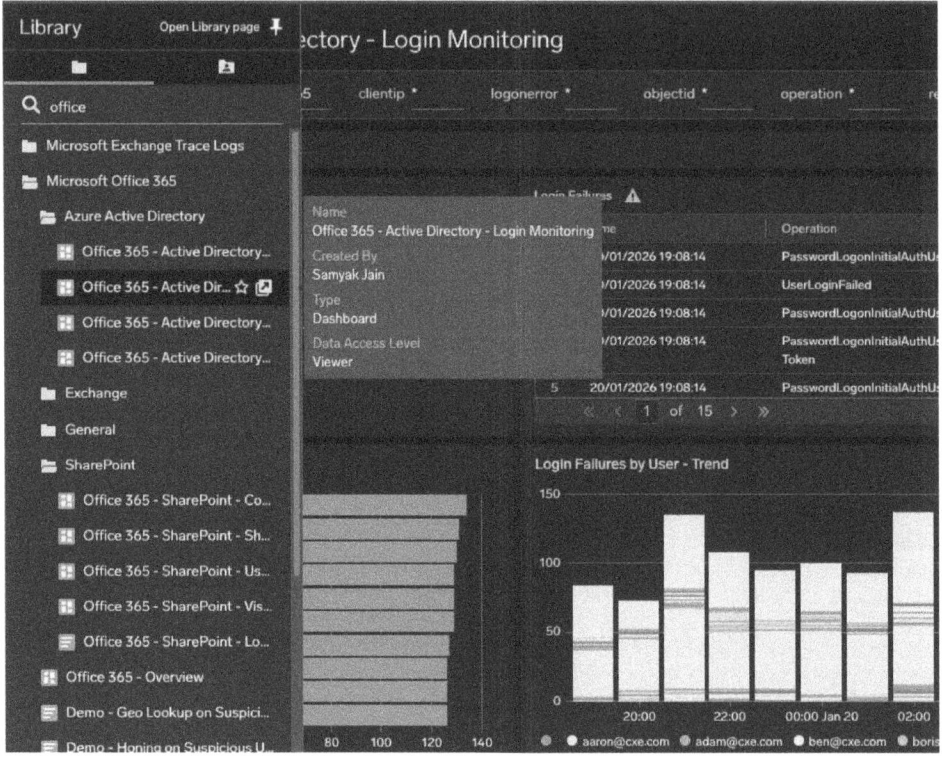

Figure 13.9 – The app contains a lot of content, including lots of auditor-ready views

This four-step process we just covered is how you can get ready for your compliance audits very quickly! The following flowchart visualizes the process:

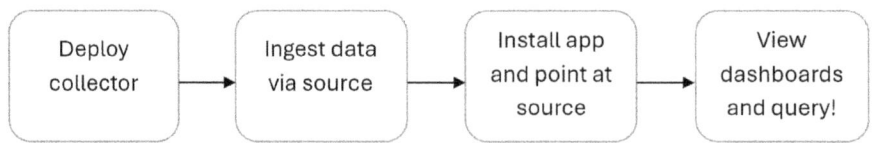

Figure 13.10 – The flow of getting started with the out-of-the-box content as quickly as possible

Step 2: Build auditor-ready master dashboards (by mixing panels)

The catalog is vendor-centric, so the evidence you need is often spread across multiple apps (Windows, Linux, Okta, Azure AD, CloudTrail, etc.). That's fine, as panels are just queries. Copy the panels you need (e.g., "successful/failed logins," "admin role assignments," "privileged actions") into a single **Enterprise Login & Authentication** dashboard. Now, you've got one URL that answers, "Are we logging *all* authentication activity across the estate?", with time ranges, filters, and drilldowns (bonus: it's live data, not a stale export).

Share it with view-only access and set the data access level so viewers only see data allowed by their role search filter. That keeps least privilege intact while still giving auditors and control owners direct visibility[11].

Here's how we do that. Let's take a panel from the **Linux – Security Analytics – Login Activity** dashboard, which shows all failed and successful logins across our Linux estate, as follows:

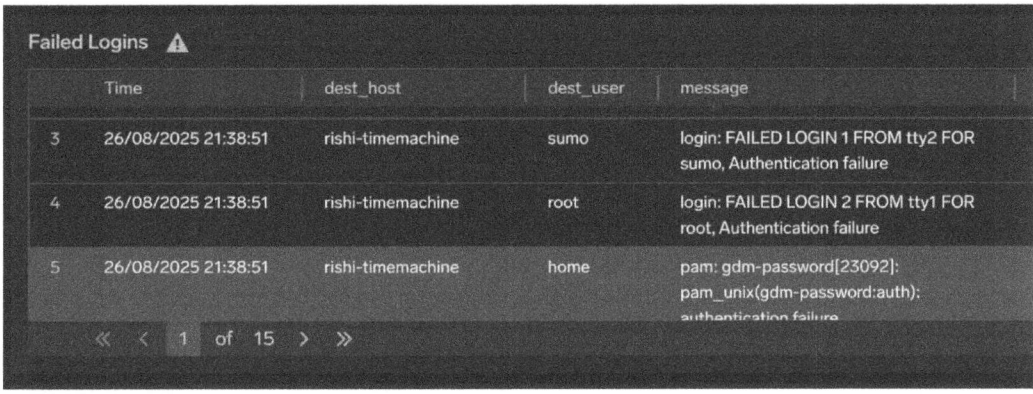

Figure 13.11 – Login activity dashboard panel

In order to save this to another dashboard, we can open this panel in a new log search, run the aggregation, and then add it to a dashboard of our choosing:

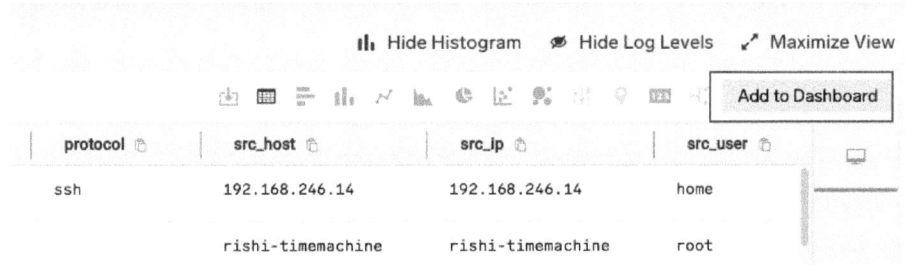

Figure 13.12 – Adding the panel to any other dashboard you want it in

Next, we take a panel about account creation on our Linux systems from the **User, Service and System Monitoring** dashboard. This panel shows us all the new users created on our Linux machines:

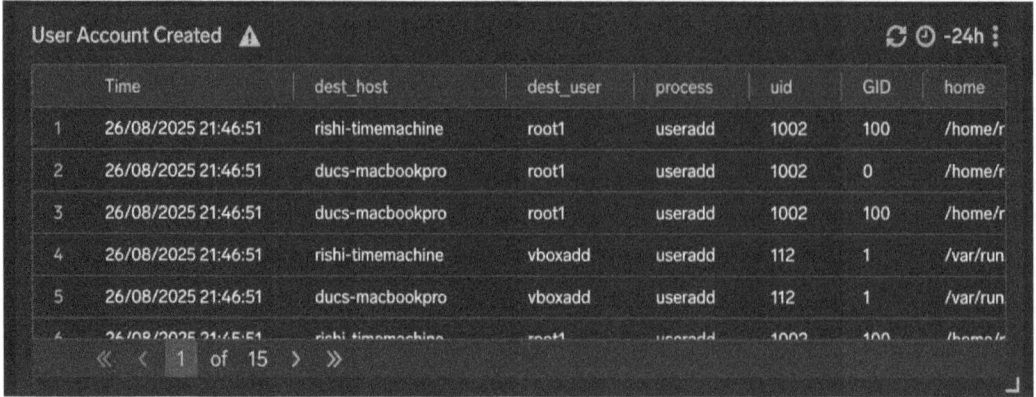

Figure 13.13 – Panel showing account creation on our Linux systems

We follow the same process as in *Figure 13.10*, and now we have a consolidated dashboard showing us a view of enterprise login, authentication, and account creation, as shown here:

Figure 13.14 – The beginning of a super compliance dashboard

Once we have our dashboard, it's easy for us to share it with those internal stakeholders who need access to it. In the following example, we're sharing it with our IT team and giving them access to look at the dashboard, but not change anything inside:

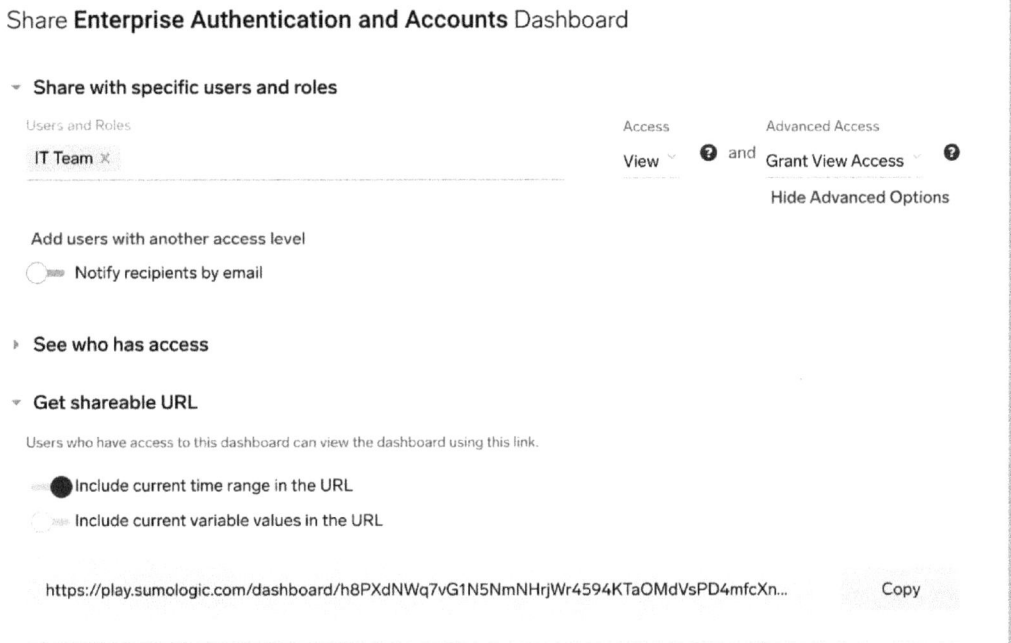

Figure 13.15 – Sharing our dashboard while being able to control access

If an auditor comes round for a check, you can either create a role for the auditor and provide login details or just share a link to the dashboards that will be used in line with compliance criteria by using the **Get shareable URL** section shown in *Figure 13.15*.

Step 3: If required, schedule the evidence so proof shows up on time

Live links beat PDF fossils, so share dashboards whenever you can. If your organization still loves attachments (or you need time-boxed evidence), here are the three workhorses for creating compliance reports with the powerful querying capabilities in Sumo Logic, and when to use each:

- **Scheduled searches**: Run compliance queries on a cadence, then (a) email results, (b) send them to a webhook (ServiceNow/Jira/etc.), or (c) save to **Lookup** to build a durable evidence table you can reuse in dashboards. Think of monthly "privileged changes" attestation or a weekly "accounts without MFA" snapshot.

  > **Tip**
  >
  > **Pro tip**: Use **monitors** for real-time alerting and **scheduled searches** for periodic attestations. When an attestation evolves into an operational alert, migrate it to a monitor for richer notifications, auto-resolution, and multi-channel routing.

Here's an example of a scheduled search on our Linux login data. After having run our query, we go to the top-right corner and click on the floppy disk to save the query. At the bottom left of the pop-up box is a **Schedule this search** option, as shown here:

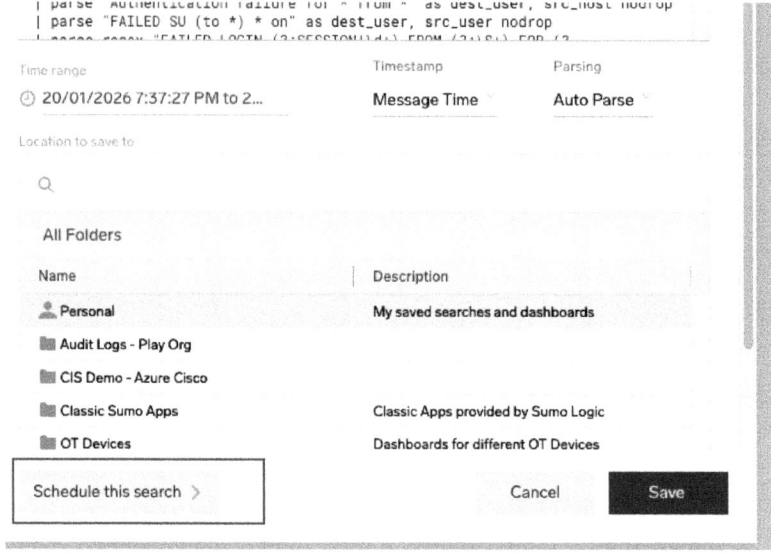

Figure 13.16 – The scheduled search option is available when you try to save a query

In the scheduling configuration, you can choose the frequency and the method (emailing results, saving to a lookup table, etc.), and it lets you then take additional actions. For example, if we select **Webhook**, as in *Figure 13.17*, we're prompted to select a connection (we covered this in *Chapter 7*), and we can choose to customize the payload that gets sent to Microsoft Teams:

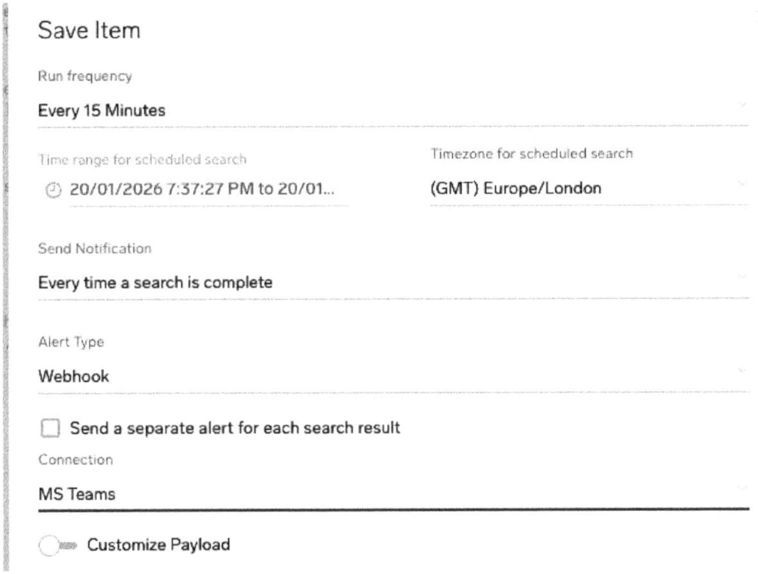

Figure 13.17 – One of the ways to send a scheduled search payload is via Webhook

- **Scheduled reports (dashboards)**: Email a PDF/PNG of a dashboard to auditors or stakeholders daily/weekly/monthly. This is great for *control-health* decks when you need a point-in-time artifact that mirrors what the live dashboard shows.

When we are looking at any dashboard, we can create a scheduled report from it by going to the top-right corner and selecting **Scheduled Reports**. A pane opens up on the right, as shown here, where you can configure how often you want the PDF or PNG report to be sent to one or a group of recipients:

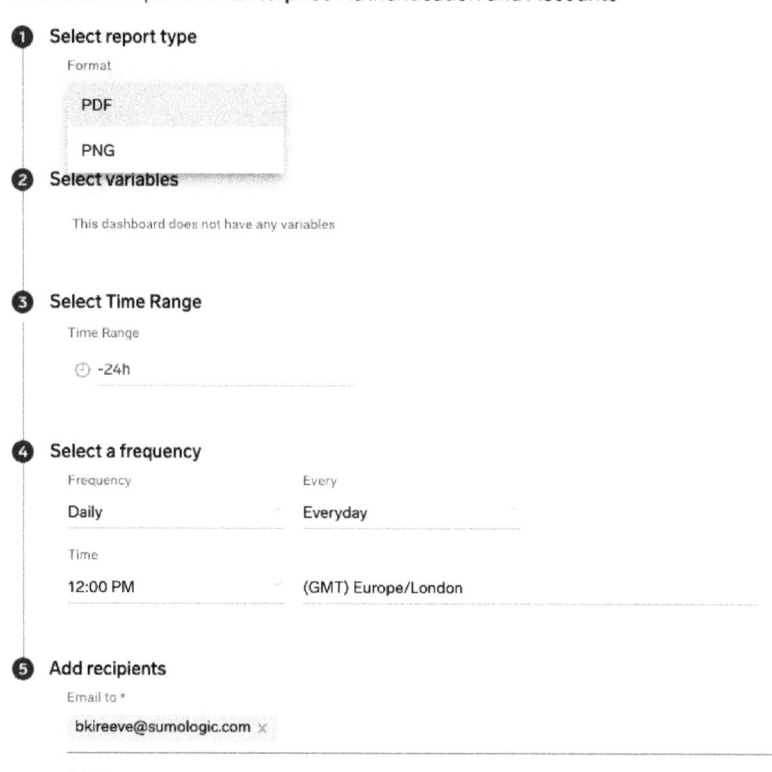

Figure 13.18 – Scheduling a report based on a dashboard view

- **Scheduled views**: This is the under-the-radar speed hack. Define a query that extracts only the compliance-critical fields (e.g., auth outcomes, actor, IP, and device), and Sumo will pre-aggregate that into a compact side index. Your evidence dashboards then load fast, even over long ranges, because they're querying a **precomputed** slice instead of your entire corpus. This is perfect for authentication evidence, admin changes, or data access exceptions (runs continuously and can be managed like any other object). It's worth pointing out that the main benefit is that you can run historical searches over very long timeframes, such as over a year or a few years, very quickly.

To create a scheduled view, go to **Data Management** > **Logs** > **Scheduled Views**. In the top-right corner, click on **+ Add Scheduled View**, and you will find this:

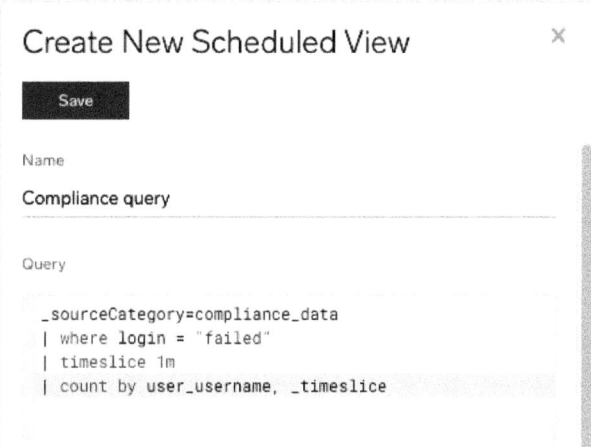

Figure 13.19 – You can create pre-aggregated views over incredibly long periods of time with great performance with scheduled views

> **Note**
>
> Want more information on scheduled views?
>
> Head to https://www.sumologic.com/help/docs/manage/scheduled-views/.

Which one to use, though? Do you need a point-in-time PDF/PNG for auditors? Use a scheduled report. Need a recurring evidence table that your dashboards can query (e.g., all critical exceptions this month)? Use scheduled search and **Save to Lookup** (or the save operator in your query). Need speed at scale for compliance dashboards over long time windows? Use a scheduled view.

> **Tip**
>
> Keep it simple. Link to live dashboards by default, and schedule artifacts only when a control, process, or auditor explicitly needs them. Your inbox and your coffee breaks will thank you!

Step 4: Log the logger to prove SIEM governance

Auditors will ask, "*Who can change alerts?*" and "*Who edited that query?*". You can answer with Sumo Logic's own **audit index** and **audit event index** (UI/API actions, scheduled job changes, and content edits), plus the **search audit index** (who ran which query). Install the **Enterprise Audit/Enterprise Search Audit** apps to visualize this quickly:

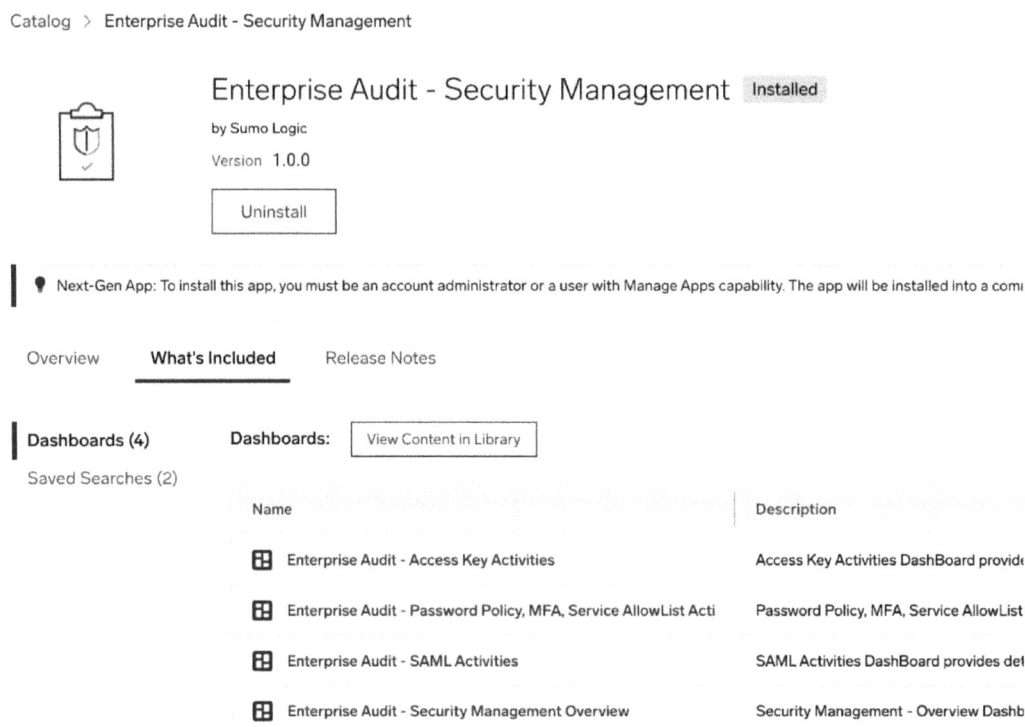

Figure 13.20 – The Enterprise Audit apps are great to see what's happening in the inner workings of the platform

You can also wire webhook notifications to ticketing (e.g., ServiceNow) so evidence chains include *when* exceptions were opened and *how* they were resolved. This can be achieved either with the automation service, which we covered in *Chapter 11, The Automation Service and Playbooks*, or with the help of connectors, which are used in monitors. These were discussed in *Chapter 8, Alerting, Monitoring, and Visualizing Data*.

> **Note**
>
> If you want a quick refresher on connectors and monitors, visit the following link: https://www.sumologic.com/help/docs/alerts/webhook-connections/set-up-webhook-connections/.

Step 5: Align retention with the rules you're under

Retention is a critical part of remaining compliant with your compliance standards, and in Sumo Logic, this is reflected in both the pricing model and the flexibility to let you choose how long you want that data stored for.

When it comes to PCI-DSS, for example, which expects one year of audit trail history with at least three months immediately available, you should configure retention and tiering accordingly; document it right on the dashboard that tracks your compliance tasks (your policy will thank you later). Unfortunately, this has to be done right from the beginning and may affect the cost of your Sumo Logic solution. If you find the indexes or partitions don't retain data long enough, either get approvals to increase the retention or find the data you need via a query and just capture it to a separate side index with a scheduled view (shhh... you didn't hear that from me).

Step 6: Share broadly, safely

Use RBAC to create Auditor, Control Owner, and Responder roles; share dashboards and folders to those roles (rather than to individuals) and let dashboards run with the viewer's access level, unless you have a specific reason otherwise. You can also expose view-only dashboards via allowlisted IPs for temporary external reviews.

To get a role like this spun up, head to **Administration** > **Roles** and click **+ Add Role** in the top-right corner. This will allow you to create a new role, as shown here:

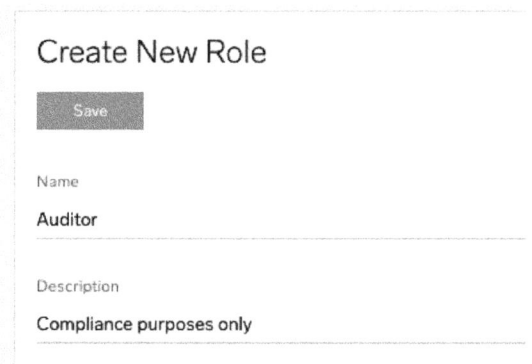

Figure 13.21 – Creating an Auditor role

You can choose to allow or deny indexes. For this example, we are limiting the **Auditor** role to certain indexes—**sumologic_audit_events** in this case:

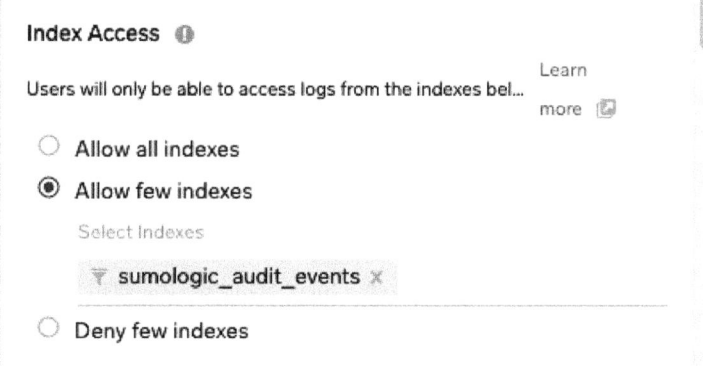

Figure 13.22 – Choosing Index Access

Below **Index Access**, you can choose **Capabilities**, or frontend permissions that the role can do in the UI. Viewing apps, installing apps, and accessing the collector page are all permissions you can permit or deny.

Ensuring regulatory (continuous) compliance

Continuous compliance exists for one simple reason: the cost of discovering gaps after the fact is always higher than the cost of proving coverage as you go.

Most organizations that fail compliance audits do not deliberately ignore the rules. They fail because they assumed evidence would be there when they needed it and only discovered it wasn't when regulators, auditors, or lawyers asked uncomfortable questions. At that point, intent no longer matters, only proof does.

This shift has become painfully clear over the last few years. In incidents involving companies such as Okta and T-Mobile, scrutiny didn't stop at *whether* controls existed. It focused on whether those controls were operating *continuously*, whether anomalies were detected in time, and whether the organization could demonstrate that it understood its own environment when challenged. Inconsistent or incomplete evidence both slowed investigations and eroded trust.

> The real purpose of continuous compliance is to reduce ambiguity under pressure.

When compliance is treated as an annual exercise, evidence tends to be reconstructed after the fact. Logs are queried retroactively, gaps are explained away, and timelines are pieced together manually. This is where organizations lose control of the narrative. In the aftermath of the MOVEit exploitation in 2023, many affected organizations weren't penalized because they used vulnerable software. Instead, they were penalized because they could not confidently answer basic questions such as *what data was accessed*, *when*, and *by whom*. The problem was not the exploit. It was the absence of durable, reviewable evidence.

Continuous compliance flips that dynamic. Controls are tested constantly, not just described. Evidence accumulates naturally as a byproduct of normal operations. When something goes wrong, and eventually something will, you are no longer guessing. You are confirming.

There is also a growing personal dimension to this. Regulators are increasingly willing to challenge security leadership directly when public assurances do not align with internal reality. Recent actions by the U.S. Securities and Exchange Commission signal a clear direction of travel: *claims about security posture must be defensible with evidence*. Dashboards, audit trails, and change history are no longer internal hygiene tools but personal liability buffers.

Retention plays a quiet but decisive role here. Many compliance failures surface months after an incident occurs, not days. If evidence has already aged out by the time questions are asked, the organization is forced into speculation. That speculation is rarely generous. If you cannot retrieve historical activity quickly and confidently, you cannot prove control effectiveness, no matter how well-designed those controls appear on paper.

We also have metrics that close the loop. Without visibility into coverage, exceptions, and response times, compliance degrades silently. Repeated failures at the same control point, which was something regulators highlighted in cases such as T-Mobile, signal not just technical weakness, but also organizational blindness.

Tracking control health over time is what distinguishes a program that is improving from one that is merely repeating itself. Remember SLOs? Use them!

Finally, access matters because credibility matters. Auditors increasingly expect transparency so when evidence is hidden behind manual exports or gatekeepers, confidence drops. When it is visible, scoped, and reproducible through role-based access, reviews move faster, and trust improves. Least privilege is not just a security principle here but is directly tied to how believable your story is under scrutiny.

Summary

In this chapter, we covered how Sumo Logic is perfectly positioned for streamlining compliance automation, audit preparation, and continuous monitoring. With the help of out-of-the-box content and the versatility of the query language, it's possible to create views that will help you stay on top of compliance and meet every audit with ease.

We covered how to hold yourself and your vendors accountable with a brief view into what to focus on and how. We looked at how to generate reports from your telemetry in the platform with a step-by-step guide, which you can start doing today! We also explored why continuous compliance is key in today's business environment and what mis-stepping looks like.

You now have a step-by-step process ready to use in order to bring this to life (creating auditor-ready dashboards, logging the logger, and helping with continuous compliance), and you can sleep easier at night!

In the final chapter, we'll cover what we think the future has in store for security intelligence. Modern technology has never evolved and adapted as quickly as it is now, and this brings about fresh challenges to security teams, including keeping track of all these changes! Join us in *Chapter 14* to cover ways for you and your team to face the future unknowns.

References

1. trust.sumologic.com
2. https://www.hhs.gov/hipaa/for-professionals/covered-entities/sample-business-associate-agreement-provisions/index.html
3. https://gdpr-info.eu/art-28-gdpr/
4. https://help.sumologic.com/docs/manage/manage-subscription/fedramp-capabilities/
5. https://help.sumologic.com/docs/alerts/monitors/
6. https://help.sumologic.com/docs/dashboards/
7. https://help.sumologic.com/docs/manage/security/audit-indexes/audit-index/
8. https://kirkpatrickprice.com/video/pci-requirement-10-7-retain-audit-trail-history-least-one-year-minimum-three-months-immediately-available/
9. https://help.sumologic.com/docs/manage/users-roles/roles/role-based-access-control/

10. https://help.sumologic.com/docs/integrations/
11. https://help.sumologic.com/docs/dashboards/share-dashboard-new/

Get this book's PDF version and more

Scan the QR code (or go to `packtpub.com/unlock`). Search for this book by name, confirm the edition, and then follow the steps on the page.

Note: Keep your invoice handy. Purchases made directly from Packt don't require an invoice.

14

The Future of Security Intelligence

Should this chapter be called *The Future of Intelligent Security*? Regardless, the future is exciting, unnerving, and, let's be honest, impossible to predict with certainty. The pace of technological change in just the past three years has been staggering, giving us glimpses of a future with extraordinary potential. But as always, every breakthrough comes with its own shadow: for every innovation that improves lives, someone finds a way to twist it into an exploit.

Nowhere is this more obvious than with **large language models** (**LLMs**), generative and agentic AI, and the infrastructure supporting them. The growth of these technologies has been nothing short of breathtaking. One thing is beyond debate: security professionals will be more crucial than ever in defending environments against an onslaught of rapidly evolving threats and attack techniques.

Defenders no longer face lone hackers with scripts; they're up against adversaries equipped with machine learning, AI-driven automation, and cheap, scalable tooling. Look at the evolution of deepfake and phishing attacks. Attackers are attacking and learning what works much quicker than before and iterating through the OODA loop (as covered in *Chapter 12, Bringing a Security Intelligence Program to Life with Sumo Logic*) dangerously fast to increase the sophistication and impact of their attacks. To stand a chance, defenders must meet fire with fire, adopting the same classes of tools, building new approaches, and weaving AI into their defenses.

This chapter explores what's happened in recent years, and more importantly, where things may be heading. We'll look at how emerging technologies are reshaping the threat landscape, and how you, as a security professional, can make sense of it, prepare for it, and maybe even get ahead of it.

This chapter will cover the following topics:

- The future of intelligent security
- The evolving role of AI in security
- Preparing for what comes next

The future of intelligent security

If the previous chapters of this book focused on *how* security intelligence is built, this chapter is about what happens when that foundation is put under pressure. The future of security is not defined by a single breakthrough technology or a new category of attack. It is defined by **acceleration**. Infrastructure spins up and down in seconds. Software ships continuously. Identities act autonomously. AI compresses tasks that once took hours into moments. Attackers are no longer limited by human speed, and defenders cannot afford to be either.

Throughout this book, we've established a core principle: intelligence does not start with data sources, tools, or vendors. It starts with questions. What matters? What is exposed? What behavior is risky in this environment? By *Chapter 12*, we had explored how telemetry, normalization, risk-based detection, and cross-team collaboration turn raw data into insight. That foundation is assumed here.

The question this chapter asks is different: What happens when everything accelerates at once?

Attackers are increasingly automated, AI-assisted, and opportunistic. They scan, test, adapt, and retry at machine speed. At the same time, defenders are drowning in telemetry, alerts, tools, and obligations. The problem is no longer simply a lack of data; it is the lack of clarity under pressure.

This shift changes the nature of defense. Security programs are no longer judged by how much they collect, but by how quickly they can reduce ambiguity. The value of intelligence is measured not in indicators ingested or alerts fired, but in decisions made with confidence.

AI further accelerates this shift. It shortens the time between signal and action for both attackers and defenders. Used well, it reduces cognitive load, exposes weak signals, and helps humans reason across complexity. Used poorly, it amplifies noise, obscures accountability, and automates mistakes at scale.

This is why it's no longer sufficient to talk about security intelligence as a collection of feeds, alerts, or dashboards. The future belongs to **intelligent security**: systems, processes, and teams that can take incomplete information, correlate it across domains, and arrive at defensible decisions faster than adversaries can exploit uncertainty.

Systems should be able to explain themselves. As environments become more autonomous, driven by pipelines, agents, APIs, and models, the ability to reconstruct *why* something happened becomes as important as detecting *that* it happened. Decisions become events. Events become evidence. And evidence must be preserved, correlated, and understood.

Now, the challenge for defenders is to build security programs that remain effective when humans are no longer in the critical path for every action.

The intelligent SOC

The term *intelligent SOC* is frequently used in marketing to describe faster alerts, more automation, or AI-powered dashboards. Stripped of the hype, however, the concept has real meaning and not as a new operating model, but as an evolution of purpose.

A traditional SOC is optimized for event handling, while an intelligent SOC is optimized for decision quality under pressure. This distinction matters and ties into the conversation in this chapter perfectly.

As environments grow more automated, security teams are no longer reacting to discrete incidents. They are navigating continuous activity streams generated by users, services, pipelines, APIs, and AI-driven systems. The limiting factor is not detection capability, but the ability to determine which signals matter, why they matter, and what to do next, quickly and confidently. These were the key concepts we covered in *Chapters 9* and *10*, which included the Cloud SIEM, the data pipelines, and the insight engine.

An intelligent SOC does not attempt to investigate everything. It accepts that perfect visibility is impossible and instead focuses on reducing uncertainty faster than adversaries can exploit it by ensuring that they have data coverage from across the key areas of their environment, no matter the source. A good way of illustrating this is referring to the **defender's dilemma**: the notion that there are always more attackers than defenders, and the attackers only need one entry point. This is illustrated here:

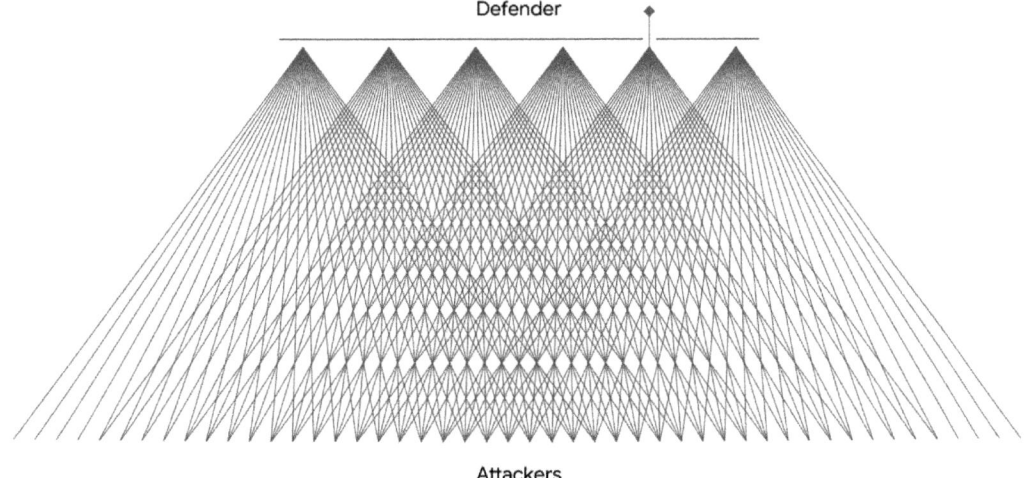

Figure 14.1 – The defender's dilemma (Google)[1]

The intelligent SOC model tries to create an environment where each defender is armed with multiple layers of defense. This isn't an old concept, as everyone who has spent time in cybersecurity knows of the **security onion** approach, which is basically defense in depth, a way of layering defensive tools to cover as much ground as possible. What needs to change is the *approach* to this old concept so that defenders can navigate the layers of their defensive tools as quickly and as easily as possible, tying together context to help drive decisions. This is illustrated here:

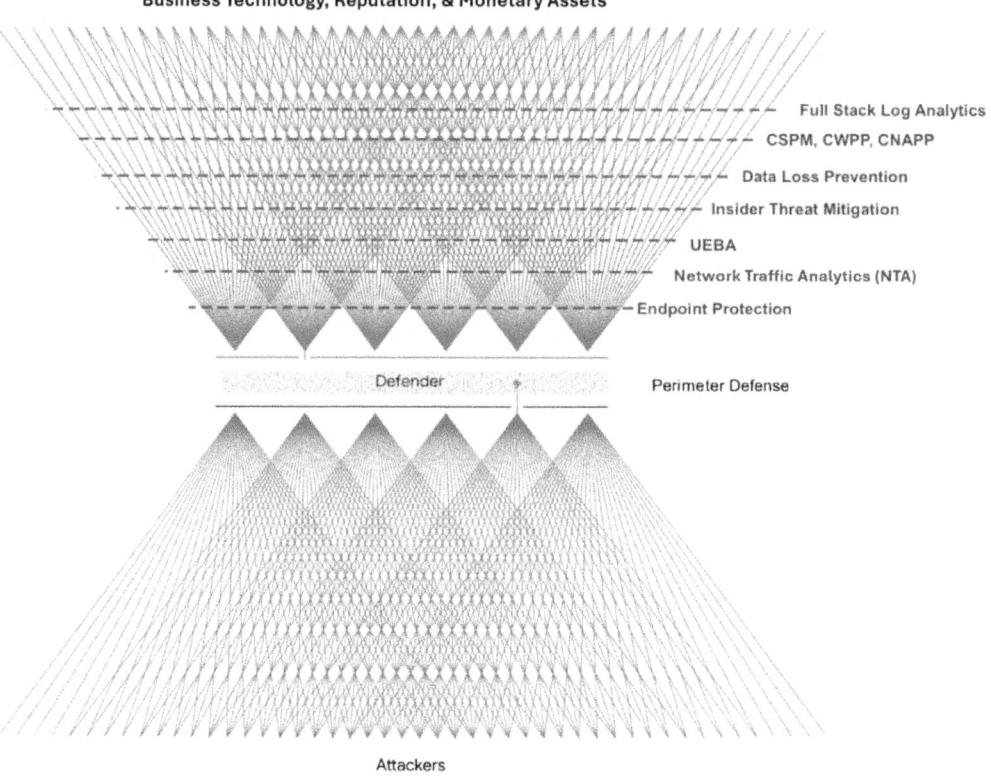

Figure 14.2 – The defender's ability to access context at scale across these layers is key to defence

Think about the OODA loop in *Chapter 12*. The quicker a defender can run through the four phases of *Observe, Orient, Decide,* and *Act*, the more likely they are to protect their environments.

What actually makes an SOC intelligent

Intelligence in this context does not come from AI alone. It emerges from how people, processes, and systems are aligned around a few core principles:

- **Entity-first thinking**: Investigations center on users, service accounts, workloads, and agents, not isolated alerts. Understanding how behavior evolves over time matters more than catching single events.
- **Correlation over collection**: Intelligence is derived from connecting signals across identity, cloud, application, and network domains, not from ingesting ever more data for the sake of it.
- **Explainability as a requirement**: Decisions, whether human or automated, must be traceable. The SOC must be able to explain why an alert was raised, why an action was taken, or why something was missed.
- **AI as an accelerator, not an authority**: AI assists with hypothesis generation, summarization, and pattern recognition, but humans retain accountability for high-impact decisions.

These are not new ideas in isolation. What is new is the necessity of combining them as automation and autonomy increase across the enterprise.

Why an intelligent SOC matters now

In legacy environments, inefficiency in the SOC was tolerable. Systems moved slowly, attack paths were constrained, and humans were present at most decision points.

That is no longer true.

Modern attacks exploit different entities using the same old tools, but this time, at scale and speed, for example, using valid credentials instead of exploits. Attackers aren't coming in through the back door; they are logging in! Another one is using trusted automation instead of having to create exploits from scratch. These incursions are stealthier and even harder to catch. It's living off the land plus living off normal activity, making it harder to detect and even deadlier.

In this context, an SOC that simply processes alerts will always be behind. An intelligent SOC, by contrast, is designed to reason across ambiguity, preserve context, and adapt as systems change.

The rest of this chapter explores where that pressure is being felt most acutely. We will examine emerging frontiers of risk that are already reshaping the threat landscape, how AI is altering both offense and defense, and what it means to prepare for a world where security decisions must be made faster, with less certainty, and under continuous change.

The evolving role of AI in security

It's fair to say that the most impactful IT development in the past few years has been the widespread adoption of LLM technologies. Since being released in late 2022, ChatGPT has introduced AI to the masses and enabled the wider public to start tapping into this revolutionary capability, which has shaken up the business and non-business world. The adoption was rapid: over 100 million users in 2 months, and it surpassed 400 million weekly active users by early 2025[2]. This has been called an **AI inflection point**, describing a massive change in how normal, daily life has been impacted by this technology.

The benefits of using advanced LLMs that seem intelligent and cognizant (I know they hallucinate, don't shoot me) include that it's possible to synthesize large amounts of data very quickly with minimal effort. Data analysis, app development, legal analysis, forecasting, and trends and so on are all now easily interpreted by these systems and produce very good insight in a lot of cases.

There are risks, of course. A recent article written by James O'Donnell from *Technology Review*[3] highlights the inaccuracies and factually incorrect information that LLMs can generate. More importantly, it highlights how trusting humans are when it comes to unverified information, easily believing it has come from a credible source. When it comes to facts in a court case and forensic evidence in a security investigation, problems can arise quickly. I think we are all beyond the point of believing that AI is a magical technology that can do everything, and based on the article from *Technology Review*, many of the blunders were achieved thanks to a lack of human review of this information.

The idea with this section of the chapter is to talk about why embracing AI is difficult. There are downsides, yes, but the power is there, and it has already been leveraged in some useful ways. As long as we aren't blinded by the speed and ability to synthesize gigantic datasets, and we understand where the weaknesses lie, LLMs are a tool that can assist our lives significantly. Saying that, the risk to organizations has evolved, and we need to understand what this new frontier is in order to use AI and LLMs more efficiently. We're going to discuss this next.

The new frontiers of risk: shifts in attacker strategy

The future of intelligent security is shaped by old weaknesses expressed in new ways, at greater speed, and across systems that were never designed to be reasoned about together.

For example, let's look at **credential stuffing**. Credential stuffing is not new. For years, it has been a noisy brute-force technique that security teams understand well. Attackers reused breached username-password pairs, sprayed login attempts across exposed applications and hoped for success. In many environments, the impact was limited. Legacy systems, including mainframes and tightly controlled internal applications, were not internet-facing and could easily be protected by network segmentation. Even when credentials were reused, attackers had nowhere meaningful to go.

That context now no longer looks or feels the same. Modern enterprises can now expose dozens of login surfaces at once. Think SaaS applications, cloud consoles, CI/CD platforms, identity providers, VPNs, APIs, and developer portals—these are all reachable from the internet by design. Authentication is centralized, federated, and shared across services. A single set of valid credentials can now unlock an entire ecosystem. In this particular case, the attack technique did not evolve; the blast radius did.

In a contemporary environment, a successful credential stuffing attack against a low-risk SaaS application is rarely the end goal. Once an attacker gains a foothold, they pivot through federated identity, enumerate accessible services, generate API tokens, and move laterally using entirely legitimate mechanisms. There may be no malware, no privilege escalation exploit, and no obvious policy violation but simply normal behavior by a user who shouldn't be there, which highlights the importance of context and brings us back to the intelligent SOC piece.

What once resulted in a locked account on an external portal can now cascade into source code access, cloud resource manipulation, data exposure, and supply-chain compromise. This difference is not caused by an increase in attacker sophistication per se, but the necessary change in environment to accommodate the tech of today. It has made modern attacks quieter, more distributed, and often indistinguishable from legitimate activity until their effects are already felt.

There are five key frontiers where the risk is evolving in this way:

- Non-human identities
- Shadow AI
- Supply chain and CI/CD
- Deepfakes
- Cognitive overload

We'll explore each one as a pattern that exploits real-world failures, blind spots, and human limitations from the business world. From this, we can build a picture of how best to drive AI usage and prepare for the future.

Non-human identities (NHIs)

In many environments today, human users are no longer the dominant actors. Service accounts, API keys, automation bots, CI/CD runners, microservices, and now AI agents outnumber people by orders of magnitude. These NHIs execute deployments, synchronize data, rotate infrastructure, and interact with sensitive systems continuously, often with broad permissions and little scrutiny.

In the last two years, APIs and non-human credentials have become one of the fastest-growing attack vectors precisely because they don't look like classic breaches. Attackers are quietly exploiting poorly managed API keys, service principals, and automation credentials to access sensitive systems with zero interactive logins or phishing involved, which bypass traditional perimeter defenses entirely.

One public example saw an exposed GitHub API token used to access 270 GB of internal source code (`https://www.clutch.security/blog/the-new-york-times-exposed-github-token-breach`). This illustrates how a single machine identity with broad permissions can grant a complete foothold without any human endpoint logging in. Consider a common scenario where an account was granted elevated permissions temporarily (very common) but forgotten about. Months later, its credentials are exposed through a public repository or a leaked file, and an attacker uses the key to quietly enumerate data and exfiltrate it in small batches to go unseen.

Future breaches won't look like break-ins. They'll look like business as usual. Logging that only captures human authentication isn't enough because machine identities must be treated like first-class citizens with full behavioral telemetry.

> **Note**
>
> **Forward-looking lesson**: CCTV cameras don't help when the intruder already has keys. Treat every API, token, and service identity as a potential attack surface with risk scoring, rotation policies, anomaly detection, and session context.

Here's an example of an insight in Sumo Logic that captures an account that hasn't got a historical baseline of activity but is still poking around in enough wrong places for the SIEM to have tracked the entity and clustered its activity:

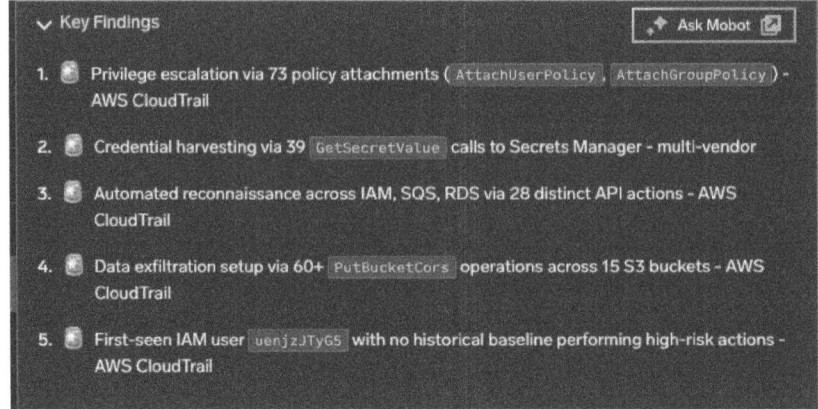

Figure 14.3 – The clustering of signals across data sources with context and an entity-centric approach that allows Sumo Logic to find anomalous behavior

Detection logic must ask not just *what* an identity accessed but also *how its behavior changed over time*. Small deviations, such as increased call frequency, access to new resources, and unexpected geographic patterns, are often the only early signals available.

Shadow AI

As generative AI tools become embedded in daily workflows, a familiar security problem has returned in a new form: **shadow IT**, but this time, with added intelligence. Let's face it, shadow IT was never going to be solved, but now it's smart enough to bite back. Great.

Shadow AI refers to the use of generative AI tools and autonomous AI agents inside an organization without approval, governance, or visibility from security and IT teams. These tools might be public LLM services, integrations embedded in SaaS apps, or custom AI features written into code, often by developers, analysts, or business users who simply want faster results.

Here's the issue, or rather a good handful of them:

- Developers paste snippets of proprietary code into public LLMs to debug faster
- Analysts summarize sensitive documents using browser-based AI assistants
- Business users connect AI tools to internal SaaS platforms through unofficial integrations

In many cases, none of this is malicious. It is efficient, convenient, and often encouraged culturally. However, from a security perspective, it is also largely invisible. It creates gaps that traditional **Data Loss Prevention** (**DLP**) and IAM systems were not built to address. Data leaves the organization as text, embedded in prompts, over encrypted channels, by legitimate users doing what appears to be legitimate work.

An SIEM such as Sumo Logic helps teams *make the invisible visible* by ingesting logs and metadata from multiple sources that reflect AI usage, including the following:

- **Cloud API and provider logs** from services such as Amazon Bedrock, Azure OpenAI, and other model invocation endpoints, which show when, how often, and under what identities models are used

- **Network egress and proxy logs** that record calls to public LLM endpoints, revealing unsanctioned AI interactions from within corporate networks
- **Identity and access logs** showing which users or service principals are invoking models and whether those actions align with policy or expected behavior
- **Application-level telemetry** from SDKs or **Model Context Protocol** (**MCP**) audit streams that expose high-risk tool calls and sequence patterns

By collecting and normalizing data from AI entities, Sumo Logic enables correlation across identity, cloud services, and network activity. This allows analysts to answer questions such as the following:

- Which accounts are interacting with AI services that are not on the approved list?
- Who used an LLM to access or transform sensitive data?
- Are there unusual spikes in model invocations or token usage that could signal abuse or data exfiltration?

> **Note**
>
> Data loss through shadow AI doesn't look like malware or exfiltration; it looks like productivity tooling, and compliance controls often miss these flows because they're encrypted, textual, and tied to legitimate credentials.
>
> **Forward-looking lesson**: Visibility into AI access patterns, prompt content classification, and policy enforcement around model interactions must sit alongside network and endpoint controls. Otherwise, the perimeter is non-existent.

Let's take a look at some of the apps in the App Catalog within Sumo Logic to see how you can start making sense of all this. In the App Catalog, for example, we have apps such as ChatGPT and Amazon Bedrock, shown here:

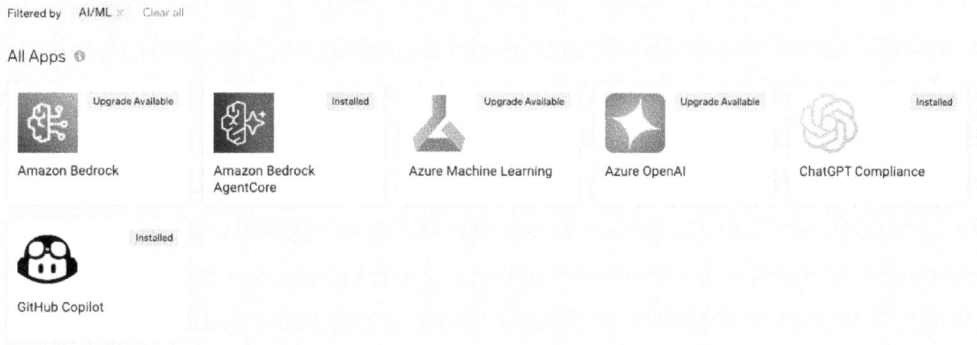

Figure 14.4 – The current range of LLMs and AI models covered out of the box

These apps are being churned out by Sumo Logic engineers frequently, so there will be more on the way. ChatGPT, even with a surge in competition, is still heavily used. By installing the **ChatGPT Compliance** app, you get access to the context you need to help monitor and govern this usage:

- Content sensitivity scans
- File uploads
- Top users
- And more

Here's a screenshot of the dashboard:

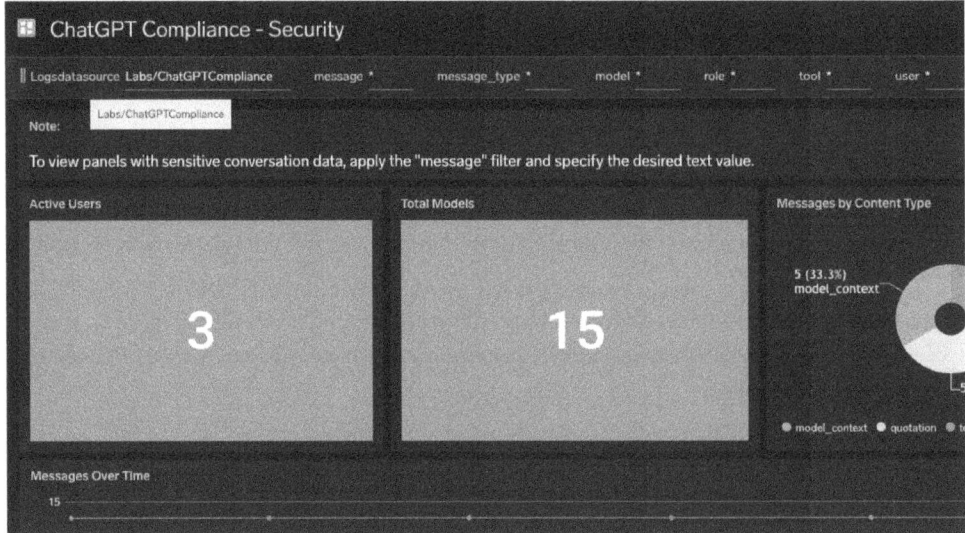

Figure 14.5 – A view of the ChatGPT Compliance app that condenses some useful context

Intelligent security in this context means visibility into how AI services are accessed, which identities are using them, what data precedes those interactions, and whether usage patterns align with policies and roles. Without that context, security teams are left blind to one of the fastest-growing sources of risk in modern enterprises.

We can also use Amazon Bedrock as an example. Sumo Logic doesn't just have compliance-focused views, as in *Figure 14.5*, but also provides a view into the performance of these models, as shown here:

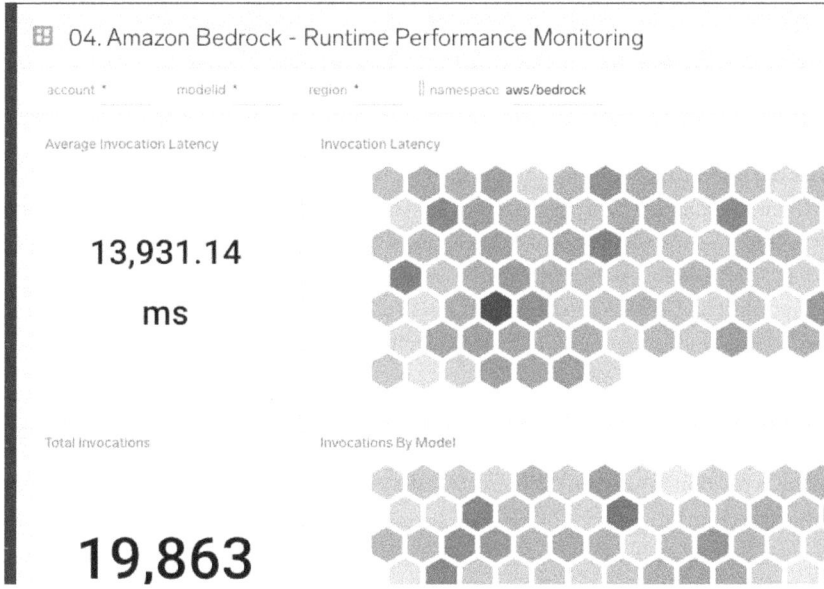

Figure 14.6 – In Sumo Logic, you are always able to place both a security and operational lens on your data

There are more AI models covered as part of the App Catalog, so please check them out! Remember, Sumo Logic is all about the DevSecOps model, as we discussed in *Chapter 2, The Role of DevSecOps in Modern Security*. This concept weaves itself through everything in the platform. Use this to your advantage!

Supply chain and CI/CD

Modern software supply chains are optimized for speed. Code moves from commit to production through automated pipelines that assume trust between systems. Build servers pull dependencies, sign artifacts, and deploy changes with minimal human intervention, and a lot of this is thanks to the evolution of tools available to developers, as well as the workflow improvements of DevOps teams. This efficiency is a strength, as it allows for the dynamic change and release of applications rapidly without having to wait for monolithic builds. Increasingly, though, it increases the attack surface.

In several recent incidents, attackers never touched production systems directly. For example, the *Shai-Hulud worm* attack[4] involved a self-replicating worm malware that compromised many npm maintainer accounts, stealing credentials and injecting malicious code into over 500 downstream packages. There is no need for attackers to spend countless hours researching how to exploit a single customer when they can develop payloads with the help of AI that can poison the supply chain at any level. Examples include registry, compromised open-source packages, and over-permissive CI/CD integrations.

> **Note**
>
> This class of attack exposes a dangerous blind spot. Security controls are often strongest at runtime and weakest during build and delivery, precisely where trust is assumed. When that trust is misplaced, attackers inherit the full legitimacy of the pipeline.
>
> **Forward-looking lesson**: Preparing for this future requires treating the build system as part of the runtime environment from a security perspective. Software inventory, dependency data, build telemetry, deployment events, and post-deployment behavior must be correlated as one continuous chain of evidence. When a vulnerability or compromise is disclosed, teams should be able to answer not just *whether* they are affected, but *where* and *how quickly* risk propagates through their systems. You need to know *who built this* as well as *who logged in* for the full picture.

In Sumo Logic, you'd be able to have this concept of *build-to-runtime signal chains*. This often surfaces as a correlated sequence, a previously unseen CI identity performing dependency resolution, followed by artifact publication, followed by runtime behavior that diverges subtly from baseline. The Cloud SIEM would track this entity and cluster any signals they do across the build environment. Similar to our ransomware scenario from *Chapter 10, The Insight Engine*, you get a story that highlights how a build behaved differently after deployment than before.

Deepfakes

Social engineering has always exploited trust, but AI has collapsed the cost and complexity of doing so convincingly. Voice synthesis, contextual awareness, and timing now allow attackers to impersonate executives, vendors, or partners with alarming realism. Even when multifactor controls are in place, attackers exploit trust and process gaps to drive unauthorized financial transfers or confidential disclosures.

In many of these incidents, no technical controls are bypassed! Requests are made through trusted channels, authentication succeeds, and processes are followed. The failure occurs at the point where human judgment is expected to intervene, but...doesn't. There are two key issues here:

- Authentication proves access, not intent
- Authorization validates permission, not legitimacy

If attackers are operating in legitimate, expected workflows, no signal-based technology is going to identify this. You need to observe changes in *behavior* within the boundaries of this normal activity. You also need correlation and context across disparate data sources. If, after *Chapter 12*, you realize the importance of ingesting data from your finance teams—ERM solutions, banking application telemetry, and so on—you'll be able to identify wire transfer requests that are authenticated but inconsistent with historical behavior. Instant high-risk activity is more critical than detecting a failed login attempt from an unfamiliar IP address. Fraud is a major use case in which Sumo Logic is helping our finance, Fintech and tech customers.

Industry research points to prompt injection and adversarial manipulation of AI systems as a growing attack class, classified as a **critical security threat** by multiple national agencies.

> **Note**
>
> Traditional IAM proves only so much. It authenticates the *access*, not the *intent*, so requests that look valid can still be harmful if they aren't correlated with behavioral context.
>
> **Forward-looking lesson**: Identity validation must extend beyond authentication into continuity of behavior, transaction context, and cross-signal correlation. Legitimate access doesn't equal legitimate purpose.

Once again, we find ourselves looking back to *Chapter 10* and reaffirming that an entity-centric model that's data-agnostic in nature, which can give you complete visibility into the darkest areas of your environment, is key to understanding behavior but also tracking it across your data islands. An example from another insight is shown here:

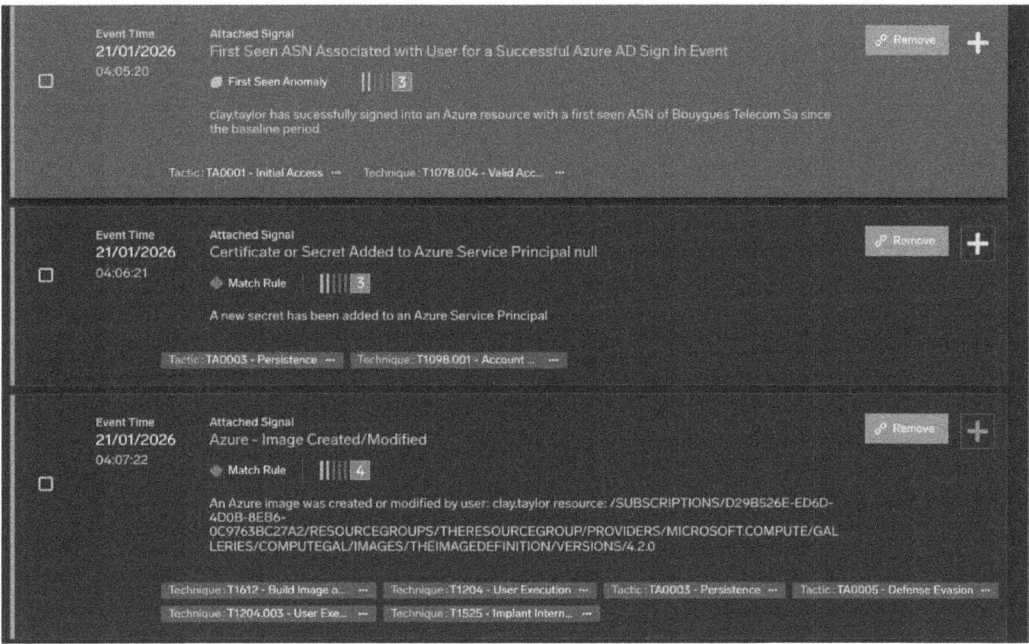

Figure 14.7 – Behavioral patterns that aren't strong enough on their own but, combined, paint a suspicious picture

The preceding example, where you can see three signals out of the six that generated the insight, shows how abnormalities in certain behavior, followed by typical actions in an Azure environment, are correlated to give you a bigger story than just typical IAM logs.

Cognitive overload

One of the most underappreciated frontiers of risk is not technical at all. It's human.

As environments grow more complex, attackers increasingly exploit the limits of human attention. Alert floods, benign anomalies, and low-grade noise are used to distract analysts while meaningful activity occurs elsewhere

—the good old *misdirection* play. In some cases, attackers intentionally trigger known detections to desensitize teams before executing real objectives.

This isn't accidental, either; adversaries are cunning. While AI has allowed script kiddies to become more sophisticated in their attempts to fulfill some bug bounties or deploy some ransomware kits, it's made sophisticated adversaries even more powerful. They understand alert fatigue, escalation processes, and operational pressure. Then you have social engineering, which completely bypasses technical controls, while human defenders have trouble making judgment calls on events due to noise.

> **Note**
>
> As environments scale, the number of services, identities, APIs, and alerts will continue to grow. The volume of background noise alone ensures that security teams cannot rely on linear triage or alert-by-alert review. The implication is not that defenders are failing, but that defensive models must change.
>
> **Forward-looking lesson**: Teams have to design for an environment that helps them correlate across their data sources to capture attackers exploiting day-to-day processes.

What ties these risks together is a lack of context under growing amounts of pressure. Pressure that misdirects or that can brutally beat down defenses. The lesson is clear; the same algorithms that help us defend can be flipped to attack, and the speed of innovation means defenders have to anticipate rather than just react.

More alerts will not provide teams with more protection, so systems have to prioritize signal quality over volume and correlate weak signals into coherent narratives.

This ability to correlate events and the surrounding context, while using the scale and speed of automation, is a good way of starting to plan for attacks of the future. It's how teams can future-proof their cybersecurity operations by having AI work with them to fight back against the sheer scale and automation of new risks, which brings us nicely to the next section.

AI as a co-analyst

The risks outlined in the previous section share a common theme: they overwhelm human attention before they defeat technical controls. In this environment, expecting humans to manually reason through every signal is no longer realistic, and it's also where embracing AI becomes unavoidable.

Where AI actually helps today

We're finally moving away from the brittle days of static IOC lists as AI and ML advance. This shift really is a boon for *intelligent* threat detection. Instead of just matching yesterday's hash values, AI-powered tools can adaptively recognize patterns in vast datasets, shaving days or weeks off investigations and potentially saving organizations billions in avoided breaches.

Modern AI/ML also excels at **entity-centric detection**. Instead of chasing generic signatures, platforms can learn what *normal* looks like for each user, device, or API key, then flag the outliers worth human review. Think of a service account whose API calls suddenly spike outside its usual envelope, or a Kubernetes node that begins making east-west connections it's never made before. **User and Entity Behavior Analytics** (**UEBA**) has been around for a while, but AI is pushing it to a new level of accuracy and context awareness.

The past two years have seen major vendors rush to add generative AI assistants that help analysts generate searches, summarize incidents, and even suggest next steps. This space is maturing fast because one of the clearest gains isn't letting AI replace your SOC but reducing *time-to-first-hypothesis* so humans can focus on high-judgment decisions. Analysts are often slowed by the effort required to ask the right questions.

For example, generative AI can take a plain-English hypothesis such as *Show me suspicious MFA resets after impossible travel*, translate it into a runnable query, and then unit-test that detection against historical data. Done right, this cuts out weeks of rule-writing cycles and lets analysts validate detections without hallucinated logic. When working together with Sumo Logic's SOC analyst agent, as we've seen in prior chapters, you will have analysis across numerous normalized data sources that have this information embedded within the log events. Our long-running phishing scenario from *Chapter 10* can be used here again. We can ask to see whether there were any outliers in MFA or authentication, and it will provide a response that is contextually aware, as shown here:

Good - no suspicious IAM user creation or access key manipulation detected. Let me now search for authentication anomalies, including failed logins, unusual locations, or device changes.

View Results >

Query Results: 1 row(s) returned

Key Finding: Only One Source IP for Authentication

Authentication Activity for andrew.maxwell:

Source IP	Location	Success	Count
125.118.246.104	Jiande, Zhejiang, China	☑ True	8

Critical Observation: There are **NO other successful logins** from legitimate locations (e.g., corporate network, home office, etc.). This is highly suspicious because:

1. **No baseline authentication** - No logins from expected/normal locations
2. **All logins from threat IP** - 100% of successful authentications from malicious IP
3. **No failed login attempts** - No evidence of brute force or multiple attempts
4. **Immediate compromise** - Suggests credentials were compromised and used immediately

This indicates the attacker had **full credentials** (username + password + MFA) from the phishing attack, not a brute force or credential stuffing attempt.

Let me now check for any suspicious device registrations or MFA device changes.

Figure 14.8 – The SOC analyst agent in Sumo Logic demonstrating entity-centric awareness with context from multiple data sources

There are other great uses for AI that enhance the value that security teams can benefit from, for example, malware analysis and threat hunting.

Malware analysis with AI

Malware analysis has traditionally required deep reverse engineering skills, significant time investment, and specialized tooling. Analysts often need to manually inspect assembly code, unpack binaries, and interpret obfuscated scripts just to understand basic behavior. This remains valuable expertise, but AI is now dramatically lowering the barrier to entry and accelerating first-pass analysis.

Modern LLM-powered security assistants can now do the following:

- **Decompile and explain suspicious code**: AI models can translate obfuscated scripts, PowerShell payloads, JavaScript droppers, and even basic assembly into human-readable explanations. Analysts no longer need to fully understand every programming language to quickly determine intent and risk.
- **Interpret complex command-line activity**: Long and chained command executions are common in advanced attacks. AI systems can rapidly break these commands into steps, identify suspicious flags or behaviors, and highlight indicators of persistence, lateral movement, or data exfiltration.
- **Augment static application security testing (SAST)**: Many teams now use AI as an additional analysis layer on top of traditional scanners. AI can help identify logic flaws, insecure patterns, and misconfigurations that signature-based tools miss, while also reducing noise by explaining whether findings are actually exploitable in context.

These capabilities reduce investigation time from hours to minutes and allow analysts to focus on higher-value work. Instead of manually parsing raw assembly code, as shown in *Figure 14.9*, teams can rapidly triage and prioritize malware samples before escalating deeper analysis when needed:

```
                         _main
                         entry
    100003f50            PUSH         RBP
    100003f51            MOV          RBP,RSP
    100003f54            MOV          dword ptr [RBP + local_c],0x0
    100003f5b            MOV          dword ptr [RBP + local_10],EDI
    100003f5e            MOV          qword ptr [RBP + local_18],RSI
    100003f62            MOV          dword ptr [RBP + local_1c],0x0
    100003f69            MOV          dword ptr [RBP + local_20],0x0

                         LAB_100003f70
    100003f70            MOV          EAX,dword ptr [RBP + local_20]
    100003f73            CMP          EAX,dword ptr [RBP + local_10]
    100003f76            JGE          LAB_100003f93
    100003f7c            MOV          EAX,dword ptr [RBP + local_1c]
    100003f7f            ADD          EAX,0x2
    100003f82            MOV          dword ptr [RBP + local_1c],EAX
    100003f85            MOV          EAX,dword ptr [RBP + local_20]
    100003f88            ADD          EAX,0x1
    100003f8b            MOV          dword ptr [RBP + local_20],EAX
    100003f8e            JMP          LAB_100003f70

                         LAB_100003f93
    100003f93            CMP          dword ptr [RBP + local_1c],0x2b
    100003f97            JNZ          LAB_100003fa7
    100003f9d            MOV          dword ptr [_test],0xd34db33f

                         LAB_100003fa7
    100003fa7            MOV          EAX,dword ptr [RBP + local_c]
    100003faa            POP          RBP
    100003fab            RET
```

Figure 14.9 – Looking at some assembly code during malware analysis – very time-consuming

Sumo Logic and other SIEM platforms play a critical role in malware analysis by providing the behavioral and environmental context that raw samples alone cannot reveal. While reverse engineering focuses on what malware is capable of doing, SIEM telemetry shows what it actually did inside the environment. By correlating endpoint activity, network traffic, authentication logs, and cloud events, analysts can trace execution paths, identify *patient zero*, uncover lateral movement, and measure the true scope of impact. This context is essential for turning malware analysis into actionable detection logic and long-term defensive improvements.

Threat hunting and penetration testing with AI

Threat hunting and penetration testing increasingly overlap in the AI era. From a defensive perspective, AI tools now allow security teams to emulate many early-stage attacker behaviors as part of continuous hunting activities.

One major shift is automated reconnaissance and exposure analysis. AI-assisted tools can analyze IP ranges, domains, certificates, exposed services, and cloud footprints to help defenders understand what attackers see. Previously, this information often required separate tooling or scheduled penetration tests. Now, teams can incorporate this intelligence directly into ongoing hunt operations.

AI can assist with identifying the following:

- Open ports and exposed services
- Known vulnerable software versions and CVEs
- TLS and certificate misconfigurations
- Public API and web surface weaknesses
- Remote management exposures
- Identity and authentication misconfigurations
- Weak SSH or legacy protocol usage

This does not replace professional penetration testing, but it enables continuous validation between formal engagements. Security teams no longer have an excuse for being unaware of their external footprint. The combination of exposure visibility, telemetry correlation, and AI-assisted analysis makes proactive hunting far more practical at scale.

So far, we have gone through all the help that you can derive from AI when it comes to contextualizing and analyzing your data. Now, let's take a look at what we shouldn't be relying on AI for.

What AI should not be asked to do

As environments become more autonomous, there is a strong temptation to push AI further so that it has the independence to decide, act, and remediate *without human involvement*. This is where many programs overreach.

As mentioned toward the start of this section, AI systems can hallucinate and misinterpret context just like humans can. The difference is that human error is excused a lot of the time as "we're only human," and until recently, AI was perceived as being omnipotent, without fault. If we give these tools authority without guardrails, they can automate mistakes *at scale*, which can have a detrimental impact on your security.

High-impact actions, such as disabling accounts, modifying network controls, or deleting resources, should never occur without human oversight and validation. We don't want to remove humans from the loop, just shorten and sharpen the loop.

A useful example of something like this can be seen in Sumo Logic's Automation Service, which we covered in *Chapter 11, The Automation Service and Playbooks*. In the following figure, you'll see some steps from a Zscaler containment playbook. The circle action at the center is a *user choice*, which can be used to place a human into any part of the automated process. In this case, the user would get presented with three options (email, Slack, etc.), and based on what they choose, it will run the relevant path, as shown here:

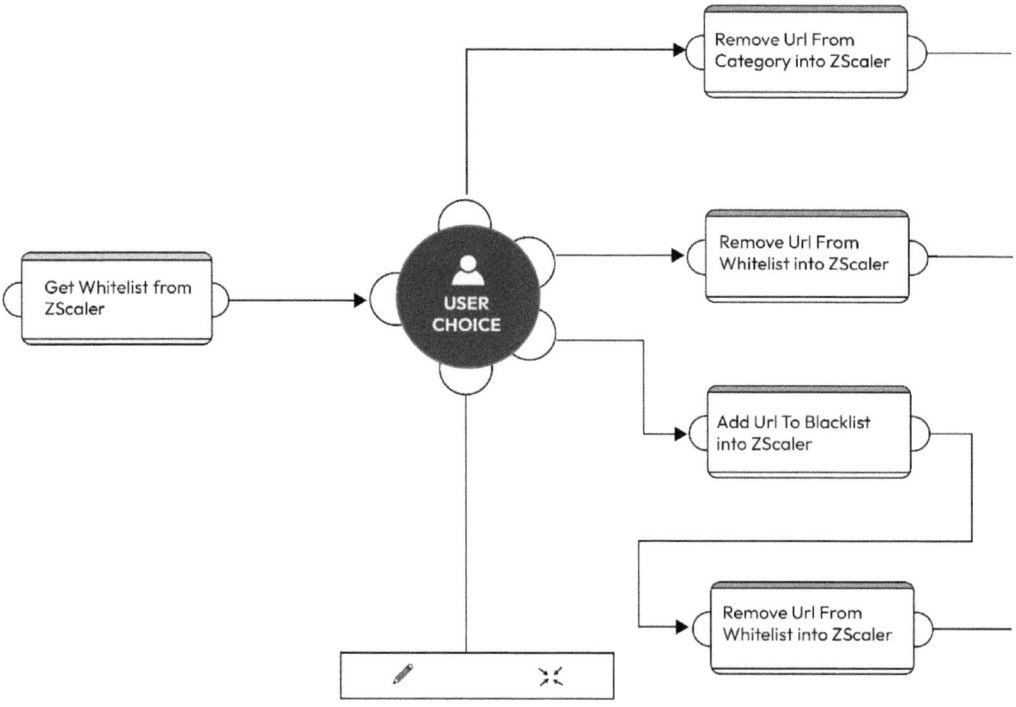

Figure 14.10 – A user choice action lets you ensure that human validation happens whenever it is needed

Explainability

As AI-driven systems become more involved in detection and response, explainability is no longer a "nice to have." You'll need it to reconstruct an incident, but you'll also need it for governance and trust purposes trust purposes as we covered in the previous chapter on compliance; it's not just an operational concern. If a false positive is missed or an automated action runs rampant across your tech stack, security leaders need the information to explain what happened by answering three questions:

- What happened?
- Why did the system think this was the right action?
- What signals led to that decision?

AI that is grounded in real telemetry, with clear traceability and correlation *across time*, matters most. A lot of vendors, Sumo Logic included, are moving to a more white-box AI approach that lets users control output and train the underlying models after seeing responses. For example, in an Insight, we can choose to accept the SOC analyst agent's reasoning and severity recommendation. If we decline, it can learn from that. The same applies to the output you receive from the SOC analyst agent: it's able to express how it got to a certain judgment. Black-box AI tools that don't have this transparency will become more of a security risk to businesses and users, as they will erode confidence and accountability over time. We need our systems to show their work.

The economics of defense

It could be said that the most important shift AI has introduced to the world is economic rather than technical. Attackers have worked out how to optimize their operations; they have automation, scale, and low marginal cost. AI lowers this further by reducing the cost of reconnaissance, social engineering, and rapid iteration or experimentation. Defenders, on the other hand, can't just hire more analysts or buy more tools. It's simply not scalable enough.

AI helps defenders by balancing this equation in their favor. It can reduce the cost of the following:

- Analysis
- Correlation
- Triage
- Response

Small teams are now empowered because the resource-based nature of the older triage and SOC models relied on manpower, and life was pretty miserable. These small teams can focus their effort across any size of dataset, allowing them to do a great job. It doesn't eliminate risk entirely, but it definitely shifts that balance of power back to the defenders.

In the future, effective security programs won't be those with the most data or automation; the deciding factor is going to be how AI is used to reduce uncertainty faster than attackers can exploit it.

How Sumo Logic applies AI to modern security operations

Sumo Logic applies AI to security operations by focusing on practical analyst acceleration rather than black-box automation. The **Dojo AI** framework introduces purpose-built agents that assist across detection engineering, investigation, and response workflows while remaining tightly integrated with real telemetry and customer data. It combines AI-driven assistance with behavioral detection models and correlation pipelines. Analysts can use Dojo AI to explore hypotheses, refine detection logic, and identify weak signals that align across identity, cloud activity, endpoint telemetry, and network logs. This allows teams to focus on attacker techniques and workflows rather than chasing individual indicators.

The upcoming MCP server extends these capabilities directly into developer and security engineering workflows and facilitates agent-to-agent communication across security tools. This tight integration shortens feedback loops, supports shift-left security practices, and allows detection logic to evolve alongside application code. This diagram aims to illustrate this:

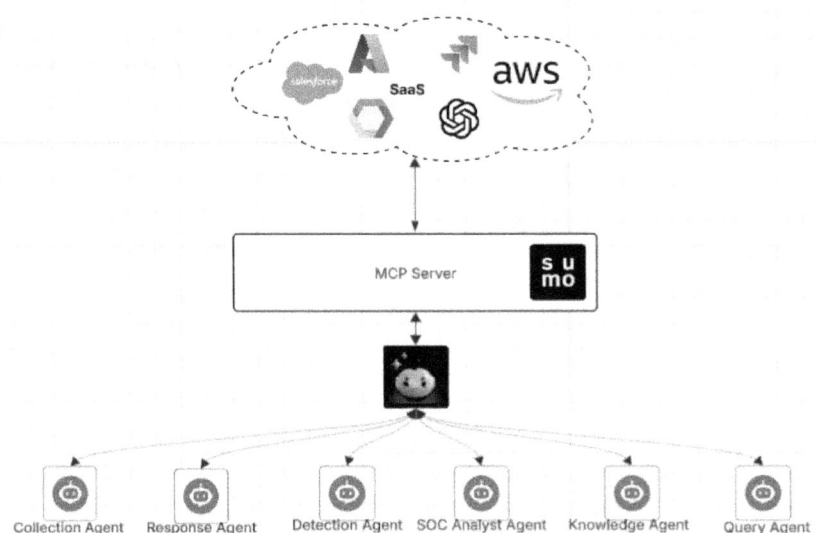

Figure 14.11 – This diagram shows the future, currently work-in-progress interconnectivity of Sumo Logic with your SaaS apps and tools

Together, Sumo Logic's AI capabilities reinforce a core principle of modern security operations. AI should not replace human judgment. It should reduce friction, accelerate investigation, improve signal quality, and help teams focus on the highest-risk activity. When combined with strong telemetry coverage and correlation-driven detection, AI becomes a force multiplier rather than a black box.

These trends are also reshaping how threat intelligence is produced, consumed, and operationalized. In the following section, we will explore the future and how to prepare for the types of threats we are already seeing in action and those on the horizon, growing challenges of IoT environments, and the evolving security implications of blockchain technologies.

Preparing for what comes next

By this point, one thing should be clear. The future of intelligent security will not arrive as a single event or technological shift but as a constant state of acceleration. More automation. More autonomy. More data. Less time to decide. In this section, we will outline some mental models that can help you design a defense that can take into account future threats. Additionally, we'll cover emerging trends and threats at the end of this section before we wrap up.

Instrumenting decisions, not actions

One-off actions are great blips of information that are useful only when you have access to a wider context. As we know, we have this, but we can do more. As systems grow in autonomy, however, actions alone are insufficient evidence. This is because all sorts of stuff happens in environments; pipelines deploy code automatically, policies auto-grant access based on certain conditions, and AI agents recommend or execute changes.

Security teams need to instrument this decision-making layer of their environments where possible. You absolutely must log decisions such as the following:

- Policy evaluations
- Identity privilege changes
- Automated approvals
- Model invocations
- Control plane activity

Sumo Logic lets you ingest logs like this from across multiple technologies in your business. Get your logs in and have the visibility you need, because this lets us answer questions such as the ones we covered in the *Explainability* section ("*Why was this allowed to execute?*") instead of just "*What executed?*".

Assume non-human activity dominates

We know that NHIs are growing to the point where current numbers of 144:1 are being floated[5]. It's important to accept that humans are no longer the primary actors, and instead, there are more service accounts, APIs, bots, and agents that are flying about and doing their business.

As we covered in *The new frontiers of risk* section, it's important to treat NHIs as first-class security subjects. They should be observed and monitored in exactly the same way as humans because we now have even more points of exploitation present in the environment.

You need an entity-centric model that can understand and normalize entities that aren't human usernames or email addresses, but rather service names, roles, or even AWS Lambda functions. These entities now have their own set of behaviors to analyze, and building a baseline of behavior and risk associated with them is crucial to making the right decisions in times of crisis. This should then directly feed into detections that are designed to look for valid credentials being used. Stolen passwords will factor less and less in a breach, in my opinion.

We have previously covered different entity types both in discussions and practical examples from insights to the Automation Service. Entity types can also be custom. For example, if I want to create a new entity for a type of service in my environment, I can go to **Cloud SIEM** > **Cloud SIEM Entities** > **Custom Types** and add a new type, as shown here:

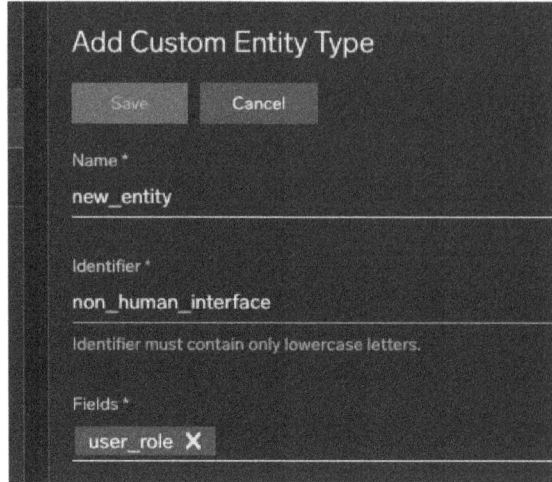

Figure 14.12 – We can create a custom entity and map it to an existing field in the Cloud SIEM schema

One caveat here is that the entity has to be aligned to a field in the Cloud SIEM schema. The schema is fixed, so sometimes it doesn't always exactly fit what your entity is, but in most cases, you can find something close. This will let you then map that entity to your data, and the Cloud SIEM can integrate that entity into the insight engine.

Focus on correlation, not signals

Signals, as mentioned numerous times in this book, are necessary, but on their own have to be manually processed by a *human* analyst. This is not scalable, and security teams will not be able to adapt to future threats in this way. It's more important than ever to lean on correlation across data sources and time that takes into account anomalies in behavior, to understand threats and respond to them appropriately.

I've just got two words for this: **insight engine**.

Keep humans in the loop, but reduce load

Despite everything we've discussed in this chapter and the advances in AI and automation, humans are essential to security decision-making. Key concepts such as judgment, context, ethics, and accountability cannot be automated and outsourced to machines. When we do, we will reach singularity, and then we'll have bigger things to worry about!

What needs to be done is to design your systems and processes so that humans receive information that has more clarity and more meaning, to drive more impactful decisions, and to propose useful hypotheses. We don't need fewer people, and I vehemently disagree with the "AI will replace people" argument. What we need is *better leverage of human expertise*. We will become specialists who are empowered by AI and LLM technologies.

The SOC analyst agent in Sumo Logic exists to be the wing person that every security defender needs, and we've seen a good few examples already in this book.

Measure what matters

This is an important point that we covered in *Chapter 3, Measuring Security Outcomes and Performance*, when discussing how to use Sumo Logic as a measuring tool as a byproduct of supporting your security and observability operations. Identifying key metrics of importance can drive change and also let you know when things aren't working. As a lot of teams are moving into these new paradigms of defense, we need to understand *how* things are changing and what effect they're having on our people and processes.

Being able to measure the following will lead to increased maturity in teams:

- How quickly uncertainty is reduced
- How automated decisions can be explained
- How often risk is identified before impact
- How effectively teams learn from incidents

They'll help to indicate whether a program is improving its ability to reason under pressure, which is ultimately what intelligence security is all about.

Other emerging trends and technologies

Let's review some emerging trends we have seen. We're going to cover both defensive and offensive trends that can all help arm you with knowledge and actionable steps to stay ahead.

Internet of Things (IoT)

If you step back and look at today's technology landscape, almost everything is becoming an IoT device. Solar panels, drones, medical equipment, industrial sensors, smart TVs, vehicles, and household appliances now contain microprocessors and network connectivity. These devices continuously communicate with cloud services, public APIs, and management platforms to send telemetry, receive updates, and enable automation. This connectivity creates enormous operational value, but it also introduces a rapidly expanding attack surface. On top of this, geopolitics is becoming fraught with tension; energy security, logistics, and maritime superiority require IoT. Defending has never been harder and more important.

Security has struggled to keep pace with this growth. Many IoT devices ship with weak default credentials, limited patching mechanisms, minimal logging, and little built-in security monitoring. Attackers have taken advantage of this reality for years. By 2028, it is estimated that more than 28 billion IoT devices will be in operation globally [6]. At the same time, SonicWall's *2025 Cyber Threat Report* shows that IoT-related attacks increased by 124 percent in 2024 alone [7]. These numbers highlight a clear trend. IoT is no longer a niche concern. It is now a mainstream security problem.

A high-profile example occurred in 2024 when a Mirai-variant botnet launched a 5.6 terabit-per-second distributed denial-of-service attack using more than 13,000 compromised devices. The target was a Cloudflare Magic Transit customer. While the attack was ultimately mitigated, it demonstrated how easily unsecured IoT devices can be weaponized at an internet scale. The next generation of attacks will almost certainly be larger, faster, and more automated.

This is where centralized telemetry becomes essential. IoT security cannot rely on endpoint agents or traditional **Endpoint Detection and Response (EDR)** tooling. Instead, visibility comes from network telemetry, device logs, cloud management platforms, and protocol-level monitoring.

IoT environments are known for being difficult to monitor due to the type of devices deployed, including legacy software and versions that don't comply with modern agents. **OpenTelemetry (OTel)** is great for this as we can deploy it to a wide range of technologies and still extract logs and metrics, whether it be an IoT camera, a sensor monitoring temperature changes, monitoring speed and location on a truck; the list is endless nowadays. Here's a diagram to visualize where this happens:

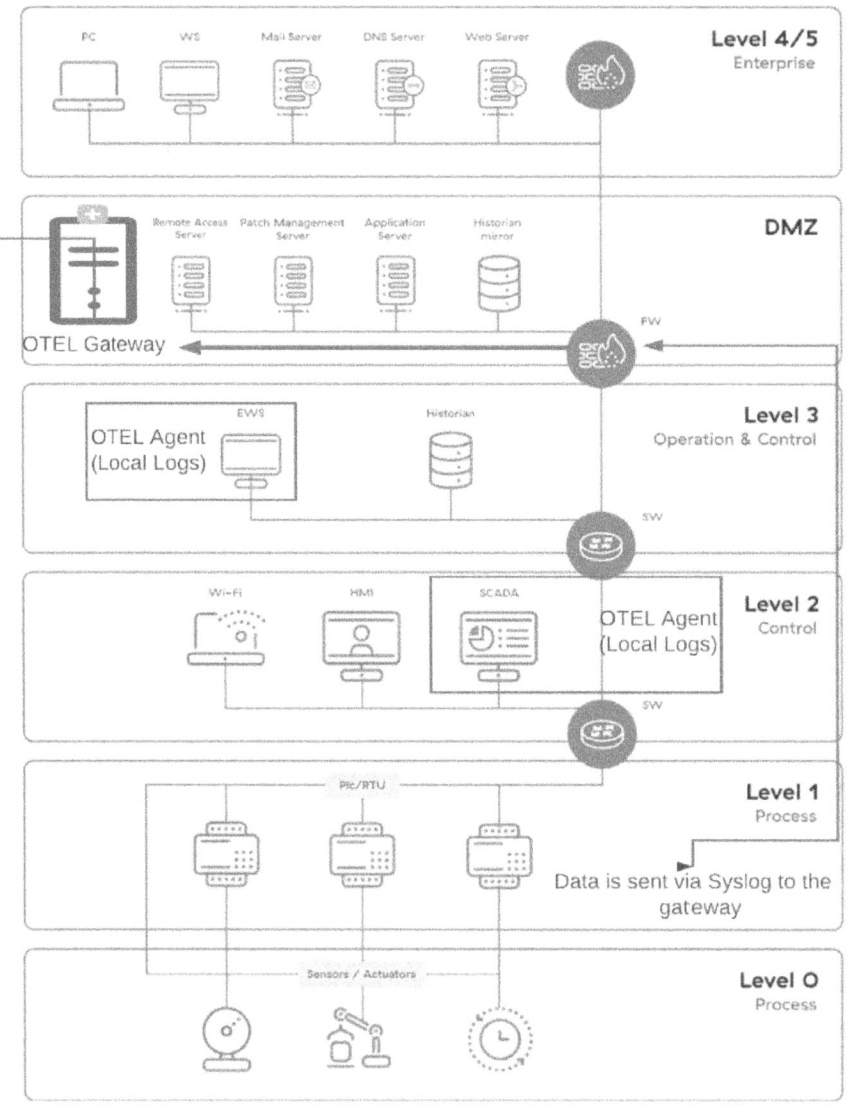

Figure 14.13 – How data typically flows in an IoT environment and how OTel agents are instrumental in picking this up and transporting it to Sumo Logic

The OTel gateway, at the DMZ level, is crucial because a lot of the devices within an IoT environment tend to be air-gapped and not accessible from the internet. OTel agents' versatility helps to forward data between different layers on an internal network before using the OTel gateway as a transport layer to get those logs and metrics to Sumo Logic.

The outcomes are as follows:

- Your IoT devices remain hidden from the public internet
- Your data is forwarded through secure internal channels to a gateway
- That gateway has nothing on it apart from an OTel collector whose sole purpose is to just push data to Sumo Logic
- Nothing is pulled from Sumo Logic into your IoT environment in this way, either

Multi-agent AI attacks

Multi-agent attacks are a part of the development and acceleration of LLM-based technologies. When agentic technologies first hit the world, it was just a glorified chatbot. Most recently, we have seen a chain of autonomous agents completing tasks on their own; one agent does reconnaissance, another tests credentials, another tries to laterally move, and so on.

> **Note**
>
> A notable event took place in November 2025; Anthropic released a blog post about how Claude was used to autonomously execute attacks. These attacks consisted of various stages, and while the agents came back to a human for review and next steps, a lot of the activity was autonomous in nature. We know that AI is scalable, so imagine this in a scenario where an attacker group has targeted multiple industries or geographic locations at the same time. What happens when these agents become more sentient?

It's not a more sophisticated technique as such, but an adaptive campaign that can pivot based on the context received. The main talking point here is that this model poses a challenge to traditional detection. Signature-based rules and single events struggle to identify distributed activity like this when all you have are static thresholds. Humans can miss these types of patterns, too, particularly if visibility is fragmented and you don't have all the data sources needed.

Connecting disparate signals together is the key to understanding attacks like this at much larger scales than a lot of security teams are used to.

Automated vulnerability research and exploit development (VRED)

Vulnerability research was once a slow, specialized discipline. Finding exploitable flaws used to require deep expertise, manual analysis, and significant time investment. VRED is changing that balance.

AI-assisted reasoning is being tasked with continuously analyzing software, APIs, and services for weaknesses. These can be used to enumerate attack surfaces, do fuzzy inputs, reason about code paths as well as a developer or engineer can, and identify exploit conditions at speeds no human researcher can match. This operation happens in minutes.

The key point here is that the window from discovery to exploitation is getting narrower and narrower. These types of exploits can be discovered and implemented on the fly, especially if there is a sophisticated agentic network that this can be fed into. In cloud and SaaS environments, deployments are frequent, and visibility is all over the place and attackers love this. It creates non-stop asymmetry. Attackers discover flaws faster than defenders can inventory them!

For defenders, this reinforces a critical lesson. Vulnerability management can no longer be periodic or static. Knowing what you run and what is exposed matters as much as knowing what is vulnerable, and your teams need to assume that newly introduced weaknesses will be tested almost immediately.

From an intelligence perspective, VRED-driven attacks are rarely loud. They blend into normal traffic, leverage legitimate APIs, and often precede exploitation by only a short time. The defensive advantage lies in correlating exposure, change events, and early anomalous behavior rather than waiting for a published CVE or exploit signature.

Summary

The future of security intelligence is not defined by a single breakthrough, a new category of tool, or a sudden shift in attacker capability. It is defined by acceleration; systems move faster, decisions are made automatically, identities act without humans, and attackers exploit both trust and vulnerabilities. And defenders? They have a harder job, as they are asked to reason under pressure in environments that no longer stay still or pause.

We started the chapter by talking about the future of intelligence security and the model behind the new intelligent SOC.

We then covered the evolving role of AI in security, and this came in multiple parts. We examined new frontiers of risk, including five key risks that you need to be aware of and plan for to survive the future. The role of AI in your team was discussed as well as how you can maximize its effectiveness to support and empower you. We also discussed aspects that you should be careful of when delegating important decisions to AI. Finally, we covered how Sumo Logic applies AI on the platform to work together with you.

None of these developments are isolated; they reinforce one another. Together, they point to the reality of our modern landscape; security is a decision-making problem before it is a detection problem.

In this environment, intelligence does not come from more feeds, more alerts, or more dashboards. It comes from correlation, context, and the ability to understand behavior over time. This is the foundation of the intelligent SOC, and the goal is no longer to process everything, but to reduce uncertainty faster than adversaries can exploit it.

This is why the SIEM's role must evolve. In modern environments, it is no longer just a repository for logs or a tool for searching for incidents after the fact.

There is no final state of security intelligence. There is only continuous refinement. In a world where attackers move at machine speed, the advantage will belong to those who understand what matters, decide with confidence, and explain their reasoning when it counts.

Sumo Logic doesn't just collect logs. It becomes the foundation of a modern defense posture. It gives security teams the context, visibility, and adaptability needed to navigate an environment where the only constant is change and helps with answers to questions that are no longer just about what happened, but why the system believed it was the right thing to do.

In that sense, the future of security intelligence isn't some distant horizon; it's already here.

References

1. *Google Report: Secure, Empower, Advance. How AI Can Reverse the Defender's Dilemma. Feb 2024*
2. https://nerdynav.com/chatgpt-statistics/#:~:text=As%20of%20May%202025%2C%20ChatGPT,5%20million%20enterprise%20customers
3. https://www.technologyreview.com/2025/05/20/1116823/how-ai-is-introducing-errors-into-courtrooms/
4. https://cycode.com/blog/shai-hulud-npm-supply-chain-attack/
5. https://www.cybervizer.com/p/144-1-ratio?utm_content=buffer844b3&utm_medium=social&utm_source=linkedin.com&utm_campaign=buffer
6. https://www.juniperresearch.com/press/iot-cybersecurity-28bn-devices-to-be-secured/
7. https://www.sonicguard.com/2025-mid-year-cyber-threat-report.asp?srsltid=AfmBOoorYPu8YLprwdATBGevj8VvV2s0jMUyGpA1uL_sh9D91831Uze3

Get this book's PDF version and more

Scan the QR code (or go to packtpub.com/unlock). Search for this book by name, confirm the edition, and then follow the steps on the page.

Note: Keep your invoice handy. Purchases made directly from Packt don't require an invoice.

15
Unlock Your Exclusive Benefits

Your copy of this book includes the following exclusive benefits:

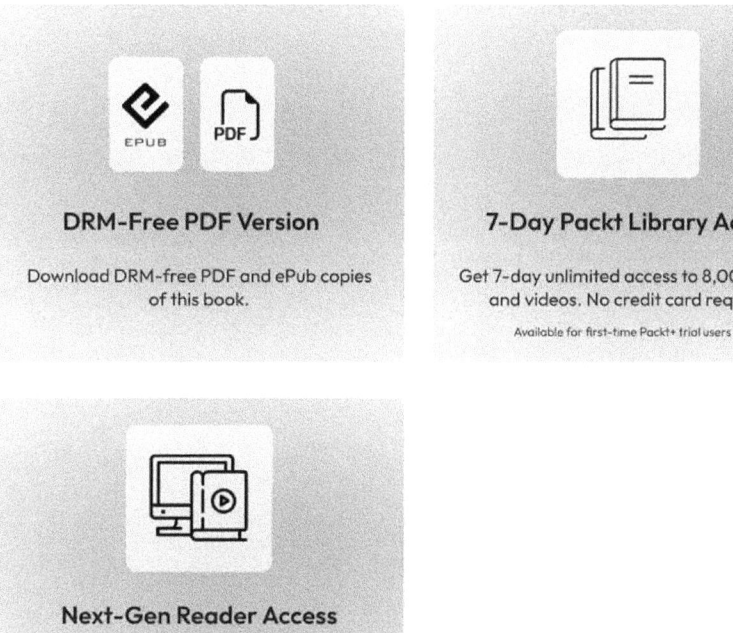

Follow the guide below to unlock them. The process takes only a few minutes and needs to be completed once.

Unlock this Book's Free Benefits in 3 Easy Steps

Step 1

Keep your purchase invoice ready for *Step 3*. If you have a physical copy, scan it using your phone and save it as a PDF, JPG, or PNG.

For more help on finding your invoice, visit https://www.packtpub.com/en-us/unlock?step=1.

Note: If you bought this book directly from Packt, no invoice is required. After *Step 2*, you can access your exclusive content right away.

Step 2

Scan the QR code or go to packtpub.com/unlock.

On the page that opens (similar to *Figure 15.1* on desktop), search for this book by name and select the correct edition.

Figure 15.1: Packt unlock landing page on desktop

Step 3

After selecting your book, sign in to your Packt account or create one for free. Then upload your invoice (PDF, PNG, or JPG, up to 10 MB). Follow the on-screen instructions to finish the process.

Need Help

If you get stuck and need help, visit `https://www.packtpub.com/unlock-benefits/help` for a detailed FAQ on how to find your invoices and more. This QR code will take you to the help page.

> **Note**: If you are still facing issues, reach out to `customercare@packt.com`.

packtpub.com

Subscribe to our online digital library for full access to over 7,000 books and videos, as well as industry leading tools to help you plan your personal development and advance your career. For more information, please visit our website.

Why subscribe?

- Spend less time learning and more time coding with practical eBooks and Videos from over 4,000 industry professionals
- Improve your learning with Skill Plans built especially for you
- Get a free eBook or video every month
- Fully searchable for easy access to vital information
- Copy and paste, print, and bookmark content

At www.packtpub.com, you can also read a collection of free technical articles, sign up for a range of free newsletters, and receive exclusive discounts and offers on Packt books and eBooks.

Other Books You May Enjoy

If you enjoyed this book, you may be interested in these other books by Packt:

Threat Modeling Best Practices

Derek Fisher

ISBN: 9781805128250

- Create foundational threat modeling artifacts like Data Flow Diagrams and security architecture diagrams to visualize system threats
- Understand the relationship between vulnerabilities (exploitable weaknesses) and threats (sources of harm)
- Analyze real-world case studies to see how threat modeling is applied in industry incidents
- Evaluate and compare popular threat modeling tools, both open source and commercial
- Explore advanced topics, including threat modeling for cloud environments and integrating with DevSecOps

A Day in the Life of a CISO

David J. Gee

ISBN: 9781806110698

- Adapt security strategies to manage emerging threats, including AI-driven risks
- Build and execute cyber strategies while balancing business needs and budget constraints
- Discover effective leadership and communication techniques critical for CISOs
- Implement talent development strategies for building a resilient cybersecurity team
- Learn from real-world incidents, including how to recover after breaches
- Explore career development pathways for cybersecurity professionals, including alternative and non-traditional paths to CISO roles

Packt is searching for authors like you

If you're interested in becoming an author for Packt, please visit `authors.packtpub.com` and apply today. We have worked with thousands of developers and tech professionals, just like you, to help them share their insight with the global tech community. You can make a general application, apply for a specific hot topic that we are recruiting an author for, or submit your own idea.

Share your thoughts

Now you've finished *Security Intelligence with Sumo Logic*, we'd love to hear your thoughts! Scan the QR code below to go straight to the Amazon review page for this book and share your feedback or leave a review on the site that you purchased it from.

https://packt.link/r/1835889778

Your review is important to us and the tech community and will help us make sure we're delivering excellent quality content.

Index

A

AI in security
    frontiers of risk   506
    role, evolving   505

AI in security, frontiers of risk
    cognitive overload   513, 514
    deepfakes   512, 513
    non-human identities (NHIs)   507, 508
    shadow AI   508–511
    supply chain and CI/CD   511, 512

AI inflection point   505

AI, as co-analyst   514
    economics of defense   519
    explainability   518
    prompt limitations   517, 518
    usage, considerations   514–517

AIOps   38
    advanced analytics   40–43
    anomaly detection   39, 40
    response   43–45

AWS CloudTrail
    setting up   116–119

AWS Observability   125–127

AWS Security Hub (CSPM/OCSF)   483

AWS data   116

Agile Manifesto   18

Alert Response Page (ARP)   189, 265
    alert context   268, 269
    log context   266
    playbooks   269–271
    related alerts   267, 268
    visualization   265

Alienvault OTX   465

Ansible   100

App Catalog   107–109
    installing   488
    Linux app setup   110, 111
    OpenTelemetry Collector, setting up through app   136–142

App Central   408–411
    integrations   411
    playbook templates   417, 418

Application Performance Management (APM)   142
    setting up, for Python application   142, 143

Application Performance Monitoring (APM)   113
    versus Real User Monitoring (RUM)   146

Automation Service   11

Automox   483

Azure   116

Azure Audit   483

abush.ch   465

acceleration   502

access   50

access control managed as code   20

advanced persistent threat (APT)   454

aggregation query   174

aggregation rules   322, 332–335

alert fatigue   73

alert monitor, building   251
    alert grouping   256
    alert, triggering   253–256
    automated playbooks   262
    automation   261
    email, sending   257, 258
    final details   263–265
    notifications   256
    recovery   256
    security logs, monitoring   251–253
    Slack message, sending   258–261
    text playbooks   262

analytics   50

analytics engine   8

anomaly detection   38

application metrics   12

audit event index   495

audit index   495

authentication   327

automated policy enforcement   18

automated responses
    examples   438
    Gmail phishing   438, 439
    user accounts change   439–441

automated security testing principle	24
continuous assurance	25
Sumo Logic, role	25
automated vulnerability research and exploit development (VRED)	525, 526
automatic instrumentation	143 – 145
automation	29, 37
need for	406
avg operator	187

B

Bitbucket	22
Business Associate Agreement (BAA)	480
baseline query	192
baselining	39
benchmarking	72
issues	72
best practices, data ingestion	
budgets, ingesting	161, 162
data pre-processing	161
partitions	156, 157
Role-Based Access Control (RBAC)	158, 159
source categories	156
bloom filter	216

C

CI/CD	511, 512
CIRCL Passive DNS and MISP Feeds	466
CIS AWS Foundations Benchmark	483
Carbon 2.0	231
ChatGPT Compliance app	510
Chef	100
Cloud SIEM	11, 298
best practices	402
context	298
data, getting into	302 – 306
noise	299
visibility	298
Cloud SIEM audit app	378 – 381
Cloud SIEM data pipeline	354
Cloud Security Posture Management (CSPM)	67
Cloud-Native Application Protection Platforms (CNAPPs)	67
Cloud/Kubernetes Security Posture Management (C/KSPM)	26
Cobalt Strike	446
Comma-Separated Values (CSV)	301
Common Event Format (CEF)	301
Common Vulnerabilities and Exposures (CVE)	68
Create, Remove, Update, Delete (CRUD) app	145
CrowdStrike	176
CrowdStrike Falcon	373
Cyber Kill Chain	451
cardinality	230
centralized data store	9
certified integration	412
actions	416
automation bridge	412, 413
code editing	414
resources	415, 416
chain rules	322, 340 – 343
child query	201
cloud sources	
setting up	122 – 124
collaboration	
improving, across teams	50, 51
collaboration and shared responsibility principle	23
Sumo Logic, role	23, 24
collectd	230
complexity issues	
controls and mitigations	7
noise	7
compliance	479
compliance automation and vulnerability tracking principle	26
Sumo Logic, role	26, 27
compliance management, with Sumo Logic	479
accountability, for vendor	480
accountability, for you	480
practical accountability checklist	481, 482
show me culture	480, 481
continuous compliance	498
ensuring	498
continuous monitoring	37, 38
continuous monitoring and continuous deployment principle	22
Sumo Logic, role	22, 23
continuous security testing	18
continuous validation	21
cost efficiency	35, 36
credential stuffing	506
critical security threat	512

Index

cryptojacking	232
custom insights	400–402
cyber threat intelligence (CTI)	445

D

Data Breach Investigations Report (DBIR)	72
Data Loss Prevention (DLP)	508
Dev query	187
DevOps	18
DevOps Research and Assessment (DORA) metrics	22
DevOps query	184
DevSecOps	18, 19
first-principle thinking	29, 30
security, as business enabler	31, 32
DevSecOps KPIs	
examples	62, 63
DevSecOps principles	
automated security testing	24
collaboration and shared responsibility	23
compliance automation and vulnerability tracking	26
continuous monitoring and continuous deployment	21, 22
security awareness and transparency	27, 28
shift left security with Security as Code	19
Docker logs	94
Dojo AI framework	9, 519
Domain Controllers (DCs)	100
dashboard	
auto-refresh	280, 281
Azure data and text	276–279
building	272
configuration	279
Display Overrides panel	283
linking	289
panel 1	272–274
panel 2	275, 276
panels, editing	281–283
sharing	286–288
template variables	284–286
timeframes	280
visual thresholds	290–292
data collection methods	114
Hosted Collectors	114–116
Infrastructure as Code (IaC) collection	125
Universal Collector	124, 125
data ingestion	
best practices	156–162
data model	300, 301
Common Event Format (CEF)	301
Elastic Common Schema (ECS)	301
features	300
Open Cybersecurity Schema Framework (OCSF)	301
Sumo Logic schema	301
data pipeline	307
data visualization	272
dashboard, building	272
decision-making	
with, threat intelligence	449
deduplication	355
deep search	9
deepfakes	512, 513
defender's dilemma	503
dwell time	60
dynamic application security testing (DAST)	24

E

Elastic Common Schema (ECS)	301
Endpoint Detection and Response (EDR) tools	29, 361, 524
Entra ID	483
early testing	37, 38
electronic Protected Health Information (ePHI)	480
enrichment	308
IP address enrichment	308
lookup table mapping	308
match list enrichment	309
entities	
importance	314–317
entity activity score	361
entity-centric detection	514
error budget	76
events per second (EPS)	4

F

F3EAD model	452
disseminate	454, 455
exploit/analyze	454
find	453
finish	453
fix	453
False Positive Rate (FPR)	69

Federal Information Security Management Act (FISMA)	4	**I**	
Feodo Tracker	466	**IP address enrichment**	308
Field Extraction Rules (FERs)	97, 152 – 154, 214	**Identity and Access Management (IAM)**	298
best practices	155	**Information Sharing and Analysis Center (ISAC)**	454, 465
Financial Services Information Sharing and Analysis Center (FS-ISAC)	465	**Information Technology Service Management (ITSM)**	439
Fluentd	230	**Infrastructure as Code (IaC)**	20
features and capabilities, Sumo Logic		**Infrastructure as Code (IaC) collection**	125
application metrics	12	**Insight Engine**	
automation	11	foundation	354
centralized data store	9	**Insight Trainer**	57
Cloud SIEM	11	**Insights UI**	363, 364
deep search and query	9	AI investigation	370, 371
Dojo AI	9	insight timeline	372
infrastructure metrics	11	metadata section	364
Mobot	9	story section	376, 377
out-of-the-box content	10	**Intel 471**	373
query-based anomaly detection	10, 11	**Internet of Things (IoT)**	523 – 525
real-time anomaly detection	10, 11	**Intrusion Kill Chain Prevention**	29
schema-on-read	10	**indicator of compromise (IOC)**	50, 176, 446
schema-on-write	10	**infrastructure metrics**	11
threat intelligence	10	**ingestion strategies**	
traces	12	air-gapped environments	164
first-seen rules	322, 338 – 340	large enterprises	163
		mid-sized organization	163
G		small organizations	163
General Data Protection Regulation (GDPR)	84	**insight**	318 – 320, 353, 354
GitHub	22	custom insight	400 – 402
Global Confidence (GC)	368	navigating	362
Google Workspace	116	**insight timeline**	372
Gramm-Leach-Bliley Act (GLBA)	4	automation	376
Graphite	231	enrichment	375
		entities	373 – 375
H		**insight use cases**	
HTTP Logs & Metrics	122, 123	phishing scenario	382 – 393
Heads-Up Display (HUD)	362	ransomware scenario	393 – 400
Health Insurance Portability and Accountability Act (HIPAA)	4	**instrumentation**	143
Host Intrusion Detection System (HIDS) tools	361	**intelligent SOC**	502 – 504
		principles	504
Hosted Collectors	114 – 116, 466	significance	505
host metrics	94	**intelligent security**	502
hostname normalization		future	520 – 523
reference link	317	**interactive application security testing (IAST)**	24

Index 541

J

Java Development Kit (JDK)	92
Jenkins	22
Jira	22

K

KPIs in SecOps	59
Key Performance Indicators (KPIs)	53, 59

L

Linux Installed Collector
- first source, adding — 93, 94
- install command, running — 91, 92
- logs, viewing — 96, 97
- operating system, selecting — 90, 91
- setting up — 87–89
- source, configuring — 95, 96

Linux app
- setting up — 110, 111

Live Tail	193 – 196

Log Search
- aggregated results — 174, 175
- log results UI — 173, 174
- navigating — 168 – 173

LogCompare	192, 193
LogReduce	188 – 191
large language models (LLMs)	501
limit operator	188
log analytics	38
log management (LM)	4
log search optimization	212

- benefits — 212
- compute — 214
- compute time best practices — 223 – 226
- extracted fields, used for reducing retrieval — 217
- FER example 1 — 218, 219
- FER example 2 — 219, 220
- key concepts — 213
- keywords, used for reducing retrieval — 216
- retrieval — 214
- scan — 213
- scheduled views, using to speed up searches — 220
- scopes, used for reducing scan — 214, 215

logs	27, 229
lookup table mapping	308
lookup tables	196

- creating — 196
- CSV creation — 198, 199
- examples — 199 – 201
- manual creation — 196 – 198
- SecOps — 199

lookupContains	183
low-and-slow attacks	360

M

MISP Threat Intelligence	466
MITRE ATT&CK	348

- foundation — 348
- matrix — 349, 350

MITRE ATT&CK coverage matrix	345
Malware Traffic Analysis	465
Mean Time to Detect (MTTD)	53, 69
Mean Time to Respond (MTTR)	53, 69
Mean time to Identify (MTTI) metric	212
Metrics Search	235 – 239
Microsoft Office 365	120

- setting up — 120, 121

Mobot	9, 205

- dev — 211, 212
- reference link — 212
- SecOps — 211
- UI — 205, 206
- usage — 206 – 210

Model Context Protocol (MCP)	21, 509
mapping	308
match list enrichment	309
match rules	322, 326

- altering on traffic, to certain countries — 328, 329
- authentication, with MFA — 326, 327
- phishing email, identifying — 329, 330

metadata section, Insights UI — 364
- case management elements — 366, 367
- entity — 365
- MITRE ATT&CK tags — 368, 369
- resolution — 364
- severity and global confidence — 367

metrics — 229, 230
- anomaly detection — 233
- application spans — 243 – 245
- benefits, to security team — 232
- for security — 232
- incident impact assessment — 233
- network traffic analytics — 232
- performance, correlating with security events — 233
- proactive defense, with metrics thresholds — 233

querying	231, 240
server CPU spike	240-242
traces	243-245
unified context, for investigation	234

metrics and logs, combining
baselines of activity	234
best practices	234
consistent metadata	234
pre-empt	234
unified dashboards	234

metrics, events, logs, and traces (MELT) 83, 297

modern security operations
Sumo Logic AI, applying to	519, 520

monitor
alert monitor, building	251
overview	249, 250

multi-agent AI attacks 525

N

Nagios	230
Network Intrusion Detection Systems (NIDSs)	4, 361
network/host intrusion detection systems (NIDSs/HIDSs)	49
next-gen SIEM architecture	299, 300
non-human identities (NHIs)	507, 508

normalized actions
reference link	327

O

OODA loop	450

OTLP/HTTP source
setting up	150, 151

OWASP Application Security Verification Standard (ASVS)	34
Okta	116
Open Cybersecurity Schema Framework (OCSF)	301
Open Integration Framework (OIF)	407
Open Policy Agent (OPA)	20
Open Source Intelligence (OSINT)	445
OpenTelemetry	85, 127, 231, 524

OpenTelemetry Collector
setting up	128-135
setting up through app, in App Catalog	136-142

OpenTelemetry collection	127
Operating Technology (OT) environments	69
OpsGenie	22

operating system logs
ingesting	86

operating system metrics
ingesting	103
source, configuring	104
source, finding	103
viewing	105, 106

operators	9
out-of-the-box content	10
outlier rules	331, 335-337
overcomplication	73

P

PCI Compliance for Linux	483
PCI Compliance for Windows JSON	483
PCI for AWS CloudTrail	483
PagerDuty	22
Payment Card Industry Data Security Standard (PCI DSS)	4
Personally Identifiable Information (PII)	133
Policy as Code tools	20
Priority Information Requirements (PIRs)	448
criteria	448
Prometheus	230, 231
Proof of Value (PoV)	70
Puppet	100

Python application
Application Performance Management (APM), setting up	142, 143

parent query	201
parse regex operator	183
parseDate operator	185
parsing	152, 308
partitions	156, 157

performance criteria
defining	59

performance measurement
automation and continuous monitoring	72, 73
benchmarking criteria	71, 72
business objectives and security goals	66
collaboration, across teams	70, 71
continuous security	57, 58
core security and DevSecOps functions, identifying	67, 68
criteria, measuring with Sumo Logic	75-78
defining, for KPIs, SLIs, and SLOs	64

Index   543

impact, of security investments and 54, 55
metrics
   need for 54
   relevant metrics, determining 68, 69
   review regularly 73, 74
   security, aligning with business goals 56
   start-left 58, 59
   step-by-step process 65
   views, differing 56, 57

playbook
   creating 408, 418 – 432
   managing 408
   testing 432 – 435

playbook templates 417, 418

process IDs (PIDs) 233

Q

Quality Assurance (QA) 31

query language 9

querying 176
   basics 176 – 181
   different queries, for different teams 182
   Live Tail 193 – 196
   LogCompare 192, 193
   LogReduce 188 – 191
   logs 167
   lookup tables 196
   Mobot 205
   problems 175
   problems resolved 182
   subqueries 201

R

Real User Monitoring (RUM) 113, 142, 145, 146
   instrumenting 147 – 150
   versus Application Performance Monitoring (APM) 146

Reliability Management 75

Resilience 29

Risk Forecasting 29

Role-Based Access Control (RBAC) 95, 156 – 159, 407

rate metrics operator
   reference link 241

real-time risk scoring 18

real-time rules 10

record 309
   types 310 – 312

reports and audit log generation 482

App Catalog, using 483, 484
auditor role, creating 497
auditor-ready master dashboards, building 489, 490
hosted collector, deploying 485
logger, logging 495, 496
logs, checking 487
Microsoft Office 365 source, adding 485, 486
retention, aligning 496
scheduled reports 493
scheduled searches 491 – 493
scheduled views 494, 495

risk mitigation 35, 36

rolling compliance window 76

rollingstd 187

routing expression 157

rule
   versus search 323 – 325

S

SIEM rules 321, 322
   aggregation rules 322, 332 – 335
   chain rules 322, 340 – 343
   first-seen rules 322, 338 – 340
   match rules 322, 326 – 330
   outlier rules 322, 335 – 337
   threshold rules 322, 331
   tuning 346, 347

SLIs in SecOps 60

SLOs in SecOps 60

Salesforce 116

Sarbanes-Oxley Act (SOX) 4

SecOps KPIs
   examples 60 – 62

SecOps query 183

Security Information and Event Management (SIEM) 4

Security Operations (SecOps) 53, 54

Security Operations Center (SOC) 354

Security Orchestration, Automation, and Response (SOAR) 406

Security as Code 20

Service-Level Agreements (SLAs) 60

Service-Level Indicators (SLIs) 53, 60, 64

Service-Level Objectives (SLOs) 53, 60, 64, 237, 247

Shadow IT 6, 508

Signals Intelligence (SIGINT) 446

Single Sign On (SSO) 120

Software Bill of Materials (SBOM) tools	67
Software Development Optimization (SDO)	34
Software Development Optimization (SDO) app	68
SolarTech Corp	32
result	33, 34
turning point	33
Source Categories	95
StatsD	230
Sumo Logic	3, 212
as nucleus of threat intelligence	456, 457
attack surface	6
basic setup	84, 85
complexity	6
complexity issues	7
core features and capabilities	9-12
digital transformation	6
digital transformation, challenges	
growing attack surface	7, 8
increased speed of development	38
instance, creating	84, 85
modern architecture	13, 14
overview	4, 5
performance criteria, measuring with	75-78
reference link	84
risk mitigation and cost efficiency	36, 37
security, as business enabler	34, 35
security-first culture	47, 48
Sumo Logic AI	
applying, to modern security operations	519, 520
Sumo Logic Audit app	483
Sumo Logic Automation Service	407
Sumo Logic schema	301
Syslog	94
scalable observability	18
scheduled query-based detections	10
scheduled view	220
aggregation example	222
scenarios	221
security example	222, 223
setting up	221
schema-on-read (schema-on-demand)	10
schema-on-write	10
search	
versus rule	323-325
search audit index	495
security awareness and transparency principle	27, 28
Sumo Logic, role	28

security intelligence program	
building, with Sumo Logic	457
intelligence flow, establishing	458-460
intelligence maturity, evolving	462
intelligence, operationalizing across teams	460, 461
security onion approach	503
security-first culture	
building	46
shadow AI	508-511
shift left security with Security as Code principle	19
automation	20
continuous validation	21
Infrastructure as Code (IaC)	20
policy and access control	20
Sumo Logic, role	21
show me culture	480
signal	312, 313, 354
creating	344
On Entity field	344
severity	344
tags	345
signal clustering	357
criticality	358-361
severity, setting	357, 358
signal index	356
signal suppression	355, 356
examples	355
fine-tuning	356
site reliability engineers (SREs)	29, 196
software bill of materials (SBOM)	34
software composition analysis (SCA)	24
source category	156
source templates	128
static application security testing (SAST)	24, 516
stats	94
stdev	183, 184
subqueries	201, 202
child query	201
child query, creating	203
creating	204
example	203
parent query	201
parent query, creating	203
sum metrics operator	
reference link	241
supply chain	511, 512

Index

suppression mechanism 317

T

Techniques, Tactics, and Procedures (TTPs) 447
Telegraf 230
Tenable 483
Ticket-Granting Tickets (TGTs) 372
Time to First Byte (TTFB) 146
ToolCity 35
Traffic Light Protocol (TLP) intelligence report 454
tags 345
target query 192
technology shift 17
telemetry 460
threat intelligence 10
   decision-making with 449
threat intelligence implementation, in Sumo Logic 463
   bring your own feed 465
   Cloud SIEM rules 474, 475
   dashboards 475
   dissemination 475
   feeds 463-465
   hosted collection, setting up 472
   intelligence API 472-474
   MISP, setting up 466-468
   STIX/TAXII collection 466
   TAXII server, setting up 469-471

threat intelligence, types
   operational 447
   strategic 447, 448
   tactical 446
threshold rules 322, 331
timeslice operator 185
traces 12, 142

U

Universal Collector 124, 125
User and Entity Behavior Analytics (UEBA) 39, 514
username normalization
   reference link 317

V

VirusTotal 417
virtual machines (VMs) 35
visibility 50

W

Windows Installed Collector
   setting up 98
   Windows Event Log source, configuring 100-102
   Windows logs, viewing 102, 103
   Windows source, adding 100

Z

Zero Trust 29

www.ingramcontent.com/pod-product-compliance
Ingram Content Group UK Ltd.
Pitfield, Milton Keynes, MK11 3LW, UK
UKHW062041230226
468321UK00006B/31